THE POEMS OF
JOHN OLDHAM

The best of Oldham's poems still deserve to please. Many are significant for the place in Augustan culture of the translation and appreciation of the classics. The majority are of value for historians of politics, social life, and literature, in particular some that use genres notably developed later by Dryden, Swift, and Pope.

A complete edition was last attempted in 1770, when the Oldham autographs in the Bodleian Library were unknown. Bell's 1854 edition is textually notorious; those published since are contaminated from it; only a few isolated poems have been printed from original sources. The present edition furnishes a complete and critical text, bibliographically prepared, with full textual apparatus. The Introduction contains a concise biography of Oldham and a critique of his work, and evaluates his evidence on the position of the man of letters, which he both discussed and exemplified in his career. A comprehensive index to Introduction and Commentary, including a classified index of topics, is designed for the use of historians and researchers as well as for students of Oldham as a poet.

Oldham's work is rich in topicalities: the detailed Commentary draws upon state papers, diaries, memoirs, private correspondence, and archives, as well as the literary and historical publications of the time, to elucidate these. Thanks to the autographs in the Bodleian, and to the identification of many of his sources, Commentary and Appendices are able to show much that was in his mind as he wrote.

HAROLD F. BROOKS is Emeritus Professor of English Literature in the University of London.

RAMAN SELDEN is Professor of English at the University of Lancaster.

JOHN OLDHAM

THE POEMS OF
JOHN OLDHAM

EDITED BY HAROLD F. BROOKS
With the collaboration of Raman Selden

CLARENDON PRESS · OXFORD
1987

Oxford University Press, Walton Street, Oxford OX2 6DP

Oxford New York Toronto
Delhi Bombay Calcutta Madras Karachi
Kuala Lumpur Singapore Hong Kong Tokyo
Nairobi Dar es Salaam Cape Town
Melbourne Auckland
and associated companies in
Beirut Berlin Ibadan Nicosia

Oxford is a trade mark of Oxford University Press

Published in the United States
by Oxford University Press, New York

British Library Cataloguing in Publication Data
Oldham, John, 1653–1683
The poems of John Oldham.
I. Title   II. Brooks, Harold F.
III. Selden, Raman
821'.4   PR3605.04
ISBN 0–19–812456–2

Printed in Great Britain
at the University Printing House, Oxford
by David Stanford
Printer to the University

TO the MEMORY of Mr. OLDHAM

Farewel, too little and too lately known,
Whom I began to think and call my own;
For sure our Souls were near ally'd; and thine
Cast in the same Poetick mould with mine.
One common Note on either Lyre did strike,
And Knaves and Fools we both abhorr'd alike:
To the same Goal did both our Studies drive,
The last set out the soonest did arrive.
Thus *Nisus* fell upon the slippery place,
While his young Friend perform'd and won the Race.
O early ripe! to thy abundant store
What could advancing Age have added more?
It might (what Nature never gives the young)
Have taught the numbers of thy native Tongue.
But Satyr needs not those, and Wit will shine
Through the harsh cadence of a rugged line.
A noble Error, and but seldom made,
When Poets are by too much force betray'd.
Thy generous fruits, though gather'd ere thy prime
Still shew'd a quickness; and maturing time
But mellows what we write to the dull sweets of Rime.
Once more, hail and farewel; farewel thou young,
But ah too short, *Marcellus* of our Tongue;
Thy Brows with Ivy, and with Laurels bound;
But Fate and gloomy Night encompass thee around.

John Dryden

*In memory of my father
the Rev. Joseph B. Brooks
Lancashire author
and a companion of my research*

PREFACE

Because the objects of this edition are bound up with the assessment of what Oldham has to offer his readers, they are described not here but early in the Introduction.

The edition is the outcome of work begun fifty years ago, and seldom long intermitted. In an early form, as my doctoral thesis, it has existed since 1939; but in the last few years, with the assistance of Dr Selden, it has been completely overhauled and brought up to date. Without his help, especially though by no means exclusively in the Commentary, the task could not have been accomplished.

In the course of fifty years' work an editor owes many debts to many people. My first is to my father, mother, and her two sisters, Dr Lillie and Miss Kathie Johnson, who for eight years maintained me as a postgraduate student never, during the depression of the thirties, in more than part-time employ; and so enabled me to pursue, mainly in the Bodleian, the research by which I laid the foundations of the edition. My father, the Revd J.B. Brooks, also accompanied me, in 1933, on a research journey, and by observing at Shipton Moyne a Hillier grave of 1917, hard by those of the Oldhams, led to the discovery, in the possession of W.I. Hillier of Kings Caple, a descendant of the poet's family, of the portrait reproduced as frontispiece. Mr Hillier contributed to my genealogy of the Oldhams and Hilliers; many years later Miss M.B. Long, of Doncaster, another descendant, supplemented his information.

It was in 1931 that as an Oxford B.Litt. student I embarked on Oldham research. I wanted to use my training in the School of Modern History where—guided by I. Deane Jones, then writing his book on *The English Revolution*—I had studied from documents the period 1653 to 1663. I also wanted to edit, a craft I was being taught in the B.Litt. course, by Percy Simpson in textual criticism and Strickland Gibson in bibliography. As a thesis subject, 'Satyrs upon the Jesuits' met both ambitions. My supervisor, H.F.B. Brett-Smith, then encouraged my proposal to edit the whole of Oldham for the D.Phil.; from the first my interest in him had

been aroused by the absence of a complete edition since 1770, and
of a scholarly edition of any part. For the doctorate, Strickland
Gibson was my supervisor: everyone who knew him would enter into
my sense of his many kindnesses. My examiners for the two degrees, H.M. Margoliouth, C.H. Wilkinson, and David Ogg, were
generous with advice and help. Margoliouth gave me access to the
Oldham and other relevant texts in his MS *m*; and Wilkinson to his
Luttrell-inscribed copies of *Garnets Ghost* and *The Clarret Drinkers Song*. I was able to tell him that his *Father Whitebread's
Walking Ghost* was the garbled piracy (till then unidentified) of
the former, which Oldham complained of.

To Brett-Smith I am indebted for the greatest experience a
Restoration scholar could have. He showed my B.Litt. thesis to
Sir Charles Firth, who then enlisted me as his literary assistant. For the last eighteen months of his life I had the run of
his collection, catalogued many of his ballads and broadsides,
and listened to many a comment that came from his incomparable
mastery of the period. To no other scholar do I owe so much as
to him, except to Geoffrey Tillotson, for over thirty years my
head of department and elder friend.

On Oldham or his background I have had the advantage of conversation or correspondence with Norman Ault, Pierre Legouis,
Professors Earl Miner, W.J. Cameron, Roger Sharrock, Howard D.
Weinbrot, Antony A. Hammond, Dr Harold Love, Dr Paul F. Hammond,
and Mr Basil Greenslade. For contributions on particular topics
I am grateful especially to Dr H. Watkins Shaw, on Blow's set-
ting of the St Cecilia Ode, Dr Leba Goldstein, who extricated me
from error on the pirated *Claret-Drinker's Song*, and Professor
John O'Neill, who collaborated with me on 'Sardanapalus'. On
'Advice-to-a-Painter' poems, I am indebted to Dr Mary Tom
Osborne. Dr Alexander C. Spence showed me the significance, for
comparison with Oldham's mock-heroic Pindariques, of Butler's
Du Val ode, and R.I. Mills in an unpublished thesis influenced
my appreciation of Oldham's ode on Morwent and the Fourth Satyr
upon the Jesuits. Miss Kathleen Eidmans documented for me his
allusion to 'Bodkins, Rings, and Spoons'. For certain points in
Cleveland and Rochester I am indebted to Professor Brian Morris
and Dr Jeremy Treglown. Consulted about the two portraits claimed
as of Oldham, Sir David Piper disposed of the authenticity of

the one from Horace Walpole's collection.

The late A.B. Emden began the generous treatment I have continued to enjoy at St Edmund Hall, when he introduced me to the
memoir (Bodl. MS Top. Oxon. f. 31) of John Friend's life and
death at the Hall in Oldham's time.

During early researches in the poet's biography, I was given
access to parish registers by the incumbent clergy at Long Newnton, Tetbury, Wootton-under-Edge, Horsley, Kingscote, Charfield,
Wickwar, Malmesbury, Bristol St John Baptist and Holy Trinity,
and Holme Pierrepont. At Shipton Moyne, visited more than once,
Canon R.F. Wilson's hospitality was memorably warm and consider-
ate. The records at the Whitgift Hospital in Croydon threw light
on Oldham's period as usher in the school there; for permission
to cite them I am indebted to the Governors of the Whitgift
Trust. It is thanks to a happy collaboration with Mr F.G.H.
Percy, historian of Whitgift School, and his friend Mr W.D.
Hussey, like himself before their retirement one of the staff,
that the identity of John Shepheard, Oldham's headmaster, has at
last been established.

To facilitate my study of Oldham's sources, a close translation of Buchanan's *Franciscanus et Fratres* was made for me by
Professor Eric Laughton, and of Phineas Fletcher's *Locustae* by
Dr Ronald Truman and Mr Geoffrey Way. With Oldham's drafts of
Latin letters I had the assistance of Mr K.J. Maidment (subsequently Vice-Chancellor, University of Auckland) and—which I am
especially glad to recall—of my friend William B. Green: his
death while still a research student cut short his exceptional
promise not only as scholar but as poet.

On a palaeographical matter, I enlisted the help of the late
Dr William Urry. Some of my bibliographical inferences and deci-
sions I tested by consulting Professors Fredson Bowers and Conor
Fahy, Dr Arthur Johnston, Dr John C. Ross, and Mr David Foxon.
I am glad of the opportunity also to thank, for examining books,
manuscripts, and microfilms on my behalf, and in some instances
furnishing me with transcripts, Mr Anthony Burton, Mr Brian
Jenkins, Dr Laurel Brake, and Miss Jean Elliott (successively
Research Assistants at Birkbeck College), Dr Clive W. Bush and
Dr A.S.G. Edwards. Certain documents were reported to me by
Mr K.E. Robinson.

From start to finish the edition has depended upon the reposi-
tories which are such vital members of the commonwealth of learning. Everything has been done by those in charge to place their
resources at my disposal. I wish particularly to thank the staffs
of the Bodleian and British Libraries and of Birkbeck College
library; Dr J.H.P. Pafford, former Goldsmith's Librarian in the
University of London, and his colleagues; and at the Cambridge
University Library, Mr Arthur Tillotson, former Deputy Librarian,
and his colleagues. Further debts are to the following libraries:
Dr Williams'; the Victoria and Albert; the Guildhall; the John
Rylands; the National Library of Scotland; Trinity College Cambridge, and at Oxford, Wadham College, Corpus Christi College,
Worcester College, and St Edmund Hall; in the States, the Hough-
ton Library (Harvard), the Beinecke Library (Yale), the Folger,
the Huntington, the W.A. Clark (Los Angeles), the Newberry
(Chicago), the Chapin (Williams College), the Princeton, Texas
(at Austin), and Ohio State University libraries; and in Vienna,
the Österreichische Nationalbibliothek. I have left till last the
University of Nottingham library, so as to keep a distinctive
place for my thanks to His Grace the Duke of Portland for permission to collate Portland manuscripts which are on deposit there,
and to print the collations.

The edition has drawn also upon the resources of the National
Portrait Gallery, the Public Record Office, Somerset House, and
Gloucester Probate Registry. For prompt and helpful answers to
enquiries, thanks are due to archivists and their assistants at
the Diocesan Record Office, Salisbury, and the County Record
Offices of Bristol, Dorset, Wiltshire, Hampshire, Surrey, and
Berkshire. At the University of Oxford archive, housed in the
Bodleian, I was given sight at once of the evidence I needed,
and copies were quickly supplied.

I should not like to close these expressions of gratitude without reference to a number of volumes which from the time of their
publication have seldom been out of my hands for long. These are
Hugh Macdonald's *John Dryden: A Bibliography*; D.M. Vieth's *Attribution in Restoration Poetry*; Rachel Trickett's *The Honest Muse*,
and Raman Selden's *English Verse Satire 1590-1765*; with the last
two volumes of the Herford and Simpson *Ben Jonson*, and the edition of Pepys by Latham and Matthews; Dryden by James Kinsley;

Hudibras, by John Wilders (and alongside his commentary, Zachary
Grey's, not wholly superseded); Rochester, by Vieth; and Cleveland, by Morris and Withington. Necessarily, because of Oldham's
discipleship to Cowley, every page of A.R. Waller's edition,
despite its imperfections, has been turned again and again.

My thanks go to Professor Roger Sharrock, for his invaluable
help in checking the commentary.

It remains to thank Methuen & Co. for permission to make use,
in some parts of the Introduction, of my essay on Oldham contributed to Harold Love's symposium, *Restoration Literature: Critical Approaches*, 1972.

Birkbeck College (University of London)   H. F. B.
May, 1983

C O N T E N T S

NOTE ON THE FRONTISPIECE

The portrait is from an oil painting, in colour, now in the possession of Mrs Cynthia Taylor and her son Mr William Taylor, of
Hartham Farm, Corsham, Wilts. It is a family heirloom. Because
of doubts raised concerning its authenticity as a likeness of
John Oldham, its provenance is of the highest importance. Mrs
Taylor is the widow of Mr William Hillier Taylor, to whom it was
willed by his uncle, Mr William Isles Hillier. Through the marriage (20 Sept. 1764) of the poet's grandniece Mary Hancock with
John Hillier, Mr William I. Hillier was descended from Daniel
Oldham, the poet's youngest brother (see my article in *Miscellanea Genealogica et Heraldica*, Sept. 1934, 'The Family of John
Oldham the Poet (1653-1683); showing also the connection between
the Oldhams and Hilliers').

The likeness engraved by Van der Gucht as the frontispiece of
Oldham's *Works* [*and*] *Remains*, 1703, is identical with that in the
painting: one was done from the other. The 1703 edition was re-
issued in 1704, with a new title-page, evidently to advertise
Oldham's 'Effigies taken from the original never done before'.
If the claim were mendacious, and the painting derived from the
engraving, it might not be an authentic likeness: Van der Gucht,
when he lacked a genuine portrait, was not above fabricating one.
The print, when compared with the painting, is not reversed; had
it been, there would be no doubt that the painting was his
original.

But although an engraving after a portrait would usually have
been reversed in the print, this was not invariably so. The
costume is of the right period: the late 1670s or early 1680s.
Another heirloom shown me by Mr W.I. Hillier went back to the
poet's time; a textbook used by his younger brother, Thomas, in
his medical studies: when (four years after John) Thomas died,
he was a fully fledged chirurgeon. It is reasonable to suppose
that the painting had likewise been in the family from before
the poet's death. His youngest brother, Daniel, survived till
1732, and his father until 1716. They could have given access to
the painting in 1703; and unless it were painted after 1732, it

would be extremely odd if the family accepted as a likeness what
bore no resemblance to him. Its provenance could not speak more
strongly for its authenticity, which, short of being absolutely
unchallengeable, I take to be all but certain.

   Another portrait reproduced as his, but clearly not of the
same man, is without comparable supporting provenance, and indeed is ruled out by the costume, which is too early, if not also
by an attribution to Dobson, the famous portrait-painter, who
died in 1646. That, however, may be a guess. It accompanies an
engraving which faces p. 17 in *The Biographical Mirrour*, 1792,
published by S. and E. Harding; and another, published by W. Walker, 1 Sept. 1820, which may be seen in an extra-illustrated copy
of Chalmers's *General Biographical Dictionary* (Montague Illustr.
65, Vol. XXIII, facing p. 329) in the Bodleian; but no artist is
named in the Horace Walpole and the Charles Wentworth Dilke sales
catalogues, 1842 and 1911. Under 'Curiosities added since this
Book was compleated', *A Description of the Villa of Mr. Horace
Walpole ... at Strawberry Hill*, 1784, records (p. 93) 'In the red
Bedchamber ... A small head of Oldham, the poet, in oil, as clear
and fine as Vandyck. It had been in the collection of Mr. Dine-
ley.' It is in fact so fine, both for the artistry and for the
personality of the sitter, that in default of the evidence here
assembled, it is not surprising it was accepted, mistakenly, as
depicting Oldham, to illustrate the *Yale Poems on Affairs of
State*, Vol. II, 1965. In 1911 the original was bought by Messrs
Wallis, The French Gallery, 11 Berkeley Square, W.1, since when
its whereabouts has remained unknown.

   I have been greatly indebted for expert advice, in 1934 to
David Piper, and in 1983 to Jacob Simons; the first then, and
the second now, of the National Portrait Gallery: and to A.C.
Cooper Ltd., especially to Mr G.H. Roberton, for art-photography.
Permissions and facilities were most generously given by Mr William and Mrs Cynthia Taylor, to whom I am warmly grateful. It is
primarily thanks to them that Oldham's college, St Edmund Hall,
has now a reproduction, full-size and in colour, of their heirloom portrait.

ABBREVIATIONS

1. BOOKS AND ARTICLES

Aubrey: John Aubrey, *Brief Lives*, ed. Andrew Clark, 2 vols. (1898)

Aubrey, *Surrey*: John Aubrey, *Natural History and Antiquities of ... Surrey*, 5 vols. (1719)

Bibliography: H.F. Brooks, *A Bibliography of John Oldham* in *Oxford Bibliographical Society, Proceedings and Papers*, v, part i (1936), Kraus Reprint, Nendeln, Liechtenstein (1969) with corrections and additions, pp. 5-36

Boileau, *L'Art Poétique*: in Nicolas Boileau Despréaux, *Oeuvres Diverses du Sieur D XXX* [sc. Despréaux] 1674

Boileau, *Satires*: *Satires* (1666), Satires I-VII, first authorized edn

Boswell, *Life*: *Boswell's Life of Johnson*, ed. G.B. Hill, rev. L.F. Powell, 6 vols. (1934-50)

Brooks, 'Contributors': H.F. Brooks, 'Contributors to Brome's *Horace*', *N&Q*, clxxiv (1938), 200

Brooks, 'Ghost': H.F. Brooks, 'The Fictitious *Ghost*: A Poetic Genre', *N&Q* (Feb. 1982), pp. 51-5

Brooks, 'Imitation': H.F. Brooks, 'The "Imitation" in English Poetry, Especially in Formal Satire, Before the Age of Pope', *RES*, xxv (1949), 124-40

Brooks, 'Oldham and Fletcher': H.F. Brooks, 'Oldham and Phineas Fletcher: An Unrecognized Source for *Satyrs upon the Jesuits*', *RES*, xxii (1971), 410-22, xxiii (1972), 19-34

Brooks, 'Oldham: Some Problems': H.F. Brooks, 'John Oldham: Some Problems of Biography and Annotation', *PQ*, liv (1975), 569-78

Browne: Sir Thomas Browne, *Works*, ed. Geoffrey Keynes, 6 vols. (1928-31)

Browne, *Pseud. Ep.*: *Pseudodoxia Epidemica*, in Keynes, ed. cit.

Buchanan, *Franciscanus*: George Buchanan, *Poemata quae extant* (Elzevir edn., 1676)

Burnet, *Some Passages*: Gilbert Burnet, *Some Passages of the Life and Death of the ... Earl of Rochester* (1680)

Burnet: Gilbert Burnet, *History of My Own Time*, ed. O. Airy, 2 vols. (1897-1900)

Burton, *Anatomy*: Robert Burton, *Anatomy of Melancholy* (6th edn., 1651)

Caraman: Philip Caraman, *Henry Garnet ... and the Gunpowder Plot* (1964)

Chamberlayne: E. Chamberlayne, *Angliae Notitia or the Present State of England* (14th edn., 1682)

Clark: A.F.B. Clark, *Boileau And The French Classical Critics in England (1660-1830)* (1925)

Cowley, *Essays*: Abraham Cowley, *Essays, Plays, and Sundry Verses*, ed. A.R. Waller (1906)

Cowley, *Poems*: Abraham Cowley, *Poems*, ed. A.R. Waller (1905)

CSPD: Calendar of State Papers, Domestic Series, 1660-1702, ed. M.E. Greene *et al.* 38 vols. (1860-1964)

Denham: Sir John Denham, *Poetical Works*, ed. T.H. Banks (1928)

De-Laune: Thomas De-Laune, *The Present State of London* (1681)

Dryden, *Essays*: John Dryden, *Essays*, ed. W.P. Ker, 2 vols. (1900, 1926)

Eachard: John Eachard, *The Grounds & Occasions Of The Contempt Of The Clergy And Religion Enquired Into* (1670)

Ebsworth: J.W. Ebsworth, ed., *The Roxburghe Ballads* (1869)

Evelyn: John Evelyn, *The Diary*, ed. E.S. de Beer, 6 vols. (1955)

Excommunicated Prince: William Bedloe (ostensibly), *The Excommunicated Prince; or, the False Relique* (1679)

Feiling: Keith Feiling, *A History of the Tory Party 1640-1714* (1924)

Fletcher, *Locustae*: Phineas Fletcher, *Locustae, Vel Pietas Jesuitica* (1627, publ. with *Locusts*)

Fletcher, *Locusts*: Phineas Fletcher, *The Locusts, Or, Apollyonists* (1627)

Foulis: Henry Foulis, *History of Romish Treasons* (1671)

The Golden Legend: [trans. William Caxton from the *Legenda Aurea* of Jacobus de Voragine] (1483), Temple Classics edn.

G. Hall: George Hall, *The Triumph of Rome over Despised Protestancy* (1667, 1st edn. 1655)

Hammond: Paul F. Hammond, *John Oldham and the Renewal of Classical Culture* (1983)

Heylyn: Peter Heylyn, *Cosmographie in Four Bookes* (1652)

HMC: *Reports of the Historical Manuscripts Commission*

Hume: R.D. Hume, *The Development of English Drama in the late Seventeenth Century* (1976)

Jonson: *Ben Jonson*, ed. C.H. Herford and P. and E.M. Simpson, 11 vols. (1925-52)

Jones: J.R. Jones, *The First Whigs. The Politics of the Exclusion Crisis* (1961)

Kenyon: John Kenyon, *The Popish Plot* (1972)

Lefèvre: Lefèvre (Tanaquillus Faber) *Epistolae. Pars Prima* (1674)

Life of Ignatius: W.M., *The Life of B. Father Ignatius of Loyola, Translated* [from Ribadeneyra] 1616

Luttrell: Narcissus Luttrell, *A Brief Historical Relation of State Affairs from September 1678 to April 1716*, 6 vols. (1857)

Luttrell, *Catalogues*: *Narcissus Luttrell's Popish Plot Catalogues*, introduced by F.C. Francis (1956)

Macdonald: Hugh Macdonald, *John Dryden: A Bibliography of Early Editions and of Drydeniana* (Oxford, 1939)

Maitland: F.W. Maitland, *Constitutional History of England* (1908)

Marvell, *Poems* (3rd edn.): Andrew Marvell, *The Poems and Letters*, ed. H.M. Margoliouth, rev. P. Legouis and E.E. Duncan-Jones, 2 vols. (3rd edn., 1971)

Miller: John Miller, *Popery and Politics in England, 1660-1688* (1973)

Milton, *Works*: John Milton, *The Works*, ed. F.A. Patterson *et al.*, 20 vols. (Columbia edn., 1931-40)

Morley: Henry Morley, *Memoirs of Bartholomew Fair* (1859)

Nichol Smith: D. Nichol Smith (ed.), *Characters from the Histories and Memoirs of the Seventeenth Century* (1918)

Nicoll: Allardyce Nicoll, *History of English Drama 1660-1900*, 6 vols. (1955-9)

North, *Examen*: Roger North, *Examen* (1740)

North, *Lives*: Roger North, *Lives of the Norths*, ed. A. Jessopp, 3 vols. (1890)

Oates: Titus Oates, *True and Exact Narration of the Horrid Plot* (1679)

Ogg: David Ogg, *England in the Reign of Charles II* (1934)

Ogg, *Europe*: David Ogg, *Europe in the Seventeenth Century* (1925)

Osborne: Mary Tom Osborne, *Advice-To-A-Painter Poems, 1633-1856* (1949)

Pascal, *Lettres*: Blaise Pascal, *Lettres Ecrites à un Provinciale* (d'après l'édition de 1754, n.d.)

Pepys: Samuel Pepys, *Diary*, ed. W. Matthews and R. Latham, 11 vols. (1970-1983)

POAS: *Poems on Affairs of State* (1689-1716): vols. specified by date

Yale *POAS*: *Poems on Affairs of State: Augustan Satirical Verse, 1660-1714*, gen. ed. G. deF. Lord (1963-75)

Pollock: Sir John Pollock, *The Popish Plot: A Study in the History of the Reign of Charles II* (1903)

R: Bodl. MS Rawlinson Poet. 123

Randolph: Thomas Randolph, *The Poems*, ed. G. Thorn-Drury [*sic*] (1929)

Ranke, *England*: Leopold von Ranke, *History of England principally in the Seventeenth Century*, 6 vols. (1875)

Ranke: Leopold von Ranke, *History of the Popes*, tr. Foster, rev. G.R. Dennis, 3 vols. (Bohn Standard Library, 1908)

Reresby: *Memoirs of Sir John Reresby* ... ed. A. Browning (1936)

Rochester, *Poems*: John Wilmot, Earl of Rochester, *Complete Poems*, ed. D.M. Vieth (1968)

Rochester, *Poems* (Pinto): John Wilmot, Earl of Rochester, *Poems*, ed. V. de Sola Pinto (2nd edn., 1964)

Rochester, *Letters*: John Wilmot, Earl of Rochester, *Letters*, ed. Jeremy Treglown (1980)

Rollins: Hyder E. Rollins, ed., *Old English Ballads, 1553-1625* (1920)

Routh: E.M.G. Routh, *Tangier, England's lost Atlantic outpost, 1661-1684* (1912)

SJ: *Satyrs Upon The Jesuits* (1681)

Spingarn: J.E. Spingarn, ed., *Critical Essays of the Seventeenth Century*, 3 vols. (1908-9)

Steele: R.R. Steele and J.L. Lindsay, Earl Crawford, *Tudor and Stuart Proclamations* (1910)

Tanner: J.R. Tanner, *Tudor Constitutional Documents* (2nd edn., 1930)

Taunton: E.L. Taunton, *The History of the Jesuits in England 1580-1773* (1901)

Thompson: Nat. Thompson, *Choice Collection of 180 Loyal Songs* (3rd edn., 1685)

Tilley: E.M. Tilley, ed., *A Dictionary of the Proverbs in England in the Sixteenth and Seventeenth Centuries* (1950)

Varenius: *Bernhardi Vareni Med. D. Descriptio Regni Japoniae et Siam. Item de Japoniorum Religione & Siamensibus* (1673)

Vieth, *Attribution*: D.M. Vieth, *Attribution in Restoration Poetry, A Study of Rochester's Poems of 1680* (1963)

Waller, *Poems*: Edmund Waller, *The Poems*, ed. G. Thorn Drury, 2 vols. (1905)

Wheatley: H.B. Wheatley, *London Past and Present* (1891)

Wiley: A.N. Wiley, *Rare Prologues and Epilogues, 1642-1700* (1940)

Wood: Anthony Wood, *Athenae Oxonienses*, ed. P. Bliss, 4 vols. (1813-20)

Wood, *Life and Times*: *The Life and Times of Anthony Wood*, ed. A. Clark, 5 vols. (1891-95)

2. PERIODICALS

DUJ: *Durham University Journal*

EHR: *English Historical Review*

HLQ: *Huntington Library Quarterly*

MLN: *Modern Language Notes*

MLR: *Modern Language Review*

MP: *Modern Philology*

N&Q: *Notes and Queries*

PQ: *Philological Quarterly*

RES: *Review of English Studies*

SB: *Studies in Bibliography*

TLS: *Times Literary Supplement*

3. OLDHAM'S POEMS

Art of Poetry (Horace His Art of Poetry, Imitated in English)

Aude aliquid. Ode (Aude aliquid brevibus Gyaris, & carcere dignum ... Ode [often known as 'A Satyr Against Vertue'])

The Author of *Sodom* (Upon the Author of the Play call'd *Sodom*)

Boileau VIII (The Eighth Satyr Of Monsieur Boileau, Imitated)

Byblis (The Passion of Byblis)

Counterpart (Counterpart to The Satyr against Vertue)

Dithyrambique (A Dithyrambique Suppos'd to be spoken by Rochester)

Homer (The Praise of Homer)

Jesuits I (Satyrs Upon the Jesuits, Satyr I; similarly Jesuits II, etc.)

Jesuits, Prologue (Prologue to Satyrs Upon the Jesuits)

Juvenal III (A Satyr in Imitation of the Third of Juvenal [other versions of classical authors are similarly abbreviated])

A Letter (A Letter from the Country to a Friend in Town)

Katharine Kingscote (On the Death of Mrs. Katharine Kingscote)

Nobility (A Satyr Touching Nobility Out of Monsieur Boileau)

Ode on Jonson (Upon the Works of Ben. Johnson. Ode)

On the Times (Satyr upon the Town and Times)

Rant (A Rant to his Mistress)

St Ambrose (Paraphrase upon the Hymn of St. Ambrose)

S. Cecilia Ode (An Ode For an Anniversary of Musick on S. Cecilia's Day)

Spencer's Ghost (A Satyr. The Person of Spencer is brought in &c.)

To a Friend (A Satyr. Adress'd to a Friend, that is about to leave the University)

To Cosmelia (Presenting a Book to Cosmelia)

Upon a Bookseller (Upon a Bookseller, that expos'd him by Printing a Piece of his grosly mangled, and faulty)

Upon a Lady (Upon a Lady, &c. Out of Voiture)

Upon a Woman (A Satyr Upon a Woman)

Upon the Marriage (Upon the Marriage of the Prince of Orange with the Lady Mary)

INTRODUCTION

The poems of John Oldham, as Dryden reminds us in the noble lines
to his memory, are the work of a young man. He died at thirty, in
1683, and wrote his poetry within the preceding decade.

> John Ouldham the sonne of John Ouldham the sonne of
> John Ouldham the elder minister was borne August 9th
> and baptized August 18th 1653.[1]

at Shipton Moyne in Gloucestershire, where his grandfather (b.
1594, d. 1657) was rector. During the interregnum, his father
(b. 1629, d. 1716) became rector of the adjoining parish of Long
Newnton, Wilts., from which he was ejected in 1662: 'he had, however, a small estate, and with keeping of a school he had a handsome livelyhood'.[2] Oldham was 'bred in grammar learning under his
father till he was nigh fit for the university, afterwards sent
to the school at Tetbury, where he spent about two years'.[3] He
matriculated at St Edmund Hall, Oxford, 17 June 1670. His first
extant composition is a copy of Latin verses on the death of John
Freind, one of his fellow-undergraduates there, written 21 March
1672/3.[4] In 1674 his BA was provisionally granted, subject to
'determination' (the performance of certain public exercises)
but as he did not comply with the condition, the degree was cancelled.[5] He had returned home,[6] doubtless to teach in his father's
school. From that time his life as schoolmaster and then tutor,
and in a brief, unsuccessful bid for independence, is closely in-
volved with his activities as a poet, and can be sketched con-
currently with it.

But first something should be said of the principal aims of
this edition. The prime need was to supply a complete and critical text, bibliographically prepared, of Oldham's poems, with the
due accompaniment of textual record and textual introduction.
Then, thanks to the identification of many of his sources, and
still more to the wealth of evidence provided by his autographs
in the Bodleian MS, Rawlinson Poet. 123, much can be shown of
what as he composed his poetry was in his mind: this is one of

the functions of the commentary and appendices. Another, which
the commentary, especially, shares with the introduction, is to
bring out his value for the historian. As a practitioner of
various genres, and in those of Augustan 'Imitation' and of
'heroic' satire an important contributor to the forms they afterwards assumed in the hands of major poets, he is significant for
the historian of literature.[7] For the social historian, he is a
leading witness on the position of the man of letters: he both
discusses it, and exemplifies it in his own career and in the
poems by which he hoped that career might be furthered. He is
rich in topical allusion and description; much of his verse might
bear the title he gave to a fragment among his drafts: 'Upon the
Town and Times'. To check and realize its precise value for historical purposes, documentation is to be sought in literature,
diaries, memoirs, private correspondence and archives, state
papers and the like, on an even wider scale than our commentary
can compass; but the essential part of the record has been
included.

The critique of the poems seeks to elucidate the qualities of
his best work, and the differences between his best and his
weakest, which cannot be properly understood apart from his
development as a poet and the various genres he attempted. The
best still deserves to please; and even in the very respects
that attract the historian, to please the ordinary reader, too.
The topicalities, once clarified by the commentary, are part of
the appeal: 'in social and moral satire of this period', as Roger
Sharrock has said, 'the sense of vivid contemporary immediacy is
often the chief pleasure to be gained from the poem'.[8] One excellent way of enjoying Oldham's pictures of metropolitan life, in
particular his imitation of Juvenal's third satire, is to treat
them as part of a series which includes scenes from Restoration
comedy, some of Dryden's prologues, Swift's 'Description of the
Morning' and 'A City Shower', Gay's *Trivia*, and Johnson's *London*.
Similarly, on the prospects of educated men with their living to
earn, whether as chaplains or poor parsons, private tutors or
schoolmasters, or precariously as dramatists and poets, Oldham
is making his contribution to a traditional subject, and it is
worth while to compare what he writes with Burton's 'Digression
of the Miseries of Scholars', Joseph Hall's Satire VI, Book II

of *Virgidemiarum*, the opening episode of Jonson's *Poetaster*,
Act III, Cowley's poem 'The Complaint', and Eachard's *Grounds and
Occasions of the Contempt of the Clergy*.

I   OLDHAM THE POET

1. *His Career*

When Oldham, in 1674, came down from Oxford, he spent the next
year or more at his father's in Shipton Moyne. His earliest extant poems in English were composed at this time: occasional
pieces likely to recommend him to families of standing in the
neighbourhood. 'To Madam L.E. upon her Recovery fròm a late Sickness' is presumably an instance. One may surmise that in the
autograph from which it was posthumously printed, the title read
'To L.E.', standing for Lady Estcourt.[9] The Estcourts were seated
hard by the Oldhams at Shipton Moyne, and were patrons of the
living Oldham's father had held at Long Newnton on the farther
side of the Estcourt park. When Joan, widow of Abraham Kingscote,
of Kingscote, lost her eleven-year-old daughter, Oldham began a
consolatory address to the mother, and wrote his complete lines
'On the Death of Mrs. Katharine Kingscote a Child of Excellent
Parts and Piety'.[10] Like those to 'L.E.', they are juvenilia; a
conventional copy of verses. Both pieces derive closely from
Waller's and Cowley's poems of compliment, and repeatedly borrow
from them. If a local tradition is to be trusted, a four-line
epitaph on the physician Abia Qui, buried at Malmesbury 8 October 1675, was by Oldham.[11] The major work of his months in
Gloucestershire was the elegy on Charles Morwent, his bosom
friend at college, who died 25 August of the same year.[12] Elaborated on the largest scale, this ode is not without literary merit,
to which we shall return. With the friendship it commemorates, it
is not unlikely to have assisted Oldham's escape from provincial
obscurity to the vicinity of the metropolis, though not so
directly as I once believed.[13] The possibility depends upon links,
one hypothetical, the other less so, between the headmaster of
Whitgift School, Croydon, under whom, by July 1676 and most likely
by May,[14] Oldham had become usher or assistant master, and Morwent's uncle, William Shepheard of Horsley, the next village to

Kingscote. The headmaster was a John Shepheard, not, however,
from Oldham's and Morwent's south-west Cotswolds, but from near
Marnhull in Dorset. One cannot help suspecting a connection between the two families of Shepheards, though because of the loss
of relevant Dorset records there is little chance this can ever
be proved. A less conjectural link between the headmaster and
William Shepheard of Horsley does exist. The patrons who had presented him in November 1667 to the rectory of Caterham near Croydon were Robert and Susan Hussey of the Cathedral Close, Salisbury,
members of the prominent family seated at Marnhull. William Shepheard, Morwent's uncle, had married as his first wife Mary Hussey
of South Newton in the diocese of Salisbury, and had further asso-
ciations with the diocese even after her death. It is thus by no
means improbable that when John Shepheard was in want of an assistant he knew or learned of Morwent's friend through the Shepheards
of Horsley and Tetbury.

   At Croydon, Oldham again pursued acquaintance with neighbouring gentry. His elegy on Harman Atwood of Sanderstead (d. 16 February 1677) eulogizes a pious benefactor of the Whitgift Foundation, whose niece the headmaster had married. The paraphrase on
the 137th Psalm was written 22 December 1676 at Beddington: evidently Oldham was spending the Christmas season in the household
of Sir Nicholas Carew.[15] He corresponded in verse and Latin prose
with a half-cousin of the Carews, John Spencer. His 'Letter from
the Country' (July 1678) was a reply to a verse-letter from
Spencer (18 March 1678).[16] Possibly a second scriptural paraphrase, 'David's Lamentation' (September 1677), was written for
a Carew audience.

   Meanwhile, however, a more dazzling opportunity presented itself, as a result of Oldham's first satiric poem (July 1676),
later christened, but not by him, 'A Satyr Against Vertue'. It
was 'Suppos'd to be spoken by a Court Hector at Breaking of the
Dial in Privy Garden'. This was a drunken exploit of Rochester's,
and the satirist's audacity and undeniably clever performance
brought him an appreciative visit from the Earl himself and some
of his fellow-wits.[17] In the sequel, Oldham appears to have composed several poems primarily for this circle: the obscene
satires 'Upon the Author of the Play call'd Sodom' and 'Sardanapalus', intended to remain in manuscript, and 'A Dithyrambique

on Drinking, Suppos'd to be spoken by Rochester at the Guinny-
Club' (5 August 1677). 'The Dream' (10 March 1677)[18] and 'Upon a
Lady: Out of Voiture' may also belong to this series. After
Rochester's death (26 July 1680), in a pastoral elegy (a version
of Moschus' *Bion*) Oldham attributed to him a decisive influence
upon his own poetic art, though this is hard to particularize.
In 1676-7, he was cherishing hopes of notice at Court, from the
household the King had set up for the Princesses Mary and Anne,
the daughters of his royal brother, James Duke of York. Drafting
a Latin letter, Oldham refers to a lady who has charge of Mary's
tresses, and perhaps, he adds slyly, of her rouge, too.[19] The
jest explains the name he bestows, pastoral-wise, on 'Cosmelia',
to whom he addresses love-verses in September 1676, sequels, evidently, of 'A Rant to his Mistress' written 15 May. Whether inspired by real emotion or not, poetically speaking these are mere
vers d'occasion, no less derivative than the Kingscote elegy,
from which indeed they borrow. The same woman is the imagined
heroine of 'The Dream', which doubly distances, as wish-fulfilment
and by pastoral convention, a scene of courtship ending in consum-
mation. That November, Cosmelia assisted the poet in a major bid
for Court favour, placing in the hands of Princess Mary[20] his ode
upon her marriage to William of Orange. But, he comments, his
pains were lost upon the recipient. They brought him, however,
his first appearance in print: the poem, written 5 November (the
morning after the marriage itself), was published within a few
days by Herringman. Perhaps through this contact, Oldham seems to
have got wind of a project Herringman did not publicly announce
until February 1679: to bring out a new edition of Ben Jonson.
For the Jonson ode, written at Croydon some time between 1 January and 24 March 1678, is optimistically entitled 'Upon the Works
of Ben Jonson, reprinted'. Oldham wrote it, no doubt, in the hope
of seeing it prefixed to the new edition;[21] but Herringman's proposal did not take effect until 1692.

October 1678 brought him a subject of passionate interest to
the religious and political public of the whole nation. With the
murder of Godfrey, following upon Oates's allegations of a Popish
plot, the Popish Terror seized upon Tories as well as Whigs.
Oldham determined to satirize the Jesuits, believed to be the
arch-champions of Counter-Reformation. Besides being topical, the

subject had tradition behind it; two of Oldham's chief sources
were satires on religious orders: Phineas Fletcher's *The Locusts*,
on the Jesuits, with reference to Gunpowder Plot;[22] and (which
he used later) George Buchanan's 'Franciscanus et Fratres'. After
two false starts, he settled down to composing *Garnet's Ghost*.
The draft of a Latin letter to John Spencer, dated December 1678,
announces the undertaking with some pardonable pride.[23] He has
drawn his pen against the traitors. Whether safely and propiti-
ously or not, remains to be seen. He has raised the ghost of
Garnet; what tidings it brings, his friend shall soon learn; they
breathe (unless he is mistaken) crime and wickedness worthy of a
Jesuit.

  Had he pursued a line to which at first he meant to give prominence, the satire would have had a party-political bent. Spencer's
relative and Oldham's local patron, Sir Nicholas Carew, was a
vehement member of the opposition in Parliament (soon to be christened Whigs), who reiterated the dangers to be apprehended from
a Popish successor, and pressed for James's exclusion.[24] In some
cancelled lines of the earliest surviving draft-opening for
'Garnet's Ghost', the apparition announces himself sent as envoy
'From Hell's dread Monarch.... First to your Royal Highness' who
'for his Cause

           Both Country, Brother, King dare sacrifice.

'Go on brave Prince', James is adjured,

           Get a crown here, another down below.

  On the following page is a note, heavily scored out: 'York
Aurengz. p. 68' which refers to a speech of Morat's in Dryden's
Aureng-Zebe, 1676:

           Birthrights a vulgar road to Kingly sway:
           'Tis evr'y dull-got Elder Brothers Way.

When a younger son takes the sceptre by violence, 'Right comes of
course,

                    Murder and usurpation are no more.

In a further draft, echoing a rant in Settle's *Cambyses*, 1671
(p. 8), Oldham has:

             ... Let lazy Princes wait
             Till their slow crowns be given by Fate....[25]

Thus he assumes (even though Oates had eschewed the far-fetched
and hazardous imputation) James's complicity in the Popish assassination plot.

    Yet the presence, in these earliest drafts, of the attack, in
keeping with Exclusionist animus, upon the Duke, is less significant than the absence of anything of the sort from the later
ones, and from the completed and published 'Garnet's Ghost' and
its sequels. Ministering to belief in the Plot, abhorrence of
the Jesuits, and scorn of Popish superstition, they are bound
thus far to have been grist to Shaftesbury's mill. But there is
nothing in them to direct the onslaught against James, the Catholic and barren Queen whom Shaftesbury hoped to prevail on Charles
to divorce, Danby, or any party target of the Whigs. On the contrary, the dissenters, to whom they were well-disposed, come in
for hostile references.[26] Oldham's anti-Catholicism, however it
may have veered briefly toward the Carew viewpoint, was not affi-
liated to party: its vehemence was straightforwardly patriotic
and Protestant.

    During the composition of the 'Satyrs upon the Jesuits', he
moved from a climate full of animosity against James to one that
favoured him. His new patron, Sir Edward Thurland, had been
James's Solicitor-General. At the end of February 1678/9 Oldham
became tutor to Thurland's grandson, in the judge's household at
Reigate.[27] Though he had been chafing at the constraints of
schoolmastering, he left Croydon, he tells a correspondent, 'with
as much concern almost as ever I left any place. Most of my boys
cried at my departure.'[28] According to the 1722 memoir, he owed
the new appointment to Harman Atwood.[29] Atwood and Thurland were
prominent members of the Inner Temple as well as near neighbours
in Surrey. Atwood may well have spoken appreciatively to his
fellow-lawyer about the young teacher and poet at the Hospital

in which he was interested. But he had been two years dead when
the tutorship was bestowed: John Spencer and Sir Nicholas Carew
may have been Oldham's sponsors. In the draft letter of December
1678, Spencer is being kept abreast of his friend's hopes, which
all rest upon 'our Rhadamanthus'. Though expecting an invitation,
Oldham, since seeing Spencer, has heard nothing: probably, however, the judge has not yet come down into the country. Like
Atwood, John Spencer and Sir Nicholas Carew moved in the same
professional and local circles as Sir Edward. They, too, were of
the Inner Temple; Sir Nicholas and he had sat in the Commons together, Sir Nicholas for Gatton, 1664-81, Sir Edward for Reigate,
1660-73, and there had been dealings between the two families.[30]

To conceive as Whiggish a series of satires written for the
most part beneath the roof of James's former Solicitor-General,
and published by Hindmarsh, bookseller under James's patronage,
and capable of being described as 'the notedst Tory in the
town',[31] is manifestly absurd. As the months passed, Tories began
to shrug off the Terror as a ploy of the Whigs,[32] who were left
the only wholehearted believers in the plot: Dryden's verdict
upon it became possible:

> Some truth there was, but dashed and brewed with lies.[33]

Oldham changed with the nation: as early as 9 March 1680, in
'The Careless Good Fellow' he treats the Terror with a humorous
detachment of which no Shaftesbury Whig would have been capable.
The Good Fellow, a loyal toper, indeed contrasts with the current image of the coffee-drinking Whig, and in a less mellow
hour may be a Tory: but at present he is in bliss, and the far
side even of Toryism. In the 'Imitation of Horace, Satire I, ix'
(June 1681), the impertinent who 'begins to plague' the poet
'with the Plot', and demands 'are you not afraid of Popery?'
(under the King's successor), is coolly answered:

> No more than my Superiors: why should I? (117 f.).

Oldham's horror of Catholic militancy and Catholic superstitions and corruptions may have been first implanted by his up-
bringing in his Presbyterian father's house; but even in the

'Satyrs upon the Jesuits' his point of view, proper to an Oxo-
nian, was that of the Church-and-King men who condemned Papist
and Covenanting Puritan alike.

Piratically published almost at once (1679), the first Satyr
upon the Jesuits had a great success. So, on their appearance in
the authorized edition—with imprint 1681, but first issued
c.November 1680—did the whole four with their prologue. *A Satyr
Against Vertue* had also been pirated early in 1679: the printer,
Mary Clark, who printed often for Hindmarsh. This piracy may have
been what brought Oldham in touch with Hindmarsh, who became his
regular publisher. The pirated text was reprinted in the authorized first edition of *Satyrs Upon The Jesuits*—reprinted with
most of its corruptions uncorrected. It was this bad text which
provoked Oldham's satire (Christmas 1680) entitled in *Some New
Pieces* 'Upon a Printer', but in the autograph 'Upon a Bookseller',
and prompted a third issue of *Satyrs Upon The Jesuits*, 1681, with
errata.[34]

At that time, Oldham was still a dependent tutor at Reigate:
but this double encouragement of having found in Hindmarsh someone likely to go on publishing his work, and of the success his
anti-Jesuit satires had met with, was no doubt what decided him
to come to London in the hope of paying his way as an author.[35]
'An Allusion to Martial' informs us that he is living in a garret at the far end of Clerkenwell. *Some New Pieces* came out by
the end of 1681, and included his Imitation of the *Ars Poetica*.
This, he says, was 'a Task imposed' on him: in answer, one may
guess, to the advice insultingly given, by Sir William Soame,
that the 'School-Master' author of 'Sardanapalus ... and ...
Other Writeings' should himself take a lesson from the precepts
Horace laid down.[36]

A second edition of *Satyrs Upon The Jesuits* was called for
c.May 1682. But to earn a competence by literary authorship,
without assistance from patronage or private means, was hardly
in Restoration times a practical proposition. Oldham had to turn
tutor again: his new pupil was the eldest son of Sir William
Hickes of Rookwood, at Low Leyton, Essex. Sir William had an
estate near the Oldhams in Gloucestershire: the poet's cousin
Mary had married into the Wickwar branch of the family, two members of which had been his contemporaries and probably his

acquaintances at Oxford.[37] While at Rookwood, he studied medicine with a distinguished physician, Richard Lower, who figures
as 'a Doctor, my deer Friend' in the 'Imitation of Horace, Satire
I, ix' (June 1681), and is paid a compliment in the Imitation of
the *Ars Poetica*.[38] When Sir William's son was judged ready to
pursue his education by foreign travel, Oldham declined the opportunity to accompany him:[39] it is uncertain whether he renewed his
attempt at independence, or whether it was without an interim that
the young William Pierrepont, from June 1682 fourth Earl of Kings-
ton, became his patron. He was invited to the Earl's mansion at
Holme Pierrepont, near Nottingham,[40] where just as his gift was
maturing and his prospects brightening, he died of smallpox. 'Mr.
John Oldham an excellent poett was buried decemb: ye 7th (83)
Humf: Perkins Rect'.[41]

Of his life from 1681 we know little. In the poet's last year,
perhaps in his last fortnight, he wrote the ode to be set to
music by Dr John Blow for St Cecilia's Day 1684; the second of
the annual celebrations inaugurated 22 November 1683. It is in
1681-3, beginning with the 'Imitation' of Horace, that Oldham is
settling into his best vein. 'A Satyr ... dissuading from ...
Poetry', 'A Satyr address'd to a Friend ... about to leave the
University', and the Imitation from Boileau's fifth satire,
'touching Nobility', can hardly be far in date from the Imitations
of Juvenal, Satires XIII and III, and Boileau, Satire VIII, composed in April, May, and October 1682. One would have liked more
biographical information about Oldham's final period, both because it was so fruitful, and because if Dryden had any personal
acquaintance with him it must have been at this time.

2. *The Poems*

In this sketch of Oldham's career as a poet, we have seen him
attempting different genres. Poets of the Restoration were much
concerned with the tone and techniques proper to the genres their
poems belonged to, deviated from, or sought to combine; that is,
with the 'decorum' fitting for each 'kind' of poetry. To assess
Oldham's work fairly and appreciate it fully, we need to look at
it according to its 'kinds' and some of its antecedents. His
short poems on several occasions of grief, congratulation, or
compliment have already been dealt with. Other short pieces are

translations from the classics, most of them amatory, but one of
them bibulous, an Anacreontique successfully emulating Cowley's.
This version of 'The Cup' has not, however, the memorable bril-
liance of Rochester's,[42] whose ear was finer, his imagination
more lyrical, and who, by 'imitating' not translating, gave his
poem a topical air. As a paraphrastic translation Oldham's is
more faithful, while running with the right ease and freedom.
Sharing this quality, his 'Catullus Epigram VII Imitated' is
again indebted to Cowley's Anacreontiques; and again, while retaining its own merit, pales beside the poem of a great lyrist;
for Jonson's 'Kiss me sweet: the wary lover' is inspired by the
same original.[43] But Jonson's 'Dialogue of Horace and Lydia'
shows the disadvantages of his literalism (or 'metaphrase') in
close translation. Neither he nor Herrick captures the graceful-
ness which makes the value of this slight ode in the Latin.
Rightly, Restoration taste would reject Herrick's epithet 'love-
cast-off Lydia' and Jonson's compound 'left-Lydia', such inversion for rhyme as Herrick's

> My heart now set on fire is,

and such phrases as Jonson's

> His arms more acceptable free,

and

> With gentle Calais, Thurine Ornith's son.

Despite a banal couplet,

> Thyrsis by me has done the same,
> The Youth burns me with mutual Flame,

Oldham's version has more 'decorum', and is preferable also to
Flatman's, where the pattern of rhyme lacks facility. This is
not to say that either in the Oldham, or indeed perhaps in the
Latin itself, we can find the fascination which made this lyric
one of the most often translated in the seventeenth century.

Ovid's *Amores*, and the Fragment then ascribed to Petronius, were
favourites too, though not to the same degree. The 'Petronius' is
echoed in Rochester's 'Platonic Lady'; and in Suckling's 'Against
Fruition' on which Oldham drew in amplifying his paraphrase.
Jonson's close version reads admirably, and, as paraphrase, Oldham's reads equally well, with the ready flow prized in such a
genre by Restoration poets. Among the *Amores*, Rochester translated II.ix with concise felicity: Oldham chose lighter pieces
and a lighter style. Not improbably it was Cowley's fantasia,
'The Inconstant', on the theme of II.iv that prompted him to try
a direct rendering. In II.v, he is less elegant and tender than
Sedley, whose narrative moves naturally where Oldham's seems
forced and is sometimes clogged with tasteless ornament. Nevertheless, Oldham's is the more dramatic; he begins and ends with
more sprightliness and vigour: he strives for effect, but sometimes obtains it.

It is not only in anacreontics and the *Amores*, and in the least
mature of the occasional poems, that Oldham shows himself a
disciple of Cowley, who in the earlier years of the Restoration
had more prestige as pioneer and model than any other contemporary or recent English poet. As innumerable conscious and unconscious borrowings testify, Oldham knew 'the beloved Cowley'[44] by
heart. With a very few exceptions, Oldham's poems are either in
the heroic couplet, or are Cowleian Pindariques. The Pindarique
appealed to baroque taste, and offered some escape from the reaction against every sort of 'enthusiasm', including *furor poeticus*', which was consequent upon the Civil War and went with the
new stress on lucidity of expression and plain good sense. Though
the regular structure of Pindar's own odes was recognized in the
earlier and the later imitations of it by Jonson, Congreve, and
Gray, Cowley ignored it. According to Cowley's 'Praise of Pindar',
he is uncircumscribed, in virtue of his unique genius, either by
Nature or by Art, and in the 'Ode. Upon Liberty' he is the type
of liberty itself. From these poems, and from the preface and
notes to the 'Pindarique Odes', we learn what Cowley finds in
him: unexhausted abundance of invention; noble extravagance; an
'enthusiastical' manner, falling boldly from one thing into another with disregard of transition and a readiness to digress; all
matched with an equal bravura in hyperbole, simile, and extended

metaphor that partakes of simile. Similar qualities were seen, by
such Orientalists as John Gregory, in Eastern poetry, and especially in the Hebrew poetry of the Bible. This perception, E.N.
Hooker points out,[45] is significant for Samuel Woodforde's choice
of Cowleian Pindarique for his paraphrases upon Psalms 18, 50,
68, and 104. 'The Psalms of David', writes Cowley, 'I believe to
have been ... the most exalted pieces of *Poesie*'; and again, 'the
manner of the *Prophets* writing, especially of *Isaiah*, seems to me
very like that of *Pindar* ...'.[46] His own sequence of 'Pindarique
Odes', which begins with Imitations of Pindar's Second Olympic
and First Nemean, ends with paraphrases on the 34th chapter of
Isaiah and on the Biblical account of the Plagues of Egypt.

Perhaps it is only in contrast with the rival or complementary
ideal so admirably embodied in the Augustan heroic-couplet styles
at their best that Pindarique verse, as actually written by Cowley and Oldham, can claim the libertarian boldness promised by
its inventor. We are acquainted with styles much bolder than the
Pindarique both in technique and imagination. In their verse,
Pindariques are free in so far as the lengths of stanza and of
line, the disposition of the shorter and longer lines in the
stanza, and the placing of the rhymes, are wholly at the discretion of the poet; the stanza need fall into no regular pattern,
nor is one stanza to repeat the pattern of another. The metre,
however, is consistently iambic. Significantly, too, in the odes
from Pindar Cowley has a note: 'the Connexion of this *Stanza* is
very obscure in the *Greek*, and could not be rendred without much
Paraphrase', and other notes to similar effect.[47] In practice,
that is, sharing the predominant tastes of his time, he supplies
more logical progression than he finds in Pindar, taking away
much of the abruptness that up to a point he admires. Something
like that abruptness does appear with effect in 'The Resurrection', but the odes which have worn best, 'To Mr. Hobs' and 'To
the Royal Society', appeal rather as essays in verse, firm in
structure, on subjects of lasting interest. Cowley was at his
best in the essay, not in metaphysical poetry, where he inherited
an ossifying tradition. For rhetorical heightening and ornamenta-
tion, Cowleian Pindarique is apt to rely on frigid conceits and
too-calculated hyperboles. Together with a prevailing dearth of
verbal music, these overworked conceits and hyperboles (often

trite to begin with) afflict the genre, as it proliferates among
imitators, with a mass of unnaturally inflated but incurably
prosaic verse.

Cowley uses the Pindarique for odes from Latin—from Horace—
as well as Greek; for paraphrases of sacred text; for poems of
moral reflection; for panegyric, in elegy and epithalamium, and
in praise of originators in the arts of civilized life and
thought and culture: Bacon, Harvey, and Hobbes. In each of these
types, Oldham follows him. Specifically, too, 'The Praise of Pindar' suggested 'The Praise of Homer'; and a note to it, on
Pindar's lost dithyrambics and on two odes of Horace that might
have an affinity with them, gave the hint for the 'Dithyrambique
on Drinking'; while 'David's Lamentation' takes up Cowley's intention to have concluded *Davideis* with a version of the same
lament.[48]

In the earliest of Oldham's Pindariques, the elegy on Morwent,
he rises in at least one stanza[49] to the genuinely metaphysical:
the stanza which begins:

> Thy Soul within such silent Pomp did keep,
> As if Humanity were lull'd asleep,
> So gentle was thy Pilgrimage beneath,
> Time's unheard Feet scarce make less noise,
> Or the soft Journey which a Planet goes....

Though most of the comparisons are hackneyed, the rhetoric has
melody, and the style looks back to the earlier and more living
phases of the metaphysical tradition. The success, however, particularly of the lines quoted, is in a vein from which Oldham,
like the age, was moving away: it has no parallel in his subsequent poems. Yet even taking the elegy as a whole, the elaboration of its forty-three stanzas was evidently a labour of love;
the borrowings are sought out from appropriate contexts and well
woven together; and the progress of the poem, as Mr R.I. Mills
has shown, is strongly organized. These merits, as he insists,
may account for Pope's listing it among 'The most Remarkable
Works in this Author'.[50]

The elegy on Atwood and the epithalamium for William and Mary,
with the 'Counterpart to the Satyr against Vertue', are competent

copies of verses, suited to their occasion. Among such things if
they are a little above average, it is in virtue of Oldham's
attention to structure, seen already on the larger scale of the
Morwent ode. In the Atwood poem, for instance, he begins with two
paradoxes concerning virtue: its mortality, and its exemplifica-
tion in the person of a lawyer. Throughout, he continues to
alternate topics which might serve in a hundred panegyrics, with
topics particular to Atwood himself: his justice, his generous
benefactions, and his piety, free from acrimonious party zeal.
He concludes, conventionally, with Atwood's reception into Heaven,
but accommodates his state of bliss to his profession, as 'the
calm ... Vacation of Eternity'. This wit may seem incongruous,
but was a decoration acceptable to baroque taste. The Atwood
elegy, and more directly the palinode or 'Counterpart' to the
'Satyr Against Vertue' ('Aude aliquid. Ode'), are poems of moral
reflection: in this, and as another competent copy of verses, the
paraphrase of Aristotle's ode upon Honour can be grouped with
them.

    The three 'sacred Odes' may be considered the weakest of Old-
ham's Pindariques. In 'David's Lamentation' and Psalm CXXXVII,
amplification, which is all that he has to contribute, drowns
the pathos of both originals and turns the fierce hatred at the
end of the Psalm into a display of 'horrid' writing. If we allow
that the original passion might be sacrificed for a different
sort of effect, we are still disappointed by the mediocrity of
the *amplificatio* itself, which employs with too little address
the stock procedures of the school or college theme. This fault,
making the poem too much of an academic exercise, extends also to
the 'Hymn of St. Ambrose'. But since the original of that (the
Te Deum) was already a public and declamatory poem, the *amplificatio* is at least not out of keeping. The 'Hymn' is more sound-
ing than the two paraphrases from Scripture, and the rhetoric is
enlivened here and there: now by a Lucretian tag—'the eternal
flaming Jail', now by a Miltonic phrase—'the bright Realms of
everlasting day'; now by baroque conceits—'an Angel-Laureat',
the Prophets as 'Envoys extraordinary'; now by the quasi-
dramatization of the Day of Wrath.

    'The Praise of Homer' and the ode on Jonson owe part of their
interest to their place in a tradition comprising two related

'kinds' of poetry. The first—to which, as I briefly indicated,
the 'Homer' and 'Jonson' directly belong—eulogizes some original
contributor to human culture, and is exemplified by Horace and
Cowley on Pindar, and Cowley on Hobbes. The second sketches the
progress of some art or craft, as, on the hint of Virgil in his
first Georgic,[51] Dryden in *Annus Mirabilis* takes occasion to
sketch the progress of navigation. This 'kind' was to culminate
in Gray's 'Progress of Poesy'. The two are combined in Cowley's
'Ode To the Royal Society', which includes a 'praise of Bacon'
within its 'progress of philosophy'; Gray's ode, also, mounts to
its great eulogies of Shakespeare, Milton, and Dryden. And though
Oldham is writing panegyrics, not 'progress poems', at the start
he hails each hero as a founder: Jonson is the 'mighty *Founder*
of our Stage'; Homer 'the unexhausted Ocean, whence / Spring
first, and still do flow th'eternal Rills of sence'. Both these
odes of Oldham's are constructed by using the recognized compo-
nents of an academically-elaborated theme, from *exordium* to *con-
clusio*; but in each ode he moves freely between *narratio, confirmatio*, and *confutatio*, so that the sequence, though firmly
controlled, is not too stereotyped.[52] In the 'Jonson', narration
of the dramatist's achievement predominates; but in stanza 3 Oldham confutes the 'meer ... Enthusiasts' who contemn the conscious
artist, and in stanzas 9 and 10 those who charge Jonson with
plagiarism and hold his slowness in composition to be a defect.
That it was not so, is confirmed by comparison with the procedure
of great painters and of God in creating the Universe. The favourite baroque analogy with the Deity is employed also in the *exordium* of 'The Praise of Homer'. Homer's descriptive power is
'narrated' in stanza 2 and the inspiring prowess of his hero,
Achilles, in stanza 3; but his greatness is affirmed chiefly by
confirmatio: by what the *Iliad* meant to Alexander; by the con-
sensus of nations and the universal currency of Homer's classical
Greek in contrast with the English poets' vernacular; and by his
power to confer a fame more lasting than any statue or royal
palace. Following the *exordium*, Oldham confutes the tradition of
Homer's blindness; and he begins the conclusion with another *confutatio*: Caligula's design of burning Homer's works only showed
his own insanity. They are imperishable, until the general conflagration at Doomsday. Thus the poem is made to end as it began,

with theological imagery. The same technique is used in concluding the Jonson ode: the image of travel transcending former
limits, applied in the *exordium* to Jonson's dramatic art, is now
applied to his more than solar glory. 'The Praise of Homer' is
diversified by a profusion of rhetorical figures: parallel phrasing; the supposed vision; apostrophe, apologia, paradox, rhetorical question, carefully-chosen epithet, periphrasis, allusion,
and analogy. The 'Jonson' has its share of these, and both odes
feature the topical conceit, as in the comparisons with contemporary finance, foreign trade, and religious extremists. Metaphor so deliberately extended that in effect it resembles simile
appears several times in the 'Homer'; but in the 'Jonson' each
stanza depends upon one or upon two such metaphors; the recur-
rence of this one figure strengthens the unity of the piece.[53]
The workmanship of the 'Homer' extorts a certain admiration; but
the 'invention' (or finding of material) draws mainly on commonplaces, and the qualities which for us give his epics their
greatness are barely touched on. The 'Jonson' is much more interesting. Its topics again were commonplaces, most of them treated
in *Jonsonus Virbius*; but Oldham has marshalled them in a verse-
essay coherently summing-up admiration of Jonson as it stood in
1678.[54]

Two Pindariques begin Oldham's career as a satirist. 'Aude
aliquid. Ode' ['A Satyr Against Vertue'] and 'A Dithyrambique
on Drinking' again belong to a recognized 'kind' of composition:
the ironic celebration of something which without irony would be
denounced or scorned; or conversely the vituperation of something
which without irony would be eulogized. The main line of the
tradition, from ancient Greek and Roman times, has been very
fully traced by H.K. Miller in his article, 'The Paradoxical Encomium with special reference to its vogue in England from 1600
to 1800'.[55] If Erasmus, in *Encomium Moriae*, might praise Folly in
prose, with all the more licence a poet might denigrate virtue
and incorporate in his *vituperatio* an encomium on vice, employing an ostensibly grand Pindarique as his vehicle. Cowley had not
turned the Pindarique to the purpose of satiric irony; Oldham's
distinguished predecessor there was Samuel Butler in his 'Pindarick Ode' 'To the Memory of the Most Renowned Du Vall' (a
notorious highwayman), published, as by the author of *Hudibras*,

in 1671, the year following its 'hero's' execution. Oldham, at
twenty-three, falls short of Butler.[56] Beside Butler's his irony
shows laboured and too often obvious, and still more so perhaps
when compared (as D.H. Vieth compares it) with Rochester's in
'A Very Heroical Epistle to Ephelia'.[57] In the comparison with
Rochester, some allowance is to be made for difference of genre:
lightness of touch is more requisite in an epistle, 'heroical'
though it may be, than in an ostensible Pindarique. As in Pindarique eulogy, Oldham has a theme to amplify, and amplifies it
by the stock rhetorical methods. The pedantry noted by Vieth
comes then, in part, from the genre in which Oldham is writing;
yet not wholly, since Butler can write his comparable Pindarique
without it. Butler's satire, too, is complex and varied in its
topical application: Oldham's topic of virtue and its opposite is
conceived for the most part in such general terms as to constitute only the tritest of subjects. For Restoration amateurs of
the paradox this would detract little from his performance: the
wit they looked for was there in the sophistical attack on the
impregnable and defence of the indefensible. This scholastic
shadow-boxing, however, is not all that the poem amounts to. It
is 'suppos'd to be spoken' by Rochester at the height of one of
his more outrageous exploits, and is best when it best lives up
to this pretence, satirizing attitudes that were genuinely part
of the libertine tradition,[58] and caricaturing sentiments which
(as we know from his conversations with Burnet and from elsewhere) the Earl might indeed have uttered: for instance, the
appeal from morals to Nature, since virtue is 'too difficult for
Flesh and Blood', and the pride in an immoralism elegant, 'studied
and elaborate'. Rochester, for a time, fostered his own legend,
in the tone of his quip to Henry Savile, adjuring him to send wine
'as ever thou dost hope to out-do Machiavel or equal me';[59] and
Oldham caught the spirit of it. Vieth rightly claims that he 'succeeds where all other satirists failed: he endows [his] mythic
image of Rochester with some of the stature the man possessed in
real life'.[60]

There is too much inclination, these days, to see ambivalence
everywhere; but ambivalent Oldham's response to Rochester and his
circle certainly was. Before he became a peripheral member of it,
he had reprobrated, in the elegy on Morwent, 'Gallants' whose

'Talent is to ... act some fine Transgression with a janty Meen',
a censure which the irony of 'A Satyr Against Vertue' (alias
'Aude aliquid. Ode') develops. Six months after writing the
'Satyr', he condemns, in commemorating Atwood, the 'Men of Sence',
or sensual men purporting to be rationalists, who 'by little
Railleries' try to make religion a thing of no account. In the
'Apology' for the 'Satyr' he has a fling at 'damn'd Placket-
Rhimes, such as our Nobles write'.[61] Two draft fragments charac-
terize Rochester as 'our witty bawdy Peer' and 'our great witty
bawdy Peer'; the second probably gives the best measure of Oldham's ambivalent appreciation.[62] Though, on being sought out by
Rochester, admiration of his genius, no less than ambition, grateful pride at the recognition of his own talent, and love of social
pleasure, must have encouraged his pursuit of the acquaintance,
he had his revulsions against 'the merry gang' and the means by
which he recommended himself to it. Addressing an old college
friend, on 22 June 1677 he writes: 'There is not an arranter fool
in nature than a rash unguarded unconsidering Sinner', and applies
the phrase to himself as he has 'formerly' been.[63] It appears also
in his unfortunately undateable 'Sunday Thought in Sickness': 'How
oft have I triumph'd in my ... seared insensibility?... Oh the
gnawing Remorse of a rash unguarded unconsidering Sinner!... How
have I abus'd and misemployed those Parts and Talents ... which
I have made the Patrons of Debauchery, and Pimps and Panders to
Vice'[64]—strictures not inapplicable to the obscene 'Sardanapalus'
and 'Upon the Author of the Play called Sodom', though only in
recoil into a mood of excessive religious penitence could he
think them warranted, as possibly he did, by 'A Satyr Against
Vertue' and 'A Dithyrambique on Drinking'.

   The 'present well-grounded inclinations' which, rather tremu-
lously for fear of ridicule, he 'whispers' to his old college
friend,[65] did not withhold him from composing the 'Dithyrambique'
six weeks later. 'Suppos'd to be spoken by Rochester at the Guinny-
Club', it sustains the image of him created in 'A Satyr Against
Vertue', magnifying him in a role he was to acknowledge (to Burnet) he had fallen into: 'the natural heate of his fancy, being
inflamed by Wine, made him so extravagantly pleasant, that many
to be more diverted by that humor, studied to engage him deeper
and deeper in Intemperance'.[66] In its truth to this vein of

extravagant fancy, the 'Dithyrambique' is genuinely amusing, and
though I admit it has less range than its predecessor, I confess
I read it with more pleasure. And while the libertine outlook
offers a worthwhile target at certain periods and in certain
circles (of which Rochester's was one)[67] the false glory of in-
toxication, by whatever drug, is more widely and constantly in
need of reduction to absurdity. One can see, though, why it was
the 'Satyr Against Vertue' that Pope listed among the 'most
Remarkable Works in this Author'.[68]

If the 'Dithyrambique' was read out where it was 'Suppos'd to
be spoken', so too, one imagines, was 'Sardanapalus'.[69] It completed Oldham's trio of mock-heroic Pindariques which invest
with ironic glamour the triple cult of the unregenerate Rochester
and his convivial associates. Libertine ethics is the subject of
'A Satyr Against Vertue', in which the 'great Rule of Sense' extends its blessing to the pleasures of 'Wine and Company', and
to 'everlasting whoring' as practised by Jove himself. In the
'Dithyrambique', 'Dionysiac' drinking, social and rhetorical, is
backhandedly glorified; and the grand archetype of promiscuous
sexual gratification is the hero or anti-hero of 'Sardanapalus'.
In such a poem, it was decorum to be indecorous. The obscenity
is made hyperbolical and in its own way artistic by the building
up of the structure and the deployment of tabooed along with
heroical vocabulary; just before the end of stanza 1 the poet
seems to be winning a wager on the number of successive lines in
which he can repeat 'c—t'. Seven side-notes, referring to learned
sources, heighten the mock-heroic effect.[70] The name of Sardanapalus, belonging to the most notorious of effete monarchs, was
also one of the nicknames satirically bestowed on Charles II. The
poem is not a sustained satire on Charles, but some implied parallels in stanzas 2 and 4 were bound to be relished by Rochester
and 'the merry gang'; sexual conquest, however, not Charles, is
the focal subject.[71] As in the other poems of the trio, an object
of their cult is being satirized throughout, but also magnified
in a vein of comic exaggeration which they could enjoy as paying
a sort of tribute to it. The tone is not wholly remote from the
'joshing' which went on among them, as in the lampoon on Rochester, probably by Dorset, 'I rise at Eleven', and from the wry
glorification of their life-style sometimes to be found in

Rochester himself.[72]

Tribute to the cult is paid once more, but now through satire
of a pretender by whom, if he were not repudiated, it would be
brought into disrepute, in the invective against the author of
'Sodom'. Here the particular brand of obscenity, disgusting in
imagery and diction, is adopted as proper for denouncing his.
For he is 'all over Devil, but in wit'; wicked with that ill
grace which in the 'Satyr Against Vertue' banishes 'dull unbred
Fools' from the élite fellowship of true antinomian gallants.
Like 'Sardanapalus', *their* pornography, it is implied, is 'studied
and elab'rate', above all witty—acceptable, in short, as creative
art.[73]

After Rochester's death (26 July 1680), Oldham, in his pastoral
elegy—a version of Moschus' *Bion*—claimed discipleship.

> If I am reckon'd not unblest in Song,
> 'Tis what I ow to thy all-teaching tongue. (191 f.).

Reading Oldham, I have never found the lessons easy to trace:
there is no sign of the sort of indebtedness he has to Cowley.
Though 'The Careless Good Fellow' was probably inspired in rhythm
and temper by the first stanza of 'Too long the wise Commons have
been in debate',[74] no poem of Oldham's is like a poem of Rochester's. He transcribed 'A Letter from Artemiza', but the complex-
ity of its satire was foreign to his own talent; and in technical
detail Rochester's art was commonly too subtle to be of much
benefit to Oldham's; though doubtless Oldham profited from his
handling in satire of inset colloquial speech and brief dramatic
scenes. Of Rochester's metaphysical cast of mind Oldham had
nothing. When in 'A Satyr against Mankind', which again Oldham
transcribed,[75] Rochester wrote his variations on a theme of
Boileau, he made them a vehicle of his own metaphysic: when Oldham 'Imitated' the same original, he communicated Boileau's point
of view, but without committing himself to it otherwise than as
translator, and within the confines of that poem. Nevertheless,
we shall find in Oldham several characteristics in respect of
which in the history of Restoration satire he and Rochester go
together.

One, when urbanity was more and more coming to be demanded of

the satirist, is their display of satiric spleen. To Burnet,
Rochester contended that 'without resentments' the satirist
'could not write with life'; and Raman Selden notes how his practice, too, shows his 'strong affinities' with the Elizabethan
doctrine: the satirist's wrath is to issue in ruggedness of
style: 'no-one', Oldham insists, 'that pretends to distinguish
the several Colours of Poetry' would expect smoothness from
Juvenal 'when he is lashing of Vice, and Villany'. The conviction
is native to Oldham's temperament and suited to his gifts, not
implanted by Rochester: yet a master is not least helpful when
he marshals a man the way that he was going.[76]

The directest form for the utterance of satiric spleen is that
of the lines on 'Sodom', or the curse with which Rochester concludes 'A Ramble in St James's Park'.[77] They belong to a genre
Puttenham calls *dirae*: 'a maner of imprecation', he writes, 'such
as Ovide [made] against Ibis',[78] the 'kind' by which, the story
went, Archilochus drove Lycambes and his daughters to suicide.
Oldham has two more *dirae*: 'Upon a Woman', his first satire in
the heroic couplet, and 'Upon a Bookseller' (or 'Printer'). Apart
from the verse-form, their interest lies chiefly in his pungent
topical allusions, and his avowal, made also in the 'Apology'
appended to the 'Satyr Against Vertue', of a vocation as satirist.

> Had he a Genius, and Poetique Rage,
> Great as the Vices of this guilty Age ...
> To noble Satyr he'd direct his Aim,

he declares in the 'Apology' (63 f., 67). The times invite satire:
and satire, he has begun to recognize, is his talent, the art in
which he can shine. The bookseller was rash to provoke a poet who
is not only

> Born to chastise the Vices of the Age, (14)

but who seeks occasion for satire

> To shew my Parts, and signalize my Muse. (20).

It was 'noble' satire that he aspired to write: what Dryden,

distinguishing Boileau's *Lutrin* from Scarron's 'travestie' of
Virgil, and his own *MacFlecknoe* or *Absalom* from Butler's burlesque
Hudibras, calls 'manly' satire. The epithets designate a genre
partaking of the grandeur of 'heroic poetry itself', of which
(Dryden claims) 'the satire is undoubtedly a species'.[79]

The first approach to this ideal was the mock-heroic. In October 1678 Oldham began a translation of *Le Lutrin* ('The Desk'),
the earliest testimony of his lasting admiration for Boileau,
caught, it may be, from Rochester, Boileau being one of the Earl's
two favourite poets.[80] Having completed Canto I in a style as
lively as the original, if less polished, in Canto II Oldham
broke off after the opening couplet. He acquired a transcript of
the pseudo-Denham's 'Second' and 'Third Advice to a Painter':
chronicle-satire in that mode was akin to the mock-heroic. He
himself made a transcript of the finest mock-heroic satire of all,
Dryden's *MacFlecknoe*, heading it, whether as the date of tran-
scription or as that given in his exemplar, 'A° 1678'.[81] Seeking
models of heightened style, he was an attentive reader of heroic
plays: ten, by Dryden, Lee, Otway, and Settle, are cited, either
in quotation or by precise reference, in his drafts for the
'Satyrs upon the Jesuits'.[82] Thus, when the subject for those
'Satyrs' presented itself, he had behind him a preparation which
enabled him to aim beyond the mock-heroic. An established form
was to be chosen for the first 'Satyr', and Oldham made two false
starts. An 'Advice to a Painter' did not get further than a few
lines. But 'The Vision', a Dream-vision of Hell, is of great
interest from its indebtedness to Phineas Fletcher's *The Locusts*,
a narrative satire of a grave and lofty kind, and to two epics,
Davideis and *Paradise Lost*.[83]

For satire could be taken beyond the mock-heroic and brought
yet closer to epic. This was to be Dryden's achievement in *Absalom*, where without forgoing the 'fine raillery' he admired in
Horace, he combined his venom in greater earnest with the 'majesty'
he found in Juvenal.[84] Towards that ideal Oldham in the 'Satyrs
upon the Jesuits' made certain advances upon *MacFlecknoe*—which
is not to pretend they can compete with it as a work of art. No
doubt it was in terms of this shared ideal of heroical satire
that Dryden, characteristically generous, could write of the
younger poet,

> To the same Goal did both our Studies drive,
> The last set out the soonest did arrive.

Oldham anticipated Dryden in taking for his subject a threat to
the nation, on the occasion of a national crisis, and treating it
with an elevation of style which is not (as in mock-heroic)
assumed in order to be laughed at. His prime model was Juvenal,
accepted as the classic master in whose satires grandeur, venom,
and a harsh vehemence were combined.[85] His allegiance was proclaimed in the very first phrase, which recalls Juvenal's: 'For
who can longer hold?' (Prologue, line 1), corresponds to 'Semper
ego auditor tantum?' (Satire I.1.1), where Juvenal, like Oldham,
begins to announce his satiric programme. A little later, the
allegiance is signalized again; Oldham's readers could be trusted
to recognize in 'indignation can create a muse' the rendering of
'Facit indignatio versum' (line 79).

Like Juvenal's, the style is everywhere heightened by rhetorical
means. Anaphora, as in 'Worthy to undertake, worthy a Plot / Like
This', or when lines or couplets are introduced, in parallel, with
repeated 'How ...' or 'Sooner ...' is no less a favourite with
Oldham than with his master. Both employ the rhetorical formula
which by a comparison to other unreckonables declares the impossibility of enumerating what he is speaking of. Another formula
of impossibilities found in these satires, as in Juvenal's, is
the list of irreconcilable contradictions.[86] Juvenalian tropes
abound: exclamation, question, apostrophe, antithesis. All, but
especially hyperbole and hyperbolical accumulation, help to
create the heroical style which for both poets is the principal
vehicle of the satire. In the 'Satyrs upon the Jesuits', oxymoron
is particularly frequent, matching the mode of 'Garnet's Ghost'
and 'Loyola's Will', where, as in 'A Satyr Against Vertue', the
reader's norms are the reverse of the spokesman's. In such
phrases as 'manly cruelty', 'sneaking modesty', one of the terms
expresses the Jesuits' perverse approval or disapproval, the
other the reader's rightminded valuation. In 'Satyr II', used by
the poet in his own person—'snivelling Hero', 'holy impudence'
—the figure is bitterly ironical.[87]

What Dryden says of Juvenal may be said of Oldham: 'he took
the method which was prescribed him by his own genius, which was

sharp and eager; he could not rally, but he could declaim'. In
the first three 'Satyrs', the monotonous gloomy hyperbole, like
Nat Lee's, creates an aesthetic effect; the grandiose declamation
animates an unnaturally imagined world of evil. That world is
conjured up partly by employing as spokesmen *personae* that belong
to it; and this is a means by which Oldham extends, as Raman
Selden has observed he does, 'the resources of the Juvenalian
voice'.[88]

Satyr II is in that voice: it is an invective uttered without
fiction by the poet himself. In 'Garnet's Ghost' (I) and 'Loyola's
Will' (III), the resources are enlarged by refraction: the satire
is conveyed in the two Jesuits' speeches, which incriminate themselves, and with them the assemblies they address. The self-
incriminating monologue had both a highly reputable ancestry in
serious literature, and currency at the popular level, and the
same was true of the forms into which Oldham cast Satyr I, the
Supposed Ghost; III, The Last Will and Testament or Dying Charge;
and IV, the Speech of an Inanimate Object.[89] Comparison with the
directions to a Painter—the pseudo-Denham's, or even Marvell's
'Last Instructions'—brings out how much these 'Satyrs' gain
from their formal unity of design: both from each being cast in
a stricter established form, and from the care taken with its
structure. Paragraph follows naturally in the wake of paragraph.
How to take care of the connections between them was something
Oldham studied in Juvenal. Among his drafts he has a note:
'Transitions Juven. S.6.', with references to fourteen places in
the sixth satire, in twelve of which editors begin new paragraphs.[90] Except for 'Loyola's Will', each 'Satyr' (and the Prologue likewise) is brought to a climax at the end by some variety,
dira-style, of threat or imprecation: 'Loyola's Will' goes beyond
threat as the fiends seize upon his soul.

The series, too, has a pattern, of calculated variation from
component part to part.[91] Satyr II returns to the poet's voice
as heard in the Prologue, except that then it was prologuizing.
Against these one may group I, III, and IV as the monologues of
personae. But where in 'Garnet's Ghost' the incrimination is entrusted wholly to the monologue itself, in 'Loyola's Will' the
true perspective is further ensured by brief narrative at the
opening and close. The monologue of 'Ignatius his Image' does

not incriminate the speaker. Like its predecessors, the Image
speaks from behind the Jesuit scenes; but it is not implicated
(except as a lay-figure) in the Jesuits' campaign: it is an un-
suspected eavesdropper, happy to blow the gaff on their malprac-
tices. Satyr IV, like I and III, is in the voice of a *persona*;
but as with II and the Prologue, the voice is a directly hostile
one: these affinities help to draw the series together at the
conclusion. Yet Satyr IV is also in contrast with the others, and
the differences are refreshing. All three *personae* are puppets:
'Garnet' and 'Loyola', unlike Dryden's MacFlecknoe or Zimri, are
not caricatures of the real men, and though the convention is
acceptable, the Image, being confessedly a puppet, has a particular aptness in that role. As objects of the satire, black vil-
lainies now give place to chicanery, superstition, and mumbo-
jumbo, topics on which our reservations are not provoked as they
are by some of the earlier onslaughts. The tone, in keeping,
moves in the direction of satiric comedy, so that this 'Satyr'
is entertaining in a way the others are not. Pope singles it out
from the rest as one of 'the most Remarkable Works in this
Author'.

   The content of the 'Satyrs' was neither narrowly limited nor
altogether lacking in genuine substance. Had it been confined to
the plot as described by Oates, it would have been both; but that
occupies a remarkably small space. Two pungent paragraphs to
launch Satyr I; a passage breathing conflagration and massacre
near the end of it, and in Satyr II the attack on the dying vows
of the Five Jesuits, are all that concern the Plot directly. The
Jesuit Order, the chief subject of the satire, is set in the context of everything which Protestants most condemned in the Church
of Rome: the doctrine of transubstantiation; idolatry in the Mass,
and in the cults of the Virgin and the Saints; veneration of
relics, and other superstitious practices; and the commercializa-
tion of sin (on which Catholics like Chaucer and Langland had had
their say). To the devout believer in the divine right of Kings,
the claims to Papal supremacy and a deposing power, of which the
Jesuits were the most vigorous champions, were peculiarly obnoxious—hence the animus against their additional fourth vow, of
obedience to the Pope. It is (primarily) as the shock-troops of
the Counter-Reformation that Oldham, like Phineas Fletcher,

denounces them. A doctrine of tyrannicide, the assassination of
heretic rulers, had been promulgated by Mariana, and where the
heretic could be regarded as lacking title, by other leading
Jesuit casuists.[92] Actual assassins, or so it was believed, had
enjoyed Jesuit blessing. In the Jesuit campaign, confession was
a powerful weapon, and calumny in their eyes a legitimate one.
Their missions, limitless in true devotion and courage, were seen
by Protestants as the spreading of a false faith and of Papal influence, and acquired, as the Society came to be active in commerce, the imputation of worldly motives. Next to their anti-
Protestant crusade, worldly or wicked default in religion or
morality is what Oldham lays to their charge. As the besetting
sin of a celibate priesthood, lechery was the age-old topic of
anti-clerical satire. In Oldham's day, the Society was, by and
large, in self-indulgent decline,[93] and had become the apologist
of a lax morality. The indictment against Jesuit casuists and
confessors for relaxing Christian ethics to attract proselytes
had been pressed home by Pascal.[94] Quite improperly, however,
Oldham treats this development, and that of commercial motives,
as inherent in the Society from the start.

In concentrating upon the bad principles attributed to the
Papists, and the historical crimes for which those principles
were held responsible; in combining anti-clerical, anti-Papal
charges as old as the Reformation or older, with others drawn
from the worst excesses of Jesuitism at the height of the Counter-
Reformation crusade and from the Order's worst weaknesses in days
of decline, Oldham provides a conspectus of the English anti-
Catholic tradition[95] as it was reflected in the mind of one
patriot and monarchist, Anglican but of Presbyterian antecedents.

The historical, no less than the doctrinal emphasis is typical
of the terms in which current religious and political controversy
were frequently conducted. The history of the Counter-Reformation
was fearsome enough, and Oldham did not fail to dwell upon the
Marian persecutions, the Armada, Gunpowder Plot, and the Irish
massacre (1640), with, in the Low Countries and France, Alva's
Council of Blood, St Bartholomew's day, and the assassinations
of Henry III and Henry IV. Elizabeth, her sea-dogs, and the
arrest of Guy Fawkes were already part of the national legend,
yet still belonged to local and family tradition. Sir Nicholas

Carew was a great-nephew of Raleigh's; on the top of a marble
table in his summer-house was painted 'the Spanish Invasion in
1588'. Howard, who commanded the fleet against it, lay buried in
the Reigate church where Thurland worshipped. Baptist Hickes,
ancestor of Sir William, a later patron with whose kinsfolk
Oldham was early acquainted, had been foreman of the jury which
convicted Garnet.[96] Nor could the satirist be accused of assail-
ing what was now a mere phantom. France, land of Popery and arbitrary government, had succeeded Spain, it seemed, as the power
aiming at 'Universal Monarchy';[97] and Huguenots were crossing to
England to escape 'increasing molestation'.[98] Though under the
Secret Treaty of Dover Charles cannot seriously have thought of
going beyond toleration for Catholics, Louis had looked to his
re-establishing Catholicism, by force if need be, the policy
favoured by James, who during the Exclusion crisis in 1679-81
urged his brother to assert the prerogatives of the crown with
the aid of the fleet, the guards, the garrisons, and forces from
Scotland and Ireland.[99] Who could say that the Counter-Reformation
was a spent force when James's Catholicizing reign, and the Revo-
cation of the Edict of Nantes which turned the trickle of Huguenot
refugees into a flood, were casting their shadows before?

   Yet, written 'upon occasion of the Plot' (however limited the
attention the Plot receives), the 'Satyrs upon the Jesuits' had
its origin in a paroxysm of ignorant, savage terror; and this is
one of the factors detracting from its status among Restoration
—and English—satires. The grounds of the Popish Terror, compared with the Exclusion crisis, the occasion and subject of
Absalom, were unreal. Furthermore, on the route to heroic satire,
Oldham had pioneered only part-way. Dryden, raising chronicle-
satire to the epic plane, was to furnish the indispensable 'series
of action',[100] for which Oldham has no equivalent, though his Garnet and Loyola do speak in situations which might belong to a
heroic poem. *MacFlecknoe*, as a personal attack, cannot escape the
category of lampoon;[101] *Absalom*, taking up its satirical portraits
into an epic catalogue of the forces, rises clear of it; and Oldham too, whose 'Satyrs' were of a generalizing not a personal
kind, had, in them, left it aside. But what the quality of his
animus gains from being without the personal rancour of lampoon,
it loses from a bigotry which in the first three 'Satyrs' is quite

unrelieved. His style, when it emulates the elevation of Juvenal,
resembles that of the rants which his drafts show him picking
out from the heroic drama; rants for the most part factitious in
their heroics. A satiric gambit, with him as with Juvenal, is the
drop into demeaning expressions; sometimes with a Juvenalian
puncturing effect, as when the sequence 'holy Banners', 'Flags',
'hallowed Swords and Daggers', culminates in 'consecrated Ratsbane'. But he is far more foul-mouthed than Juvenal. Though much
of his demeaning diction comes from the commercial and plebeian
worlds, half as much again is from the sordid underworld of
criminals, charlatans, whores, gamesters, drinkers, and debtors,
and from repulsive bodily functions and diseases. In the heroic
satire of *Absalom* such diction would be unthinkable; and there
indeed the pejorative vocabulary never ranges so low as it can
in Juvenal, let alone Oldham. Oldham's is part of the violence in
which he is akin to that Juvenal of whom Dryden wrote, approv-
ingly, 'his spleen is raised, and he raises mine';[102] and perhaps,
after all, the comparison with Juvenal is fairer than with the
ideal of heroic satire. But in the violence of the 'Satyrs upon
the Jesuits', especially the first, second, and third, he is
Juvenalian to a fault.

'Oldham has strong rage' was Pope's verdict, 'but 'tis too
much like Billingsgate'.[103] Not improbably Dryden's friend Mulgrave had Oldham in mind when he wrote in 1682:

> Some think if sharp enough, they cannot fail
> As if their only business was to rail:
> Rage you must hide, and prejudice lay down,
> A Satyr's smile is sharper than his frown.

The theory of harshness in satire, which Oldham perpetuated, is
rebuked:

> Of well-chose words some take not care enough
> And think they may be, as the subject, rough.
> This great work must be more exactly made
> And sharpest thoughts in smoothest words conveyed.[104]

In the Advertisement to *Some New Pieces*, 1681, Oldham responds

to 'a report that some persons found fault with the roughness of
my Satyrs formerly publisht'. The attack by Sir William Soame
has every appearance of being written while Oldham was still
usher at Croydon: it would in any case have been impossible after
his version of the *Ars Poetica* had appeared in *Some New Pieces*.
It is addressed 'To the Author of Sardanapalus upon that, & his
other Writeings':

> Tho teaching thy peculiar Bus'ness be
> Learn this one Lesson, (School-master) of me,
> Where ere Sence fails, the best Descriptions Vile,
> And a rough Verse, the noblest Thought will spoil;
> Think it not Genius, to know how to scan,
> Nor great to Shew a Monster for a Man;
> Wound not the Ear, with ill turn'd Prose in Rhyme,
> Nor mistake furious Fustian for Sublime.
> Beleive this Truth, & thy vain Rumbling quit,
> What is not Reason, never can be Wit.
> From the Boys hands, take Horace into Thine,
> And thy rude Satyrs, by his Rules, refine.
> See thy gross Faults in Boileau's faithfull glass,
> And get the Sence to know thy Self an Ass.[105]

To such censure—probably indeed to these actual lines—Oldham's response was twofold. On the one hand he made and published
his version of the *Ars Poetica*—'a Task impos'd upon me'—acknowledging himself 'in some measure recompenc'd for my pains by the
advantage ... of fixing these admirable Rules of Sense so well in
my memory'. But he accompanied this soft answer (if that is what
it is) by a fighting self-justification, claiming, with justice,
that his vocabulary *was* carefully chosen: 'I confess, I did not
so much mind the Cadence, as the Sense and expressiveness of my
words, and therefore chose not those which were best dispos'd to
placing themselves in Rhyme, but rather the most keen, and tuant',
according, he contends, to satiric decorum as exemplified by
Juvenal. Youth-like, he was reluctant to accept a limitation in
his potentialities, and despite his former dedication of himself
to satire—

>   ... my only Province and delight
>   For whose dear sake alone I've vow'd to write,

resisted the idea that he was not gifted for more harmonious
poetry. 'To shew that way I took', when writing satire, had been
'out of choice', and that he could compass a far different style,
he made versions of two pastoral elegies, from Bion and Moschus,
'some of the softest and tenderest of all antiquity'. He had
translated, likewise, the Passion of Byblis, from the *Metamorphoses*, in emulation of *Ovid's Epistles*, 1680. Practised in teaching
translation with good heed to 'decorum' of vocabulary, he had
small trouble in changing from his hoard of 'tuant' words to his
hoard of 'soft' ones; but that did not re-tune his verse, or alter
his addiction to imperfect rhymes. 'Byblis' he confessed a
failure, though 'now tis done, he is loath to burn it'.[106] 'Delicacy and a good ear', Dennis was to pronounce, 'none but blockheads can grant him', though 'wit and genius none can deny
him'.[107] Magnanimously, Dryden absolved the youthful satirist:
'Wit', he declares, 'will shine

>   Through the harsh cadence of a rugged line.
>   A noble Error, and but seldom made,
>   When Poets are by too much force betray'd.[108]

In our literature, 'Oldham was the last major satirist to cultivate successfully the cankered muse'.[109] Both his achievements
in that style, and the faults of it censured by Pope, Soame, and
the rest, culminate in the 'Satyrs upon the Jesuits', his best-
known and most ambitious work, but not his best. It is to this
first period of his as a satirist that the censures principally
apply. The subsequent satires are much less violent, a change
attributable to two developments: besides the response to Horace,
Oldham's discovery of 'Imitation' as a form especially suited to
his gifts.
    As early as 'Ignatius His Image' he went to Horace for the
originating hint, and furthermore, in content and tone moved in
a Horatian direction from what was still the basically Juvenalian
cast of the satire.[110] This initiates something like a Horatian
phase in his work. He writes versions not only of the *Ars Poetica*,

but the satire (I.ix) on 'The Impertinent', and two of the
Odes.[111] All are 'Imitations': that is, the Roman allusions are
altered to English ones such as Oldham might have made in an
original poem, so that the Latin poet is given the air of writing
in the times and circumstances of his translator or adapter.[112]
Oldham knew the form as practised by Cowley, Sprat, Boileau, and
Rochester, and the theory as formulated by Cowley. He had pon-
dered the objection to it taken by Dryden in discussing the
principles of translation in the preface to *Ovid's Epistles*,
1680, for the type of Imitation he decides on is calculated to
meet that objection. Dryden had written, of Cowley's and Denham's theory,

> I take imitation of an author, in their sense, to be an endeavour of a later
> poet to write like one who has written before him, on the same subject; that
> is, not to translate his words, or to be confined to his sense, but only ...
> to write as he supposes that author would have done, had he lived in our age,
> and in our country.... To add or to diminish what we please ... ought only to
> be granted to Mr. Cowley, and that too only in his translation of Pindar ...
> but if ... any regular intelligible authors be thus used, tis no longer to be
> called their work (;) ... he who is inquisitive to know an author's thoughts
> will be disappointed of his expectation.... [I]t would be unreasonable to
> limit a translator to the narrow compass of his author's words: 'tis enough
> if he choose out some expression which does not vitiate the sense. I suppose
> he may stretch his chain to such a latitude; but by innovation of thoughts,
> methinks he breaks it.[113]

Oldham resolved to abjure the claim to add and to diminish what
he pleased. To secure the essential advantages of Imitation—the
freshness and immediacy, the scope for self-expression—he need
not do more than 'alter the scene from *Rome* to *London*, and ...
make use of *English* names of Men, Places, and Customs'. By taking
no other liberties, he would give his readers an adequate reflection of his author's thoughts. Of his Imitation of the *Ars Poetica*
he says 'I have not ... been over-nice in keeping to the words of
the original.... Nevertheless, I have been religiously strict to
its sense.'[114] This last phrase is somewhat too strong: but it
represents the principle of his method, still discernible even in
subsequent Imitations which are not altogether so faithful.[115]

His earliest essay in the genre was probably the refashioning of Moschus' 'Bion' into an elegy on Rochester; but in two odes of Horace he succeeds much better. 'Quid dedicatum', with its theme of the happy man, and 'Eheu fugaces' with its moral senti- ment of time and morality, and its satiric parting shot, are congenial to him; and the acclimatization is well managed by felicitous modern allusions and by casting the odes into the Pindarique form, free however from the faults which spoil so many Pindariques: inept hyperbole, and contrariwise a flatness of sense and sound. Oldham's cadences here, if not especially melodious, run fitly and agreeably.

But it is the Imitations in heroic couplets which by contrast with the *dirae* and the 'Satyrs upon the Jesuits' show how the commitment to the sense of another poet supplied the curb he needed, and as Rachel Trickett observes, 'chastened and digni- fied' his violent style.[116] That the first of these Imitations were of Horace told in the same direction: for Horace, conceiv- ing himself heir to Lucilius yet deprecating his acrimony and want of polish, had made it his aim to refine the art and civil- ize the spirit of satire.[117] Among Oldham's poems from Horace, the masterpiece is his rendering of the satire (I.ix) on the im- pertinent bore. Sprat had written a lively Imitation of this;[118] and it had helped to inspire Donne's First and Fourth Satires, and Marvell's on Flecknoe. From comparison with these predeces- sors, good as they are, Oldham's poem has nothing to fear: in- deed, it is no mean forerunner of the Imitations of Horace by Swift and Pope. Needless to say, it has not the qualities which make Pope unique as a satirist: the nuance, fine sensibility, virtuosity of versification; the bloom of poetry and the some- times intimate personal note. Nor does Oldham, here or elsewhere, attain the Horatian elegance. But his version does not fall short of the original in humour, and evokes the world of Restoration London with no less sure a touch than Horace the world of Augus- tan Rome. Like Swift and Pope (nor should we forget Rochester, Boileau, even Sprat) Oldham can match the couplet to the rhythms of dialogue:

> 'Sir, I perceive you stand on Thorns' (said he)
> 'And fain would part: but faith, it must not be:

Come, let us take a Bottle.' (I cried) 'No;
Sir, I am in a Course, and dare not now.'
'Then tell me whether you desire to go:
I'll wait upon you.' 'O! Sir, 'tis too far:
I visit cross the Water; therefore spare
Your needless trouble.' 'Trouble! Sir, 'tis none:
'Tis more, by half, to leave you here alone.
I have no present business to attend,
At least which I'll not quit, for such a Friend ...'
                                          (38 ff.).

Pope lists this satire and the 'Art of Poetry' among the five
'most remarkable' (viz. best worth noting) of Oldham's works.[119]
To speak of no other debts, his colloquialisms owe something to
Oldham's: when he writes

The things, we know, are neither rich nor rare,
But wonder how the Devil they got there,[120]

he is recalling the 'Art of Poetry, Imitated':

When such a lewd incorrigible sot
Lucks by meer chance upon some happy thought;
Among such filthy trash, I vex to see't,
And wonder how (the Devil) he came by't.   (578 ff.).

Oldham is well suited by the recurrent mockery, in the *Ars
Poetica*, of literary faults and fools: the satiric and the colloquial in his 'Imitation' are responsible for much of its liveliness. Despite one howler, originally Dryden's, about Gorboduc,[121]
his allusions to English life and English and French literature
are apt, as usual; and he imparts movement to the verse-paragraph.
He worked from Jonson's very literal and Roscommon's freer translation as well as the Latin, and drew on Boileau's *L'Art Poétique*:
to follow his use of them enhances one's appreciation.
  The Horatian middle style was proper for verse-epistles. 'A
Letter from the Country', an earlier success of Oldham's (July
1678) has affinity with his 'Art of Poetry' in tone as in subject. Answering, closely at first, the epistle on poetry from his

friend Spencer, he depicts himself in revulsion against his unprofitable Muse, but then reaffirms his inescapable passion for
her. The felicity of the erotic parallel is admirably brought
out by Rachel Trickett. 'The old image of the muse as the mistress' has 'been given a new significance': 'like an intrigue,
the art of writing' involves 'frequent tedium', yet also 'desire,
pursuit, attainment';[122] poetry, seen as 'This vile and wicked
lust' is denounced, but then rehabilitated and cherished as the
irresistible object of a true devotion. Skilful transitions help
to give the 'Letter' its shape and easy progression. As it comes
to a climax, Oldham develops from a few phrases of Dryden's dedication to *The Rival Ladies*[123] a fine introspective account of
his habits of composition, and asserts his vocation in ringing
lines which Pope, again, remembered:[124]

> In Youth, or Age, in Travel, or at Home,
> Here, or in Town, at *London*, or at *Rome*,
> Rich, or a Begger, Free, or in the *Fleet*,
> What ere my fate is, 'tis my Fate to write.   (224 ff.).

His vocation as poet or satirist is a subject on which he
always writes well, as in passages of the 'Apology' for 'A Satyr
Against Vertue' and 'Upon a Bookseller'. He returns to it in 'A
Satyr ... dissuading ... from Poetry': the dissuader is Spenser's
ghost and his argument the meagre prospects of a modern poet.
Even more significantly than Oldham's earlier use of the dis-
approved spokesman, Garnet, Loyola, or the Court Hector, the
personal accent of these poems 'extends the resources of the
Juvenalian voice'.[125] The subjective voice of Juvenal is 'a de-
personalised declamatory one', like Oldham's in the Prologue and
Satyr II of the 'Satyrs upon the Jesuits', and in 'Upon a Woman'
(though even there it is 'the Death of my Friend'—*his friend*—
that he is avenging). But the 'Letter' is a reply to one, about
poetry, which in sober fact he has received; 'Upon a Bookseller'
is provoked by a wrong done him, damaging to his poetical reputation; and the lines in the 'Apology' are a pointer to what he
aspires to write; they are a counterpart to his recognition, as
he reflects upon 'Byblis', that 'his vein' lies 'another way'. His
'Allusion to Martial' characterizes both Hindmarsh his real-life

publisher, and his own lodging, during his attempt to live by his
pen; and 'Spencer's Ghost' broods on the poets' situation, complained of already in the 'Letter', but which the failure of that
attempt must have brought more forcibly home to him. Sprat, in
his Imitation of Horace on the bore, had written in his own person as chaplain to 'his Grace';[126] but Oldham, when he is 'the
poet speaking about his most intimate concern—poetry', goes
further, taking us into his personal confidence; and though
Horace, too, writes of his art,[127] it is not with the same emotion.

Whatever Oldham may have owed to Horace, his satire remained
predominantly Juvenalian. Paying heed to his author, he does for
the most part eschew, in his Imitations of Horace, Juvenalian
procedures he had employed in the 'Satyrs upon the Jesuits'.[128]
But of the six satires, evidently subsequent, published in *Poems,
And Translations*, 1683, five have connections with Juvenal. His
Third and Thirteenth satires are Imitated. The 'Satyr touching
Nobility' is on a topic of his: the satire of Boileau it 'imitates' is an Imitation of Juvenal VIII. And rather as Rochester
twice takes a theme from Boileau and improvises upon it, so
'Spencer's Ghost' and 'A Satyr Address'd to a Friend' are varia-
tions upon the theme of Juvenal VII. There was warrant for the
title bestowed on Oldham of 'the English Juvenal',[129] and for the
place the affiliation is given by three of his elegists: Robert
Gould (an avowed disciple), Tom Durfey, and Thomas Andrews.[130]

The five satires, with the Imitation of Boileau, Satire VIII,
which opens the volume, are the major pieces evidently written
for it. His reference to some of the contents being 'printed just
as he finished them off'[131] cannot be understood of the other
major poems: the 'Dithyrambique' and 'David's Lamentation' were
composed in September 1677 and the Jonson ode in the first three
months of 1678. The six, together with the 'Art of Poetry' and
'The Impertinent', show him writing in the genre which suits his
talents best: presumably this was 'the vein' he foresaw as
'lying another way' than in 'Byblis'. He seems now to have
settled down to write in it, though he will not, of course, decline the commission for the 'Ode on S. Cecilia's Day'. There are
no more endeavours to demonstrate his capacity for the 'softer'
styles of verse, emulating tender pastoral elegy or Ovidian

epistle of female passion (the 'Amores' chosen for rendering are
not tender, and the conventional love-verses to Cosmelia belong
to 1676 and 1677). Neither are there any more Pindariques
('David's Lamentation' being likewise of 1677). Gone too, are
the rants of the 'Satyrs upon the Jesuits', the frantic curses
of the *dirae*: Spencer's ghost pronounces a parting curse, but it
is in practical terms, without the former hyperbole. Some hyperbole survives, from the original, in 'Juvenal XIII'; but in
'Juvenal III' there are only two really hyperbolical passages;
and when Oldham is composing freely, in 'Spencer's Ghost', there
is only one, and in 'To a Friend' none at all.

In these and other ways the vehemence is toned down, yet not so
far as to incur the reproach satire must fall under 'when you
take away

> That Rage, in which his Noble Vigour lay'.[132]

As before, Oldham barbs his lines with derogatory verbs—the
aliens 'wriggle' into advantageous employ—and pungent epithets:
'her tawdry Grace', 'gaping Prentices', 'sharping Courtiers',
the 'gaudy flutt'ring Race of English now'. He continues fertile
in demeaning expressions: the learned dispute 'About black-
pudding'; the clergy are 'the Sacred Herd', engaged in 'hawkering
Divinity'; the smugglers' cargo is 'prohibited Goods, and Dildoes'; nowadays, Sappho would have to 'let her Tail to hire, as
well as Brains'; Butler was 'interr'd on tick'.[133] In the Imitation of Boileau, Satire VIII, the demeaning expressions are
thicker-sown than in the French. The comparison is instructive.
Boileau's satire obeys a canon of dignity from which, within that
neo-classical limit, one of its merits, an urbane 'keeping',
derives. One of the merits of Oldham's is in being under less
restraint, and enjoying, therefore, a greater alacrity in sink-
ing. His pejorative vocabulary is extended in its lower range.
And Boileau could never have dropped, even once, into burlesque,
as Oldham does when he describes as 'turn spit Angels'[134] the
intelligences that rule the spheres.

Diction is not his only weapon. Where either his author, or he
himself on his own account, is attacking a general characteristic
or presenting something typical, he is in the habit of embodying

it in acutely-realized particulars. Satiric use of examples thus
given sharp definition has been noted by Rachel Trickett as perhaps his strongest means of arousing the emotions of the reader.[135] In 'To a Friend', the private chaplain's status is
defined in all its ignominy by the details of his treatment at
table. Joseph Hall, Oldham's source here,[136] had devoted several
graphic lines to this, but Oldham's fuller dramatization brings
home the humiliations more painfully. Among these examples of
his, deservedly the best-remembered is the narration, in 'Spencer's Ghost', of Butler's fate, where even more than on the chaplain's behalf 'pity as well as indignation is aroused':[137] the
chaplain is a typical figure; Butler was flesh-and-blood.

Oldham's style is now at its most fully developed. In his versification, he everywhere commands variety in the medial pauses:
a good instance is the opening of 'Spencer's Ghost'. Of his trip-
lets (the other licence, the alexandrine, he does not employ)
almost a third are strategically positioned to conclude or begin
a paragraph; 'Boileau VIII' and 'To a Friend' are brought to a
full close with a triplet, and 'Spencer's Ghost' with a triplet
and final couplet. The placing of the rest does not appear structural; but besides diversifying the succession of couplets (themselves more freely handled than in the tautest of Augustan
styles), they are used when without them the sense must have
been cramped into a couplet or diffused over two, and so they
liberate the poet's phrasing from a constraint the measure would
otherwise have imposed. This, with the skilful management of the
pauses, and of syntactical links, enables him to sustain the deployment of his sense for eight or ten or as many as fourteen
lines at a time.[138] In turn, the sustaining of the sense has a
main share in the building of his paragraphs, for which he had
already shown a talent in his earlier poems.

For the most part, his words are disposed in a natural order;
when not the order of prose, it has a clear rhetorical purpose,
either for emphasis, or to bring the ideas to the reader in the
best sequence: there are some forced inversions for rhyme, but
not many.[139] At will, and frequently, he is colloquial. Livelihood is needed

                To fill a Bladder, and twelve yards of Gut;

'Son fils' is translated 'his hopeful brat', 'senior bulla dig-
nissime', 'gray-headed Boy', 'Fonteio consule', 'good King
Jemmy's days'; treasonably, the date has been predicted when 'the
King shall die

> And you know what [sc. Popery] come in'.

Colloquialism may be increased by an expansion: Alexander 'lack'd
elbow-room'; was he

> 'A fool belike?' 'Yes, faith, sir, much the same ...'[140]

That 'Yes, faith, sir' is typical of many terms of address and
retorts, which heighten the impression of speakers answering one
another. Brisk dialogue, as Dryden shows in epilogues of 1668 and
1682, can be conducted in Augustan couplets, but even in Oldham's
less tight form of them, it is a feat of no mean skill: one which
the exchanges between the poet and the Impertinent proved he had,
not only when following Horace, but in the talk he interpolated
on the Plot. He displays it again when confronted with a brilliant
passage of Boileau VIII, of which his version begins:

> *Up!* (strait says Avarice) *tis time to rise.*
> Not yet: one minute longer. *Up:* (she cries).
> Th' Exchange and Shops are hardly open yet.
> *No matter: Rise!* But after all, for what?
> *D'ye ask?* . . . . (95-9)

Aided by his mastery of the paragraph, both as verse and as
rhetoric, he is no less at home in the long set speech, the
miserly merchant's, for instance, in the same satire, or those of
the principal *personae*, such as Spencer's Ghost, or the poet himself in the address 'To a Friend'. More briefly, the speaking
voice is admirably caught when in 'Juvenal III' a victim is
hustled from the pew, or another assaulted by a drunken 'Scow-
rer'.[141]

The Imitations of Boileau and Juvenal do not entirely conform
to the method Oldham described himself adopting for the 'Art of
Poetry'. The description was accurate: except for an omission and

one local divergence, when he was not acclimatizing he furnished
a translation. In the present Imitations, however, he skips and
diverges more often, and adds English references beyond those
which replace references in the Latin and French. Hence they cannot be read as complete English equivalents of their originals.
He does—'Juvenal III' is a good example—follow the originals
topic by topic; but he goes further, now, towards creating new
Restoration poems on the foundations of Boileau or Juvenal than
he had with the *Ars Poetica*.

Yet simply as translations, when he is translating, his versions are almost always acceptable, often outstanding. As with
'shuns and disavows' for 'fuit et ... renie' or 'how demure and
grave a look' for 'quae sit ficti constantia vultus', his choice
of English equivalents is well-judged; sometimes it is notably
felicitous: in 'Boileau VIII', for example, 'hampered in the
knot ('dans le piège arresté'). 'Why all this Rant?' ('Que sert
de s'emporter?'), 'This is our image, just' ('Voilà l'homme en
effet'); or in 'Boileau V', for 'naufrage des temps', 'the
general wreck of time', where *general* wreck' makes good the loss
of the French plural.[142] He satisfies the canon that the genius
of the language translated into must be paramount: he had read,
though he would hardly have needed to, what Dryden said on the
subject in the preface to *Ovid's Epistles*, 1680: 'since every
language is so full of its own proprieties, that what is beautiful in one, is often barbarous, nay sometimes nonsense in another', it is enough if a translator 'choose out some expression
which does not vitiate the sense'.[143] These Imitations read as
wholly English poems. Negatively, Oldham retains no Latinisms or
Gallicisms. Positively, he makes good use of English idioms:
'dance attendance', 'ill-gotten gold' ('Boileau V'); 'hand and
seal' ('Juvenal XIII'); 'More changing than a weathercock' for
'Il tourne au moindre vent' ('Boileau VIII'). A particularly
interesting example reflects the place in English literature of
the Authorized Version; a place the vernacular *Sainte Bible* does
not hold in French: Boileau's 'autant de témoins' (Satire V)
becomes Oldham's 'cloud of witnesses'.[144]

Writing Imitations, Oldham is not tied at every point to translate: he omits, adds, and expands. Even in the 'Art of Poetry',
he judiciously omitted the account of Latin metres, as incompat-

ible with his plan; and in the Imitations of Boileau and Juvenal
he makes omissions on the same score. He interpolates in 'Juvenal
XIII' some well-turned lines on the aloofness of the Epicurean
gods. In 'Boileau V' he expands 'fuiez-vouz l'injustice?' and
'Respectez-vous les lois?'; and in 'Juvenal III' the clamour
which denies the dweller in the capital his night's rest.[145] That
description illustrates the scope Imitation affords him for graphic detail. As there, when acclimatizing he is no less happy
than when translating in the equivalents he finds. It was 'the
imitator's skill' to find particulars which as in the original
'relate ... to the general theme of the work', and as Rachel
Trickett says further, Oldham never lacks 'a precise contemporary
example' for the purpose.[146]

The wider significance of Oldham's Imitations has been greatly
illuminated by her studies. From the Renaissance onwards, 'to
join a classical and a modern inspiration' had been a recurrent
literary endeavour, and she indicates how by his Imitations he
was contributing to the Augustan phase of it, seeking to couple
the authority of tradition with 'a pressing sense of immediate
events and opinions', assessed by an 'honest muse'. To acclimat-
ize the ancient classical or foreign neo-classical poem, topicalities were requisite, while the classical heritage ensured
that the topicality would not render the Imitation ephemeral.
Most topical satires of the period were partisan, but as an Imitator—and indeed (like Rochester in various of his satires) in
'Spencer's Ghost' and 'To a Friend'—Oldham showed how 'good use
of topical material' could be made by a poet without primary
allegiance to 'a party or a cause'; how he could 'remain independent' and 'yet concerned with the life of his time'.[147]

He bestows censure where he considers censure is due: on 'the
horrid Plot' but also on 'all the Perjuries to make it out, or
make it nothing'; on both 'Fanatick' and 'Churchman' for their
feud; and on those who 'tack about [their] conscience, whensoe're
To a new Point, [they] see Religion veer'.[148] Warm Monarchist
though he is, subscribing to the cult of Charles the Martyr, that
does not prevent his condemning sycophantic clergy who

> ... sooth the Court, and preach up Kingly Right,
> To gain a Prebendr'y, and Mitre by't.[149]

No Whig, he is no establishment man either: his reference to
'Halifax, or Hide' when they were two of 'the great Triumvirate',
is not particularly respectful, and he adverts to the government's
patronage, through Warcup, of the Irish witnesses, with the
withering contempt it deserves.[150] In the Imitations, the
acclimatizing references are numerous enough—there are almost
forty in 'Juvenal XIII'—to afford room for much that he has observed, and his judgements upon it.

    Imitating Horace, Satire I.ix, Sprat had given the patron the
title of 'his Grace'; Oldham, making the refuser of rescue 'a
Doctor, my dear Friend', would, if the allusion stood alone, have
been personalizing the poem to exactly the same extent, for it is
to his friend Dr Lower, and so he is endowing the narrator, as
Sprat did, with a relationship which is his own in real life. But
by interpolating the dialogue on the Plot, Oates, and Fitzharris,
he takes the personalization further, endowing the narrator not
only with his own situation—as a friend of Dr Lower—but with
his own attitude of detachment from the political hysteria now
subsiding. In the Imitations of Juvenal XIII and Boileau V, the
suggestion of 'a personality behind the verse' has not the support of references such as these: the personality is felt, nevertheless, in the tone of the poems, 'lively, ... informal, fluent',
and the arguing of traditional truths in a manner at least as
characteristic of Oldham himself as of his authors.[151] As we
shall see, it is felt even more strongly in 'Juvenal III' and in
'Boileau VIII', so that it pervades even the four Imitations
among the recently-written satires of the 1683 volume, besides
being directly expressed in the other two: 'To a Friend', which
the poet speaks as the good counsellor, and 'Spencer's Ghost', in
which he is the recipient of the ghost's admonition.

    Each of the six in this or that particular or passage shows
Oldham at his best; yet there are reasons to place some of them
above the others. 'Juvenal XIII' has many of his happiest modern-
izing allusions; but it suffers from the broken-backed morality
of the original: thoughts of revenge, the wronged man is told,
are unworthy; but the final satisfaction offered him is the prospect of gloating over the offender's fate.[152] In the Imitation of
Boileau's Fifth satire, on true nobility, no such flaw spoils the
working-out of the theme, which had had a fascinating history:[153]

Oldham would be aware of its treatment by Juvenal (Satire VIII.
Stemmata quid faciunt?) and by Joseph Hall (*Virgidemiarum*, IV.
iii). But the subject, like that of 'Juvenal XIII', does not lie
close to Oldham's experience or vocation; his concern does not
go much beyond the making of the two versions, brought vigor-
ously to life in Restoration terms. To this end, in 'Boileau V',
the expansion of the analogue of the racehorse, particularized
as *Dragon*, admirably contributes.[154] 'Spencer's Ghost' is distinguished by passages as fine and finer; on the peer with his
empty praise and commiseration but tight-shut purse, the authors
sunk in their reputation, the neglected genius of Spenser himself, of Cowley, above all of Butler, a neglect so feelingly ex-
claimed against—

> On *Butler* who can think without just rage?[155]

In no poem of Oldham's is he more engaged with his themes: 'the
miseries of scholars' was a time-honoured *topos*, but in his
Clerkenwell garret he had lived with them. And in the lines

> So many now and bad, the Scriblers be
> 'Tis scandal to be of the Company, (52 f.)

he speaks his disgust at seeing his vocation debased by inter-
lopers. The disgust is not unrelated to the perception which
justifies *MacFlecknoe* and *The Dunciad*: that duncery and scribbling
endanger the commonwealth of letters, and are therefore a threat
to civilization. In point of its personal emotion, 'Spencer's
Ghost' must stand with the 'Satyr Address'd to a Friend' and 'A
Letter from the Country' at the head of Oldham's poems. And yet,
comparing it with 'A Letter', one is conscious of an inadequacy,
almost amounting to misrepresentation, in what it conveys of his
attitude to his poetic calling. Admitting that his addiction is
very likely incurable, it purports to condemn it. One cannot believe that he endorsed this apparent moral of the piece: the
'Letter' likewise depicts a revolt against his dedication to
poetry, but subsequently reaffirms it. The two poems, it is true,
are of different genres. From an epistle, a more frankly personal expression is expected, and in the 'Letter' this even takes

on a confessional tone:

> Thus have I made my shrifted Muse confess ...

writes Oldham in conclusion. In a satire like 'Spencer's Ghost',
dominated by the admonitory *persona*-spokesman, it was not ille-
gitimate to concentrate on the revulsion from her. Yet because
it is not written out of the whole of Oldham's feeling about its
subject, speaking for myself I am left faintly dissatisfied, and
disinclined to place it quite on a level with the three satires
which, together with the Imitation of Horace's on the Impertinent,
and with 'A Letter', I regard as the peaks of his achievement.

   The three are the Imitations of Boileau VIII, and Juvenal III,
and the 'Satyr Address'd to a Friend'. Each is prompted by one
of his strongest inspirations: 'Boileau VIII' by his admiration
for Rochester and especially for Rochester's masterpiece developed from the same original, his 'Satyr against Reason and Mankind' which Oldham had taken the trouble to transcribe. To that
original he turned, not to compete with Rochester, but to furnish
a close Imitation· of what Rochester had transmuted. Among its
highlights are the dialogue (praised already) which leads into
Avarice's discourse; that discourse itself; and the merchant's
to his 'hopeful brat': Oldham has lost none of his skill at the
set speech which discredits what it advocates. But the whole debate loses nothing in his hands, even though, as in Boileau, the
defence counsel for mankind is present only that he may be
refuted: at least, thanks to the French, he gets more of a look-
in than any other *adversarius* in Oldham, bar the Horatian Impertinent. But while the debate is as well conducted by Oldham as
by Boileau, he is not committed, further than as translator, to
the thesis advanced; whereas for Rochester it had been one to be
explored more deeply, on the lines of his own metaphysic. Yet the
theme of human reason so-called, contrasted with the 'true'
rationality of sense-experience and animal instinct, was not new
in Oldham: it was part of the *libertin* creed dealt with in his
poems on the cults of Rochester's circle. 'Boileau VIII', in its
subject, is by no means so little connected with Oldham's personal interests as 'Boileau V' and 'Juvenal XIII' in theirs. In
its allusions, the wide range of those interests is reflected.

Among other topicalities, they comprehend faction-fighting over
politics and religion, philosophical dispute, the activities
(absurd or otherwise) of the Royal Society, astrological superstition, abuses in law and medicine, the sordid preference of
commercial to liberal education, evils of patronage, and Ned
Howard as type of the irrepressible bad poet and dramatist. One
is constantly aware of Oldham's love-and-hate relationship with
the town and times, which culminates in his comprehensive London
satire 'In Imitation of the Third of Juvenal'.

Here and in 'To a Friend' the subjects themselves are central
to Oldham's experience, and are the source of his inspiration.
In 'Juvenal III' the evils prevalent in Restoration London as in
ancient Rome—the expense, the noise, the jerry-building, the
dangers from traffic by day and sons of Belial or professional
footpads by night, the snobbery, the extorted bribery, and the
rest—are made vivid by modern particulars: the poetaster Pordage
in his wretched garret, for instance, or the huge Portland stone
impending from its vehicle in transit to St Paul's. The satire is
often sharpened by the diction:

> What will you give to have the quarter-face,
> The squint and nodding go-by of his *Grace*? (283 f.)

The Latin gave opportunity for dwelling on two of the topics
which came home most personally to the Imitator: Oldham's lines
are never more heartfelt than when describing the contempt to
which poverty exposes a man in London, or keener than in the
attack on sycophancy.

Hatred of dependence, next to his vocation as a poet, was Oldham's dearest passion: and he had found them incompatible. He
had tried and failed to live in London without other employment
and without a patron. In 'Spencer's Ghost', the scanty reward a
poet might expect was for him no mere traditional commonplace.
He broadened it in the satire 'Address'd to a *Friend*, that is
about to leave the University, and come abroad in the World'. At
the time when, having left Oxford, he was aspiring beyond Gloucestershire and his father's school, to 'come abroad in the World',
he must have reviewed his prospects much as the Friend is adjured
to do. 'Let me hear

What course your Judgement counsels you to steer:
Always consider'd that your whole Estate
And all your Fortune lies beneath your Hat. (24-6)

Unemployment faces the would-be parson; the ill-paid schoolmaster
must 'beat Greek and Latin for [his] life'. Even a post in a
noble household (comparable with Oldham's tutorships) offers
nothing better than the existence of a superior menial, and after
seven years' service a miserable chaplainship, with not even a
Leah, but

My ladies antiquated Waiting-maid (101),

as an imposed bride.

For meer Board-Wages such their Freedom sell,
Slaves to an Hour, and Vassals to a Bell. (90 f.)

The poet's resolve for independence is pointed by a concluding
apologue, the fable of the dog and the wolf principally from
Romulus and Phaedrus. In this effective structural device Oldham
is following the satire (II.vi) that Horace ended with his fable
of the Town and Country Mice, and that Cowley and Sprat, between
them, had imitated.

   To earn a competence by literature alone, Oldham was born too
early: but in his other great ambition he was not wholly thwarted.
When, just after he had found himself as satirist and Imitator,
'Fate and gloomy night' encompassed him, he had 'established a
Reputation', and, as he rather wistfully phrased it, left behind
him 'something to make me survive myself'.[156]

II THE TEXT

The present edition is the first to include all Oldham's poems,
and the first[157] in which the text is based on the original
authorities. The anonymous editor in 1722, and Captain Edward
Thompson in 1770, gave everything that had been collected in *The
Works of Mr. John Oldham Together with his Remains*, 1684, of
which the parts represented *Satyrs Upon the Jesuits*, 1681, 1682;

Some New Pieces, 1681; *Poems And Translations*, 1683; and *Remains*,
1684.[158] Apart from adding two uncollected pieces in the Fourth
part (1687),[159] the *Works* from 1686 to 1710 are simply a deteri-
orating series of reprints. The *1722* editor drew his text from
more than one of these; Thompson used only *1722*. Since 1770 the
only extensive collection published has been Robert Bell's in
1854, with its derivatives, a new issue in 1871 (where pp. 117-
19 have been re-set), and the Centaur Press edition in 1960, the
text of which is photographically reproduced from the *1854*.[160]
Bell has thirty-four and omits nineteen of the poems Thompson
printed. His copy-text was Thompson, though he evidently consulted an edition of the *Works*, probably of 1686, and certainly
not the first edition (*1684*), let alone any substantive text.
His text has some 170 corrupt readings (accumulated errors and
his own bowdlerizations), which the Centaur necessarily per-
petuates. Neither Bell, nor Thompson, nor the *1722* editor knew
of Oldham's autograph drafts and fair copies now preserved in
MS Rawlinson Poet 123 in the Bodleian. From these have been
printed the translation of *Le Lutrin*, Canto 1, in A.F.B. Clark's
Boileau and the French Classical Critics in England, 1925, and
the text of the ode on Jonson in Vol. xi of the Herford and
Simpson *Ben Jonson*. Apart from Ken Robinson's *Selected Poems*
(1980), soundly intentioned, but contaminated through the use of
the *Works*, third edition, 1686, and of the Centaur, imperfectly
corrected, as copy-texts,[161] the only critical edition of any
portion of Oldham's work so far published is Elias F. Mengel
Jr's of the 'Satyrs upon the Jesuits' and 'The Careless Good
Fellow' in *Poems on Affairs of State*, ed. G.deF. Lord and others,
Vol. ii, 1965.[162] In his commentary, Mengel cites the drafts in
the Rawlinson manuscript six times on textual and twice on other
matters. Otherwise, so far as I know, they have remained unused.

1. *The Authorities: the Canon*

For almost the whole of Oldham's text, the authorities are admirable. First, there are the autographs in the Rawlinson MS: fair
copies of eight poems, and drafts which provide supplementary
evidence for others. The manuscript (which I designate *R*) begins
with what was probably a notebook: Oldham was transcribing fair
copies into it. The rest once consisted of loose leaves. Its

provenance, before it came into the Rawlinson collection, is un-
traced. The contents, it is reasonable to guess, were the papers
left, out of those Oldham had with him at the time of his brief
illness and death, when others were taken away to supply the
copy for the *Remains*, 1684.[163] The manuscript is calendared in
my unpublished doctoral thesis (1939), an edition of Oldham, in
the Bodleian. The drafts (omitting a few obscene passages, then
unacceptable for the projected publication) are there transcribed.
To find, from any draft, whatever corresponding passages there
may be in the edited text, one uses the footnotes; to find, from
any passage of the text, whatever drafts of it there may be, one
uses the index.

Half-a-dozen excepted, all Oldham's poems appear in the five
volumes published by Hindmarsh: four, though anonymous, under
the poet's own auspices, with his prefatory 'Advertisements',
commenting upon them.[164] They are the first (1681) and second
(1682) editions of *Satyrs Upon The Jesuits*, and—both 'By the
Author of the Satyrs upon the Jesuits'—the first of *Some New
Pieces*, 1681, and *Poems, And Translations*, 1683. The fifth volume,
the posthumous *Remains*, 1684, contains (to anticipate) nothing
not authentic.[165] The third issue of *Satyrs Upon the Jesuits*,
1681, and the second of *Some New Pieces*, 1681, lists errata,
supplied (again to anticipate) by the author.[166] A second edition (1687) of the *Remains* collects the epithalamium to William
and Mary brought out by Herringman in a single sheet folio, 1677,
at the time of the marriage, and the 'Ode for S. Cecilia's Day'
printed, 'The Words by ... Mr. John Oldham ... Set ... by Dr.
John Blow', as *A Second Musical Entertainment*, 1685.[167] Publication of three poems antedates their inclusion in authorized
volumes. 'The Careless Good Fellow' was printed in a single leaf,
as *The Clarret Drinker's Song: or, The Good Fellow's Design*,
1680.[168] Whether or not this was a piracy, the single sheet folio
Garnets Ghost [1679] and quarto *Satyr Against Vertue*, 1679, certainly were;[169] yet, taken from manuscript copies in circulation,
they derive independently from Oldham's original, though by an
unsatisfactory process of transmission. Other texts of this
'Satyr', similarly derived, are found in six manuscripts,[170] and
in the pirated *Poems On Several Occasions By ... E. of R[oches-
ter]*, 1680, which D.M. Vieth has shown to depend upon the arche-

type of one of the six, the famous Yale MS b. 105 in the Osborn
Collection.[171] It is to this manuscript and the Rochester volume
we must go for a completed text of 'Upon the Author of the Play
call'd Sodom', since the Rawlinson manuscript has drafts only,
though they cover a good deal of it. Like this piece, 'Sardanapalus' is an obscene performance absent from Oldham's collections
and the *Remains*. As it has left no trace of a text among the
autographs either, it is the only item in the canon for which we
have to rely wholly upon circulating manuscripts, represented by
twelve copies which are extant. Fortunately, one in particular
yields a sound version.[172]

That 'Sardanapalus' does belong to the canon requires to be
shown, and the same is true of the *Remains*: the authenticity of
the other poems, published on the author's own initiative, or
extant in holograph, often in course of composition, is unchallengeable. 'Sardanapalus' is ascribed to Oldham in seven manuscripts, and nowhere to any other author. Of the seven, six
cannot be relied on as witnesses independent of each other; they
all emanate from the same scriptorium.[173] These are MSS Firth,
Dyce, Portland (PwV 42), Taylor, Vienna, and Wentworth. The
seventh, Harley[3] (Harl. 7913) is not from the scriptorium, and
there is reason to suppose its ascription is of independent
descent. Further, following Oldham's poem, it has the attack by
Sir William Soame, 'To the Author of Sardanapalus upon that, &
his other Writeings', which though it does not name the author,
points to Oldham by calling him 'School-master'. The attack is
also included with 'Sardanapalus' in MSS Harvard (Eng. 585) and
Portland[2] (PwV 45); one of the scriptorium group, Dyce, has the
first eight lines. It was eventually printed, anonymously, in
Examen Poeticum, 1693 (p. 328). Since it is to be dated with
virtual certainty no later than 1681, and in all probability
before Spring 1679,[174] the manuscript datings of 'Sardanapalus',
'1683' in Harley[3], Firth, and Portland[1], '1683/4' in Wentworth,
cannot record the date of composition: but they might be connected with Oldham's death in December 1683, if that released a
copy. One other feature, present to a varying extent in eight of
the manuscripts, helps to confirm Oldham's authorship. They
carry, in the margin, abbreviated references to authorities.[175]
Nowhere else, it is true, does Oldham retain such marginalia in

the finished form of a poem; but they are just the sort he sometimes notes down for his own benefit in a draft; and the reason
for retaining them in this instance is obvious: to heighten the
mock-heroic gravity of the piece. Other internal evidence makes
assurance doubly sure. The style has Oldham's characteristic
heavy irony and imperfect rhymes. He was in the habit of repeat-
ing turns of thought and phrase from earlier compositions in
later ones, particularly if the earlier were unpublished, as he
destined 'Sardanapalus' to remain. Sure enough, expressions in
'Sardanapalus' are echoed in this way.

'T'have fought, or F——d for Universal Monarchy' has its parallel in 'A Dithyrambique', 1. 50:

> And Drunk as well as Fought for Universal Monarchy.

'Satyrs upon the Jesuits' yields five: with

> ——Much more thou wouldst have said, but the ascending Smoak
>   Broke of thy Pray'r and did its uttrance choke ...
>
> ——Beauties which profess the Trade ...
>
> ——Great was the bold Resolve, and firm as Fate it stood ...
>
> ——Wise Mannag'ry ...

compare

> ——Much more I had to say, but now grow faint (III.635).
>
> ——But in the utt'rance choak't (I.308)
>
> ——How many whores in Rome profess the Trade (IV.215)
>
> ——Bravely resolved! and 'twas as bravely dar'd (II.183)

and the identical 'Wise Manag'ry' at III.366. The metaphor of
'unprohibited commodities' (1. 57) occurs in two drafts R93 and
103) where no one but the author could have located it. Of two
parallels with the 'Counterpart to the Satyr against Vertue',
the second would be all but decisive in itself. The first is the
metaphor of 'Pay custom' ('Sardanapalus', 1. 57; 'Counterpart',
1. 111). The second is an identical line ('Sardanapalus', 9;

'Counterpart', 178):

>   And all the undershrievalties of life, not worth a name.

'*Under-Sheriffries*' is Bacon's translation of '*Sbirrerie*', applied
by the '*Cardinals* of *Rome*' as a 'Phrase of ... Scorne' to 'Civill
Businesse ... As if they were but matters for Under-Sheriffes
and Catchpoles';[176] 'undershrievalties' is so rare a form of the
term as to be unrecorded in *OED*. Here it is evidently taken from
Marvell's *Rehearsal Transpros'd: the Second Part*, 1673; which,
bantering Samuel Parker's use of it, has 'the *Undershrievalties
of that* [sc. secular] *life*'.[177] That the identical echoes should
not be by the same author is obviously most improbable.
   That 'Sardanapalus' is Oldham's would be apparent even without
this last piece of evidence; and so that is evidence that the
'Counterpart', the first poem in the *Remains*, is his, too. The
'Counterpart' has similar links with others undoubtedly authentic: three lines (33-5) are identical with three (132-4) in the
'Hymn of St. Ambrose', and ll. 30-1 almost so with 19-20 in
'Presenting a Book to Cosmelia'. Numerous debts to Cowley—to the
essay and ode on Liberty, 'The Complaint' and other pieces—are
further signs of Oldham's hand. All but one of the other poetical 'Remains' are occasional. There is an autograph draft for the
St Cecilia Ode. For the epithalamium to William and Mary there
are a number; and the autograph letter describing its composition
has already been quoted.[178] Another autograph, the trial opening
of a consolatory poem to the bereaved mother of Katharine Kingscote, authenticates the elegy on the eleven-year-old girl herself.[179] 'To Madam L.E.', if as is probable L.E. stands for Lady
Estcourt, is, like the last, intended for a potential patron hard
by the poet's family home (see above, p. xxvii). By far the most
elaborate of the *Remains* is his ode to the memory of Charles
Morwent, the bosom friend of his youth. Harman Atwood, commemorated in another, was a patron of Whitgift Hospital when Oldham
was usher at the school; the headmaster was husband of Atwood's
niece.[180] As in the 'Counterpart', these occasional poems have
links of expression with undoubted compositions of Oldham's. The
Morwent ode has a line (see l. 554 n.) almost identical with one
in the autograph fragment of 'Horace B[ook] 4. Ode 13', undated,

and another (724, see n.) virtually repeated in the unprinted
autograph 'Rant to his Mistress'. The author who in 'Madam L.E.'
(11. 1 ff., 68) borrowed from Cowley the 'joys that hinder one
another in the crowd', and the 'Post Angel' is clearly the same
who made the identical borrowings in the 'Letter from the Country' and 'A Sunday Thought in Sickness'. The 'Sunday Thought' is
itself one of the *Remains*,[181] and two of the others are similarly
cross-linked: some of the lines on Atwood (207-10) are a variant
of some on Katharine Kingscote.

Every poem in the *Remains* is thus accounted for, with one exception, the translation of Virgil's eighth eclogue. This resembles Oldham's straight translations from Ovid's *Metamorphoses*
and *Amores*, and has over twenty of his imperfect rhymes. It is
not known outside this volume, of which the whole character confirms the genuineness of what it contains, assembled by or for
Oldham's regular publisher, and prefaced by memorial verses from
Dryden and eight other poets. In such tributes the writers were
not on oath, yet there is nothing improbable in the claims of
Flatman, Tom Durfey, and Nahum Tate to have been Oldham's friends;
Thomas Wood and Robert Gould were disciples. The *Remains* is no
piece of bookseller's hackwork. At the provenance of its copy,
as of the papers collected in the Rawlinson manuscript, a probable guess has already been made. In the manuscript there is no
fair copy or complete draft of any poem included in the 1684
Remains, which suggests that such completed poems as were thought
publishable were taken to furnish copy for the volume, while the
rest of the papers remained to become the manuscript we have. The
conjecture requires us, however, to assume the selectors passed
over among the autographs two poems which were complete: that on
William and Mary and 'A Rant to his Mistress'.[182]

Because the 'Rant' is complete and a fair copy, it might
theoretically—like Oldham's transcripts of *MacFlecknoe*, *A Satyr
against Mankind*, and 'A Letter from Artemisa', besides 'The Epicure', subscribed 'Philomusus', and a Latin paraphrase on Job
XXXIX, 19-26; subscribed A.S.A.B.C.C.[183]—not be his. The date,
however, 15 May 1676, groups it with his other love-verses of
four months later, and it has no subscription such as assigns the
minor transcripts to other authors. 'The Desk', Canto I, is likewise a fair copy, but it is seen also in the course of composi-

tion. The remaining items similarly given in the present edition
from their sole texts in the Rawlinson manuscript are all autograph fragments.

From outside the manuscript and Hindmarsh's volumes, two further pieces, besides 'Sardanapalus', can be added to the canon,
the first with certainty, the second plausibly. When John Freind,
Oldham's fellow-student, died at St Edmund Hall, 20 March 1673,
and was buried next day, his heartbroken father 'procured
[through] Mr. John Webbe of Edmund Hall June 27, 1673' and transcribed, the Latin verses written by scholars of the Hall and
'fixed to his Herse cloth'; among them Oldham's.[184] A believable
tradition, not however recorded until 1805 (by the Revd J.M.
Moffat in his *History of ... Malmesbury and its ... Abbey*) assigns
to him a four-line epitaph in the Abbey churchyard, on Dr Abia
Qui, an eminent physician.[185] The tradition may be a family one:
the husband of one of Oldham's nieces was living at Westport,
adjoining Malmesbury, till 1787. Two others survived at Shipton
Moyne till 1795 and 1798. Christopher Qui, Abia's eldest son,
was married at Shipton in 1695; and an acquaintance between the
Quis and the Oldhams is the more probable since the poet's brother
Thomas, aged 20 in 1675, was applying himself to medicine.[186]
Abia was buried 8 October 1675, when the poet was living at Shipton in the interval between leaving college and becoming usher at
Croydon: in the same year he commemorated Charles Morwent and
Katharine Kingscote, two other neighbours. The tradition would
have invited rejection had it referred to any other time; as it
is, it is consonant with his biography. Direct confirmation, however, is lacking.

The Oldham canon has proved to harbour no serious problems; and
it is unlikely to receive additions. I know of no further poems
anywhere ascribed to him.

2. *The Character of the Texts*

In establishing the text, the first step is to determine the
character of Hindmarsh's volumes: the nature of the copy from
which they were set up, and the relevant features of their printing and publication.[187] The first edition of *Satyrs Upon The
Jesuits* (1681)—with the exception of 'A Satyr Against Vertue'—
and those of *Some New Pieces* (1681) and *Poems, And Translations*

(1683), were printed, it is safe to assume, from autograph: Oldham could not have paid a scribe, nor had he need of one, being
capable, as can be seen in the Rawlinson manuscript, of exemplary
fair copy. The presumption is confirmed by the numerous instances
in which habits of spelling and punctuation exhibited in the
autographs, and contrary to those of the compositors, are reflected in the prints.[188] The instances persist in the *Remains*,
1684: 'sence', 'sences', 'shew'd', 'shewd'st', 'badge', 'knowledge', 'Priviledge', 'Judge', 'judgement', 'ows', 'lye', 'human'
(against compositorial 'humane'), 'Eccho', are authorial spellings. In contrast with the compositor's 'whom soe're' we find
'whatsoe're' (twice); and with his practice of hyphenating pre-
fixes, 'offspring', 'overheating': authorial, too, are half-a-
dozen 'y'd' endings ('bely'd' etc.). Though the volume was posthumous, the copy, one concludes, was again autograph.[189] By 1687,
the date of the second edition, the already published but uncollected poems on William and Mary and St Cecilia's Day had come to
notice, and it was from the printed texts that they were added.

All five Oldham volumes, from 1681 to 1684, were printed for
Joseph Hindmarsh by Mary Clark.[190] Except for *Satyrs Upon The
Jesuits* (1681), compositor-analysis shows only that they were
set either by the workman responsible for the greater part of
that text, or by others with habits so similar as to make them
virtually impossible to differentiate.[191] The first edition of
Satyrs Upon The Jesuits, however, was being hastened out, and
was divided between two compositors, who even shared Sheets D and
E, meeting in E5^r. The bibliographical units set by the second
man leap to the eye, because of his lavish use of italics: I
therefore call him L, using M for the main compositor. The contrast in italicization has nothing to do with the copy.[192] Nor
does M's anomalous treatment of the fourth 'Satyr upon the
Jesuits', which he separates from its predecessors by a half-
title, leaving the verso blank. At one time, ignorant of the
three issues of the edition,[193] I was inclined to think Oldham
might have supplied the manuscript of this 'Satyr' later than
that of the first three. But in fact M is simply spreading out
his copy to fill his allotted space. The title-page of the volume
announces 'other Pieces' as included after 'the *Satyr* against
Vertue'; but in the first issue only 'The Passion of Byblis'

follows, ending on K8^V with 'Finis'.[194] Evidently the casting-
off, necessary for the division between compositors, reckoned on
the inclusion of 'Upon a Woman'. When, to save time, the work
was to be issued without it, M, from F6^r to K8^V, expended on the
half-title with inner titles and blank leaves the nine pages
which approximate very fairly to the space 'Upon a Woman' would
have occupied.[195] It was added in a second issue, so that now
'Finis' appeared both on K8^V and L6^V.[196]

   The textual history of 'A Satyr Against Vertue' has next to be
unravelled. As 'Aude aliquid. Ode', it was written July 1676.[197]
Manuscript copies were passed round, and from one of them a corrupt text was piratically published: the 1679 Quarto. When, near
the end of 1680, *Satyrs Upon The Jesuits* was being rushed through
the press, this poem was set up from the corrupt Quarto, which
Mary Clark had by her, since it was she who had printed it: an
elaborate ornament on the title-page, a woodcut bowl of flowers,
belongs to her stock. *Satyrs Upon The Jesuits* was set up as far
as sheet H in 1680, as the internal title-page to 'A Satyr Against
Vertue' testifies, and was advertised in the Term Catalogues for
November; its 1681 imprint is postdated to prevent the publication
soon seeming stale.[198] Before the end of the year, therefore, the
bad text was given renewed and wider circulation, and that in the
very volume where Oldham had vindicated the inclusion of the
'Satyr' as 'a justice done to his own Reputation, to have it come
forth without those faults, which it has suffered from transcribers and the Press hitherto'.[199] Holding Hindmarsh responsible,
in the invective written at Christmas he vented his fury 'Upon
a Bookseller, that expos'd him by Printing a Piece of his grosly
mangled, and faulty'. (For Hindmarsh even to have had a hand in
the pirated Quarto is not impossible: the T.A. who subscribed its
address 'To the Reader' may be Thomas Ashington, who frequented
his shop, and signed a *Letter* to him in the same way; alternatively, however, T.A. may be Thomas Andrews, who was to be one
of Oldham's elegists in the *Remains*.) Before Oldham's onslaught
was printed in *Some New Pieces*, Hindmarsh may have satisfied him
that the use of the bad text was to be blamed on Mary Clark
alone: 'Upon a Bookseller' became 'Upon a Printer'. But the
change may have been merely to avoid the objectionableness of
denouncing the publisher in his own publication.[200]

Oldham's indignant intervention had a practical result of great textual consequence: a third issue of the book, with an errata list. Errata were supplied, too, in a second issue of *Some New Pieces*, 1681.[201] Both lists are Oldham's: each contains a new revision, which in an errata list none but the author would make. In *Some New Pieces*, this is at l. 596 of 'Horace, His Art of Poetry, Imitated', a version in which he is consulting Jonson's and Boileau's while constructing his own. At first he printed:

> Most Callings else do difference allow

following Boileau, who has:

> Il est dans tout autre art des degrez differens;

then to give a clearer sense, in the errata he substituted 'In-difference' for 'do difference', taking a hint from Jonson's:

> ... neither men, nor gods, nor Pillars meant
> Poets should ever be indifferent.

Of the other four errata, two are confirmed by his extant fair copies. In *Satyrs Upon The Jesuits*, at l. 254 of 'A Satyr Against Vertue' not only the 1679 and 1681 texts (with Rochester, *Poems*, 1680, and the five manuscripts from copies in circulation: Yale b. 105; Yale, Osborn Chest II, No. 14; Gyldenstolpe;[202] Portland PwV 40, and *m*—formerly *apud* Margoliouth),[203] but also the auto-graph fair copy (MS *R* 3 ff.), read 'Unthought, unknown, unpat-tern'd'. There is no error here, yet the erratum revises the phrase to 'Unknown, unheard, unthought of'. The reading of BL MS Additional 14047 (MS *A*),[204] 'Unthought, unknown, unpractic'd' is probably Oldham's too, a variant prior to *R*'s, so that from an early stage he was unsatisfied with the wording. In two further instances, the errata vary from what was originally written in *R*, agreeing with revisions in the margin. At p. 260 of the 'Satyr', the erratum, like *R*, notes 'down' for insertion. In the 'Apology', l. 72, the 1679 and 1681 editions have a hiatus, the result of a copyist's inability to recognize the recently imported and rare word, 'tuant', Oldham's first choice, as *R* shows. The

margin and the erratum have his revision, 'pointed'. Two lines
above, 'it' is corrected to 'them', where *R* has 'em'. The remaining forty-six corrections to the 'Satyr' and 'Apology' restore
R's reading. In the 'Satyr' at 1. 137 the erratum alone agrees
with *R* against the texts of *1679*, *1681*, Rochester's *Poems*, *1680*,
and the six manuscripts cited above. From correcting the text
reprinted from the corrupt Quarto, Oldham turned, evidently, to
that of the 'Satyrs upon the Jesuits': the errata-list, authoritative as has just been demonstrated, rectifies it in seventeen
places. For these corrections are no less sound than the other
fifty. Some restore a harder reading: 'made' for 'make' at
III.201; 'write' for 'writ' at III.207; 'shamelesness' for
'shamefulness' at III.213. The obvious 'there' for 'these' in
1. 28 of the 'Prologue' agrees with an autograph draft. At II.20,
where 'cure' is corrected to 'curse', a draft has 'plague'; at
II.119 'little' is corrected to 'title', and a draft has 'name'.
That is, the word in the Errata gives the true sense, indicated
in the manuscript; and is yet so near in form to the wrong reading in the text as to make the error easy to understand. Finally,
no one correcting by the mere light of nature would have suspected corruption in II.235:

> Than Bullies common Oaths and canting Lies?

Yet in the Errata 'canting' is changed to 'bant'ring' and
'bantring' is also the reading of two autograph drafts.

   The second (*1682*) edition of *Satyrs Upon The Jesuits* claims on
the title-page to be 'more corrected', and the claim is true. It
was set line-by-line from the first (*1681*) edition, except for
three passages where corrections are made in the 'Satyr Against
Vertue', an extra line given to p. 37 to avoid splitting a couplet, and the re-setting of p. 39 in italic as part of a new
typographical distinction between the introductory narrative and
Loyola's speech. This change produces a bibliographical link
which exhibits the compositor wrongly following his *1681* copy.
The italic gave him an additional line on the page, but on adding the catchword he overlooked this and reproduced the old and
now erroneous one. He does the same on p. 109 in the 'Satyr
Against Vertue', and on p. 113, in its 'Apology', repeats the

wrong catchword of the 1681 compositor. As the 1682 text of
these poems is corrected in some fifty places compared with that
of *1681*, besides the forty-seven where it profits from the *1681*
errata, the bibliographical proof that it was nevertheless set
up from a copy of the 1681 edition is of consequence.

Whether Oldham's corrections and revisions were effected by
marking a copy of *1681*, or by supplying a list, I have failed to
determine. That he did one or the other, the fresh amendments in
the 'Satyr' and 'Apology' are part of the evidence. In forty-one
instances the reading of his fair copy is restored; in two of
these a whole line is reintroduced. In at least half-a-dozen
more the superseded reading was not visibly corrupt: thus 'beyond' in p. 178 of the 'Satyr', and 'more' in l. 73 of the
'Apology' made sense and metre, yet they are changed to 'above'
and 'worse'. The *1682* text of 'Upon a Woman' also agrees, in its
six corrections, with the autograph fair copy; but none of these
(though two restore an omitted word) would have been beyond conjecture. Similarly, the four practically certain corrections in
'The Passion of Byblis', and twenty-two of the twenty-six in the
'Satyrs upon the Jesuits' are of the most obvious kind, and even
the remaining four would not demand knowledge of the true text.[205]

But besides the corrections in the 'Satyr Against Vertue' and
'Apology', the volume contains even clearer instances of Oldham's
amendments. Of six readings which show him attempting to improve
on what he had previously written and printed, four occur in the
'Satyrs upon the Jesuits'. At I.254-7 *1681* has:

> Let the full clouds, which a long time did wrap
> Your gathering thunder, now with sudden clap
> Break out upon your *Foes*: dash and confound,
> And scatter wide destruction all around.

In *1682* the last line becomes

> And spread avoidless ruine all around.

A draft in *R* 250 reads

> Let Clouds a while your <u>breeding</u> thunder wrap

> Still gathering strength, till with a sudden clap
> It break upon your Fos, dash & confound
> And scatter bolts of Vengeance all around.

In the margin are the revisions 'gathering' for 'breeding'; 'Till big & ripe', and 'deal its wide destruction', with a reference to Don C[arlos] p. 21, quoting part of a passage which runs:

> Full charg'd with rage and with my vengeance hot
> Like a Granado from a Cannon shot,
> Which lights at last upon the Enemies ground
> Then breaking deals destruction all around.

Evidently in 1682 Oldham revised to get rid of the tautology in 'wide destruction all around' and of the verbal dependence on Otway. At III.296 f., *1681* reads

> Ravish at th' Altar, kill when you have done,
> Make them your Rapes the Victims to attone.

In *1682* the second line becomes:

> Make them your Rapes, and victims too in one

A draft (*R* 260) has

> Make them your Guilt the victims to attone   Rapes

Another (*R* 265) agrees exactly with *1681*; but *Garnets Ghost* [1679] agrees with *1682*. Since there is not the least sign nor likelihood that the *1679* text was consulted in setting up the *1682*, the conclusion must be that disliking the harsh inversion he had adopted in *1681*, Oldham reverted in *1682* to his earlier phrasing, which *1679*, though piratical, preserves. At II.235, according to *1681* the Jesuits hold solemn perjuries more light

> Than *Bullies* common Oaths and canting Lies,

where 'canting', the Errata and two drafts bear witness, should
be 'bant'ring'. In *1682* the line takes the revised form,

> Than a Town-Bullie common Oaths, and Lies.

Again, at III.601, where no draft is extant, the readings are:
1681

> But if ill fortune should your Plot betray,
> And you to mercy of your Foes a prey:

and *1682*, for the second line:

> And leave you to the Rage of Foes a prey;

eliminating, compared with the former syntax, the awkward ellip-
sis of 'betray' 'And [betray] you'.

The other two clear instances of authorial revision are in the
'Satyr Against Vertue'. The rhythm of 1. 137 had given trouble.
Oldham's fair copy has

> Her Quiet and Calm and Peace of Mind.

In *1681* the first 'and' is rejected, I suspect by the compositor's
ear, for the Errata restores it. Perhaps someone warned Oldham
that a quasi-monosyllabic pronunciation of 'Quiet'[206] was unacceptable; the word disappears in *1682*:

> Her boasted calm, and peace of mind,

which regularizes the line and makes it more pregnant. At 1. 38,
1679 and *1681* read

> We (thanks to Heaven) more cheaply can offend.

'Heaven' is most likely an authentic early reading, but it is
awkwardly repeated four lines below: hence the autograph fair
copy and the Errata substitute 'Providence' making the line into
an alexandrine, which Oldham perhaps then decided he did not want

at this point, for *1682* brings back the pentameter by changing
Providence to Fate. Oldham's original title is also brought back,
'A Satyr Against Vertue' having been thrust upon it: the rever-
sion to

> *Aude aliquid brevibus Gyaris, & carcere dignum,*
> *Si vis esse aliquis*—Juven. Sat.
> Ode.

will have been his doing.

   How far did his revision extend? We cannot saddle him with every
variant of the *1682* edition which makes sense; set up from the
1681, it suffers from all the deterioration in detail characteristic of a reprint. It is heavily and mechanically re-punctuated,
with apostrophes replacing vowels so as to reduce the lines to
an obvious scansion, and commas inserted before almost every
'and'.[207] The lighter pointing of *1681* is more in accordance with
Oldham's practice in his fair copies in the Rawlinson MS. At least
once the *1682* punctuation obscures the meaning. In 'Satyrs upon
the Jesuits', III.297, *1681* reads

> Empty whole *Surius,* and the *Talmud* drain,
> Saint *Francis* and Saint *Mahomet's Alcoran*

Oldham is referring to *L'Alcoran des Cordeliers*, as well as to
Mahomet's. But in *1682* the couplet was punctuated:

> Empty whole *Surius* and the *Talmud*: drain
> St. *Francis,* and Saint *Mahomet's Alcoran*

The colon, getting rid of the inversion, may be the author's; but
with the compositor's habitual comma before 'and', the allusion
is destroyed. The same satire furnishes two good examples of
altered words which do not make obvious nonsense, yet are certainly wrong. At 1. 37, *'Genevah's Rebel'* becomes *'Geneva's
Rebels'*, though Calvin is meant. At 1. 471, Loyola extols 'direction of the intention', enabling one to enjoy the fruits of
simony without incurring the guilt, so long as

thoughts and *Ducats* well directed be.

1682 corrupts 'well' to 'will'. Perhaps it was by Oldham's deliberate choice that in the *1682* 'Satyr against Vertue' and
'Apology' sixteen readings, good in themselves but differing from
the autograph, were retained from the unreliable *1681* text used
as copy. Yet one doubts it. An obviously wrong reading (at 'Satyr',
263) is kept in the same way, and two of the sixteen are manifestly suspicious. In 1. 7 of the 'Satyr', 'wild' is repeated
from *1681*, despite the correction to 'vile', the reading of the
autograph, in the *1681* Errata. And in 1. 107, which we should expect to be a long one, *R* has:

>   And kindly sent him to the Gods, and better company

with 'quickly' for 'kindly' in the margin. Neither epithet figures
in *1679, 1681*, or *1682*, so the line is shortened. At 1. 258 there
is what looks like progressive corruption. *R* reads:

>   I travail with a glorious Mischief, for whose Birth
> My Soul's too narrow, and weak Fate too feeble yet to bring it forth.

The clumsiness of the last phrase caused 'it' to be dropped in
the *1679* and *1681* editions; in *1682* the metre, thus injured, was
repaired by the omission of 'yet'. That edition has in fact a
considerable number of doubtful variants, possibly authorial, but
for the most part at least equally likely to be inadvertent errors
or unauthorized emendations in the printing-house. In 'The Passion
of Byblis' the compositor who in 1. 122 produced nonsense by turning 'to him make known' into 'to make him known' would no doubt
be as capable as the author of transposing 'Shame and Blood' into
'Blood and Shame' in 1. 10. In 'Satyrs upon the Jesuits', III.100,
where *1681*, agreeing with a rough draft, has

>   Chast, Gentle, Meek, a Saint, a God, what not?

and *1682* substitutes 'who not?', one immediately suspects the
sophisticating hand of compositor or corrector. Other doubtful
readings are merely altered pronouns or conjunctions, very minor

changes to be made in revision, unless as corrections; and that
some of them are not simply corrections is clear, since in four
or five instances the *1681* reading concurs with an autograph
draft.

In drawing upon the autograph fair copies of 'Aude aliquid.
Ode' ('A Satyr Against Vertue') and 'Upon a Woman' to help elucidate the relationship between the *1681* and *1682* editions, it has
been assumed that the corrections in the 'Ode', and the autograph of 'Upon a Woman', from which in *1681* they must have been
printed, were later than those versions in *R*. The priority between the manuscript and published texts not only of these poems,
but of the other seven of which *R* contains similar copies, has
now to be investigated, so as to establish which authorial
variants are the revisions, those in the extant autographs or
those in the first editions. With one exception—the epithalamium to William and Mary—the published text gives the later
version.

The evidence is plainest in 'A Dithyrambique'. Here *Poems, And
Translations, 1683*, discards twenty lines of the manuscript,
twelve of which Oldham had meanwhile turned to account elsewhere.[208] In the ode upon Jonson, it substitutes 'And' for the
unpleasing contraction ''Bove' in l. 5, and changes l. 142 into
an alexandrine to break a long run of pentameters. In *Some New
Pieces, 1681*, there are similar revisions of the manuscript
readings in the 'Hymn of St. Ambrose' and the satire 'Upon a Bookseller'. In l. 38 of the 'Hymn', 'Vast' is altered to 'Huge'
because 'vast' occurred twelve lines above and twice below. In
l. 53 of the satire, the edition has 'sensless' drone: Oldham
had to change the more pregnant 'stingless' of the manuscript
because it clashed with 'stung' in the previous sentence. Again,
in l. 92 the manuscript has 'chows'd Bubble', with 'Cully' in
the margin; the edition adopts 'Cully', and extends the revision,
with 'pawn'd' for 'chows'd'. The print of the 'Paraphrase upon
the 137 Psalm' has only one major variant from the fair copy:
l. 57

    When nought, Jerusalem, can claim our thoughts, but thou,

is transposed to

When nought can claim our thoughts, Jerusalem, but thou

so that the parts of the phrase fall in a more natural order.

The *1681* version of 'Upon a Woman' twice agrees with the marginal reading, and not the text, as first written, of the autograph. Evidently the marginal revisions were incorporated in the manuscript sent to the press. The *1682* text of 'A Satyr Against Vertue' and its 'Apology'—the first to embody Oldham's corrections and revisions of the bad *1679, 1681* version—similarly agrees with four of the autograph marginal readings. It ignores two others: but there, in preparing the list of alterations or the marked copy of *1681*, whichever it was, that he supplied for the printer, Oldham evidently preferred his original version to his marginal alternative.

In the seven poems discussed, the direction of revision is from the manuscript to the published texts. In the pindarique on William and Mary, it is the reverse. That is not surprising. Oldham sent it to be published immediately it was written. Herringman, evidently the publisher concerned, brought out a good text in a single sheet folio, licensed 8 November 1677, only three days after the lines, Oldham himself relates, were not so much composed, as hastily poured out: he had hardly the time to transcribe them, much less to correct them: at another time he would have made them more polished.[209] As from this account one would expect, his fair copy proves to have been made later; it contains revisions of the *1677* version. At l. 66, *1677* reads 'fair' and repeats the word two lines below: reading 'soft', the autograph gets rid of the repetition. Again at l. 91, *1677* has

But what in Pity you to others show,

altered only a little from a rough draft—

But what for others you in Pitty show.

the autograph, with

But what you must to others in Compassion show,

revised more radically. In three instances out of four, *1677*
agrees with the autograph as originally fair-copied, not with
the marginal revisions, whereas in the seven comparable texts,
the count is seven against two the other way. For this poem, the
autograph embodies Oldham's latest intentions, since the text in
the *1687 Remains* is merely a reprint of *1677*; not only without
revisions, but with a bare dozen variants in punctuation, spelling, and capitals.

Before Oldham included it in *Poems, And Translations, 1683*,
'The Careless Good Fellow' had appeared, as *The Clarret Drinker's
Song*, in a single leaf, dated 1680 and by Luttrell 14 July; and
as 'The Claret Bottle' in John Playford's *Choice Ayres and Songs*,
Book III, 1681.[210] These publications of the Song are of uncertain status. They are anonymous: the texts are reasonably good
(in the *1680* there is only one manifest error (in 1. 34) though
three or four of its other readings are inferior). But that need
not mean they were authorized: the Song is comparatively short,
and if it were circulating in manuscript had not had, from the
time it was written, more than about four months to suffer from
transcriptions before reaching print. There is nothing to show
that Playford's text or a transcript in manuscript are independent of the *1680*. Neither that nor Playford's was used as copy
in *1683*. Still more uncertain is the status of the text of 'An
Ode of Anacreon. The Cup' in the Oxford *Anacreon*,[211] which may
or may not predate its inclusion in the same Oldham volume. The
Anacreon is dated 1683, so that it might be prior or subsequent
to *Poems, And Translations*, which was advertised in *The Observator* for 14 July; indeed, since the *Anacreon* date might be Old
Style, its publication might have been after Oldham's death. The
other odes not newly translated for it by Thomas Wood and Francis
Willis—Cowley's, to wit—were from print, and it seems probable
that so was 'The Cup'. Wood, as an admirer of Oldham's, was most
likely responsible for its inclusion. Oldham's verses 'Upon a
Lady' were first published in *Poems, And Translations*; and this
yields possible evidence, which, however, there is some diffi-
culty in accepting, that Wood knew the book by 26 July. That is
Luttrell's date, recorded by Thorn Drury, on his copy of *Juvenalis Redivivus*, where Wood alludes to 'Upon a Lady'.[212] If he read
those verses in Oldham's volume, no doubt he read 'The Cup' there

too. But unless the *Observator* advertisement of 14 July was somewhat belated, his allusion, if he first met with 'Upon a Lady'
in that volume, was uncommonly quick work. Being indecent, 'Upon
a Lady' was just the sort of thing to circulate in manuscript,
and Wood may have met it earlier in such a copy. Yet I have never
encountered it elsewhere than in Oldham's own text, and must
still doubt whether Wood did so.

   No doubts like these attach to the publications in 1679, prior
to Oldham's authorized *Satyrs Upon The Jesuits, 1681*, of *Garnets
Ghost* and *Father Whitebread's Walking Ghost*, each in a single
sheet folio, and the quarto of *A Satyr Against Vertue*.[213] It is
these which he stigmatizes in two 'Advertisements'; the first,
an abortive draft, composed when he contemplated bringing out
the first two 'Satyrs upon the Jesuits' in advance of the rest;
the second prefixed to the *1681* volume itself. The draft begins:

The author of these trifles [*margin* Satyrs] had not consented to their publishing as yet (he having design'd more on the same subject, & to have them
come out altogether [*sic*]) but that he is now forc'd to do it in his own
defence.

Garnets Ghost [*1679*] is then described:

One of them was lately printed without his knowledge out of the stragling
copies that past about the town, which besides the uncorrectness it went with
from his hands, was so miserably mangled and abused by the ignorance & mistakes of transcribers, that twas becom a greater satyr upon himself than
those upon whom it was design'd [*margin* written].

Next comes a deserved diatribe against *Father Whitebread's Walking Ghost, 1679*:

Another lewd Rhymer had foisted good part of it into a thing of his own
[*interlined* among some doggrel of his own] & coupled it with worse sence
than what we have sung in Churches, & cried at Fleetbrigde [*sic*].

The rest, with memoranda which follow and are taken up in 'Satyrs
upon the Jesuits' III.469 f., 490 ff., IV.84 f., enable us to
date the draft during the composition of Satyr III and before

Satyr IV was begun.

To prevent the spreading of these he is fain hasten out this true edition,
wherein he had added another Satyr upon the same subject. If these find any
liking in the world he will shortly make some more adjoinders of the like
nature.[214]

In the 'Advertisement' to *Satyrs Upon The Jesuits, 1681, A Satyr
Against Vertue, 1679,* is the target.

At first he intended it not for the publick, nor to pass beyond the privacy
of two or three Friends, but seeing it had the Fate to steal abroad in Manuscript, and afterwards in print, without his knowledge; he now thinks it a
justice due to his own Reputation, to have it come forth without those faults,
which it has suffered from Transcribers and the Press hitherto, and which
make it a worse Satyr upon himself than upon what it was design'd.[215]

Written originally of *Garnets Ghost*, the final phrase is much
more justly applicable to the thoroughly corrupt text of *A Satyr
Against Vertue*. Even so, that piracy, and some extant representatives of the manuscripts which 'stole abroad', do seem to preserve a number of authentic discarded readings. That *Garnets
Ghost* does so follows from what Oldham says about 'the uncorrectness [the satire] went with from his hands', and in fact some
twenty-five of its variants appear to be of this kind. Though its
bad readings are numerous enough to confirm Oldham's account of
its origin, textually it is in a different class from *A Satyr
Against Vertue*, and the stolen lines in *Father Whitebread's
Walking Ghost*, which last are too garbled to be worth collating
in the apparatus.

There remain to be assessed the means for establishing the
texts of 'Sardanapalus' and 'Upon the Author of the Play call'd
Sodom'. A copy of the 'Sodom' verses, complete, and correctly
attributed to Oldham, existed in the archetype common to the
1680 Rochester and Yale MS b. 105. Their versions are substan-
tially identical, except that the Rochester has two bad readings
(in ll. 47-8 and 49), and omits the attribution. The Yale text
is excellent, supported in so many of its readings by the autograph drafts that one has no hesitation, since it must represent

a subsequent final version, in trusting it for the seven lines
without equivalent in the drafts, the fifteen or so where its
form appears to supersede theirs, and its indication of which
phrases in them were dropped from the finished piece.

Readings endorsed by these drafts carry the unchallengeable
stamp of the author's intention. In 'Sardanapalus' no readings
are similarly authenticated: the manuscript to be chosen as copy-
text has to be arrived at by comparing the twelve possibilities,[216]
and its variants must be weighed, each of them, against the alter-
natives elsewhere. Happily, the result is unequivocal: Harvard
MS Eng. 585 emerges as markedly the best text.[217] Several of its
features are in its favour. It is independently descended, not
one of the six manuscripts emanating from one and the same scriptorium. Though it does not assign the piece to Oldham, it is one
of the three to have, in full, Soame's verses upon the author.[218]
Still more significantly, in common only with MS Dyce 43 it
carries all seven of the marginal references, evidently Oldham's,
to learned sources. Collation, however, is the decisive test. The
Harvard manuscript is found unique in one important and one minor
correct reading. It avoids a specious mispunctuation which traps
seven of the twelve manuscripts. Twice elsewhere, in company with
a different pair of manuscripts each time, it is right where the
rest are wrong. Again with two companions, one a new one, it has
what is evidently an authorial revision. Coupled with this it
preserves the original where the archetype of eight manuscripts
had a blank. No other manuscript has the right (or in the case of
the revision the best) reading in all five places. Wentworth has
it in four, Portland PwV 42 in two, Harley 7319, in general the
most reliable after Harvard, in none of them. With Harvard as
copy-text, an editor is obliged to emend it on seven occasions,
two of them trivial; and is likely to judge its reading inferior
in three more. For Harley 7319 the corresponding figures are
eleven (four trivial), and four. Its unique variants 'great' for
'kind' (1. 155) and 'Triumph shown' for 'Banner hung' (1. 149)
appear to be authentic early readings, like three different ones
in which Vienna and Harley 6914 agree, and 'grasping' (1. 181)
shared by these three manuscripts and five others.

3. *The Present Edition: Text and Textual Apparatus*

For thirty-one poems the sole authorities are the first editions
of *Some New Pieces*, or *Poems, And Translations*, or the *Remains*,
from which accordingly they are edited, with acceptance of the
errata, undoubtedly Oldham's, in three of them. Four more are
only partial or doubtful exceptions. The last twenty-five lines
of the 'Lamentation for Adonis' and the first thirty-five of the
Imitation of Juvenal III survive in autograph fair copy in the
Rawlinson manuscript. In substantive readings these exactly confirm the published texts, and though in accidentals they represent Oldham's practice where the prints vary from it, for con-
sistency's sake within those poems the prints are kept as
copy-texts throughout, though the opportunity of the autographs
is taken to remove three intrusive compositorial commas. Texts
of 'The Careless Good Fellow' printed earlier than *Poems, And
Translations*, lack any mark of authorization; and that of 'The
Cup' in the Oxford *Anacreon* may (as we have seen) be subsequent
to it and derive from it. None of their few variants, in any
event, are of a kind to bear on a textual decision.

   Five poems in *Some New Pieces* and *Poems, And Translations* have
two texts of the highest authority: besides the first editions,
the autograph fair copies. The autographs, not extant, from
which they were set up superseded those in the Rawlinson manuscript, which nevertheless in accidentals give us Oldham's
practice, and which take us behind the possible errors of the
printing-house. They are therefore made the copy-text, with the
substitution from the editions of every recognizably authorial
variant, as representing Oldham's revised intentions.[219] The
regular seventeenth-century contractions, as everywhere when
manuscript is being followed, are silently expanded.

   'Upon the Marriage of the Prince of Orange' likewise exists in
an authorized first edition—Herringman's in 1677—and an autograph fair copy. But this time it is the autograph which revises
the published text, and is to be followed, as combining with
Oldham's accidentals his finally preferred readings. The reprint
of *1687*, when the poem was first included in Oldham's *Remains*,
is wholly dependent on the first edition, and textually of no
account.

In *Satyrs Upon The Jesuits, 1681*, 'Upon a Woman', like the five poems noted in *Some New Pieces* and *Poems, And Translations* exists in an autograph fair copy antedating the published text. So far, the editorial principle is the same: to take the autograph as copy-text, but to accept from the published version any variant discernible as what the author eventually intended. Now, however, there is a further text to reckon with, for the second edition of the *Satyrs (1682)* underwent authorial revision. To decide whether a variant does represent the eventual intention, both the *1681* and the *1682* texts have to be considered—a process that establishes beyond doubt certain *1681* readings as unwarrantable departures from the autograph.

With the 'Satyrs upon the Jesuits'—'Garnet's Ghost' ('Satyr I') excepted—and 'The Passion of Byblis', we are back to two authorities, the first edition, and the second—'corrected'. For the sake of the accidentals, the earlier is taken as copy-text, apart from L's italics, so alien to Oldham's practice. These, imposed by the compositor upon his copy, are stripped away,[220] and the passages concerned (all in the 'Satyrs upon the Jesuits') conformed, to the best of the editor's judgement, with the habits of compositor M. As regards the variant readings, with no help from autograph except occasionally from the drafts, the problem is the familiar one where a second authority combines revisions with the corruptions characteristic of a reprint.[221] When manifest corruptions have been rejected in favour of the *1681* reading, and manifest revisions in *1682* adopted, there is a remainder of variants which it baffles editorial discrimination to assign to either category. Some are practically sure to belong to one and some to the other, yet there are no rational grounds for treating any of them differently from the rest. One can either accept them all from the later text, thus making certain that no revision or correction is excluded, at the price of replacing with corruptions what were sound readings in the earlier; or one can retain all the earlier readings, so that none is corrupted, but in the certainty that some revisions and corrections are being rejected. Counting the sin of omission the less heinous of the two, in these indifferent variants I have preferred to keep the text of *1681*; the apparatus enables a reader, if so minded, to make the opposite choice. My own is to adopt readings

from *1682* only when convinced the changes are Oldham's. These
include its adoption of all but one of the *1681* errata, and its
further revision of that one.

So far as establishing the text is concerned, 'Garnet's Ghost'
is on the same footing, and is treated in the same way, as the
rest of the 'Satyrs upon the Jesuits': in the *1681* and *1682*
editions no use was made of the *1679* piracy, whose variants, like
those of a transcript in MS *m*, consist of corruptions and authentic but discarded readings.

The remaining piece in *Satyrs Upon The Jesuits* is 'A Satyr
Against Vertue' and its 'Apology'. In view of its textual vicis-
situdes, our good fortune in having the aid of an autograph fair
copy and the *1681* errata is great indeed. In the present edition,
on the principle it follows elsewhere, the autograph supplies the
copy-text, and Oldham's subsequent changes, where one can be confident of them, are introduced, wholly (since *1681* virtually
reproduces the bad text of *1679*) from *1682*, including its adoption of forty-five of the *1681* errata, and its revisions of the
other two.

The uncollected (and save for 'The Desk. Canto I' hitherto unpublished) poems and fragments in the Rawlinson manuscript are
given direct from the autographs. The two drafts of 'The Vision'
and the two of the 'Satyr on the Town and Times', being unsuited
for collation, are each printed. 'In Praise of Poetry' must be
confessed a construction by the editor, assembled from scattered
drafts, and arranged partly at his discretion, though partly with
the guidance of overlaps between several of the fragments, and
of gaps left, for subsequent filling, in one of them.

For the verses on the author of 'Sodom', in substantive readings there is no clash of testimony between Oldham's drafts, and
the two witnesses to the archetype of a completed version, the
Yale MS b. 105 and the Rochester *Poems 1680* (which differs from
Yale only by two minimal manifest errors). There are no drafts
for 11. 12, 32, 38, and at 11. 19-21 a draft couplet was expanded
into a triplet. The edited text relies for the final form of the
piece upon the Yale manuscript, but invokes the drafts to authen-
ticate that unauthorized version, and for the accidentals, takes
them into account. The text being so well established by these
witnesses, it seemed needless (with one exception) to record the

seventeen variants of the Portland MS (PwV 40) which comprise
fourteen obvious scribal errors and two other readings certainly
wrong: but 'poore' (1. 19) is apparently, like 'dull' in a draft
(*R*98), an epithet tried out before Oldham settled on 'meer'.

   To reach the position from which 'Sardanapalus' could be
edited was a matter of some time and trouble; but once the
manuscripts had been found, collated, and assessed, the task was
simple: to follow the Harvard manuscript, emending it in ten
places with the aid of the others. Since the assessment depends
wholly on the collation, it was desirable to record the evidence,
the variants of all twelve manuscripts, in full.

   Three of these manuscripts owe their special interest to what
appear to be authentic but superseded readings.[222] Such readings,
in versions of 'A Satyr Against Vertue' and 'Garnet's Ghost'
which against the autograph or authorized texts have no authority,
constitute the decisive reason for bringing even those versions
within the scope of the textual apparatus. On which variants are
of this kind there is room for difference of opinion; and so the
record must be sufficiently comprehensive. For *Garnets Ghost*
(*1679*) and the transcript of that poem in MS *m* it can be complete. For 'A Satyr Against Vertue' and its 'Apology' to have
made it so would have been neither practicable nor useful. Besides the autograph and two authorized texts, one with errata,
eight others were concerned: not only those of *1679* and *1681*,
which were links in the chain of transmission, but the *1680*
Rochester and five manuscripts which were not.[223] To keep the
apparatus within bounds, it is so far selective that where one
text alone departs from the rest, and in what is a manifest copyist's error, that reading is ignored. Such readings have nothing
to tell us about relationships between the texts, and would have
swelled the tide of insignificant variants in which the possibly
significant are liable to be drowned.

   The prints of 'The Careless Good Fellow' (as *The Clarret
Drinker's Song*) and of 'The Cup' in the Oxford *Anacreon* are alike
in being doubtfully related to those in *Poems, And Translations,
1683*. On the remote chance that a couple of readings in each,
not in themselves inferior, might come from an authorial transcript prior to the Hindmarsh edition, their variants are
recorded.

The apparatus is intended to record all substantive readings
in which there are variants between texts having authority, with
the editor's decisions between them; and all which he has emended.
Where a change made on his responsibility has been anticipated in
an unauthoritative edition this is specified in a form such as
'Ed. (1722)'. A few variant formes have been found: the corrected
and uncorrected states are noted.[224] In support of a reading,
autograph drafts are sometimes cited. Some longer ones for
'A Letter from the Country' are printed in Appendix II, with passages Oldham excised from the 'Dithyrambique' and the ode on
Jonson.

Variants in punctuation, capitals, and spelling are recorded
only if sense or versification is affected, or if they bear on
some textual question in dispute. Long 's' is used neither by
Oldham nor by the scribes of the Harvard 'Sardanapalus' or Yale
'Upon the Author of ... "Sodom"', and their treatment of i and j,
u and v, is modern. Where in other manuscripts the older forms
occur, they are ignored in collation. So are such printing-house
errors as the want of a full stop at the end of a paragraph, a
wrong letter yielding no conceivably acceptable word, or a lapse
in an otherwise consistent series of italics or quotation marks
to indicate the speaker in a dialogue. Silent emendation of accidentals has been extended to two recurrent features undoubtedly
compositorial. Normalization of the lavish use of italics by
compositor L in his share (bibliographically identified) of
Satyrs Upon The Jesuits, 1681, has been noted earlier. Also compositorial is a particular class of commas frequent in *Some New
Pieces, 1681*, and *Poems, And Translations, 1683*, but not in
Satyrs Upon The Jesuits, 1681, or *Remains, 1684* (the compositors,
setting from similar copy, are evidently not the same). In his
fair copies, it is no practice of Oldham's to divide doublets,
like 'Art & Nature', 'strengthen & establish', 'ready & unerring',
'in duty and in love', by a comma before the 'and'. In the three
poems in *Some New Pieces* and the two in *Poems, And Translations*,
where the first editions can be compared with autograph fair
copies, every one of the eighty-nine such commas (thirty-three
in *Some New Pieces*, fifty-six in *Poems, And Translations*) is
absent from the autographs. This category of comma, beyond doubt
obtruded on the text of Oldham's manuscript from which the first

editions were set up, has therefore been expunged from all the poems where we depend for the accidentals upon those editions. (In similar doublets, Oldham does regularly have a comma before 'or': those in the editions have accordingly been retained.) Finally, punctuation has been emended, but not without record, in the small number of instances where it impedes a self-evident run-on at the end of a line, or where a premature full stop interrupts the syntax.

Two notations in the textual apparatus had better perhaps be interpreted. Such a siglum as *MSS -Y1* means that all the manuscripts minus (viz. with the exception of) *Y1* have the reading in question; the reading of *Y1* will be given as a variant. *P3 absent*, or the like, means that *P3* does not include the passage in which the reading occurs, and so has no evidence to offer concerning it.

NOTES

[1] Parish Register, Shipton Moyne.

[2] Bodl. MS J. Walker, c. 7, fol. 16. Confusion between Oldham's father and grandfather persists from Wood's *Athenae Oxonienses* to the *DNB*. See Sybil Rosenfeld and myself in *N&Q*, clxiv. 112, clxvii. 30, and *Miscellanea Genealogica*, Sept. 1934. Since even the *Victoria County History, Gloucestershire,* xi (1976), p. 249, makes the father curate of Shipton Moyne, it must be emphasized that he never enjoyed Anglican emoluments except at Long Newnton, to which he was admitted by the Triers, 6 May 1659. He may have acted from the d. of his predecessor, John Trotman, Feb. 1656/7. He is 'John Ouldham junior' in the Shipton parish register 8 Nov. 1655, but 'Cler.' 29 Dec. 1658, and 'Rector' in the Newnton register 8 Feb. 1661. Upon deprivation (not till after 8 Nov. 1662) he sometimes 'conventicled it', prior to the Toleration Act (1689), when he 'professedly set up' as a Presbyterian minister: MS J. Walker, loc. cit.; Alexander Gordon, *Freedom After Ejection*, pp. 44, 322, citing MS Minutes in the archives of the Presbyterian Board in Dr Williams's Library.

[3] Wood, *Ath. Oxon.*, ed. Bliss, iv.119-22.

[4] Bodl. MSS Wood F. 28, fol. 283^r; Top. Oxon. f. 31, 287 f.

[5] Oxford University Archives: Congregation Register 1669-80, pp. 45, 54.

[6] 'Living for some time after with his father, much against his humour and inclinations' (Wood, op. cit., iv.120).

[7] See my history of 'The "Imitation" in English Poetry, Especially in Formal Satire, before the Age of Pope', *RES*, xxv (1949), 124-40; and above, pp. xlvi f., lvi f., lxxxiii-v.

[8] 'Modes of Satire', in *Restoration Theatre*, ed. J.R. Brown and B. Harris, Stratford-upon-Avon Studies, 1965, p. 128.

[9] Cf. 'To L.G.', the heading of a draft for 'Upon a Woman', MS *R*99.

[10] Aged eleven, she d. 2 Dec. 1675. Cf. Kingscote Parish Register; MS *R*238.

[11] See my 'Bibliography of John Oldham', *Oxford Bibliographical Society Proceedings of Papers*, v.i, 1936, Kraus Reprint, with addenda and corrigenda, 1969 (hereafter *Bibliography*), ii.42, Revd J.M. Moffatt, *The History of the Town of Malmesbury*, 1805, p. 72. Three principal considerations favour the tradition: it would be suspect if it referred to any later year, when Oldham had left the neighbourhood; his brother, Thomas, aged 20, was applying himself to medicine; two of the poet's nieces survived at Shipton till 1795 and 1798, and the husband of a third was living at Westport adjoining Malmesbury until 1787, well within Moffatt's lifetime (see my 'Family of John Oldham the Poet', *Miscellanea Genealogica et Heraldica*, Sept. 1934).

[12] Wood, op. cit., iv.121; anon. memoir, *Works of Mr. John Oldham*, 1722, p. v (hereafter, *1722* Memoir); T.D. Fosbroke, *An Original History of the City of Gloucester*, p. 136.

[13] See my 'John Shepheard, Master of Whitgift School when John Oldham the Poet was Under-Master', *Notes & Queries for Somerset and Dorset*, Sept. 1979, pp. 435-44, recording the research by which F.H.G. Percy, W.D. Hussey, and I establish the Master's identity: where n. 22 gives the authorities for Morwent's kinship with the Shepheards of Horsley and Tetbury.

[14] The dates of 'Aude aliquid. Ode' and 'A Rant to his Mistress'.

[15] For confirmation of the Carews as patrons of Oldham, a fact I deduced from MS *R*, see D.M. Vieth, 'John Oldham, the Wits, and *A Satyr against Vertue*', *PQ* xxxii (1953), 91-3.

[16] Printed, from Spencer's autograph (MS *R*198-204) as Appendix I. My identification of Spencer from the pedigrees of Carew and Spencer in Manning and
Bray, *History ... of ... Surrey*, ii.253, Clutterbuck, *History ... of ... Hertford*, iii.97, and *GEC Baronetage*, ii.200, is rendered certain by the agree-
ment of the signature to the verse-letter with that of a letter from this John
Spencer preserved in the Berkshire Record Office.

[17] See, for the vandalism, 'Aude aliquid. Ode', headnote; for the visit, id.
with the variant accounts in the *1722 Memoir*, pp. v f., and the Osborn MS,
Chest II, No. 14, at Yale, quoted by Vieth, loc. cit., and his discussion.

[18] MS *R*, p. 206; *Poems, And Translations*, 1683, p. 206.

[19] MS *R*, p. 106.

[20] Not her mother, as I absurdly suggested in Harold Love's symposium,
Restoration Literature; Critical Approaches, 1972, p. 180: the recipient is
Cosmelia's 'Hera', and Mary is alluded to as Hera in the poem.

[21] See 'Ode on Jonson', headnote.

[22] See my 'Oldham and Phineas Fletcher: An Unrecognized Source for Satyrs
Upon The Jesuits', *RES* n.s. xxii.88, 89 (Nov. 1971, Feb. 1972), pp. 19-34,
410-22. Cooper R. Mackin, 'The Satiric Technique of John Oldham's *Satyrs
Upon The Jesuits*', *SP*, lxii, 1965 (thin on its announced subject), quoted two
parallels from Fletcher's *The Locusts* (p. 84, n. 8, p. 88, n. 11) but without
recognizing it as a major source. On Buchanan and 'Franciscanus', see *Satyrs
Upon The Jesuits*, 'Advertisement', l. 23, n., and 'Jesuits III', headnote.

[23] MS *R*, p. 279.

[24] Anchitel Grey, *Debates in the House of Commons, 1667-1694*, 1763, viii.295;
cf. vi.116, 21, 23, 24, 25, 42, 52, 81, 82, 89, etc.; Danby to the King, 21
May 1679: henchmen of Monmouth's 'cry up Sir Nicholas Carew and his associates' for 'theire great earnestnesse to have a successor named' (Andrew
Browning, *Thomas Osborne Earl of Danby* (1951), ii.83).

[25] MS *R*, pp. 246 f., 260.

[26] 'Jesuits I', 31 ff., II.241; cf. the odes to Atwood, st. VIII, and Jonson, l. 52 ff. For Opposition attitudes, even on the Covenanters' rising, see
J.R. Jones, *The First Whigs* (1961), pp. 79 f.; H.C. Foxcroft, *Life and Letters of ... Halifax* (1898), i.166, 168; Pollock, pp. 234-6.

[27] *Pace DNB*, there was one grandson only, also named Edward, *aet.* 9. For
both him and his grandfather, see Manning and Bray, *Surrey*, i.40, 292, 317;
ii.234, 498; F.A. Inderwick (ed.), *A Calendar of the Inner Temple Records*,
ii.324, iii.232, and *passim* (index p. 526); Foss, *Judges of England*, vii.173;
Surrey Archaeological Society, Collections, xiv.27, 31, 34; *Visitations of
Surrey* (Harleian Soc. Publications) xliii.191; *Surrey Record Society*, xxxi.
161; *Victoria County History ... Surrey*, iii.232; H.M. Margoliouth (ed.),
Poems and Letters of Andrew Marvell, i.145; J. Foster, *Alumni Oxonienses*.

[28] Draft, MS *R*187, printed J.L. Hill, *St. Edmund Hall Magazine*, 1931, p. 68.

[29] i. p. vi.

[30] MS *R*279; Manning and Bray, *Surrey*, i.292, ii.234, 498; F.A. Inderwick
(ed.), *Calendar of the Inner Temple Records*, iii.105, 117; Sir Nicholas's
relatives, ii.120, 133, 234, 296, iii.49.

[31] 'An Allusion to Martial', l. 20.

[32] Cf. e.g. the awakening (cited Jones, p. 168) of Lionel Duckett, Exclusionist MP in 1680, who wrote (30 July 1683) that he had then been young and innocent, but shortly saw that his colleagues were not actuated by disinterested
zeal against Popery.

[33] *Absalom and Achitophel*, 1. 114. Cf. John Kenyon, *The Popish Plot* (1972), pp. 151, 154, 182-4, 187, 191, 204, 224 f., 242 f.; John Miller, *Popery and Politics in England 1660-1688* (1973), pp. 174-9; J.R. Jones, *The First Whigs*, pp. 107 f., 112, 122 f.

[34] See *Bibliography*, ii.2, 3 (the note by Dr Leba Goldstein and myself in the revised reprint, 1969, pp. 38 d, e, supersedes the 1936 version); and my 'Chief Substantive Editions of Oldham's Poems, 1679-1684: Printer, Compositors, and Publication', *Studies in Bibliography* (1974), xxvii, especially pp. 190-2. For the changed title of 'Upon a Bookseller', see headnote.

[35] According to Wood, iv.120, he was with Thurland 'till 1681; then 'out of ... employ'.

[36] See above, pp. lii, liv, and n. 101 below.

[37] Sir William, and the poet's uncle Thomas Oldham (Will, 1695, in Gloucester Probate Registry, Monumental Inscription at Didmarton, in Bigland, *Historical Collections ... relative to the County of Gloucester*), both had property in Beverstone, close by Tetbury and Kingscote. The likely Oxford acquaintances are John Hickes, s. of Arthur of Charfield (St Edmund Hall, 1673-9), and William Hickes of West End, Wickwar (Magdalen Hall, 1669-72, but in touch with John Freind of St Edmund Hall and his father, whose pupil he had been). Mary, dtr. of Oldham's uncle Phanuel, m. a Charles Hickes of Wickwar. See Mrs William Hicks-Beach, *A Cotswold Family: Hicks and Hicks-Beach*, pp. 45-9; Wood, loc. cit.; *Biographia Britannica* (under Oldham, 3265-8); *GEC Baronetage*, i.125; J. Foster, *Alumni Oxonienses*; Bodl. MS Top. Oxon. f. 31, pp. 172, 353; Parish Registers, Shipton, Charfield (John Hickes, b. 1656, d. 1684); Monumental Inscriptions, Charfield and Wickwar (Bigland, op. cit.); Hickes Wills, and Phanuel and Mary (*née* Hort) Oldham's, in Gloucester Probate Registry (see *The Index Library*, xxxiv, *Gloucester Wills, 2*, 1660-1800); Robert Atkyns, *Ancient and Present State of Gloucestershire*, 1712, p. 376; *Bristol and Gloucestershire Archaeological Society, Transactions*, xi.264.

[38] According to the memoir in Oldham's *Works, 1722*, i.vii, Lower's friendship with the poet arose from his intimate acquaintance with Hickes, and it was 'for about a Year' that under him Oldham studied medicine. Wood (iv.297), whose friend and for a time physician he was, gives an account of him; see further, *DNB*; E.C. and Phebe M. Hoff, 'The Life and Times of Dr. Richard Lower', *Bulletin of the Institute of the History of Medicine*, iv (Mar. 1936), 517-35; J.F. Fulton, *Bibliography of Two Oxford Physicists* (Oxford Bibliographical Society, 1934); Lower, *De Corde*, tr. J.J. Franklin, 1932. B. 1631, he was educated at Westminster School, and Christ Church, Oxford. Becoming junior partner to the famous Dr Willis (cf. 'Art of Poetry', 1. 598, n.), in 1666 he followed him to London, and after Willis's death in 1675 was esteemed the leading physician there, in Westminster, and at Court. On his income, see 'Juvenal XIII', 197 n. But from 1678, on adhering to the Whigs, he lost much of his fashionable practice. When at College's trial (17 Aug. 1681), Dugdale, former Whig witness now a turncoat, denied he had had pox, Lower, who had treated him, subsequently nailed the lie before the Council (Luttrell, i.136). From the Sackville manuscripts (information from Mrs Teri Musman), we learn (0269. A 404, L 11) that Lower was attending the Dorset household as early as May 1674 and as late as Feb. 1684/5; and (T 101/3) that the house in Bow Street, Covent Garden, in 1682 'now or late in the tenure of ... Richard Lower' and to be transferred to Philippa Waldegrave (Dorset's mistress), belonged to Will Richards, close friend of Dorset, and one of the two men deputed by Rochester's representatives to reward anyone who informed against the printer of his pirated *Poems* (*London Gazette*, 22-5 November, 1680). Lower, when Oldham knew him, was probably living here, and then in near-by King Street, where he d. 17 Jan. 1691.

At Oxford, with Willis, Boyle, Wren, and Wallis he belonged to the group who

were to inaugurate the Royal Society: he was FRS, 1667-78, and FRCP from 1675.
He assisted Willis in anatomical research on the nervous system, and published
a defence of Willis's discourse on fevers. In the history of medicine, he is
remembered for his experiments in blood-transfusion, before the Royal Society
(canine, Feb. 1665; human, Nov. 1667), and for locating in the lungs the
change from venous to arterial blood (Pepys, vii.21, n. 3, and authorities
there cited).

Personally, says White Kennet (quoted Bliss, in Wood, loc. cit.), he was
a great lover of news, often going for it to Nell Gwyn. For his characteristic
borrowing of the bullets with which Tom Thynne was assassinated, see 'Juvenal
XIII', 249, n. Somewhat surprisingly, he is described as 'of humour most
austere' in verses 'On Dr. Lower's growing good-natur'd before his death'
(Tom Brown, *Works* (1744), ii.82). He was lampooned for membership of the Whig
clubs, *POAS* (1704) iii.144; and in 'Utile Dulce' (BL MS Harl. 6913 f. 76),
where rowdies' 'noise and serenade' are supposed to have

Forc'd Lower from his Bed which h'as deny'd
To many Patients tho' the wretches died.

[39] *1722* Memoir, i.ix. The future Sir Harry was about 15; Sir William about
52. See Philip Morant, *History ... of ... Essex*, 1768, pp. 24 f.; *GEC Baronetage*, i.125; Le Neve's *Knights* (Harleian Society Publications, viii), pp. 70,
204, 329; Clutterbuck, *History of ... Hertford*, i.444; Venn, *Alumni Canta-
brigienses*.

[40] Wood, iv.121. The Earl was only 21 when Oldham died: see *Complete Peerage*, ed. Vicary Gibbs, viii.306 (IV. Earl: s. of Elizabeth, dau. of Sir John
Evelyn, West Dene, Wilts.).

[41] Wood's date, 'die Decembris nono' is a mistake, perhaps for the nones,
the 5th. The present tablet bearing the inscription, which gives 19 April, is
not the original (see *Gentleman's Magazine*, lxiv (1794), i.115). Evidently
the tablet became detached; for the surrounding ornament *is* original, and
Pevsner's praise of it, in the Penguin *Buildings of England: Nottinghamshire*,
1951, pp. 84 f., is just.

[42] Which, however, though indirectly from Anacreon, are directly from Ronsard; see D.M. Vieth's edn. of Rochester's *Poems*, 1968, p. 52, citing Curt A.
Zimansky.

[43] For this poem, and others cited in this paragraph, see *Ben Jonson*, ed.
Herford and Simpson, vii.103; Robert Herrick, *Poetical Works*, ed. L.C. Martin,
p. 70; Sir John Suckling, *Works*, ed. A.A. Hamilton Thompson, p. 18; Abraham
Cowley, *Poems*, ed. A.R. Waller, p. 133; Rochester, ed. cit., pp. 25, 35, 54;
Sir Charles Sedley, *Poetical and Dramatic Works*, ed. V. de Sola Pinto, i.95;
Minor Poets of the Caroline Period, ed. G. Saintsbury, iii.396 (Flatman).

[44] 'A Letter from the Country', 1. 129.

[45] 'The Early Poetical Career of Samuel Woodforde', in *Essays Critical and
Historical Dedicated to Lily B. Campbell*, 1950, pp. 100-2.

[46] Ed. cit., pp. 146, 214.

[47] Ed. cit., pp. 166, 168, 177.

[48] Cowley, *Poems*, pp. 178, 180 f., 188, 192, 201, 209, 211, 219, 413, 416,
441, 450; *Essays*, pp. 11, 388, 434, 441, 462; edd. cit.

[49] St. xxi.

[50] In his unpublished MA thesis, University of Adelaide. For Pope's n., see
below, n. 68.

[51] 11. 125-49.

[52] For theme-rhetoric, see T.W. Baldwin, *Shakspere's Small Latine & Lesse
Greeke*, 1944, pp. 281, 291, 327 ff.

[53] As remarked by R.I. Mills, op. cit.

[54] Given that the Ode is panegyric, and Dryden's characterization of Jonson in *Of Dramatick Poesie* (*Essays*, i.81-3) judicial criticism, Dryden's appreciation, in final effect, is hardly less high. The panegyrist echoes three of the favourable observations, and ignores the unfavourable ones, the reservations of the judge. Nor of course does he give Jonson a rival in Shakespeare.

[55] *MP*, lii (1956), pp. 145-78.

[56] Cf. Alexander C. Spence (ed.), *Samuel Butler. Three Poems* (Augustan Reprint Society, No. 88), 1961, and his unpublished London MA thesis, 'Samuel Butler (1613-1680): Four Satires on Social Folly', 1958, pp. 41-3, 206-35, especially 228.

[57] *Attribution in Restoration Poetry: A Study of Rochester's 'Poems' of 1680*, 1963, p. 185.

[58] See below, headnote.

[59] *The Letters of ... Rochester*, ed. Jeremy Treglown, 1980, p. 95; cf. the horrified and horrifying bravado of 'To the Postboy' (*Poems*, ed. Vieth, pp. 130 f.; quoted Treglown, p. 2).

[60] Loc. cit.

[61] On Morwent, ll. 450-61; Atwood, 161-6; 'Apology', 38 f.

[62] MS *R*, pp. 95, 225; 90 (margin); cf. on p. 91 a fragment satirizing a debauched gathering:

> Another strait did in the talk succeed ...
> Studied he was in Sodom (which by heart
> H'ad got & cou'd rehearse in every Part)
> And many of its filthy scenes had tried
> And seen them acted ore or els he lied.
> Much of L'Escole de Filles was mentioned there
> [See Pepys 8 Feb. 1667/8.]
> And more of our great witty bawdy Peer.

[63] Bodl. MS Ballard, xx.23, pp. 36 f.; printed in Seward, *Supplement to the Anecdotes of some Distinguished Persons*, 1797, v.91 ff.

[64] *Remains*, 1684, pp. 38 f., 42 f.

[65] MS Ballard, xx.23, p. 37.

[66] Burnet, *Some Passages*, 1680, p. 12.

[67] See 'Aude aliquid. Ode', headnote.

[68] *Bibliography*, ii.23 (Pope's copy).

[69] See John H. O'Neill, 'Oldham's "Sardanapalus". A Restoration Mock-Encomium and its Topical Implications', *Clio*, 1976, 193-210. In studying 'Sardanapalus', we joined forces. He found for us eight manuscripts additional to those in the BL and Bodleian, traced the passages referred to in the side-notes, and contributed much to their elucidation; further, we discussed the piece in all its bearings.

[70] See n. 175 below.

[71] O'Neill, agreeing (p. 206) that 'the most important satirical theme ... is not the sexual *mores* of the King but the libertine life generally', nevertheless (p. 203) calls Charles 'the indirect subject of the ode'. But just as the presence of political and historical allegory in *Hudibras* Part I, or *The Faerie Queene*, does not mean that that allegory is sustained, so here the practice of discontinuous or local topicality should be recognized.

[72] See Vieth, *Attribution*, pp. 169-74, 198-203; and e.g. the former feats Rochester's 'Disabled Debauchee' will propose for emulation.

[73] 'Aude aliquid. Ode', ll. 169 f., 267 f. It is therefore impossible that Oldham should have believed Rochester the author of 'Sodom'. See 'Upon the Author', headnote.

[74] *Poems*, ed. Vieth, p. 46.

[75] The transcriptions are in MS *R*108-23.

[76] See further, above, pp. liii-v; and R. Selden, *English Verse Satire 1590-1765*, p. 96.

[77] *Poems*, ed. Vieth, pp. 45 f.

[78] *The Arte of English Poesie*, ed. G.D. Willcock and A. Walker, 1936, pp. 57 f.

[79] *Essays*, ed. Ker, ii.105, 108.

[80] Burnet, *Some Passages*, 1680, p. 8.

[81] These transcripts are in MS *R*, 105, 214, 232-5; in *MacFlecknoe* two leaves are missing. *MacFlecknoe* was composed before 12 Dec. 1677; and after May 1676, probably in the late summer. D.M. Vieth's article 'The Discovery of the Date of *MacFlecknoe*' (*Evidence in Literary Scholarship*, ed. René Wellek and A. Ribeira, 1979) makes good its title. Hugh Macdonald (*John Dryden. A Bibliography*, 1939, pp. 28 f.) states with exactness what research had up to then established: that the contents of the satire were more or less common knowledge for at least three years before 4 October 1682, the date marked by Luttrell on his copy of the first (pirated) edition.

[82] See above, p. liii, and Appendix III.

[83] Cf. 'The Vision', nn.

[84] *Essays*, ed. Ker, ii.92, 101, 108; cf. 84, 86.

[85] On Juvenal, especially his style, I am much indebted to R. Selden, *English Verse Satire 1590-1765*, 1978, pp. 28-44, 84-9, and 'Juvenal and Restoration Modes of Translation', *MLR*, lxviii, 1973.

[86] Prologue, ll. 38-50; II.241-9.

[87] I.192; II.91, 190; III.216.

[88] *English Verse Satire*, p. 86.

[89] Cf. my 'Poems of John Oldham' (*Restoration Literature*, ed. Love), p. 193, see headnotes to the three Satyrs.

[90] MS *R*, 180. Regarding Augustan concern for transitions, cf. Geoffrey Tillotson, *On the Poetry of Pope*, 1950, pp. 49-54.

[91] I owe this observation to Raman Selden.

[92] See J.N. Figgis, *The Divine Right of Kings* (2nd edn., 1914), pp. 180-4, and *Studies of Political Thought from Gerson to Grotius* (2nd edn., 1923), pp. 138 f., 141 f., 146, 151 f., especially on the Catholic Ligueur polemicists Jean Boucher and Rossaeus (William Reynolds) and Jesuit extremist Juan Mariana, approving the assassination of Henri III. 'No government is legitimate without the admission of the true religion' (141); 'a Catholic King turning heretic becomes *ipso facto* a tyrant' (when 'his deposition may be justified' (138 f.); 'nearly all were agreed that a tyrant *absque titulo* may be slain by anyone' (148). But 'from the close of the religious wars in 1648 we may almost date [the Jesuits'] tacit surrender of the claim to pronounce on these questions' (151). See 'Jesuits II', 57 f., n.

[93] L. von Ranke, *History of the Popes* (Bohn's Popular Library), ii.428, 430, 431-4; D. Ogg, *Europe in the Seventeenth Century*, pp. 333 f., 340-51; G.N. Clark, *The Seventeenth Century*, pp. 302, 313 f.

[94] *Lettres Provinçiales*, 1656-7, which Oldham knew: see *Jesuits*, II.188, III.459, 469, 476, 478, 484, 609, 617, nn.

[95] On which see John Miller's chapter in *Popery and Politics in England 1660-1688*, 1973, pp. 67 ff.

[96] Manning and Bray, *Surrey*, i.317 f., 320 f., ii.527, pedigree facing 523; John Aubrey, *Natural History and Antiquities of ... Surrey*, ii.160 f.; Mrs W. Hicks Beach, *A Cotswold Family*, p. 87.

[97] Cf. e.g., *The buckler of state and justice against the design manifestly discovered of the universal monarchy under the vain pretext of the Queen of France her pretensions*, 1668 (see Pepys, *Diary*, ix.61, n. 2). And see below, 'Upon the Marriage', l. 68 n.

[98] G.N. Clark, *The Seventeenth Century*, p. 308; E. and E. Haag, *La France Protestante*, i (1848), and David C.A. Agnew, *Protestant Exiles from France*, i (1886), cited 'Juvenal III', 130 nn. Cf. Foxcroft, *Halifax* (1898), i.211, 310.

[99] D. Ogg, *England in the Reign of Charles II*, i.352-5, 592; John Miller, *Popery and Politics in England 1660-1688*, 1973, p. 119; James to Legge, 28 May 1679, Dartmouth MSS 33, 34, cited John Pollock, *The Popish Plot*, 1903, p. 217.

[100] Dryden (*Essays*, ii.100) quotes Heinsius' definition of satire as being 'without a series of action'.

[101] Cf. Dryden (id., ii.80) on lampoon, fully justifiable only when the subject of it 'is become a public nuisance'.

[102] Id., p. 84.

[103] Joseph Spence, *Observations, Anecdotes, and Characters of Books and Men*, ed. J.M. Osborn, 1966, i.202 (No. 473).

[104] 'An Essay upon Poetry', *Critical Essays of the Seventeenth Century*, ed. J.E. Spingarn, ii.220.

[105] BL MS Harley 7319 fol. 128^r-132^v; for other texts, see above, p. lxxiii.

[106] Below, Advertisements to *Satyrs Upon The Jesuits*, 1681, and *Some New Pieces*, 1681; and 'Upon a Bookseller', ll. 17 f.

[107] *The Impartial Critick*, in Spingarn, op. cit., iii.177.

[108] 'To the Memory of Mr. Oldham', ll. 15 ff. As regards both tone and metrics, see R. Selden, 'Roughness in Satire from Horace to Dryden', *MLR* lxvi (1971).

[109] R. Selden, *English Verse Satire 1590-1765*, 1978, p. 89.

[110] R.I. Mills, op. cit., made me more aware of the difference between this satire and the other three.

[111] The start of a third is in MS *R*, but there is no indication of its date.

[112] For this, and the rest of the paragraph, see my article, 'The "Imitation" in English Poetry, especially in Formal Satire, before the Age of Pope', *RES* xxv (1949).

[113] *Essays*, ed. W.P. Ker, i.240 f.

[114] Advertisement, *Some New Pieces*, 1681.

[115] Re-examination of the subsequent Imitations leads me to qualify what

I wrote in 1949. In method they differ less from Rochester's in *An Allusion to Horace* than I then concluded.

[116] R. Trickett, *The Honest Muse*, 1967, p. 102.

[117] R. Selden, op. cit., pp. 17 f., 28.

[118] Oldham's attribution to Sprat (Advertisement, *Some New Pieces*, 1681) is confirmed in my 'Contributors to Brome's Horace', *N&Q* clxxiv, 19 Mar. 1938.

[119] See above, p. xliv and n.

[120] 'Epistle ... to Dr. Arbuthnot', ll. 171 f., *Poems*, ed. John Butt, 1963, p. 603.

[121] See l. 341 n.

[122] Trickett, op. cit., p. 101.

[123] *Essays*, ed. Ker, i.1.

[124] 'Imitations of Horace, Epistle I. i.', l. 184; *Poems*, ed. cit., p. 630.

[125] See above, p. xlix, n. 88.

[126] See Brooks, 'Contributors', as above, n. 118.

[127] Trickett, op. cit., p. 102; Selden, *English Verse Satire*, p. 17.

[128] Cf. Selden, 'Oldham's Versions of the Classics', *Poetry and Drama 1570–1700*, ed. A. Coleman and A. Hammond, 1981, pp. 118 f.

[129] *Biographia Britannica*, art. Oldham, by Philip Morant, ad init.

[130] Oldham, *Remains*, 1684, 1687.

[131] Advertisement, *Poems, And Translations*, 1683.

[132] Dryden, Prologue to *Amphitryon*, 1690, quoted Trickett, op. cit., p. 58.

[133] 'Boileau VIII', 230; 'Juvenal III', 44, 96, 105, 126; 'To a Friend', 45, 46; 'Spencer's Ghost', 80, 149, 164, 188.

[134] 'Boileau VIII', 75.

[135] Trickett, op. cit., p. 189.

[136] *Virgidemiarum*, II.vi.

[137] Trickett, op. cit., p. 92.

[138] Cf. e.g., 'Juvenal III', 205-18, 331-44; 102-18 (running for seventeen lines).

[139] e.g. in 'Juvenal III', ll. 13 ff., he has one such inversion in twenty-one lines and if we continue to l. 183, no more than three or four more.

[140] 'Boileau VIII', 138, 143, 286; 'Juvenal III', 60-2; 'Juvenal XIII', 26, 52; 'To a Friend', 110.

[141] ll. 238 ff., 427 ff.

[142] 'Boileau V', 112, 172; 'Boileau VIII', 56, 61, 212; 'Juvenal XIII', 110.

[143] *Essays*, ed. Ker, i.241.

[144] 'Boileau V', 88, 158, 165; 'Boileau VIII', 63; 'Juvenal XIII', 218.

[145] 'Boileau V', 65-8; 'Juvenal III', 364 ff.; 'Juvenal XIII', 131 ff.

[146] Trickett, op. cit., pp. 94, 103.

[147] Id., pp. 21, 59, 104 f., 139.

[148] 'Boileau VIII', 174; 'Juvenal III', 62-4; 'Juvenal XIII', 247.

[149] 'Spencer's Ghost', 259 f.

[150] 'On the Times'.

[151] Cf. Trickett, op. cit., pp. 99 f., 104.

[152] Cf. Selden, *English Verse Satire*, p. 31.

[153] See G.K. Hunter (ed.), *All's Well that Ends Well*, p. xxxviii, n. 1, and references there given.

[154] ll. 37-50.

[155] ll. 93-107, 129-46; 167-90.

[156] The quoted phrases are from Dryden's memorial ode, and Oldham's 'Sunday Thought in Sickness', *Remains*, 1684, pp. 7, 36.

[157] Except for the five poems edited by J.F. Mengel, 1965 (see p. lxxi and n. 162). On Ken Robinson, *John Oldham: Selected Poems* (1980), ibid. and n. 161.

[158] See my Oldham *Bibliography*, Kraus reprint (revised) 1969, ii.17, 29, 30.

[159] Ibid., under ii.21.

[160] Ibid., ii.31. 32; addenda, pp. 38 a, i, j: nn. 4, 34, 36.

[161] Robinson gives fourteen poems. *Works*, 1686, a derivative reprint, and Centaur, were used to print from, and though he had made corrections in them from authoritative texts, these, contrary to his intention, were incomplete: inevitably, corrupt readings (in fact some thirty) survived.

[162] Careful lists are furnished of the variants in the original editions, and also (rather oddly) in two merely derivative (from which, however, only one reading is accepted). Of five readings in *Satyrs upon the Jesuits*, 1682, inexplicable save as authorial revisions, three are accepted and two rejected. Its corrections originating in the *1681* errata are adopted, with seven others undoubtedly correct, and eleven which in my view cannot safely be assumed to be other than printing-house variants (see above, pp. lxxxv-vii, xciii-v.

[163] Doubtless Oldham's publisher, Hindmarsh, received from his patron, William Pierrepont, the manuscripts found at Holme Pierrepont when he died. Patron and publisher had dealings in 1684-7: Pierrepont paid Hindmarsh £10, 11 Dec. 1684; £60, 6 June 1685; £10, 24 Jan. 1686-7 (see University of Nottingham Library, Manvers Collection, MS M, 4210 fol. 3V and BL MS Egerton, fols. 17-70 b under these dates).

[164] He refers to Hindmarsh as his bookseller (which comprehended publisher) in 'An Allusion to Martial'. 'Upon a Bookseller' concerns Hindmarsh's first issue of *Satyrs Upon The Jesuits*, 1681 (see above, p. lxxix).

[165] *Bibliography*, ii.6, 7, 8, 10, 12; addenda, pp. 38 f, g, nn. 17-19, 21 f.

[166] See p. lxxx.

[167] *Bibliography*, ii.1-13, 21.

[168] Ibid., ii.4. See the corrigenda, pp. 38 d-f, n. 16, for ii.5, *The Claret-Drinker's Song*, n.d., the black-letter ballad published by J. Jordan, with Oldham's seven stanzas clumsily altered, and five spurious ones added. Thanks to research undertaken for me by Dr Leba M. Goldstein, the corrigenda refutes the hypothesis and supersedes the discussion regarding the ballad in the first issue of the *Bibliography* (1936), and dates it, probably, *c.*1685, viz. after Oldham's death.

[169] Ibid., ii.2, 3.

[170] See above, p. lxxix f.

[171] See the facsimile ed. James Thorpe, 1950; and Vieth, *Attribution in Restoration Poetry*, 1963, ch. 3.

[172] See above, p. xcii.

[173] See W.J. Cameron, 'A Late Seventeenth Century Scriptorium', *Renaissance and Modern Studies*, viii (1963); D.M. Vieth, *Attribution*, pp. 25 f.

[174] See above, p. liv.

[175] See headnote and 11. 2 f., 22 f., 45 f., 75-8, 86 f., 99 f., 123 f., nn.

[176] 'Of Praise', *Essays*, ed. W. Aldis Wright, 1865 (1920), p. 215.

[177] p. 255 of D.I.B. Smith's edn. of both Parts, 1971.

[178] See above, pp. xxix and n. 19, lxxxviii.

[179] See 'Katharine Kingscote', headnote.

[180] For all four poems, see above, pp. xxvii f.

[181] Essentially a prose work, it is not included in the present edition. One of its phrases occurs also in a draft letter (*R*166); a mark of its genuineness.

[182] *R*27-31, 228, 230.

[183] *R*64^{c-d}, 236-7 (the minor pieces); 108-16 (Rochester's); 214, 232-5 (*MacFlecknoe*: two leaves are missing).

[184] See above, p. xxv.

[185] *Bibliography*, ii.42.

[186] See my 'Family of John Oldham', *Miscellanea Genealogica et Heraldica*, September 1934, ii.2, iii.1, 2, 11. The poet's grandniece, Mary Hillier, *née* Hancock (iii.7.iv), did not die until 1830—at Shipton. His brother inscribed a copy of James Cooke, *Melliscium Chirurgiae*, 1676, 'Thomas Oldham 1677': it was among the heirlooms shown me in 1934 by William I. Hillier.

[187] See my detailed investigation of these (and *A Satyr Against Vertue*, 1679) in *Studies in Bibliography*, xxvii (1974), pp. 188-226: 'The Chief Substantive Editions of Oldham's Poems, 1679-1684: Printer, Compositors, and Publication', cited below as 'Editions (SB)'.

[188] See 'Editions (SB)', pp. 204-19; for Oldham's spellings, pp. 204-6 with Table III; for their persistence, pp. 208 f., 211 f., 215, 218 f.

[189] Id., pp. 211, 215, 218 f.

[190] Id., pp. 188-90.

[191] Id., pp. 206-19; 220 (the habits summed up); 223-5 (the types of compositorial error). See, for a differentiation between the compositors of *Some New Pieces 1681* and *Poems, And Translations 1683*, and those of *Satyrs Upon The Jesuits 1681* and *Remains 1684*, below, p. xcvii.

[192] Id., pp. 194-9.

[193] Id., pp. 190 f.; 192.

[194] Oldham's Advertisement treats 'Byblis' as the last poem.

[195] 'Editions (SB)', pp. 200 f.

[196] Id., p. 191.

[197] *R*3.

[198] 'Editions (SB)', pp. 188-90, 213 f., 220 f.; *Bibliography*, ii.3, addenda, 38c., n. 14.

[199] Advertisement, ll. 63-6.

[200] 'Editions (SB)', pp. 190-2; *Bibliography*, ii.2, addenda, p. 38 f., n. 17; ii.6, corrigenda p. 38 e-f, n. 16 *ad fin.*

[201] *Bibliography*, ii.6, 8; 'Editions (SB)', pp. 192-4.

[202] See Bror Danielsson and D.M. Vieth (eds.), *The Gyldenstolpe Manuscript Miscellany*, 1967.

[203] See H.M. Margoliouth (ed.), *The Poems and Letters of Andrew Marvell*, 2nd edn., i.208, 318.

[204] *Bibliography*, i.11.

[205] Where variants are categorized but not identified, they can be traced in the textual apparatus.

[206] It is rhymed to 'pate' in the 'Good Fellow', l. 6. It is dissyllabic, however, in 'The Dream', l. 5, and the ode on Atwood, l. 176.

[207] Cf. 'Editions (SB)', p. 207.

[208] See Appendix II, 21.

[209] See above, p. lxxv and n. 178.

[210] *Bibliography*, ii.4, 33.

[211] Id., ii.35; addenda, p. 38j., n. 38.

[212] Id., ii.10 (Remarks).

[213] Id., ii.2 addenda, p. 38c, n. 13; and above, pp. viii, xxxiii, lxxii.

[214] *R256*.

[215] ll. 59-68.

[216] Harvard MS Eng. 585; BL MSS Harley 6913, 6914, 7319; Bodl. MS Firth C 15; V & A MS Dyce 43; Portland MSS PwV 42, 45 (deposited Nottingham UL); MS Advocate 19.1.12 (Natnl. L. of Scotland); Taylor MS 2 (Princeton UL); Öster-reichische Nationalbibliothek MS 14090 (Vienna); the Wentworth MS (Ohio State UL). Those not in BL or Bodley were brought to my attention by John H. O'Neill (see above, n. 69), who furnished me with a diagram of affinities among the twelve.

[217] Like my own collation, O'Neill's, computer-aided, singled it out as such.

[218] For the six and the three, see above, p. lxxiii and n. 173.

[219] This accords with 'The Rationale of Copy-Text', as discussed by W.W. Greg (*Collected Papers*, ed. J.C. Maxwell, 1966).

[220] See 'Editing (SB)', pp. 195, 225; and above, p. lxxviii.

[221] Considered in 'The Editor and the Literary Text', my contribution to *Librarianship and Literature* (the Pafford Festschrift), ed. A.T. Milne, 1970: pp. 107 f. and n. 50.

[222] See above, pp. lxxxiv, xci.

[223] A fairly comprehensive record is justified by a history so illustrative of what may befall a text. Is there another poem in the period for which we have an autograph fair copy; manuscripts transcribed from copies in circula-tion, and preserving authentic early readings; a piratical bad text printed from such a copy, reprinted in the first issue of what was otherwise an authorized volume; in the third issue errata with revision as well as correc-tion; and in a second edition a good text with further revision as well as further correction?

[224] 'Editions (SB)', pp. 199 f.

LIST OF SIGLA,
including all Authorities for the Text

1. *The Autograph manuscript*

R	Bodleian MS Rawlinson Poetry 123: fair copies.
*R*178 (or other numeral)	Draft on that page
R^1	First version
R^2, R^3	Revised reading; further revision
Rm	In the margin (reading or note)
Rs	Superscript; interlined

2. *Substantive Editions* (with references to the Bibliography)

1677   *Upon the Marriage of the Prince of Orange with the Lady Mary*, 1677 (ii.1)

1679   *Garnets Ghost*, n.d. (piracy: ii.2)

1679   *A Satyr Against Vertue* (piracy of 'Aude aliquid. Ode' ii.3)
Note: *The Clarret Drinker's Song*, 1680 (ii.4) has no significant variants from the text printed as 'The Careless Good Fellow' in *Poems, And Translations*, 1683

1680   *Poems on Several Occasions by the Right Honourable, The E of R[ochester]*, the Huntington copy, *Bibliography*, ii.33; see p. 38j.

1681   *Satyrs Upon The Jesuits ... and Some Other Pieces* (ii.6) for the Advertisement and poems in that volume

1681   *Some New Pieces ... By the Author of the Satyrs upon the Jesuites* (ii.8) for the Advertisement and poems in that volume

1682   *Satyrs Upon The Jesuits ... and some other Pieces ... The Second Edition more Corrected* (ii.7)

1683   *Poems, And Translations. By the Author of the Satyrs upon the Jesuits* (ii.10: the true first edition, with the sprig of flowers ornament on the title page)

1684   *Remains of Mr. John Oldham In Verse and Prose* (ii.12)

1685   *A Second Musical Entertainment Perform'd On St. Cecilia's day. November XXII. 1684. The Words by the late ingenious Mr. John Oldham ... Set to Music ... by Dr. John Blow* (ii.13)

E   Errata in *Satyrs Upon The Jesuits*, 1681, *Some New
            Pieces*, 1681, and J.M. Moffatt, *The History of* ...
            Malmesbury, 1805 (source for the 'Epitaph on Dr.
            Abia Qui')
            Note: the sole, and highly authoritative text for
                  'In Obitum ... Johanis Frend' is his father
                  Nathaniel's memoir, Bodl. MS Top. Oxon.
                  f. 31.

3. *Manuscripts with texts of 'Garnet's Ghost', 'A Satyr Against
   Vertue', 'Upon the Author of* ... *Sodom', and 'Sardanapalus',
   from copies in circulation*

m   The late H.M. Margoliouth's MS m, collated by his
            kindness. It was 'writt' (apparently) 'wth a
            woman's hand': see his edn. of Marvell, i.318
            (*Bibliography*, i.16)

F   Bodleian MS Firth C 15

A   BL MS Additional 14047 (*Bibliography*, i.11)

H1   BL MS Harley 6914 (*Bibliography*, i.8)

H2   BL MS Harley 6913 (*Bibliography*, i.8)

H3   BL MS Harley 7319 (*Bibliography*, i.7)

D   Victoria and Albert Museum MS Dyce 43

P1   At the University of Nottingham, Portland MS PwV
            40. With the next two manuscripts, this was col-
            lated by kind permission of the Duke of Portland

P2   At the University of Nottingham, Portland MS PwV 42

P3   At the University of Nottingham, Portland MS PwV 45

S   National Library of Scotland, MS Adv. 19. 1. 12

Y1   Yale (Osborn Collection) MS b. 105

Y2   Yale, Osborn MS Chest II. No. 14

Hv   Harvard MS Eng. 585

T   Princeton University Library, Robert H. Taylor Col-
            lection, MS Taylor 2

W   Ohio State University Library, Wentworth MS

V   Österreichische Nationalbibliothek, Vienna, MS
            14090

G   The Gyldenstolpe MS Miscellany, ed. Bror Danielsson
            and D.M. Vieth, 1967

4. *Editions not substantive, anticipating but not responsible for
   amendments in the present one* (with references to *Bibliography*)

1684a   *The Works of Mr. John Oldham, Together with his
            Remains* (ii.17, 18; cf. 9: the first collected
            edition: has 2nd edns. of *Some New Pieces* and *Poems*,

And Translations, the latter with type-ornaments replacing sprig of flowers

'1683'   In the *Works and Remains*, 1686 (ii.21), the false-dated 3rd edn. of *Poems, And Translations*, with crowned rose ornament instead of sprig of flowers

1687   *Remains*, 2nd edn., in *Works and Remains* (ii.20, 21)

1697   In *Works and Remains*, 1698, all but *Poems, And Translations* (Part III); (ii.25)

1703   *Works and Remains* (ii.26, cf. 27); first edition to have portrait

1722   *The Works of Mr. John Oldham Together with his Remains. In Two Volumes With Memoirs of his Life, and Explanatory Notes.* (ii.29); first edited edition

1770   *The Compositions In Prose and Verse of Mr John Oldham. To which are added Memoirs of his Life, and Explanatory Notes upon some obscure passages of his writings. By Edward Thompson* (ii.30). There was no later attempt at a complete edition

1854   *Poetical Works of John Oldham. Edited by Robert Bell* (ii.31, cf. 32). A selection, in Bell's annotated series of English poets

1

SATYRS UPON THE JESUITS
AND SOME OTHER PIECES

S A T Y R S
UPON THE
J E S U I T S :

Written in the YEAR 1679.
Upon occasion of the
PLOT,
Together with the
Satyr against Vertue,
AND
Some other PIECES by
The same HAND.

———————————

LONDON:
Printed for *Joseph Hindmarsh*, at the *Black
Bull* in *Cornhill*. 1681.

A D V E R T I S E M E N T .

THE Author might here (according to the laudable
custom of Prefaces) entertain the Reader with a
Discourse of the Original, Progress, and Rules of
Satyr, *and let him understand, that he has lately Read* Casaubon,
and several other Criticks upon the Point, but at present he is   5
minded to wave it, as a vanity he is in no wise fond of. His
only intent now is to give a brief account of what he Publishes,
in order to prevent what censures he foresees may colourably be
past thereupon: And that is, as followeth:
  What he calls the Prologue, *is in imitation of* Persius, *who has* 10
prefix'd somewhat by that Name before his Book of Satyrs, and
may serve for a pretty good Authority. The first Satyr he drew
by Sylla's Ghost *in the great* Johnson, *which may be perceiv'd by*
some strokes and touches therein, however short they come of the
Original. In the second, he only follow'd the swing of his own   15
Genius. The Design, and some passages of the third were taken
out of the Franciscan *of* Buchanan. *Which Ingenuous confession he*
thinks fit to make, to shew he has more modesty than the common
Padders in Wit of these times. He doubts, there may be some few
mistakes in Chronology therein, which for want of Books he could 20
not inform himself in. If the skilful Reader meet with any such,
he may the more easily pardon them upon that score. Whence he
had the hint of the fourth, is obvious to all, that are any
thing acquainted with Horace. *And without the Authority of so*
great a President, the making of an Image speak, is but an ordi- 25
nary Miracle in Poetry. He expects, that some will tax him of
Buffoonery, and turning holy things into ridicule. But let them
Read, how severely Arnobius, Lactantius, Minutius Felix, *and the*
gravest Fathers, *have railly'd the fopperies and superstitions*
of the Heathen, and then consider, whether those, which he has   30
chosen for his Argument, are not as worthy of laughter. The only
difference is, that they did it in Prose, as he does in Verse,
where perhaps 'tis the more allowable.
  As for the next Poem (which is the most liable to censure)
though the World has given it the Name of the Satyr *against*   35

Vertue, *he declares 'twas never design'd to that intent, how apt*
soever some may be to wrest it. And this appears by what is said
after it, and is discernable enough to all, that have the sence
to understand it. 'Twas meant to abuse those, who valued them-
40 *selves upon their Wit and Parts in praising Vice, and to shew,*
that others of sober Principles, if they would take the same
liberty in Poetry, could strain as high rants in Profaness as
they. At first he intended it not for the publick, nor to pass
beyond the privacy of two or three Friends, but seeing it had the
45 *Fate to steal abroad in Manuscript, and afterwards in Print,*
without his knowledge; he now thinks it a justice due to his own
Reputation, to have it come forth without those faults, which it
has suffer'd from Transcribers and the Press hitherto, and which
make it a worse Satyr upon himself, than upon what it was de-
50 *sign'd.*

Something should be said too of the last Trifle, if it were
worth it. 'Twas occasion'd upon Reading the late Translations of
Ovid's Epistles, *which gave him a mind to try what he could do*
upon a like Subject. Those being already forestal'd, he thought
55 *fit to make choice of this of the same Poet, whereon perhaps he*
has taken too much liberty. Had he seen Mr. Sandys *his Transla-*
tion before he begun, he never durst have ventur'd: Since he has,
and finds reason enough to despair of his undertaking. But now
'tis done, he is loath to burn it, and chooses rather to give
60 *somebody else the trouble. The Reader may do as he pleases,*
either like it, or put it to the use of Mr. Jordan's *Works. 'Tis*
the first attempt, he ever made in this kind, and likely enough
to be the last, his vein (if he may be thought to have any)
lying another way.

42 *Profaness*] *1681; Profaneness 1682*   55 *of this of the*] *1681; of the*
1682

SATYRS
UPON THE
JESUITS.

———————

PROLOGUE.

For who can longer hold? when every Press,
The Bar and Pulpit too has broke the peace?
When every scribling Fool at the alarms
Has drawn his Pen, and rises up in Arms?
And not a dull Pretender of the Town,   5
But vents his gall in pamphlet up and down?
When all with license rail, and who will not, ⎫
Must be almost suspected of the *PLOT*,   ⎬
And bring his Zeal, or else, his parts in doubt? ⎭
   In vain our Preaching Tribe attack the Foes,   10
In vain their weak Artillery oppose:
Mistaken honest Men, who gravely blame,
And hope that gentle Doctrine should reclaim.
Are Texts and such exploded trifles fit
T'impose and sham upon a *Jesuit?*   15
Would they the dull Old *Fisher-men* compare
With mighty *Suarez* and great *Escobar?*
Such threadbare proofs and stale Authorities
May Us poor simple *Hereticks* suffice:
But to a sear'd *Ignatian's* conscience,   20
Harden'd, as his own Face, with Impudence,
Whose faith is contradiction-bore, whom lies,
Nor nonsence, nor impossibilities,
Nor shame, nor death, nor damning can assail;
Not these mild fruitless methods will avail.   25
   'Tis pointed Satyr and the sharps of wit
For such a prize are th' only weapons fit:

22 faith is] *1681*; Faith in *1682*

Nor needs there art or genious here to use,
Where indignation can create a muse:
Should Parts and Nature fail, yet very spite   30
Would make the arrant'st *Wild*, or *Withers* write.
   It is resolv'd: henceforth an endless War,
I and my Muse with them and theirs declare;
Whom neither open malice of the Foes,
Nor private daggers, nor *Saint Omer's* dose,   35
Nor all that *Godfrey* felt, or Monarchs fear,
Shall from my vow'd and sworn revenge deter.
   Sooner shall false Court favourites prove just
And faithful to their King's and Country's trust:
Sooner shall they detect the tricks of State,   40
And knav'ry suits and bribes and flatt'ry hate:
Bawds shall turn Nuns, Salt D——s grow chast,
And paint and pride and lechery detest:
Popes shall for Kings supremacy decide,
And *Cardinals* for *Huguenots* be tried: 45
Sooner (which is the great'st impossible)
Shall the vile brood of *Loyola* and Hell
Give o're to Plot, be villains, and rebel;
Than I with utmost spite and vengeance cease
To prosecute and plague their cursed race.   50
   The rage of Poets damn'd, of Women's Pride
Contemn'd and scorn'd, or proffer'd lust denied:
The malice of religious angry Zeal,
And all cashier'd resenting statesmen feel:
What prompts dire Hags in their own blood to write,   55
And sell their very souls to Hell for spite:
All this urge on my rank envenom'd spleen,
And with keen Satyr edge my stabbing Pen:
That its each home-set thrust their blood may draw,
Each drop of Ink like *Aquafortis* gnaw.   60
   Red hot with vengeance thus, I'll brand disgrace
So deep, no time shall e're the marks deface:
Till my severe and exemplary doom

28 there] *E, 1682*; *R*174; these *1681*   39 King's and Country's] *1681*,
*R*186; Kings, and Countreys *1682*·   50 prosecute] *1682*; persecute *1681, R*181

Spread wider than their guilt, till it become
   More dreaded than the Bar, and frighten worse   65
   Than damning *Popes* Anathema's and curse.

64 it become] *E, 1682 (see R*178); I become *1681*

S A T Y R   I .

Garnet's Ghost *addressing to the*
Jesuits, *met in private Cabal just*
after the Murder of Godfrey.

By hell 'twas bravely done! what less than this? ⎫
What sacrifice of meaner worth and price   ⎬
Could we have offer'd up for our success?   ⎭
So fare all they, whoe're provoke our hate,
Who by like ways presume to tempt their fate;   5
Fare each like this bold medling Fool, and be
As well secur'd, as well dispatch'd as he:
Would he were here, yet warm, that we might drain
His reeking gore, and drink up ev'ry vein!
That were a glorious sanction, much like thine,   10
Great *Roman!* made upon a like design:
Like thine? we scorn so mean a *Sacrament*, ⎫
To seal and consecrate our high intent,   ⎬
We scorn base blood should our great league cement: ⎭
Thou didst it with a slave, but we think good   15
To bind our Treason with a bleeding God.
   Would it were His (why should I fear to name,
Or you to hear't?) at which we nobly aim!
Lives yet that hated en'my of our cause?
Lives He our mighty projects to oppose?   20
Can His weak innocence and Heaven's care
Be thought security from what *we* dare?

4 whoe're] Ed.; who're *1681*; who e're *1682*; who dare *1679, m*

Are you then *Jesuits?* are you so for nought?
In all the *Catholick* depths of Treason taught?
In orthodox and solid pois'ning read?   25
In each profounder art of killing bred?
And can *you* fail, or bungle in your trade?
Shall one poor life your cowardice upbraid?
Tame dastard slaves! who your profession shame,
And fix disgrace on our great *Founder*'s name.   30
  Think what late *Sect'ries* (an ignoble crew, ⎤
Not worthy to be rank'd in sin with you)   ⎬
Inspir'd with lofty wickedness, durst do: ⎦
How from his throne they hurl'd a Monarch down,
And doubly eas'd him of both Life and Crown: 35
They scorn'd in covert their bold act to hide, ⎤
In open face of heav'n the work they did,   ⎬
And brav'd its vengeance, and its pow'rs defied. ⎦
This is his Son, and mortal too like him,
Durst you usurp the glory of the crime;   40
And dare ye not? I know, you scorn to be
By such as they outdone in villany,
Your proper province; true, you urg'd them on, ⎤
Were engins in the fact, but they alone   ⎬
Share all the open credit and renoun.   ⎦   45
  But hold! I wrong our Church and Cause, which need
No foreign instance, nor what others did:
Think on that matchless Assassin, whose name
We with just pride can make our happy claim;
He, who at killing of an Emperour,   ⎤   50
To give his poison stronger force and pow'r   ⎬
Mix't a *God* with't, and made it work more sure: ⎦
Blest memory! which shall thro' Age to come
Stand sacred in the lists of Hell and *Rome*.
  Let our great *Clement,* and *Ravillac*'s name,   55
Your Spirits to like heights of sin inflame;

---

26 In] *1681, 1682*; And *1679, m, R*248   bred?] *1682*; bread? *1681*; bred:
1679; bred. *R*248   31 (an ignoble] *E, 1682, m*; (and ignoble *1679, 1681*;
and a Rascal *R*250   35 doubly ... both] *1681, 1682*; bravely ... his *1679,
m*   38 brav'd] *1681, 1682*; dar'd *1679, m, R*250   its pow'rs] *1681, R*250
subst.; it pow'rs *1682*; its powers *1679*; its power *m*

Those mighty Souls, who bravely chose to die
T'have each a Royal Ghost, their company:
Heroick Act! and worth their tortures well,   ⎫
Well worth the suff'ring of a double Hell,   ⎬   60
That they felt here, and that below they feel. ⎭
   And if these cannot move you, as they shou'd,
Let me and my example fire your blood:
Think on my vast attempt, a glorious deed,
Which durst the Fates have suffer'd to succeed,   65
Had rival'd Hell's most proud exploit and boast,
Ev'n that, which wou'd the *King of fates* depos'd,
Curst be the day, and ne're in time inrol'd,   ⎫
And curst the Star, whose spiteful influence rul'd ⎬
The luckless Minute, which my project spoil'd: ⎭   70
Curse on that *Pow'r*, who, of himself afraid,
My glory with my brave design betray'd:
Justly he fear'd, lest I, who strook so high
In guilt, should next blow up his Realm and Sky:
And so I had; at least I would have durst,   75
And failing, had got off with Fame at worst.
   Had you but half my bravery in Sin,
Your work had never thus unfinish'd bin:
Had I bin Man, and the great act to do;
H'ad dy'd by this, and bin what I am now,   80
Or what His Father is: I would leap Hell
To reach His Life, tho in the midst I fell,
And deeper than before.——
   Let rabble Souls of narrow aim and reach
Stoop their vile Necks, and dull Obedience preach: 85
Let them with Slavish aw (disdain'd by me) ⎫
Adore the purple Rag of Majesty,   ⎬
And think't a sacred Relick of the Sky: ⎭

57-8 who bravely chose to die | T'have each] *1681, 1682*; who each durst
bravely die | To have *1679*; which each durst bravely die | To have *m*
64 on my vast] *1681, 1682*; what I durst *1679, m, R260*   71 Curse on that
Pow'r, who of himself] *1681, 1682, m subst., R260*; What meant that pow'r,
which of it self *1679*   73 Justly] *1681, 1682, m*; Was't that *1679*   And
so I had] *1681, 1682, m subst.*; Or if that fail'd *1679*   76 failing,]
1681, 1682, m subst.; missing *1679*   77 bravery] *1681, 1682*; daringness
1679, m subst.

Well may such Fools a base Subjection own,
Vassals to every Ass, that loads a Throne: 90
Unlike the soul, with which proud *I* was born,
Who could that sneaking thing a Monarch scorn,
Spurn off a Crown, and set my foot in sport
Upon the head, that wore it, trod in dirt.
   But say, what is't, that binds your hands? do's fear   95
From such a glorious action you deter?
Or is't Religion? but you sure disclaim
That frivolous pretence, that empty name:
Meer bugbare-word, devised by Us to scare   ⎫
The sensless rout to slavishness and fear,   ⎬   100
Ne're known to aw the brave, and those that dare. ⎭
Such weak and feeble things may serve for checks
To rein and curb base-mettled *Hereticks*;
Dull creatures, whose nice bogling consciences
Startle, or strain at such slight crimes as these;   105
Such, whom fond inbred honesty befools,
Or that old musty piece the *Bible* gulls:
That hated Boak, the bulwark of our foes,
Whereby they still uphold their tott'ring cause.
   Let no such toys mislead you from the road   110
Of glory, nor infect your Souls with good:
Let never bold incroaching Virtue dare
With her grim holy face to enter there,
No, not in very Dream: have only will
Like Fiends and Me to covet and act ill: 115
Let true substantial wickedness take place, ⎫
Usurp and Reign; let it the very trace   ⎬
(If any yet be left) of good deface.   ⎭
If ever qualms of inward cowardice
(The things, which some dull sots call conscience) rise   120
Make them in steams of Blood and slaughter drown,

89-90 a base Subjection own, | Vassels to every Ass, that loads a Throne]
1681, 1682; be subject to controul; | To every scepter'd wretch that dares
but rule *1679*; bee Subjects to controule | To every sceptered ass that dares
but Rule *m*; (*cf. R262*: & slaves to everything that reigns)   103 rein]
1682; reign *1681*   115 covet and act ill:] *1681, 1682 subst.*; Act and
covet ill *1679, m subst., R253, R260, R261 subst.*   121 Make] *1681, 1679,
m*; Let *1682*   steams] *1681, 1682*; streams *1679, m subst.*

Or with new weights of guilt still press 'em down.
Shame, faith, religion, honour, loyalty, ⎫
Nature it self, whatever checks there be ⎬
To loose and uncontroul'd impiety,   ⎭   125
Be all extinct in you; own no remorse
But that you've balk'd a sin, have bin no worse,
Or too much pitty shewn.——
Be diligent in mischief's Trade, be each
Performing as a Dev'l; nor stick to reach   130
At Crimes most dangerous; where bold despair, ⎫
Mad lust and heedless blind revenge would ne're ⎬
Ev'n look, march you without a blush, or fear, ⎭
Inflam'd by all the hazards, that oppose,
And firm, as burning Martyrs, to your Cause.   135
    Then you're true *Jesuits*, then you're fit to be
Disciples of great *Loyola* and Me:
Worthy to undertake, worthy a Plot
Like this, and fit to scourge an *Huguenot*.
    Plagues on that Name! may swift confusion seize,   140
And utterly blot out the cursed Race:
Thrice damn'd be that *Apostate Monk*, from whom
Sprung first these Enemies of Us and *Rome*:
Whose pois'nous Filth dropt from ingendring Brain,
By monstrous Birth did the vile Insects spawn,   145
Which now infest each Country, and defile
With their o'respreading swarms this goodly Ile.
Once it was ours, and subject to our Yoke,
'Till a late reigning Witch th' Enchantment broke:
It shall again: Hell and I say't: have ye   150
But courage to make good the Prophesie:
Not Fate it self shall hinder.——

122 'em] *1681*, *1682*; them *1679*, *m*   down.] *1682*; down *1681*   123 Shame,
faith] *1681*, *1682*; *Faith, shame 1679*, *m subst.*   132-3 Mad lust and
heedless blind revenge would ne're │ Ev'n look] *1681*, *1682 subst.*; And heedless blind Revenge would never dare │ To look *1679*, *m subst.*; And blind
Revenge more heedless wou'd not dare │ To go *R288*[1]; And headlong fierce
R[evenge] wou'd hardly dare │ To lead *R288*[2]; (*cf*. *R288*[3] to throw a look)
135 your] *1681*, *1682*, *m*; our *1679*; their *R288* (*twice*)   141 the] *1681*,
1682, *m*, *R281*; that *1679*, *cf*. *R282*   142 that] *1681*, *1682*, *m*, *R286*; your
1679   146 infest] *1681*, *1682*; infect *1679*; infects *m*   150-1 Hell and
I say't: have ye │ But courage to] *1681*, *1682 subst.*; tis Hell and I decree
│ If you but dare *1679*, *m subst.*

Too sparing was the time, too mild the day,
When our great *Mary* bore the *English* sway:
Unqueen-like pity marr'd her Royal Pow'r,   155
Nor was her Purple dy'd enough in Gore.
Four or five hundred, such-like petty sum
Might fall perhaps a Sacrifice to *Rome*,
Scarce worth the naming: had I had the Pow'r, ⎫
Or bin thought fit t'have bin her Councellor, ⎬   160
She should have rais'd it to a nobler score. ⎭
Big Bonfires should have blaz'd and shone each day,
To tell our Triumphs, and make bright our way:
And when 'twas dark, in every Lane and Street ⎫
Thick flaming *Hereticks* should serve to light ⎬   165
And save the needless Charge of Links by night: ⎭
Smithfield should still have kept a constant fire,
Which never should be quench'd, never expire,
But with the lives of all the miscreant rout,
Till the last gasping breath had blown it out.   170
  So *Nero* did, such was the prudent course ⎫
Taken by all his mighty successours,   ⎬
To tame like *Hereticks* of old by force: ⎭
They scorn'd dull reason and pedantick rules
To conquer and reduce the harden'd Fools: 175
Racks, gibbets, halters were their arguments,
Which did most undeniably convince:
Grave bearded Lions manag'd the dispute,
And reverend Bears their doctrins did confute:
And all, who would stand out in stiff defence,   180
They gently claw'd and worried into sence:
Better than all our *Sorbon* dotards now,
Who would by dint of words our Foes subdue.
This was the riged discipline of old,
Which modern sots for Persecution hold: 185
Of which dull Annalists in story tell ⎤

157 such-like] *1681*; such like *1682*; some such *1679*   160 t'have bin]
1681, 1682 subst.; to be *1679*   162 Bonfires should ... blaz'd and shone]
1681, 1682; Bonefires ... blazed; shone *1679*   171 the] *1681, 1682*; his
1679, R287   172 Taken] *1681, 1682*; Us'd too *1679, R287*   180 would
stand] *1681, 1682*; durst hold *1679, R287*   182 than] *1681, 1682*; then
1679

Strange legends, and huge bulky volumns swell
With Martyr'd Fools, that lost their way to hell.

   From these, our Church's glorious Ancestours,
We've learnt our arts and made their methods ours: 190
Nor have we come behind, the least degree,
In acts of rough and manly cruelty:
Converting faggots and the pow'rful stake
And Sword resistless our *Apostles* make.

   This heretofore *Bohemia* felt, and thus   195
Were all the num'rous proselites of *Huss*
Crush'd with their head: So *Waldo*'s cursed rout,
And those of *Wickliff* here were rooted out,
Their names scarce left. Sure were the means, we chose,
And wrought prevailingly: Fire purg'd the dross   200
Of those foul heresies, and soveraign Steel
Lopt off th'infected limbs the Church to heal.

   Renown'd was that *French Brave*, renown'd his deed,
A deed, for which the day deserves its red
Far more than for a paltry Saint, that died: 205
How goodly was the Sight! how fine the Show!
When *Paris* saw through all its Channels flow
The blood of *Huguenots*; when the full *Sein*,
Swell'd with the flood, its Banks with joy o'reran!
He scorn'd like common Murderers to deal   210
By parcels and piecemeal; he scorn'd Retail
I'th' Trade of Death: whole Myriads died by th'great,
Soon as one single life; so quick their Fate,
Their very Pray'rs and Wishes came too late.

   This a King did: and great and mighty 'twas,   215
Worthy his high Degree, and Pow'r, and Place,
And worthy our *Religion* and our Cause:
Unmatch'd 't had bin, had not *Macguire* arose,
The bold *Macguire* (who, read in modern Fame,
Can be a Stranger to his Worth and Name?)   220
Born to outsin a Monarch, born to Reign

191 least] *1681, 1682*; first *1679*   198 And] *1681, 1682*; With *1679*
205 than] *1681, 1682*; then *1679, R283*   212 I' th' Trade] *1681, R283 subst.*;
I' th' Trace *1682*; Th' trade *1679*   219 *Macguire*] Ed., *R283*; *Mac-quire*
1681, 1682, 1679

In Guilt, and all Competitors disdain:
Dread Memory! whose each mention still can make
Pale *Hereticks* with trembling Horrour quake.
T'undo a Kingdom, to atchieve a crime   225
Like his, who would not fall and die like him?
Never had *Rome* a nobler service done,
Never had Hell; each day came thronging down
Vast shoals of Ghosts, and mine was pleas'd and glad,
And smil'd, when it the brave revenge survey'd.   230
   Nor do I mention these great Instances
For bounds and limits to your wickedness:
Dare you beyond, something out of the road
Of all example, where none yet have trod,
Nor shall hereafter: what mad *Catiline*   235
Durst never think, nor's madder *Poet* feign.
Make the poor baffled Pagan Fool confess,
How much a *Christian* Crime can conquer his:
How far in gallant mischief overcome,
The old must yield to new and modern *Rome*.   240
Mix Ills past, present, future, in one act;
One high, one brave, one great, one glorious Fact,
Which Hell and very I may envy—
Such as a *God* himself might wish to be
A Complice in the mighty villany   245
And barter's heaven, and vouchsafe to die.
   Nor let Delay (the bane of Enterprize)
Marr yours, or make the great importance miss.
This fact has wak'd your Enemies and their fear;
Let it your vigour too, your haste, and care.   250
Be swift, and let your deeds forestall intent, ⎤

---

234 have trod] *1681, 1682, 1679,* R293, R161[2]; ever trod *m*; have went R161[1]
237 baffled Pagan Fool confess] *1681, 1682, m subst.,* R293; buffled pagan-
fool to own *1679*; baffled Pagan Know y[t] he R261   238] *Not in 1679*
242 brave,] *1682*; brave *1681*   243 very I] *1681, 1682, m subst.* (*cf.*
R293[2]); even I *1679*; I myself R293[1]   244 a *God*] *1681, 1682,* R293; that
Jove 1679, m subst.   245 A Complice] *1681, 1682, 1679 subst.,* R293
(*altered from* Accomplice); A Complices *m*   246 Barter's] *1681, 1682, m*
subst., R293 subst.; barters *1679*   250 it your,] *1681, 1682, m*; it be
your *1679*   your haste, and care] *1681, 1682*; be swift to dare *1679, m*
251 Be swift] *1681, 1682*; Hasten *1679, m*

Forestall even wishes ere they can take vent,
Nor give the Fates the leisure to prevent.
Let the full Clouds, which a long time did wrap
Your gath'ring thunder, now with sudden clap   255
Break out upon your Foes; dash and confound,
And spread avoidless ruine all around.

  Let the fir'd City to your Plot give light;
You raz'd it half before, now raze it quite.
Do't more effectually; I'd see it glow   260
In flames unquenchable as those below.
I'd see the Miscreants with their houses burn,
And all together into ashes turn.

  Bend next your fury to the curst Divan,
That damn'd *Committee*, whom the Fates ordain   265
Of all our well-laid Plots to be the bane.
Unkennel those State-Foxes, where they ly
Working your speedy fate and destiny.
Lug by the ears the doting *Prelates* thence,
Dash Heresie together with their Brains   270
Out of their shatter'd heads. Lop off the *Lords*
And *Commons* at one stroke, and let your Swords
Adjourn 'em all to th' other world—

  Would I were blest with flesh and bloud again,
But to be Actor in that happy Scene!   275
Yet thus I will be by, and glut my view;
Revenge shall take its fill, in state I'le go
With captive Ghosts t'attend me down below.

  Let these the Handsells of your vengeance be,
Yet stop not here, nor flag in cruelty.   280
Kill like a Plague or *Inquisition*; spare
No Age, Degree, or Sex; onely to wear
A Soul, onely to own a Life, be here

---

253 prevent] *1681, 1682, 1679* (*cf*. *R250, R252*); repent *m* (*cf*. *R288*)
257 spread avoidless ruine] *1682*; scatter wide destruction *1681, 1679, m*;
scatter bolts of Vengeance *R250*[1]; deal its wide Destruction *R250*[2]
260 I'd see] *1681, 1682, R261*; I'd have *1679*; Ile see *m*   263 all] *1681,*
1682; both *1679, m, R261*   276 thus I will] *1681, 1682, m*; still I may
1679   280 Yet] *1681, 1679, m*; But *1682*   flag] *1681, 1682, 1679*; stay *m*
282-4 wear | A Soul, only to own a Life, be here | Thought] *1681, 1682*; dare
| To own a life; only a soul to wear| Be *1679, m subst., R265*

Thought crime enough to lose't: no time nor place
Be Sanctuary from your outrages.   285
Spare not in Churches kneeling Priests at pray'r,
Though interceding for you, slay ev'n there.
Spare not young Infants smiling at the brest,
Who from relenting Fools their mercy wrest:
Rip teeming Wombs, tear out the hated Brood   290
From thence, and drown 'em in their Mothers bloud.
Pity not Virgins, nor their tender cries,
Though prostrate at your feet with melting eyes
All drown'd in tears; strike home as 'twere in lust,
And force their begging hands to guide the thrust.   295
Ravish at th' Altar, kill when you have done,
Make them your Rapes, and Victims too in one.
Nor let gray hoary hairs protection give
To Age, just crawling on the verge of Life:
Snatch from its leaning hands the weak support,   300
And with it knock't into the grave with sport;
Brain the poor Cripple with his Crutch, then cry,
You've kindly rid him of his misery.

  Seal up your ears to mercy, lest their words
Should tempt a pity, ram 'em with your Swords   305
(Their tongues too) down their throats; let 'em not dare ⎫
To mutter for their Souls a gasping pray'r,   ⎬
But in the utt'rance choak't, and stab it there.   ⎭
'Twere witty handsom malice (could you do't)
To make 'em die, and make 'em damn'd to boot.   310
  Make Children by one fate with Parents die,
Kill ev'n revenge in next Posterity:
So you'll be pester'd with no Orphans cries,
No childless Mothers curse your memories.

289 their] 1681, 1682, m, R265[1]; may 1679; fond R265[2]   295 begging hands
... thrust] 1681, 1682, m subst., R265 (cf. R262); hands ... fatal thrust 1679
297 and] 1682, 1679; the 1681, R260, R265; your m   too in one] 1682, 1679;
to attone 1681, m subst., R260, R265   300 the] 1681, 1682; their 1679,
R265; its m (cf. also R262)   301 with sport] 1681, 1682; in sport 1679,
m subst., R265   308 in the utt'rance choak't] 1681, 1682; choak't in th'
utterance 1679; Check it in the utterance m; choack it in y[e] utterance R265
312 ev'n revenge in] 1681, 1682, m; in revenge, the 1679   313 So you'll]
1681, 1682; You'l so 1679, m, R286   cries] 1681, 1682, m subst.; cry 1679,
R286   314 memories] 1681, 1682, m subst.; Memory 1679, R286

Make Death and Desolation swim in bloud   315
Throughout the Land, with nought to stop the floud
But slaughter'd Carcasses; till the whole Isle
Become one tomb, become one funeral pile;
Till such vast numbers swell the countless summ,
That the wide Grave and wider Hell want room.   320
   Great was that Tyrants wish, which should be mine,
Did I not scorn the leavings of a sin;
Freely I would bestow't on *England* now,   ⎫
That the whole Nation with one neck might grow, ⎬
To be slic'd off, and you to give the blow.   ⎭   325
What neither *Saxon* rage could here inflict,
Nor *Danes* more savage, nor the barbarous *Pict*;
What *Spain* nor *Eighty eight* could ere devise,
With all its fleet and fraight of cruelties;
What ne're *Medina* wish'd, much less could dare,   330
And bloudier *Alva* would with trembling hear;
What may strike out dire Prodigies of old,
And make their mild and gentler acts untold.
What Heav'ns Judgments, nor the angry Stars,
Forein Invasions, nor Domestick Wars,   335
Plague, Fire, nor Famine could effect or do;
All this and more be dar'd and done by you.
   But why do I with idle talk delay
Your hands, and while they should be acting, stay?
Farewell—   340
If I may waste a pray'r for your success,
Hell be your aid, and your high projects bless!
May that vile Wretch, if any here there be,
That meanly shrinks from brave Iniquity;
If any here feel pity or remorse,   345
May he feel all I've bid you act, and worse!

326 neither] *1681, 1682*; never *1679, m*   here] *1681, 1682*; ere *1679*
329 fraight of] *1682*; fraught of *1681, 1679, R261, R293*; fraught w^th *m*
330 ne're *Medina* wish'd] *1681, 1682*; *Medina* nere wish't *1679, m subst.*, *R293*
subst.   332 strike out dire] *1681*; strike our dire *1682*; outdo all *1679*;
strick out Diriest *m*; strike out dir'st *R293*   333 mild and gentler acts]
1681, 1682 subst.; milder cruelties *1679, m subst.*, *R293 subst.*   341 waste]
1681, 1682, m subst., *R288*; waft *1679*   344 meanly] *1681, 1682, 1679, R288*;
basely *m*   345 here] *1681, 1682*; dare *1679, m, R288*   346 Ive bid you
act] *1681, 1682, 1679*; I haue bid him act *m* (*cf. R288*)

May he by rage of Foes unpitied fall,
And they tread out his hated Soul to Hell.
   May's Name and Carcase rot, expos'd alike to be
   The everlasting mark of grinning infamy.   350

350 The] *1681, 1682*; An *1679, m*

S A T Y R   I I .

Nay, if our sins are grown so high of late,
That Heav'n no longer can adjourn our fate;
May't please some milder vengeance to devise,
Plague, Fire, Sword, Dearth, or any thing but this.
Let it rain scalding showres of Brimstone down,   5
To burn us, as of old the lustful Town:
Let a new deluge overwhelm agen,
And drown at once our Land, and Lives, and Sin.
Thus gladly we'll compound, all this we'll pay,
To have these worst of Ills remov'd away.   10
   Judgments of other kinds are often sent
In mercy onely, not for punishment:
But where these light, they shew a Nations fate
Is given up and past for reprobate.
   When God his stock of wrath on *Egypt* spent,   15
To make a stubborn Land and King repent,
Sparing the rest, had he this one Plague sent;
For this alone his People had been quit,
And *Pharoah* circumcis'd a Proselyte.
   Wonder no longer why no curse like these   20
Was known or suffer'd in the primitive days:
They never sinn'd enough to merit it,
'Twas therefore what Heavens just pow'r thought fit,

3 devise,] *1682*; devise *1681*   8 and Lives, and] *1681, R*190; our Lives,
our *1682*   10 these] *1681, R*190 (*altered from* this); this *1682*
20 curse] *E, 1682 subst.*; cure *1681 subst.*; plagues *R*188

To scourge this latter and more sinful age
With all the dregs and squeesings of his rage.   25
   Too dearly is proud *Spain* with *England* quit
For all her loss sustain'd in *Eighty eight*;
For all the Ills our warlike *Virgin* wrought,
Or *Drake* and *Rawleigh* her great Scourges brought.
Amply was she reveng'd in that one birth,   30
When Hell for her the *Biscain* Plague brought forth;
Great Counter-plague! in which unhappy we
Pay back her sufferings with full usury:
Than whom alone none ever was design'd   ⎫
T'entail a wider curse on Human kind,   ⎬   35
But he who first begot us, and first sinn'd. ⎭
   Happy the World had been, and happy Thou,
(Less damn'd at least, and less accurst than now)
If early with less guilt in War th'hadst dy'd,
And from ensuing mischiefs Mankind freed.   40
Or when thou view'dst the *Holy Land* and *Tomb*,
Th'hadst suffer'd there thy brother Traytors doom.
Curst be the womb that with the Firebrand teem'd,
Which ever since has the whole Globe inflam'd;
More curst that ill-aim'd Shot, that basely mist ⎫   45
That maim'd a limb, but spar'd thy hated brest, ⎬
And made th'at once a Cripple and a Priest.   ⎭
   But why this wish? The Church if so might lack
Champions, Good works, and Saints for the *Almanack*.
These are the *Janizaries* of the Cause,   ⎫   50
The *Life Guard* of the *Roman Sultan*, chose ⎬
To break the force of *Huguenots* and Foes.   ⎭
The Churches Hawkers in Divinity,
Who 'stead of Lace and Ribbons, Doctrine cry:
Romes Strowlers, who survey each Continent,   55
Its trinkets and commodities to vent.
Export the *Gospel* like mere ware for sale,
And truck't for Indigo and Cutchineal,

24 latter] *1682 subst.*, *R*188; later *1681*   29 Drake and] *Ed.*, *R*292
subst.; Drake or *1681*, Drake, and *1682*   45 that basely] *1681*, *R*178, *R*292;
which basely *1682*   46 That] *1681*; Which *1682*   49 the] *1681*; th' *1682*
58 truck't] *1682*, *R*245; truck'd *1681*   Cutchineal,] *Ed.* (*1854 subst.*);
Cutchineal. *1681*, *1682 subst.*

As the known Factors here the Brethren once
Swopt *Christ* about for Bodkins, Rings, and Spoons.   60
     And shall these great *Apostles* be contemn'd,
And thus by scoffing Hereticks defam'd?
They by whose means both *Indies* now enjoy
The two choice blessings Pox and Popery;
Which buried else in ignorance had been,   65
Nor known the worth of Beads and *Bellarmine*.
     It pitied holy Mother Church to see
A world so drown'd in gross Idolatry.
It griev'd to see such goodly Nations hold
Bad Errors, and unpardonable Gold.   70
Strange! what a godly zeal can Coyn infuse!
What charity Pieces of Eight produce!
So you were chose the fittest to reclaim
The Pagan World, and give't a *Christian* Name.
And great was the success; whole Myriads stood   75
At Font, and were baptiz'd in their own bloud.
Millions of Souls were hurl'd from hence to burn
Before their time, be damn'd before their turn.
     Yet these were in compassion sent to Hell,
The rest reserv'd in spite, and worse to feel,   80
Compell'd instead of Fiends to worship you,
The more inhuman Devils of the two.
     Rare way and method of conversion this,
To make your Votaries your Sacrifice!
If to destroy be Reformation thought,   85
A Plague as well might the good work have wrought.
     Now see we why your *Founder* weary grown,
Would lay his former Trade of Killing down;
He found 'twas dull, he found a Gown would be
A fitter case and badge of cruelty.   90
Each snivelling Hero Seas of Bloud can spil,
When wrongs provoke, and Honour bids him kill.
Each tiny Bully Lives can freely bleed,
When prest by Wine or Punk to knock o'th' head:
Give me your through-pac'd Rogue, who scorns to be ⎫   95
Prompted by poor Revenge or Injury,   ⎬
But does it of true inbred cruelty: ⎭

Your cool and sober Murderer, who prays ⎫
And stabs at the same time, who one hand has ⎬
Stretch'd up to Heav'n, t'other to make the Pass. ⎭   100
  So the late *Saints* of blessed memory,
Cut throats in godly pure sincerity:
So they with lifted hands and eyes devout
Said Grace, and carv'd a slaughter'd Monarch out.
  When the first Traitor *Cain* (too good to be   105
Thought Patron of this black Fraternity)
His bloudy Tragedy of old design'd, ⎫
One death alone quench'd his revengful mind, ⎬
Content with but a quarter of Mankind: ⎭
Had he been *Jesuit*, had he but put on   110
Their savage cruelty, the rest had gone:
His hand had sent old *Adam* after too,
And forc'd the Godhead to create anew.
  And yet 'twere well, were their foul guilt but thought
Bare sin: 'tis something ev'n to own a fault.   115
But here the boldest flights of wickedness
Are stampt *Religion*, and for currant pass.
The blackest, ugliest, horrid'st, damned'st deed, ⎫
For which Hell flames, the Schools a Title need, ⎬
If done for *Holy Church* is sanctified. ⎭   120
This consecrates the blessed Work and Tool,
Nor must we ever after think 'em foul.
To undo Realms, kill Parents, murder Kings,
Are thus but petty trifles, venial things,
Not worth a Confessor; nay Heav'n shall be   125
It self invok'd t' abet th' impiety.
  "Grant, gracious Lord (*Some reverend Villain prays*)
"That this the bold Assertor of our Cause
"May with success accomplish that great end,
"For which he was by thee and us design'd.   130
"Do thou t'his Arm and Sword thy strength impart,
"And guide 'em steddy to the Tyrants heart.
"Grant him for every meritorious thrust
"Degrees of bliss above among the Just;

   119 Title] *E, 1682*; little *1681*; name *R*191

"Where holy *Garnet* and S. *Guy* are plac'd,   135
"Whom works like this before have thither rais'd;
"Where they are interceding for us now;
"For sure they're there. Yes questionless, and so
Good *Nero* is and *Dioclesian* too,
And that great ancient Saint *Herostratus*,   140
And the late godly Martyr at *Tholouse*.
    Dare something worthy *Newgate* and the *Tow'r*,
If you'l be canoniz'd and Heav'n ensure.
Dull primitive Fools of old! who would be good!
Who would by vertue reach the blest abode!   145
Far other are the ways found out of late,
Which Mortals to that happy place translate:
Rebellion, Treason, Murder, Massacre,
The chief Ingredients now of *Saintship* are,
And *Tyburn* onely stocks the *Calendar*.   150
    Unhappy *Judas*, whose ill fate or chance
Threw him upon gross times of ignorance;
Who knew not how to value or esteem
The worth and merit of a glorious crime!
Should his kind Stars have let him acted now,   155
H'ad dy'd absolv'd, and dy'd a Martyr too.
    Hear'st thou, great God, such daring blasphemy,
And letst thy patient Thunder still lie by?
Strike and avenge, lest impious Atheists say,
Chance guides the world, and has usurp'd thy sway;   160
Lest these proud prosperous Villains too confess,
Thou'rt sensless, as they make thy Images.
Thou just and sacred Power! wilt thou admit
Such Guests should in thy glorious presence sit?
If Heav'n can with such company dispense,   165
Well did the *Indian* pray, Might he keep thence.
    But this we onely feign, all vain and false,
As their own Legends, Miracles, and Tales;
Either the groundless calumnies of spite,
Or idle rants of Poetry and Wit.   170

136 rais'd;] *Ed.*, *Mengel* (rais'd,); rais'd. *1681, 1682*   144 good!] *Ed.*;
good? *1681*; good, *1682*; good *R194*   145 abode!] *Ed.*; abode? *1681*; abode:
1682; abode. *R194*

We wish they were; but you hear *Garnet* cry,
"I did it, and would do't again; had I
"As much of Bloud, as many Lives as *Rome*
"Has spilt in what the Fools call Martyrdom;
"As many Souls as Sins; I'de freely stake   175
"All them and more for Mother Churches sake.
"For that I'll stride o're Crowns, swim through a Flood,
"Made up of slaughter'd Monarch's Brains and Blood.
"For that no lives of *Hereticks* I'll spare,
"But reap 'em down with less remorse and care   180
"Than *Tarquin* did the poppy-heads of old,
"Or we drop beads, by which our prayer's are told.
   Bravely resolved! and 'twas as bravely dar'd ⎫
But (lo!) the Recompence and great Reward,   ⎬
The wight is to the *Almanack* preferr'd.   ⎭   185
Rare motives to be damn'd for holy Cause,
A few red letters, and some painted straws.
Fools! who thus truck with Hell by *Mohatra*
And play their Souls against no stakes away.
   'Tis strang with what an holy impudence   190
The Villain caught, his innocence maintains:
Denies with oaths the fact untill it be
Less guilt to own it then the perjury:
By th' Mass and blessed *Sacraments* he swears, ⎫
This *Mary's Milk*, and t'other *Mary's Tears*, ⎬   195
And the whole muster-roll in *Calendars*.   ⎭
Not yet swallow the Falsehood? if all this   ⎫
Won't gain a resty Faith; he will on's Knees   ⎬
The *Evangelists* and *Ladie's Psalter* kiss   ⎭
To vouch the Lye: nay more, to make it good   200
Mortgage his Soul upon't, his Heaven and God.
Damn'd faithless *Hereticks*, hard to convince,
Who trust no Verdict, but dull obvious Sense.
Unconscionable Courts, who Priests deny
Their Benefit o'th Clergy, Perjury.   205
   Room for the *Martyr'd Saints*! behold they come!

183 resolved!] *Ed.*; resolved? *1681*; resolv'd *1682*, *R*174   191 Villain]
1682; Villian *1681*   193 then] *1681*; than *1682*, *R*293   199 The] *1681*;
Th' *1682*

With what a noble Scorn they meet their Doom!
Not Knights o'th Post, nor often carted Whores
Shew more of Impudence, or less Remorss.
  O glorious and heroick Constancy!   210
That can forswear upon the Cart, and die
With gasping Souls expiring in a Lye.
None but tame Sheepish Criminals repent,
Who fear that idle Bugbear Punishment:
Your Gallant Sinner scorns that Cowardice,   215
The poor regret of having done amiss:
Brave he, to his first Principles still true,
Can face Damnation, Sin with Hell in view:
And bid it take the Soul, he does bequeath
And blow it thither with his dying Breath.   220
Dare such as these profess *Religions* Name?
Who, should they own't, and be believed, would shame
It's Practice out o'th World, would Atheists make
Firm in their Creed, and vouch it at the Stake?
Is Heaven for such, whose Deeds make Hell too good   225
Too mild a Penance for their cursed Brood?
For whose unheard-of Crimes and damned Sake
Fate must below new sorts of Torture make,
Since, when of old it fram'd that place of Doom,
'Twas thought no Guilt like this could thither come.   230
  Base recreant Souls! would you have Kings trust you?
Who never yet kept your Allegiance true
To any but Hell's Prince? who with more ease
Can swallow down most solemn Perjuries
Than a Town-Bullie common Oaths, and Lies?   235
Are the *French Harries* Fates so soon forgot?
Our last blest *Tudor*? or the *Powder Plot*?
And those fine Streamers that adorned so long
The *Bridge* and *Westminster*, and yet had hung,
Were they not stoln, and now for Relicks gone?   240
  Think *Tories* loyal, or *Scotch Covenanters*;
Rob'd Tygers gentle; courteous, fasting Bears,

207 Doom!] *Ed.*; Doom? *1681, 1682*   214 that] *1681*; the *1682*
230 come.] Ed.; come *1681, 1682, R*195   235 a Town-Bullie] *1682*; *Bullies*
1681   Lies] *1682*; canting Lies *1681*; bantring Lies *E subst., R*193, *R*281

Atheists devout, and thrice-wrack'd Mariners: ⎤
Take Goats for Chast, and cloyster'd Marmosites,
For plain and open two-edg'd Parasites: 245
Believe Bawds modest, and the shameless Stews,
And binding Drunkards Oaths, and Strumpet's Vows:
And when in time these Contradictions meet,
Then hope to find 'em in a *Loyolite*:
To whom, tho gasping, should I credit give,   250
I'd think 'twere Sin, and damn'd like unbelief.
    Oh for the *Swedish* Law enacted here!
No Scarecrow frightens like a Priest-Guelder:
Hunt them, as Beavers are, force them to buy
Their Lives with Ransom of their Lechery: 255
Or let that wholsome Statute be reviv'd,
Which *England* heretofore from Wolves reliev'd:
Tax every Shire instead of them to bring
Each Year a certain tale of *Jesuits* in:
And let their mangled Quarters hang the Ile   260
To scare all future Vermin from the Soil.
Monsters avaunt! may some kind Whirlwind sweep
Our Land and drown these *Locusts* in the deep:
Hence ye loth'd Objects of our Scorn and Hate,
With all the Curses of an injur'd State: 265
Go foul Impostors, to some duller Soil,
Some easier Nation with your Cheats beguile:
Where your gross common Gulleries may pass,
To slur and top on bubbled Consciences:
Where Ignorance and th' *Inquisitian* Rules,   270
Where the vile Herd of poor Implicit Fools
Are damn'd contentedly, where they are led
Blindfold to Hell, and thank and pay their Guide.
    Go where all your black Tribe, before are gon,
Follow *Chastel, Ravillac, Clement* down,   275
Your *Catesby, Faux,* and *Garnet*, thousands more,

---

247 Drunkards] *Ed.* (*1685*b, *R285 twice*); Drunkard *1681, 1682*   248 in
time] *1682*; in them *1681*; you find *R285*   259 tale] *1681* (*corr.*), *1682*;
Call *1681* (*uncorr.*)   271 Implicit] *1681* (*corr.*), *1682*; Impluicit *1681*
(*uncorr.*)   276 thousands] *1681* (*corr.*), *1682, R285* (*twice*); thousand *1681*
(*uncorr.*)

And those, who hence have lately rais'd the Score.
Where the *Grand Traitor* now and all the Crew
Of his Disciples must receive their Due:
Where Flames and Tortures of Eternal Date   280
Must punish you, yet ne're can expiate:
Learn duller Fiends your unknown Cruelties,
Such as no Wit, but yours could ere devise,
  No Guilt but yours deserve; make Hell confess
  It self out done, its Devils damn'd for less.   285

S A T Y R   I I I .

———————

Loyola's *Will*

Long had the fam'd *Impostor* found Success,
Long seen his damn'd Fraternitie's increase,
In Wealth and Power, Mischief and Guile improv'd
By Popes, and Pope-rid Kings upheld and lov'd:
Laden with Years, and Sins, and numerous Skars,   5
Got some i'th Field, but most in other Wars,
Now finding Life decay, and Fate draw near, ⎫
Grown ripe for Hell, and *Roman* Calendar,   ⎬
He thinks it worth his Holy Thoughts and Care,⎭
Some hidden Rules and Secrets to impart,   10
The Proofs of long Experience, and deep Art,
Which to his Successors may useful be
In conduct of their future Villany.
Summon'd together, all th' Officious Band
The Orders of their Bed-rid Chief attend;   15
Doubtful, what Legacy he will bequeath,
And wait with greedy Ears his dying Breath:

2 Fraternitie's] *Ed.*; Fraternities *1681*; Fraterniti's *1682*; Fraternity's
*R*164, *R*184

With such quick Duty Vassal Fiends below
To meet commands of their Dread Monarch go.
   On Pillow rais'd, he do's their Entrance greet,   20
And joys to see the Wish'd Assembly meet:
They in glad Murmurs tell their Joy aloud,
Then a deep Silence stills th' expecting Croud.
Like *Delphick* Hag of old by Fiend possest,
He swells, wild Frenzy heaves his panting Brest,   25
His bristling Hairs stick up, his Eye-Balls glow,
And from his Mouth long flakes of Drivel flow:
Thrice with due Reverence he himself doth cross,
Then thus his Hellish Oracles disclose.
   Ye firm Associates of my great Design,   30
Whom the same Vows, and Oaths, and Order joyn,
The faithful Band, whom I, and *Rome* have chose,
The last Support of our declining Cause:
Whose Conquering Troops I with Success have led
Gainst all Opposers of our Church and Head;   35
Who e're to the mad *German* owe their Rise,
Geneva's Rebel, or the hot brain'd *Swiss*;
Revolted Hereticks, who late have broke,
And durst throw off the long-worn Sacred Yoke:
You, by whose happy Influence *Rome* can boast   40
A greater Empire, than by *Luther* lost:
By whom wide Nature's far-stretch't Limits now,
And utmost *Indies* to its Crosier Bow:
   Go on, ye mighty Champions of our Cause,
Maintain our Party, and subdue our Foes: 45
Kill Heresy, that rank and poisonous Weed,
Which threatens now the Church to overspread:
Fire *Calvin*, and his Nest of Upstarts out,
Who tread our Sacred Mitre under Foot;
Stray'd *Germany* reduce; let it no more   50
Th' incestuous *Monk* of *Wittenburge* adore:
Make Stubborn *England* once more stoop its Crown,
And Fealty to our Priestly Soveraign own:

37 *Geneva's Rebel*] *1681* (*corr.*); *Genevah's Rebel 1681* (*uncorr.*); *Geneva's Rebels 1682*   51 *Wittenburge*] *1681*; *Wittemberg 1682*

Regain our Church's Rights, the *Island* clear
From all remaining Dregs of *Wickliff* there.   55
Plot, enterprize, contrive, endeavour: spare
No toil nor Pains: no death nor Danger fear:
Restless your Aims pursue: let no defeat
Your sprightly Courage and Attempts rebate,
But urge to fresh and bolder, ne're to end   60
Till the whole world to our great *Califf* bend:
Till he thro' every Nation every where
Bear Sway, and Reign as absolute as here:
Till *Rome* without Controul and Contest be
The Universal Ghostly Monarchy.   65
  Oh! that kind Heaven a longer Thread would give,
And let me to that happy Juncture live:
But 'tis decreed!—at this he paus'd and wept,
The rest alike time with his Sorrow kept:
Then thus continued he—Since unjust Fate   70
Envies my race of Glory longer date;
Yet, as a wounded General, e're he dies,
To his sad Troops, sighs out his last Advice,
Who tho' they must his fatal Absence moan,
By those great Lessons conquer when he's gone;   75
So I to you my last Instructions give,
And breath out Counsel with my parting Life:
Let each to my important words give Ear,
Worth your Attention, and my dying Care.
  First, and the chiefest thing by me enjoyn'd,   80
The Solemn'st tie, that must your Order bind,
Let each without demur, or scruple pay
A strict Obedience to the *Roman* Sway:
To the unerring Chair all Homage Swear,
Altho' a Punk, a Witch, a Fiend sit there: 85
Who e're is to the Sacred Mitre rear'd,
Believe all Vertues with the place conferr'd:
Think him establish'd there by Heaven, tho' he ⎫
Has Altars rob'd for Bribes the choice to buy, ⎬
Or pawn'd his Soul to Hell for Simony: ⎭   90

74-5] *1681*; (Who, ... gone) *1682*

Tho' he be Atheist, Heathen, *Turk*, or *Jew*,
Blaspheamer, Sacriligious, Perjured too:
Tho' Pander, Bawd, Pimp, Pathick, Buggerer,
What e're Old *Sodoms* Nest of Lechers were:
Tho' Tyrant, Traitor, Pois'oner, Parricide,   95
Magician, Monster, all that's bad beside:
Fouler than Infamy; the very Lees,
The Sink, the Jakes, the Common-shore of Vice:
Strait count him Holy, Vertuous, Good, Devout,
Chast, Gentle, Meek, a Saint, a God, what not?   100
  Make Fate hang on his Lips, nor Heaven have
Pow'r to Predestinate without his leave:
None be admitted there, but who he please,
Who buys from him the Patent for the Place.
Hold these amongst the highest rank of Saints,   105
Whom e're he to that Honour shall advance,
Tho' here the Refuse of the Jail and Stews,
Whom Hell it self would scarce for lumber chuse:
But count all Reprobate, and Damn'd, and worse,
Whom he, when Gout, or Tissick Rage, shall curse: 110
Whom he in anger Excommunicates
For *Fryday* meals and abrogating Sprats,
Or in just Indignation spurnes to Hell
For jeering holy Toe and Pantofle.
  What e're he sayes esteem for Holy Writ,   115
And text Apocryphal if he think fit:
Let arrant Legends, worst of Tales and Lies,
Falser than *Capgraves* and *Voragines*,
Than *Quixot*, *Rablais*, *Amadis de Gaul*,   ⎫
If signed with Sacred Lead, and Fisher's Seal,   ⎬   120
Be thought Authentick and Canonical.   ⎭
Again, if he ordain't in his Decrees,
Let very Gospel for meer Fable pass:
Let Right be Wrong, Black White, and Vertue Vice,
No Sun, no Moon, nor no Antipodes: 125

  100 what] *1681*, *R253*; who *1682*   105 these] *1681*; those *1682*
108 Whom] *1681*; Which *1682*   112 meals] *E*, *1682 subst.*; Meale *1681*
120 If] *1681*; Is *1682*   121 Canonical] *1681 (corr.)*, *1682*; Cononical *1681*
(*uncorr.*)

Forswear your Reason, Conscience, and your Creed,
Your very Sense, and *Euclid*, if he bid.
    Let it be held less heinous, less amiss,
To break all Gods Commands, than one of his:
When his great Missions call, without delay, ⎫   130
Without reluctance readily Obey,   ⎬
Nor let your Inmost Wishes dare gainsay: ⎭
Should he to *Bantam*, or *Japan* command,
Or farthest Bounds of *Southern* unknown Land,
Farther than Avarice its Vassals drives,   135
Thro' Rocks and Dangers, loss of Blood and Lives;
Like great *Xavier's* be your Obedience shown,
Outstrip his Courage, Glory and Renown;
Whom neither yawning Gulphs of deep Despair,
Nor scorching Heats of Burning Line could scare: 140
Whom Seas nor Storms, nor Wracks could make refrain
From propagating Holy Faith and Gain.
    If he but nod Commissions out to kill,
But becken Lives of Hereticks to spill;
Let th' *Inquisition* rage, fresh Cruelties   145
Make the dire Engins groan with tortured Cries:
Let *Campo Flori* every Day be strow'd
With the warm Ashes of the *Lutheran* Brood:
Repeat again *Bohemian* Slaughters ore,
And *Piedmont* Vallies drown with floating Gore: 150
Swifter than Murthering Angels, when they fly
On Errands of avenging Destiny.
Fiercer than Storms let loose, with eager hast,
Lay Cities, Countries, Realms, whole Nature wast.
Sack, ravish, burn, destroy, slay, massacre,   155
Till the same Grave their Lives and Names interr.
    These are the Rights to our great *Mufty* due,
The sworn Allegience of your Sacred Vow:
What else we in our Votaries require,
What other Gifts next follows to enquire.   160
    And first it will our great Advice befit,

  140 Line] *E* (line), *1682*; Lime *1681*   147 strow'd] *E, 1682*; show'd *1681*
160 Gifts] *1681*; Gift *1682*

What Souldiers to your Lists you ought admit,
To Natives of the Church and Faith, like you,
The foremost rank of Choice is justly due
'Mongst whom the chiefest place assign to those,   165
Whose Zeal has mostly Signaliz'd the Cause.
But let not Entrance be to them denied,
Who ever shall desert the adverse Side:
Omit no Promises of Wealth and Power,
That may inveigled Hereticks allure: 170
Those whom great learning, parts, or wit renowns ⎫
Cajole with Hopes of Honours, Scarlet Gowns,   ⎬
Provincialships, and Palls, and Triple Crowns.   ⎭
This must a Rector, that a Provost be,
A third succeed to the next Abbacy: 175
Some Princes Tutors, others Confessors
To Dukes, and Kings, and Queens, and Emperors:
These are strong Arguments, which seldom fail,
Which more than all your weak disputes prevail.
   Exclude not those of less desert, decree   180
To all Revolters your Foundation free:
To all whom Gaming, Drunkenness, or Lust
To Need and Popery shall have reduc'd:
To all, whom slighted Love, Ambition crost,
Hopes often bilk't, and Sought Preferment lost,   185
Whom Pride, or Discontent, Revenge or Spite,
Fear, Frenzy, or Despair shall Proselite:
Those Powerful Motives, which the most bring in,
Most Converts to our Church and Order win.
Reject not those, whom Guilt and Crimes at home   190
Have made to us for Sanctuary come:
Let Sinners of each Hue, and Size, and Kind
Here quick admittance, and safe Refuge find:
Be they from Justice of their Country fled
With Blood of Murders, Rapes, and Treasons dy'd: 195
No Varlet, Rogue, or Miscreant refuse,
From Gallies, Jails, or Hell it self Broke loose.

163 Natives] *E*, *1682*; Natures *1681*   169 and] *1681*; or *1682*
174 Provost] *1682*; Provest *1681*   189 to] *1681* (*corr.*), *1682*; ro *1681* (*uncorr.*)   195 dy'd] *Ed.* (*1722*); died *1681, 1682*

By this you shall in Strength and Numbers grow
And shoals each day to your throng'd Cloysters flow:
So *Rome's* and *Mecca's* first great Founders did,   200
By such wise Methods made their Churches spread.
  When shaven Crown, and hallowed Girdle's Power
Has dub'd him Saint, that Villain was before;
Enter'd, let it his first Endeavour be
To shake off all remains of Modesty,   205
Dull sneaking Modesty, not more unfit
For needy flattering Poets, when they write,
Or trading Punks, than for a *Jesuit*:
If any Novice feel at first a blush,
Let Wine, and frequent converse with the Stews   210
Reform the Fop, and shame it out of Use,
Unteach the puling Folly by Degrees,
And train him to a well-bred Shamelesness.
Get that great Gift and Talent, Impudence,
Accomplish't Mankind's highest Excellence: 215
'Tis that alone prefers, alone makes great,
Confers alone Wealth, Titles, and Estate:
Gains Place at Court, can make a Fool a Peer,
An Ass a Bishop, can vilest Blockheads rear
To wear Red Hats, and sit in Porph'ry Chair.   220
'Tis Learning, Parts, and Skill, and Wit, and Sense,
Worth, Merit, Honour, Vertue, Innocence.
  Next for *Religion*, learn what's fit to take,
How small a Dram does the just Compound make.
As much as is by Crafty *States-men* worn   225
For Fashion only, or to serve a turn:
To bigot Fools its idle Practice leave,
Think it enough the empty Form to have:
The outward Show is seemely, cheap and light,
The Substance Cumbersome, of Cost and Weight: 230
The Rabble judge by what appears to th' Eye,
None, or but few the Thoughts within Descry.

  198 Numbers] *E, 1682*; Members *1681*   201 made] *E, 1682*; make *1681* (*corr.*);
may *1681* (*uncorr.*)   205 off] *1681*; of *1682*   207 write] *E, 1682*; writ
1681   213 Shamelesness] *E, 1682*; Shamefulness *1681*   225 by] *1681*; by
the *1682*

Make't you an Engine to ambitious Pow'r
To stalk behind, and hit your Mark more sure:
A Cloak to cover well-hid *Knavery*,   235
Like it when us'd, to be with ease thrown by:
A shifting Card, by which your Course to steer,
And taught with every changing *Wind* to veer.
Let no nice, holy Conscientious Ass ⎫
Amongst your better Company find place, ⎬   240
Me and your great Foundation to disgrace: ⎭
Let Truth be banish't, ragged Vertue fly,
And poor unprofitable Honesty;
Weak Idols, who their wretched Slaves betray;
To every Rook, and every Knave a Prey: 245
These lie remote and wide from Interest, ⎫
Farther than Heaven from Hell, or *East* from *West*, ⎬
Far as they e're were distant from this brest. ⎭
    Think not your selves t'Austerities confin'd,
Or those strict Rules, which other Orders bind: 250
To *Capuchins, Carthusians, Cordeliers*
Leave Penance, meager abstinence, and Prayers:
In lousy rags let *begging Friers* ly,
Content on straw, or Boards to mortify:
Let them with Sackcloth discipline their Skins,   255
And scourge them for their madness and their Sins:
Let pining *Anchorets* in Grotto's starve,
Who from the Liberties of Nature swerve:
Who make't their chief *Religion* not to eat,
And place't in nastiness and want of Meat: 260
Live you in Luxury and pamper'd Ease,
As if whole Nature were your Cateress.
Soft be your Beds, as those, which Monarch's Whores
Ly on, or Gouts of Bed-rid Emperours:
Your Wardrobes stor'd with choice of Suits, more Dear   265
Than Cardinals on High Processions wear:
With Dainties load your Board, whose every Dish,
May tempt cloy'd Gluttons, or *Vitellius'* Wish,

233 Make't] *1682*; Mak't *1681*; Make it *R254*   241 your great] *1681*; your
1682   260 place't] *1682*; plac't *1681*   267 Board] *1681*; Boards *1682*
268 *Vitellius'*] Ed.; *Vitellius's 1681*; *Vitellius 1682*

Each fit a longing Queen: let richest Wines
With Mirth your Heads Inflame, with Lust your Veins: 270
Such as the Friends of Dying *Popes* would give
For Cordials to prolong their gasping Life.
   Ner'e let the *Nazarene*, whose Badge and Name
You wear, upbraid you with a Conscious Shame:
Leave him his slighted Homilies and Rules,   275
To stuff the Squabbles of the wrangling Schooles:
Disdain that he and the poor angling Tribe,
Should Laws and Government to you prescribe:
Let none of those good Fools your Patterns make;
Instead of them, the mighty *Judas* take.   280
Renown'd *Iscariot*, fit alone to be
Th' Example of our great Society:
Whose daring Guilt despis'd the common Road,
And scorn'd to stoop at Sin beneath a God.
   And now 'tis time I should Instructions give,   285
What Wiles and Cheats the Rabble best deceive:
Each Age and Sex their Different Passions wear,
To suit with which requires a prudent Care:
Youth is Capricious, Headstrong, Fickle, Vain,
Given to Lawless Pleasure, Age to gain: 290
Old Wives in Superstition over-grown,
With Chimny Tales and Stories best are won:
Tis no mean Talent rightly to descry,
What several Baits to each you ought apply.
The Credulous, and easy of Belief,   295
With Miracles, and well fram'd Lies deceive.
Empty whole *Surius*, and the *Talmud* drain,
Saint *Francis'* and Saint *Mahomet's Alcoran*:
Sooner shall *Popes* and Cardinals want Pride,
Than you a Stock of Lies and Legends need.   300
   Tell how blest *Virgin* to come down was seen,
Like Play-House Punk descending in Machine:
How she writ Billets Doux, and Love-Discourse,
Made Assignations, Visits, and Amours:

270 Inflame,] *1682*; Inflame *1681*   271 Friends] *1681*; Fiends *1682*
297 *Talmud* drain,] *1681*; *Talmud*: drain *1682*   298 *Francis'*] *Ed.*; *Francis*
1681; *Francis, 1682*

How Hosts distrest, her Smock for Banner bore,   305
Which vanquish't Foes, and murdered at twelve Score.
Relate how Fish in Conventicles met,
And Mackril were with Bait of Doctrine caught:
How Cattle have Judicious Hearers been,
And Stones pathetically cryed Amen: 310
How consecrated Hive with Bells was hung,
And Bees kept Mass, and Holy Anthems Sung:
How Pigs to th' *Rosary* kneel'd, and sheep were taught
To bleat *te Deum* and *Magnificat*:
How Fly-Flap of Church-Censure, Houses rid   315
Of Insects, which at Curse of *Fryer* dy'd:
How travelling Saint, well mounted on a Switch,
Rid Journies thro' the Air, like *Lapland* Witch:
And ferrying Cowls *Religious Pilgrims* bore
O're waves without the help of Sail or Oar.   320
Nor let *Xaviers* great Wonders pass conceal'd,
How Storms were by th' Almighty Wafer quell'd;
How zealous Crab the sacred Image bore,
And Swam a Cath'lick to the distant Shore.
With Shams like these, the giddy Rout mislead,   325
Their Folly and their Superstition feed.
   'Twas found a good and gainful Art of Old
(And much it did our Churches Power uphold)
To feign Hobgoblings, Elves and walking Sprites,
And Fairies dancing Salenger a Nights: 330
White Sheets for Ghosts, and Will-a-wisps have past
For Souls in Purgatory unreleast:
And Crabs in Church-Yards crawl'd in Masquerade,
To cheat the Parish, and have Masses said.
By this our Ancestors in happier Dayes,   335
Did store of Credit and Advantage raise:
But now the Trade is fall'n, decay'd and Dead,
Ere since contagious Knowledge has or'e-spread:

308 Mackril were] *E, 1682 subst.*; *Mackril 1681, R*173 *subst.*   311 Hive]
*1681, R*172; Hives *1682*   320 without] *1681, R*173; with *1682*   325 mis-
lead] *1682, R*172; misled *1681*   332 unreleast:] *Ed.* (unreleas'd, *1722*);
unreleast *1681*; unreleast. *1682*   335 Ancestors] *1681*; Ancestor *1682*
338 or'e-spread:] *1682*; ore spread *1681*

With Scorn the grinning Rabble now hear tell
Of *Hecla, Patricks hole,* and *Mongibel*;   340
Believ'd no more than Tales of *Troy,* unless
In Countries drown'd in Ignorance like this.
Henceforth be wary how such things you feign,
Except it be beyond the *Cape,* or *Line*:
Except at *Mexico, Brazile, Peru,*   345
At the *Molucco's, Goa,* or *Pegu,*
Or any distant or remoter Place,
Where they may currant and unquestion'd pass:
Where never poching *Hereticks* resort,
To spring the Lye, and make't their Game and Sport.   350
    But I forget (what should be mention'd most)
Confession our chief Priviledge and Boast:
That Staple ware which ne're returns in vain,
Ne're balks the Trader of expected Gain.
'Tis this that spies through Court-intrigues and   355
Admission to the Cabinets of Kings: [brings
By this we keep proud Monarchs at our Becks,
And make our Foot-stools of their Thrones and Necks:
Give 'em Commands, and if they Disobey,
Betray 'em to th' Ambitious Heir a Prey: 360
Hound the Officious Curs on Hereticks,
The Vermin which the Church infest and vex:
And when our turn is served, and Business done,
Dispatch 'em for Reward, as useless grown.
    Nor are these half the Benefits and Gains,   365
Which by wise Manag'ry accrue from thence:
By this w' unlock the Misers hoarded Chests,
And Treasure, though kept close as States-mens Brests:
This does rich Widows to our Nets decoy,
Lets us their Jointers, and themselves enjoy: 370
To us the Merchant does his Customes bring,
And payes our Duty tho he cheats his King:
To us Court-Ministers refund, made great
By Robbery and Bank-rupt of the State:

345 *Peru*] *1681*; *Pegu 1682*   347 or] *1681*; and *1682*   350 make't]
1682; mak't *1681*   360 Betray 'em] Ed.; Betray'm *1681*; Betray them *1682*

Ours is the Souldiers Plunder, Padders Prize,   375
Gabels on Letchery, and the Stews Excise:
By this our Colledges in Riches shine,
And vy with *Becket*'s and *Loretto's* Shrine.
  And here I must not grudge a word or two
(My younger Vot'ries) of Advice to you: 380
To you whom Beautie's Charms and generous Fire
Of boiling Youth to sports of Love inspire:
This is your Harvest, here secure and cheap
You may the Fruits of unbought Pleasure reap:
Riot in free and uncontroull'd Delight,   385
Where no dull Marriage clogs the Appetite.
Tast every dish of Lust's variety,   ⎫
Which *Popes*, and Scarlet Lechers dearly buy,   ⎬
With Bribes and Bishopricks, and Simony.   ⎭
But this I ever to your care commend,   390
Be wary how you openly Offend:
Lest scoffing lewd Buffoons descry our shame,
And fix disgrace on the great Order's fame.
  When the ungarded Maid alone repairs
To ease the burthen of her Sins and cares;   395
When youth in each, and privacy conspire
To kindle wishes, and befriend desire;
If she has Practis'd in the Trade before,
(Few else of Proselytes to us brought o're)
Little of Force, or artifice will need   400
To make you in the victory succeed:
But if some untaught Innocence she be,   ⎫
Rude, and unknowing in the mystery;   ⎬
She'l cost more labour to be made comply.   ⎭
Make her by Pumping understand the sport,   405
And undermine with secret trains the Fort.
Somtimes, as if you'd blame her gaudy dress,   ⎫
Her Naked Pride, her Jewels, Point, and Lace;   ⎬
Find Opportunity her Breasts to Press: ⎭
Oft feel her Hand, and whisper in her ear   410

---

395 burthen] *1681*; burthens *1682*   403 unknowing] *E, 1682*; unknown *1681*
410 ear] *Ed.*; ear, *1681, 1682*

You find the secret marks of lewdness there:
Somtimes with naughty sence her blushes raise,
And make 'em guilt, she never knew, confess:
"Thus (may you say) with such a leering smile,
"So Languishing a look you hearts beguile: 415
"Thus with your foot, hand, eye, you tokens speak,
"These Signs deny, these Assignations make:
"Thus 'tis you clip, with such a fierce embrace
"You clasp your Lover to your Brest and Face:
"Thus are your hungry lips with Kisses cloy'd,   420
"Thus is your Hand, and thus your Tongue employ'd.
    Ply her with talk like this; and, if sh'encline,
To help devotion give her *Aretine*
Instead o'th' Rosary: never despair,
She, that to such discourse will lend an Ear,   425
Tho' chaster than cold cloyster'd Nuns she were,
Will soon prove soft and pliant to your use,
As Strumpets on the *Carnaval* let loose.
Credit experience; I have tri'd 'em all,
And never found th' unerring methods fail: 430
Not *Ovid*, tho' 'twere his cheif Mastery,
Had greater Skill in these Intrigues, than I:
Nor *Nero's* learned *Pimp*, to whom we ow
What choice Records of Lust are extant now.
This heretofore, when youth, and sprightly Blood   435
Ran in my Veins. I tasted and enjoy'd:
Ah those blest days!—(here the old Lecher smil'd,
With sweet remembrance of past pleasure fill'd)
But they are gone! Wishes alone remain,
And Dreams of joy ne're to be felt again: 440
To abler Youth I now the Practice leave,
To whom this counsel and advice I give.
    But the dear mention of my gayer days
Has made me farther, than I would, digress:
'Tis time we now should in due Place expound,   445
How guilt is after shrift to be atton'd:
Enjoyn no sow'r Repentance, Tears and Grief;

415 you] *1681, R291*; your *1682*   447 Tears] *1681*; Tear *1682*

Eys weep no cash, and you no profit give:
Sins, tho' of the first rate, must punish'd be,
Not by their own, but th' Actor's Quality: 450
The Poor, whose purse cannot the Penance bear,
Let whipping serve, bare feet, and shirts of hair:
The richer Fools to *Compostella* send,
To *Rome, Monserrat*, or the *Holy Land*:
Let Pardons, and th' Indullgence-Office drain   455
Their Coffers, and enrich the *Pope's* with gain:
Make 'em build Churches, Monasteries found,
And dear bought Masses for their crimes compound.
 Let Law and Gospel rigid precepts set,
And make the paths to Bliss rugged and strait: 460
Teach you a smooth and easier way to gain
Heavn's joys, yet sweet and useful sin retain:
With every frailty, every lust comply,
T'advance your Spiritual Realm and Monarchy:
Pull up weak Vertue's fence, give scope and space   465
And Purlieus to out-lying Consciences:
Shew that the Needle's eye may stretch, and how
The largest Camel-vices may go thro'.
 Teach how the *Priest* Pluralities may buy,
Yet fear no odious Sin of Simony,   470
While Thoughts and Ducats well directed be:
 Let Whores adorn his exemplary life,
But no lewd heinous Wife a Scandal give.
Sooth up the Gaudy Atheist, who maintains
No Law, but Sense, and owns no *God*, but Chance.   475
Bid Thieves rob on, the Boistrous Ruffian tell,
He may for Hire, Revenge, or Honour kill:
Bid Strumpets persevere, absolve 'em too,
And take their dues in kind for what you do:
Exhort the painful and Industrious Bawd   480
To Diligence and Labour in her Trade:
Nor think her innocent Vocation ill,

454 To] *1681*; Tome *1682*   *Monserrat*] *1681*; *Monferrat 1682*   455 th']
1681; the *1682*   461 smooth and] *1681*, *R*167; smooth, an *1682*   468 The
... may] *1682*; For ... to *1681*, *R*167   469 *Priest*] *1682*; *Priests 1681*
471 well] *1681*; will *1682*   478 persevere] *1682*; preseverse *1681*

Whose income do's the sacred Treasure fill:
Let Griping Usurers Extortion use,
No Rapine, Falshood, Perjury refuse,   485
Stick at no Crime, which covetous *Popes* would scarce
Act to enrich themselves and Bastard-Heirs:
A small Bequest to th' Church can all attone,
Wipes off all scores, and Heav'n and all's their own.
Be these your Doctrins, these. the Truths you preach, ⎤ 490
But no forbiden *Bible* come in reach,   ⎟
Your cheats and Artifices to Impeach;   ⎦
Lest thence lay-Fools Pernicious knowledge get,
Throw off Obedience, and your Laws forget:
Make 'em belive't a spell more dreadfull far   495
Than *Bacon, Haly* or *Albumazar.*
Happy the time, when th' unpretending Crowd
No more, than I, its Language understood.
When the worm-eaten Book, link'd to a chain,
In dust lay moulding in the *Vatican*;   500
Despis'd, neglected, and forgot, to none,
But poring *Rabbies*, or the *Sorbon* known:
Then in full pow'r our Soveraign Prelate sway'd,
By Kings and all the Rabble-World Obey'd:
Here humble Monarch at his feet kneel'd down,   505
And beg'd the Alms and Charity of a Crown:
There, when in Solemn State he pleas'd to ride,
Poor Scepter'd slaves ran Henchboys by his side:
None, tho' in thought, his Grandeur durst Blasphem,
Nor in their very sleep a Treason Dream.   510
   But since the broaching that mischeivous Piece,
Each Alderman a *Father Lumbard* is:
And every Cit dares impudently know
More than a Council, *Pope* and Conclave too.
Hence the late *Damned Frier*, and all the crew   515
Of former Crawling Sects their poison drew:
Hence all the Troubles, Plagues, Rebellions breed,

483 income] *1681*; incomes *1682*   491 reach,] Ed. *(1722)*; reach: *1681*,
1682   492 Impeach;] *Ed. (1722)*; Impeach. *1681, 1682*   493 get] *1682*;
gets *1681*   495 Make 'em] *1682*; Mak' em *1681*   509 Grandeur] *1682*;
Grandure *1681*

We've felt, or feel, or may hereafter dread:
Wherefore enjoyn, that no Lay-coxcomb dare
About him that unlawful Weapon wear;   520
But charge him chiefly not to touch at all
The dangerous Works of that old *Lollard, Paul*;
That arrant *Wickliffist*, from whom our Foes
Take all their Batt'ries to attack our Cause;
Would he in his first years had Martyr'd been,   525
Never *Damascus* nor the Vision seen;
Then he our Party was, stout, vigorous,
And fierce in chase of Hereticks like us:
Till he at length by th' Enemies seduc'd,
Forsook us, and the hostile side espous'd.   530
  Had not the mighty *Julian* mist his aims,
These holy Shreds had all consum'd in flames:
But since th' immortal Lumber still endures,
In spite of all his industry and ours;
Take care at least it may not come abroad,   535
To taint with catching Heresie the Crowd:
Let them be still kept low in sence, they'l pay
The more respect, more readily obey.
Pray that kind Heav'n would on their hearts dispense
A bounteous and abundant Ignorance,   540
That they may never swerve, nor turn awry
From sound and orthodox Stupidity.
  But these are obvious things, easie to know,
Common to every *Monk* as well as you:
Greater Affairs and more important wait   545
To be discuss'd, and call for our debate:
Matters that depth require, and well befit
Th' Address and Conduct of a *Jesuit*.
How Kingdoms are embroil'd, what shakes a Throne,
How the first seeds of Discontent are sown   550
To spring up in Rebellion; how are set
The secret snares that circumvent a State:
How bubbled Monarchs are at first beguil'd,
Trepann'd and gull'd, at last depos'd and kill'd.
  When some proud Prince, a Rebel to our Head,   555
For disbelieving Holy Churches Creed

And *Peter-pence* is Heretick decreed; ⌉

And by a solemn and unquestion'd Pow'r

To Death, and Hell, and You, deliver'd o're:

Chuse first some dext'rous Rogue well tried and known, 560

(Such by Confession your Familiars grown;)

Let him by Art and Nature fitted be

For any great and gallant Villany,

Practis'd in every Sin, each kind of Vice,

Which deepest Casuists in their searches miss,   565

Watchful as Jealousie, wary as Fear,   ⌉

Fiercer than Lust, and bolder than Despair,   ⎬

But close as plotting Fiends in Council are.   ⌋

To him in firmest Oaths of Silence bound,

The worth and merit of the Deed propound: 570

Tell of whole Reams of Pardon new come o're,

Indies of Gold, and Blessings endless store:

Choice of Preferments, if he overcome,

And if he fail, undoubted Martyrdom:

And Bills for Sums in Heav'n, to be drawn   575

On Factors there, and at first sight paid down.

With Arts and Promises like these allure,

And make him to your great design secure.

   And here to know the sundry ways to kill,

Is worth the *Genius* of a *Machiavel:*   580

Dull *Northern* Brains in these deep Arts unbred,

Know nought but to cut Throats or knock o'th' Head.

No slight of Murder of the subt'lest shape,

Your busie search and observation scape:

Legerdemain of Killing, that dives in,   585

And juggling steals away a Life unseen:

How gawdy Fate may be in Presents sent,

And creep insensibly by Touch or Scent:

How Ribbands, Gloves, or Saddle Pomel may

An unperceiv'd but certain Death convey;   590

Above the reach of Antidotes, above the pow'r

Of the fam'd *Pontick Mountebank* to cure.

What er'e is known to quaint *Italian* spite,

In studied Pois'ning skill'd and exquisite:

What e're great *Borgia* or his *Sire* could boast,   595

Which the Expence of half the Conclave cost.
   Thus may the business be in secret done, ⎫
Nor Authors nor the Accessaries known,   ⎬
And the slurr'd guilt with ease on others thrown. ⎭
But if ill Fortune should your Plot betray,   600
And leave you to the rage of Foes a prey;
Let none his Crime by weak confession own,
Nor shame the Church, while he'd himself attone.
Let varnish'd Guile and feign'd Hypocrisies, ⎫
Pretended Holiness and useful Lies,   ⎬   605
Your well-dissembled Villany disguise.   ⎭
A thousand wily Turns and Doubles try,
To foil the Scent, and to divert the Cry:
Cog, shamm, outface, deny, equivocate,
Into a thousand shapes your selves translate: 610
Remember what the crafty *Spartan* taught,
"Children with Rattles, Men with Oaths are caught:
Forswear upon the Rack, and if you fall,
Let this great comfort make amends for all,
Those whom they damn for Rogues next Age shall see   615
Made Advocates i'th' Church's Litany.
   Who ever with bold Tongue or Pen shall dare
Against your Arts and Practices declare;
What Fool shall e're presumptuously oppose,
Your holy Cheats and godly Frauds disclose;   620
Pronounce him Heretick, Firebrand of Hell,
Turk, Jew, Fiend, Miscreant, Pagan, Infidel;
A thousand blacker Names, worse Calumnies,
All Wit can think, and pregnant Spite devise:
Strike home, gash deep, no Lies nor Slanders spare;   625
A Wound though cur'd, yet leaves behind a Scar.
   Those whom your Wit and Reason can't decry,
Make scandalous with Loads of Infamy:
Make *Luther* Monster, by a Fiend begot,
Brought forth with Wings, and Tail, and Cloven Foot: 630
Make Whoredom, Incest, worst of vice and shame,

601 leave you to the rage of] *1682*; you to mercy of your *1681*
626 leaves] *1682*, *R*169; leave *1681*

Pollute and foul his Manners, Life and Name.
Tell how strange Storms usher'd his fatal end,
And Hells black Troops did for his Soul contend.
  Much more I had to say, but now grow faint,   635
And strength and Spirits for the Subject want:
Be these great Mysteries I here unfold,
Amongst your Order's Institutes enroll'd:
Preserve them sacred, close, and unreveal'd;
As ancient *Rome* her *Sybils* Books conceal'd.   640
Let no bold Heretick with sawcy eye
Into the hidden unseen Archives pry;
Lest the malicious flouting Rascals turn
Our Church to Laughter, Raillery, and Scorn.
Let never Rack or Torture, Pain or Fear,   645
From your firm Brests th' important Secrets tear.
If any treacherous Brother of your own   ⎫
Shall to the World divulge and make them known,   ⎬
Let him by worst of Deaths his Guilt attone.   ⎭
Should but his Thoughts or Dreams suspected be,   ⎫   650
Let him for safety and prevention die,   ⎬
And learn i'th' Grave the Art of Secresie.   ⎭
  But one thing more, and then with joy I go,
Nor ask a longer stay of Fate below:
Give me again once more your plighted Faith,   655
And let each seal it with his Dying Breath:
As the great *Carthaginian* heretofore   ⎫
The bloudy reeking Altar touch'd, and swore   ⎬
Eternal Enmity to th' *Roman* Pow'r: ⎭
Swear you (and let the Fates confirm the same)   660
An endless Hatred to the *Lutheran* Name:
Vow never to admit or League, or Peace,
Or Truce, or Commerce with the cursed Race:
Now through all Age, when Time or Place soe're
Shall give you pow'r, wage an immortal War: 665
Like *Theban* Feuds let yours your selves survive,
And in your very Dust and Ashes live.
Like mine, be your last Gasp their Curse—At this

635 grow] *1681*; grown *1682*

They kneel, and all the Sacred Volum kiss;
Vowing to send each year an Hecatomb   670
Of *Huguenots* an Offering to his Tomb.
  In vain he would continue—Abrupt Death
A Period puts, and stops his impious Breath:
In broken Accents he is scarce allow'd
To faulter out his Blessing on the Crowd.   675
   Amen is echo'd by Infernal Howl,
  And scrambling Spirits seize his parting Soul.

S A T Y R   I V .

———————

S. Ignatius *his Image brought in, discovering the Rogueries of the* Jesuits, *and ridiculous Superstition of
the* Church of Rome.

Once I was common Wood, a shapeless Log,
Thrown out a Pissing-post for every Dog:
The Workman yet in doubt what course to take,
Whether I'd best a Saint or Hog-trough make,
After debate resolv'd me for a Saint,   5
And thus fam'd *Loyola* I represent:
And well I may resemble him, for he
As stupid was, as much a Block as I.
My right Leg maim'd at halt I seem to stand,
To tell the Wounds at *Pampelune* sustain'd.   10
My Sword and Souldiers Armour here had been,
But they may in *Monserrats* Church be seen:
Those there to *blessed Virgin* I laid down
For Cassock, Surcingle, and shaven Crown,
The spiritual Garb in which I now am shown.   15
  With due Accoutrements and fit disguise
I might for Centinel of Corn suffice:

As once the well-hung *God* of old stood guard,
And the invading Crows from Forrage scar'd.
Now on my Head the Birds their Reliques leave,   20
And Spiders in my mouth their Arras weave:
And persecuted Rats oft find in me
A Refuge and religious Sanctuary.
But you profaner *Hereticks*, who e're
The *Inquisition* and its vengeance fear,   25
I charge stand off, at peril come not near:
None at twelve score untruss, break wind, or piss;
He enters *Fox* his Lists that dares transgress:
For I'm by Holy Church in reverence had,
And all good Catholick Folk implore my aid.   30
    These Pictures which you see my Story give,
The Acts and Monuments of me alive:
That Frame wherein with Pilgrims weeds I stand,
Contains my Travels to the *Holy Land*.
This me and my Decemvirate at *Rome*,   35
When I for Grant of my great Order come.
There with Devotion rapt I hang in Air,
With Dove (like *Mahomets*) whisp'ring in my ear.
Here *Virgin* in Galesh of Clouds descends,
To be my safeguard from assaulting Fiends.   40
    Those Tables by, and Crutches of the lame,
My great Atchievments since my death proclaim:
Pox, Ague, Dropsie, Palsie, Stone, and Gout,
Legions of Maladies by me cast out,
More than the *College* know, or ever fill   45
Quacks Wiping Paper and the Weekly Bill.
What *Peter*'s shadow did of old, the same
Is fancied done by my all pow'rful Name;
For which some wear't about their Necks and Arms,
To guard from Dangers, Sicknesses, and Harms;   50
And some on Wombs the barren to relieve,
A Miracle I better did alive.
    Oft I by crafty *Jesuit* am taught
Wonders to do, and many a juggling Feat.
Sometimes with Chaffing Dish behind me put,   55
I sweat like Clapt Debauch in Hot House shut,

And drip like any Spitchcock'd *Huguenot.* ⎤

Sometimes by secret Springs I learn to stir,

As Paste-Board Saints dance by miraculous Wire:

Then I *Tradescant*'s Rarities outdo,   ⎤   60

Sands Waterworks and *German* Clockwork too,   ⎬ .

Or any choice Device at *Barthol'mew.*   ⎦

Sometimes I utter Oracles by Priest,

Instead of a Familiar possest.

The Church I vindicate, *Luther* confute,   65

And cause Amazement in the gaping Rout.

   Such holy Cheats, such *Hocus* Tricks as these,

For Miracles amongst the Rabble pass.

By this in their Esteem I daily grow,

In Wealth enrich'd, increas'd in Vot'ries too.   70

This draws each year vast Numbers to my Tomb,

More than in Pilgrimage to *Mecca* come.

This brings each week new Presents to my Shrine,

And makes it those of *Indian* Gods outshine.

This gives a Chalice, that a Golden Cross,   75

Another massie Candlesticks bestows:

Some Altar Cloths of costly work and price,   ⎤

Plush, Tissue, Ermin, Silks of noblest Dies, ⎬

The *Birth* and *Passion* in Embroideries: ⎦

Some Jewels, rich as those th' *Egyptian* Punk   80

In Jellies to her *Roman* Stallion drunk.

Some offer gorgeous Robes, which serve to wear

When I on Holydays in state appear;

When I'm in pomp on high Processions shown,

Like Pageants of Lord Mayor or *Skimmington.*   85

Lucullus could not such a Wardrobe boast,

Less those of Popes at their Election cost;

Less those, which *Sicily*'s Tyrant heretofore

From plunder'd Gods and *Jove*'s own Shoulders tore.

   Hither as to some Fair the Rabble come,   90

To barter for the Merchandize of *Rome*;

Where Priests like Mountebanks on Stage appear,

T'expose the Frippery of their hallow'd Ware:

This is the Lab'ratory of their Trade,

The Shop where all their staple Drugs are made;   95

Prescriptions and Receipts to bring in Gain,
All from the Church Dispensatories ta'en.
    The Pope's Elixir, Holy Water's here,
Which they with Chymick Art distill'd prepare:
Choice above *Goddards* Drops, and all the Trash   100
Of modern Quacks; this is that Sovereign Wash
For fetching Spots and Morphew from the Face,
And scowring dirty Cloaths and Consciences.
One drop of this, if us'd, had pow'r to fray
The Legion from the Hogs of *Gadara:*   105
This would have silenc'd quite the *Wiltshire Drum,*
And made the prating Fiend of *Mascon* dumb.
    That Vessel consecrated Oyl contains,
Kept sacred as the fam'd *Ampoulle of France;*
Which some profaner *Hereticks* would use   110
For liquoring Wheels of Jacks, and Boots, and Shooes:
This makes the Chrism, which mixt with Snot of Priests,
Anoints young Catholicks for the Church's lists;
And when they're crost, confest, and die; by this
Their lanching Souls slide off to endless Bliss: 115
As *Lapland* Saints when they on Broomsticks fly,
By help of Magick Unctions mount the Sky.
    Yon Altar-Pix of Gold is the Abode
And safe Repository of their God.
A Cross is fix't upon't the Fiends to fright,   120
And Flies which would the Deity beshite;
And Mice, which oft might unprepar'd receive,
And to lewd Scoffers cause of scandal give.
    Here are perform'd the Conjurings and Spells,
For Christning Saints, and Hawks and Carriers Bells;   125
For hallowing Shreds, and Grains, and Salts, and Bawms,
Shrines, Crosses, Medals, Shells, and Waxen Lambs:
Of wondrous virtue all (you must believe)
And from all sorts of Ill preservative;
From Plague, Infection, Thunder, Storm, and Hail,   130
Love, Grief, Want, Debt, Sin, and the Devil and all.

111 and Boots] *1681;* of Boots *1682*   112 makes] *1681;* make *1682*
113 Anoints] *1681;* Anoint *1682*   122 might] *1681 (corr.), 1682;* wight *1681*
(*uncorr.*)

Here Beads are blest, and *Pater nosters* fram'd,
(By some the Tallies of Devotion nam'd)
Which of their Prayr's and Oraisons keep tale,
Lest they and Heav'n should in the reck'ning fail.   135
Here Sacred Lights, the Altars graceful Pride,
Are by Priests breath perfum'd and sanctified;
Made some of Wax, of *Hereticks* Tallow some,
A gift which *Irish Emma* sent to *Rome:*
For which great Merit worthily (we're told)   140
She's now amongst her Country Saints inroll'd.
Here holy Banners are reserv'd in store,
And Flags, such as the fam'd *Armado* bore:
And hallow'd Swords and Daggers kept for use
When resty Kings the Papal Yoke refuse: 145
And consecrated Ratsbane, to be laid
For *Heretick* Vermin which the Church invade.
  But that which brings in most of Wealth and Gain,
Does best the Priests swoln Tripes and Purses strain;
Here they each week their constant Auctions hold   150
Of Reliques, which by Candles Inch are sold:
Saints by the dozen here are set to sale,
Like Mortals wrought in Gingerbread on Stall.
Hither are loads from emptied Charnels brought,
And Voiders of the Worms from *Sextons* bought,   155
Which serve for Retail through the World to vent,
Such as of late were to the *Savoy* sent:
Hair from the Skulls of dying Strumpets shorn,
And Felons Bones from rifled Gibbets torn;
Like those which some old Hag at midnight steals,   160
For Witchcrafts, Amulets, and Charms, and Spells,
Are past for sacred to the cheap'ning Rout;
And worn on Fingers, Breasts, and Ears about.
This boasts a Scrap of me, and that a Bit
Of good S. *George*, S. *Patrick*, or S. *Kit*.   165
These Locks S. *Bridgets* were, and those S. *Clares*;
Some for S. *Catherines* go, and some for *hers*
That wip'd her *Saviours* feet, wash'd with her tears.

    134 and] *1681 (corr.)*, *1682*; aud *1681 (uncorr.)*

Here you may see my wounded Leg, and here
Those which to *China* bore the great *Xavier*.   170
Here may you the grand *Traitor*'s Halter see,
Some call't the Arms of the Society:
Here is his Lanthorn too, but *Faux* his not,
That was embezl'd by the *Huguenot*.
Here *Garnet*'s Straws, and *Becket*'s Bones and Hair,   175
For murd'ring whom some Tails are said to wear,
As learned *Capgrave* does record their fate,
And faithful *British* Histories relate.
Those are S. *Laurence* Coals expos'd to view,
Strangly preserv'd and kept alive till now.   180
That's the fam'd *Wildefortis* wondrous Beard,
For which her Maidenhead the Tyrant spar'd.
Yon is the *Baptist*'s Coat, and one of's Heads,
The rest are shewn in many a place besides;
And of his Teeth as many Sets there are,   185
As on their Belts six Operators wear.
Here Blessed *Maries* Milk, not yet turn'd sour, ⎫
Renown'd (like Ass's) for its healing pow'r, ⎬
Ten *Holland* Kine scarce in a year give more. ⎭
Here is her *Manteau*, and a Smock of hers,   190
Fellow to that which once reliev'd *Poictiers*;
Besides her *Husbands* Utensils of Trade,
Wherewith some prove that Images were made.
Here is the Souldiers Spear, and Passion Nails,
Whose quantity would serve for building *Pauls*:   195
Chips some from Holy Cross, from *Tyburn* some,
Honour'd by many a *Jesuits* Martyrdom:
All held of special and miraculous Pow'r,
Not *Tabor* more approv'd for Agues cure:
Here Shooes, which once perhaps at *Newgate* hung,   200
Angled their Charity that past along,
Now for S. *Peter*'s go, and th' Office bear
For Priests, they did for lesser Villains there.
    These are the Fathers Implements and Tools,

188 Ass's] *1681*; Ass'es *1682*   197 *Jesuits*] *1681*; *Jesuit's 1682*
201 their] *1682*; for *1681*

Their gawdy Trangums for inveigling Fools: 205
These serve for Baits the simple to ensnare,
Like Children spirited with Toys at Fair.
Nor are they half the Artifices yet,
By which the Vulgar they delude and cheat:
Which should I undertake, much easier I   ⎫   210
Much sooner might compute what Sins there be   ⎬
Wip'd off and pardon'd at a *Jubilee*:   ⎭
What Bribes enrich the *Datary* each year,
Or Vices treated on by *Escobar:*
How many Whores in *Rome* profess the Trade,   215
Or greater numbers by Confession made.
  One undertakes by Scale of Miles to tell
The Bounds, Dimensions, and Extent of Hell;
How far and wide th'Infernal Monarch reigns,
How many *German* Leagues his Realm contains: 220
Who are his Ministers, pretends to know,
And all their several Offices below:
How many Chaudrons he each year expends
In Coals for roasting *Huguenots* and Fiends:
And with as much exactness states the case,   225
As if h'ad been Surveyor of the place.
  Another frights the Rout with ruful Stories,
Of wild *Chimaera's, Limbo's, Purgatories,*
And bloated Souls in smoaky durance hung,   ⎫
Like a *Westphalia* Gammon or Neats Tongue,   ⎬   230
To be redeem'd with Masses and a Song.   ⎭
A good round Summ must the Deliverance buy,
For none may there swear out on poverty.
Your rich and bounteous Shades are onely eas'd,
No *Fleet* or *Kings Bench* Ghosts are thence releas'd.   235
  A third the wicked and debauch'd to please,   ⎫
Crys up the vertue of Indulgences,   ⎬
And all the rates of Vices does assess;   ⎭
What price they in the *holy Chamber* bear,
And Customs for each Sin imported there: 240
How you at best advantages may buy

    212 Jubilee:] *Ed. (1770)*; Jubilee. *1681, 1682*

Patents for Sacrilege and Simony.
What Tax is in the Leach'ry-Office laid
On Panders, Bawds, and Whores, that ply the Trade:
What costs a Rape, or Incest, and how cheap   245
You may an Harlot or an Ingle keep;
How easie Murder may afforded be
For one, two, three, or a whole Family;
But not of *Hereticks*, there no Pardon lacks,
'Tis one o'th' Churches meritorious Acts.   250
   For venial Trifles less and slighter Faults,
They ne're deserve the trouble of your thoughts.
Ten *Ave Maries* mumbled to the Cross
Clear scores of twice ten thousand such as those:
Some are at sound of christen'd Bell forgiven,   255
And some by squirt of Holy Water driven:
Others by Anthems plaid are charm'd away,
As men cure Bites of the *Tarantula*.
   But nothing with the Crowd does more enhance
The value of these holy *Charlatans*,   260
Than when the Wonders of the Mass they view,
Where spiritual Jugglers their chief Mast'ry shew:
Hey Jingo, Sirs! What's this? 'tis Bread you see;
Presto be gone! tis now a Deity.
Two grains of Dough, with Cross and stamp of Priest,   265
And five small words pronounc'd, make up their Christ.
To this they all fall down, this all adore,
And strait devour what they ador'd before;
Down goes the tiny *Saviour* at a bit,
To be digested, and at length beshit: 270
From Altar to Close Stool or Jakes preferr'd,
First Wafer, next a God, and then a ——
   'Tis this that does th' astonish'd Rout amuse,
And Reverence to shaven Crown infuse:
To see a silly, sinful, mortal Wight   275
His Maker make, create the Infinite.
None boggles at th' impossibility;
Alas, 'tis wondrous heavenly Mystery!

273 th'] 1681; the 1682

None dares the mighty God-maker blaspheme,
Nor his most open Crimes and Vices blame: 280
Saw he those hands that held his God before,
Strait grope himself, and by and by a Whore;
Should they his aged Father kill or worse,
His Sisters, Daughters, Wife, himself too force.

   And here I might (if I but durst) reveal   285
What pranks are plaid in the Confessional:
How haunted Virgins have been dispossest,
And Devils were cast out to let in Priest:
What Fathers act with Novices alone,
And what to Punks in shriving Seats is done;   290
Who thither flock to Ghostly Confessor,
To clear old debts, and tick with Heav'n for more.
Oft have I seen these hallow'd Altars stain'd
With Rapes, those Pews with Buggeries profan'd:
Not great *Cellier*, nor any greater Bawd,   295
Of Note and long experience in the Trade,
Has more and fouler Scenes of Lust survey'd.
But I these dang'rous Truths forbear to tell,
For fear I should the *Inquisition* feel.

   Should I tell all their countless Knaveries,   300
Their Cheats, and Shamms, and Forgeries, and Lies,
Their Cringings, Crossings, Censings, Sprinklings, Chrisms,
Their Conjurings, and Spells, and Exorcisms;
Their motly Habits, Maniples, and Stoles,
Albs, Ammits, Rochets, Chimers, Hoods, and Cowls.   305
Should I tell all their several Services,
Their Trentals, Masses, Dirges, Rosaries:
Their solemn Pomps, their Pageants, and Parades,
Their holy Masques, and spiritual Cavalcades,
With thousand Antick Tricks and Gambols more;   310
'Twould swell the summ to such a mighty score,
That I at length should more volum'nous grow,
Than *Crabb*, or *Surius*, lying *Fox*, or *Stow*.

   Believe what e're I have related here,
As true as if 'twere spoke from Porph'ry Chair.   315

         304 Maniples] *E, 1682*; Manciples *1681*

If I have feign'd in ought or broach'd a Lie,
Let worst of Fates attend me, let me be
Pist on by Porter, Groom, and Oyster-whore,
Or find my Grave in Jakes and Common-shore:
Or make next Bonfire for the *Powder-plot*,   320
The sport of every sneering *Huguenot*.
   There like a Martyr'd Pope in Flames expire,
   And no kind Catholick dare quench the Fire.

[Title-page in *Satyrs Upon The Jesuits, 1681*]

A

S A T Y R

AGAINST

V E R T U E .

Aude aliquid brevibus Gyaris et carcere dignum
Si vis esse aliquis—Juven. Sat.

[ORNAMENT]

LONDON,
Printed for *Jo. Hindmarsh*, 1680.

Aude aliquid brevibus Gyaris, & carcere dignum,
Si vis esse aliquis.—Juven. Sat.

O D E .

Suppos'd to be spoken by a Court-Hector at Breaking of the Dial in Privy-
Garden.

July 1676 at Croydon

1.

    Now Curses on you all! ye vertuous Fools,
        Who think to fetter free-born Souls,
  And ty 'em up to dull Morality and Rules:
    The Stagyrite be damn'd, and all the Crew
    Of learned Ideots, who his Steps pursue,   5
And those more silly Proselytes, whom his fond Precepts drew:
  Oh! had his Ethicks bin with their vile Author drownd,
    Or a like Fate with those lost Writings found,
    Which that grand Plagiary doom'd to Fire,
      And made by unjust Flames expire!   10
    They ne'er had then seduc'd Mortality,
Ne'er lasted to debauch the World with their Lewd Pedantry.
But damn'd and more (if Hell can do't) be that thrice-cursed
    Whoe're the Rudiments of Law design'd,   [Name,
    Whoe're did the first Model of Religion frame,   15
    And by that double Vassalage inthral'd Mankind,
    By nought before but their own Pow'r or Will confin'd;
    Now quite abridg'd of all their primitive Liberty,
    And Slaves to each caprichious Monarch's Tyranny:
    More happy Brutes! who the great Rule of Sence observe,   20

  0.4-5 Suppos'd ... Court Hector ... Privy-Garden] *R, A, G, P1*; Suppos'd ...
Court Hector 1680, m subst., Y1, Y2; Suppos'd ... Town-Hector *1679*; *not in*
1681, 1682   0.6 July ... Croydon] *R only*   1 you] *R, 1682, A, m*; ye
1679, 1681, 1680, G, P1, Y1, Y2   3 'em up] *R, 1680, G, m, P1, Y1*; them up
A; 'um *1679, Y2*; 'um up *1681*; 'em *1682*   Morality] *R, 1679, 1681, 1682, 1680,*
A, G; moralitis *m*; Mortality *P1*   7 vile] *R, E, A*; wild *1679, 1681, 1682,*
1680, MSS −A   8 with] *R, E, 1682, 1680, MSS −Y2*; which *1679, 1681, Y2*
11 Mortality] *R, E, 1682, 1680, A, G, P1, Y1*; Morality *1679, 1681, m, Y2*
13 thrice-cursed] *R, E, 1682, 1680, MSS −Y2 (E, 1680, G, A, Y1, unhyphenated)*;
their cursed *1679, 1681, Y2*   16 *R, 1682, 1680, MSS −Y2*; *not in 1679, 1681,*
Y2   20 who the great] *R, 1679, 1682, 1680, MSS −A*; which the first *A*

And ne'er from their first Charter swerve;
Happy! whose Lives are meerly to Enjoy,
And feel no stings of Sin that may their Bliss annoy;
Still unconcern'd at Epithets of Ill or Good,
Distinctions, unadult'rate Nature never understood.   25

2.

Hence hated Vertue from our goodly Ile!
No more our Joys beguile;
No more with thy loth'd Presence plague our happy State,
Thou Enemy to all thats brisk, or gay, or brave, or great:
Begone! with all thy pious meager Train   30
To some unfruitful unfrequented Land,
And there an Empire gain,
And there extend thy rigorous Command;
There, where illiberal Nature's Niggardice
Has set a Tax on Vice;   35
Where the lean barren Region dos enhance
The Worth of dear Intemperance,
And for each pleasurable Sin exacts Excise:
We (thanks to Fate) more cheaply can Offend,
And want no tempting Luxuries,   40
No good convenient sinning Opportunities,
Which Nature's Bounty could bestow, or Heaven's Kindness lend.
Go, follow that nice Goddess to the Skies,
Who heretofore, disgusted at encreasing Vice,
Dislik'd the World, and thought it too Profane   45
And timely hence retir'd, and kindly ne'er return'd again:
Hence to those airy Mansions rove,
Converse with Saints and holy Folks above;
Those may thy Presence woo,
Whose lazy Ease affords 'em nothing els to do;   50
Where haughty scornful I,

23 stings] *R, 1682, 1680, G, m, P1, Y1*; sting *1679, 1681, Y2*   26 goodly]
R, E, 1682, 1680, MSS; godly *1679, 1681*   38 pleasurable sin exacts] *R,
1679, 1681, 1682, 1680, MSS −A*; pleasure does exact *A*   39 Fate] *1682*;
Providence *R, E, A, G, P1*; Heaven *1679, 1681, 1680, m, Y1, Y2*   44 heretofore, disgusted] *R*; heretofore disgusted *E, 1682, 1680, A, G, P1, Y1*;
hearetofore disgusting *m, Y2*; here too sore disgusting *1679, 1681*
48 Folks] *R, 1679, 1681, 1682, 1680, MSS −A*; fooles *A*

And my great Friends will ne'er vouchsafe Thee Company;
    Thou'rt now an hard unpracticable Good,
        Too difficult for Flesh and Blood,
Were I all Soul, like them, perhaps I'de learn to practise   55
                                  [Thee.

3.

    Vertue! thou solemn grave Impertinence,
    Abhor'd by all the Men of Wit and Sence!
    Thou damn'd Fatigue! that clogst Life's journy here,
    Tho thou no weight of Wealth or Profit bear!
    Thou puling fond Greensicknes of the Mind!   60
    That mak'st us prove to our own selves unkind,
    Whereby we Coals and Dirt for Diet chuse,
    And Pleasure's better Food refuse!
    Curst Jilt! that leadst deluded Mortals on,
    Till they too late perceive themselves undone,   65
    Chows'd by a Dowry in Reversion!
    The greatest Votarie, thou ere couldst boast
(Pitty so brave a Soul was on thy Service lost,
    What Wonders he in Wickednes had done,
Whom thy weak Pow'r could so inspire alone?)   70
    Tho long with fond Amours he courted Thee,
Yet dying did recant his vain Idolatry;
    At length, tho' late, he did Repent with shame,
    Forc'd to confess thee nothing but an empty Name:
    So was that Lecher gull'd, whose haughty Love   75
Design'd a Rape on the Queen regent of the Gods above;
    When he a Goddes thought he had in chase,
    He found a gawdy Vapor in the place,
    And with thin Air beguil'd his starv'd Embrace,

52 great ... will ne're] *R, 1679, 1681, 1682, 1680, MSS −P1*; deare ... nere
will *P1*   53 an] *R, 1682, P1*; a *1679, 1681, 1680, MSS −P1*   55 like
them, perhaps] *R, 1679, 1681, 1682, 1680, MSS −A*; perhaps *A*   56 solemn]
R², 1679, 1681, 1682, 1680, MSS; solid *R¹*   61 mak'st] *R, 1682, Y1, Y2*;
makest *1679, 1681, A, G, m, P1*; makes *1680*   63 Pleasure's] *R, 1682, Y1*;
Pleasures *1680, A, G, m, P1, Y2*; Pleasure, *1679, 1681*   better] *R², 1679,
1681, 1682, 1680, MSS*; sweeter *R¹ (deleted)*   Food] *R, 1682, 1680, MSS −Y1*;
food, *1679, 1681, Y1*   64 Jilt] *R, E, 1682, 1680, A, G, P1, Y1*; ill *1679,
1681, m, Y2*   65 perceive] *R, 1682, 1680, A, G, m, P1, Y1*; do find *1679,
1681, Y2*   68 (Pitty] *R, 1682, Y1*; Pity *1679, 1681, 1680, MSS −Y1*
70 inspire alone?)] *R, 1682*; inspire alone! *1679, 1681, 1680, MSS −A subst.*;
inspire *A*   71 Tho] *R, E, 1682, 1680, MSS*; There *1679, 1681*

Idly he spent his Vigor, spent his Bloud,   80
And tir'd himself t'oblige an unperforming Cloud.

                              4.

If human kind to Thee ere worship paid,
            They were by Ignorance misled,
That only them devout, and Thee a Goddes made:
Known haply in the World's rude untaught Infancy,   85
Before it had outgrown its childish Innocence,
            Before it had arriv'd at Sence,
Or reach'd the Manhood and Discretion of Debauchery:
      Known in those ancient godly duller Times,
      When crafty Pagans had ingrost all Crimes;   90
      When Christian Fools were obstinately Good,
      Nor yet their Gospel-Freedom understood;
Tame easy Fops! who could so prodigally bleed,
To be thought Saints, and dy a Calendar with Red!
      No prudent Heathen ere seduc'd could be   95
            To suffer Martyrdom for Thee;
Only that arrant Ass, whom the false Oracle call'd wise,
      (No wonder if the Devil utter'd Lies)
That sniveling Puritan, who spite of all the Mode
            Would be unfashionably Good,   100
And exercis'd his whining Gifts to Rail at Vice;
            Him all the Wits of Athens damn'd,
            And justly with Lampoons defam'd;
But when the mad Fanatick could not silenc'd be
      From broaching dangerous Divinity,   105
The wise Republique made him for Prevention dy,
And quickly sent him to the Gods and better Company.

   81 t' oblige] *R, 1682, 1680, G, P1 subst., Y1*; to oblige *1679, 1681, A, m,*
Y2   82 kind] *R, E, 1682, 1680, MSS*; bend *1679, 1681*   85 Known] *R, E,*
1682, 1680, A, G, m, Y1; Know *P1*; None *1679, 1681, Y2*   88 reach'd] *R, E,*
1682, 1680, MSS; watch't *1679, 1681*   89 Known] *R, E, 1682, 1680*; know *P1*;
None *1679, 1681, Y2*   94 and dy ... with] *R, 1679, 1681, 1682, 1680, MSS*
—P1; and ... in *P1*   97 arrant] *R, 1682, 1680, MSS —A*; errant, *1679, 1681, A*
98 (No ... Lies)] *R, 1682, 1680, A, G, Y1*; No ... lies. *1679, 1681, m, P1, Y2*
99 spite] *R, 1682, 1680, A, G, P1, Y1*; in spight *1679, 1681, m, Y2*
101 exercis'd] *R, 1679, 1681, 1682, 1680, m*; exercise *A, G, P1, Y1, Y2*
107 quickly sent] R^2; kindly sent R^1, *1680, MSS —Y2*; sent *1679, 1681, 1682,*
Y2

5.

Let fumbling Age be grave and wise,
  And Vertue's poor contemn'd Idea prize,
Who never knew, or now are past the Sweets of Vice,   110
      While we, whose active Pulses beat
      With lusty Youth and vigorous Heat,
  Can all their Beards and Morals too despise:
  While my plump Veins are fill'd with Lust and Blood,
      Let not one Thought of her Intrude,   115
          Or dare approach my Breast;
          But know 'tis all possest
          By a more welcom Guest;
And know I have not yet the Leisure to be Good:
      If ever unkind Destiny   120
          Shall force long Life on me;
    If ere I must the Curse of Dotage bear,
Perhaps I'll dedicate those Dregs of Time to her,
And come with Crutches her most humble Votary.
          When sprightly Vice retreats from hence   125
      And quits the Ruins of decayed Sence,
      She'll serve to usher in a fair Pretence
And varnish with her Name a well-dissembled Impotence.
      When Ptisick, Rheums, Catarrhs, and Palsies seize,
          And all the Bill of Maladies,   130
  Which Heav'n to punish overliving Mortals sends,
Then let her enter with the numerous Infirmities,
Her self the greatest Plague, which Wrinkles and grey Hairs
                                          [attends.

6.

  Tell me, ye venerable Sots, who court her most,
      What small Advantage can she boast,   135

113 Beards] *R*, *E*, *1682*, *G*, *P1*; Bards— *1679*, *1681*, *Y2*; Birds *1680*, *Y1*;
Lawes *m*; Morals *A*   Morals] *R*, *1679*, *1681*, *1682*, *1680*, *MSS* –*A*; Beards *A*
116 *R*, *1679*, *1681*, *1682*, *1680*, *MSS* –*m*; *not in m*   117 'tis] *R*, *1682*, *1680*,
MSS; its *1679*, *1681*   121 on] *R*, *E*, *1682*, *1680*, *MSS*; of *1679*, *1681*
123 I'll] *R*, *1681*, *1682*, *1680*, *MSS* –*m*; I will *1679*; I'de *m*   126 decayed]
R, *1682*, *1680*, *G*, *P1*, *Y1*, *Y2*; decay'd *1679*, *1681*, *A*, *m*   128 varnish] *R*,
E, *1682*, *1680*, *MSS* –*A*; varnish't *A*; banish *1679*, *1681*   her] *R*, *E*, *1682*,
1680, *MSS*; the *1679*, *1681*   131 Mortals] *R*, *1679*, *1681*, *1682*, *1680*, *MSS* –*G*;
Monsters *G*   132 numerous] *R*, *1679*, *1681*, *1682*, *1680*, *MSS* –*A*; innumerous *A*
133 Plague] *R*, *1681*, *1682*, *1680*, *MSS*; place *1679*

Which her great Rival has not in a greater Store ingrost?
        Her boasted Calm and Peace of Mind
     In Wine and Company we better find,
        Find it with Pleasure too combin'd,
     In mighty Wine, where we our Sences steep,   140
     And lull our Cares and Consciences asleep;
        But why do I that wild Chimera name?
        Conscience! that giddy airy Dream,
Which dos from brainsick Heads, or ill-digesting Stomachs steam!
        Conscience! the vain fantastick Fear   145
     Of Punishments we know not when, or where!
   Project of crafty Statesmen! to support weak Law,
        Whereby they slavish Spirits aw,
     And dastard Souls to forc'd Obedience draw!
     Grand Wheadle! which our gown'd Impostors use   150
     The poor unthinking Rabble to abuse!
   Scarecrow! to fright from the forbidden Fruit of Vice,
        Their own beloved Paradice!
     Let those vile Canters Wickednes decry,
        Whose mercenary Tongues take Pay   155
             For what they say,
   And yet commend in Practice what their Words deny;
     While we discerning Heads, who farther pry,
             Their holy Cheats defy,
And scorn their Frauds, and scorn their sanctified Cajolery. 160

    136 has not] R, 1680, A, m, P1, Y1; hath not 1679, 1681, 1682, Y2; cannot G
137 Her boasted] 1682; Her Quiet and R, E; Her Quiet 1679, 1681, 1680, MSS -A;
For Calme and A   Calm and] R, 1681, 1682, 1680, MSS -A; claim and 1679;
quiet A   139 Pleasure too combin'd,] R, E, 1682, 1680, MSS -A; pleasures
too combin'd A; pleasure to combine, 1679, 1681   141 And lull our Cares
and] R, 1679, 1681, 1682, 1680, MSS -A; In which we lull our A   144 or]
R, 1682, 1680, G, m; and 1679, 1681, A, P1, Y1, Y2   steam] R, 1679, 1681,
1682, 1680, G, P1, Y1, Y2; streame A, m   146 when, or] R, 1680, G, P1,
Y1; when nor 1679, 1681, 1682, m, Y2; whence or A   147 Project] R, E,
1682, 1680, G, Y1; Projects 1679, 1681, A, m, P1, Y2   148 they ... aw] R,
1679, 1681, 1682, 1680, MSS -P1; the ... draw P1   149 R, 1679, 1681,
1682, 1680, MSS -P1, not in P1   152 fright] R, 1682, 1680, MSS; fright's
1679, 1681   from the forbidden Fruit of] R, 1679, 1681, 1682, 1680, MSS -A;
them from forbidden Sins and A   154 Canters] R, 1679, 1681, 1682, 1680,
MSS -A; Teachers A   158 farther] R, 1682, 1680, G, P1, Y1; further A; farthest m; furthest 1679, 1681, Y2   159 defy] R, E, 1682, 1680, MSS; deny
1679, 1681   160 And ... Frauds,] As R, 1682, &c.; separate line 1679,
1681   And scorn] 1679, 1681, 1682, 1680, MSS; And scorns R   Cajolery] R,
1679, 1681, 1682, 1680, MSS -A; Lie A

7.

None, but dull unbred Fools, discredit Vice,
Who act their Wickednes with an ill Grace;
    Such their Profession scandalize,
    And justly forfet all that Praise,
All that Esteem, that Credit, and Applause,   165
Which we by our wise Menage from a Sin can raise:
    A true and brave Transgressor ought
To sin with the same Height of Spirit Caesar fought.
Mean-soul'd Offenders now no Honour gain,
    Only Debauches of the nobler Strain;   170
    Vice well improv'd yields Bliss and Fame beside,
And some for Sinning have bin deified:
      Thus the lewd Gods of old did move
By these brave Methods to the Seats above;
Ev'n Jove himself, the Soveraign Deity,   175
Father and King of all th' immortal Progeny,
      Ascended to that high Degree
By Crimes above the reach of weak Mortality.
      He Heav'n one large Seraglio made,
    Each Goddes turn'd a glorious Punk o'th' Trade,   180
      And all that sacred Place
Was fill'd with Bastard-Gods of his own Race;
Almighty Lech'ery got his first Repute,
And everlasting Whoring was his chiefest Attribute.

8.

How gallant was that Wretch whose happy Guilt   185
A Fame upon the Ruins of a Temple built;

---

161 dull unbred Fools] *R, E, 1682, 1680, A, G, m, Y1*; ill bred fooles *P1*;
dull Souls *1679, 1681, Y2*   166 Menage] *R, 1682, G, Y1*; Manage *1679, 1681,*
1680, A, m, P1, Y2   168 sin] R^1, *1679, 1681, 1682, 1680, MSS*; write R^2
(deleted)   Height of Spirit *R, E, 1682, 1680, G, m, Y1*; heat of spirit *A*;
hight of pleasurs *P1*; spirit *1679, 1681, Y2*   169 Mean-soul'd] *R, E, 1682,*
1680, MSS -Y2; Mean Souls *1679, 1681, Y2*   Honour] *R, 1680, MSS*; honours
1679, 1681, 1682   170 Debauches] *R, E, 1682, A, G, m, Y1*; Debauchees
1680; debaucher *1679, P1*; debauchers *1681, Y2*   172 *R, 1679, 1681, 1682,*
1680, MSS -A; not in A   174 these] *R, 1682, 1680, A, G, m, Y1*; those
1679, 1681, P1, Y2   175 Ev'n] *R, E, 1682, 1680, A, G, Y1*; Even *Y2*; Ere
1679, 1681, m, P1   176 all th'] *R, 1682, 1680, Y1*; all the *A, G, m, P1*;
all that *Y2*; the *1679, 1681*   178 above] *R, 1682, 1680, MSS*; beyond *1679,*
1681   179 large] *R, 1679, 1681, 1682, 1680, MSS -A*; great *A*

Let Fools (said he) Impiety alledge,
And urge the no-great Fault of Sacriledge;
 I'll set the sacred Pile on Flame,
And in it's Ashes write my lasting Name,   190
     My Name, which thus shall be
  Deathless as it's own Deity;
 Thus the vain-glorious Carian I'll outdo,
  And Ægypt's proudest Monarchs too,
Those lavish Prodigals, who idly did consume 195
 Their Lives and Treasures to erect a Tomb,
And only great by being buried would become;
At cheaper Rates then their's Ill buy Renown,
And my loud Fame shall all their Silent Glories drown:
So spake the daring Hector, so did prophesy, 200
 And so it prov'd;—in vain did envious Spite
    By fruitless Methods try
 To raze his well-built Fame and Memory
    Amongst Posterity;
The Boutefeu can now Immortal write,   205
While the inglorious Founder is forgotten quite.

      9.

 Yet greater was that mighty Emperour
 (A greater Crime befitted his high Pow'r)
 Who sacrific'd a City to a Jest,
And shew'd he knew the grand Intrigues of Humour 210
  He made all Rome a Bonfire to his Fame, [best:
  And sung and play'd and danc'd amidst the Flame.
 Bravely begun! yet pity there he staid,

187 Impiety] R, 1682, 1680, MSS −Y2; quietly 1679, Y2; now quietly 1681
191 thus] R, 1682, 1680, MSS −Y2; thence 1679, 1681, Y2 193 Carian] R,
E, 1682, 1680, G, P1, Y1; Curran Y2; Carrin m; Caron 1679, 1681; left blank A
194 Monarchs] R, E, 1682, 1680, A, G, P1, Y1; Monarch 1679, 1681, m, Y2
198 their's] R; they 1679, 1681, 1682, 1680, MSS −Y2; theyle Y2 199 R,
1682, 1680, MSS; not in 1679, 1681 201 so] R, 1679, 1681, 1682, 1680,
MSS −A; thus A envious Spite] R, E, 1682, P1; envie's spite, A, G; envious
Fate 1679, 1681, 1680, m, Y1, Y2 203 raze] R, 1679, 1681, 1682, MSS −P1;
raise 1680, P1 205 Boutefeu] R, 1679, 1681, 1682, m; Beautifeu 1680, G,
Y2; Beaucifeu Y1; -few P1 208 (A greater Crime ... Pow'r)] R, 1682,
1680, Y1, Y2; A greater Crime ... Power, 1679, 1681, G, P1; So great a crime
... power. m; As greater Crimes ... Power A 211 to his] R, E, 1682,
1680, A, G, P1, Y1; for loud 1679, 1681, m, Y2

One step to Glory more he should have made,
He should have heav'd the noble Frolick higher,   215
And made the People on that Fun'eral Pile expire,
Or providently with their Blood put out the Fire.
           Had this bin done,
The utmost Pitch of Glory he had won,
       No greater Monument could be   220
    To consecrate him to Eternity,
Nor should there need another Herald of his Praise, but Me.

                          10.

And thou yet greater *Faux*, the Glory of our Ile,
    Whom baffled Hell esteems its chiefest Foile;
    'Twere Injury should I omit thy Name,   225
    Whose Action merits all the breath of Fame;
    Methinks I see the trembling Shades below
        Around in humble Rev'erence bow,
    Doubtful they seem, whether to pay their Loyalty
        To their dread Monarch, or to Thee;   230
No wonder he, grown jealous of thy fear'd Success,
Envied Mankind the Honour of thy Wickednes,
And spoil'd that brave Attempt, which must have made his Grandeur
        Howe're regret not, mighty Ghost,   [less.
        Thy Plot by treach'erous Fortune crost,   235
    Nor think thy well-deserved Glory lost;
Thou the full Praise of Villany shalt ever share,
And all will judge thy Act compleat enough, when thou couldst
    So thy great Master far'd, whose high Disdain   [dare.
    Contemn'd that Heaven, where he could not Reign; 240
        When He with bold Ambition strove

---

216 that Fun'ral Pile] *R, 1682, 1680, MSS −A*; the funeral pile *A*; that Funeral *1679, 1681*   219 utmost Pitch] *R, E, 1682, 1680, MSS*; utmost *1679,
1681*   he had won] *R, 1682, 1680, MSS −A*; he had run *1679, 1681*; had been won
A   226 Action merits] *R, 1682, 1680, G, m, P1, Y1*; Actions merit *1679,
1681, A, Y2*   228 *R, 1679, 1681, 1682, 1680, MSS −A; not in A*   Around] *R,
E, 1682, 1680, MSS*; All round *1679, 1681*   231 grown] *R, E, 1680, A, G, Y1*;
(grown *1682*; grew *1679, 1681, m, P1, Y2*   Success] *R, 1679, 1681, 1680, MSS*;
success) *1682*   233 must have] *R, 1682, 1680, G, P1, Y1*; would have *A, m*;
should have *1679, 1681, Y2*   235 Thy Plot by] *R, 1679, 1681, 1682, 1680,
MSS −A*; The Plot thy *A*   237 full Praise] *R, 1679, 1681, 1682, 1680, MSS
−A*; just prise *A*   238 thy Act] *R, E, 1682, 1680, A, G, P1, Y1*; thou art
1679, 1681, Y2; thou wert *m*   239 far'd] *R, 1679, 1681, 1682*; fear'd *1680, MSS*

T'usurp the Throne above,
And led against the Deity an armed Train;
        Tho' from his vast Designs he fell,
        Orepow'r'd by his Almighty Fo;   245
    Yet gain'd he Vict'ry in his Overthrow,
He gain'd sufficient Triumph, that he durst Rebell,
And 'twas some Pleasure to be thought the great'st in Hell.

                        11.
Tell me, ye great Triumvirate, what shall I do
        To be illustrious as You?   250
Let your Examples move me with a gen'erous Fire,
    Let them into my daring Thoughts inspire
Somewhat compleatly Wicked, some vast giant Crime,
Unknown, unheard, unthought of by all past and present Time:
    'Tis done, 'tis done;—methinks I feel the pow'rfull   255
        And a new Heat of Sin my Spirits warms;   [Charms,
    I travail with a glorious Mischief, for whose Birth
My Soul's too narrow, and weak Fate too feeble yet to bring it
        Let the unpittied Vulgar tamely go,   [forth:
And stock for Company the wide Plantations down below;   260
        Such their vile Souls for viler Barter sell,
        Scarce worth the Damning, or their Room in Hell:
We are its Grandees, and expect as high Preferment there
        For our good Service, as on Earth we share:
    In them Sin is but a meer Privative of Good,   265
        The Frailty and Defect of Flesh and Blood;
        In Us 'tis a Perfection, who profess
        A studied and elab'rate Wickednes:

248 great'st] R, E, 1680, G, Y1; great's 1682; greatest A; greatest tho' m;
greatest one 1679, 1681, Y2   249 ye] R, 1680, MSS −P1; you 1679, 1681, P1
251 Examples] R, E, 1682, Y1; example 1679, 1681, 1680, MSS −Y1   254 Unknown, unheard, unthought of] E, 1682; Unthought, unknown, unpattern'd R, 1679,
1681, 1680, MSS −A; Unthought, unknown, unpractic'd A   255 methinks] R,
E, 1682, 1680, MSS −Y2; I think 1679, 1681, Y2   258 yet to bring it] R,
1680, A, G, P1, Y1; yet to bring 1679, 1681; to bring 1681, 1682, m
260 stock] R, E, 1682, 1680, MSS −Y2; stalk 1679, 1681, Y2   the wide] R,
1679, 1681, 1682, 1680, MSS −A; those rude A   Plantations down] R², E,
1682, m; Plantations R¹, 1680, A, G, Y1; Plantation, 1679, 1681, 1680, Y2
263 its] R, 1680, MSS; his 1679, 1681, 1682   Preferment] R, 1682, 1680,
MSS; Preferments 1679, 1681

We're the great *Roya'l Society* of Vice,
Whose Talents are to make Discoveries,   270
And advance Sin like other Arts and Sciences:
   'Tis I, the bold Columbus, only I,
     Who must new Worlds in Vice descry,
And fix the Pillars of unpassable Iniquity:

             12.

   How sneaking was the first Debauch, that Sin'd,   275
   Who for so small a Crime sold human kind?
     How undeserving that high Place,
   To be thought Parent of our Sin and Race,
Who by low Guilt our Nature doubly did debase?
     Unworthy was he to be thought   280
Father of the great First-born Cain, which he begot,
   The noble Cain, whose bold and gallant Act
     Proclaim'd him of more high Extract;
         Unworthy Me,
And all the braver Part of his Posterity: 285
   Had the just Fates design'd me in his stead,
   I'd done some great and unexampled Deed;
     A Deed, which should decry
    The Stoicks dull Equality,
And shew that Sin admits Transcendency;   290
A Deed, wherein the Tempter should not share,
Above what Heav'n could punish, and above what he could dare;
   For greater Crimes then his I would have fell,
And acted somewhat, which might merit more then Hell.

269 We're] *R, 1682, 1680, A, G, Y1*; W'are *P1*; Wee'ar *m*; We are *1679, 1681,
Y2*   271 Sin] *R, 1679, 1681, 1682, 1680, MSS* –*A*; this *A*   272 'Tis] *R,
1682, 1680, MSS* –*A*; It's *1679, 1681, A*   275 that Sin'd] *R, E, 1682, 1680,
A, G, m, Y1*; we find *1679, 1681, P1, Y2*   276 Crime] *R, E, 1682, A, G, P1*;
sin *1679, 1681, 1680, Y1, Y2*   280-3 *R, 1679, 1681, 1682, 1680, A, m, Y1,
Y2*; not in *G, P1*   281 he begot] *R, E, 1682, 1680, A, Y1*; got *1679, 1681,
m, Y2*   282 and gallant] *R*[1]*, 1679, 1681, 1682, 1680, MSS (G, P1, absent)*;
heroick *R*[2]   287 I'd] *R, 1682, 1680, MSS* –*Y2*; I had *1679, 1681, Y2*
289 Equality] *R, 1681, 1682, 1680, MSS* –*Y2*; Eznallity *1679, Y2*   293 his]
R, 1682, 1680, A, G, Y1; this *1679, 1681, m, P1, Y2*

AN APOLOGY FOR THE FOREGOING ODE,
BY WAY OF EPILOGUE.

My Part is done, and you'l (I hope) excuse
Th' Extravagance of a repenting Muse;
Pardon whatere she has too boldly said,
She only acted here in Masquerade;
And the slight Arguments, she did produce,   5
Were not to Flatter Vice, but to Traduce;
So we Buffoons in Princely Dress expose
Not to be Gay, but more Ridiculous:
When she a Hector for her Subject had,
She thought she must be Termagant and mad;   10
That made her speak like a lewd Punk o'th' Town, ⎫
Who, by Converse with Bullies wicked grown,   ⎬
Has learnt the Mode to cry all Vertue down;   ⎭
But now the Vizard's off, she changes Scene,
And turns a modest civil Girle agen.   15
  Our Poet has a diff'rent Tast of Wit,
Now will to th' common Vogue himself submit;
Let some admire the Fops, those Talents ly
In venting dull insipid Blasphemy;
He swears he cannot with those terms dispence,   20
Nor will be damn'd for the Repute of Sence:
Wit's Name was never to Profaness due,
For then you see he could be witty too:
  He cou'd lampoon the State and libel Kings, ⎫
But that he's Loyal and knows better things,   ⎬   25
Then Fame, whose guilty Birth from Treason springs. ⎭
He likes not Wit, which can't a Licence claim,

1 you'l] R^1, 1679, 1681, 1682, 1680, m, Y1, P1; all R^2 3 has] R,
1680, MSS; hath 1679, 1681, 1682   5 And] R, 1680, MSS; For 1679, 1681,
1682   9 a] R, 1680, MSS; an 1679, 1681, 1682   11 her speak] R, E,
1682, 1680, MSS; our Spark 1679, 1681   14 Vizard's] R, 1682; vizards
1679, 1681, m; Vizor's 1680, P1, Y1   16 Tast] R, 1679, 1681, 1682, 1680,
MSS -m; sort m   17 to th'] R, 1679, 1681, 1680, Y1; to them m; th' P1; to
1682   22 Profaness] R, 1680, P1; prophaness m, Y1; profaneness 1679,
1681, 1682   25 he's] R, 1681, 1682, 1680, MSS; he is 1679   27 can't
a] R, 1679, 1681, 1682, MSS -P1; can no 1680, P1

To which the Author dares not set his Name;
Wit should be open, court each Reader's Ey,
Not lurk in sly unprinted Privacy;   30
But Criminal Writers, like dull Birds of Night,
For Weakness, or for Shame avoid the Light;
May such a Jury for their Audience have,
And from the Bench, not Pit, their Doom receive.
May they the Tow'r for their due merit share,   35
And a just Wreath of Hemp, for Laurel, wear.
  He could be Bawdy too, and nick the Times
In what they dearly love, damn'd Placket-Rhimes,
Such as our Nobles write,—
Whose nauseous Poetry can reach no higher,   40
Then what the Codpiece and its God inspire;
So lewd, they spend at Quill, you'd justly think,
They wrote with something nastier then Ink:
But he still thought that little Wit, or none, ⎫
Which a just Modesty must never own,   ⎬   45
And the meer Reader with a blush attone: ⎭
If Ribaldry deserv'd the Praise of Wit,   ⎫
He must resign to each Illiterate Cit,   ⎬
And Prentices and Carmen challenge it;   ⎭
Ev'n they too can be smart and Witty there   50
For all Men on that Subject Poets are:
  Henceforth, he says, if ever more he find
Himself to the base Itch of Verse inclin'd,
If e're he's given up so far to write,
He never means to make his End Delight;   55
Should he do so, he must despair Success, ⎫
For he's not now debaucht enough to Please, ⎬
And must be damn'd for want of Wickedness; ⎭
He'l therefore use his Gift another Way,

33 their] *R, 1682, m*; the *1679, 1681, 1680, P1, Y1*   35 merit] R^2, *P1*;
merits *1679, 1681, 1682, 1680, m, Y1*; Guerdon R^1 (*deleted*)   36 for] *R*;
not *1679, 1681, 1682, 1680, MSS*   41 and] *R*; or *1679, 1681, 1682, 1680,
MSS*   44 thought that] *R, 1679, 1682, 1680, MSS*; that *1681*   46 attone]
R, 1682, 1680, MSS −m; a Tone *1679*; at one *1681*; a Lone *m*   47 deserv'd]
R, 1679, 1681, 1682, Y1; deserve *1680, P1*; deserues *m*   50 Ev'n] *R, 1682,
1680, Y1*; Eu'en *P1*; Even *1679, 1681, m*   52 says] *R, 1680, MSS*; vows *1679,
1681, 1682*   53 the base] *R, E, 1682, 1680, MSS*; th' busie *1679, 1681*
59 Gift] *R, 1680, MSS*; Wit *1679, 1681, 1682*

And next the Ugliness of Vice display;   60
Tho against Vertue once he drew his Pen,
He'll ne'er for ought, but her Defence agen:
   Had he a Genius and Poetique Rage,
Great as the Vices of this guilty Age;
Were he all Gall, and arm'd with store of Spite,   65
'Twere worth his Pains to undertake to write;
To noble Satyr he'd direct his Aim,
And by't, Mankind and Poetry reclaim;
He'd shoot his Quills, just like a Porcupine,
At Vice, and make 'em stab in ev'ry Line: 70
The World should learn to blush,—
And dread the Vengeance of his pointed Wit,
Which worse then their own Consciences should fright,
   And all should think him Heav'ns just Plague, design'd
To Visit for the Sins of lewd Mankind.   75

63 a] *R, E, 1682, 1680, MSS*; the *1679, 1681*   68 by't] *R, E, 1682, 1680,*
MSS; bite *1679, 1681*   69 He'd] *R, E, 1682, 1680, MSS*; And *1679, 1681*
Quills] *R, E, 1682, 1680, MSS*; Quill *1679, 1681*   70 'em] *R, 1680, P1, Y1*;
them *E, 1682*; it *1679, 1681*   Line] *R, E, 1682, 1680, MSS*; Vein *1679, 1681*
72 pointed Wit] *R², E, 1682*; tuant Wit *R¹*; — Wit *1679, 1681*; angry Wit *1680,*
P1, Y1; curse *m*   73 worse] *R, 1682*; more *1679, 1681, 1680, MSS*   74 And
all] *R, E, 1682, 1680, MSS*; And *1679, 1681*   Heav'ns] *R, E, 1682, 1680, Y1*;
heauens *m, P1*; for Heavens *1679, 1681*

                              THE
                      Passion of Byblis
                          OUT OF
           Ovid's Metamorphosis, *B.9.F.II.*
                       Beginning at
    Byblis in exemplo est, ut ament concessa puellæ
                     And ending with

                             —*Modumque*
          Exit, & infelix committit sæpe repelli.

You heedless Maids, whose young and tender hearts
Unwounded yet, have scap'd the fatal darts;
Let the sad tale of wretched *Byblis* move,
And learn by her to shun forbidden Love.

Not all the plenty, all the bright resort   5
Of gallant Youth, that grac'd the *Carian* Court,
Could charm the haughty Nymphs disdainful heart,
Or from a Brother's guilty Love divert;
Caunus she lov'd, not as a Sister ought,
But Honour, Shame and Blood alike forgot: 10
Caunus alone takes up her Thoughts and Eyes,
For him alone she wishes, grieves and sighs.
   At first her new-born Passion owns no name,
A glim'ring Spark scarce kindling into flame;
She thinks it no offence, if from his Lip   15
She snatch an harmless bliss, if her fond clip
With loose embraces oft his Neck surround,
And Love is yet in debts of Nature drown'd.
   But Love at length grows naughty by degrees,
And now she likes, and strives her self to please: 20
Well-drest she comes and arms her Eyes with darts, ⎤
Her Smiles with charms and all the studied arts,   ⎬
Which practis'd Love can teach to vanquish hearts. ⎦
Industrious now she labours to be fair,
And envies all whoever fairer are.   25
   Yet knows she not, she loves, but still does grow,
Insensibly that thing she does not know:
Strict honour yet her check'd desires does bind,
And modest thoughts on this side wish confin'd:
Only within she sooths her pleasing flames,   30
And now the hated terms of Blood disclaims:
Brother sounds harsh; she the unpleasing word
Strives to forget and oftner calls him *Lord*:
And when the name of *Sister* grates her ear,
Could wish't unsaid, and rather *Byblis* hear.   35
   Nor dare she yet with waking Thoughts admit
A wanton hope: but when returning night
With Sleep's soft gentle spell her Senses charms,
Kind Fancy often brings him to her Arms:
In them she oft does the lov'd Shadow seem   40

10 Shame and Blood] *1681*; Blood, and shame *1682*   16 snatch] *1682*;
snatcht *1681*   27 that] *1681*; the *1682*

To grasp, and joys, yet blushes too in Dream.
She wakes, and long in wonder silent lies,
And thinks on her late pleasing Extasies:
Now likes and now abhors her guilty flame,
By turns abandon'd to her Love and Shame: 45
At length her struggling thoughts an utt'rance find,
And vent the wild disorders of her mind.

   "Ah me! (she cries) kind Heaven avert! what means
"This boading form, that nightly rides my dreams?
"Grant 'em untrue! why should lewd hope divine?   50
"Ah! why was this too charming Vision seen?
"'Tis true, by the most envious wretch that sees, ⎤
"He's own'd all fair and lovely, own'd a prize   ⎬
"Worthy the conquest of the brightest eyes: ⎦
"A prize that wou'd my high'st ambition fill,   55
"All I could wish;—but he's my Brother still!
"That cruel word for ever must disjoyn,
"Nor can I hope, but thus, to have him mine.

   "Since then I waking never must possess, ⎤
"Let me in sleep at least enjoy the bliss,   ⎬   60
"And sure nice Vertue can't forbid me this: ⎦
"Kind sleep does no malicious spies admit,
"Yet yields a lively semblance of delight:
"Gods! what a scene of joy was that! how fast
"I clasp'd the Vision to my panting breast!   65
"With what fierce bounds I sprung to meet my bliss,
"While my rapt soul flew out in every kiss!
"Till breathless, faint and softly sunk away,
"I all dissolv'd in reeking pleasures lay!
"How sweet is the remembrance yet! though night   70
"Too hasty fled, drove on by envious light.

   "O that we might the Laws of Nature break! ⎤
"How well could *Caunus* me an Husband make!   ⎬
"How well to Wife might he his *Byblis* take!   ⎦
"Wou'd God! in all things we had partners bin   75
"Besides our Parents and our fatal Kin:
"Wou'd thou wert nobler, I more meanly born,

67 rapt] *1682*; wrapt *1681*   73 could] *1681*; would *1682*

"Then guiltless I'd despair'd and suffer'd scorn:
"Happy that Maid unknown, whoe're shall prove
"So blest, so envied, to deserve thy love.   80
"Unhappy me! whom the same womb did joyn,
"Which now forbids me ever to be thine:
"Curst fate! that we alone in that agree,
"By which we ever must divided be.
"And must we be? what meant my Visions then?   85
"Are they and all their dear presages vain?
"Have dreams no credit but with easie love?
"Or do they hit sometimes and faithful prove?
"The Gods forbid! yet those whom I invoke,
"Have lov'd like me, have their own Sisters took: 90
"Great *Saturn* and his greater Off-spring *Jove*,
"Both stock'd their Heaven with incestuous love:
"Gods have their priviledge; why do I strive
"To strain my hopes to their Prerogative?

  "No, let me banish this forbidden fire,   95
"Or quench it with my blood, and with't expire:
"Unstain'd in honour, and unhurt in fame,
"Let the same Grave bury my Love and Shame:
"But when at my last hour I gasping lie,
"Let only my kind *Murderer* be by: 100
"Let him, while I breath out my soul in sighs,
"Or gaze't away, look on with pittying eyes:
"Let him (for sure he can't deny me this)
"Seal my cold Lips with one dear parting Kiss.

  "Besides, 'twere vain should I alone agree   105
"To what another's will must ratifie:
"Cou'd I be so abandon'd to consent,   ⎫
"What I have pass'd for good and innocent,   ⎬
"He may perhaps as worst of Crimes resent.   ⎭
"Yet we amongst our race examples find   110
"Of Brothers, who have been to Sisters kind:
"Fam'd *Canace* cou'd thus successful prove,
"Cou'd crown her wishes in a Brother's love.
"But whence cou'd I these instances produce?

  78 I'd] *1682*; I *1681*   108 pass'd] *1681*; pass *1682*

"How 'came I witty to my ruine thus?   115
"Whither will this mad frenzy hurry on?
"Hence, hence, you naughty flames, far hence be gone,
"Nor let me e're the shameful Passion own.
  "And yet shou'd he address I shou'd forgive,
"I fear, I fear, I shou'd his suit receive: 120
"Shall therefore I, who cou'd not love disown
"Offer'd by him, not mine to him make known?
"And canst thou speak? can thy bold tongue declare?
"Yes, Love shall force:—and now methinks I dare.
"But lest fond modesty at length refuse,   125
"I will some sure and better method chuse:
"A Letter shall my secret flames disclose,
"And hide my Blushes, but reveal their cause.
  This takes, and 'tis resolv'd as soon as said,
With this she rais'd her self upon her bed,   130
And propping with her hand her leaning head:
"Happen what will (says she) I'le make him know
"What pains, what raging pains I undergo:
"Ah me! I rave! what tempests shake my breast?
"And where? O where will this distraction rest?   135
Trembling, her Thoughts endite, and oft her Eye
Looks back for fear of conscious spies too nigh:
One hand her Paper, t'other holds her Pen,
And Tears supply what Ink her Lines must drain.
  Now she begins, now stops, and stopping frames   140
New doubts, now writes, and now her Writing damns.
She writes, defaces, alters, likes and blames:
Oft throws in haste her Pen and Paper by,
Then takes 'em up again as hastily:
Unsteady her resolves, fickle and vain,   145
No sooner made, but strait unmade again:
What her desires wou'd have she does not know,
Displeas'd with all what e're she goes to do:
At once contending, shame and hope and fear
Wrack her tost mind, and in her looks appear.   150
Sister was wrote; but soon mis-giving doubt

122 to him make] *1681*; to make him *1682*   139 what] *1681*; that *1682*

Recals it, and the guilty word blots out:
Again she pauses, and again begins,
At length her Pen drops out these hasty Lines.
  "Kind health, which you and only you can grant,   155
"Which, if deny'd, she must for ever want;
"To you your Lover sends: ah! blushing shame
"In silence bids her Paper hide her name:
"Wou'd God! the fatal message might be done
"Without annexing it, nor *Byblis* known,   160
"E're blest success her hopes and wishes crown.
  "And had I now my smother'd grief conceal'd,
"It might by tokens past have been reveal'd:
"A thousand proofs were ready to impart
"The inward anguish of my wounded heart: 165
"Oft, as your sight a sudden blush did raise,
"My blood came up to meet you at my face:
"Oft (if you call to mind) my longing Eyes
"Betray'd in looks my souls too thin disguise:
"Think how their Tears, think how my heaving Breast   170
"Oft in deep sighs some cause unknown confest:
"Think how these Arms did oft with fierce embrace,
"Eager as my desires, about you press:
"These Lips too (when they cou'd so happy prove,
"Had you but mark'd) with close warm kisses strove   175
"To whisper something more than Sisters love.
  "And yet, though rankling grief my mind distrest,
"Though raging flames within burnt up my breast,
"Long time I did the mighty pain endure,
"Long strove to bring the fierce disease to cure: 180
"Witness ye cruel Pow'rs, who did inspire
"This strange, this fatal, this resistless fire,
"Witness what pains (for you alone can know)
"This helpless wretch to quench't did undergo:
"A thousand Racks, and Martyrdoms, and more   185
"Than a weak Virgin can be thought, I bore:
"O'rematch'd in pow'r at last I'm forc'd to yield,
"And to the conqu'ring God resign the field:

   178 burnt] *1681*; burn *1682*   181 ye] *1682*; the *1681*

"To you, dear cause of all, I make address,
"From you with humble pray'rs I beg redress: 190
"You rule alone my arbitrary fate,
"And life and death on your disposal wait:
"Ordain, as you think fit; deny, or grant,
"Yet know no stranger is your suppliant;
"But she, who, though to you by Blood allied   195
"In nearest bonds, in nearer wou'd be tied.
   "Let doating age debate of Law and Right,
"And gravely state the bounds of just and fit;
"Whose wisdom's but their envy, to destroy
"And bar those pleasures which they can't enjoy: 200
"Our blooming years, more sprightly and more gay,
"By Nature were design'd for love and play:
"Youth knows no check, but leaps weak Vertues fence,
"And briskly hunts the noble chase of sence:
"Without dull thinking we enjoyment trace,   205
"And call that lawful, whatsoe're does please.
"Nor will our guilt want instances alone,
"'Tis what the glorious Gods above have done:
"Let's follow where those great examples went,
"Nor think that Sin, where Heaven's a precedent.   210
   "Let neither aw of Father's frowns, nor shame ⎫
"For ought that can be told by babbling fame,   ⎬
"Nor any gastlier fantom, fear can frame,   ⎭
"Frighten or stop us in our way to bliss,
"But boldly let us rush on happiness: 215
"Where glorious hazzards shall enhance delight,
"And that, that makes it dangerous make it great.
   "Relation too, which does our fault increase,
"Will serve that fault the better to disguise;
"That lets us now in private often meet   220
"Bless'd opportunities for stoln delight:
"In publick often we embrace and kiss,
"And fear no jealous, no suspecting eyes.
"How little more remains for me to crave!
"How little more for you to give! O save   225

194 suppliant;] *Ed.* (*1770* suppliant:); suppliant. *1681, 1682*

"A wretched Maid undone by love and you,
"Who does in tears and dying accents sue;
"Who bleeds that Passion she had ne're reveal'd,
"If not by love, almighty love compel'd:
"Nor ever let her mournful Tomb complain,   230
"Here *Byblis* lies, kill'd by your cold disdain.
   Here forc'd to end, for want of room, not will
To add, her lines the crowded Margin fill,
Nor space allow for more: she trembling, folds
The Paper, which her shameful message holds;   235
And sealing, as she wept with boading fear,
She wet her Signet with a falling Tear.
This done, a trusty Messenger she call'd,
And in kind words the whisper'd Errand told:
"Go, carry this with faithful care, she said,   ⎫   240
"To my dear,—there she paus'd a while, and staid, ⎬
And by and by—*Brother*—was heard to add: ⎭
As she deliver'd it with her commands,
The Letter fell from out her trembling hands,
Dismay'd with the ill *Omen*, she anew   245
Doubted success, and held, yet bad him go.
   He goes, and after quick admission got
To *Caunus* hands the fatal secret brought:
Soon as the doubtful Youth a glance had cast   ⎫
On the first lines, and guest by them the rest, ⎬   250
Strait horror and amazement fill'd his breast: ⎭
Impatient with his rage he could not stay
To see the end, but threw't half read away.
Scarce could his hands the trembling wretch forbear,
Nor did his tongue these angry threatnings spare: 255
"Fly hence, nor longer my chaf'd fury trust,
"Thou cursed Pander of detested lust;
"Fly quickly hence, and to thy swiftness owe
"Thy life, a forfeit to my vengeance due:
"Which, had not danger of my Honour crost,   260
"Thou'dst paid by this, and been sent back a ghost.
   He the rough orders strait obeys, and bears

255 these] *1681*; those *1682*

The killing news to wretched *Byblis* ears;
Like striking thunder the fierce tidings stun,
And to her heart quicker than light'ning run: 265
The frighted blood forsakes her gastly face,
And a short death does every member seize:
But soon as sense returns, her frenzy too
Returns, and in these words breaks forth anew.

　　"And justly serv'd;——for why did foolish I   270
"Consent to make this rash discovery?
"Why did I thus in hasty lines reveal
"That dang'rous secret, Honour wou'd conceal?
"I shou'd have first with art disguis'd the hook,   ⎫
"And seen how well the gawdy bait had took,   ⎬   275
"And found him hung at lest, before I strook: ⎭
"From shore I shou'd have first descri'd the wind,   ⎫
"Whether 'twould prove to my adventure kind,   ⎬
"E're I to untry'd Seas my self resign'd: ⎭
"Now dash'd on Rocks unable to retire,   280
"I must i'th' wreck of all my hopes expire.

　　"And was not I by tokens plain enough
"Forewarn'd to quit my unauspicious Love?
"Did not the Fates my ill success foretel,
"When from my hands th' unhappy Letter fell?   285
"So should my hopes have done, and my design,
"That, or the day should then have alter'd bin;
"But rather the unlucky day; when Heaven
"Such ominous proofs of its dislike had given:
"And so it had, had not mad Passion sway'd,   290
"And Reason been by blinder Love misled.

　　"Besides (alas!) I shou'd my self have gone,
"Nor made my Pen a proxy to my Tongue;
"Much more I could have spoke, much more have told,
"Than a short Letters narrow room would hold: 295
"He might have seen my Looks, my wishing Eyes,
"My melting Tears, and heard my begging Sighs;
"About his Neck I could have flung my Arms,
"And been all over Love, all over Charms;
"Grasp'd and hung on his Knees, and there have dyed,   300
"There breath'd my gasping Soul out if denied:

"This and ten thousand things I might have done
"To make my Passion with advantage known;
"Which if they each could not have bent his mind,
"Yet surely all had forc'd him to be kind.   305
    "Perhaps he whom I sent was too in fault,
"Nor rightly tim'd his Message, as he ought;
"I fear he went in some ill-chosen hour,
"When cloudy weather made his temper lour.
"Not those calm seasons of the mind, which prove   310
"The fittest to receive the seeds of love.
    "These things have ruin'd me; for doubtless he
"Is made of humane flesh and blood like me;
"He suck'd no Tygress sure, nor Mountain Bear,
"Nor does his breast relentless Marble wear.   315
"He must, he shall consent, again I'le try,
"And try again, if he again deny:
"No scorn, no harsh repulse, or rough defeat
"Shall ever my desires, or hopes rebate.
"My earnest suits shall never give him rest,   320
"While Life, and Love more durable, shall last:
"Alive I'le press, till breath in pray'rs be lost,
"And after come a kind beseeching ghost.
    "For, if I might, what I have done, recall,
"The first point were, not to have done't at all;   325
"But since 'tis done, the second to be gain'd
"Is now to have, what I have sought, attain'd:
"For he, though I should now my wishes quit,
"Can never my unchaste attempts forget:
"Should I desist, 'twill be believ'd that I   330
"By slightly asking, taught him to deny;
"Or that I tempted him with wily fraud,
"And snares for his unwary Honour laid:
"Or, what I sent (and the belief were just)
"Were not th' efforts of Love, but shameful Lust.   335
    "In fine, I now dare any thing that's ill;
"I've writ, I have solicited, my will
"Has been debauch'd; and shou'd I thus give out,

325 done't] *Ed.*; don't *1681, 1682*

"I cannot chast and innocent be thought:
"Much there is wanting still to be fulfill'd,   340
"Much to my wish, but little to my guilt.
    She spoke; but such is her unsetled mind,   ⎫
It shifts from thought to thought, like veering wind, ⎬
Now to this point and now to that inclin'd: ⎭
What she could wish had unattempted been,   345
She strait is eager to attempt agen:
What she repents, she acts; and now lets loose
The reins to Love, nor any bounds allows:
Repulse upon repulse unmov'd she bears,
And still sues on, while she her suit despairs.   350

A

S A T Y R

Upon a Woman, who by her Falshood and
Scorn was the Death of my Friend.
Whitsuntide 1678. at Croydon.

No, she shall ne'er escape, if Gods there be,
Unless they perjur'd grow and false as she;
Tho no strange Judgement yet the Murd'ress seize,
To punish her and quit the partial Skies:
Tho no revenging Lightning yet has flasht   5
From thence, that might her criminal Beauties blast:
Tho they in their old Lustre still prevail,
By no Disease, nor Guilt it self made pale,
Guilt, which should blackest Moors themselves but own,
Would make thro all their Night new Blushes dawn: 10
Tho that kind Soul, who now augments the Blest,
Thither too soon by her unkindness chas't
(Where, may it be her smalst and lightest Doom

0.1-0.3 A | SATYR | Upon] *1681, 1682*; Some pieces of Satyr. | On *R*
0.5 Whitsuntide ... Croydon] *R* (-78); *not in 1681, 1682*   6 criminal] *R²*,
1681, 1682; guilty *R¹*, *R*99   9 should blackest] *R, 1682, R*99; blackest *1681*
13 smalst] *R, 1682 subst.*; smallest *1681*

(For thats not half my Curse) never to come)
Tho he when prompted by the highst Despair   15
Ne'er mention'd her without an Hymn, or Pray'r,
And could by all her scorn be forc'd no more
Then Martyrs to revile what they adore;
Who, had he curst her with his dying Breath,
Had done but just, and Heaven had forgave: 20
Tho ill-made Law no Sentence has ordain'd
For her, no Statute has her Guilt arraign'd
(For Hangmen, Women's Scorn, and Doctor's Skill
All by a licens'd way of Murder kill)
Tho she from Justice of all these go free, ⎫   25
And boast perhaps in her Success, and cry, ⎬
'Twas but a little harmless Perjury;   ⎭
Yet think she not she still secure shall prove,
Or that none dare avenge an injur'd Love:
I rise in Judgement, am to be to her   30
Both Witness, Judge, and Executioner:
Arm'd with dire Satyr, and resentful Spite,
I come to haunt her with the Ghosts of Wit:
My Ink unbid starts out and flies on her,
Like Blood upon some touching Murderer: 35
And should that fail, rather then want I wou'd
(Like Hags) to curse her write in my own Blood:
   Ye spiteful Pow'rs (if any there can be
That boast a worse and keener Spite then I)
Assist with Malice and your mighty Aid   40
My sworn Revenge, and help me rhime her dead:
Grant I may fix such brands of Infamy,
So plain, so deeply grav'd on her, that she,
Her skill, Patches, nor Paint all join'd can hide,
And which shall lasting as her Soul abide: 45
Grant my rank Hate may such strong Poison cast,
That ev'ry Breath may taint and rot and blast,
Till one large Gangren quite orespread her Fame
With foul Contagion, till her odious Name,

16 mention'd] *R*², *1681*, *1682*; spoke of *R*¹   28 think] *R*, *1682*; thinks
1681   38 there can be] *1681*, *1682*; now there be *R*

Spit at and curst by evry Mouth like mine,   50
Be Terror to her self and all her Line:
   Vil'st of that viler Sex, who damn'd us all,
Ordain'd to cause and plague us for our Fall!
Woman! nay worse! for she can nought be said
But Mummy by som Dev'l inhabited!   55
Not made in Heaven's Mint, but basely coin'd,
She wears an human Image stampt on Fiend;
And whoso Marriage would with her contract,
Is Witch by Law, and that a meer Compact:
Her Soul (if any Soul in her there be)   60
By Hell was breath'd into her in a Ly,
And its whole Stock of Falshood there was lent,
As if hereafter to be true it meant:
Bawd Nature taught her Jilting, when she made
And by her Make design'd her for the Trade;   65
Hence 'twas she daub'd her with a painted Face,
That she at once might better cheat and please;
All those gay charming Looks, that court the Ey,
Are but an Ambush to hid Treachery,
Mischief adorn'd with Pomp and smooth Disguise,   70
A Painted Skin stuff'd full of Guile and Lies,
Within a gawdy Case a nasty Soul,
Like T— of Quality in a guilt Closestool:
Such on a Cloud those flattring Colours are,
Which only serve to dress a Tempest fair,   75
So Men upon this Earth's fair surface dwell,
Within are Fiends and at the Centre Hell.
Court-Promises, the Leagues, which Statesmen make
With more Convenience and more ease to break,
The Faith a Jesuit in Allegiance swears,   ⎫   80
Or a Town-Jilt to keeping Coxcombs bears,   ⎬
Are firm and certain all compar'd with hers: ⎭
Early in Falshood, at her Font she lied,
And should ev'n then for Perjury bin tried:
Her Conscience stretch'd, and open as the Stews,   85
But laughs at Oaths and plays with solemn Vows,

56 basely] *R, 1681*; base *1682*   65 design'd her] *R, 1682*; designed *1681*
70 Disguise,] *1681, 1682, subst.*; Disguise *R*

And at her Mouth swallows down perjur'd Breath
More glib then Bits of Lechery beneath:
Less serious known, when she dos most protest,
Then Thoughts of arrantest Buffoons in jest: 90
More cheap then the vile mercenariest Squire,   ⎫
Who plies for half-crown Fees at Westminster,   ⎬
And trades in Staple Oaths and swears to hire: ⎭
Less Guilt then hers, less Breach of Oath and Word,
Has stood aloft and look'd thro Penance-board: 95
And he, that trusts her in a Death-bed Pray'r,
Has Faith to merit, and save any thing but her.
  But since her Guilt description dos outgo,
I'le try if it outstrip my Curses too,
Curses, which may they equal my just Hate,   ⎫ 100
My Wish, and her Desert; be each so great,   ⎬
Each heard like Pray'rs, and Heaven make 'em Fate. ⎭
  First for her Beauties which the Mischief brought, ⎫
May she affected, they be borrow'd thought,   ⎬
By her own Hand, not that of Nature wrought: ⎭ 105
Her Credit, Honour, Portion, Health, and those
Prove light and frail as her broke Faith and Vows:
Some base unnam'd Disease her Carcase foul,
And make her Body ugly as her Soul:
Cankers and Ulcers eat her, till she be   110
Shun'd like Infection, loth'd like Infamy:
Strength quite expir'd may she alone retain   ⎫
The Snuff of Life, may that unquench'd remain, ⎬
As in the Damn'd, to keep her fresh for Pain: ⎭
Hot Lust light on her, and the Plague of Pride   115
On that, this ever scorn'd as that denied:
Ach, Anguish, Horror, Grief, Dishonour, Shame,
Pursue at once her Body, Soul, and Fame:
If ere the Devil Love must enter her
(For nothing sure but Fiends can enter there)   120
May she a just and true Tormentor find,
And that like an ill Conscience wrack her Mind:

87 perjur'd] *R*¹, *1681, 1682*; forsworn *R*² (*crossed out*)   89 dos] *R*; doth
1681, 1682   92 Who] *R*; That *1681, 1682*   94 Oath] *1681, 1682 subst.*;
Oaths *R*   Word,] *1681, 1682*; Word *R*

Be some diseas'd and ugly Wretch her Fate,
She doom'd to Love of one, whom all els hate,
May he hate her, and may her Destiny   125
Be to despair, and yet love on, and dy:
Or to invent some wittier Punishment,
May he to plague her out of Spite consent:
May the old Fumbler, tho' disabled quite,
Have strength to give her Claps, but no Delight: 130
May he of her unjustly jealous be,
For one that's worse and uglier far then he:
May's Impotence balk and torment her Lust,
Yet scarcely her to Dreams or Wishes trust:
Forc'd to be chast, may she suspected be,   135
Share none o'th' Pleasure, all the Infamy.
   In fine, that I all Curses may compleat,
(For I've but curst in jest and railly'd yet)
Whatere the Sex deserves, or feels, or fears,
May all those Plagues be hers and only hers: 140
Whatere great Favorites, turn'd out of doors,
Sham'd Cullies, bilk'd and disappointed Whores,
Or losing Gamesters vent, what Curses ere
Are spoke by Sinners raving in Despair,
All those fall on her, as they're all her due,   145
Till Spite can't think, nor Heav'n inflict anew:
May then (for once I will be kind and pray)
No Madness take her use of Sence away,
But may she in full Strength of Reason be,
To feel and understand her Misery: 150
Plagu'd so, till she think Damning a Release
And humbly pray to go to Hell for Ease:
Yet may not all these Suff'rings here attone
Her Sin, and may she still go Sinning on,
Tick up in Perjury and run o'th' Score   155
Till on her Soul she can get Trust no more:
   Then may she stupid and repentless dy,   ⎫
   And Heav'n it self forgive no more then I,   ⎬
   But so be damn'd of mere Necessity.   ⎭

124 one] *R, 1682*; me *1681*   157 she] *R, 1682*; the *1681*

2

SOME NEW PIECES

SOME NEW
P I E C E S
Never before Publisht.

By the AUTHOR of the
Satyrs upon the Jesuites.

Nos otia vitae
Solamur cantu, ventosaque gaudia famae
Quaerimus. ——————— Stat. Sylv.

LONDON:
Printed by *M.C.* for *Jo. Hindmarsh,*
at the Black Bull in *Cornhil,* 1681.

ADVERTISEMENT.

Being to appear anew in the world, it may be expected, that I
should say something concerning these ensuing Trifles, which I
shall endeavour to do with as much briefness, as I did before
what I last publish'd in this kind.

   I doubt not but the Reader will think me guilty of an high   5
presumption in adventuring upon a Translation of The Art of
Poetry, *after two such great Hands as have gone before me in the*
same attempt: I need not acquaint him, that I mean Ben Johnson,
and the Earl of Roscommon, *the one being of so establisht an*
Authority, that whatever he did is held as sacred, the other   10
having lately perform'd it with such admirable success, as al-
most cuts off all hope in any after Pretenders of ever coming
up to what he has done. Howbeit, when I let him know, that it
was a Task impos'd upon me, and not what I voluntarily engag'd
in; I hope, he will be the more favourable in his Censures. I   15
would indeed very willingly have wav'd the undertaking upon the
foremention'd account, and urg'd it as a reason for my declining
the same, but it would not be allow'd as sufficient to excuse
me. Wherefore, being prevail'd upon to make an Essay, I fell to
thinking of some course, whereby I might serve my self of the   20
Advantages, which those, that went before me, have either not
minded, or scrupulously abridg'd themselves of. This I soon
imagin'd was to be effected by putting Horace *into a more modern*
dress, than hitherto he has appear'd in, that is, by making him
speak, as if he were living, and writing now. I therefore   25
resolv'd to alter the Scene from Rome *to* London, *and to make use*
of English *names of Men, Places, and Customs, where the Parallel*
would decently permit, which I conceiv'd would give a kind of
new Air to the Poem, and render it more agreeable to the relish
of the present Age.   30

   With these considerations I set upon the work, and pursued it
accordingly. I have not, I acknowledg, been over-nice in keeping
to the words of the Original, for that were to transgress a Rule
therein contained. Nevertheless I have been religiously strict
to its sence, and exprest it in as plain and intelligible a   35

manner, as the Subject would bear. Where I may be thought to have
varied from it (which is not above once or twice, and in Passages
not much material) the skilful Reader will perceive 'twas neces-
sary for carrying on my propos'd design, and the Author himself,
40 *were he again alive, would (I believe) forgive me. I have been*
careful to avoid stiffness, and made it my endeavour to hit (as
near as I could) the easie and familiar way of writing, which is
peculiar to Horace *in his Epistles, and was his proper talent*
above any of mankind. After all, 'tis submitted to the judgment
45 *of the truly knowing, how I have acquitted my self herein. Let*
the success be what it will, I shall not however wholly repent
of my undertaking, being (I reckon) in some measure recompenc'd
for my pains by the advantage I have reap'd of fixing these
admirable Rules of Sense so well in my memory.
50   *The* Satyr *and* Odes *of the Author, which follow next in order,*
I have translated after the same libertine way. In them also I
labour'd under the disadvantages of coming after other persons.
The Satyr *had been made into a Scene by* B. Johnson, *in a Play of*
his, called the Poetaster. *After I had finish'd my Imitation*
55 *thereof, I came to learn, that it had been done likewise by Dr.*
Sprat, *and since I have had the sight of it amongst the Printed*
Translations of Horace's *Works. The* Odes *are there done too, but*
not so excellently well, as to discourage any farther endeavours.
If these of mine meet with good entertainment in the world, I may
60 *perhaps find leisure to attempt some other of them, which at*
present suffer as much from their Translaters, as the Psalms of
David *from* Sternhold *and* Hopkins.
The two sacred Odes *I design'd not to have made publick now,*
forasmuch as they might seem unfit to appear among Subjects of
65 *this nature, and were intended to come forth apart hereafter in*
company of others of their own kind. But, having suffer'd Copies
of them to straggle abroad in Manuscript, and remembring the Fate
of some other Pieces of mine, which have formerly stoln into the
Press without my leave, or knowledg, and been expos'd to the
70 *world abominably false and uncorrect; to prevent the same mis-*
fortune likely enough to befal these, I have been persuaded to
yield my consent to their Publishing amongst the rest. Nor is the
Printing of such Miscellanies altogether so unpresidented, but
that it may be seen in the Editions of Dr. Donne, *and Mr.* Cowley's

Works, whether done by their own appointment, or the sole direc-   75
tion of the Stationers, I am not able to determine.

As for the two Essays out of Greek, *they were occasion'd by a*
report, that some persons found fault with the roughness of my
Satyrs formerly publisht, tho, upon what ground they should do
it, I could be glad to be inform'd. Unless I am mistaken, there   80
are not many lines but will endure the reading without shocking
any Hearer, that is not too nice and censorious. I confess, I
did not so much mind the Cadence, as the Sense and expressiveness
of my words, and therefore chose not those, which were best dis-
pos'd to placing themselves in Rhyme, but rather the most keen   85
and tuant, as being the suitablest to my Argument. And certainly
no one that pretends to distinguish the several Colours of
Poetry, would expect that Juvenal, *when he is lashing of Vice*
and Villany, should flow so smoothly as Ovid, *or* Tibullus, *when*
they are describing Amours and Gallantries, and have nothing to   90
disturb and ruffle the evenness of their Stile.

Howbeit, to shew that the way I took, was out of choice, not
want of judgment, and that my Genius is not wholly uncapable of
performing upon more gay and agreeable Subjects, if my humor
inclin'd me to exercise it, I have pitch'd upon these two, which   95
the greatest men of sense have allow'd to be some of the softest
and tenderest of all Antiquity. Nay, if we will believe Rapin,
one of the best Criticks which these latter Ages have produc'd;
they have no other fault, than that they are too exquisitely
delicate for the Character of Pastoral, which should not seem   100
too labour'd, and whose chief beauty is an unaffected air of
plainness and simplicity.

That, which laments the Death of Adonis *has been attempted in*
Latin *by several great Masters, namely,* Vulcanius, Douza, *and*
Monsieur le Fevre. *The last of them has done it Paraphrastically,* 105
but left good part of the Poem toward the latter end untouch'd,
perhaps because he thought it not so capable of Ornament, as the
rest. Him I chiefly chose to follow, as being most agreeable to
my way of translating, and where I was at a loss for want of his
guidance, I was content to steer by my own Fancy.   110

The Translation of that upon Bion *was begun by another Hand,*
as far as the first fifteen Verses, but who was the Author I
could never yet learn. I have been told that they were done by

the Earl of Rochester; *but I could not well believe it, both*

115 *because he seldom meddled with such Subjects, and more especially*
by reason of an uncorrect line or two to be found amongst them,
at their first coming to my hands, which never us'd to flow from
his excellent Pen. Conceiving it to be in the Original, a piece
of as much Art, Grace, and Tenderness, as perhaps was ever

120 *offered to the Ashes of a Poet, I thought fit to dedicate it to*
the memory of that incomparable Person, of whom nothing can be
said or thought so choice and curious, which his Deserts do not
surmount. If it be thought mean to have borrow'd the sense of
another to praise him in, yet at least it argues at the same time

125 *a value and reverence, that I durst not think any thing of my*
own good enough for his Commendation.

This is all, which I judg material to be said of these follow-
ing Resveries. As for what others are to be found in the parcel,
I reckon them not worth mentioning in particular, but leave them

130 *wholly open and unguarded to the mercy of the Reader; let him*
make his Attaques how and where he please.

HORACE
His ART of
POETRY,
Imitated in *English*.

Addrest by way of Letter to a Friend.

Should some ill Painter in a wild design
To a mans Head an Horses shoulders joyn,
Or Fishes Tail to a fair Womans Waste,
Or draw the Limbs of many a different Beast,
Ill match'd, and with as motly Feathers drest;   5
If you by chance were to pass by his Shop;
Could you forbear from laughing at the Fop,
And not believe him whimsical, or mad?
Credit me, Sir, that Book is quite as bad,
As worthy laughter, which throughout is fill'd   10
With monstrous inconsistencies, more vain and wild
Than sick mens Dreams, whose neither head, nor tail,
Nor any parts in due proportion fall.
But 'twill be said, *None ever did deny*
Painters and Poets their free liberty   15
Of feigning any thing: We grant it true,
And the same privilege crave and allow:
But to mix natures clearly opposite,
To make the Serpent and the Dove unite,
Or Lambs from Savage Tygers seek defence,   20
Shocks Reason, and the rules of common Sence.
   Some, who would have us think they meant to treat
At first on Arguments of greatest weight,
Are proud, when here and there a glittering line
Does through the mass of their coarse rubbish shine: 25
In gay digressions they delight to rove,
Describing here a Temple, there a Grove,
A Vale enamel'd o're with pleasant streams,
A painted Rainbow, or the gliding *Thames*.
But how does this relate to their design?   30

Though good elsewhere, 'tis here but foisted in.
A common Dawber may perhaps have skill
To Paint a Tavern Sign, or Landskip well:
But what is this to Drawing of a Fight,
A Wrack, a Storm, or the *last Judgment* right?   35
When the fair Model and Foundation shews   ⎫
That you some great *Escurial* would produce, ⎬
How comes it dwindled to a Cottage thus?   ⎭
In fine, whatever work you mean to frame,
Be uniform, and every where the same.   40
    Most Poets, Sir, ('tis easie to observe)
Into the worst of faults are apt to swerve
Through a false hope of reaching excellence:
Avoiding length, we often cramp our Sense,
And make't obscure; oft, when we'd have our stile   45
Easie and flowing, lose its force the while:
Some, striving to surmount the common flight,
Soar up in airy Bombast out of sight:
Others, who fear to a bold pitch to trust
Themselves, flag low, and humbly sweep the dust: 50
And many fond of seeming marvellous,
While they too carelesly transgress the Laws
Of likelihood, most odd *Chimera's* feign,
Dolphins in Woods, and Boars upon the Main.
Thus they, who would take aim, but want the skill,   55
Miss always, and shoot wide, or narrow still.
    One of the meanest Workmen in the Town
Can imitate the Nails, or Hair in Stone,
And to the life enough perhaps, who yet
Wants mastery to make the work complete: 60
Troth, Sir, if 'twere my fancy to compose,   ⎫
Rather than be this bungling wretch, I'd choose ⎬
To wear a crooked and unsightly Nose   ⎭
'Mongst other handsome features of a Face
Which only would set off my ugliness.   65
    Be sure all you that undertake to write,
To choose a Subject for your Genius fit:
Try long and often what your Talents are;
What is the burthen, which your parts will bear,

And where they'l fail: he that discerns with skill   70
To cull his Argument and matter well,
Will never be to seek for Eloquence
To dress, or method to dispose his Sense.
They the chief Art and Grace in order show
(If I may claim any pretence to know)   75
Who time discreetly what's to be discourst,
What should be said at last, and what at first:
Some passages at present may be heard,
Others till afterward are best deferr'd:
Verse, which disdains the Laws of History,   80
Speaks things not as they are, but ought to be:
Whoever will in Poetry excel,
Must learn and use this hidden secret well.
  'Tis next to be observ'd, that care is due,
And sparingness in framing words anew: 85
You shew your mast'ry, if you have the knack
So to make use of what known word you take,
To give't a newer sense: if there be need
For some uncommon matters to be said;
Pow'r of inventing terms may be allow'd,   90
Which *Chaucer* and his Age ne're understood:
Provided always, as 'twas said before,
We seldom, and discreetly use that pow'r.
Words new and forein may be best brought in,
If borrow'd from a Language near akin: 95
Why should the pievish Criticks now forbid
To *Lee* and *Dryden*, what was not deny'd
To *Shakespear, Ben,* and *Fletcher* heretofore,
For which they praise and commendation bore?
If *Spencer*'s Muse be justly so ador'd   100
For that rich copiousness, wherewith he stor'd
Our Native Tongue; for Gods sake why should I ⎫
Straight be thought arrogant, if modestly   ⎬
I claim and use the self-same liberty?   ⎭
This the just Right of Poets ever was,   ⎫   105
And will be still to coin what words they please, ⎬
Well fitted to the present Age and Place.   ⎭
  Words with the Leaves of Trees a semblance hold

In this respect, where every year the old
Fall off, and new ones in their places grow: 110
Death is the Fate of all things here below:
Nature her self by Art has changes felt,
The *Tangier* Mole (by our great *Monarch* built)
Like a vast Bulwark in the Ocean set,
From Pyrates and from Storms defends our Fleet: 115
Fens every day are drain'd, and men now Plow,
And Sow, and Reap, where they before might Row;
And Rivers have been taught by *Middleton*   ⎫
From their old course within new Banks to run,   ⎬
And pay their useful Tribute to the Town.   ⎭   ˙   120
If Mans and Natures works submit to Fate,
Much less must words expect a lasting date:
Many which we approve for currant now,
In the next Age out of request shall grow:
And others which are now thrown out of doors,   125
Shall be reviv'd, and come again in force,
If custom please: from whence their vogue they draw,
Which of our Speech is the sole Judg and Law.
  Homer first shew'd us in Heroick strains
To write of Wars, of Battles and Campaigns,   130
Kings and great Leaders, mighty in Renown,
And him we still for our chief Pattern own.
  Soft Elegy, design'd for grief and tears,
Was first devis'd to grace some mournful Herse:
Since to a brisker note 'tis taught to move,   135
And cloaths our gayest Passions, Joy and Love.
But, who was first Inventer of the kind,
Criticks have sought, but never yet could find.
  Gods, Heroes, Warriors, and the lofty praise
Of peaceful Conquerors in *Pisa*'s Race,   140
The Mirth and Joys, which Love and Wine produce, ⎫
With other wanton sallies of a Muse,   ⎬
The stately Ode does for its Subjects choose.   ⎭
  Archilochus to vent his Gall and spite,
In keen Iambicks first was known to write: 145
Dramatick Authors us'd this sort of Verse
On all the *Greek* and *Roman* Theaters,

As for Discourse and Conversation fit,
And aptst to drown the noises of the Pit.
  If I discern not the true stile and air,   150
Nor how to give the proper Character
To every kind of work; how dare I claim,
And challenge to my self a Poets Name?
And why had I with awkard modesty,
Rather than learn, always unskilful be?   155
Volpone and *Morose* will not admit
Of *Catiline*'s high strains, nor is it fit
To make *Sejanus* on the Stage appear
In the low dress, which Comick persons wear.
What e're the Subject be, on which you write,   160
Give each thing its due place and time aright:
  Yet Comedy sometimes may raise her stile,
And angry *Chremes* is allow'd to swell,
And Tragedy alike sometimes has leave
To throw off Majesty, when 'tis to grieve: 165
Peleus and *Telephus* in misery,
Lay their big words, and blust'ring language by, ⎫
If they expect to make their Audience cry. ⎭
'Tis not enough to have your Plays succeed,
That they be elegant: they must not need   170
Those warm and moving touches which impart ⎫
A kind concernment to each Hearers heart, ⎬
And ravish it which way they please with art. ⎭
Where Joy and Sorrow put on good disguise,
Ours with the persons looks straight sympathize: 175
Would'st have me weep? thy self must first begin; ⎫
Then, *Telephus*, to pity I incline, ⎬
And think thy case, and all thy suff'rings mine; ⎭
But if thou'rt made to act thy part amiss,
I can't forbear to sleep, or laugh, or hiss.   180
Let words express the looks, which speakers wear;
Sad, fit a mournful and dejected air;
The passionate must huff, and storm, and rave;
The gay be pleasant, and the serious grave.

     169 succeed,] *Ed.* (*1770*); succeed; *1681*

For Nature works and moulds our Frame within,   185
To take all manner of Impressions in:
Now makes us hot, and ready to take fire,
Now hope, now joy, now sorrow does inspire,
And all these passions in our face appear,
Of which the Tongue is sole interpreter: 190
But he whose words and Fortunes do not suit,
By Pit and Gall'ry both, is hooted out.
    Observe what Characters your persons fit,
Whether the Master speak, or *Jodolet*:
Whether a man, that's elderly in growth,   195
Or a brisk Hotspur in his boiling youth:
A roaring Bully, or a shirking Cheat,
A Court-bred Lady, or a tawdry Cit:
A prating Gossip, or a jilting Whore,
A travell'd Merchant, or an homespun Bore: 200
Spaniard, or *French, Italian, Dutch*, or *Dane*;
Native of *Turky, India*, or *Japan*.
    Either from History your persons take,
Or let them nothing inconsistent speak:
If you bring great *Achilles* on the Stage,   205
Let him be fierce and brave, all heat and rage,
Inflexible, and head-strong to all Laws,
But those, which Arms and his own will impose.
Cruel *Medea* must no pity have,   ⎫
Ixion must be treacherous, *Ino* grieve,   ⎬   210
Io must wander, and *Orestes* rave.   ⎭
But if you dare to tread in paths unknown,
And boldly start new persons of your own;
Be sure to make them in one strain agree,
And let the end like the beginning be.   215
    'Tis difficult for Writers to succeed
On Arguments, which none before have tri'd:
The *Iliad*, or the *Odyssee* with ease
Will better furnish Subjects for your Plays
Than that you should your own Invention trust,   220
And broach unheard-of things yourself the first.

        194 *Jodelet*] *Ed.*; *Todelet 1681*

In copying others works, to make them pass,
And seem your own, let these few rules take place:
When you some of their Story represent,
Take care that you new Episodes invent: 225
Be not too nice the Authors words to trace,
But vary all with a fresh air and grace;
Nor such strict rules of imitation choose,
Which you must still be tied to follow close,
Or forc'd to a retreat for want of room,   230
Give over, and ridiculous become.
  Do not like that affected Fool begin,
King Priam's *Fate, and* Troy's *fam'd War, I sing.*
What will this mighty Promiser produce?
You look for Mountains, and out creeps a Mouse.   235
How short is this of *Homer*'s fine Address
And Art, who ne're says any thing amiss?
Muse, speak the man, who since Troy's *laying waste* ⎫
Into such numerous Dangers has been cast   ⎬
So many Towns, and various People past: ⎭   240
He does not lavish at a blaze his Fire,
To glare a while, and in a snuff expire:
But modestly at first conceals his light,
In dazling wonders, then breaks forth to sight;
Surprizes you with Miracles all o're,   ⎫   245
Makes dreadful *Scylla* and *Charybdis* roar, ⎬
Cyclops, and bloody *Lestrygons* devour: ⎭
Nor does he time in long Preambles spend,
Describing *Meleager*'s ruful end,
When he's of *Diomed*'s return to treat; ⎫   250
Nor when he would the *Trojan* War relate, ⎬
The Tale of brooding *Leda*'s Eggs repeat. ⎭
But still to the design'd event hasts on,
And at first dash, as if before 'twere known,
Embarques you in the middle of the Plot,   255
And what is unimprovable leaves out,
And mixes Truth and Fiction skilfully,
That nothing in the whole may disagree.
  Who e're you are, that set your selves to write,
If you expect to have your Audience sit   260

Till the fifth Act be done, and Curtain fall;
Mind what Instructions I shall further tell:
Our Guise and Manners alter with our Age,
And such they must be brought upon the Stage.
    A Child, who newly has to Speech attain'd,   265
And now can go without the Nurses hand,
To play with those of his own growth is pleas'd,
Suddenly angry, and as soon appeas'd,
Fond of new Trifles, and as quickly cloy'd,
And loaths next hour what he th'last enjoy'd.   270
    The beardless Youth from Pedagogue got loose,
Does Dogs and Horses for his pleasures choose;
Yielding and soft to every print of vice,
Resty to those who would his faults chastise,
Careless of profit, of expences vain,   ⎫   275
Haughty, and eager his desires t'obtain,   ⎬
And swift to quit the same desires again. ⎭
    Those, who to manly years, and sense are grown,
Seek Wealth and Friendship, Honor and Renown:
And are discreet, and fearful how to act   280
What after they must alter and correct.
    Diseases, Ills, and Troubles numberless
Attend old Men, and with their Age increase:
In painful toil they spend their wretched years,
Still heaping Wealth, and with that wealth new cares: 285
Fond to possess, and fearful to enjoy,
Slow and suspicious in their managry,
Full of Delays, and Hopes, lovers of ease,
Greedy of life, morose, and hard to please,
Envious at Pleasures of the young and gay,   290
Where they themselves now want a stock to play:
Ill natur'd Censors of the present Age,
And what has past since they have quit the Stage:
But loud Admirers of Queen *Besse's* time,
And what was done when they were in their prime.   295
    Thus, what our tide of flowing years brings in,
Still with our ebb of life goes out agen:
The humors of Fourscore will never hit
One of Fifteen, nor a Boy's part befit

A full-grown man: it shews no mean Address,   300
If you the tempers of each Age express.
   Some things are best to act, others to tell;
Those by the ear convey'd, do not so well,
Nor half so movingly affect the mind,
As what we to our eyes presented find.   305
Yet there are many things, which should not come
In view, nor pass beyond the Tiring Room:
Which, after in expressive Language told,
Shall please the Audience more, than to behold:
Let not *Medea* shew her fatal rage,   310
And cut her Childrens Throats upon the Stage:
Nor *Oedipus* tear out his eye-balls there,
Nor bloody *Atreus* his dire Feast prepare:
Cadmus, nor *Progne* their odd changes take,
This to a Bird, the other to a Snake: 315
Whatever so incredible you show,
Shocks my Belief, and straight does nauseous grow.
   Five Acts, no more, nor less, your Play must have,
If you'l an handsome Third days share receive.
Let not a God be summon'd to attend   320
On a slight errand, nor on Wire descend,
Unless th' importance of the Plot engage;
And let but three at once speak on the Stage.
   Be sure to make the *Chorus* still promote
The chief Intrigue and business of the Plot: 325
Betwixt the Acts there must be nothing Sung,
Which does not to the main design belong:
The praises of the Good must here be told,
The Passions curb'd, and foes of Vice extoll'd:
Here Thrift and Temperance, and wholesome Laws, ⎫   330
Strict Justice, and the gentle calms of Peace ⎬
Must have their Commendations and Applause: ⎭
And Prayers must be sent to Heaven to guide   ⎫
Blind Fortunes blessings to the juster side,   ⎬
To raise the Poor, and lower prosp'rous Pride. ⎭   335
   At first the Musick of our Stage was rude,
Whilst in the *Cock-Pit* and *Black-Friers* it stood:
And this might please enough in former Reigns,

A thrifty, thin, and bashful Audience:
When *Bussy d' Ambois* and his Fustian took,   340
And men were ravish'd with Queen *Gorboduc*.
But since our Monarch by kind Heaven sent,
Brought back the Arts with him from Banishment,
And by his gentle influence gave increase
To all the harmless Luxuries of peace: 345
Favour'd by him, our Stage has flourisht too,
And every day in outward splendor grew:
In Musick, Song, and Dance of every kind,
And all the grace of Action 'tis refin'd;
And since that Opera's at length came in,   350
Our Players have so well improv'd the Scene
With gallantry of Habit and Machine;
As makes our Theater in Glory vie
With the best Ages of Antiquity:
And mighty *Roscius* were he living now,   355
Would envy both our Stage and Acting too.
   Those, who did first in Tragedy essay
(When a vile Goat was all the Poets day)
Us'd to allay their Subjects gravity
With enterludes of Mirth and Raillery: 360
Here they brought rough and naked Satyrs in,
Whose Farce-like Gesture, Motion, Speech, and Meen
Resembled those of modern *Harlequin*.
Because such antick Tricks, and odd grimace,
After their drunken Feasts on Holidays,   365
The giddy and hot-headed Rout would please:
As the wild Feats of *Merry Andrews* now
Divert the sensless Crowd at *Bartholmew*.
   But he, that would in this Mock-way excel,
And exercise the Art of Rallying well,   370
Had need with diligence observe this Rule
In turning serious things to ridicule:
If he an Hero, or a God bring in,
With Kingly Robes and Scepter lately seen,

341 *Gorboduc*] *Ed.* (*1722*); *Gordobuc 1681*   342 kind] *1681* (*corr.*); klnd
1681 (*uncorr.*)

Let them not speak, like Burlesque Characters,   375
The wit of *Billinsgate* and *Temple-stairs*:
Nor, while they of those meannesses beware,
In tearing lines of *Bajazet* appear.
Majestick Tragedy as much disdains
To condescend to low and trivial strains: 380
As a Court-Lady thinks her self disgrac'd
To Dance with Dowdies at a May-pole-Feast.

  If in this kind you will attempt to write,
You must no broad and clownish words admit:
Nor must you so confound your Characters,   385
As not to mind what person 'tis appears.
Take a known Subject, and invent it well,
And let your stile be smooth and natural:
Though others think it easie to attain,
They'l find it hard, and imitate in vain: 390
So much does method and connexion grace
The common'st things, the plainest matters raise.

  In my opinion 'tis absurd and odd,
To make wild Satyrs, coming from the Wood,
Speak the fine Language of the *Park* and *Mall*,   395
As if they had their Training at *Whitehall*:
Yet, tho I would not have their Words too quaint,
Much less can I allow them impudent:
For men of Breeding, and of Quality
Must needs be shock'd with fulsom Ribaldry: 400
Which, tho it pass the Footboy and the Cit,
Is always nauseous to the Box and Pit.

  There are but few, who have such skilful ears
To judg of artless and ill-measur'd Verse.
This till of late was hardly understood,   405
And still there's too much liberty allow'd,
But will you therefore be so much a fool
To write at random, and neglect a Rule?
Or, while your faults are set to general view,
Hope all men should be blind, or pardon you?   410
Who would not such fool-hardiness condemn, ⎤

    390 They'l] *1681* (*corr.*); TheyI *1681* (*uncorr.*)

Where, tho perchance you may escape from blame, ⎫
Yet praise you never can expect, or claim?   ⎭
Therefore be sure your study to apply
To the great patterns of Antiquity: 415
Ne're lay the Greeks and Romans out of sight,
Ply them by day, and think on them by night.
Rough hobbling numbers were allow'd for Rhime,
And clench for deep conceit in former time:
With too much patience (not to call it worse)   420
Both were applauded in our Ancestors:
If you, or I have sense to judg aright
Betwixt a Quibble, and true sterling Wit:
Or ear enough to give the difference
Of sweet well-sounding Verse from doggrel strains.   425
   Thespis ('tis said) did Tragedy devise,
Unknown before, and rude at its first rise:
In Carts the Gypsie Actors strowl'd about,   ⎫
With faces smear'd with Lees of Wine and Soot,   ⎬
And through the Towns amus'd the wondring rout: ⎭   430
Till *Æschylus* appearing to the Age,
Contriv'd a Play-house, and convenient Stage,
Found out the use of Vizards, and a Dress
(An handsomer and more gentile Disguise)
And taught the Actors with a stately Air   ⎫   435
And Meen to speak and Tread, and whatsoe're   ⎬
Gave Port and Grandeur to the Theater.   ⎭
   Next this succeeded ancient Comedy,
With good applause, till too much liberty
Usurp'd by Writers had debauch'd the Stage,   440
And made it grow the Grievance of the Age:
No merit was secure, no person free
From its licentious Buffoonery:
Till for redress the Magistrate was fain
By Law those Insolencies to restrain.   445
   Our Authors in each kind their praise may claim,
Who leave no paths untrod, that lead to fame:
And well they merit it, who scorn'd to be
So much the Vassals of Antiquity,
As those, who know no better than to cloy   450

With the old musty Tales of *Thebes* and *Troy*:
But boldly the dull beaten track forsook,
And Subjects from our Country-story took.
Nor would our Nation less in Wit appear,
Than in its great Performances of War;   455
Were there encouragements to bribe our care:
Would we to file and finish spare the pains,
And add but justness to our manly sence.
But, Sir, let nothing tempt you to bely
Your skill and judgment, by mean flattery: 460
Never pretend to like a piece of Wit,
But what, you're certain, is correctly writ:
But what has stood all Tests, and is allow'd
By all to be unquestionably good.

  Because some wild Enthusiasts there be   465
Who bar the Rules of Art in Poetry,
Would have it rapture all, and scarce admit
A man of sober sense to be a Wit;
Others by this conceit have been misled
So much, that they're grown statutably mad: 470
The Sots affect to be retir'd alone,
Court Solitude and Conversation shun,
In dirty Cloaths, and a wild Garb appear,
And scarce are brought to cut their Nails and Hair,
And hope to purchase credit and esteem,   475
When they, like *Cromwel's Porter*, frantick seem.
Strange! that the very height of Lunacy,
Beyond the cure of *Allen*, e're should be
A mark of the Elect in Poetry.
How much an Ass am I that us'd to Bleed,   480
And take a Purge each Spring to clear my Head?
None otherwise would be so good as I,
At lofty strains and rants of Poetry:
But, faith, I am not yet so fond of Fame,
To lose my Reason for a Poets name.   485
Tho I my self am not dispos'd to write;
In others I may serve to sharpen Wit:

      480 us'd] *1681*; use *conj. Ed.*

Acquaint them what a Poet's duty is,
And how he shall perform it with success:
Whence the materials for his work are sought,   490
And how with skilful Art they must be wrought:
And shew what is and is not decency,
And where his faults and excellencies lie.

   Good sense must be the certain standard still
To all that will pretend to writing well: 495
If you'l arrive at that, you needs must be
Well vers'd and grounded in Philosophy:
Then choose a Subject, which you throughly know,
And words unsought thereon will easie flow.
Who e're will write, must diligently mind   500
The several sorts and ranks of humane kind:
He that has learnt, what to his Country's due,
What we to Parents, Friends, and Kindred owe,
What charge a Statesman, or a Judg does bear,
And what the parts of a Commander are;   505
Will never be at loss (he may be sure)
To give each person their true portraiture.
Take humane life for your original,
Keep but your Draughts to that, you'l never fail.
Sometimes in Plays, tho else but badly writ,   ⎫   510
With nought of Force, or Grace, of Art, or Wit,   ⎬
Some one well humor'd Character we meet,   ⎭
That takes us more than all the empty Scenes,
And jingling toys of more elaborate Pens.

   Greece had command of Language, Wit and Sence: 515
For cultivating which she spar'd no pains:
Glory her sole design, and all her aim
Was how to gain her self immortal Fame:
Our *English* Youth another way are bred,   ⎫
They're fitted for a Prentiship and Trade,   ⎬   520
And *Wingate*'s all the Authors, which they've read. ⎭
The Boy has been a year at Writing-School,   ⎫
Has learnt Division, and the Golden Rule;   ⎬
Scholar enough! cries the old doating Fool,   ⎭
I'le hold a piece, he'l prove an Alderman,   525
And come to sit at Church with's Furs and Chain.

This is the top design, the only praise,
And sole ambition of the booby Race:
While this base spirit in the Age does reign,
And men mind nought but Wealth and sordid gain,   530
Can we expect or hope it should bring forth
A work in Poetry of any worth,
Fit for the learned *Bodley* to admit
Among its Sacred Monuments of Wit?
  A Poet should inform us, or divert,   535
But joyning both he shews his chiefest Art:
Whatever Precepts you pretend to give,
Be sure to lay them down both clear and brief:
By that they're easier far to apprehend,
By this more faithfully preserv'd in mind: 540
All things superfluous are apt to cloy
The Judgment, and surcharge the Memory.
  Let whatsoe're of Fiction you bring in,
Be so like Truth, to seem at least akin:
Do not improbabilities conceive,   545
And hope to ram them into my belief:
Ne're make a Witch upon the Stage appear,
Riding enchanted Broomstick through the Air:
Nor Canibal a living Infant spew,
Which he had murther'd, and devour'd but now.   550
The graver sort dislike all Poetry,
Which does not (as they call it) edifie:
And youthful sparks as much that Wit despise,
Which is not strew'd with pleasant Gaieties.
But he, that has the knack of mingling well   555
What is of use with what's agreeable,
That knows at once how to instruct and please,
Is justly crown'd by all mens suffrages:
These are the works, which valued every where,
Enrich *Paul's Church-yard* and the Stationer: 560
These admiration through all Nations claim,
And through all Ages spread their Author's Fame.
  Yet there are faults wherewith we ought to bear;
An Instrument may sometimes chance to jar
In the best hand, in spight of all its care: 565

Nor have I known that skilful Marks-man yet
So fortunate, who never mist the White.
But where I many excellencies find,
I'm not so nicely critical to mind
Each slight mistake an Author may produce,   570
Which humane frailty justly may excuse.
Yet he, who having oft been taught to mend
A Fault, will still pursue it to the end,
Is like that scraping Fool, who the same Note
Is ever playing, and is ever out,   575
And silly as that bubble every whit,
Who at the self-same blot is always hit.
When such a lewd incorrigible sot
Lucks by meer chance upon some happy thought;
Among such filthy trash, I vex to see't,   580
And wonder how (the Devil!) he came by't.
In works of bulk and length we now and then
May grant an Author to be overseen:
Homer himself, how sacred e're he is,
Yet claims not a pretence to Faultlesness.   585
    Poems with Pictures a resemblance bear;
Some (best at distance) shun a view too near:
Others are bolder and stand off to sight;
These love the shade, those choose the clearest light,
And dare the survey of the skilfull'st eyes: 590
Some once, and some ten thousand times will please.
    Sir, though your self so much of knowledg own ⎫
In these affairs, that you can learn of none,   ⎬
Yet mind this certain truth which I lay down: ⎭
Most Callings else Indifference allow,   595
Where ordinary Parts and Skill may do:
I've known Physicians, who respect might claim,
Tho they ne're rose to *Willis* his great fame:
And there are Preachers, who have just renown,
Yet ne're come up to *Sprat*, or *Tillotson*:   600
And Counsellors, or Pleaders in the Hall
May have esteem and practice, tho they fall

            595 Indifference] *E*; do difference *1681*

Far short of smooth-tongu'd *Finch* in Eloquence,
Tho they want *Selden*'s Learning, *Vauhan*'s sence.
But Verse alone does of no mean admit,   605
Whoe're will please, must please us to the height:
He must a *Cowley* or a *Fleckno* be,
For there's no second Rate in Poetry:
A dull insipid Writer none can bear, ⎫
In every place he is the publick jeer, ⎬   610
And Lumber of the Shops and Stationer. ⎭

   No man that understands to make a Feast,
With a coarse Dessert will offend his Guest,
Or bring ill Musick in to grate the ear,
Because 'tis what the entertain might spare: 615
'Tis the same case with those that deal in Wit,
Whose main design and end should be delight:
They must by this same sentence stand, or fall,
Be highly excellent, or not at all.

   In all things else, save only Poetry,   620
Men shew some signs of common modesty:
You'l hardly find a Fencer so unwise,
Who at *Bear-garden* e're will fight a Prize,
Not having learnt before: nor at a Wake
One, that wants skill and strength, the Girdle take;   625
Or be so vain the pond'rous Weight to fling,
For fear they should be hiss'd out of the Ring.
Yet every Coxcomb will pretend to Verse,
And write in spight of nature, and his Stars:
All sorts of Subjects challenge at this time   630
Their Liberty and Property of Rhime.
The Sot of honor, fond of being great
By something else than Title and Estate,
As if a Patent gave him claim to sence,
Or 'twere entail'd with an inheritance,   635
Believes a cast of Foot-boys, and a set
Of *Flanders* must advance him to a Wit.
But you who have the judgment to descry
Where you excel, which way your Talents lie,
I'm sure, will never be induc'd to strain   640
Your Genius, or attempt against your vein.

Yet (this let me advise) if e're you write,
Let none of your composures see the light,
Till they've been throughly weigh'd, and past the Test
Of all those Judges who are thought the best: 645
While in your Desk they're lock'd up from the Press,
You've power to correct them as you please:
But when they once come forth to view of all,
Your Faults are chronicled, and past recall.

  Orpheus the first of the inspired Train,   650
By force of powerful numbers did restrain
Mankind from rage, and bloody cruelty,
And taught the barbarous world civility.
Hence rose the Fiction, which the Poets fram'd,
That Lions were by's tuneful Magick tam'd,   655
And Tygers, charm'd by his harmonious lays,
Grew gentle, and laid by their savageness:
Hence that, which of *Amphion* too they tell,
The pow'r of whose miraculous Lute could call
The well-plac'd stones into the *Theban* Wall.   660
Wondrous were the effects of primitive Verse,
Which setled and reform'd the Universe:
This did all things to their due ends reduce,
To publick, private, sacred, civil use:
Marriage for weighty causes was ordain'd,   665
That bridled lust, and lawless Love restrain'd:
Cities with Walls and Rampiers were inclos'd,
And Property with wholsom Laws dispos'd:
And bounds were fix'd of Equity and Right,
To guard weak Innocence from wrongful might.   670
Hence Poets have been held a sacred name,
And plac'd with first Rates in the Lists of Fame.
Next these, great *Homer* to the world appear'd,
Around the Globe his loud alarms were heard,
Which all the brave to war-like action fir'd: 675
And *Hesiod* after him with useful skill
Gave Lessons to instruct the Plough-mans toil.
Verse was the language of the gods of old,
In which their sacred Oracles were told:
In Verse were the first rules of vertue taught,   680

And Doctrine thence, as now from Pulpits sought:
By Verse some have the love of Princes gain'd, ⎫
Who oft vouchsafe so to be entertain'd,   ⎬
And with a Muse their weighty cares unbend. ⎭
Then think it no disparagement, dear Sir, ⎫   685
To own your self a Member of that Quire, ⎬
Whom Kings esteem, and Heaven does inspire. ⎭
   Concerning Poets there has been contest,
Whether they're made by Art, or Nature best:
But if I may presume in this Affair,   690
Amongst the rest my judgment to declare,
No Art without a Genius will avail,
And Parts without the help of Art will fail:
But both ingredients joyntly must unite
To make the happy Character complete.   695
   None at *New-market* ever won the Prize,
But us'd his Airings, and his Exercise,
His Courses and his Diets long before,
And Wine and Women for a time forbore:
Nor is there any Singing-man, we know,   700
Of good Repute in either *Chappel* now,
But was a Learner once (he'l freely own)
And by long Practice to that Skill has grown:
But each conceited Dunce, without pretence ⎫
To the least grain of Learning, Parts, or sense, ⎬   705
Or any thing but harden'd impudence, ⎭
Sets up for Poetry, and dares engage
With all the topping Writers of the Age:
"Why should not he put in amongst the rest?
"Damn him! he scorns to come behind the best: 710
"Declares himself a Wit, and vows to draw
"On the next man, who e're disowns him so.
   Scriblers of Quality who have Estate,
To gain applauding Fools at any rate,
Practise as many tricks as Shop-keepers   715
To force a Trade, and put off naughty wares:
Some hire the House their Follies to expose,
And are at charge to be ridiculous:
Others with Wine and Ordinaries treat

A needy Rabble to cry up their Wit: 720
'Tis strange, that such should the true diff'rence find
Betwixt a spunging Knave and faithful Friend.
Take heed how you e're prostitute your sence
To such a fawning crew of Sycophants:
All signs of being pleas'd the Rogues will feign, ⎤   725
Wonder and bless themselves at every line,   ⎬
Swearing, "'*Tis soft! 'tis charming! 'tis Divine!* ⎦
Here they'l look pale, as if surpriz'd, and there
In a disguise of grief squeeze out a tear:
Oft seem transported with a sudden joy,   730
Stamp and lift up their hands in extasie:
But, if by chance your back once turn'd appear, ⎤
You'l have 'em strait put out their tongues in jeer, ⎬
Or point, or gibe you with a scornful sneer.   ⎦
As they who truly grieve at Funerals, shew   735
Less outward sorrow than hir'd mourners do;
So true Admirers less concernment wear
Before your face than the sham-Flatterer.
   They tell of Kings, who never would admit
A Confident, or bosom-Favourite,   740
Till store of Wine had made his secrets float,
And by that means they'd sound his temper out:
'Twere well if Poets knew some way like this,
How to discern their friends from enemies.
   Had you consulted learned *Ben* of old,   745
He would your faults impartially have told:
"*This Verse correction wants* (he would have said) ⎤
"*And so does this*: If you replied, you had   ⎬
To little purpose several trials made;   ⎦
He presently would bid you strike a dash   750
On all, and put in better in the place:
But if he found you once a stubborn sot,
That would not be corrected in a fault;
He would no more his pains and counsel spend
On an abandon'd Fool that scorn'd to mend,   755
But bid you in the Devils name go on,

742 sound] *1681*; found (*1684a*)

And hug your dear impertinence alone.

  A trusty knowing Friend will boldly dare
To give his sence and judgment, wheresoe're
He sees a Fault: *"Here, Sir, good faith you're low,*   760
"And must some heightning on the place bestow:
"There, if you mind, the Rhime is harsh and rough,
"And should be soften'd to go smoothlier off:
"Your strokes are here of Varnish left too bare,
"Your Colours there too thick laid on appear: 765
"Yon Metaphor is coarse, that Phrase not pure,
"This Word improper, and that sence obscure.
In fine, you'l find him a strict Censurer,
That will not your least negligences spare
Through a vain fear of disobliging you: 770
They are but slight and trivial things, 'tis true:
Yet these same Trifles (take a Poets word)
Matter of high importance will afford,
When e're by means of them you come to be
Expos'd to Laughter, Scorn and Infamy.   775
  Not those with *Lord have mercy* on their doors,
Venom of Adders, or infected Whores,
Are dreaded worse by men of sence and Wit,
Than a mad Scribler in his raving fit:
Like Dog, whose tail is pegg'd into a bone, ⎫   780
The hooting Rabble all about the Town,   ⎬
Pursue the Cur, and pelt him up and down. ⎭
Should this poor Frantick, as he past along,
Intent on's Rhiming work amidst the throng,
Into *Fleet-Ditch*, or some deep Cellar fall, ⎫ 785
And till he rent his throat for succor bawl, ⎬
No one would lend an helping hand at call: ⎭
For who (the Plague!) could guess at his design,
Whether he did not for the nonce drop in?
I'd tell you, Sir, but questionless you've heard   790
Of the odd end of a *Sicilian* Bard:
Fond to be deem'd a god, this fool (it seems)
In's fit leapt headlong into *Ætna*'s Flames.
Troth, I could be content an Act might pass, ⎫
Such Poets should have leave, when e're they please, ⎬ 795

To die, and rid us of our Grievances: ⎤

A God's name let 'em hang, or drown, or choose ⎞

What other way they will themselves dispose, ⎬

Why should we life against their wills impose? ⎠

Might that same fool I mention'd, now revive,   800

He would not be reclaim'd, I dare believe,

But soon be playing his old freaks again,

And still the same capricious hopes retain.

  'Tis hard to guess, and harder to alledg

Whether for Parricide, or Sacriledg,   805

Or some more strange, unknown, and horrid crime, ⎞

Done in their own, or their Fore-fathers time,   ⎬

These scribling Wretches have been damn'd to Rhime: ⎠

But certain 'tis, for such a crack-brain'd race

Bedlam, or *Hogsdon* is the fittest place: 810

Without their Keepers you had better choose

To meet the Lions of the *Tower* broke loose,

Than these wild savage Rhymers in the street,

Who with their Verses worry all they meet:

In vain you would release your self; so close   815

The Leeches cleave, that there's no getting loose.

  Remorsless they to no entreaties yield,

  Till you are with inhumane non-sense kill'd.

An imitation of

H O R A C E .

B O O K   I .   S A T Y R   I X .

Written in *June*, 1681.

_____

Ibam fortè viâ sacrâ, &c.

As I was walking in the *Mall* of late,

Alone, and musing on I know not what;

Comes a familiar Fop, whom hardly I
Knew by his name, and rudely seizes me:
Dear Sir, I'm mighty glad to meet with you: }   5
And pray, how have you done this Age, or two?
"*Well I thank God* (said I) *as times are now:*
"*I wish the same to you.* And so past on,
Hoping with this the Coxcomb would be gone.
But when I saw I could not thus get free;   10
I ask'd, what business else he had with me?
Sir (answer'd he) *if Learning, Parts, or Sence*
Merit your friendship; I have just pretence.
"*I honor you* (said I) *upon that score,*
"*And shall be glad to serve you to my power.*   15
Mean time, wild to get loose, I try all ways
To shake him off: Sometimes I walk apace,
Sometimes stand still: I frown, I chafe, I fret,
Shrug, turn my back, as in the *Bagnio,* sweat:
And shew all kind of signs to make him guess   20
At my impatience and uneasiness.
"*Happy the folk in* Newgate! (whisper'd I)
"*Who, tho in Chains are from this torment free:*
"*Wou'd I were like rough* Manly *in the Play,*
"*To send Impertinents with kicks away!*   25
   He all the while baits me with tedious chat, }
Speaks much about the drought, and how the rate }
Of Hay is rais'd, and what it now goes at: }
Tells me of a new Comet at the *Hague,*
Portending God knows what, a Dearth, or Plague: 30
Names every Wench, that passes through the Park,
How much she is allow'd, and who the Spark
That keeps her: points, who lately got a Clap,
And who at the *Groom-Porters* had ill hap
Three nights ago in play with such a Lord: }   35
When he observ'd, I minded not a word,   }
And did no answer to his trash afford;   }
Sir, I perceive you stand on Thorns (said he)
And fain would part: but, faith, it must not be:

19 *Bagnio,*] *Ed.* (*1697*); *Baigno, 1681*   32 Spark] *Ed.* (*1722*); Spark, *1681*

Come, let us take a Bottle. (I cried) *"No;* ⎫   40
"Sir, I am in a Course, and dare not now. ⎬
Then tell me whether you design to go: ⎭
I'll wait upon you. "Oh! Sir, 'tis too far:
"I visit cross the Water: therefore spare
"Your needless trouble. Trouble! Sir, 'tis none: 45
'Tis more by half to leave you here alone.
I have no present business to attend,
At least which I'll not quit for such a Friend:
Tell me not of the distance: for I vow,
I'll cut the Line, double the Cape for you,   50
Good faith, I will not leave you: make no words:
Go you to Lambeth? *Is it to my* Lords?
His Steward I most intimately know,
Have often drunk with his Comptroller too.
By this I found my wheadle would not pass,   55
But rather serv'd my suff'rings to increase:
And seeing 'twas in vain to vex, or fret,
I patiently submitted to my fate.
   Strait he begins again: *Sir, if you knew*
My worth but half so throughly as I do;   60
I'm sure, you would not value any Friend,
You have, like me: but that I won't commend
My self, and my own Talents; I might tell
How many ways to wonder I excel.
None has a greater gift in Poetry,   65
Or writes more Verses with more ease than I:
I'm grown the envy of the men of Wit,
I kill'd ev'n Rochester *with grief and spight:*
Next for the Dancing part I all surpass,
St. André *never mov'd with such a grace:*   70
And 'tis well known, when e're I sing, or set,
Humphreys, *nor* Blow *could ever match me yet.*
   Here I got room to interrupt: *"Have you*
"A Mother, Sir, or Kindred living now?
Not one: they are all dead. "Troth, so I guest: 75
"The happier they (said I) *who are at rest.*

70 André] *Ed.* (*1854*); Andrew *1681*

"Poor I am only left unmurder'd yet:
"Hast, I beseech you, and dispatch me quite:
"For I am well convinc'd, my time is come:
"When I was young, a Gypsie told my doom: 80
This Lad (said she, and look'd upon my hand)
Shall not by Sword, or Poison come to's end,
Nor by the Fever, Dropsie, Gout, or Stone,
But he shall die by an eternal Tongue:
Therefore, when he's grown up, if he be wise,   85
Let him avoid great Talkers, I advise.

By this time we were got to *Westminster,*
Where he by chance a Trial had to hear,
And, if he were not there, his Cause must fall:
Sir, if you love me, step into the Hall   90
For one half hour. "The Devil take me now,
"(Said I) *if I know any thing of Law:*
"Besides I told you whither I'm to go.
Hereat he made a stand, pull'd down his Hat
Over his eyes, and mus'd in deep debate: 95
I'm in a straight (said he) *what I shall do:*
"Whether forsake my business, Sir, or you.
"Me by all means (say I). *No* (says my Sot)
I fear you'l take it ill, if I should do't:
I'm sure, you will. "Not I, by all that's good.   100
"But I've more breeding, than to be so rude.
"Pray, don't neglect your own concerns for me:
"Your Cause, good Sir! My Cause be damn'd (says he)
I value't less than your dear Company.
With this he came up to me, and would lead   105
The way; I sneaking after hung my head.

Next he begins to plague me with the *Plot,*
Asks, whether I were known to *Oats* or not?
"Not I, 'thank Heaven! I no Priest have been:
"Have never Doway *nor* St. Omers *seen.*   110
What think you, Sir? will they Fitz-Harris *try?*
Will he die, think you? "Yes, *most certainly.*
I mean, be hang'd. "Would thou wert so (wish'd I).
Religion came in next; tho he'd no more
Than the *French* King, his Punk, or Confessor.   115

Oh! the sad times, if once the King should die!
Sir, are you not afraid of Popery?
"No more than my Superiors: why should I?
"I've no Estate in Abby-Lands to lose.
But Fire and Faggot, Sir, how like you those?   120
"Come Inquisition, *any thing* (thought I)
"So Heav'n would bless me to get rid of thee:
"But 'tis some comfort, that my Hell is here:
"I need no punishment hereafter fear.

  Scarce had I thought, but he falls on anew   125
How stands it, Sir, betwixt his Grace, and you?
"Sir, he's a man of sense above the Crowd,
"And shuns the Converse of a Multitude.
Ay, Sir, (says he) *you're happy, who are near*
His Grace, and have the favour of his ear: 130
But let me tell you, if you'l recommend
This person here, your point will soon be gain'd.
Gad, Sir, I'll die, if my own single Wit
Don't Fob his Minions, and displace 'em quite,
And make your self his only Favourite.   135
"No, you are out abundantly (said I)
"We live not, as you think: no Family
"Throughout the whole three Kingdoms is more free
"From those ill Customs, which are us'd to swarm
"In great mens houses; none e're does me harm,   140
"Because more Learned, or more rich, than I:
"But each man keeps his Place, and his Degree.
'Tis mighty strange (says he) *what you relate,*
"But nothing truer, take my word for that.
You make me long to be admitted too   145
Amongst his Creatures: Sir, I beg, that you
Will stand my Friend: Your Interest is such,
You may prevail, I'm sure, you can do much.
He's one, that may be won upon, I've heard,
Tho at the first approach access be hard.   150
I'll spare no trouble of my own, or Friends,
No cost in Fees and Bribes to gain my ends:
I'll seek all opportunities to meet
With him, accost him in the very street:

Hang on his Coach, and wait upon him home,   155
Fawn, Scrape and Cringe to him, nay to his Groom.
Faith, Sir, this must be done, if we'll be great:
Preferment comes not at a cheaper rate.
    While at this Savage rate he worried me;
By chance a Doctor, my dear Friend came by,   160
That knew the Fellow's humor passing well:
Glad of the sight, I joyn him; we stand still:
Whence came you, Sir? and whither go you now?
And such like questions past betwixt us two:
Strait I begin to pull him by the sleeve,   165
Nod, wink upon him, touch my Nose, and give
A thousand hints, to let him know, that I
Needed his help for my delivery:
He, naughty Wag, with an arch fleering smile
Seems ignorant of what I mean the while: 170
I grow stark wild with rage. *"Sir, said not you,*
"You'd somewhat to discourse, not long ago,
"With me in private? I remember't well:
Some other time, be sure, I will not fail:
Now I am in great hast upon my word: 175
A Messenger came for me from a Lord,
That's in a bad condition, like to die.
"Oh! Sir, he can't be in a worse, than I:
"Therefore for Gods sake do not stir from hence.
Sweet Sir! your pardon: 'tis of consequence: 180
I hope you're kinder than to press my stay,
Which may be Heav'n knows what out of my way.
This said, he left me to my murderer:
Seeing no hopes of my relief appear;
"Confounded be the Stars (said I) *that sway'd*   185
"This fatal day! would I had kept my Bed
"With sickness, rather than been visited
"With this worse Plague! what ill have I e're done
"To pull this curse, this heavy Judgment down?
    While I was thus lamenting my ill hap,   190
Comes aid at length: a brace of Bailiffs clap
The Rascal on the back: *"Here take your Fees,*
"Kind Gentlemen (said I) *for my release.*

He would have had me Bail. *"Excuse me, Sir,*
"I've made a Vow ne're to be surety more:
"My Father was undone by't heretofore.   195
  Thus I got off, and blest the Fates that he
  Was Pris'ner made, I set at liberty.

Paraphrase upon
H O R A C E .

B O O K   I .   O D E   XXXI.

Quid dedicatum poscit Apollinem
Vates? &c. ——

_____

I
  What does the Poet's modest Wish require?
  What Boon does he of gracious Heav'n desire?
  Not the large Crops of *Esham*'s goodly Soil,
  Which tire the Mower's and the Reaper's toil:
  Not the soft Flocks, on hilly *Cotswold* fed,   5
  Nor *Lemster* Fields with living Fleeces clad:
  He does not ask the Grounds, where gentle *Thames*,
      Or *Seavern* spread their fat'ning Streams.
    Where they with wanton windings play,
And eat their widen'd Banks insensibly away: 10
    He does not ask the Wealth of *Lombard-street*,
    Which Consciences and Souls are pawn'd to get.
      Nor those exhaustless Mines of Gold,
Which *Guinny* and *Peru* in their rich bosoms hold.

2
  Let those that live in the *Canary* Isles,   15
  On which indulgent Nature ever smiles,
  Take pleasure in their plenteous Vintages,

And from the juicy Grape its racy Liquor press:
        Let wealthy Merchants, when they Dine,
        Run o're their costly names of Wine,   20
    Their Chests of *Florence*, and their *Mont-Alchine.*
    Their *Mants, Champagns, Chablees, Frontiniacks* tell,
    Their Aums of *Hock*, of *Backrag* and *Moselle:*
        He envies not their Luxury
    Which they with so much pains and danger buy: 25
    For which so many Storms and Wrecks they bear,
    For which they pass the *Streights* so oft each year,
And scape so narrowly the Bondage of *Argier.*

                            3

    He wants no *Cyprus* Birds, nor *Ortolans*,
    Nor Dainties fetch'd from far to please his Sence,   30
    Cheap wholsom Herbs content his frugal Board,
        The Food of unfaln Innocence,
    Which the mean'st Village Garden does afford:
    Grant him, kind Heav'n, the sum of his desires,
    What Nature, not what Luxury requires: 35
    He only does a Competency claim,
    And, when he has it, wit to use the same:
    Grant him sound Health, impair'd by no Disease,
        Nor by his own Excess:
    Let him in strength of Mind and Body live,   40
    But not his Reason, nor his Sense survive:
    His Age (if Age he e're must live to see)
    Let it from want, Contempt, and Care be free,
But not from Mirth, and the delights of Poetry.
    Grant him but this, he's amply satisfi'd,   45
And scorns whatever Fate can give beside.

        22 *Mants,*] *1681*; *Nants (1697)*

120

Paraphrase upon
H O R A C E .

B O O K   II.   O D E   XIV.

Eheu fugaces, Posthume, Posthume,
Labuntur anni, &c. ———

1.

Alas! dear Friend, alas! time hasts away,
Nor is it in our pow'r to bribe its stay:
The rolling years with constant motion run,
Lo! while I speak, the present minute's gone,
And following hours urge the foregoing on.   5
          'Tis not thy Wealth, 'tis not thy Power,
     'Tis not thy Piety can thee secure:
          They're all too feeble to withstand
Grey Hairs, approaching Age, and thy avoidless end.
          When once thy fatal Glass is run,   10
          When once thy utmost Thred is spun,
     'Twill then be fruitless to expect Reprieve:
          Could'st thou ten thousand Kingdoms give
     In purchase for each hour of longer life,
          They would not buy one gasp of breath,   15
     Not move one jot inexorable Death.

2.

All the vast stock of humane Progeny,
          Which now like swarms of Insects crawl
     Upon the Surface of Earth's spacious Ball,
Must quit this Hillock of Mortality,   20
          And in its Bowels buried lie.
The mightiest King, and proudest Potentate,
     In spight of all his Pomp, and all his State,
Must pay this necessary Tribute unto Fate.
The busie, restless *Monarch* of the times, which now   25

Keeps such a pother, and so much ado
        To fill Gazettes alive,
And after in some lying Annal to survive;
Ev'n He, ev'n that great mortal Man must die,
And stink, and rot as well as thou, and I,   30
As well as the poor tatter'd wretch, that begs his bread,
And is with Scraps out of the Common Basket fed.

3.

In vain from dangers of the bloody Field we keep,
     In vain we scape
   The sultry *Line*, and stormy *Cape*,   35
  And all the treacheries of the faithless Deep:
In vain for health to forein Countries we repair,
  And change our *English* for *Mompellier* Air,
  In hope to leave our fears of dying there:
  In vain with costly far-fetch'd Drugs we strive   40
  To keep the wasting vital Lamp alive:
  In vain on Doctors feeble Art rely;
Against resistless Death there is no remedy:
  Both we, and they for all their skill must die,
And fill alike the Bedrols of Mortality.   45

4.

  Thou must, thou must resign to Fate, my Friend,
And leave thy House, thy Wife, and Family behind:
  Thou must thy fair and goodly Mannors leave,
  Of these thy Trees thou shalt not with thee take,
  Save just as much as will thy Coffin make: 50
Nor wilt thou be allow'd of all thy Land, to have,
  But the small pittance of a six-foot Grave.
    Then shall thy prodigal young Heir
  Lavish the Wealth, which thou for many a year
  Hast hoarded up with so much pains and care: 55

Then shall he drain thy Cellars of their Stores,
Kept sacred now as Vaults of buried Ancestors:
   Shall set th'enlarged Butts at liberty,
   Which there close Pris'ners under durance lie,
   And wash these stately Floors with better Wine   60
Than that of consecrated Prelates when they dine.

The PRAISE of
H O M E R .
_____

O D E .
_____

1.

Hail God of Verse! pardon that thus I take in vain
      Thy sacred, everlasting Name,
      And in unhallow'd Lines blaspheme:
Pardon that with strange Fire thy Altars I profane.
Hail thou! to whom we mortal Bards our Faith submit.   5
Whom we acknowledg our sole Text, and holy Writ:
    None other Judg infallible we own,
But Thee, who art the Canon of authentick Wit alone.
    Thou art the unexhausted Ocean, whence
Sprung first, and still do flow th'eternal Rills of sence: 10
    To none but Thee our Art Divine we owe,
From whom it had its Rise, and full Perfection too.
Thou art the mighty Bank, that ever do'st supply
Throughout the world the whole Poetick Company:
    With thy vast stock alone they traffick for a name,   15
And send their glorious Ventures out to all the Coasts of Fame.

2

   How trulier blind was dull Antiquity,
   Who fasten'd that unjust Reproach on Thee?

        Who can the sensless Tale believe?
      Who can to the false Legend credit give?   20
Or think thou wantedst sight, by whom all others see?
      What Land, or Region, how remote so e're,
Does not so well describ'd in thy great Draughts appear,
      That each thy native Country seems to be,
And each t'have been survey'd and measur'd out by Thee?   25
Whatever Earth does in her pregnant Bowels bear,
            Or on her fruitful Surface wear;
      What e're the spacious Fields of Air contain,
Or far extended Territories of the Main;
Is by thy skilful Pencil so exactly shown,   30
We scarce discern where Thou, or Nature best has drawn.
            Nor is thy quick all-piercing Eye
                  Or check'd, or bounded here;
But farther does surpass, and farther does descry:
      Beyond the Travels of the Sun and Year,   35
Beyond this glorious Scene of starry Tapestry,
            Where the vast Purliews of the Sky,
            And boundless wast of Nature lies,
Thy Voyages thou mak'st, and bold Discoveries.
      What there the Gods in Parliament debate,   40
      What Votes, or Acts i'th'Heav'nly Houses pass,
      By Thee so well communicated was;
      As if thou'dst been of that Cabal of State,
As if Thou hadst been sworn the Privy-Counsellor of Fate.

                        3.

What Chief, who does thy Warrior's great Exploits survey,   45
      Will not aspire to Deeds as great as they?
      What generous Readers would he not inspire
With the same gallant Heat, the same ambitious Fire?
Methinks from *Ida*'s top with noble Joy I view
The warlike Squadrons by his daring Conduct led,   50
I see th'immortal Host engaging on his side,
            And him the blushing Gods out-do.
      Where e're he does his dreadful Standards bear,
Horror stalks in the Van, and Slaughter in the Rere.
      Whole Swarths of Enemies his Sword does mow,   55

And Limbs of mangled Chiefs his passage strow,
And Floods of reeking Gore the Field o're-flow:
While Heaven's dread Monarch from his Throne of State,
With high concern upon the Fight looks down,
And wrinkles his majestick Brow into a Frown,   60
To see bold Man, like him, distribute Fate.

4.

While the great *Macedonian* Youth in Non-age grew,
Not yet by Charter of his years set free
From Guardians, and their slavish tyranny,
No Tutor, but the Budg Philosophers he knew: 65
And well enough the grave and useful Tools
Might serve to read him Lectures, and to please
With unintelligible Jargon of the Schools,
And airy Terms and Notions of the Colleges:
They might the Art of Prating and of Brawling teach,   70
And some insipid Homilies of Vertue preach:
But when the mighty Pupil had outgrown
Their musty Discipline, when manlier Thoughts possest
His generous Princely Breast,
Now ripe for Empire, and a Crown,   75
And fill'd with lust of Honor and Renown;
He then learnt to contemn
The despicable things, the men of Flegm:
Strait he, to the dull Pedants gave release,
And a more noble Master strait took place: 80
Thou, who the *Grecian* Warriour so could'st praise,
As might in him just envy raise,
Who (one would think) had been himself too high
To envy any thing of all Mortality,
'Twas thou that taughtst him Lessons loftier far,   85
The Art of Reigning, and the Art of War:
And wondrous was the Progress, which he made,
While he the Acts of thy great Pattern read:
The world too narrow for his boundless Conquests grew,
He Conquer'd one, and wish'd and wept for new: 90
From thence he did those Miracles produce,
And Fought and Vanquish'd by the Conduct of a Muse.

                              5.

No wonder rival Nations quarrel'd for thy Birth,
     A Prize of greater and of higher worth
     Than that which led whole *Greece* and *Asia* forth,   95
     Than that, for which thy mighty Hero fought,
And *Troy* with ten years War, and its Destruction bought.
Well did they think it noble to have bore that Name,
Which the whole world would with ambition claim:
                              Well did they Temples raise   100
To Thee, at whom Nature her self stood in amaze,
     A work, she never tried to mend, nor cou'd,
In which mistaking Man, by chance she form'd a God.
     How gladly would our willing *Isle* resign
Her fabulous *Arthur*, and her boasted *Constantine*,   105
     And half her Worthies of the *Norman* Line,
     And quit the honor of their Births to be ensur'd to Thine?
     How justly might it the wise choice approve,
Prouder in this than *Crete* to have brought forth Almighty *Jove*?

                              6

     Unhappy we, thy *British* Off-spring here,   110
Who strive by thy great Model Monuments to rear:
     In vain for worthless Fame we toil,
That's pent in the strait limits of a narrow *Isle*:
     In vain our Force and Art we spend
     With noble labors to enrich our Land,   115
Which none beyond our Shores vouchsafe to understand.
     Be the fair structure ne'r so well design'd,
     The parts with ne'r so much proportion joyn'd;
Yet forein Bards (such is their Pride, or Prejudice)
All the choice Workmanship for the Materials sake despise.   120
     But happier thou thy Genius didst dispence
     In Language universal as thy sence:
All the rich Bullion, which thy Sovereign Stamp does wear
On every Coast of Wit does equal value bear,
     Allow'd by all, and currant every where.   125
     No Nation yet has been so barbarous found,

                    96 Than] *E*; That's *1681*

Where thy transcendent Worth was not renown'd.
Throughout the World thou art with Wonder read,
Where ever Learning does its Commerce spread,
Where ever Fame with all her Tongues can speak,   130
Where ever the bright God of Wit does his vast Journies take.

7

Happy above Mankind that envied Name,
Which Fate ordain'd to be thy glorious Theme:
What greater Gift could bounteous Heaven bestow
          On its chief Favourite below?   135
What nobler Trophy could his high Deserts befit,
Than these thy vast erected Pyramids of Wit?
          Not Statues cast in solid Brass,
Nor those, which Art in breathing Marble does express,
    Can boast an equal Life, or lastingness   140
    With their well-polish'd Images, which claim
A Nich in thy majestick Monuments of Fame.
Here their embalm'd incorruptible memories
Can proudest *Louvres* and *Escurials* despise,
And all the needless helps of *Egypts* costly Vanities.   145
    No Blasts of Heaven, or Ruin of the Spheres,
    Not all the washing Tides of rolling years,
Nor the whole Race of batt'ring time shall e're wear out
    The great Inscriptions, which thy Hand has wrought.
Here thou and they shall live, and bear an endless date,   150
Firm, as enroll'd in the eternal Register of Fate.
    For ever curst be that mad *Emperor*,
          (And curst enough he is be sure)
    May future Poets on his hated Name
    Shed all their Gall, and foulest Infamy,   155
And may it here stand branded with eternal shame,
          Who thought thy Works could mortal be,
And sought the glorious Fabrick to destroy:
    In this (could Fate permit it to be done)
    His damned *Successor* he had out-gone,   160
Who *Rome* and all its Palaces in Ashes laid,
And the great Ruins with a Savage Joy survey'd:
He burnt but what might be re-built and richer made.

But had the impious Wish succeeded here,
  'T had raz'd what Age, nor Art could e're repair.   165
        Not that vast universal Flame,
          Which at the final Doom
  This beauteous Work of Nature must consume,
And Heav'n and all its Glories in one Urn entomb,
  Will burn a nobler, or more lasting Frame: 170
  As firm and strong as that it shall endure,
     Through all the Injuries of Time secure,
Nor die, till the whole world its Funeral Pile become.

Two Pastorals out of the Greek.

B I O N .

A Pastoral, in Imitation of the Greek
of Moschus, *bewailing the Death*
of the Earl of ROCHESTER.

Mourn all ye Groves, in darker shades be seen,
Let Groans be heard, where gentle Winds have been:
Ye *Albion* Rivers, weep your Fountains dry,
And all ye Plants, your moisture spend, and die:
Ye melancholy Flowers, which once were Men,   5
Lament, until you be transform'd agen:
Let every Rose pale as the Lilly be,
And Winter Frost seize the Anemone:
But thou, O *Hyacinth*, more vigorous grow
In mournful Letters thy sad glory show,   10
Enlarge thy grief, and flourish in thy wo:
For *Bion*, the beloved *Bion*'s dead,
His voice is gone, his tuneful breath is fled.

Come all ye Muses, *come, adorn the Shepherd's Herse*
With never-fading Garlands, never-dying Verse.   15
Mourn ye sweet Nightingales in the thick Woods,
Tell the sad news to all the *British* Floods:
See it to *Isis*, and to *Cham* convey'd,
To *Thames*, to *Humber*, and to utmost *Tweed*:
And bid them waft the bitter tidings on,   20
How *Bion*'s dead, how the lov'd Swain is gone,
And with him all the Art of graceful Song.
   Come all ye Muses, *come, adorn the Shepherd's Herse*
   With never-fading Garlands, never-dying Verse.
Ye gentle Swans, that haunt the Brooks and Springs,   25
Pine with sad grief, and droop your sickly Wings:
In doleful notes the heavy loss bewail,
Such as you sing at your own Funeral,
Such as you sung, when your lov'd *Orpheus* fell.
Tell it to all the Rivers, Hills, and Plains,   30
Tell it to all the *British* Nymphs and Swains,
And bid them too the dismal tydings spread
Of *Bion*'s fate, of *England*'s *Orpheus* dead,
   Come all ye Muses, *come, adorn the Shepherd's Herse,*
   With never-fading Garlands, never-dying Verse.   35
No more, alas! no more that lovely Swain
Charms with his tuneful Pipe the wondring Plain:
Ceast are those lays, ceast are those sprightly airs,
That woo'd our Souls into our ravisht Ears:
For which the list'ning streams forgot to run,   40
And Trees lean'd their attentive branches down:
While the glad Hills, loth the sweet sounds to lose,
Lengthen'd in Echoes every heav'nly close.
Down to the melancholy Shades he's gone,
And there to *Lethe*'s Banks reports his moan: 45
Nothing is heard upon the Mountains now
But pensive Herds that for their Master low:
Straggling and comfortless about they rove,
Unmindful of their Pasture, and their Love.
   Come all ye Muses, *come, adorn the Shepherd's Herse,*   50

23 *all ye*] Ed. (*1684a*); *ye all 1681*

With never-fading Garlands, never-dying Verse.
For thee, dear Swain, for thee, his much-lov'd Son,
Does *Phœbus* Clouds of mourning black put on:
For thee the *Satyrs* and the rustick *Fauns*
Sigh and lament through all the Woods and Lawns: 55
For thee the *Fairies* grieve, and cease to dance
In sportful Rings by night upon the Plains:
The water *Nymphs* alike thy absence mourn,
And all their Springs to tears and sorrow turn:
Sad *Echo* too does in deep silence moan,   60
Since thou art mute, since thou art speechless grown:
She finds nought worth her pains to imitate,
Now thy sweet breath's stopt by untimely fate:
Trees drop their Leaves to dress thy Funeral,
And all their Fruit before its *Autumn* fall: 65
Each Flower fades, and hangs its wither'd head,
And scorns to thrive, or live, now thou art dead:
The bleating Flocks no more their Udders fill,
The painful Bees neglect their wonted toil:
Alas! what boots it now their Hives to store   ⎫   70
With the rich spoils of every plunder'd Flower,   ⎬
When thou, that wast all sweetness, art no more?   ⎭
    Come all ye Muses, *come, adorn the Shepherd's Herse*
    With never-fading Garlands, never-dying Verse.
Ne're did the Dolphins on the lonely Shore   75
In such loud plaints utter their grief before:
Never in such sad Notes did *Philomel*
To the relenting Rocks her sorrow tell:
Ne'r on the Beach did poor *Alcyone*
So weep, when she her floating Lover saw: 80
Nor that dead Lover, to a Sea-fowl turn'd,
Upon those Waves, where he was drown'd, so mourn'd:
Nor did the Bird of *Memnon* with such grief
Bedew those Ashes, which late gave him life:
As they did now with vying grief bewail,   85
As they did all lament dear *Bion*'s fall.
    Come all ye Muses, *come, adorn the Shepherd's Herse*
    With never-fading Garlands, never-dying Verse.
In every Wood, on every Tree and Bush

The Lark, the Linnet, Nightingale, and Thrush,   90
And all the feather'd Choire, that us'd to throng
In listning Flocks to learn his well-tun'd Song,
Now each in the sad Consort bear a part,
And with kind Notes repay their Teachers Art:
Ye Turtles too (I charge you) here assist,   95
Let not your murmurs in the crowd be mist:
To the dear Swain do not ungrateful prove,
That taught you how to sing, and how to love.
    Come all ye Muses, *come, adorn the Shepherd's Herse*
    With never-fading Garlands, never-dying Verse.   100
Whom hast thou left behind thee, skilful Swain,
That dares aspire to reach thy matchless strain?
Who is there after thee, that dares pretend
Rashly to take thy warbling Pipe in hand?
Thy Notes remain yet fresh in every ear,   105
And give us all delight, and all despair:
Pleas'd *Echo* still does on them meditate,
And to the whistling Reeds their sounds repeat.
Pan only ere can equal thee in Song,
That task does only to great *Pan* belong: 110
But *Pan* himself perhaps will fear to try,
Will fear perhaps to be out-done by thee.
    Come all ye Muses, *come, adorn the Shepherd's Herse*
    With never-fading Garlands, never-dying Verse.
Fair *Galatea* too laments thy death,   115
Laments the ceasing of thy tuneful breath:
Oft she, kind Nymph, resorted heretofore
To hear thy artful measures from the shore:
Not harsh like the rude *Cyclops* were thy lays,
Whose grating sounds did her soft ears displease: 120
Such was the force of thy enchanting tongue,
That she for ever could have heard thy Song,
And chid the hours, that did so swiftly run,
And thought the Sun too hasty to go down,
Now does that lovely *Nereid* for thy sake   125
The Sea, and all her fellow Nymphs forsake:
Pensive upon the Beach, she sits alone,
And kindly tends the Flocks from which thou'rt gone.

Come all ye Muses, *come, adorn the Shepherd's Herse,*
    With never-fading Garlands, never-dying Verse.   130
With thee, sweet *Bion*, all the grace of Song,
And all the *Muses* boasted Art is gone:
Mute is thy Voice, which could all hearts command,
Whose pow'r no Sheperdess could e're withstand:
All the soft weeping *Loves* about thee moan,   135
At once their Mothers darling, and their own:
Dearer wast thou to *Venus* than her *Loves*,
Than her charm'd Girdle, than her faithful Doves,
Than the last gasping Kisses, which in death
Adonis gave, and with them gave his breath.   140
This, *Thames*, ah! this is now the second loss,
For which in tears thy weeping Current flows:
Spencer, the Muses glory, went before,
He past long since to the *Elysian* shore:
For him (they say) for him, thy dear-lov'd Son,   ⎫   145
Thy Waves did long in sobbing murmurs groan,   ⎬
Long fill'd the Sea with their complaint, and moan: ⎭
But now, alas! thou do'st afresh bewail,
Another Son does now thy sorrow call:
To part with either thou alike wast loth,   150
Both dear to thee, dear to the fountains both:
He largely drank the rills of sacred *Cham*,
And this no less of *Isis* nobler stream:
He sung of Hero's, and of hardy Knights
Far-fam'd in Battles, and renown'd Exploits: 155
This meddled not with bloody Fights, and Wars, ⎫
Pan was his Song, and Shepherds harmless jars, ⎬
Loves peaceful combats, and its gentle cares.   ⎭
Love ever was the subject of his lays,
And his soft lays did *Venus* ever please.   160
    Come, all ye Muses, *come, adorn the Shepherd's Herse*
    With never-fading Garlands, never-dying Verse.
Thou, sacred *Bion*, art lamented more
Than all our tuneful Bards, that dy'd before:
Old *Chaucer*, who first taught the use of Verse,   165
No longer has the tribute of our tears:
Milton, whose Muse with such a daring flight

Led out the warring *Seraphims* to fight:
Blest *Cowley* too, who on the banks of *Cham*
So sweetly sigh'd his wrongs, and told his flame: 170
And *He*, whose Song rais'd *Cooper*'s Hill so high,
As made its glory with *Parnassus* vie:
And soft *Orinda*, whose bright shining name
Stands next great *Sappho*'s in the ranks of fame:
All now unwept and unrelented pass,   175
And in our grief no longer share a place:
Bion alone does all our tears engross,
Our tears are all too few for *Bion*'s loss.
     Come all ye Muses, *come, adorn the Shepherd's Herse*
     With never-fading Garlands, never-dying Verse.   180
Thee all the Herdsmen mourn in gentlest lays,
And rival one another in thy praise:
In spreading Letters they engrave thy Name
On every Bark, that's worthy of the same:
Thy Name is warbled forth by every tongue,   185
Thy Name the Burthen of each Shepherd's Song:
Waller, the sweet'st of living Bards, prepares
For thee his tender'st, and his mournful'st airs:
And I, the meanest of the British Swains,
Amongst the rest offer these humble strains: 190
If I am reckon'd not unblest in Song,
'Tis what I ow to thy all-teaching tongue:
Some of thy Art, some of thy tuneful breath
Thou didst by Will to worthless me bequeath:
Others thy Flocks, thy Lands, thy Riches have,   195
To me thou didst thy Pipe and Skill vouchsafe.
     Come all ye Muses, *come, adorn the Shepherd's Herse,*
     With never-fading Garlands, never-dying Verse.
Alas! by what ill Fate, to man unkind,
Were we to so severe a lot design'd?   200
The meanest Flowers which the Gardens yield,
The vilest Weeds, that flourish in the Field,
Which must ere long lie dead in Winter's Snow,
Shall spring again, again more vigorous grow:
Yon Sun, and this bright glory of the day,   205
Which night is hasting now to snatch away,

Shall rise anew more shining and more gay: 」
But wretched we must harder measure find,
The great'st, the brav'st, the witti'st of mankind,
When Death has once put out their light, in vain   210
Ever expect the dawn of Life again:
In the dark Grave insensible they lie,
And there sleep out endless eternity.
There thou to silence ever art confin'd,
While less deserving Swains are left behind: 215
So please the Fates to deal with us below,
They cull out thee, and let dull *Maevius* go:
Maevius still lives; still let him live for me,
He, and his Pipe shall ne'r my envy be:
None ere that heard thy sweet, thy artful tongue,   220
Will grate their ears with his rough untun'd Song.
     Come, all ye Muses, *come, adorn the Shepherd's Herse*
     With never-fading Garlands, never-dying Verse.
A fierce Disease, sent by ungentle Death,
Snatch'd *Bion* hence, and stop'd his hallow'd breath: 225
A fatal damp put out that heav'nly fire,
That sacred heat which did his breast inspire.
Ah! what malignant ill could boast that pow'r,
Which his sweet voice's magick could not cure?
Ah cruel Fate! how couldst thou chuse but spare?   230
How couldst thou exercise thy rigor here?
Would thou hadst thrown thy Dart at worthless me,
And let this dear, this valued life go free:
Better ten thousand meaner Swains had dy'd,
Than this best work of Nature been destroy'd.   235
     Come, all ye Muses, *come, adorn the Shepherd's Herse*
     With never-fading Garlands, never-dying Verse.
Ah! would kind Death alike had sent me hence;
But Grief shall do the work, and save its pains:
Grief shall accomplish my desired doom,   240
And soon dispatch me to *Elysium*:
There, *Bion*, would I be, there gladly know,
How with thy voice thou charm'st the shades below.
Sing, Shepherd, sing one of thy strains divine,
Such as may melt the fierce *Elysian* Queen: 245

She once her self was pleas'd with tuneful strains,
And sung and danc'd on the *Sicilian* Plains:
Fear not, thy Song should unsuccessful prove,
Fear not, but 'twill the pitying Goddess move:
She once was won by *Orpheus* heav'nly lays,   250
And gave his fair *Eurydice* release.
And thine as pow'rful (question not, dear Swain)
Shall bring thee back to these glad Hills again.
    Ev'n I my self, did I at all excel,
    Would try the utmost of my voice and skill,   255
    Would try to move the rigid King of Hell.

The   Lamentation   for
A D O N I S .

Imitated out of the *Greek* of *Bion*
of *Smyrna.*

P A S T O R A L .

I mourn *Adonis*, fair *Adonis* dead,
He's dead, and all that's lovely, with him fled:
    Come all ye Loves, come hither and bemoan
    The charming sweet *Adonis* dead and gone:
Rise from thy Purple Bed, and rich Alcove,   5
Throw off thy gay attire, great Queen of Love:
Henceforth in sad and mournful weeds appear,
And all the marks of grief and sorrow wear,
And tear thy locks, and beat thy panting breast,
And cry, *My dear* Adonis *is deceast.*   10
    I mourn *Adonis*, the soft Loves bemoan
    The gentle sweet *Adonis* dead and gone.

On the cold Mountain lies the wretched Youth,
Kill'd by a Savage Boar's unpitying tooth:
In his white thigh the fatal stroke is found,   15
Not whiter was that tooth, that gave the wound:
From the wide wound fast flows the streaming gore,
And stains that skin which was all snow before:
His breath with quick short tremblings comes and goes,
And Death his fainting eyes begins to close: 20
From his pale lips the ruddy colour's fled,
Fled, and has left his kisses cold and dead:
Yet *Venus* never will his kisses leave,
The Goddess ever to his lips will cleave:
The kiss of her dear Youth does please her still,   25
But her poor Youth does not the pleasure feel:
Dead he feels not her love, feels not her grief,
Feels not her kiss, which might ev'n life retrive.
    I mourn *Adonis*, the sad Loves bemoan
    The comely fair *Adonis* dead and gone.   30
Deep in his Thigh, deep went the killing smart,
But deeper far it goes in *Venus* heart:
His faithful Dogs about the Mountain yell,
And the hard fate of their dead Master tell:
The troubled Nymphs alike in doleful strains   35
Proclaim his death through all the Fields and Plains:
But the sad Goddess, most of all forlorn,
With love distracted, and with sorrow torn,
Wild in her look, and ruful in her air,
With garments rent, and with dishevel'd hair,   40
Through Brakes, through Thickets, and through pathless ways,
Through Woods, through Haunts and Dens of Savages,
Undrest, unshod, careless of Honor, Fame,
And Danger, flies, and calls on his lov'd name.
Rude Brambles, as she goes, her body tear,   45
And her cut feet with blood the stones besmear.
She thoughtless of the unfelt smart flies on,
And fills the Woods and Vallies with her moan,

21 colour's] *Ed.* (*1684a*); colours *1681*   29 *Adonis*,] *Ed.* (*1697*); *Adonis*
1681

Loudly does on the Stars and Fates complain,
And prays them give *Adonis* back again: 50
But he, alas; the wretched Youth, alas!
Lies cold and stiff, extended on the grass:
There lies he steep'd in gore, there lies he drown'd
In purple streams, that gush from his own wound.
 All the soft band of Loves their Mother mourn, 55
At once of beauty, and of love forlorn.
Venus has lost her Lover, and each grace,
That sate before in triumph in her face,
By grief chas'd thence, has now forsook the place.
That day which snatch'd *Adonis* from her arms, 60
That day bereft the Goddess of her charms.
 The Woods and Trees in murmuring sighs bemoan
 The fate of her *Adonis* dead and gone.
The Rivers too, as if they would deplore
His death, with grief swell higher than before: 65
The Flowers weep in tears of dreary dew,
And by their drooping heads their sorrow shew:
But most the *Cyprian* Queen with shrieks and groans,
Fills all the neighb'ring Hills, and Vales, and Towns:
The poor Adonis *dead*! is all her cry,   70
Adonis *dead*! sad *Echo* does reply.
 What cruel heart would not the Queen of Love
To melting tears, and soft compassion move,
When she saw how her wretched Lover fell,
Saw his deep wound, saw it incurable?   75
Soon as her eyes his bleeding wound survey'd,
With eager clips she did his limbs invade,
And these soft, tender, mournful things she said:
"Whither, O whither fli'st thou, wretched Boy,
"Stay my *Adonis*, stay my only joy,   80
"O stay, unhappy Youth, at least till I
"With one kind word bespeak thee, ere thou die,
"Till I once more embrace thee, till I seal
"Upon thy dying lips my last farewel.
"Look up one minute, give one parting kiss,   85
"One kiss, dear Youth, to dry these flowing eyes:
"One kiss as thy last legacy I'd fain

"Preserve, no God shall take it off again.
"Kiss, while I watch thy swimming eye-balls roul,
"Watch thy last gasp, and catch thy springing soul.   90
"I'll suck it in, I'll hoard it in my heart,
"I with that sacred pledg will never part.
"But thou wilt part, but thou art gone, far gone
"To the dark shades, and leav'st me here alone.
"Thou dy'st, but hopeless I must suffer life,   95
"Must pine away with easless endless grief.
"Why was I born a Goddess? why was I
"Made such a wretch to want the pow'r to die?
"If I by death my sorrows might redress,
"If the cold Grave could to my pains give ease;   100
"I'd gladly die, I'd rather nothing be
"Than thus condemn'd to immortality:
"In that vast empty void, and boundless wast,
"We mind not what's to come, nor what is past.
"Of life, or death we know no difference,   105
"Nor hopes, nor fears at all affect our sence:
"But those who are of pleasure once bereft,
"And must survive, are most unhappy left:
"To ravenous sorrow they are left a prey,
"Nor can they ever drive despair away.   110
    "Take, cruel *Proserpine*, take my lov'd Boy,
"Rich with my spoils, do thou my loss enjoy.
"Take him relentless Goddess, for thy own,
"Never till now wast thou my envy grown.
"Hard fate! that thus the best of things must be   115
"Always the plunder of the Grave, and thee:
"The Grave, and thou now all my hopes engross,
"And I for ever must *Adonis* lose.
"Thou'rt dead, alas! alas! my Youth, thou'rt dead,
"And with thee all my pleasures too are fled: 120
"They're all like fleeting vanisht dreams past ore, ⎫
"And nought but the remembrance left in store,   ⎬
"Of tasted joys ne're to be tasted more: ⎭
"With thee my *Cestos*, all my charms are gone,   ⎫
"Thy *Venus* must thy absence ever moan,   ⎬   125
"And spend the tedious live-long nights alone.   ⎭

"Ah! heedless Boy, why would'st thou rashly choose
"Thy self to dang'rous pleasures to expose?
"Why would'st thou hunt? why would'st thou any more
"Venture with Dogs to chase the foaming Boar?   130
"Thou wast all fair to mine, to humane eyes,   ·
"But not (alas!) to those wild Savages.
"One would have thought thy sweetness might have charm'd
"The roughest kind, the fiercest rage disarm'd:
"Mine (I am sure) it could; but wo is thee!   135
"All wear not eyes, all wear not breasts like me.
    In such sad words the Dame her grief did vent,
While the wing'd Loves kept time with her complaint:
As many drops of Blood as from the wound
Of slain *Adonis* fell upon the ground,   140
So many tears, and more you might have told,
That down the cheeks of weeping *Venus* roul'd:
Both tears and blood to new-born flow'rs give rise,
Hence Roses spring, and thence Anemones.
    Cease, *Venus*, in the Woods to mourn thy Love,   145
Thou'st vented sighs, thou'st lavisht tears enough:
See! Goddess, where a glorious bed of State
Does ready for thy dear *Adonis* wait:
This bed was once the Scene of Love and Joy,
But now must bear thy wretched, murder'd Boy: 150
There lies he, like a pale and wither'd Flower,
Which some rude hand had cropt before its hour:
Yet smiles and beauties still live in his face,
Which death can never frighten from their place.
There let him lie upon that conscious bed,   155
Where you loves mysteries so oft have tried:
Where you've enjoy'd so many an happy night,
Each lengthen'd into ages of delight.
There let him lie, there heaps of Flowers strow,
Roses and Lilies store upon him throw,   160
And myrtle Garlands lavishly bestow:
Pour Myrrh, and Balm, and costliest Oyntments on,
Flowers are faded, Ointments worthless grown,
Now thy *Adonis*, now thy Youth is gone,
Who was all sweetnesses compriz'd in one.   165

In Purple wrapt, *Adonis* lies in state,
A troop of mourning Loves about him wait:
Each does some mark of their kind sorrow show,
One breaks his Shafts, t'other unstrings his Bow,
A third upon his Quiver wreaks his hate,   170
As the sad causes of his hasty fate:
This plucks his bloody garments off, that brings ⎫
Water in Vessels from the neighb'ring Springs, ⎬
Some wash his Wound, some fan him with their Wings: ⎭
 All equally their Mothers loss bemoan,   175
 All moan for poor *Adonis* dead and gone.
Sad *Hymen* too the fatal loss does mourn, ⎫
His Tapers all to Funeral Tapers turn, ⎬
And all his wither'd Nuptial Garlands burn: ⎭
His gay and airy Songs are heard no more,   180
But mournful Strains, that hopeless love deplore.
Nor do the *Graces* fail to bear a part
With wretched *Venus* in her pain and smart:
The poor Adonis *dead!* by turns they cry,
And strive in grief the Goddess to out-vie.   185
The *Muses* too in softest lays bewail
The hapless Youth, and his fled Soul recal:
But all in vain;——ah! numbers are too weak
To call the lost, the dead *Adonis* back:
Not all the pow'rs of Verse, or charms of Love   190
The deaf remorsless *Proserpine* can move.
 Cease then, sad Queen of Love, thy plaints give o're,
 Till the next year reserve thy grief in store:
 Reserve thy Sighs and tears in store till then,
 Then thou must sigh, then thou must weep agen.   195

170-95 *1681*, *R* (*but see* 191) 191 deaf] *1681*, *R²*; fierce *R¹*

Paraphrase upon the 137. Psalm.

December 22. 1676. at Bedington.

---

(1)

V.1.   Far from our pleasant native Palestine,
Where great Euphrates with a mighty current flows,
And dos in watry limits Babylon confine,
Curst Babylon! the cause and author of our Woes;
          There on the Rivers side   5
          Sate wretched captive We,
And in sad Tears bewail'd our Misery,
Tears, whose vast Store increast the neighb'ring Tide:
We wept, and strait our Griefe before us brought
A thousand distant Objects to our Thought;   10
As oft as we survey'd the gliding Stream,
Lov'd Jordan did our sad Remembrance claim:
As oft as we th' adjoining City view'd,
Dear Sion's razed Walls our Griefe renew'd:
We thought on all the Pleasures of our happy Land,   15
      Late ravish'd by a cruell Conqu'rors hand:
We thought on every piteous, every mournful Thing,
That might Access to our enlarged Sorrows bring.

2.   Deep Silence told the greatness of our Griefe,
Of Griefe too great by Vent to find reliefe: 20
          Our Harps, as mute and dumb as we,
          Hung useless and neglected by,
And now and then a broken String would lend a Sigh,
As if with us they felt a Sympathy,
And mourn'd their own and our Captivity: 25
The gentle River too, as if compassionate grown,
      As 'twould its Natives' Cruelty attone,
      As it pass'd by, in murmurs gave a pittying Groan.

0.1 *upon*] *1681*; on *R*   Psalm.] *1681*; Psalm./Pindarique./*R*   0.2 *R* (10ber ... 76); *not in 1681*   27 Natives'] *Ed.*; Native's *R*; Natives *1681*

(2)

3.   There the proud Conquerors, who gave us Chains,
          Who all our Suff'rings and Misfortunes gave,   30
          Did with rude Insolence our Sorrows brave,
      And with insulting Raillery thus mock'd our Pains:
          Play us (said they) some brisk and airy strain,
          Such as your Ancestors were wont to hear
                  On Shilo's pleasant Plain,   35
      Where all the Virgins met in Dances once a year:
                  Or one of those,
          Which your illustrious David did compose,
                  Whilst he fill'd Israel's happy Throne,
      Great Souldier, Poet, and Musician all in one: 40
          Oft (have we heard) he went with Harp in hand,
                  Captain of all th' harmonious Band,
      And vanquisht all the Quire with's single Skill alone:
4.   Forbid it Heav'n! forbid thou great thrice-hallow'd Name!
                  We should thy sacred Hymns defame,   45
                  Or them with impious Ears profane:
          No, no, Inhuman Slaves, is this a time?
          (Oh cruell and preposterous Demand!)
          When every Joy, and every Smile's a crime,
      A Treason to our poor unhappy native Land?   50
                  Is this a time for sprightly Airs,
          When every Look the Badge of Sorrow wears,
                  And Livery of our Miseries,
      Sad miseries, that call for all our Breath in sighs,
                  And all the Tribute of our Eys,   55
      And moisture of our veins, our very Blood in Tears?
      When nought can claim our Thoughts, Jerusalem, but Thou,
      Nought, but thy sad Destruction, Fall, and Overthrow?

(3)

5.   Oh dearest City! late our Nation's justest Pride!
          Envy of all the wond'ring World beside!   60
      Oh sacred Temple! once th' Almighty's blest Abode!

57 nought can] *1681*; nought, Jerusalem, can *R*   Thoughts, Jerusalem] *1681*
(Thoughts, *Jerusalem*); Thoughts, *R*

Now quite forsaken by our angry God!
      Shall ever distant Time or Place
Your firm Ideas from my Soul deface?
      Shall they not still take up my Brest,   65
As long as that, and Life, and I shall last?
Grant Heav'n (nor shall my Pray'rs the Curse withstand)
      That this my learned skilful Hand,
(Which now o're all the tuneful Strings can boast Command,
Which dos as quick, as ready and unerring prove,   70
As Nature, when it would its Joints or Fingers move)
    Grant it forget its Art and Feeling too,
When I forget to think, to wish, and pray for You:
6.   For ever tied with Dumbness be my Tongue,   74
When it speaks ought that shall not to your Praise belong,
If that be not the constant Subject of my Muse and Song.

(4)

7.   Remember, Heav'n, remember Edom on that day,
      And with like Sufferings their Spite repay,
Who made our Miseries their cruel Mirth and Scorn,
      Who laugh'd to see our flaming City burn, 80
      And wish'd it might to Ashes turn:
      Raze, raze it (was their cursed Cry)
      Raze all its stately Structures down,
And lay its Palaces and Temple level with the Ground,
    Till Sion buried in its dismal Ruins lie,   85
    Forgot alike its Place, its Name, and Memory.
8.   And thou, proud Babylon! just Object of our Hate,
      Thou too shalt feel the sad Reverse of Fate,
      Tho' thou art now exalted high,
      And with thy lofty Head oretopst the Sky, 90
      As if thou wouldst the Powr's above defie;
      Thou (if those Powr's (and sure they will)
                 prove just,
      If my prophetick Griefe can ought foresee)
      Ere long shalt lay that lofty Head in dust,
And Blush in Blood for all thy present Cruelty: 95

73 and pray] *R*; to pray *1681*

How loudly then shall we retort these bitter Taunts!
How gladly to the Musick of thy Fetters dance!

(5)

    A day will come (oh might I see't!) ere long
      That shall revenge our mighty Wrong;
      Then blest, for ever blest be he,   100
      Whoever shall return't on thee,
And grave it deep, and pay't with bloody Usury:
      May neither Aged Groans, nor Infant-Cries
Nor piteous Mother's Tears, nor ravish'd Virgin's Sighs
      Soften thy unrelenting Enemies: 105
Let them, as thou to us, inexorable prove,
      Nor Age, nor Sex their deaf Compassion move:
      Rapes, Murders, Slaughters, Funerals,
And all thou durst attempt within our Sion's Walls,
      Mayst thou endure and more, till joyful   110
Confess thy self outdone in artful Cruelty: [we
      Blest, yea thrice-blessed be that barb'arous
                            Hand
      (Oh Griefe! that I such dire Revenge commend)
      Who tears out Infants from their Mothers Womb,
      And hurls 'em yet unborn unto their Tomb: 115
      Blest he, who plucks 'em from their Parents
                            Arms,
    That Sanctuary from all common Harms;
Who with their Skuls and Bones shall pave thy Streets
                       all ore
And fill thy glutted Channels with their scatter'd
                    Brains and Gore.

9.

101 return't] *R*, *E*; return *1681*   115 'em] *R*; them *1681*   116 'em] *R*;
them *1681*

Paraphrase upon the *HYMN*
of St. AMBROSE

ODE.
Writ Febr. 1680 at Rygate:

1.

To thee, o God, we thy just praises sing,
  To thee we thy great Name rehearse;
We are thy Vassals, and this humble Tribute bring
  To thee, acknowledg'd only Lord and King,
Acknowledg'd sole and soverain Monarch of the Universe.   5
  All parts of this wide Universe adore,
  Eternal Father, thy almighty pow'er:
  The skies and stars, fire, air and earth and sea,
  With all their numerous nameless progeny,
  Confess, and their due homage pay to thee;   10
For why? thou spak'st the word, and mad'st them all from
                      Nothing be.
  To thee all Angels, all thy glorious Court on high,
    Seraph and Cherub, the Nobility,
      And whatsoever Spirits be
      Of lesser Honour, less Degree;   15
        To thee in heav'nly lays
    They sing loud Anthems of immortal praise.
Still holy, holy, holy Lord of hosts, they cry,
    This is their bus'iness, this their sole employ,
And thus they spend their long and blest Eternity.   20

2.

Farther than Nature's utmost Shores and limits stretch
    The streams of thy unbounded Glory reach;
    Beyond the Straits of scanty Time and Place,
  Beyond the ebbs and flows of Matter's narrow seas

0.2 St.] *1681*; S./ R   0.4 R; *not in 1681*

They reach, and fill the Ocean of Eternity and Space.   25
          Infus'd like som vast mighty soul,
    Thou dost inform and actuate this spatious Whole:
    Thy unseen hand dos the well-jointed Frame sustain,
    Which els would to its primitive Nothing shrink again.
          But most thou dost thy Majesty display   30
          In the bright Realms of everlasting day:
    There is thy Residence, there dost thou reign,
          There on a State of dazling lustre sit,
          There shine in robes of pure refined light;
    Where Sun's coarse rays are but a foil and stain, 35
And refuse Stars the sweepings of thy glorious train.

                     3.

    There all thy Family of menial Saints,
    Huge Colonies of blest Inhabitants,
Which Death thro countless ages has transplanted hence,
          Now on thy Throne forever wait   40
And fill the large Retinue of thy heav'nly State.
There reverend Prophets stand, a pompous goodly Show,
Of old thy Envoys extraordinary here,
Who brought thy sacred Embassies of peace and war,
That to th' obedient, this the rebel World below: 45
          By them the mighty Twelve have their abode,
Companions once of the incarnate suff'ring God,
          Partakers now of all his Triumphs there,
          As they on earth did in his miseries share:
          Of Martyrs next a crown'd and glorious Quire,   50
          Illustrious Hero's, who have gain'd
Thro dangers and Red Seas of blood, the Promis'd Land,
And past thro ordeal Flames to the Eternity in fire:
    These all make up the Consort of thy praise,
          To thee they sing, and never cease,   55
    Loud Hymns and Hallelujahs of applause;
An Angel-Laureat dos the sence and strains compose,
    Sence far above the reach of mortal Verse,

    38 Huge] *1681*; Vast *R*   40 forever] *R*; for ever *1681*

Strains far above the reach of mortal Ears,
And all a Muse unglorified can fancy, or rehearse.   60

4.

Nor is this consort only kept above,
Nor is it to the Blest alone confin'd;
But Earth and all thy Faithful here are join'd,
And strive to vy with them in duty and in love,
And, tho they cannot equal notes and measures raise,   65
Strive to return th' imperfect Ecchos of thy praise:
They thro all Nations own thy glorious Name,
And every where the great *Three-One* proclaim,
Thee, Father of the World and Us and Him,
Who must Mankind, whom thou didst make, redeem: 70
Thee, blessed Saviour, the ador'd, true, only Son,
To Man debas'd to rescue Man undon:
And Thee, eternal holy Pow'r,
Who dost by grace exalted Man restore
To all, he lost by the old Fall and Sin before: 75
You blest and glorious Trinity,
Riddle to baffled Knowledge and Philosophy
Which cannot comprehend the mighty Mystery
Of numerous One and the unnumber'd Three.
Vast topless pile of Wonders! at whose sight   80
Reason it self turns giddy with the height,
Above the fluttring pitch of human Wit,
And all but the strong wings of Faith, that Eagles towring flight.

5.

Blest Jesu! how shall we enough adore
Or thy unbounded Love, or thy unbounded Power?   85
Thou art the Prince of Heav'n, thou art th'Almighty's Heir,
Thou art th' eternal Offspring of th' eternal Sire:
Hail thou the World's Redeemer! whom to free
From bonds of Death and endless misery,
Thou thoughtst it no disdain to be   90
Inhabiter in low mortality:
Th' Almighty thought it no disdain
To dwell in the pure Virgin's spotless Womb,

There did the boundless Godhead and whole Heav'n find room,
And a small Point the Circle of Infinity contain.   95
    Hail Ransom of Mankind, all-great, all-good!
      Who didst attone us with thy blood
    Thy self the Off'ring, Altar, Priest and God:
    Thy self didst dy to be our glorious Bail
From Death's Arrests and the eternal flaming Jail: 100
    Thy self thou gav'st th' inestimable price
To purchase and redeem our mortgag'd Heav'n and Happiness.
    Thither, when thy great work on earth had end,
      When Death it self was slain and dead,
    And Hell with all its Powers captive led,   105
    Thou didst again triumphantly ascend:
There dost thou now by thy great Father sit on high,
    With equal glory, equal Majesty,
Joint Ruler of the everlasting Monarchy.

       6.

Again from thence thou shalt with greater triumph come, 110
    When the last Trumpet sounds the general doom:
And (lo!) thou com'st, and (lo!) the direful sound dos make
    Thro Death's vast realm mortality awake:
      And (lo!) they all appear
        At thy dread Bar,   115
And all receive th' unalterable sentence there:
Affrighted Nature trembles at the dismal day,
    And shrinks for fear, and vanishes away:
Both that and Time breath out their last, and now they dy,
And now are swallow'd up and lost in vast Eternity.   120
      Mercy, O mercy, angry God!
Stop, stop thy flaming wrath, too fierce to be withstood,
    And quench it with the deluge of thy Blood,
    Thy pretious blood, which was so freely spilt
    To wash us from the stains of sin and guilt: 125
    O write us with it in the book of Fate
    Amongst thy chosen and predestinate,
Free Denizons of Heav'n, of the immortal State.

    98 Off'ring] *R, E*; Off-spring *1681*

7.

Guide us, O Saviour, guide thy Church below,
Both Way and Star, Compass and Pilot Thou: 130
Do thou this frail and tottring Vessel steer
    Thro Life's tempestuous Ocean here,
    Thro all the tossing Waves of Fear,
    And dang'rous Rocks of black despair:
Safe under thee we shall to the wish'd Haven move   135
And reach the undiscover'd Lands of Bliss above.
    Thus low (behold!) to thy great Name we bow
    And thus we ever wish to grow:
Constant as Time dos thy fixt laws obey,
To thee our Worship and our Thanks we pay;   140
    With these we wake the cheerful light,
    With these we rest and sleep invite,
And thus we spend our breath, and thus we spend our days,
And never cease to sing, and never cease to praise.

8.

While thus each brest and mouth and ear   145
Are filled with thy praise and love and fear,
Let never Sin get room or entrance there.
Vouchsafe, O Lord, thro this and all our days
    To guard us with thy powr'ful grace:
Within our hearts let no usurping Lust be found,   150
    No rebel Passion tumult raise,
    To break thy laws, or break our peace,
But set thy Watch of Angels on the place,
And keep the Tempter still from that forbidden ground.
    Ever, O Lord, to us thy Mercies grant,   155
    Never, O Lord, let us thy Mercies want
Ne're want thy Favour, Bounty, Liberality,
    But let them ever on us be,
Constant as our own hope and trust on thee:
On thee we all our hope and trust repose;   160
    O never leave us to our Foes,
    Never, O Lord, desert our Cause:

142 rest and sleep] *R*; Sleep, and Rest *1681*

Thus aided and upheld by thee,
We'll fear no danger, death, or misery:
Fearless we thus will stand a falling World   165
With crushing ruins all about us hurld,
And face wide gaping Hell and all its slighted Pow'rs defy.

164 or] *R*; nor *1681*

*A Letter from the Country to a Friend
in Town, giving an Account of the
Author's Inclinations to* Poetry.

Written in July, 1678

As to that *Poet* (if so great a one, as he,
May suffer in comparison with me)
When heretofore in *Scythian* exile pent,
To which he by ungrateful *Rome* was sent,
If a kind Paper from his Country came,   5
And wore subscrib'd some known and faithful Name;
That like a pow'rful Cordial, did infuse
New life into his speechless gasping Muse,
And strait his Genius, which before did seem
Bound up in Ice, and frozen as the Clime,   10
By its warm force, and friendly influence thaw'd,
Dissolv'd apace, and in soft numbers flow'd:
Such welcome here, dear Sir, your Letter had
With me shut up in close constraint as bad:
Not eager Lovers, held in long suspence,   15
With warmer Joy, and a more tender sence
Meet those kind Lines, which all their wishes bless,
And Sign and Seal deliver'd Happiness:

0.1-0.4 *1681*; In Answer to Mr. Spencer: *R87*

My grateful Thoughts so throng to get abroad,
They over-run each other in the crowd: 20
To you with hasty flight they take their way,
And hardly for the dress of words will stay.
       Yet pardon, if this only fault I find,
That while you praise too much, you are less kind:
Consider, Sir, 'tis ill and dang'rous thus   25
To over-lay a young and tender Muse:
Praise, the fine Diet, which we're apt to love,
If given to excess, does hurtful prove:
Where it does weak, distemper'd Stomachs meet,
That surfeits, which should nourishment create.   30
Your rich Perfumes such fragrancy dispense,
Their sweetness overcomes and palls my sence:
On my weak head you heap so many Bays,
I sink beneath 'em, quite opprest with Praise,
And a resembling fate with him receive,   ⎫   35
Who in too kind a triumph found his Grave,   ⎬
Smother'd with Garlands, which Applauders gave.   ⎭
       To you these Praises justlier all belong,
By alienating which, your self you wrong:
Whom better can such commendations fit   40
Than you, who so well teach and practise Wit?
Verse, the great boast of drudging Fools, from some,
Nay most of Scriblers with much straining come:
They void 'em dribling, and in pain they write,
As if they had a Strangury of Wit: 45
Your Pen uncall'd they readily obey,
And scorn your Ink should flow so fast as they:
Each strain of yours so easie does appear,   ⎫
Each such a graceful negligence does wear,   ⎬
As shews you have none, and yet want no care.   ⎭   50
None of your serious pains or time they cost,
But what thrown by, you can afford for lost:
If such the fruits of your loose leisure be,
Your careless minutes yield such Poetry;
We guess what proofs your Genius would impart,   55

43 Nay] *Ed.* (*1684a*); May *1681*

Did it employ you, as it does divert:
But happy you, more prudent and more wise,
With better aims have fixt your noble choice.
While silly I all thriving Arts refuse,
And all my hopes, and all my vigor lose,   60
In service on that worst of Jilts, a Muse,
For gainful business court ignoble ease,
And in gay Trifles wast my ill-spent days,
      Little I thought, my dearest Friend, that you
Would thus contribute to my Ruine too: 65
O're-run with filthy Poetry and Rhyme,
The present reigning evil of the time,
I lack'd, and (well I did my self assure)
From your kind hand I should receive a cure:
When (lo!) instead of healing Remedies,   70
You cherish and encourage the Disease:
Inhumane you help the Distemper on,
Which was before but too inveterate grown.
As a kind looker on, who intrest shares,
Tho not in's stake, yet in his hopes and fears,   75
Would to his Friend a pushing Gamester do,
Recal his Elbow when he hasts to throw;
Such a wise course you should have took with me,
A rash and vent'ring fool in Poetry.
Poets are Cullies, whom Rook Fame draws in,   80
And wheadles with deluding hopes to win:
But, when they hit, and most successful are,
They scarce come off with a bare saving share.
      Oft (I remember) did wise Friends dissuade,
And bid me quit the trifling barren Trade.   85
Oft have I tried (Heav'n knows) to mortifie
This vile and wicked lust of Poetry:
But still unconquer'd it remains within,
Fixt as an Habit, or some darling Sin.
In vain I better studies there would sow,   90
Often I've tried, but none will thrive, or grow:
All my best thoughts, when I'd most serious be,
Are never from its foul infection free:

Nay (God forgive me) when I say my Prayers,
I scarce can help polluting them with Verse: 95
That fabulous *Wretch* of old reverst I seem,
Who turn what e're I touch to Dross and Rhyme.
    Oft to divert the wild Caprice, I try ⎫
If Sovereign Wisdom and Philosophy   ⎬
Rightly applied, will give a remedy: ⎭   100
Strait the great *Stagyrite* I take in hand,
Seek Nature and my Self to understand:
Much I reflect on his vast Worth and Fame,
And much my low and groveling aims condemn,
And quarrel, that my ill-pack'd fate should be   105
This vain, this worthless thing call'd Poetry:
But when I find this unregarded Toy
Could his important Thoughts and Pains employ,
By reading there I am but more undone,
And meet that danger, which I went to shun.   110
Oft when ill Humor, Shagrin, Discontent ⎫
Give leisure my wild Follies to resent, ⎬
I thus against my self my Passion vent. ⎭
"Enough, mad rhiming Sot, enough for shame,
"Give o're, and all thy Quills to Tooth-picks damn: 115
"Didst ever thou the Altar rob, or worse,   ⎫
"Kill the Priest there, and Maids Receiving force? ⎬
"What else could merit this so heavy Curse?   ⎭
"The greatest curse, I can, I wish on him,
"(If there be any greater than to rhime)   120
"Who first did of the lewd invention think,
"First made two lines with sounds resembling clink,
"And, swerving from the easie paths of Prose,
"Fetters and Chains did on free Sense impose:
"Curst too be all the fools, who since have went   125
"Misled in steps of that ill President:
"Want be entail'd their lot:—and on I go,
Wreaking my spight on all the jingling Crew:
Scarce the beloved *Cowley* scapes, tho I

94 say] *Ed.* (*1684a*); say say *1681*   128 jingling] *E*; jugling *1681*

Might sooner my own curses fear, than he: 130
And thus resolv'd against the scribling vein,
I deeply swear never to write again.
    But when bad Company and Wine conspire
To kindle and renew the foolish Fire,
Straitways relaps'd, I feel the raving fit   135
Return, and strait I all my Oaths forget:
The Spirit, which I thought cast out before, ⎫
Enters again with stronger force and power, ⎬
Worse than at first, and tyrannizes more.   ⎭
No sober good advice will then prevail,   140
Nor from the raging Frenzy me recal:
Cool Reason's dictates me no more can move
Than men in Drink, in *Bedlam*, or in Love:
Deaf to all means which might most proper seem
Towards my cure, I run stark mad in Rhime: 145
A sad poor haunted wretch, whom nothing less
Than Prayers of the Church can dispossess.
    Sometimes, after a tedious day half spent,
When Fancy long has hunted on cold Scent,
Tir'd in the dull and fruitless chase of Thought,   150
Despairing I grow weary, and give out:
As a dry Lecher pump'd of all my store,
I loath the thing, 'cause I can do't no more:
But, when I once begin to find again,
Recruits of matter in my pregnant Brain,   155
Again more eager I the haunt pursue,
And with fresh vigor the lov'd sport renew:
Tickled with some strange pleasure, which I find,
And think a secresie to all mankind,
I please my self with the vain, false delight,   160
And count none happy, but the Fops that write.
    'Tis endless, Sir, to tell the many ways,
Wherein my poor deluded self I please:
How, when the Fancy lab'ring for a Birth,
With unfelt Throws brings its rude issue forth: 165
How after, when imperfect shapeless Thought
Is by the Judgment into Fashion wrought.
When at first search I traverse o're my mind,

Nought but a dark and empty Void I find:
Some little hints at length, like sparks, break thence,   170
And glimm'ring Thoughts just dawning into sence:
Confus'd a while the mixt Idea's lie,
With nought of mark to be discover'd by,
Like colours undistinguisht in the night,
Till the dusk images, mov'd to the light,   175
Teach the discerning Faculty to chuse,
Which it had best adopt, and which refuse.
Here rougher strokes, touch'd with a careless dash,
Resemble the first sitting of a face:
There finisht draughts in form more full appear,   180
And to their justness ask no further care.
Mean while with inward joy I proud am grown,
To see the work successfully go on:
And prize my self in a creating power,
That could make something, what was nought before.   185
      Sometimes a stiff, unwieldy thought I meet,
Which to my Laws will scarce be made submit:
But, when, after expence of pains and time,
'Tis manag'd well, and taught to yoke in Rhime,
I triumph more, than joyful Warriours wou'd,   190
Had they some stout and hardy Foe subdu'd:
And idly think, less goes to their Command,
That makes arm'd Troops in well-plac'd order stand,
Than to the conduct of my words, when they
March in due ranks, are set in just array.   195
      Sometimes on wings of Thought I seem on high, ⎫
As men in sleep, tho motionless they lie,   ⎬
Fledg'd by a Dream, believe they mount and fly: ⎭
So Witches some enchanted Wand bestride,   ⎫
And think they through the airy Regions ride,   ⎬   200
Where Fancy is both Traveller, Way and Guide: ⎭
Then strait I grow a strange exalted thing,
And equal in conceit, at least a King:
As the poor Drunkard, when Wine stums his brains,
Anointed with that liquor, thinks he reigns.   205
Bewitch'd by these Delusions 'tis I write,
(The tricks some pleasant Devil plays in spight)

And when I'm in the freakish Trance, which I
Fond silly wretch, mistake for Ecstasie,
I find all former Resolutions vain,
And thus recant them, and make new again.   210
    "What was't, I rashly vow'd? shall ever I
"Quit my beloved Mistress, Poetry?
"Thou sweet beguiler of my lonely hours,
"Which thus glide unperceiv'd with silent course:
"Thou gentle Spell, which undisturb'd do'st keep   215
"My Breast, and charm intruding care asleep:
"They say, thou'rt poor and unendow'd, what tho?
"For thee I this vain, worthless world forego:
"Let Wealth and Honor be for Fortunes slaves,
"The Alms of Fools, and prize of crafty Knaves: 220
"To me thou art, what ere th' ambitious crave,
"And all that greedy Misers want, or have:
"In Youth, or Age, in Travel, or at Home,
"Here, or in Town, at *London*, or at *Rome*,
"Rich, or a Beggar, free, or in the Fleet,   225
"What ere my fate is, 'tis my fate to write.
    Thus I have made my shrifted Muse confess,
Her secret Feebles, and her weaknesses:
All her hid Faults she sets expos'd to view,
And hopes a gentle Confessor in you: 230
She hopes an easie pardon for her sin,⎫
Since 'tis but what she is not wilful in, ⎬
Nor yet has scandalous nor open been.⎭
Try if your ghostly counsel can reclaim
The heedless wanton from her guilt and shame: 235
At least be not ungenerous to reproach
That wretched frailty, which you've help'd debauch.
    'Tis now high time to end, for fear I grow
More tedious than old Doaters, when they woo,
Than travel'd Fops, when far-fetch'd lies they prate,   240
Or flatt'ring Poets, when they dedicate.
No dull forgiveness I presume to crave,
Nor vainly for my tiresom length ask leave:
Lest I, as often formal Coxcombs use,
Prolong that very fault, I would excuse: 245

May this the same kind welcome find with you,
As yours did here, and ever shall; Adieu.

Upon a Bookseller, *that expos'd him by*
Printing a Piece of his grosly man-
gled, and faulty.

Christmas 1680 Rygate.

Dull and unthinking! had'st thou none but me
To plague and urge to thine own Infamy?
Had I some tame and sneaking Author bin,
Whose Muse to Love and softness did incline,
Some small Adventurer in Song, that whines   5
Phyllis and *Chloris* out in charming lines
Fit to divert mine Hostess, and mislead
The heart of some poor tawdry Waiting-maid;
Perhaps I might have then forgiven thee,
And thou hadst scap'd from my Resentments free.   10
    But I, whom spleen, and manly rage inspire,
Brook no Affront, at each Offence take fire:
Born to chastise the Vices of the Age,
Which Pulpits dare not, nor the very Stage,
Sworn to lash Knaves of all degrees, and spare   15
None of the kind, however great they are:
Satyr's my only Province and delight,
For whose dear sake alone I've vow'd to write:
For this I seek Occasions, court Abuse,
To shew my Parts, and signalize my Muse: 20
Fond of a quarrel as young Bullies are
To make their mettle and their skill appear.
And didst thou think, I would a Wrong acquit,

0.1 Bookseller,] *R*; Printer *1681*   0.4 *R*; *not in 1681*   6 *Phyllis* and
Chloris] *R*; *Chloris* and *Phyllis 1681*

That touch'd my tenderst part of Honour, Wit?
No Villain, may my Sins ne're pardon'd be   25
By Heav'n it self, if ere I pardon thee.
      Members from breach of Priviledge deterr
By threatning *Topham* and a Messenger:
Scroggs and the Brothers of the Coif oppose
The force and dint, of Statutes and the Laws: 30
Strumpets of *Bilinsgate* redress their wrongs
By the sole Noise and foulness of their Tongues:
And I go always arm'd for my defence,
To punish and revenge an Insolence:
I wear my Pen, as others do their Sword,   35
To each affronting Sot, I meet, the word
Is satisfaction; strait to Thrusts I go
And pointed Satyr runs him thro and thro.
      Perhaps thou hop'dst that thy Obscurity
Should be thy safeguard, and secure thee free: 40
No, Wretch, I mean from thence to fetch thee out,
Like sentenc'd Felons to be drag'd about.
Torn, mangled, and expos'd to scorn and shame
I mean to hang and gibbet up thy Name:
If thou to live in Satyr so much thirst;   )   45
Enjoy thy Wish and Fame, till Envy burst,   }
Renown'd as he, whom banish'd *Ovid* curst,   )
Or he, whom old *Archilochus* so stung
In Verse, that he for shame and madness hung:
Deathless in Infamy do thou so live,   50
And let my Rage like his to Halters drive.
      Thou thoughtst perhaps my Gaul was spent and gone
My Venom drain'd, and I a sensless Drone:
Thou thoughtst I had no Curses left in store,
But to thy sorrow know and find, I've more: 55
More, and more dreadful yet, able to scare
Like Hell, and urge to Daggers and Despair:
Such, thou shalt feel, are still reserv'd by me
To vex and force thee to thy Destiny:
Since thou hast brav'd my Vengeance thus, prepare   60

53 sensless] *1681*; stingless *R*   59 vex] *R²*, *1681* (vex,); plague *R¹*
60 brav'd] *R²*, *1681*; dar'd *R¹*

And tremble from my Pen thy Doom to hear.
  Thou, who with spurious Nonsence durst profane
The genuin Issue of a Poet's brain,
May'st thou hereafter never deal in Verse,
But what hoarse Bellmen in their Walks rehearse,   65
Or *Smithfield* Audience sung on Crickets hears.
Mayst thou print *Howard*, or some duller Ass,
Jordan, or Him, that wrote *Dutch Hudibrass*,
Or next vile Scribler of the House, whose Play
Will scarce for Candles and their Snuffing pay.   70
May you each other curse; thy self undone,
And He the laughing-stock of all the Town.
  Mayst thou ne'er rise to History, but what
Poor *Grubstreet* penny Chronicles relate,
Memoirs of *Tyburn* and the mournful state   75
Of Cutpurses in *Holborn* Cavalcade,
Till thou thy self be the same Subject made.
Compell'd by want, mayst thou print Popery,
For which be the Cart's Arse and Pillory
Turnips and rotten Eggs thy Destiny,   80
Maul'd worse than *Reading*, *Christian*, or *Cellier*,
Till thou dawb'd ore with loathsom filth appear
Like Brat of some vile Drab, in Privy found,
Which there has layn three months in Ordure drown'd.
  The Plague of Poets, Rags and Poverty,   85
Debts, Writs, Arrests, and Serjeants light on thee;
For others bound, mayst thou to Durance go,
Condemn'd to Scraps and begging with a Shoe.
And mayst thou never from the Goal get free,
Till thou swear out thy self by Perjury.   90
Forlorn, abandon'd, pittyless, and poor
As a pawn'd Cullie, or a mortgag'd Whore,
Mayst thou an Halter want for thy redress,
Forc'd to steal hemp to end thy miseries,
And damn thy self to balk the Hangman's Fees: 95
  And may no sawcy Fool have better fate
  That dares pull down the vengeance of my Hate.

92 pawn'd] *1681*; chows'd *R* Cullie] *R²*, *1681* (Cully); Bubble *R¹*

3

POEMS AND TRANSLATIONS

P O E M S ,

AND

Translations.

By the AUTHOR of
The Satyrs upon the Jesuits.

[ORNAMENT]

LONDON:
Printed for *Jos. Hindmarsh*, Bookseller to his Royal
Highness, at the Black Bull in *Cornhil*, 1683.

THE Author of the following Pieces must be excused for their
being huddled out so confusedly. They are Printed just as he
finished them off, and some things there are which he design'd
not ever to expose, but was fain to do it, to keep the Press at
work, when it was once set a going. If it be their Fate to   5
perish, and go the way of all mortal Rhimes, 'tis no great matter in what method they have been plac'd, no more than whether
Ode, Elegy, or *Satyr* have the honor of Wiping first. But if they,
and what he has formerly made Publick, be so happy as to live,
and come forth in an Edition all together; perhaps he may then   10
think them worth the sorting in better Order. By that time belike
he means to have ready a very Sparkish Dedication, if he can but
get himself known to some Great Man, that will give a good parcel of Guinnies for being handsomly flatter'd. Then likewise the
Reader (for his farther comfort) may expect to see him appear   15
with all the Pomp and Trappings of an Author; his Head in the
Front very finely cut, together with the Year of his Age, Commendatory Verses in abundance, and all the Hands of the Poets of
Quorum to confirm his Book, and pass it for Authentick. This at
present is content to come abroad naked, Undedicated, and Un-   20
prefac'd, without one kind Word to shelter it from Censure; and
so let the Criticks take it amongst them.

Written in *October*, 1682

The POET brings himself in, as discoursing with a
Doctor of the University upon the Subject ensuing.

OF all the Creatures in the world that be,
Beast, Fish, or Fowl, that go, or swim, or fly
Throughout the Globe from *London* to *Japan*,
The arrant'st Fool in my opinion's Man.
   What? (strait I'm taken up) *an Ant, a Fly,*   5
A Tiny Mite, which we can hardly see
Without a Perspective, a silly Ass,
Or freakish Ape? Dare you affirm, that these
Have greater sense than Man? Ay, questionless.
Doctor, I find you're shock'd at this discourse: 10
Man is (you cry) *Lord of the Universe*;
For him was this fair frame of Nature made,
And all the Creatures for his use and aid:
To him alone of all the living kind,
Has bounteous Heav'n the reas'ning gift assign'd.   15
True Sir, that Reason ever was his lot,
But thence I argue Man the greater Sot.
   This idle talk, (you say) *and rambling stuff*
May pass in Satyr, and take well enough
With Sceptick Fools, who are dispos'd to jeer   20
At serious things: but you must make't appear
By solid proof. Believe me, Sir, I'll do't:
Take you the Desk, and let's dispute it out.

Then by your favour, tell me first of all,
What 'tis, which you grave Doctors Wisdom call?   25
You answer: *'Tis an evenness of Soul,*
A steddy temper, which no cares controul,
No passions ruffle, nor desires inflame,
Still constant to its self, and still the same,
That does in all its slow Resolves advance,   30
With graver steps, than Benchers, when they dance.
Most true; yet is not this, I dare maintain,
Less us'd by any, than the Fool, call'd Man.
    The wiser Emmet, quoted just before,   ⎫
In Summer time ranges the Fallows o're   ⎬   35
With pains and labour, to lay in his store: ⎭
But when the blust'ring North with ruffling blasts
Saddens the year, and Nature overcasts;
The prudent Insect, hid in privacy,
Enjoys the fruits of his past industry.   40
No Ant of sense was e're so awkard seen,
To drudg in Winter, loiter in the Spring.
    But sillier Man, in his mistaken way,
By Reason, his false guide, is led astray:
Tost by a thousand gusts of wavering doubt,   45
His restless mind still rolls from thought to thought:
In each resolve unsteddy and unfixt,
And what he one day loaths, desires the next.
    Shall I, so fam'd for many a tuant jest
On wiving, now go take a jilt at last?   50
Shall I turn Husband, and my station choose,
Amongst the reverend Martyrs of the Noose?
No, there are fools enough besides in Town,
To furnish work for Satyr and Lampoon:
Few months before cried the unthinking Sot,   55
Who quickly after, hamper'd in the knot,
Was quoted for an instance by the rest,
And bore his Fate, as tamely as the best,
And thought, that Heav'n from some miraculous side,
For him alone had drawn a faithful Bride.   60
    This is our image just: such is that vain,
That foolish, fickle, motly Creature, Man:

More changing than a Weathercock, his Head
Ne'er wakes with the same thoughts, he went to bed,
Irksome to all beside, and ill at ease,   65
He neither others, nor himself can please:
Each minute round his whirling humors run, ⎫
Now he's a Trooper, and a Priest anon,   ⎬
Today in Buff, to morrow in a Gown.   ⎭

   Yet, pleas'd with idle whimsies of his brain,   70
And puft with pride, this haughty thing would fain
Be thought himself the only stay and prop,
That holds the mighty frame of Nature up:
The Skies and Stars his properties must seem,
And turn-spit Angels tread the spheres for him: 75
Of all the Creatures he's the Lord (he cries)
More absolute, than the *French* King of his.
And who is there (say you) *that dares deny*
So own'd a truth? That may be, Sir, do I.

   But to omit the controversie here,   ⎫   80
Whether, if met, the Passenger and Bear,   ⎬
This or the other stands in greater fear: ⎭
Or, if an Act of Parliament should pass
That all the *Irish* Wolves should quit the place,
They'd strait obey the Statutes high command,   85
And at a minutes warning rid the Land:
This boasted Monarch of the world, that aws
The Creatures here, and with his beck gives laws;
This titular King, who thus pretends to be
The Lord of all, how many Lords has he?   90
The lust of Mony, and the lust of Power, ⎫
With Love, and Hate, and twenty passions more, ⎬
Hold him their slave, and chain him to the Oar. ⎭

   Scarce has soft sleep in silence clos'd his eyes,
Up! (strait says Avarice) *'tis time to rise.*   95
Not yet: one minute longer. *Up!* (she cries)
Th'Exchange, and Shops are hardly open yet.
No matter: Rise! But after all, for what?
D'ye ask? go, cut the Line, *double the* Cape,

              82 fear:] *Ed.* *(1854)*; fear. *1683*

THE EIGHTH SATYR OF MONSIEUR BOILEAU

Traverse from end to end the spacious deep: 100
Search both the Indies, Bantam, *and* Japan:
Fetch Sugars from Barbadoes, *Wines from* Spain.
What need all this? I've wealth enough in store,
I thank the Fates, nor care for adding more.
You cannot have too much, this point to gain   105
You must no Crime, no Perjury refrain,
Hunger you must endure, Hardship, and Want,
Amidst full Barns keep an eternal Lent,
And, tho you've more than B[uckingha]m *has spent,*
Or C[layto]n *got, like stingy* B[eth]el *save,*   110
And grudg your self the charges of a Grave,
And the small Ransom of a single Groat,
From Sword, or Halter to redeem your Throat.
And pray, why all this sparing? *Don't you know?*
Only t'enrich a spendthrift Heir, or so: 115
Who shall, when you are timely dead and gone,
With his gilt Coach and Six amuse the Town,
Keep his gay brace of Punks, and vainly give
More for a night, than you to fine for Shrieve.
But you lose time! The Wind and Vessel waits,   120
Quick, let's aboard! Hey for the Downs *and* Streights.
    Or, if all-powerful Mony fail of charms
To tempt the wretch, and push him on to harms:
With a strong hand does fierce Ambition seize,
And drag him forth from soft repose and ease: 125
Amidst ten thousand dangers spurs him on,
With loss of Blood and Limbs to hunt renown.
Who for reward of many a wound and maim,
Is paid with nought but wooden Legs, and Fame;
And the poor comfort of a grinning Fate,   130
To stand recorded in the next Gazette.
    But hold (cries one) *your paltry gibing wit,*
Or learn henceforth to aim it more aright:
If this be any, 'tis a glorious fault,
Which through all ages has been ever thought   135

105 *gain*] *Ed.*; *gain,* *1683*   109 B[uckingha]m] *Ed.* (*1722*); B—m *1683*
110 C[layto]n] *Ed.*; C—n *1683*; Cuddon (*1722*)   B[eth]el] *Ed.* (*1722*); B—el
1683   134 *any,*] *Ed.* (*1854*); *any; 1683*

The Hero's virtue, and chief excellence:
Pray, what was Alexander *in your sence?*
A Fool belike. Yes, faith, Sir, much the same:
A crack-brain'd Huff, that set the world on flame:
A Lunatick broke loose, who in his fit   140
Fell foul on all, invaded all, he met:
Who, Lord of the whole Globe, yet not content,
Lack'd elbow-room, and seem'd too closely pent.
What madness was't, that, born to a fair Throne,
Where he might rule with Justice and Renown,   145
Like a wild Robber, he should choose to roam,
A pitied wretch, with neither house, nor home,
And hurling War and Slaughter up and down,
Through the wide world make his vast folly known?
Happy for ten good reasons had it been,   150
If *Macedon* had had a *Bedlam* then:
That there with Keepers under close restraint
He might have been from frantick mischief pent.

But that we mayn't in long digressions now
Discourse all *Rainolds,* and the Passions through,   155
And ranging them in method stiff and grave,
Rhime on by Chapter and by Paragraph;
Let's quit the present Topick of dispute,
For *More* and *Cudworth* to enlarge about:
And take a view of man in his best light,   160
Wherein he seems to most advantage set.

   'Tis he' alone (you'l say) *'tis happy he,*
That's fram'd by Nature for Society:
He only dwells in Towns, is only seen
With Manners and Civility to shine;   165
Does only Magistrates and Rulers choose,
And live secur'd by Government and Laws.

   'Tis granted, Sir; but yet without all these, ⎫
Without your boasted Laws and Policies,   ⎬
Or fear of Judges, or of Justices;   ⎭   170
Who ever saw the Wolves, that he can say, ⎫
Like more inhuman Us, so bent on prey,   ⎬
To rob their fellow Wolves upon the way?   ⎭
Who ever saw *Church* and *Fanatick* Bear,

Like savage Mankind one another tear?   175
What Tyger e're, aspiring to be great,
In Plots and Factions did embroil the State?
Or when was't heard upon the *Libyan* Plains,
Where the stern Monarch of the Desert reigns,
That *Whig* and *Tory* Lions in wild jars   180
Madly engag'd for choice of Shrieves and May'rs?
The fiercest Creatures, we in Nature find,
Respect their figure still in the same kind;
To others rough, to these they gentle be,
And live from Noise, from Feuds, from Actions free.   185
   No Eagle does upon his Peerage sue,
And strive some meaner Eagle to undo:
No Fox was e're suborn'd by spite, or hire,
Against his brother Fox his life to swear:
Nor any Hind, for Impotence at Rut,   190
Did e're the Stag into the Arches put;
Where a grave Dean the weighty Case might state,
What makes in Law a carnal Job complete:
They fear no dreadful *Quo Warranto* Writ,
To shake their ancient privilege and right: 195
No Courts of Sessions, or Assize are there,
No *Common-Pleas, Kings-Bench,* or *Chancery-Bar*:
But happier they, by Natures Charter free,
Secure and safe in mutual peace agree,
And know no other Law, but Equity.   200
   'Tis Man, 'tis Man alone, that worst of Brutes,
Who first brought up the trade of cutting Throats,
Did Honor first, that barbarous term, devise,
Unknown to all the gentler Savages;
And, as 'twere not enough t'have fetch'd from Hell,   205
Powder and Guns, with all the arts to kill,
Farther to plague the world, he must ingross
Huge Codes and bulky Pandects of the Laws,
With Doctors Glosses to perplex the Cause,
Where darken'd Equity is kept from light,   210
Under vast Reams of non-sense buried quite.
Gently, good Sir! (cry you) *why all this rant?*
Man has his freaks and passions; that we grant:

He has his frailties, and blind sides; who doubts?
But his least Virtues balance all his Faults.   215
Pray, was it not this bold, this thinking Man,
That measur'd Heav'n, and taught the Stars to scan,
Whose boundless wit, with soaring wings durst fly,
Beyond the flaming borders of the sky;
Turn'd Nature o're, and with a piercing view   220
Each cranny search'd, and lookt her through and through:
Which of the Brutes have Universities?   ⎫
When was it heard, that they e're took Degrees,   ⎬
Or were Professors of the Faculties?   ⎭
By Law, or Physick were they ever known   225
To merit Velvet, or a Scarlet Gown?

   No questionless; nor did we ever read,   ⎫
Of Quacks with them, that were Licentiates made,   ⎬
By Patent to profess the pois'ning Trade: ⎭
No Doctors in the Desk there hold dispute   ⎫   230
About Black-pudding, while the wond'ring Rout   ⎬
Listen to hear the knotty Truth made out: ⎭
Nor Virtuoso's teach deep mysteries
Of Arts for pumping Air, and smothering Flies.
   But not to urge the matter farther now,   ⎫   235
Nor search it to the depth, what 'tis to know,   ⎬
And whether we know any thing or no: ⎭
Answer me only this, What man is there
In this vile thankless Age, wherein we are,
Who does by Sense and Learning value bear?   240
Would'st thou get Honour, and a fair Estate,
And have the looks and favours of the Great?
Cries an old Father to his blooming Son,
Take the right course, be rul'd by me, 'tis done.
Leave mouldy Authors to the reading Fools,   245
The poring crowds in Colleges and Schools:
How much is threescore Nobles? Twenty pound.
Well said, my Son, the Answer's most profound:
Go, thou know'st all that's requisite to know:
What Wealth on thee, what Honors haste to flow!   250

237 no:] *Ed.* ('*1683*'); no. *1683*

In these high Sciences thy self employ,
Instead of Plato, *take thy* Hodder, Boy.
Learn there the art to audit an Account,
To what the Kings Revenue does amount:
How much the Customs and Excise bring in, 255
And what the Managers each year purloin.
Get a Case-harden'd Conscience, Irish *proof,*
Which nought of pity, sense, or shame can move:
Turn Algerine, Barbarian, Turk, *or* Jew,
Unjust, inhuman, treacherous, base, untrue; 260
Ne'r stick at wrong; hang Widows sighs and tears,
The cant of Priests to frighten Usurers:
Boggle at nothing to encrease thy Store,
Not Orphans spoils, nor plunder of the Poor:
And scorning paltry rules of Honesty, 265
By surer methods raise thy Fortune high.
 When shoals of Poets, Pedants, Orators,
Doctors, Divines, Astrologers, and Lawyers,
Authors of every sort, and every size,
To thee their Works and Labors shall address, 270
With pompous Lines their Dedications fill,
And learnedly in Greek *and* Latin *tell*
Lies to thy face, that thou hast deep insight,
And art a mighty judg of what they write.
He, that is rich, is every thing, that is, 275
Without one grain of Wisdom he is wise,
And knowing nought, knows all the Sciences:
He's witty, gallant, virtuous, generous, stout,
Well-born, well-bred, well-shap'd, well-drest, what not?
Lov'd by the Great, and courted by the Fair, 280
For none that e're had Riches, found despair:
Gold to the loathsom'st object gives a grace,
And sets it off, and makes ev'n Bovey *please:*
But tatter'd Poverty they all despise,
Love stands aloof, and from the Scare-crow flies. 285
 Thus a stanch Miser to his hopeful Brat
Chalks out the way that leads to an Estate;
Whose knowledg oft with utmost stretch of Brain
No high'r than this vast secret can attain,

Five and four's nine, take two, and seven remain. ⌉   290
   Go, Doctor, after this, and rack your Brains,
Unravel *Scripture* with industrous pains:
On musty *Fathers* wast your fruitless hours,
Correct the Criticks and Expositors:
Out-vie great *Stillingfleet* in some vast Tome,   295
And there confound both *Bellarmin* and *Rome*;
Or glean the *Rabbies* of their learned store,
To find what Father *Simon* has past o're:
Then at the last some bulky piece compile,
There lay out all your time, and pains, and skill;   300
And when 'tis done and finish'd for the Press,
To some Great name the mighty Work address:
Who for a full reward of all your toil,
Shall pay you with a gracious nod or smile:
Just recompence of life too vainly spent!   305
An empty *Thank you Sir*, and Complement.
   But, if to higher Honors you pretend,
Take the advice and counsel of a Friend;
Here quit the Desk, and throw your Scarlet by,
And to some gainful course your self apply.   310
Go, practise with some Banker how to cheat,
There's choice in Town, enquire in *Lombard-street*.
Let *Scot* and *Ockam* wrangle as they please, ⌉
And thus in short with me conclude the case, ⎬
A Doctor is no better than an Ass. ⌋   315
   A Doctor, Sir? your self: Pray have a care,
This is to push your Raillery too far.
But not to lose the time in trifling thus,
Beside the point, come now more home and close:
That Man has Reason is beyond debate,   320
Nor will your self, I think, deny me that:
And was not this fair Pilot giv'n to steer,
His tott'ring Bark through Life's rough Ocean here?
   All this I grant: But if in spite of it
The wretch on every Rock he sees will split,   325
To what great purpose does his Reason serve,
But to mis-guide his course, and make him swerve?

What boots it *H[oward]* when it says, *Give o're*
Thy scribling itch, and play the fool no more,
If her vain counsels, purpos'd to reclaim,   330
Only avail to harden him in shame?
Lampoon'd, and hiss'd, and damn'd the thousandth time,
Still he writes on, is obstinate in Rhime:
His Verse, which he does every where recite,
Put all his Neighbors, and his Friends to flight: 335
Scar'd by the rhiming Fiend, they hast away,
Nor will his very Groom be hir'd to stay.
   The Ass, whom Nature Reason has deny'd,
Content with Instinct for his surer guide,
Still follows that, and wiselier does proceed: 340
He ne'er aspires with his harsh braying Note,
The Songsters of the Wood to challenge out:
Nor, like this awkard smatterer in Arts,
Sets up himself for a vain Ass of parts;
Of Reason void, he sees and gains his end,   345
While Man, who does to that false light pretend,
Wildly gropes on, and in broad day is blind.
By whimsie led he does all things by chance,
And acts in each against all common sense.
With every thing pleas'd, and displeas'd at once,   350
He knows not what he seeks, nor what he shuns:
Unable to distinguish good, or bad,
For nothing he is gay, for nothing sad:
At random loves, and loaths, avoids, pursues,
Enacts, repeals, makes, alters, does, undoes.   355
   Did we, like him, e're see the Dog, or Bear,
Chimera's of their own devising fear?
Frame needless doubts, and for those doubts forego
The Joys which prompting Nature calls them to?
And with their Pleasures awkardly at strife,   360
With scaring Fantoms pall the sweets of Life?
Tell me, grave Sir, did ever Man see Beast
So much below himself, and sense debas'd,
To worship Man with superstitious Fear,

328 *H[oward]*] *Ed.* (*1722 footnote*); *H. 1683*   329 *more,*] *Ed.* ('*1683*');
more. 1683

And fondly to his Idol Temples rear?   365
Was he e're seen with Pray'rs and Sacrifice ⎫
Approach to him, as Ruler of the Skies,   ⎬
To beg for Rain, or Sun-shine on his knees? ⎭
No never: but a thousand times has Beast
Seen Man, beneath the meanest Brute debas'd,   370
Fall low to Wood and Metal heretofore,
And madly his own Workmanship adore:
In *Egypt* oft has seen the Sot bow down,
And reverence some deified Baboon:
Has often seen him on the Banks of *Nile*   375
Say Pray'rs to the Almighty Crocodile:
And now each day in every street abroad
Sees prostrate Fools adore a breaden God.
    But why (say you) *these spiteful Instances*
Of Egypt, *and its gross Idolatries?*   380
Of Rome, *and hers as much ridiculous?*
What are these lewd Buffooneries to us?
How gather you from such wild proofs as these,
That Man, a Doctor is beneath an Ass?
An Ass! that heavy, stupid, lumpish Beast,   385
The Sport and mocking-stock of all the rest?
Whom they all spurn, and whom they all despise,
Whose very name all Satyr does comprize?
    An Ass, Sir? Yes: Pray what should make us laugh?
Now he unjustly is our jeer and scoff.   390
But, if one day he should occasion find
Upon our Follies to express his mind;
If Heav'n, as once of old, to check proud Man,
By miracle should give him Speech again;
What would he say, d'ye think, could he speak out,   395
Nay, Sir, betwixt us two, what would he not?
    What would he say, were he condemn'd to stand
For one long hour in *Fleetstreet*, or the *Strand*,
To cast his eyes upon the motly throng,
The two-leg'd Herd, that daily pass along;   400
To see their old Disguises, Furs, and Gowns,
Their Cassocks, Cloaks, Lawn-sleeves and Pantaloons?
What would he say to see a Velvet Quack

Walk with the price of forty kill'd on's Back;
Or mounted on a Stage, and gaping loud,   405
Commend his Drugs and Ratsbane to the Crowd?
What would he think, on a Lord Mayor's day,
Should he the Pomp and Pageantry survey?
Or view the Judges, and their solemn Train,
March with grave decency to kill a Man?   410
What would he think of us, should he appear ⎤
In Term amongst the crowds at *Westminster*, ⎬
And there the hellish din and Jargon hear,   ⎦
Where *J[efferies]* and his pack with deep-mouth'd Notes
Drown *Billinsgate*, and all its Oyster-Boats?   415
There see the Judges, Sergeants, Barristers,
Attorneys, Counsellors, Solicitors,
Criers, and Clerks, and all the Savage Crew
Which wretched man at his own charge undo?
If after prospect of all this, the Ass   420
Should find the voice he had in *Esop*'s days;
Then, Doctor, then, casting his eyes around
On human Fools, which every where abound,
    Content with Thistles, from all envy free,
    And shaking his grave head, no doubt he'd cry   425
    Good faith, Man is a Beast as much as we.

414 *J[efferies]*]] *Ed.* (*1722*); *J.* *1683*   423 abound,] *Ed.* (*1722*); abound.
1683

THE THIRTEENTH
S   A   T   Y   R
OF
J U V E N A L ,
Imitated.

Written in *April*, 1682

ARGUMENT.

The POET comforts a Friend, that is overmuch concerned for the loss of a con-
siderable Sum of Money, of which he has lately been cheated by a person, to

whom he intrusted the same. This he does by shewing, that nothing comes to
pass in the world without Divine Providence, and that wicked Men (however
they seem to escape its Punishment here) yet suffer abundantly in the tor-
ments of an evil Conscience. And by the way takes occasion to lash the
Degeneracy and Villany of the present Times.

THere is not one base Act, which Men commit, ⎫
But carries this ill sting along with it,   ⎬
That to the Author it creates regret: ⎭
And this is some Revenge at least, that he ⎫
Can ne'r acquit himself of Villany,   ⎬   5
Tho a Brib'd Judg and Jury set him free.   ⎭
    All people, Sir, abhor (as 'tis but just)
Your faithless Friend, who lately broke his Trust,
And curse the treacherous Deed: But, thanks to Fate,
That has not bless'd you with so small Estate,   10
But that with patience you may bear the Cross,
And need not sink under so mean a Loss.
Besides your Case for less concern does call,
Because 'tis what does usually befal:
Ten thousand such might be alledg'd with ease,   15
Out of the common crowd of Instances.
    Then cease for shame, immoderate regret,
And don't your Manhood and your Sense forget:
'Tis womanish and silly to lay forth
More cost in Grief than a Misfortune's worth.   20
You scarce can bear a puny trifling ill,
It goes so deep, pray Heav'n! it does not kill:
And all this trouble, and this vain ado,
Because a Friend (forsooth) has prov'd untrue.
Shame o' your Beard! can this so much amaze?   25
Were you not born in good King *Jemmy*'s days?
And are not you at length yet wiser grown,
When threescore Winters on your head have snown?
    Almighty Wisdom gives in Holy Writ
Wholsom Advice to all, that follow it: 30
And those, that will not its great Counsels hear,
May learn from meer experience how to bear
(Without vain strugling) Fortune's yoke, and how

They ought her rudest shocks to undergo.
There's not a day so solemn thro the year,   35
Not one red Letter in the Calendar,
But we of some new Crime discover'd hear.
Theft, Murder, Treason, Perjury, what not?
Moneys by Cheating, Padding, poisoning got.
Nor is it strange; so few are now the Good,   40
That fewer scarce were left at *Noah*'s Flood:
Should *Sodom*'s Angel here in Fire descend,
Our Nation wants ten Men to save the Land.
Fate has reserv'd us for the very Lees
Of Time, where Ill admits of no degrees: 45
An Age so bad old Poets ne'er could frame,
Nor find a Metal out to give't a name.
This your Experience knows, and yet for all
On faith of God and Man aloud you call,
Louder than on Queen *Besse*'s day the Rout   50
For *Antichrist* burnt in Effigie shout:
But, tell me, Sir, tell me, grey-headed Boy,
Do you not know what Lech'ry men enjoy
In stollen Goods? For Gods sake don't you see ⎫
How they all laugh at your simplicity,   ⎬   55
When gravely you forewarn of Perjury?   ⎭
Preach up a God and Hell, vain empty names,
Exploded now for idle thredbare shams,
Devis'd by Priests, and by none else believ'd,
E're since great *Hobbes* the world has undeceiv'd?   60
     This might have past with the plain simple Race
Of our Forefathers in King *Arthur*'s days:
E're, mingling with corrupted forein Seed,
We learnt their Vice, and spoil'd our native Breed.
E're yet bless'd *Albion*, high in ancient Fame,   65
With her first Innocence resign'd her Name.
Fair dealing then, and downright Honesty,
And plighted Faith were good Security:
No vast Ingrossments for Estates were made,
Nor Deeds, large as the Lands, which they convey'd: 70
To bind a Trust there lack'd no formal ties ⎫
Of Paper, Wax, and Seals, and Witnesses,   ⎬

Nor ready Coin, but sterling Promises: ⎫
Each took the other's word, and that would go
For currant then, and more than Oaths do now: 75
None had recourse to *Chanc'ry* for defence,
Where you forego your Right with less Expence:
Nor traps were yet set up for Perjurers,
That catch men by the Heads, and whip off Ears.
Then Knave and Villain, things unheard of were, ⎫   80
Scarce in a Century did one appear,   ⎬
And he more gaz'd at than a Blazing-Star: ⎭
If a young Stripling put not off his Hat
In high respect to every Beard he met,
Tho a Lord's Son and Heir, 'twas held a crime,   85
That scarce deserv'd its Clergy in that time:
So venerable then was four years odds,
And grey old Heads were reverenc'd as Gods.
      Now if a Friend once in an Age prove just,
If he miraculously keep his Trust,   90
And without force of Law deliver all
That's due, both Interest and Principal:
Prodigious wonder! fit for *Stow* to tell,
And stand recorded in the Chronicle;
A thing less memorable would require   95
As great a Monument as *London* Fire.
A man of Faith and Uprightness is grown ⎫
So strange a Creature both in Court and Town, ⎬
That he with Elephants may well be shown; ⎭
A Monster, more uncommon than a Whale   100
At *Bridg*, the last great Comet, or the Hail,
Than *Thames* his double Tide, or should he run
With Streams of Milk, or Blood to *Gravesend* down.
You're troubled that you've lost five hundred pound
By treacherous Fraud: another may be found,   105
Has lost a thousand: and another yet,
Double to that; perhaps his whole Estate.
      Little do folks the heav'nly Powers mind,
If they but scape the knowledg of Mankind:

99 shown;] *Ed.* *(1854)*; shown. *1683*

Observe, with how demure and grave a look   110
The Rascal lays his hand upon the Book:
Then with a praying Face, and lifted Eye
Claps on his Lips, and Seals the Perjury:
If you persist his Innocence to doubt,
And boggle in Belief; he'l strait rap out   115
Oaths by the volley, each of which would make
Pale Atheists start, and trembling Bullies quake;
And more than would a whole Ships crew maintain
To the *East-Indies* hence, and back again.
As God shall pardon me, Sir, I am free   120
Of what you charge me with: let me ne'er see
His Face in Heaven else: may these hands rot, ⎫
These eyes drop out; if I e're had a Groat   ⎬
Of yours, or if they ever touch'd, or saw't. ⎭
Thus he'l run on two hours in length, till he   125
Spin out a Curse long as the Litany:
Till Heav'n has scarce a Judgment left in store
For him to wish, deserve, or suffer more.

  There are, who disavow all Providence,
And think the world is only steer'd by chance: 130
Make God at best an idle looker on,
A lazy Monarch lolling in his Throne;
Who his Affairs does neither mind, or know,
But leaves them all at random here below:
And such at every foot themselves will damn,   135
And Oaths no more than common Breath esteem:
No shame, nor loss of Ears can frighten these,
Were every Street a Grove of Pillories.

  Others there be, that own a God, and fear
His Vengeance to ensue, and yet forswear: 140
Thus to himself, says one, *Let Heaven decree*
What Doom soe're, its pleasure will, of me:
Strike me with Blindness, Palsies, Leprosies, ⎫
Plague, Pox, Consumption, all the Maladies   ⎬
Of both the Spittles; so I get my Prize,   ⎭   145
And hold it sure; I'll suffer these, and more;
All Plagues are light to that of being poor.
There's not a begging Cripple in the streets

(Unless he with his Limbs has lost his Wits,
And is grown fit for Bedlam*) but no doubt,*   150
To have his Wealth would have the Rich man's Gout.
Grant Heavens Vengeance heavy be; what tho?
The heaviest things move slowliest still we know:
And, if it punish all, that guilty be,
'Twill be an Age before it come to me: 155
God too is merciful, as well as just;
Therefore I'll rather his forgiveness trust,
Than live despis'd and poor, as thus I must:
I'll try, and hope, he's more a Gentleman
Than for such trivial things as these, to damn.   160
Besides, for the same Fact we've often known
One mount the Cart, another mount the Throne:
And foulest Deeds, attended with success,
No longer are reputed wickedness,
Disguis'd with Virtues Livery and Dress.   165

With these weak Arguments they fortifie
And harden up themselves in Villany:
The Rascal now dares call you to account,
And in what Court you please, joyn issue on't:
Next Term he'l bring the Action to be tri'd,   170
And twenty Witnesses to swear on's side:
And, if that Justice to his Cause be found,
Expects a Verdict of five hundred pound.
Thus he, who boldly dares the Guilt out-face,
For innocent shall with the Rabble pass: 175
While you, with Impudence and sham run down,
Are only thought the Knave by all the Town.
    Mean time, poor you at Heav'n exclaim and rail,
Louder than J[efferies] at the Bar does bawl:
Is there a Pow'r above? and does he hear?   180
And can he tamely Thunderbolts forbear?
To what vain end do we with Pray'rs adore?
And on our bended knees his aid implore?
Where is his Rule, if no respect be had,
Of Innocence, or Guilt, of Good, or Bad?   185

179 J[efferies]] Ed. (1722); J. 1683

THE THIRTEENTH SATYR OF JUVENAL

And who henceforth will any credit show
To what his lying Priests teach here below?
If this be Providence; for ought I see,
Bless'd Saint, Vaninus! *I shall follow thee:*
Little's the odds 'twixt such a God, and that,   190
Which Atheist Lewis *us'd to wear in's Hat.*

   Thus you blaspheme and rave: But pray, Sir, try
What Comforts my weak Reason can apply,
Who never yet read *Plutarch*, hardly saw,
And am but meanly vers'd in *Seneca*.   195
In cases dangerous and hard of cure
We have recourse to *Scarborough*, or *Lower*:
But if they don't so desperate appear,
We trust to meaner Doctors skill and care.

   If there were never in the world before   200
So foul a deed; I'm dumb, not one word more:
A God's name then let both your sluces flow,
And all th'extravagance of sorrow show;
And tear your Hair, and thump your mournful Breast,
As if your dearest First-born were deceas'd.   205
'Tis granted that a greater Grief attends
Departed Moneys than departed Friends:
None ever counterfeits upon this score,   ⎫
Nor need he do't; the thought of being poor ⎬
Will serve alone to make the eyes run o're. ⎭   210
Lost Money's griev'd with true unfeigned Tears,
More true, than Sorrow of expecting Heirs
At their dead Father's Funerals, tho here
The Back and Hands no pompous Mourning wear.

   But if the like Complaints be daily found   215
At *Westminster*, and in all Courts abound;
If Bonds and Obligations can't prevail,
But Men deny their very Hand and Seal,
Sign'd with the Arms of the whole Pedegree
Of their dead Ancestors to vouch the Lye,   220
If *Temple-Walks*, and *Smithfield* never fail
Of plying Rogues, that set their Souls to sale
To the first Passenger, that bids a price,
And make their livelihood of Perjuries;

For God's sake why are you so delicate,   225
And think it hard to share the common Fate?
And why must you alone be Fav'rite thought
Of Heav'n, and we for Reprobates cast out?
    The wrong you bear, is hardly worth regard,
Much less your just resentment, if compar'd   230
With greater out-rages to others done,
Which daily happen, and alarm the Town:
Compare the Villains who cut Throats for Bread, ⎫
Or Houses fire, of late a gainful Trade,   ⎬
By which our City was in Ashes laid: ⎭   235
Compare the sacrilegious Burglary,
From which no place can Sanctuary be,
That rifles Churches of Communion-Plate,
Which good King *Edward*'s days did dedicate:
Think, who durst steal S. *Alban*'s Font of Brass,   240
That Christen'd half the Royal *Scotish* Race:
Who stole the Chalices at *Chichester*,
In which themselves receiv'd the day before:
Or that bold daring Hand, of fresh Renown,
Who, scorning common Booty, stole a Crown: 245
Compare too, if you please, the horrid Plot,
With all the Perjuries to make it out,
Or make it nothing, for these last three years;
Add to it *Thinne's* and *Godfrey*'s Murderers:
And if these seem but slight and trivial things,   250
Add those, that have, and would have murder'd Kings.
    And yet how little's this of Villany
To what our Judges oft in one day try?
This to convince you, do but travel down,
When the next Circuit comes, with *Pemberton*,   255
Or any of the Twelve, and there but mind,
How many Rogues there are of Human kind,
And let me hear you, when you're back again,
Say, you are wrong'd, and, if you dare, complain.
    None wonder, who in *Essex* Hundreds live,   260
Or *Sheppy* Island, to have Agues rife:
Nor would you think it much in *Africa*,
If you great Lips, and short flat Noses saw:

Because 'tis so by Nature of each place;
And therefore there for no strange things they pass.   265
In Lands, where Pigmies are, to see a Crane
(As Kites do Chickens here) sweep up a Man
In Armour clad, with us would make a show,
And serve for entertain at *Bartholmew:*
Yet there it goes for no great Prodigy,   270
Where the whole Nation is but one foot high:
Then why, fond Man, should you so much admire,
Since Knave is of our Growth, and common here?
　　But must such Perjury escape (say you)
　　And shall it ever thus unpunish'd go?   275
Grant, he were dragg'd to Jail this very hour,
To starve and rot; suppose it in your Pow'r
To rack and torture him all kind of ways,
To hang, or burn, or kill him, as you please;
(And what would your Revenge it self have more?)   280
Yet this, all this would not your Cash restore:
And where would be the Comfort, where the Good,
If you could wash your Hands in's reaking Blood?
　　But, Oh, Revenge more sweet than Life! 'Tis true,
So the unthinking say, and the mad Crew   285
Of hect'ring Blades, who for slight cause, or none,
At every turn are into Passion blown:
Whom the least Trifles with Revenge inspire,
And at each spark, like Gun-powder, take fire:
These unprovok'd kill the next Man they meet,   290
For being so sawcy, as to walk the street;
And at the summons of each tiny Drab,
Cry, *Damme! Satisfaction!* draw, and stab.
　　Not so of old, the mild good *Socrates,*
(Who shew'd how high without the help of Grace,   295
Well-cultivated Nature might be wrought)
He a more noble way of suff'ring taught,
And, tho he Guiltless drank the poisonous Dose,
Ne'er wish'd a drop to his accusing Foes.
Not so our great good *Martyr'd King* of late   300

267 Man] *Ed.* (*1854*); Man, *1683*   298 he] *Ed.* (*1684a*); the *1683*

(Could we his bless'd Example imitate)
Who, tho the great'st of mortal sufferers,
Yet kind to his rebellious Murderers,
Forgave, and bless'd them with his dying Pray'rs.

Thus, we by sound Divinity, and Sense   305
May purge our minds, and weed all Errors thence:
These lead us into right, nor shall we need
Other than them thro Life to be our Guide.
Revenge is but a Frailty, incident
To craz'd and sickly minds, the poor Content   310
Of little Souls, unable to surmount
An Injury, too weak to bear Affront:
And this you may infer, because we find,
'Tis most in poor unthinking Woman-kind,
Who wreak their feeble spite on all they can,   315
And are more kin to Brute than braver Man.

But why should you imagin, Sir, that those
Escape unpunish'd, who still feel the Throes
And Pangs of a rack'd Soul, and (which is worse
Than all the Pains, which can the Body curse)   320
The secret gnawings of unseen Remorse?
Believe't, they suffer greater Punishment
Than *Rome*'s Inquisitor's could e're invent:
Nor all the Tortures, Racks, and Cruelties,
Which ancient Persecutors could devise,   325
Nor all, that *Fox* his Bloody Records tell,
Can match what *Bradshaw* and *Ravilliac* feel,
Who in their Breasts carry about their Hell.

I've read this story, but I know not where,
Whether in *Hackwel*, or *Beard*'s Theatre: 330
A certain Spartan, *whom a Friend, like you,*
Had trusted with a Hundred pound or two,
Went to the Oracle to know if he
With safety might the Sum in trust deny.
'Twas answer'd, No, *that if he durst forswear,*   335
He should e're long for's knavery pay dear:
Hence Fear, not Honesty, made him refund;

332 *two,*] *Ed.* (*1684a*); *two.* *1683*; *two*; ('*1683*')

Yet to his cost the Sentence true he found:
Himself, his Children, all his Family,
Ev'n the remot'st of his whole Pedegree,   340
Perish'd (as there 'tis told) *in misery.*
Now to apply: if such be the sad end
Of Perjury, tho but in Thought design'd,
Think, Sir, what Fate awaits your treach'rous Friend,
Who has not only thought, but done to you   345
All this, and more; think, what he suffers now,
And think, what every Villain suffers else,
That dares, like him, be faithless, base, and false.
   Pale Horror, ghastly Fear, and black Despair
Pursue his steps, and dog him wheresoe're   350
He goes, and if from his loath'd self he fly,
To herd, like wounded Deer, in company,
These strait creep in and pall his mirth and joy.
The choicest Dainties, ev'n by *Lumly* drest,
Afford no Relish to his sickly Tast,   355
Insipid all, as *Damocles* his Feast.
Ev'n Wine, the greatest Blessing of Mankind,
The best support of the dejected mind,
Applied to his dull spirits, warms no more
Than to his Corps it could past Life restore.   360
Darkness he fears, nor dares he trust his Bed
Without a Candle watching by his side:
And, if the wakeful Troubles of his Breast
To his toss'd Limbs allow one moments Rest,
Straitways the groans of Ghosts, and hideous Screams   365
Of tortur'd Spirits haunt his frightful Dreams:
Strait there return to his tormented mind
His perjur'd Act, his injur'd God, and Friend:
Strait he imagins you before his Eyes,
Ghastly of shape, prodigious of size,   370
With glaring Eyes, cleft Foot, and monstrous Tail,
And bigger than the Giants at *Guild-hall*,
Stalking with horrid strides across the Room,

340 *Ev'n the remot'st*] *Ed.*; *Ev'n the remotest 1683*; The most remote (*1710,*
1722)   366 haunt] *Ed.* (*1684a*); haunts *1683*

And guards of Fiends to drag him to his Doom:
Hereat he falls in dreadful Agonies,   375
And dead cold sweats his trembling Members seize:
Then starting wakes, and with a dismal cry,
Calls to his aid his frighted Family;
There owns the Crime, and vows upon his knees
The sacred Pledg next morning to release.   380
 These are the men, whom the least Terrors daunt,
Who at the sight of their own shadows faint;
These, if it chance to Lighten, are agast,
And quake for fear, lest every Flash should blast:
These swoon away at the first Thunder-clap,   385
As if 'twere not, what usually does hap,
The casual cracking of a Cloud, but sent
By angry Heaven for their Punishment:
And, if unhurt they scape the Tempest now,
Still dread the greater Vengeance to ensue: 390
These the least Symptoms of a Fever fright,
Water high-colour'd, want of rest at night,
Or a disorder'd Pulse strait makes them shrink,
And presently for fear they're ready sink
Into their Graves: their time (think they) is come,   395
And Heav'n in judgment now has sent their Doom.
Nor dare they, tho in whisper, waft a Prayer,
Lest it by chance should reach th' Almighty's ear,
And wake his sleeping Vengeance, which before
So long has their impieties forbore.   400
 These are the thoughts which guilty wretches haunt,
Yet enter'd, they still grow more impudent:
After a Crime perhaps they now and then ⎫
Feel pangs and strugglings of Remorse within, ⎬
But strait return to their old course agen: ⎭   405
They, who have once thrown Shame and Conscience by,
Ne'er after make a stop in Villany:
Hurried along, down the vast steep they go,
And find, 'tis all a Precipice below.
 Ev'n this perfidious Friend of yours, no doubt,   410
Will not with single wickedness give out;
Have patience but a while, you'l shortly see

His hand held up at Bar for Felony:
You'l see the sentenc'd wretch for Punishment
To *Scilly* Isles, or the *Caribbes* sent: 415
Or (if I may his surer Fate divine)
Hung like *Boroski*, for a Gibbet-Sign:
Then may you glut Revenge, and feast your Eyes
With the dear object of his Miseries:
And then at length convinc'd, with joy you'l find   420
That the just God is neither deaf, nor blind.

D   A   V   I   D'S
LAMENTATION
For the DEATH of
SAUL and *JONATHAN*,
PARAPHRAS'd.

Written in *September*, 1677.

O   D   E
I

AH wretched *Israel!* once a bless'd, and happy State,
The Darling of the Stars, and Heavens Care,
Then all the bord'ring world thy Vassals were,
And thou at once their Envy and their Fear,
How soon art thou (alas!) by the sad turn of Fate   5
    Become abandon'd and forlorn?
How art thou now become their Pity, and their scorn?
Thy Lustre all is vanish'd, all thy Glory fled,
    Thy Sun himself set in a blood red,
    Too sure Prognostick! which does ill portend   10
    Approaching Storms on thy unhappy Land,
Left naked and defenceless now to each invading Hand.

9 blood] *1683*; bloody *conj. Ed.*

A fatal Battel, lately fought,
Has all these Mis'ries and Misfortunes brought,
Has thy quick Ruin and Destruction wrought: 15
There fell we by a mighty Overthrow
A Prey to an enrag'd, relentless Foe,
The toil and labour of their wearied Cruelty,
Till they no more could kill, and we no longer die:
Vast slaughter all around th' enlarged Mountain swells,   20
And numerous Deaths increase its former Hills.

                              II

In *Gath* let not the mournful News be known,
Nor publish'd in the streets of *Askalon*;
    May Fame it self be quite struck dumb!
Oh may it never to *Philistia* come,   25
Nor any live to bear the cursed Tidings home!
    Lest the proud Enemies new Trophies raise,
    And loudly triumph in our fresh Disgrace:
No captive *Israelite* their pompous Joy adorn,
    Nor in sad Bondage his lost Country mourn: 30
    No Spoils of ours be in their Temples hung,
        No Hymns to *Ashdod*'s Idol sung,
Nor thankful Sacrifice on his glad Altars burn.
Kind Heav'n forbid! lest the base Heathen Slaves blaspheme
    Thy sacred and unutterable Name,   35
    And above thine extol their *Dagon*'s Fame;
    Lest the vile *Fish*'s Worship spread abroad,
Who fell a prostrate Victim once before our conqu'ring God:
And you, who the great Deeds of Kings and Kingdoms write,
Who all their Actions to succeeding Age transmit,   40
        Conceal the blushing Story, ah! conceal
        Our Nations loss, and our dread Monarch's fall:
        Conceal the Journal of this bloody Day,
    When both by the ill Play of Fate were thrown away:
    Nor let our wretched Infamy, and Fortune's Crime   45
Be ever mention'd in the Registers of future Time.

                36 Fame;] *Ed. (1854)*; Fame. *1683*

III

For ever, *Gilboa*, be curst thy hated Name,
Th'eternal Monument of our Disgrace and Shame!
   For ever curst be that unhappy Scene,
   Where Slaughter, Blood, and Death did lately reign!   50
No Clouds henceforth above thy barren top appear,
      But what may make thee mourning wear:
      Let them ne're shake their dewy Fleeces there,
         But only once a year
On the sad Anniverse drop a remembring Tear: 55
   No Flocks of Off'rings on thy Hills be known,
Which may by Sacrifice our Guilt and thine attone:
No Sheep, nor any of the gentler kind hereafter stay
   On thee, but Bears, and Wolves, and Beasts of prey,
   Or men more savage, wild, and fierce than they;   60
   A Desart may'st thou prove, and lonely wast,
   Like that, our sinful, stubborn Fathers past,
Where they the Penance trod for all, they there transgrest:
   Too dearly wast thou drench'd with precious Blood
   Of many a *Jewish* Worthy, spilt of late,   65
   Who suffer'd there by an ignoble Fate,
And purchas'd foul Dishonour at too high a rate:
   Great *Saul's* ran there amongst the common Flood,
   His Royal self mixt with the baser Crowd:
   He, whom Heav'ns high and open suffrage chose,   70
   The Bulwark of our Nation to oppose
      The Pow'r and Malice of our Foes;
   Ev'n He, on whom the Sacred Oyl was shed,
   Whose mystick drops enlarg'd his hallow'd Head,
   Lies now (oh Fate, impartial still to Kings!)   75
Huddled and undistinguish'd in the heap of meaner things.

IV.

   Lo! there the mighty Warriour lyes,
   With all his Lawrels, all his Victories,
To ravenous Fowls, or worse, to his proud Foes, a Prize:
How chang'd from that great *Saul!* whose generous Aid,   80
A conqu'ring Army to distressed *Jabesh* led,
   At whose approach *Ammon's* proud Tyrant fled:

How chang'd from that great *Saul*! whom we saw bring
From vanquish'd *Amalek* their captive Spoils and King;
  When unbid Pity made him *Agag* spare;   85
Ah Pity! more than Cruelty found guilty there:
  Oft has he made these conquer'd Enemies bow,
    By whom himself lies conquer'd now:
  At *Micmash* his great Might they felt and knew,
    The same they felt at *Dammin* too: 90
  Well I remember, when from *Helah*'s Plain
  He came in triumph, met by a numerous Crowd,
  Who with glad shouts proclaim'd their Joy aloud;
A Dance of beauteous Virgins led the solemn Train,
And sung and prais'd the man *that had his Thousands slain*.   95
  Seir, Moab, Zobah felt him, and where e're
    He did his glorious Standards bear,
  Officious Vict'ry follow'd in the rere:
  Success attended still his brandish'd Sword,
  And, like the Grave, the gluttonous Blade devour'd: 100
  Slaughter upon its point in triumph sate,
  And scatter'd Death, as quick and wide as Fate.

V

Nor less in high Repute and Worth was his great Son,
  Sole Heir of all his Valour and Renown,
Heir too (if cruel Fate had suffer'd) of his Throne: 105
  The matchless *Jonathan* 'twas, whom loud-tongu'd Fame
  Amongst her chiefest Heroes joys to name,
  E're since the wond'rous Deeds at *Seneh* done,
Where he, himself an Host, o'recame a War alone:
  The trembling Enemies fled, they try'd to fly,   110
  But fixt amazement stopt, and made them die.
Great Archer He! to whom our dreaded skill we owe,
Dreaded by all, who *Israel*'s warlike Prowess know;
  As many Shafts, as his full Quiver held,
  So many Fates he drew, so many kill'd: 115
Quick and unerring they, as darted Eye-beams, flew,
  As if he gave 'em sight, and swiftness too.
Death took her Aim from his, and by't her Arrows threw.

86 than] *Ed.* ('*1683*'); can *1683*

VI

Both excellent they were, both equally alli'd
    On Nature, and on Valour's side: 120
  Great *Saul*, who scorn'd a Rival in Renown,
  Yet envied not the Fame of's greater Son,
  By him endur'd to be surpass'd alone:
  He gallant Prince, did his whole Father shew,
And fast, as he could set, the well-writ Copies drew,   125
  And blush'd, that Duty bid him not out-go:
Together they did both the paths to Glory trace,
  Together hunted in the noble Chace,
  Together finish'd their united Race:
  There only did they prove unfortunate,   130
    Never till then unbless'd by Fate,
    Yet there they ceas'd not to be great;
  Fearless they met, and brav'd their threaten'd fall,
And fought when Heav'n revolted, Fortune durst rebel.
  When publick safety, and their Countries care   135
Requir'd their Aid, and call'd them to the toils of War;
As Parent-Eagles, summon'd by their Infants cries
    Whom some rude hands would make a Prize,
Hast to Relief, and with their wings out-fly their eyes;
  So swift did they their speedy succour bear,   140
    So swift the bold Aggressors seize,
So swift attack, so swift pursue the vanquish'd enemies:
  The vanquish'd enemies with all the wings of Fear
     Mov'd not so quick as they,
    Scarce could their souls fly fast enough away.   145
  Bolder than Lions, they thick Dangers met,
Thro Fields with armed Troops, and pointed Harvests set,
Nothing could tame their Rage, or quench their generous Heat:
  Like those, they march'd undaunted, and like those,
  Secure of Wounds, and all that durst oppose,   150
So to Resisters fierce, so gentle to their prostrate Foes.

VII

  Mourn, wretched *Israel*, mourn thy Monarch's fall,
  And all thy plenteous stock of sorrow call,
    T'attend his pompous Funeral:

Mourn each, who in this loss an int'rest shares,   155
　　Lavish your Grief, exhaust it all in Tears:
　　　　　　You *Hebrew* Virgins too,
Who once in lofty strains did his glad Triumphs sing,
Bring all your artful Notes, and skilful Measures now,
　　　Each charming air of Breath and string,   160
　　Bring all to grace the Obsequies of your dead King,
And high, as then your Joy, let now your Sorrow flow.
　　　　Saul, your great *Saul* is dead,
　　Who you with Natures choicest Dainties fed,
　　Who you with Natures gayest Wardrobe clad,   165
By whom you all her Pride, and all her Pleasures had:
　　For you the precious Worm his Bowels spun,
　　For you the *Tyrian* Fish did Purple run,
　　For you the blest *Arabia*'s Spices grew,
　　And *Eastern* Quarries harden'd Pearly dew;   170
　　The Sun himself turn'd Labourer for you:
　　For you he hatch'd his golden Births alone,
Wherewith you were array'd, whereby you him out-shone,
All this and more you did to *Saul*'s great Conduct owe,
All this you lost in his unhappy overthrow.   175

VIII

Oh Death! how vast an Harvest hast thou reap'd of late!
　　　Never before hadst thou so great,
　　Ne'er drunk'st before so deep of *Jewish* Blood,
　　Ne're since th'embattled Hosts at *Gibeah* stood;
　　When three whole days took up the work of Fate,   180
　　When a large Tribe enter'd at once thy Bill,
And threescore thousand Victims to thy Fury fell.
　　　Upon the fatal Mountains Head,
　　　Lo! how the mighty Chiefs lie dead:
　　There my beloved *Jonathan* was slain,   185
　　The best of Princes, and the best of Men;
Cold Death hangs on his Cheeks like an untimely Frost
On early Fruit, there sits, and smiles a sullen Boast,
And yet looks pale at the great Captive, she has ta'en.
My *Jonathan* is dead (oh dreadful word of Fame!   190
Oh grief! that I can speak't, and not become the same!)

He's dead, and with him all our blooming Hopes are gone,
  And many a wonder, which he must have done,
  And many a Conquest which he must have won,
  They're all to the dark Grave and Silence fled   195
  And never now in story shall be read,
      And never now shall take their date,
Snatch'd hence by the preventing hand of envious Fate.

             IX
  Ah, worthy Prince! would I for thee had dyed!
  Ah, would I had thy fatal place supplied!   200
I'd then repaid a Life, which to thy gift I owe,
Repaid a Crown, which Friendship taught thee to forgo;
      Both Debts, I ne'er can cancel now:
Oh, dearer than my Soul! if I can call it mine,
  For sure we had the same, 'twas very thine,   205
  Dearer than Light, or Life, or Fame,
Or Crowns, or any thing, that I can wish, or think, or name:
  Brother thou wast, but wast my Friend before,
  And that new Title then could add no more:
Mine more than Blood, Alliance, Natures self could make,   210
    Than I, or Fame it self can speak:
  Not yearning Mothers, when first Throes they feel
To their young Babes in looks a softer Passion tell:
  Not artless undissembling Maids express
  In their last dying sighs such Tenderness: 215
Not thy fair Sister, whom strict Duty bids me wear
  First in my Breast, whom holy Vows make mine,
Tho all the Virtues of a loyal Wife she bear,
    Could boast an Union so near,
Could boast a Love so firm, so lasting, so Divine.   220
  So pure is that which we in Angels find
  To Mortals here, in Heav'n to their own kind:
So pure, but not more great must that blest Friendship prove
(Could, ah, could I to that wisht Place, and Thee remove)
Which shall for ever joyn our mingled Souls above.   225

X

Ah wretched *Israel*! ah unhappy state!
Expos'd to all the Bolts of angry Fate!
Expos'd to all thy Enemies revengeful hate!
   Who is there left their Fury to withstand?
   What Champions now to guard thy helpless Land?   230
   Who is there left in listed Fields to head
Thy valiant Youth, and lead them on to Victory?
      Alas! thy valiant Youth are dead,
      And all thy brave Commanders too:
Lo! how the Glut and Riot of the Grave thus lie,   235
   And none survive the fatal Overthrow,
To right their injur'd Ghosts upon the barbarous Foe!
Rest, ye bless'd shades, in everlasting Peace,
   Who fell your Country's bloody Sacrifice:
   For ever Sacred be your Memories,   240
   And may e're long some dread Avenger rise
      To wipe off Heav'ns and your Disgrace:
      May then these proud insulting Foes
Wash off our stains of Honor with their Blood.
   May they ten thousand-fold repay our loss.   245
For every Life a Myriad, every Drop a Flood.

235 thus] *1683*; they *conj. Ed.*

THE

O   D   E

OF

Aristotle in *Athenæus*,

PARAPHRAS'D.

_____

I

Honour! thou greatest Blessing in the gift of Heaven,
   Which only art to its chief Darlings given:
   Cheaply with Blood and Dangers art thou sought,
   Nor canst at any rate be over-bought.

Thou, shining Honor, art the noblest chase   5
Of all the braver part of Human Race:
   Thou only art worth living for below,
     And only worth our dying too.
   For thee, bright Goddess, for thy charming sake,
   Does *Greece* such wond'rous Actions undertake: 10
   For thee no Toils, nor Hardships she forgoes,
And Death amidst ten thousand ghastly Terrors wooes.
   So powerfully do'st thou the mind inspire,
   And kindlest there so generous a fire,
     As makes thy zealous Votaries   15
       All things, but Thee despise;
     Makes them the love of Thee prefer
   Before th'enchantments of bewitching Gold,
   Before th'embraces of a Parent's arms,
   Before soft ease, and Love's enticing Charms,   20
And all, that Men on Earth most valuable hold.

II

   For Thee the Heav'n-born *Hercules*
   And *Leda*'s faithful Twins, in Birth no less,
   So many mighty Labours underwent,
And by their God-like Deeds proclaim'd their high Descent.
     By thee they reach'd the blest Abode,   26
The worthy Prize, for which in Glory's paths they trod.
   By thee great *Ajax*, and the greater Son
   Of *Peleus* were exalted to Renown:
   Envied by the Immortals did they go,   30
   Laden with triumph to the shades below.
     For thee, and thy dear sake
Did the young *Hermias* worthy of *Atarna* lately stake
   His Life in Battel to the chance of Fate,
   And bravely lost, what he so boldly set: 35
     Yet lost he not his glorious aim,
   But by short Death purchas'd eternal Fame:
The grateful Muses shall embalm his Memory,
       And never let it die:
     They shall his great Exploits rehearse,   40
And consecrate the Hero in immortal Verse.

Upon the WORKS of BEN. JOHNSON.

Written at Croyden. Anno $16\frac{7}{8}$

ODE.

(1)

Great Thou! whom 'tis a crime almost to dare to praise;
Whose firm, establisht and unshaken glories stand,
    And proudly their own fame command,
  Above our pow'r to lessen, or to raise,
And all, but the few heirs of thy brave Genius and thy Bays;   5
Hail mighty *Founder* of our Stage! for so I dare
Entitle thee, nor any modern censures fear,
  Nor care what thy unjust detractors say:
They'll say perhaps that others did materials bring,
  That others did the first foundations lay;   10
  And glorious 'twas (we grant) but to begin:
  But thou alone could'st finish the Design,
All the fair Model and the workmanship was thine.
  Some bold *Advent'rers* might have bin before,
    Who durst the unknown world explore: 15
  By them it was survey'd at distant view,
  And here and there a Cape and Line they drew
  Which only serv'd as hints and marks to thee,
Who wast resersv'd to make the full Discovery.
  Art's Compass to thy painfull search we ow,   20
Whereby thou wentst so far, and we may after go;
By that we may Wit's vast and trackless Ocean try,
    Content no longer as before
    Dully to coast along the shore,

0.1 Johnson.] *1683*; Jonson, / reprinted. / Pindarique. *R*; Johnson / Reprinted, *R224*   0.2 *R* (*A⁰*); *not in 1683*   1 whom 'tis a] *1683*; who
maks't it *R*   5 And] *1683*; 'Bove *R*   11 (we grant)] *R²*, *1683*; *not
in R¹*

But steer a course more unconfin'd and free,   25
Beyond the narrow bounds, that pent Antiquity.

(2)

Never till thee the Theater possest
A Prince with equal pow'r and greatness blest:
    No Government, or Laws it had,
    To strengthen and establish it,   30
    Till thy great hand the Scepter sway'd,
But groan'd under a wretched Anarchy of wit.
    Unform'd and void was then it's Poesy,
    Only some preexisting matter we
                    Perhaps could see   35
    That might foretel what was to be:
    A rude and undigested lump it lay,
Like the old Chaos ere the birth of light and day,
Till thy brave Genius like a new Creator came,
    And undertook the mighty frame;   40
No shuffled Atoms did the well-built work compose,
It from no lucky hit of blund'ring chance arose
    (As some of this great Fabrick idly dream)
    But wise all-seeing judgement did contrive,
    And knowing art its graces give.   45
No sooner did thy Soul with active force and fire
    The dull and heavy mass inspire,
    But strait throwout it let us see
    Proportion, order, harmony,
And every part did to the whole agree,   50
And strait appear'd a beauteous new-made World of Poetry.

(3)

Let dull and ignorant Pretenders Art condemn
    (Those only foes to Art and Art to them)
The meer Fanaticks and Enthusiasts in Poetry
    (For Schismaticks in that, as in Religion be)   55
    Who make't all Revelation, Trance and Dream,

31 the] *1683*; it's *R*   42 It] *R*; If *1683*

   Let them despise her laws, and think
   That Rules and Forms the Spirit stint:
Thine was no mad unruly frenzy of the brain
    Which justly might deserve the chain: 60
  'Twas brisk and mettled, but a manag'd rage,
Sprightly as vig'rous youth, and cool as temp'erate age.
  Free, like thy Will, it did all force disdain
  But suffer'd Reason's loose and easy rein,
    By that it suffer'd to be led   65
Which did not curb poetique liberty, but guide.
  Fancy, that wild and haggard Faculty,
  Untam'd in most and let at random fly,
  Was wisely govern'd and reclaim'd by thee,
  Restraint and discipline was made endure,   70
And by thy calm and milder Judgement brought to lure:
  Yet when 'twas at some nobler Quarry sent
  With bold and towring wings it upwards went,
    Not lessen'd at the greatest height,
Not turn'd by the most giddy flights of dazling Wit. 75

(4)

  Nature and Art, together met and joyn'd,
  Made up the character of thy great mind:
   That, like a bright and glorious sphere,
   Appear'd with num'erous stars embellish'd o're,
And much of light to thee, and much of influence bore: 80
   This was the strong intelligence, whose pow'r
Turn'd it about, and did th'unerring motions steer.
  Concurring both, like vital seed and heat,
  The noble births they joyntly did beget,
   And hard 'twas to be thought,   85
Which most of force to the great generation brought.
So mingling Elements compose our Body's frame
   Fire, Water, Earth and Air
  Alike their just proportions share:
  Each undistinguish'd still remains the same,   90
  Yet can't we say that either's here, or there,
But all we know not how are scatter'd every where.
   73 upwards] *R*; upward *1683*   87 Body's] *R*; Bodies *1683*

(5)

Sober and grave was still the garb thy Muse put on,
 No tawdry, careless, slattern dress,
 Nor starch'd and formal with affectedness,   95
Nor the cast Mode and Fashion of the Court and Town:
 But neat, agreeable and janty 'twas,
 Well-fitted it sate close in every place,
And all became with an uncommon Air and Grace.
 Rich, costly and substantial was the Stuff,   100
Not barely smooth, nor yet too coarsely rough:
  No refuse ill-patch'd Shreds o'th' Schools,
 The motly wear of read and learned Fools.
No French Commodity, which now so much do's take,
 And our own better manufacture spoil;   105
  Nor was it ought of forein Soil;
But staple all, and all of English growth and make:
 What Flow'rs soe're of art it had, were found
  No tinsel'd slight embroideries;
 But all appear'd, either the native ground,   110
Or twisted, wrought and interwoven with the piece.

(6)

 Plain Humour, shewn with her whole various face,
  Not mask'd with any antick dress,
 Nor screw'd in forc'd ridiculous grimace
  (The gaping Rabble's dull delight,   115
 And more the Actor's than the Poet's wit)
  Such did she enter on thy Stage,
And such was represented to the wondring Age.
 Well wast thou skill'd and read in human kind,
In every wild fantastick Passion of his mind: 120
Did'st into all his hidden inclinations dive,
  What each from Nature do's receive,
Or Age, or Sex, or Quality, or Country give:
 What Custom too, that mighty Sorceress,
  Whose powr'ful Witchcraft do's transform   125
Inchanted Man to several monstrous images,

101 barely smooth, ... coarsely rough:] *1683*; coarsely rough, ... barely
smooth: *R* 119 wast] *1683*; was *R*

Makes this an odd and freakish Monkey turn,
    And that a grave and solemn Ass appear,
And all a thousand beastly shapes of folly wear:
    Whate're Caprice, or Whimsy leads awry   130
    Perverted and seduc'd Mortality;
        Or do's incline and byass it
From what's discreet and wise and right and good and fit;
    All in thy faithful glass were so exprest,
    As if they were reflections of thy brest,   135
    As if they had bin stamp'd on thy own mind,
And thou the universal vast Idea of Mankind.

                          (7)

Never didst thou with the same Dish repeated cloy,
    Tho every Dish, well-cook'd by thee,
    Contain'd a plentiful variety,   140
    To all, that could sound relishing palats be:
Each Regale with new Delicacies did invite,
    Courted the tast, and rais'd the appetite:
    Whate're fresh dainty Fops in season were,
    To garnish and set out thy bill of fare   145
    (Those never found to fail throwout the year,
    For seldom that ill-natur'd Planet rules,
    That plagues a Poet with a dearth of Fools)
    What thy strict observation e're survey'd,
From the fine luscious Spark of high and courtly breed,   150
        Down to the dull insipid Cit,
    Made thy pleas'd Audience entertainment fit,
Serv'd up with all the grateful poignancies of Wit.

                          (8)

Most Plays are writ like Almanacks of late,
And serve one only year one only State;   155
Another makes them useless, stale and out of date;
    But thine were wisely calculated fit
    For each Meridian, every Clime of wit:

---

137 Mankind.] *1683*; the kind: *R*   142 Regale] *1683*; Treat *R*   Delica-
cies] *1683*; Regalios *R*

For all succeeding time and after-age,
And all Mankind might thy vast Audience sit,   160
And the whole World be justly made thy Stage.
Still they shall taking be, and ever new,
Still keep in vogue in spite of all the damning crew,
   Till the last Scene of this great Theater
                 Clos'd and shut down,   165
     The num'erous Actours all retire,
  And the grand Play of human Life be done.

(9)

Beshrew their envious tongues, who seek to blast thy Bays,
  Who Spots in thy bright fame would find, or raise,
  And say it only shines with borrow'd Rays.   170
  Rich in thy self, to whose unbounded store
  Exhausted Nature could vouchsafe no more;
Thou couldst alone the Empire of the Stage maintain,
  Couldst all its grandeur and its port sustain,
  Nor neededst others Subsidies to pay,   175
Neededst no Tax on forein, or thy native Country lay,
  To bear the charges of thy purchas'd fame;
    But thy own stock could raise the same,
Thy sole Revenue all the vast expence defray.
Yet, like some mighty Conquerour in Poetry,   180
    Design'd by Fate of choice to be
Founder of its new Universal Monarchy,
  Boldly thou didst the learned World invade;
  Whil'st all around thy pow'rful Genius sway'd:
  Soon vanquisht *Rome* and *Greece* were made submit,   185
  Both were thy humble tributaries made,
And thou returnd'st in triumph with their captive Wit.

(10)

  Unjust and more ill-natur'd those,
  Thy weak, but spiteful and malicious Foes,
  Who on thy happiest Talent fix a lye,   190
And call that slowness, which was care and industry.

Let me (with pride so to be guilty thought)
Share all thy wish'd Reproach, and share thy shame,
 If diligence be deem'd a fault
If to be faultless must deserve their blame.   195
Judge of thy self alone (for none there were,
Could be so just, or could be so severe)
 Thou thy own Works didst strictly try
By known and uncontested Rules of Poetry,
And gav'st thy Sentence still impartially.   200
With rigour thou arraign'dst each guilty line,
And didst of each offending word define,
And spar'dst no criminal Sence, because 'twas thine.
Unbrib'd by Favour, Love, or Self-conceit
  (For never, or too seldom we,   205
Objects too near us, our own blemishes can see)
 Thou didst no smalst delinquencies acquit,
 But saw'st them to Correction all submit,
Saw'st Execution done on all convicted crimes of Wit.

(11)

Some curious Painter, taught by Art to dare,   210
(For they with Poets in that title share)
When he would undertake a glorious Frame
Of lasting worth, and fadeless as his fame;
Long he contrives and weighs the bold design,
Long holds his doubting hand, ere he begin,   215
And justly then proportions every stroke and line,
 And oft he brings it to review,
And oft he do's deface, and dashes oft anew,
And mixes oil to make the flitting colours dure,
To keep 'em from the tarnish of injurious time secure: 220
Finish'd at length in all, that care and skill can do,
 The matchless Piece is set to publick view,
 And all surpriz'd about it wondring stand,
  And tho no name be found below,
 Yet strait discern th' unimitable hand,   225
And strait they cry, 'tis *Titian*, or 'tis *Angelo*:

199 Rules] *1683*; Laws *R* 202 *R; not in 1683* 204 by] *R*; with *1683*
209 Wit.] *1683*; Wit *R* 219 oil] *R*; Oyls *1683*

So thy brave Soul, that scorn'd all cheap and easy ways,
            And trod no common road to praise,
Would not with rash and speedy negligence proceed
    (For who e're saw Perfection grow in hast?   230
    Or that soon done, which must for ever last?)
    But gently did advance with wary heed,
And shew'd that Mastery is most in justness read.
    Nought ever issued from thy teeming brest,
But what had gone full time, could write exactly best,   235
And stand the sharpest censure, and defy the rigidst Test.

                            (12)

    Twas thus th' Almighty Poet (if we dare
    Our weak and meaner Acts with his compare)
When He the World's fair Poem did of old design,
That Work, which now must boast no longer date than thine,
    Tho twas in him alike to will and do,   241
    Tho the same word, that spoke, could make it too:
Yet would he not such quick and hasty methods use,
Nor did an instant (which it might) the great Effect produce;
    But when th' All-wise himself in councel sate,   245
    Vouchsaf'd to think and be deliberate;
When Heav'n consider'd, and th' Eternal Wit and sence
        Seem'd to take time and care and pains
        It shew'd that some uncommon birth
That something worthy of a *God* was coming forth.   250
    Nought uncorrect there was, nought faulty there,
No Point amiss did in the large voluminous Piece appear:
    And when the glorious Author all survey'd,
    Survey'd whatere his mighty labours made,
        Well-pleas'd he was to find   255
All answer'd the great Model and Idea of his Mind
    Pleas'd at himself he in high wonder stood,
And much his pow'r and much his wisdom did applaud,
To see how all was perfect, all transcendent good.

    234 teeming] *R*; seeming *1683*   237 Twas thus] *R²*, *1683*; As when *R¹*
cancelled   254 made,] *1683* (made *R cropped*)

(13)

Let meaner Spirits stoop to low precarious fame,   260
    Content on gross and coarse applause to live,
    And what the dull and sensless Rabble give,
    Thou didst it still with noble scorn contemn,
    Nor wouldst that wretched Alms receive,
The poor Subsistence of some bankrupt sordid name.   265
    Thine was no empty vapour, rais'd beneath,
                    And form'd of common breath,
    The false and foolish fire, that's whisk'd about
By popular Air, and glares a while, and then go's out:
But 'twas a solid, whole and perfect globe of light,   270
    That shone all over, was all over bright,
And dar'd all sully'ing clouds, and fear'd no dark'ning night.
    Like the gay Monarch of the Stars and Sky,
        Who wheresoe're he do's display
    His Soverain lustre and majestick ray,   275
    Strait all the less and petty glories nigh
                    Vanish and shrink away,
O'rewhelm'd and swallow'd by the greater blaze of day:
With such a strong, an awfull and victorious beam
    Appear'd (and ever shall appear) thy Fame,   280
View'd and ador'd by all th' undoubted race of wit,
    Who only can endure to look on it,
        The rest o'recome with too much light,
With too much brightness dazled, or extinguish'd quite.
    Restless and uncontroul'd it now shall pass   285
    As wide a course about the world as he,
    And when his long-repeated travels cease,
        Begin a new and vaster race,
And still tread round the endless circle of Eternity.

273 the Stars] *1683*; Stars *R*   281 ador'd] *R²*, *1683*; admir'd *R¹ cancelled*

THE NINTH
O D E
Of the Third Book of
H O R A C E,
IMITATED.

A Dialogue betwixt the Poet and *Lydia*.

Donec gratus eram tibi, &c.

I.

Hor.   While you for me alone had Charms,
And none more welcome fill'd your Arms,
Proud with content, I slighted Crowns,
And pitied Monarchs on their Thrones.

II.

Lyd.   While you thought *Lydia* only fair,   5
And lov'd no other Nymph but her,
Lydia was happier in your Love,
Than the bless'd Virgins are above.

III.

Hor.   Now *Chloes* charming Voice and Art
Have gain'd the conquest of my Heart: 10
For whom, ye Fates, I'd wish to die,
If mine the Nymphs dear Life might buy.

IV.

Lyd.   *Thyrsis* by me has done the same,
The Youth burns me with mutual Flame:
For whom a double Death I'd bear;   15
Would Fate my dearest *Thyrsis* spare.

V.

Hor.   But say, fair Nymph, if I once more
Become your Captive as before?
Say, I throw off my *Chloes* chain,
And take you to my Breast again?   20

VI.

Lyd.   Why then, tho he more bright appear,
More constant than a fixed Star;
Tho you than Wind more fickle be,
And rougher than the stormy Sea;
     By Heav'n, and all its Pow'rs I vow   25
     I'd gladly live, and die with you.

24 Sea;] *Ed.* (*1710* Sea,); Sea. *1683*

UPON A

L A D Y,

Who by overturning of a
Coach, had her Coats behind
flung up, and what was under
shewn to the View of the
Company.

Out of *Voiture.*

I.

Phillis, 'tis own'd, I am your Slave,
This happy moment dates your Reign;
No force of Human Pow'r can save
My captive Heart, that wears your chain:
But when my Conquest you design'd;   5
Pardon, bright Nymph, if I declare,
It was unjust, and too severe,
Thus to attack me from behind.

II.

Against the Charms, your Eyes impart,
With care I had secur'd my Heart;   10
On all the wonders of your Face
Could safely and unwounded gaze:
But now entirely to enthral
My Breast, you have expos'd to view
Another more resistless Foe,   15
From which I had no guard at all.

III.

At first assault constrain'd to yield,
My vanquish'd Heart resign'd the Field,
My Freedom to the Conqueror
Became a prey that very hour: 20
The subtle Traitor, who unspied
Had lurk'd till now in close disguise,
Lay all his life in ambush hid
At last to kill me by surprize.

IV.

A sudden Heat my Breast inspir'd,   25
The piercing Flame, like Light'ning, sent
From that new dawning Firmament
Thro every Vein my Spirits fir'd;
My Heart, before averse to Love,
No longer could a Rebel prove;   30
When on the Grass you did display
Your radiant B U M to my survey,
And sham'd the Lustre of the Day.

V.

The Sun in Heav'n, abash'd to see
A thing more gay, more bright than He,   35
Struck with disgrace, as well he might,
Thought to drive back the Steeds of Light:
His Beams he now thought useless grown,
That better were by yours supplied,
But having once seen your Back-side,   40
For shame he durst not shew his own.

VI.

Forsaking every Wood and Grove,
The *Sylvans* ravish'd at the sight,
In pressing Crowds about you strove,
Gazing, and lost in wonder quite: 45
Fond *Zephyr* seeing your rich store
Of Beauty, undescried before,
Enamor'd of each lovely Grace,   ⎫
Before his own dear *Flora*'s face,   ⎬
Could not forbear to kiss the place.   ⎭   50

VII.

The beauteous Queen of Flow'rs, the Rose,
In blushes did her shame disclose:
Pale Lillies droop'd, and hung their heads,
And shrunk for fear into their Beds:
The amorous *Narcissus* too,   55
Reclaim'd of fond self-love by you,
His former vain desire cashier'd,
And your fair Breech alone admir'd.

VIII.

When this bright Object greets our sight,
All others lose their Lustre quite: 60
Your Eyes that shoot such pointed Rays,
And all the Beauties of your Face,
Like dwindling Stars, that fly away
At the approach of brighter Day,
No more regard, or value bear,   65
But when its Glories disappear.

IX.

Of some ill Qualities they tell,
Which justly give me cause to fear;
But that, which most begets despair,
It has no sense of Love at all: 70
More hard than Adamant it is,
They say, that no Impression takes,

It has no Ears, nor any Eyes,
And rarely, very rarely speaks.

X.

Yet I must love't, and own my Flame,   75
Which to the world I thus rehearse,
Throughout the spacious coasts of Fame
To stand recorded in my Verse:
No other subject, or design
Henceforth shall be my Muses Theme,   80
But with just Praises to proclaim
The fairest ARSE, that e're was seen.

XI.

In pity gentle *Phillis* hide
The dazling Beams of your Back-side;
For should they shine unclouded long,   85
All human kind would be undone.
Not the bright Goddesses on high,
That reign above the starry Sky,
Should they turn up to open view   ⎫
All their immortal Tails, can shew   ⎬   90
An *Arse-h—* so divine as you.   ⎭

75 love't] *Ed.*; lov't *1683*

C A T U L L U S
E P I G R.   V I I.
IMITATED.

_____

Quæris quot mihi Basiationes, &c.

NAY, *Lesbia*, never ask me this,
How many Kisses will suffice?
Faith, 'tis a question hard to tell,

Exceeding hard; for you as well
May ask what sums of Gold suffice   5
The greedy Miser's boundless Wish:
Think what drops the Ocean store,
With all the Sands, that make its Shore:
Think what Spangles deck the Skies,
When Heaven looks with all its Eyes: 10
Or think how many Atoms came
To compose this mighty Frame:
Let all these the Counters be,
To tell how oft I'm kiss'd by thee:
Till no malicious Spy can guess   15
To what vast height the Scores arise;
Till weak Arithmetick grow scant,
And numbers for the reck'ning want:
All these will hardly be enough
For me stark staring mad with Love.   20

SOME
E L E G I E S
OUT OF
OVID'S Amours,
IMITATED.

BOOK II.   ELEGY IV.

That he loves Women of all sorts and sizes.

Non ego mendosos ausim defendere mores, &c.

Not I, I never vainly durst pretend
My Follies and my Frailties to defend:
I own my Faults, if it avail to own,
While like a graceless wretch I still go on:

I hate my self, but yet in spite of Fate   5
Am fain to be that loathed thing I hate:
In vain I would shake off this load of Love,
Too hard to bear, yet harder to remove:
I want the strength my fierce Desires to stem,
Hurried away by the impetuous stream.   10
'Tis not one Face alone subdues my Heart,
But each wears Charms, and every Eye a Dart:
And wheresoe're I cast my Looks abroad,
In every place I find Temptations strow'd.
The modest kills me with her down-cast Eyes,   15
And Love his ambush lays in that disguise.
The Brisk allures me with her gaity,
And shews how Active she in Bed will be:
If Coy, like cloyster'd Virgins, she appears,
She but dissembles, what she most desires: 20
If she be vers'd in Arts, and deeply read,
I long to get a Learned Maidenhead:
Or if Untaught and Ignorant she be,
She takes me then with her simplicity:
One likes my Verses, and commends each Line,   25
And swears that *Cowley*'s are but dull to mine:
Her in mere Gratitude I must approve,
For who, but would his kind Applauder love?
Another damns my Poetry, and me,
And plays the Critick most judiciously: 30
And she too fires my Heart, and she too charms,
And I'm agog to have her in my arms.
One with her soft and wanton Trip does please,
And prints in every step, she sets, a Grace:
Another walks with stiff ungainly tread;   35
But she may learn more pliantness abed.
This sweetly sings; her Voice does Love inspire,
And every Breath kindles and blows the fire:
Who can forbear to kiss those Lips, whose sound
The ravish'd Ears does with such softness wound?   40
That sweetly plays: and while her Fingers move, ⌉

36 abed.] *Ed.*; abed, *1683*

While o're the bounding Strings their touches rove, ⎫
My Heart leaps too, and every Pulse beats Love: ⎬
What Reason is so pow'rful to withstand   ⎭
The magick force of that resistless Hand?   45
Another Dances to a Miracle,
And moves her numerous Limbs with graceful skill:
And she, or else the Devil's in't, must charm,
A touch of her would bed-rid Hermits warm.
If tall; I guess what plenteous Game she'l yield,   50
Where Pleasure ranges o're so wide a Field:
If low; she's pretty: both alike invite,
The Dwarf, and Giant both my wishes fit.
Undress'd; I think how killing she'd appear,
If arm'd with all Advantages she were: 55
Richly attir'd; she's the gay Bait of Love,
And knows with Art to set her Beauties off.
I like the Fair, I like the Red-hair'd one,
And I can find attractions in the Brown:
If curling Jet adorn her snowy Neck,   60
The beauteous *Leda* is reported Black:
If curling Gold; *Aurora*'s painted so:
All sorts of Histories my Love does know.
I like the Young with all her blooming Charms,
And Age it self is welcom to my Arms: 65
There uncropt Beauty in its flow'r assails,
Experience here, and riper sense prevails.
In fine, whatever of the Sex are known
To stock this spacious and well-furnish'd Town;
Whatever any single man can find   70
Agreeable of all the num'rous kind:
At all alike my haggard Love does fly,
And each is Game, and each a Miss for me.

53 fit.] *Ed.*; fit, *1683*

BOOK II. ELEGY V

To his Mistriss that jilted him.

Nullus amor tanti est: abeas pharetrate Cupido, &c.

Nay then the Devil take all Love! if I
So oft for its damn'd sake must wish to die:
What can I wish for but to die, when you,
Dear faithless Thing, I find, could prove untrue?
Why am I curs'd with Life? why am I fain   5
For thee, false Jilt, to bear eternal Pain?
'Tis not thy Letters, which thy Crimes reveal,
Nor secret Presents, which thy Falshood tell:
Would God! my just suspicions wanted cause,
That they might prove less fatal to my ease: 10
Would God! less colour for thy guilt there were,
But that (alas!) too much of proof does bear:
Bless'd he, who what he loves can justifie, ⎫
To whom his Mistriss can the Fact deny,   ⎬
And boldly give his Jealousie the lye.   ⎭   15
Cruel the Man, and uncompassionate,
And too indulgent to his own Regret,
Who seeks to have her guilt too manifest,
And with the murd'ring secret stabs his Rest.
I saw, when little you suspected me,   20
When sleep, you thought, gave opportunity,
Your Crimes I saw, and these unhappy eyes
Of all your hidden stealths were Witnesses:
I saw in signs your mutual Wishes read,
And Nods the message of your Hearts convey'd: 25
I saw the conscious Board, which writ all o're
With scrawls of Wine, Love's mystick Cypher bore:
Your Glances were not mute, but each bewray'd,
And with your Fingers Dialogues were made:
I understood the Language out of hand,   30

(For what's too hard for Love to understand?)
Full well I understood for what intent
All this dumb Talk, and silent Hints were meant:
And now the Ghests were from the Table fled,
And all the Company retir'd to bed.   35
I saw you then with wanton Kisses greet,
Your Tongues (I saw) did in your Kisses meet:
Not such as Sisters to their Brothers give,
But Lovers from their Mistrisses receive:
Such as the God of War, and *Paphian* Queen   40
Did in the height of their Embraces joyn.
Patience, ye Gods! (cried I) *what is't I see?*
Unfaithful! why this Treachery to me?
How dare you let another in my sight
Invade my native Property and Right?   45
He must not, shall not do't: by Love I swear
I'll seize the bold usurping Ravisher:
You are my Free-hold, and the Fates design,
That you should be unalienably mine:
These Favours all to me impropriate are: 50
How comes another then to trespass here?
This, and much more I said, by Rage inspir'd,
While conscious shame her Cheeks with Blushes fir'd:
Such lovely stains the face of Heav'n adorn
When Light's first blushes paint the bashful Morn: 55
So on the Bush the flaming Rose does glow,
When mingled with the Lillies neighb'ring Snow:
This, or some other Colour much like these,
The semblance then of her Complexion was:
And while her Looks that sweet Disorder wore   60
Chance added Beauties undisclos'd before:
Upon the ground she cast her jetty Eyes,
Her Eyes shot fiercer Darts in that Disguise:
Her Face a sad and mournful Air express'd,
Her Face more lovely seem'd in sadness dress'd: 65
Urg'd by Revenge, I hardly could forbear,
Her braided Locks and tender Cheeks to tear:
Yet I no sooner had her Face survey'd,
But strait the tempest of my Rage was laid:

A look of her did my Resentments charm,   70
A look of her did all their Force disarm:
And I, that fierce outrageous thing e're-while,
Grow calm as Infants, when in sleep they smile:
And now a Kiss am humbly fain to crave,
And beg no worse than she my Rival gave: 75
She smil'd, and strait a throng of Kisses prest, ⎫
The worth of which, should *Jove* himself but taste, ⎬
The brandish'd Thunder from his Hand would wrest: ⎭
Well-pleas'd I was, and yet tormented too,
For fear my envied Rival felt them so: 80
Better they seem'd by far than I e're taught,
And she in them shew'd something new methought:
Fond jealous I my self the Pleasure grutch,
And they displeas'd, because they pleas'd too much:
When in my mouth I felt her darting Tongue,   85
My wounded Thoughts it with suspicion stung:
Nor is it this alone afflicts my mind,
More reason for complaint remains behind:
I grieve not only that she Kisses gave,
Tho that affords me cause enough to grieve: 90
Such never could be taught her but in Bed,
And Heav'n knows what Reward her Teacher had.

BOOK II. ELEGY X.

To a Friend,
Acquainting him, that he is in Love with
two at one time.

Tu mihi, tu certè (memini) Græcine, negabas, &c.

I've heard, my Friend, and heard it said by you,
No Man at once could ever well love two:
But I was much deceiv'd upon that score,

For single I at once love one, and more:
Two at one time reign joyntly in my Breast,   5
Both handsom are, both charming, both well-dress'd,
And hang me, if I know, which takes me best:
This Fairer is than that, and that than this,
That more than this, and this than that does please:
Tost, like a Ship, by diff'rent gusts of Love,   10
Now to this point, and now to that I move.
Why, Love, why do'st thou double thus my pains?
Was't not enough to bear one Tyrant's chains?
Why, Goddess, do'st thou vainly lavish more
On one, that was top-full of Love before?   15
Yet thus I'd rather love, than not at all,
May that ill Curse my Enemies befal:
May my worst Foe be damn'd to love of none,
Be damn'd to Continence, and lie alone:
Let Loves alarms each night disturb my Rest,   20
And drowsie sleep never approach my Breast,
Or strait-way thence be by new Pleasure chas'd.
Let Pleasures in succession keep my Sense
Ever awake, or ever in a Trance:
Let me lie melting in my fair One's Arms,   25
Riot in Bliss, and surfeit on her Charms:
Let her undo me there without controul,
Drain nature quite, suck out my very Soul:
And, if by one I can't enough be drawn,
Give me another, clap more Leeches on.   30
The Gods have made me of the sporting kind,
And for the Feat my Pliant Limbs design'd:
What Nature has in Bulk to me denied,
In Sinews and in vigor is supplied:
And should my Strength be wanting to Desire,   35
Pleasure would add new Fewel to the Fire:
Oft in soft Battles have I spent the Night,
Yet rose next Morning vig'rous for the Fight,
Fresh as the Day, and active as the Light:
No Maid, that ever under me took pay,   40
From my Embrace went unoblig'd away.
Bless'd he, who in Loves service yields his Breath,

Grant me, ye Gods, so sweet, so wish'd a Death!
In bloody Fields let Souldiers meet their Fate,
To purchase dear-bought Honor at the rate: 45
Let greedy Merchants trust the faithless Main,
And shipwrack Life and Soul for sordid gain:
Dying, let me expire in gasps of Lust,
And in a gush of Joy give up the ghost:
    And some kind pitying Friend shall say of me,   50
    So did he live, and so deserv'd to die.

A FRAGMENT of
P E T R O N I U S,
PARAPHRAS'D.

Fœda est in coitu, & brevis voluptas, &c.

I hate Fruition, now 'tis past,
'Tis all but nastiness at best;
The homeliest thing, that man can do,
Besides, 'tis short and fleeting too:
A squirt of slippery Delight,   5
That with a moment takes its flight:
A fulsom Bliss, that soon does cloy,
And makes us loath what we enjoy.
Then let us not too eager run,
By Passion blindly hurried on,   10
Like Beasts, who nothing better know,
Than what meer Lust incites them to:
For when in Floods of Love we're drench'd,
The Flames are by enjoyment quench'd:
But thus, let's thus together lie,   15
And kiss out long Eternity:
Here we dread no conscious spies,
No blushes stain our guiltless Joys:
Here no Faintness dulls Desires,
And Pleasure never flags, nor tires: 20

This has pleas'd, and pleases now,
And for Ages will do so:
   Enjoyment here is never done,
   But fresh, and always but begun.

AN
O   D   E
OF
ANACREON,
PARAPHRAS'D.

The C U P.

Τὸν ἄργυρον τορεύσας, &c.

Make me a Bowl, a mighty Bowl,
Large, as my capacious Soul,
Vast, as my thirst is; let it have
Depth enough to be my Grave;
I mean the Grave of all my Care,   5
For I intend to bury't there,
Let it of Silver fashion'd be,
Worthy of Wine, worthy of me,
Worthy to adorn the Spheres,
As that bright Cup amongst the Stars: 10
That Cup which Heaven deign'd a place;
Next the Sun its greatest Grace.
Kind Cup! that to the Stars did go,
To light poor Drunkards here below:
Let mine be so, and give me light,   15
That I may drink and revel by't:
Yet draw no shapes of Armour there,
No Cask, nor Shield, nor Sword, nor Spear,
Nor Wars of *Thebes*, nor Wars of *Troy*,
Nor any other martial Toy: 20

For what do I vain Armour prize,
Who mind not such rough Exercise,
But gentler Sieges, softer Wars,
Fights, that cause no Wounds, or Scars?
I'll have no Battles on my Plate,   25
Lest sight of them should Brawls create,
Lest that provoke to Quarrels too,
Which Wine it self enough can do.
Draw me no Constellations there,
No Ram, nor Bull, nor Dog, nor Bear,   30
Nor any of that monstrous fry
Of Animals, which stock the sky:
For what are Stars to my Design,   ⎫
Stars, which I, when drunk, out-shine,   ⎬
Out-shone by every drop of Wine?   ⎭   35
I lack no Pole-Star on the Brink,
To guide in the wide Sea of Drink,
But would for ever there be tost;
And wish no Haven, seek no Coast.
Yet, gentle Artist, if thou'lt try   40
Thy Skill, then draw me (let me see)
Draw me first a spreading Vine,
Make its Arms the Bowl entwine,
With kind embraces, such as I
Twist about my loving she.   45
Let its Boughs o're-spread above
Scenes of Drinking, Scenes of Love:
Draw next the Patron of that Tree,
Draw *Bacchus* and soft *Cupid* by;
Draw them both in toping Shapes,   50
Their Temples crown'd with cluster'd Grapes:
Make them lean against the Cup,
As 'twere to keep their Figures up:
And when their reeling Forms I view,
I'll think them drunk, and be so too: 55
    The Gods shall my examples be,
    The Gods, thus drunk in Effigy.

24 or Scars?] *1683*; nor Scars. *1683A*   39 And wish] *1683*; Wish *1683A*
48 that] *1683*; the *1683A*

218

An Allusion to
M A R T I A L.

BOOK I. EPIG. 118.

As oft, Sir *Tradewel*, as we meet,
You're sure to ask me in the street,
When you shall send your Boy to me,
To fetch my Book of Poetry,
And promise you'l but read it o're,   5
And faithfully the Loan restore:
But let me tell ye as a Friend,
You need not take the pains to send:
'Tis a long way to where I dwell,
At farther end of *Clarkenwel*:   10
There in a Garret near the Sky,
Above five pair of Stairs I lie.
But, if you'd have, what you pretend,
You may procure it nearer hand:
In *Cornhil*, where you often go,   15
Hard by th' *Exchange*, there is, you know,
A Shop of Rhime, where you may see
The Posts all clad in Poetry;
There H[*indmarsh*] lives of high renown,
The noted'st T O R Y in the Town: 20
Where, if you please, enquire for me,
And he, or's Prentice, presently,
From the next Shelf will reach you down
The Piece well bound for half a Crown:
The Price is much too dear, you cry,   25
To give for both the Book, and me:
Yes doubtless, for such vanities,
We know, Sir, you are too too wise.

19 H[*indmarsh*]] *Ed.* *(1722)*; *H— 1683*

THE

D R E A M.

Written, *March* 10. 1677.

Late as I on my Bed reposing lay,
And in soft sleep forgot the Toils of Day,
My self, my Cares, and Love, all charm'd to Rest,
And all the Tumults of my waking Breast,
Quiet and calm, as was the silent Night,   5
Whose stillness did to that bless'd sleep invite;
I dreamt, and strait this visionary Scene
Did with Delight my Fancy entertain.
    I saw, methought, a lonely Privacy,
Remote alike from man's and Heavens Eye,   10
Girt with the covert of a shady Grove,
Dark as my thoughts, and secret as my Love:
Hard by a Stream did with that softness creep,
As 'twere by its own murmurs husht asleep;
On its green Bank under a spreading Tree,   15
At once a pleasant, and a shelt'ring Canopy,
There I, and there my dear *Cosmelia* sate,
Nor envied Monarchs in our safe Retreat:
So heretofore were the first Lovers laid
On the same Turf of which themselves were made.   20
A while I did her charming Glories view,
Which to their former Conquests added new;
A while my wanton hand was pleas'd to rove
Thro all the hidden Labyrinths of Love;
Ten thousand Kisses on her Lips I fix'd,   25
Which she with interfering Kisses mix'd,
Eager as those of Lovers are in Death,
When they give up their Souls too with the Breath.
    Love by these Freedoms first became more bold,

16 At once a pleasant, and a] *1683*; A pleasant, and a *conj. Ed.*; At once a
pleasant, and (*1698*); At once a pleasant, (*1703*)

At length unruly, and too fierce to hold: 30
See then (said I) *and pity, charming Fair,* ⎫
Yield quickly, yield; I can no longer bear   ⎬
Th'impatient Sallies of a Bliss so near: ⎭
You must, and you alone these storms appease,
And lay those Spirits which your Charms could raise;   35
Come, and in equal Flouds let's quench our Flame,
Come let's—and unawares I went to name
The Thing, but stopt and blusht methought in Dream.
    At first she did the rude Address disown,
And check'd my Boldness with an angry Frown,   40
But yielding Glances, and consenting Eyes
Prov'd the soft Traitors to her forc'd Disguise;
And soon her looks with anger rough e're while,
Sunk in the dimples of a calmer smile:
Then with a sigh into these words she broke,   45
And printed melting Kisses as she spoke:
Too strong, Philander, *is thy pow'rful Art*
To take a feeble Maids ill-guarded Heart:
Too long I've struggled with my Bliss in vain,
Too long oppos'd what I oft wish'd to gain,   50
Loath to consent, yet loather to deny,
At once I court, and shun Felicity:
I cannot, will not yield;—and yet I must,
Lest to my own Desires I prove unjust:
Sweet Ravisher! what Love commands thee, do;   55
Tho I'm displeas'd, I shall forgive thee too,
Too well thou know'st;—and there my hand she press'd,
And said no more, but blush'd and smil'd the rest.
    Ravish'd at the new grant, fierce eager I
Leap'd furious on, and seiz'd my trembling Prey;   60
With guarding Arms she first my Force repell'd,
Shrunk, and drew back, and would not seem to yield;
Unwilling to o'recome, she faintly strove,
One hand pull'd to, what t'other did remove:
So feeble are the struglings, and so weak   65
In sleep we seem, and only seem to make:
Forbear! (she said) *ah, gentle Youth, forbear*
      66 only seem] *Ed.* (*1684a*); only sleep *1683*

(And still she hug'd, and clasp'd me still more near)
Ah! will you? will you force my Ruin so?
Ah! do not, do not, do not; - let me go.   70
      What follow'd was above the pow'r of Verse,
Above the reach of Fancy to rehearse:
Not dying Saints enjoy such Extasies,
When they in Vision antedate their Bliss;
Not Dreams of a young Prophet are so bless'd, ⎫   75
When holy Trances first inspire his Breast,   ⎬
And the God enters there to be a Guest.   ⎭
Let duller Mortals other Pleasures prize,
Pleasures which enter at the waking Eyes,
Might I each Night such sweet Enjoyments find,   80
I'd wink for ever, be for ever blind.

A
S A T Y R
TOUCHING
N O B I L I T Y .

Out of Monsieur *B O I L E A U.*

'Tis granted, that Nobility in Man,
Is no wild flutt'ring Notion of the Brain,
Where he, descended of an ancient Race,
Which a long train of numerous Worthies grace,
By Virtues Rules guiding his steddy Course,   5
Traces the steps of his bright Ancestors.
      But yet I can't endure an haughty Ass,
Debauch'd with Luxury, and slothful Ease,
Who besides empty Titles of high Birth,
Has no pretence to any thing of Worth,   10
Shoud proudly wear the Fame, which others sought,
And boast of Honor which himself ne'er got.
      I grant, the Acts which his Fore-fathers did
Have furnish'd matter for old *Hollinshead*,

For which their Scutcheon, by the *Conqu'ror* grac'd   15
Still bears a *Lion Rampant* for its Crest:
But what does this vain mass of Glory boot
To be the Branch of such a noble Root,
If he of all the Heroes of his Line
Which in the Register of Story shine,   20
Can offer nothing to the World's regard,
But mouldy Parchments which the Worms have spar'd?
If sprung, as he pretends, of noble Race,
He does his own Original disgrace,
And, swoln with selfish Vanity and Pride,   25
To greatness has no other claim beside,
But squanders life, and sleeps away his days,
Dissolv'd in Sloth, and steep'd in sensual ease?
   Mean while to see how much the Arrogant
Boasts the false Lustre of his high Descent,   30
You'd fancy him Comptroller of the Sky,
And fram'd by Heaven of other Clay than me.
   Tell me, great Hero, you, that would be thought
So much above the mean and humble Rout.
Of all the Creatures which do men esteem?   35
And which would you your self the noblest deem?
Put case of Horse: No doubt, you'l answer strait,
The Racer, which has often'st won the Plate:
Who full of mettle, and of sprightly Fire,
Is never distanc'd in the fleet Career: 40
Him all the Rivals of *New-market* dread,
And crowds of Vent'rers stake upon his Head:
But if the Breed of *Dragon*, often cast,
Degenerate, and prove a Jade at last;
Nothing of Honor, or respect (we see)   45
Is had of his high Birth and Pedigree:
But maugre all his great Progenitors,
The worthless Brute is banish'd from the Course,
Condemn'd for Life to ply the dirty Road,
To drag some Cart, or bear some Carrier's Load.   50
   Then how can you with any sense expect
That I should be so silly to respect
The ghost of Honor, perish'd long ago,

That's quite extinct, and lives no more in you?
Such gaudy Trifles with the Fools may pass,   55
Caught with mere shew, and vain Appearances:
Virtue's the certain Mark, by Heav'n design'd,
That's always stamp'd upon a noble mind:
If you from such illustrious Worthies came,
By copying them your high Extract proclaim: 60
Shew us those generous Heats of Gallantry,
Which Ages past did in those Worthies see,
That zeal for Honor, and that brave Disdain,
Which scorn'd to do an Action base, or mean:
Do you apply your Interest aright,   65
Not to oppress the Poor with wrongful Might?
Would you make Conscience to pervert the Laws,
Tho brib'd to do't, or urg'd by your own Cause?
Dare you, when justly call'd, expend your Blood
In service for your King's and Countries good?   70
Can you in open Field in Armour sleep,
And there meet danger in the ghastliest shape?
    By such illustrious Marks as these, I find,
You're truly issued of a noble kind:
Then fetch your Line from *Albanact*, or *Knute*,   75
Or, if these are too fresh, from older *Brute*:
At leisure search all History to find
Some great and glorious Warriour to your mind:
Take *Caesar, Alexander*, which you please,
To be the mighty Founder of your Race;   80
In vain the World your Parentage bely,
That was, or should have been your Pedegree.
    But, if you could with ease derive your Kin
From *Hercules* himself in a right Line;
If yet there nothing in your Actions be,   85
Worthy the name of your high Progeny;
All these great Ancestors, which you disgrace,
Against you are a cloud of Witnesses:
And all the Lustre of their tarnish'd Fame
Serves but to light and manifest your Shame: 90
In vain you urge the merit of your Race,
And boast that Blood, which you your selves debase.

In vain you borrow, to adorn your Name,
The Spoils and Plunder of another's Fame;
If, where I look'd for something Great and Brave, ⎫   95
I meet with nothing but a Fool, or Knave,   ⎬
A Traitor, Villain, Sycophant, or Slave,   ⎭
A freakish Madman, fit to be confin'd,
Whom *Bedlam* only can to order bind,
Or (to speak all at once) a barren Limb   100
And rotten Branch of an illustrious Stem.
    But I am too severe, perhaps you'l think,
And mix too much of Satyr with my Ink:
We speak to men of Birth and Honor here,
And those nice Subjects must be touch'd with care: 105
Cry mercy, Sirs! Your Race, we grant, is known;
But how far backwards can you trace it down?
You answer: For at least a thousand year,   ⎫
And some odd hundreds you can make't appear: ⎬
'Tis much: But yet in short the proofs are clear: ⎭   110
All Books with your Fore-fathers Titles shine,
Whose names have scap'd the general wreck of Time:
But who is there so bold, that dares engage
His Honor, that in this long Tract of Age
No one of all his Ancestors deceas'd   115
Had e're the fate to find a Bride unchast?
That they have all along *Lucretia*'s been,   ⎫
And nothing e're of spurious Blood crept in,   ⎬
To mingle and defile the Sacred Line?   ⎭
    Curss'd be the day, when first this vanity   120
Did primitive simplicity destroy,
In the bless'd state of infant time, unknown,
When Glory sprung from Innocence alone:
Each from his merit only Title drew,
And that alone made Kings, and Nobles too: 125
Then, scorning borrow'd Helps to prop his Name,
The Hero from himself deriv'd his Fame:
But Merit by degenerate time at last,
Saw Vice ennobled, and her self debas'd:
And haughty Pride false pompous Titles feign'd,   130
T'amuse the World, and Lord it o're mankind:

Thence the vast Herd of Earls and Barons came,
For Virtue each brought nothing but a Name:
Soon after Man, fruitful in Vanities,
Did Blazoning and Armory devise,   135
Founded a College for the Herald's Art,
And made a Language of their Terms apart,
Compos'd of frightful words, of *Chief*, and *Base*,
Of *Chevron, Saltier, Canton, Bend*, and *Fess*,
And whatsoe're of hideous Jargon else   140
Mad *Guillim*, and his barbarous Volume fills.

    Then farther the wild Folly to pursue,
Plain down-right Honor out of fashion grew:
But to keep up its Dignity and Birth,
Expence and Luxury must set it forth: 145
It must inhabit stately Palaces,
Distinguish Servants by their Liveries,
And carrying vast Retinues up and down,
The Duke and Earl be by their Pages known.

    Thus Honor to support it self is brought   ⎫ 150
To its last shifts, and thence the Art has got ⎬
Of borrowing every where, and paying nought: ⎭
'Tis now thought mean, and much beneath a Lord
To be an honest man, and keep his Word;
Who, by his Peerage and Protection safe,   155
Can plead the Privilege to be a Knave:
While daily Crowds of starving Creditors
Are forc'd to dance attendance at his doors:
Till he at length with all his mortgag'd Lands
Are forfeited into the Banker's hands: 160
Then to redress his wants, the bankrupt Peer
To some rich trading Sot, turns Pensioner:
And the next News, you're sure to hear that he
Is nobly wed into the Company:
Where for a Portion of ill gotten Gold,   165
Himself and all his Ancestors are sold:
And thus repairs his broken Family
At the expence of his own Infamy.

    141 *Guillim*] *1683* (*corr.*); *Guilliam 1683* (*uncorr.*)

For if you want Estate to set it forth,
In vain you boast the splendor of your Birth: 170
Your priz'd Gentility for madness goes,
And each your Kindred shuns and disavows:
But he that's rich is prais'd at his full rate,
And tho he once cry'd *Small-coal* in the street,
Tho he, nor none of his e're mention'd were,   175
But in the Parish-Book, or Register,
    D[ugda]le by help of Chronicle shall trace
An hundred Barons of his ancient Race.

176 Register,] *Ed.* (*1722*); Register. *1683*   177 D[ugda]le] *Ed.* (*1722*);
D-*le 1683*

A

S A T Y R.

Address'd to a Friend, *that is about to
leave the University, and come
abroad in the World.*

If you're so out of love with Happiness,
To quit a College-life, and learned ease;
Convince me first, and some good Reasons give,
What methods and designs you'l take to live:
For such Resolves are needful in the Case,   5
Before you tread the worlds mysterious Maze:
Without the Premisses in vain you'l try
To live by Systems of Philosophy:
Your *Aristotle, Cartes*, and *Le-Grand*,
And *Euclid* too in little stead will stand.   10
    How many men of choice and noted parts,
Well fraught with Learning, Languages, and Arts,
Designing high Preferment in their mind,
And little doubting good success to find,
With vast and tow'ring thoughts have flock'd to Town, 15
But to their cost soon found themselves undone,
Now to repent, and starve at leisure left,
Of miseries last Comfort, Hope, bereft?
    These fail'd for want of good Advice, you cry,

Because at first they fix'd on no employ: 20
Well then, let's draw the Prospect and the Scene
To all advantage possibly we can:
The world lies now before you, let me hear,
What course your Judgment counsels you to steer:
Always consider'd, that your whole Estate,   25
And all your Fortune lies beneath your Hat:
Were you the Son of some rich Usurer,
That starv'd and damn'd himself to make his Heir
Left nought to do, but to interr the Sot,
And spend with ease what he with pains had got;   30
'Twere easie to advise how you might live,
Nor would there need instruction then to give:
But you, that boast of no Inheritance,
Save that small stock, which lies within your Brains,
Learning must be your Trade, and therefore weigh   35
With heed, how you your Game the best may play;
Bethink your self a while, and then propose
What way of Life is fitt'st for you to choose.
   If you for Orders, and a Gown design,
Consider only this, dear Friend of mine,   40
The Church is grown so overstock'd of late, ⎫
That if you walk abroad, you'l hardly meet ⎬
More Porters now than Parsons in the street. ⎭
At every Corner they are forc'd to ply
For Jobs of hawkering Divinity: 45
And half the number of the Sacred Herd
Are fain to strowl and wander unpreferr'd:
   If this, or thoughts of such a weighty Charge
Make you resolve to keep your self at large;
For want of better opportunity,   50
A School must your next Sanctuary be:
Go, wed some Grammar-Bridewel, and a Wife,
And there beat *Greek* and *Latin* for your life:
With birchen Scepter there command at will,
Greater than *Busby*'s self, or Doctor *Gill*:   55
But who would be to the vile Drudg'ry bound
Where there so small encouragement is found?

Where you for recompence of all your pains
Shall hardly reach a common Fidler's gains?
For when you've toil'd and labour'd all you can,   60
To dung and cultivate a barren Brain:
A Dancing-Master shall be better paid,
Tho he instructs the Heels, and you the Head:
To such Indulgence are kind Parents grown,
That nought costs less in Breeding than a Son: 65
Nor is it hard to find a Father now,
Shall more upon a Setting-dog allow:
And with a freer hand reward the Care
Of training up his Spaniel, than his Heir.
    Some think themselves exalted to the Sky,   70
If they light in some noble Family:
Diet, an Horse, and thirty pounds a year,
Besides th'advantage of his Lordships ear,
The credit of the business, and the State,
Are things that in a Youngster's Sense sound great.   75
Little the unexperienc'd Wretch does know,
What slavery he oft must undergo:
Who tho in silken Skarf and Cassock drest,
Wears but a gayer Livery at best:
When Dinner calls the Implement must wait   80
With holy Words to consecrate the Meat:
But hold it for a Favour seldom known,
If he be deign'd the Honor to sit down.
Soon as the Tarts appear, Sir *Crape*, withdraw!
Those Dainties are not for a spiritual Maw: 85
Observe your distance, and be sure to stand
Hard by the Cistern with your Cap in hand:
There for diversion you may pick your Teeth,
Till the kind Voider comes for your Relief:
For meer Board-wages such their Freedom sell,   90
Slaves to an Hour, and Vassals to a Bell:
And if th'enjoyment of one day be stole,
They are but Pris'ners out upon Parole:
Always the marks of slavery remain,
And they, tho loose, still drag about their Chain.   95
    And where's the mighty Prospect after all,

A Chaplainship serv'd up, and seven years Thrall?
The menial thing perhaps for a Reward
Is to some slender Benefice preferr'd,
With this Proviso bound, that he must wed ⎤
My Ladies antiquated Waiting-maid,   ⎬   100
In Dressing only skill'd, and Marmalade. ⎦

    Let others who such meannesses can brook,
Strike Countenance to every Great man's Look:
Let those that have a mind, turn slaves to eat,   105
And live contented by another's Plate:
I rate my Freedom higher, nor will I
For Food and Rayment truck my Liberty.
But, if I must to my last shifts be put,
To fill a Bladder, and twelve yards of Gut: 110
Rather with counterfeited wooden Leg,
And my right Arm tied up, I'll chuse to beg:
I'll rather chuse to starve at large, than be
The gawdiest Vassal to Dependency.

    'T has ever been the top of my Desires,   115
The utmost height to which my wish aspires,
That Heav'n would bless me with a small Estate,
Where I might find a close obscure retreat;
There, free from Noise, and all ambitious ends,
Enjoy a few choice Books, and fewer Friends,   120
Lord of my self, accountable to none,
But to my Conscience, and my God alone:
There live unthought of, and unheard of, die,
And grudg Mankind my very memory.
But since the Blessing is (I find) too great   125
For me to wish for, or expect of Fate:
Yet, maugre all the spight of Destiny,
My Thoughts and Actions are, and shall be free.
A certain Author, very grave and sage,
This Story tells: no matter, what the Page.   130

    One time, as they walk'd forth e're break of day,
The Wolf and Dog encounter'd on the way:
Famish'd the one, meager, and lean of plight,

115 'T has] *1683* (*corr.*); 'Tas *1683* (*uncorr.*)

As a cast Poet, who for Bread does write:
The other fat and plump, as Prebend, was,   135
Pamper'd with Luxury, and holy Ease.
    Thus met, with Complements, too long to tell,
Of being glad to see each other well:
How now, Sir Towzer? (said the Wolf) *I pray,*
Whence comes it, that you look so sleek and gay?   140
While I, who do as well (I'm sure) deserve,
For want of Livelihood am like to starve?
Troth Sir (replied the Dog) *'thas been my Fate,*
I thank the friendly Stars, to hap of late
On a kind Master, to whose care I owe   145
All this good Flesh, wherewith you see me now:
From his rich Voider every day I'm fed
With Bones of Fowl, and Crusts of finest Bread:
With Fricassee, Ragoust, *and whatsoe're*
Of costly Kickshaws now in fashion are,   150
And more variety of Boil'd and Roast,
Than a Lord Mayor's *Waiter e're could boast.*
Then, Sir, 'tis hardly credible to tell,
How I'm respected and belov'd by all:
I'm the Delight of the whole Family,   155
Not darling Shock *more Favorite than I:*
I never sleep abroad, to Air expos'd,
But in my warm apartment am inclos'd:
There on fresh Bed of Straw, with Canopy
Of Hutch above, like Dog of State I lie.   160
Besides, when with high Fare, and Nature fir'd,
To generous Sports of Youth I am inspir'd,
All the proud shees are soft to my Embrace
From Bitch of Quality down to Turn-spit Race:
Each day I try new Mistrisses and Loves,   165
Nor envy Sovereign Dogs in their Alcoves.
Thus happy I of all enjoy the best,
No mortal Cur on Earth yet half so bless'd:
And farther to enhance the Happiness,
All this I get by idleness and ease.   170
    Troth! (said the Wolf) *I envy your Estate*
Would to the Gods it were but my good Fate,

That I might happily admitted be
A Member of your bless'd Society!
I would with Faithfulness discharge my place 175
In any thing that I might serve his Grace:
But, think you, Sir, it would be feasible,
And that my Application might prevail?
   Do but endeavour, Sir, you need not doubt;
I make no question but to bring't about: 180
Only rely on me, and rest secure,
I'll serve you to the utmost of my Pow'r;
As I'm a Dog of Honor, Sir:——but this
I only take the Freedom to advise,
That you'd a little lay your Roughness by, 185
And learn to practise Complaisance, like me.
   For that let me alone: I'll have a care,
And top my part, I warrant, to a hair:
There's not a Courtier of them all shall vie
For Fawning and for Suppleness with me. 190
And thus resolv'd at last, the Travellers
Towards the House together shape their course:
The Dog, who Breeding well did understand,
In walking gives his Ghest the upper hand:
And as they walk along, they all the while 195
With Mirth, and pleasant Raillery beguile
The tedious Time and Way, till Day drew near,
And Light came on; by which did soon appear
The Mastiff's Neck to view all worn and bare.
   This when his Comrade spi'd, *What means* (said he) 200
This Circle bare, which round your Neck I see?
If I may be so bold;——Sir, you must know,
That I at first was rough and fierce, like you,
Of Nature curs'd, and often apt to bite
Strangers, and else, who ever came in sight: 205
For this I was tied up, and underwent
The Whip sometimes, and such light Chastisement:
Till I at length by Discipline grew tame,
Gentle and tractable, as now I am:
'Twas by this short and slight severity 210
I gain'd these Marks and Badges, which you see:

But what are they? Allons Monsieur! *let's go.*
Not one step farther: Sir, excuse me now.
Much joy t'ye of your envied, bless'd Estate:
I will not buy Preferment at that rate: 215
  A Gods name, take your golden Chains for me:
  Faith, I'd not be a King, not to be free:
  Sir Dog, your humble Servant, so Godbw'y.

S O M E
V E R S E S
Written in *Septemb.* 1676

Presenting a Book to *C O S M E L I A.*

Go, humble Gift, go to that matchless Saint,
Of whom thou only wast a Copy meant:
And all, that's read in thee, more richly find
Compriz'd in the fair Volume of her mind;
That living System, where are fully writ   5
All those high Morals, which in Books we meet:
Easie, as in soft Air, there writ they are,
Yet firm, as if in Brass they graven were.
Nor is her Talent lazily to know
As dull Divines, and holy Canters do;   10
She acts what they only in Pulpits prate,
And Theory to Practice does translate:
Not her own Actions more obey her Will,
Than that obeys strict Virtues dictates still:
Yet does not Virtue from her Duty flow,   15
But she is good, because she will be so:
Her Virtue scorns at a low pitch to flie,
'Tis all free Choice, nought of Necessity:
By such soft Rules are Saints above confin'd,
Such is the Tie, which them to Good does bind.   20

The scatter'd Glories of her happy Sex
In her bright Soul as in their Center mix:
And all, that they possess but by Retail,
She hers by just Monopoly can call;
Whose sole Example does more Virtues shew,   25
Than Schoolmen ever taught, or ever knew.
No Act did e're within her Practice fall,
Which for th' atonement of a Blush could call:
No word of hers e're greeted any ear,
But what a Saint at her last gasp might hear: 30
Scarcely her Thoughts have ever sullied been
With the least print, or stain of native Sin:
Devout she is, as holy Hermits are,
Who share their time 'twixt Extasie, and Prayer:
Modest, as infant Roses in their Bloom,   35
Who in a Blush their fragrant Lives consume:
So chast, the Dead themselves are only more,
Who lie divorc'd from Objects, and from Power:
So pure, could Virtue in a Shape appear,
'Twould chuse to have no other Form, but Her: 40
So much a Saint, I scarce dare call her so,
For fear to wrong her with a name too low:
Such the Seraphick Brightness of her mind,
I hardly can believe her Womankind:
But think some nobler Being does appear,   ⎫   45
Which to instruct the World, has left the Sphere,   ⎬
And condescends to wear a Body here.   ⎭
Or, if she mortal be, and meant to show
The greater Art by being form'd below;
  Sure Heaven preserv'd her by the Fall uncurs'd,   50
  To tell how good the Sex was made at first.

        28 Blush] *Ed.* (*'1683'*); Bush *1683*

THE

P A R T I N G.

———————————

Too happy had I been indeed, if Fate
Had made it lasting, as she made it great;
But 'twas the Plot of unkind Destiny,
To lift me to, then snatch me from my Joy:
She rais'd my Hopes, and brought them just in view,   5
And then in spight the pleasing Scene withdrew.
So *He* of old the *promis'd Land* survey'd,
Which he might only see, but never tread:
So Heav'n was by that damned *Caitiff* seen,   ⎫
He saw't, but with a mighty Gulf between,   ⎬   10
He saw't to be more wretched, and despair agen: ⎭
Not Souls of dying Sinners, when they go,
Assur'd of endless Miseries below,
Their Bodies more unwillingly desert,
Than I from you, and all my Joys did part.   15
As some young Merchant, whom his Sire unkind
Resigns to every faithless Wave and Wind;
If the kind Mistriss of his Vows appear,
And come to bless his Voyage with a Prayer,
Such Sighs he vents as may the Gale increase,   20
Such Floods of Tears as may the Billows raise:
And when at length the launching Vessel flies,
And severs first his Lips, and then his Eyes;
Long he looks back to see what he adores,
And, while he may, views the beloved Shores.   25
Such just concerns I at your Parting had,
With such sad Eyes your turning Face survey'd:
Reviewing, they pursu'd you out of sight,
Then sought to trace you by left Tracks of Light:
And when they could not Looks to you convey,   ⎫   30
Tow'rds the lov'd Place they took delight to stray, ⎬
And aim'd uncertain Glances still that way.   ⎭

Complaining of
A B S E N C E.

Ten days (if I forget not) wasted are
(A year in any Lover's Calendar)
Since I was forc'd to part, and bid adieu
To all my Joy and Happiness in you:
And still by the same Hindrance am detain'd,   5
Which me at first from your lov'd Sight constrain'd:
Oft I resolve to meet my Bliss, and then
My Tether stops, and pulls me back agen:
So, when our raised Thoughts to Heav'n aspire,
Earth stifles them, and choaks the good desire.   10
Curse on that Man, who Bus'ness first design'd,
And by't enthral'd a free-born Lover's mind:
A curse on Fate, who thus subjected me,
And made me slave to any thing but thee!
Lovers should be as unconfin'd as Air,   15
Free as its wild Inhabitants from Care:
So free those happy Lovers are above,
Exempt from all Concerns but those of Love:
But I, poor Lover militant below,
The Cares and Troubles of dull Life must know;   20
Must toil for that, which does on others wait,
And undergo the drudgery of Fate:
Yet I'll no more to her a Vassal be,
Thou now shalt make, and rule my Destiny:
Hence troublesom Fatigues! all Bus'ness hence!   25
This very hour my Freedom shall commence:
Too long that Jilt has thy proud Rival been,
And made me by neglectful Absence sin;
But I'll no more obey its Tyranny,   ⎫
Nor that, nor Fate it self shall hinder me,   ⎬   30
Henceforth from seeing and enjoying thee.   ⎭

20 know;] *Ed.* (*1684a*); know? *1683*

Promising a
V I S I T.

Sooner may Art, and easier far divide
The soft embracing waters of the Tide,
Which with united Friendship still rejoyn,
Than part my Eyes, my Arms, or Lips from thine:
Sooner it may Time's headlong motion force,   5
In which it marches with unalter'd course,
Or sever this from the succeeding Day,
Than from thy happy Presence force my stay.
Not the touch'd Needle (emblem of my Soul)
With greater Rev'rence trembles to its Pole,   10
Nor Flames with surer instinct upwards go,
Than mine, and all their motives tend to you.
Fly swift, ye minutes, and contract the space
Of Time, which holds me from her dear Embrace:
When I am there I'll bid you kindly stay,   15
I'll bid you rest, and never glide away.
Thither when Bus'ness gives me a Release
To lose my Cares in soft and gentle Ease,
I'll come, and all arrears of Kindness pay,
And live o're my whole Absence in one day.   20
Not Souls, releas'd from human Bodies, move
With quicker hast to meet their Bliss above;
Than I, when freed from Clogs, that bind me now,
Eager to seize my Happiness, will go.
Should a fierce Angel arm'd with Thunder stand,   25
And threaten Vengeance with his brandish'd hand,
To stop the entrance to my Paradise;
I'll venture, and his slighted Bolts despise.
Swift as the wings of Fear, shall be my Love,
And me to her with equal speed remove: 30
Swift, as the motions of the Eye, or Mind,
I'll thither fly, and leave slow Thought behind.

THE CARELESS
Good   Fellow.

Written, *March* 9. 1680.

S O N G.

I.

A Pox of this fooling and plotting of late,
What a pother and stir has it kept in the State!
Let the Rabble run mad with Suspicions and Fears,
Let them scuffle and jar, till they go by the ears:
  Their Grievances never shall trouble my pate,   5
  So I can enjoy my dear Bottle at quiet.

II.

What Coxcombs were those, who would barter their ease
And their Necks for a Toy, a thin Wafer and Mass?
At old *Tyburn* they never had needed to swing,
Had they been but true Subjects to Drink, and their King;   10
  A Friend and a Bottle is all my design;
  He has no room for Treason, that's top-full of Wine.

III.

I mind not the Members and makers of Laws,
Let them sit or Prorogue, as his Majesty please:
Let them damn us to Woollen, I'll never repine   15
At my Lodging, when dead, so alive I have Wine:
  Yet oft in my Drink I can hardly forbear
  To curse them for making my Claret so dear.

IV.

I mind not grave Asses, who idly debate
About Right and Succession, the trifles of State;   20
We've a good King already: and he deserves laughter
That will trouble his head with who shall come after:

Come, here's to his Health, and I wish he may be
As free from all Care and all Trouble, as we.

V.

What care I how Leagues with the *Hollander* go?   25
Or Intrigues betwixt *Sidney*, and Monsieur *D'Avaux*?
What conerns it my Drinking, if *Casel* be sold,
If the Conqueror take it by Storming, or Gold?
  Good *Bordeaux* alone is the place that I mind,
  And when the Fleet's coming, I pray for a Wind.   30

VI.

The Bully of *France*, that aspires to Renown
By dull cutting of Throats, and vent'ring his own;
Let him fight and be damn'd, and make Matches, and Treat,
To afford the News-mongers, and Coffee-house Chat:
  He's but a brave wretch, while I am more free,   35
  More safe, and a thousand times happier than He.

VII.

Come He, or the Pope, or the Devil to boot,
Or come Faggot and Stake; I care not a Groat;
Never think that in *Smithfield* I Porters will heat:
No, I swear, Mr. *Fox*, pray excuse me for that.   40
  I'll drink in defiance of Gibbet and Halter,
  This is the Profession, that never will alter.

A

S A T Y R.

The Person of Spencer *is brought in,*
Dissuading the Author from the
Study of POETRY, *and shewing how*
little it is esteem'd and encourag'd in
this present Age.

One night, as I was pondering of late
On all the mis'ries of my hapless Fate,
Cursing my rhiming Stars, raving in vain

At all the Pow'rs, which over Poets reign:
In came a ghastly Shape, all pale and thin,   5
As some poor Sinner, who by Priest had been
Under a long Lent's Penance, starv'd and whip'd,
Or par-boil'd Lecher, late from Hot-house crept:
Famish'd his Looks appear'd, his Eyes sunk in,
Like Morning-Gown about him hung his Skin: 10
A Wreath of Lawrel on his Head he wore,
A Book, inscrib'd the *Fairy Queen*, he bore.
  By this I knew him, rose, and bow'd, and said,
Hail reverend Ghost! all hail most sacred Shade!
Why this great Visit? why vouchsaf'd to me,   15
The meanest of thy British Progeny?
Com'st thou in my uncall'd, unhallow'd Muse,
Some of thy mighty Spirit to infuse?
If so; lay on thy Hands, ordain me fit
For the high Cure and Ministry of Wit: 20
Let me (I beg) thy great Instructions claim,
Teach me to tread the glorious paths of Fame.
Teach me (for none does better know than thou)
How, like thy self, I may immortal grow.
  Thus did I speak, and spoke it in a strain,   25
Above my common rate, and usual vein;
As if inspir'd by presence of the Bard,
Who with a Frown thus to reply was heard,
In stile of Satyr, such wherein of old
He the fam'd Tale of *Mother Hubberd* told.   30
  I come, fond Ideot, e're it be too late,
Kindly to warn thee of thy wretched Fate:
Take heed betimes, repent, and learn of me
To shun the dang'rous Rocks of Poetry:
Had I the choice of Flesh and Blood again,   35
To act once more in Life's tumultuous Scene;
I'd be a Porter, or a Scavenger,
A Groom, or any thing, but Poet here:
Hast thou observ'd some Hawker of the Town,
Who thro the Streets with dismal Scream and Tone,   40

36 tumultuous] *Ed.* (*1684a*, '*1683*'); tumultous *1683*

Cries Matches, Small-coal, Brooms, Old Shoes and Boots,
Socks, Sermons, Ballads, Lies, Gazetts, and Votes?
So unrecorded to the Grave I'd go,
And nothing but the Register tell, who:
Rather that poor unheard-of Wretch I'd be,   ⎫   45
Than the most glorious Name in Poetry,   ⎬
With all its boasted Immortality: ⎭
Rather than He, who sung on *Phrygia*'s Shore,
The *Grecian* Bullies fighting for a Whore:
Or He of *Thebes*, whom Fame so much extols   50
For praising Jockies, and *New-market* Fools.

    So many now, and bad the Scriblers be,
'Tis scandal to be of the Company:
The foul Disease is so prevailing grown,
So much the Fashion of the Court and Town,   55
That scarce a man well-bred in either's deem'd,
But who has kill'd, been clapt, and often rhim'd:
The Fools are troubled with a Flux of Brains,
And each on Paper squirts his filthy sense:
A leash of Sonnets, and a dull Lampoon   ⎫   60
Set up an Author, who forthwith is grown   ⎬
A man of Parts, of Rhiming, and Renown: ⎭
Ev'n that vile *Wretch*, who in lewd Verse each year
Describes the Pageants, and my good *Lord May'r*,
Whose Works must serve the next Election-day   65
For making Squibs, and under Pies to lay,
Yet counts himself of the inspired Train,
And dares in thought the sacred Name profane.
    But is it nought (thou'lt say) *in Front to stand,*
With Lawrel crown'd by White, *or* Loggan's *hand?*   70
Is it not great and glorious to be known,   ⎫
Mark'd out, and gaz'd at thro the wond'ring Town,   ⎬
By all the Rabble passing up and down?   ⎭
So *Oats* and *Bedloe* have been pointed at,
And every busie Coxcomb of the State: 75
The meanest Felons who thro *Holborn* go,
More eyes and looks than twenty Poets draw:

---

57 clapt, and often rhim'd] *Ed.* (*1722*); often clapt, and oft has rhim'd *1683*

If this be all, go, have thy posted Name
Fix'd up with Bills of Quack, and publick Sham;
To be the stop of gaping Prentices,   80
And read by reeling Drunkards, when they piss;
Or else to lie expos'd on trading Stall,
While the bilk'd Owner hires Gazetts to tell,
'Mongst Spaniels lost, that Author does not sell.

  Perhaps, fond Fool, thou sooth'st thy self in dream, 85
With hopes of purchasing a lasting Name?
Thou think'st perhaps thy Trifles shall remain,
Like sacred *Cowley*, and immortal *Ben?*
But who of all the bold Adventurers,
Who now drive on the trade of Fame in Verse   90
Can be ensur'd in this unfaithful Sea,
Where there so many lost and shipwrack'd be?
How many Poems writ in ancient time,
Which thy Fore-fathers had in great esteem,
Which in the crowded Shops bore any rate,   95
And sold like News-Books, and Affairs of State,
Have grown contemptible and slighted since,
As *Pordidg, Fleckno,* or the *British Prince?*
Quarles, Chapman, Heywood, Withers had Applause,
And *Wild*, and *Ogilby* in former days;   100
But now are damn'd to wrapping Drugs and Wares,
And curs'd by all their broken Stationers:
And so may'st thou perchance pass up and down,
And please a while th'admiring Court and Town,
Who after shalt in *Duck-lane* Shops be thrown,   105
To mould with *Silvester* and *Shirley* there,
And truck for pots of Ale next *Stourbridg*-Fair.
Then who'l not laugh to see th'immortal Name
To vile *Mundungus* made a Martyr Flame?
And all thy deathless Monuments of Wit,   110
Wipe Porters Tails, or mount in Paper-kite?

  But, grant thy Poetry should find success,
And (which is rare) the squeamish Criticks please;
Admit it read, and prais'd, and courted be
By this nice Age, and all Posterity;   115
If thou expectest ought but empty Fame;

Condemn thy Hopes and Labors to the Flame:
The rich have now learn'd only to admire, ⎫
He, who to greater Favours does aspire,   ⎬
Is mercenary thought, and writes to hire: ⎭   120
Would'st thou to raise thine, and thy Countries Fame,
Chuse some old *English* Hero for thy Theme,
Bold *Arthur*, or great *Edward*'s greater *Son*,
Or our fifth *Harry*, matchless in Renown,
Make *Agincourt* and *Cressy* Fields outvie   125
The fam'd *Lavinian* Shores, and Walls of *Troy*;
What *Scipio*, what *Mæcenas* would'st thou find,
What *Sidney* now to thy great Project kind?
Bless me! how great Genius! how each Line   ⎫
Is big with Sense! how glorious a Design   ⎬   130
Does thro the whole, and each Proportion shine! ⎭
How lofty all his Thoughts, and how inspir'd!
Pity, such wond'rous Parts are not preferr'd:
Cries a gay wealthy Sot, who would not bail
For bare five Pounds the Author out of Jail,   135
Should he starve there, and rot; who if a Brief ⎫
Came out the needy Poets to relieve,   ⎬
To the whole Tribe would scarce a Tester give. ⎭
But fifty Guinnies for a Whore and Clap!
The Peer's well us'd, and comes off wond'rous cheap; 140
A Poet would be dear, and out o'th'way,
Should he expect above a Coach-man's pay:
For this will any dedicate, and lye,
And dawb the gaudy Ass with Flattery?
For this will any prostitute his Sense   145
To Coxcombs void of Bounty, as of Brains?
Yet such is the hard Fate of Writers now,
They're forc'd for Alms to each great Name to bow:
Fawn, like her Lap-dog, on her tawdry Grace, ⎫
Commend her Beauty, and bely her Glass,   ⎬   150
By which she every morning primes her Face: ⎭
Sneak to his Honor, call him Wity, Brave,
And Just, tho a known Coward, Fool, or Knave,

129 *great*] *1683*; *great a conj. Ed.*; *great his* ('*1683*')

And praise his Lineage, and Nobility,
Whose Arms at first came from the Company.   155
   'Tis so, 'twas ever so, since heretofore ⎫
The blind old *Bard*, with Dog and Bell before, ⎬
Was fain to sing for bread from door to door: ⎭
The needy Muses all turn'd Gipsies then,
And of the begging Trade e're since have been: 160
Should mighty *Sappho* in these days revive,
And hope upon her stock of Wit to live;
She must to *Creswel*'s trudg to mend her Gains,
And let her Tail to hire, as well as Brains.
What Poet ever fin'd for Sheriff? or who   165
By Wit and Sense did ever Lord Mayors grow?
   My own hard Usage here I need not press, ⎫
Where you have every day before your face ⎬
Plenty of fresh resembling Instances: ⎭
Great *Cowley*'s Muse the same ill Treatment had, ⎫   170
Whose Verse shall live for ever to upbraid ⎬
Th'ungrateful World, that left such Worth unpaid. ⎭
Waller himself may thank Inheritance
For what he else had never got by Sense.
On *Butler* who can think without just Rage,   175
The Glory and the Scandal of the Age?
Fair stood his hopes, when first he came to Town,
Met every where with welcomes of Renown,
Courted and lov'd by all, with wonder read,
And promises of Princely Favour fed: 180
But what Reward for all had he at last,
After a Life in dull expectance pass'd?
The Wretch at summing up his mis-spent days
Found nothing left, but Poverty, and Praise:
Of all his Gains by Verse he could not save   185
Enough to purchase Flannel, and a Grave:
Reduc'd to want, he in due time fell sick,
Was fain to die, and be interr'd on tick:
And well might bless the Fever that was sent,
To rid him hence, and his worse Fate prevent.   190
   You've seen what fortune other Poets share;
View next the Factors of the Theatre:

That constant Mart, which all the year does hold,
Where Staple Wit is barter'd, bought, and sold;
Here trading Scriblers for their Maintainance   195
And Livelihood trust to a Lott'ry-chance:
But who his Parts would in the Service spend,
Where all his hopes on vulgar Breath depend?
Where every Sot, for paying half a Crown,
Has the Prerogative to cry him down?   200
Sidley indeed may be content with Fame,
Nor care should an ill-judging Audience damn:
But *Settle*, and the Rest, that write for Pence,
Whose whole Estate's an ounce, or two of Brains,
Should a thin House on the third day appear,   205
Must starve, or live in Tatters all the year.
And what can we expect that's brave and great, ⎫
From a poor needy Wretch, that writes to eat? ⎬
Who the success of the next Play must wait   ⎭
For Lodging, Food, and Cloaths, and whose chief care   210
Is how to spunge for the next Meal, and where?
  Hadst thou of old in flourishing *Athens* liv'd,
When all the learned Arts in Glory thriv'd,
When mighty *Sophocles* the Stage did sway,
And Poets by the State were held in pay;   215
'Twere worth thy Pains to cultivate thy Muse,
And daily wonders then it might produce;
But who would now write Hackney to a Stage,
That's only thought the Nuisance of the Age?
Go after this, and beat thy wretched Brains,   220
And toil to bring in thankless Ideots means:
Turn o're dull *Horace*, and the Classick Fools,
To poach for Sense, and hunt for idle Rules:
Be free of Tickets, and the Play-houses,   ⎫
To make some tawdry Act'ress there thy Prize,   225 ⎬
And spend thy third Days gains 'twixt her clap'd Thighs. ⎭
  All Trades and all Professions here abound,
And yet Encouragement for all is found:
Here a vile Emp'rick, who by Licence kills,

225 thy] *R94 (1703)*; by *1683*

Who every week helps to increase the Bills,   230
Wears Velvet, keeps his Coach, and Whore beside,
For what less Villains must to *Tyburn* ride.
There a dull trading Sot, in Wealth o'regrown
By thriving Knavery, can call his own
A dozen Mannors, and if Fate still bless,   235
Expects as many Counties to possess.
Punks, Panders, Bawds, all their due Pensions gain,
And every day the Great Mens Bounty drain:
Lavish expence on Wit, has never yet
Been tax'd amongst the Grievances of State.   240
The *Turky, Guinny, India* Gainers be,
And all but the Poetick Company:
Each place of Traffick, *Bantam, Smyrna, Zant,*
Greenland, Virginia, Sevil, Alicant,
And *France*, that sends us Dildoes, Lace, and Wine,   245
Vast profit all, and large Returns bring in:
Parnassus only is that barren Coast,
Where the whole Voyage and Adventure's lost.
  Then be advis'd, the slighted Muse forsake,
And *Cook* and *Dalton* for thy study take: 250
For Fees each Term sweat in the crowded Hall,
And there for Charters, and crack'd Titles bawl:
Where *M[aynar]d* thrives, and pockets more each year
Than forty Laureats of the Theater.
Or else to Orders, and the Church betake   255
Thy self, and that thy future Refuge make:
There fawn on some proud Patron to engage
Th'Advowson of cast Punk and Parsonage:
Or sooth the Court, and preach up Kingly Right,
To gain a Prebend'ry and Mitre by't.   260
In fine, turn Pettifogger, Canonist,
Civilian, Pedant, Mountebank, or Priest,
Soldier, or Merchant, Fidler, Painter, Fencer,
Jack-pudding, Juggler, Player, or Rope-dancer:
Preach, Plead, Cure, Fight, Game, Pimp, Beg, Cheat,   265
Be all but Poet, and there's way to live.   [or Thieve;

253 *M[aynar]d*] *Ed. (1722); M—d 1683*

But why do I in vain my Counsel spend
On one whom there's so little hope to mend?
Where I perhaps as fruitlesly exhort,
As Lenten Doctors, when they Preach at Court?   270
Not enter'd Punks from Lust they once have tried,
Not Fops and Women from Conceit and Pride,
Not Bawds from Impudence, Cowards from Fear,
Nor sear'd unfeeling Sinners past Despair,
Are half so hard, and stubborn to reduce,   275
As a poor Wretch, when once possess'd with Muse.
   If therefore, what I've said, cannot avail,
Nor from the Rhiming Folly thee recal,
But spight of all thou wilt be obstinate,
And run thy self upon avoidless Fate;   280
May'st thou go on unpitied, till thou be
Brought to the Parish, Bridg, and Beggary:
Till urg'd by want, like broken Scriblers, thou ⎫
Turn Poet to a Booth, a *Smithfield*-Show,   ⎬
And write Heroick Verse for *Bartholmew*.   ⎭   285
   Then slighted by the very Nursery,
May'st thou at last be forc'd to starve, like me.

275 half so] *Ed.* (*1684a*); half *1683*

A

S A T Y R,

In Imitation of the Third of

J U V E N A L.

Written, *May*, 1682.

The Poet brings in a Friend of his, giving him
an account why he removes from London *to*
live in the Country.

Tho much concern'd to leave my dear old Friend,
I must however his Design commend
Of fixing in the Country: for were I
As free to chuse my Residence, as he;
The *Peake*, the *Fens*, the *Hundreds*, or *Lands-end*,   5
I would prefer to *Fleetstreet*, or the *Strand*.
What place so desart, and so wild is there, ⎫
Whose Inconveniencies one would not bear,   ⎬
Rather than the Alarms of midnight Fire,   ⎭
The falls of Houses, Knavery of Cits,   10
The Plots of Factions, and the noise of Wits,
And thousand other Plagues, which up and down
Each day and hour infest the cursed Town?
  As Fate wou'd have't, on the appointed day
Of parting hence, I met him on the way,   15
Hard by *Mile-end*, the place so fam'd of late,
In Prose and Verse for the great *Factions Treat*;
Here we stood still, and after Complements
Of course, and wishing his good Journey hence,
I ask'd what sudden causes made him flie   20
The once-lov'd Town, and his dear Company:
When, on the hated Prospect looking back,
Thus with just rage the good old *Timon* spake.
  Since Virtue here in no repute is had,   ⎫
Since Worth is scorn'd, Learning and Sense unpaid, ⎬   25
And Knavery the only thriving Trade;   ⎭
Finding my slender Fortune every day
Dwindle and wast insensibly away,
I, like a losing Gamester, thus retreat,
To manage wiselier my last stake of Fate: 30
While I have strength, and want no staff to prop
My tott'ring Limbs, e're Age has made me stoop
Beneath its weight, e're all my Thread be spun, ⎫
And Life has yet in store some Sands to run,   ⎬
'Tis my Resolve to quit the nauseous Town.   ⎭   35

1-35 *1683*, *R* (*but see* 17, 28, 35)   17 Prose and] *R*; Prose, and *1683*
28 Dwindle and] *R*; Dwindle, and *1683*   35 nauseous] *1683*; plotting *R227*

Let thriving *Morecraft* chuse his dwelling there,
Rich with the Spoils of some young spend-thrift Heir:
Let the Plot-mongers stay behind, whose Art
Can Truth to Sham, and Sham to Truth convert:
Who ever has an House to Build, or Set   40
His Wife, his Conscience, or his Oath to let:
Who ever has, or hopes for Offices,
A Navy, Guard, or Custom-house's Place:
Let sharping Courtiers stay, who there are great
By putting the false Dice on King, and State.   45
Where they, who once were Grooms and Foot-boys known,
Are now to fair Estates and Honors grown;
Nor need we envy them, or wonder much
At their fantastick Greatness, since they're such,
Whom Fortune oft in her capricious freaks   50
Is pleas'd to raise from Kennels, and the Jakes,
To Wealth and Dignity above the rest,
When she is frolick, and dispos'd to jest.
    I live in *London*? What should I do there?
I cannot lye, nor flatter, nor forswear: 55
I can't commend a Book, or Piece of Wit,
(Tho a Lord were the Author) dully writ:
I'm no Sir *Sydrophel* to read the Stars,
And cast Nativities for longing Heirs,
When Fathers shall drop off: no *Gadbury*   60
To tell the minute, when the King shall die,
And you know what—come in: nor can I steer ⎫
And tack about my Conscience, whensoe're,   ⎬
To a new Point, I see Religion veer.   ⎭
Let others pimp to Courtier's Lechery,   65
I'll draw no City-Cuckold's Curse on me:
Nor would I do it, tho to be made great,
And rais'd to the chief Minister of State.
Therefore I think it fit to rid the Town
Of one, that is an useless member grown.   70
    Besides, who has pretence to Favour now, ⎫
But he, who hidden Villany does know,   ⎬

40 Set] *Ed.* (*1722*); Set, *1683*   68 Minister] *Ed.* ('*1683*'); Ministers *1683*

Whose Breast does with some burning Secret glow? ⌉
By none thou shalt preferr'd, or valued be,
That trusts thee with an honest Secresie: 75
He only may to great men's Friendship reach,
Who Great Men, when he pleases, can impeach.
Let others thus aspire to Dignity;
For me, I'd not their envied Grandeur buy
For all th'*Exchange* is worth, that *Pauls* will cost,   80
Or was of late in the *Scotch* Voyage lost.
What would it boot, if I, to gain my end,   ⌉
Forego my Quiet, and my ease of mind,   ⌡
Still fear'd, at last betray'd by my great Friend. ⌡

   Another Cause, which I must boldly own,   85
And not the least, for which I quit the Town,
Is to behold it made the Common-shore,
Where *France* does all her Filth and Ordure pour:
What Spark of true old *English* rage can bear
Those, who were Slaves at home, to Lord it here?   90
We've all our Fashions, Language, Complements,
Our Musick, Dances, Curing, Cooking thence;
And we shall have their Pois'ning too e're long,
If still in the improvement we go on.   94

   What would'st thou say, great *Harry*, should'st thou view
Thy gawdy flutt'ring Race of *English* now,
Their tawdry Cloaths, Pulvilio's, Essences,   ⌉
Their *Chedreux* Perruques, and those Vanities, ⌡
Which thou, and they of old did so despise?   ⌡
What would'st thou say to see th' infected Town   100
With the fowl Spawn of Foreigners o're-run?
Hither from *Paris*, and all Parts they come,
The Spue and Vomit of their Goals at home;
To Court they flock, and to *S. James* his Square,
And wriggle into Great Mens Service there: 105
Foot-boys at first, till they, from wiping Shooes,
Grow by degrees the Masters of the House:
Ready of Wit, harden'd of Impudence,   ⌉
Able with ease to put down cither *H*[*ains,*]   ⌡

   109 *H*[*ains,*]] *Ed.* (*1854 subst.*); *Hans,* (*1722*); *H—— 1683*

Both the King's Player, and King's Evidence: ⎤   110
Flippant of Talk, and voluble of Tongue,
With words at will, no Lawyer better hung:
Softer than flattering Court-Parasite,
Or City-Trader, when he means to cheat:
No Calling, or Profession comes amiss,   115
A needy *Monsieur* can be what he please,
Groom, Page, Valet, Quack, Operator, Fencer,
Perfumer, Pimp, Jack-pudding, Juggler, Dancer:
Give but the word; the Cur will fetch and bring,
Come over to the *Emperor*, or *King*:   120
Or, if you please, fly o're the Pyramid,
Which [*Asto*]*n* and the rest in vain have tried.
    Can I have patience, and endure to see
The paltry Forein Wretch take place of me,
Whom the same Wind and Vessel brought ashore,   125
That brought prohibited Goods and Dildoes o're?
Then, pray, what mighty Privilege is there
For me, that at my Birth drew *English* Air?
And where's the Benefit to have my Veins
Run *Brittish* Blood, if there's no difference   130
'Twixt me, and him, the Statute Freedom gave,
And made a Subject of a true-born Slave?
    But nothing shocks, and is more loath'd by me,
Than the vile Rascal's fulsom Flattery:
By help of this false Magnifying Glass,   135
A Louse, or Flea shall for a Camel pass:
Produce an hideous Wight, more ugly far   ⎤
Than those ill Shapes, which in old Hangings are, ⎬
He'l make him strait a *Beau Garçon* appear: ⎦
Commend his Voice and Singing, tho he bray   140
Worse than Sir *Martin Marr-all* in the Play:
And if he Rhime; shall praise for Standard Wit,
More scurvy sense than *Pryn* and *Vickars* Writ.
    And here's the mischief, tho we say the same,
He is believ'd, and we are thought to sham: 145
Do you but smile, immediately the Beast

122 [*Asto*]*n*] *Ed.*; *J——n 1683*; *Johnston 1722*

Laughs out aloud, tho he ne'er heard the jest;
Pretend, you're sad, he's presently in Tears,
Yet grieves no more than Marble, when it wears
Sorrow in Metaphor: but speak of Heat;   150
O God! how sultry 'tis! he'l cry, and sweat
In depth of Winter: strait, if you complain
Of Cold; the Weather-glass is sunk again:
Then he'l call for his Frize-Campaign, and swear,
'Tis beyond *Eighty*, he's in *Greenland* here.   155
Thus he shifts Scenes, and oft'ner in a day
Can change his Face, than Actors at a Play:
There's nought so mean, can scape the flatt'ring Sot,
Not his Lord's Snuff-box, nor his Powder-Spot:
If he but Spit, or pick his Teeth; he'l cry, ⎫   160
How every thing becomes you! let me die,   ⎬
Your Lordship does it most judiciously: ⎭
And swear, 'tis fashionable, if he Sneeze,
Extremely taking, and it needs must please.

    Besides, there's nothing sacred, nothing free   165
From the hot Satyr's rampant Lechery:
Nor Wife, nor Virgin-Daughter can escape,
Scarce thou thy self, or Son avoid a Rape:
All must go pad-lock'd: if nought else there be,
Suspect thy very Stables Chastity.   170
By this the Vermin into Secrets creep,
Thus Families in awe they strive to keep.
What living for an *English* man is there,   ⎫
Where such as these get head, and domineer,   ⎬
Whose use and custom 'tis, never to share   ⎭   175
A Friend, but love to reign without dispute,
Without a Rival, full, and absolute?
Soon as the Insect gets his *Honor's* ear,
And fly-blows some of's pois'nous malice there,
Strait I'm turn'd off, kick'd out of doors, discarded, 180
And all my former Service dis-regarded.
    But leaving these *Messieurs*, for fear that I

151 *'tis!*] *Ed.* (*'1683'*); *'tis?* *1683*   161 *you!*] *Ed.* (*'1683'*); *you?*
1683

Be thought of the *Silk-Weavers Mutiny*,
From the loath'd subject let us hasten on,
To mention other Grievances in Town: 185
And further, what Respect at all is had
Of poor men here? and how's their Service paid,
Tho they be ne'r so diligent to wait,
To sneak, and dance attendance on the Great?
No mark of Favour is to be obtain'd   190
By one, that sues, and brings an empty hand:
And all his merit is but made a sport,
Unless he glut some Cormorant at Court.
  'Tis now a common thing, and usual here,
To see the Son of some rich Usurer   195
Take place of Nobless, keep his first-rate Whore,
And for a Vaulting bout, or two give more
Than a Guard-Captains Pay: mean while the Breed
Of Peers, reduc'd to Poverty and Need,
Are fain to trudg to the *Bank-side*, and there   200
Take up with Porters leavings, Suburb-Ware,
There spend that Blood, which their great Ancestor ⎤
So nobly shed at *Cressy* heretofore,   ⎬
At Brothel Fights in some foul Common-shore.   ⎦
  Produce an Evidence, tho just he be,   205
As righteous *Job*, or *Abraham*, or *He*,
Whom Heaven, when whole Nature shipwrack'd was,
Thought worth the saving, of all human Race,
Or *t'other*, who the flaming Deluge scap'd,
When *Sodom*'s Lechers Angels would have rap'd;   210
How rich he is, must the first question be,
Next for his Manners, and Integrity,
They'l ask, *what Equipage he keeps, and what*
He's reckon'd worth in Money and Estate,
For Shrieve how oft he has been known to fine,   215
And with how many Dishes he does dine:
For look what Cash a person has in store,
Just so much Credit has he, and no more:
Should I upon a thousand Bibles Swear, ⎤

212 Integrity,] *Ed.*; Integrity: *1683*

And call each Saint throughout the Calendar, }   220
To vouch my Oath; it won't be taken here;
The Poor slight Heav'n and Thunderbolts (they think)
And Heav'n it self does at such Trifles wink.

  Besides, what store of gibing scoffs are thrown
On one, that's poor, and meanly clad in Town;   225
If his Apparel seem but overworn,
His Stockings out at heel, or Breeches torn?
One takes occasion his ript Shooe to flout,
And swears 'thas been at Prison-grates hung out:
Another shrewdly jeers his coarse Crevat,   230
Because himself wears *Point*: a third his Hat,
And most unmercifully shews his Wit,
If it be old, or does not cock aright:
Nothing in Poverty so ill is born,
As its exposing men to grinning scorn,   235
To be by tawdry Coxcombs piss'd upon,
And made the jesting-stock of each Buffoon.
Turn out there, Friend! (cries one at Church) *the Pew*
Is not for such mean scoundrel Curs, as you:
'Tis for your Betters kept: Belike, some Sot,   240
That knew no Father, was on Bulks begot:
But now is rais'd to an Estate, and Pride,
By having the kind Proverb on his side:
Let *Gripe* and *Cheatwel* take their Places there,
And *Dash* the Scriv'ners gawdy sparkish Heir,   245
That wears three ruin'd Orphans on his back:
Mean while you in the Alley stand, and sneak:
And you therewith must rest contented, since
Almighty Wealth does put such difference.
What Citizen a Son-in-law will take,   250
Bred ne'er so well, that can't a Joynter make?
What man of sense, that's poor, e'er summon'd is
Amongst the Common-Council to advise?
At Vestry-Consults when does he appear, }
For choosing of some Parish Officer,   255

220 Calendar,] *Ed.* (*1683b*); Calendar: *1683*   224 thrown] *1683* (*some
copies*) hrown (*others*)

Or making Leather-Buckets for the Choire? ⎦
  'Tis hard for any man to rise, that feels
His Virtue clog'd with Poverty at heels:
But harder 'tis by much in *London*, where   ⎤
A sorry Lodging, coarse, and slender Fare,   ⎬   260
Fire, Water, Breathing, every thing is dear: ⎦
Yet such as these an earthen Dish disdain,
With which their Ancestors, in *Edgar*'s Reign,
Were serv'd, and thought it no disgrace to dine,
Tho they were rich, had store of Leather-Coin.   265
Low as their Fortune is, yet they despise
A man that walks the streets in homely Frize:
To speak the truth, great part of *England* now
In their own Cloth will scarce vouchsafe to go:
Only, the Statutes Penalty to save,   270
Some few perhaps wear Woollen in the Grave.
Here all go gaily drest, altho it be
Above their Means, their Rank, and Quality:
The most in borrow'd Gallantry are clad,
For which the Tradesmen's Books are still unpaid: 275
This Fault is common in the meaner sort,   ⎤
That they must needs affect to bear the Port ⎬
Of Gentlemen, tho they want Income for't.   ⎦
  Sir, to be short, in this expensive Town
There's nothing without Mony to be done: 280
What will you give to be admitted there,
And brought to speech of some Court-Minister?
What will you give to have the quarter-face,
The squint and nodding go-by of his *Grace*?
His Porter, Groom, and Steward must have Fees,   285
And you may see the *Tombs* and *Tow'r* for less:
Hard Fate of Suitors! who must pay, and pray
To Livery-slaves, yet oft go scorn'd away.
  Who e're at *Barnet*, or *S. Albans* fears
To have his Lodging drop about his ears,   290
Unless a sudden Hurricane befal,
Or such a Wind as blew old *Noll* to Hell?
Here we build slight, what scarce out-lasts the Lease,
Without the help of Props and Buttresses:

And Houses now adays as much require   295
To be ensur'd from Falling, as from Fire.
There Buildings are substantial, tho less neat,
And kept with care both Wind and Water-tight:
There you in safe security are blest,
And nought, but Conscience, to disturb your Rest.   300
   I am for living where no Fires affright,
No Bells rung backward break my sleep at night:
I scarce lie down, and draw my Curtains here,
But strait I'm rous'd by the next House on Fire:
Pale, and half-dead with Fear, my self I raise,   305
And find my Room all over in a blaze:
By this 'thas seiz'd on the third Stairs, and I ⎫
Can now discern no other Remedy,   ⎬
But leaping out at Window to get free: ⎭
For if the Mischief from the Cellar came,   310
Be sure the Garret is the last, takes flame.
   The moveables of P[orda]ge were a Bed   ⎫
For him, and's Wife, a Piss-pot by its side,   ⎬
A Looking-glass upon the Cupboards Head,   ⎭
A Comb-case, Candlestick, and Pewter-spoon,   315
For want of Plate, with Desk to write upon:
A Box without a Lid serv'd to contain
Few Authors, which made up his *Vatican*:
And there his own immortal Works were laid,
On which the barbarous Mice for hunger prey'd: 320
P[ordage] had nothing, all the world does know;
And yet should he have lost this Nothing too.
No one the wretched Bard would have suppli'd
With Lodging, House-room, or a Crust of Bread.
   But if the Fire burn down some Great Man's House,   325
All strait are interessed in the loss:
The Court is strait in Mourning sure enough,
The Act, Commencement, and the Term put off:
Then we Mischances of the Town lament,
And Fasts are kept, like Judgments to prevent.   330
Out comes a Brief immediately, with speed

312 *P[orda]ge*] *Ed. (1722)*; P—ge *1683*   321 *P[ordage]*] *Ed. (1722)*; P— *1683*

To gather Charity as far as *Tweed*.
Nay, while 'tis burning, some will send him in
Timber and Stone to build his House agen:
Others choice Furniture: here some rare piece   335
Of *Rubens*, or *Vandike* presented is:
There a rich Suit of *Moreclack*-Tapestry,
A Bed of Damask, or Embroidery:
One gives a fine Scritore, or Cabinet,
Another a huge massie Dish of Plate,   340
Or Bag of Gold: thus he at length gets more
By kind misfortune than he had before:
And all suspect it for a laid Design,
As if he did himself the Fire begin.
Could you but be advis'd to leave the Town,   345
And from dear Plays, and drinking Friends be drawn,
An handsom Dwelling might be had in *Kent*,
Surrey, or *Essex*, at a cheaper Rent
Than what you're forc'd to give for one half year
To lie, like Lumber, in a Garret here: 350
A Garden there, and Well, that needs no Rope,
Engin, or Pains to Crane its Waters up:
Water is there thro Natures Pipes convey'd,
For which no Custom, or Excise is paid:
Had I the smallest Spot of Ground, which scarce   355
Would Summer half a dozen Grasshoppers,
Not larger than my Grave, tho hence remote, ⎫
Far as *S. Michaels Mount*, I would go to't, ⎬
Dwell there content, and thank the Fates to boot. ⎭
   Here want of Rest a nights more People kills   360
Than all the College, and the weekly Bills:
Where none have privilege to sleep, but those,
Whose Purses can compound for their Repose:
In vain I go to bed, or close my eyes, ⎫ `
Methinks the place the Middle Region is, ⎬   365
Where I lie down in Storms, in Thunder rise: ⎭
The restless Bells such Din in Steeples keep,
That scarce the Dead can in their Church-yards sleep:
Huzza's of Drunkards, Bell-mens midnight-Rhimes,
The noise of Shops, with Hawkers early Screams,   370

Besides the Brawls of Coach-men, when they meet
And stop in turnings of a narrow Street,
Such a loud Medley of confusion make,
As drowsie A[rche]r on the Bench would wake.

If you walk out in Bus'ness ne'er so great,   375
Ten thousand stops you must expect to meet:
Thick Crowds in every Place you must charge thro,
And storm your Passage, wheresoe're you go:
While Tides of Followers behind you throng,
And, pressing on your heels, shove you along: 380
One with a Board, or Rafter hits your Head,
Another with his Elbow bores your side;
Some tread upon your Corns, perhaps in sport,
Mean while your Legs are cas'd all o're with Dirt.
Here you the March of a slow Funeral wait,   385
Advancing to the Church with solemn State:
There a Sedan and Lacquies stop your way,
That bears some Punk of Honor to the Play:
Now you some mighty piece of Timber meet,
Which tott'ring threatens ruin to the Street: 390
Next a huge *Portland* Stone, for building *Pauls*,
It self almost a Rock, on Carriage rowls:
Which, if it fall, would cause a Massacre,
And serve at once to murder, and interr.

If what I've said can't from the Town affright,   395
Consider other dangers of the Night:
When Brickbats are from upper Stories thrown,
And emptied Chamber-pots come pouring down
From Garret Windows: you have cause to bless
The gentle Stars, if you come off with Piss: 400
So many Fates attend, a man had need
Ne'er walk without a Surgeon by his side:
And he can hardly now discreet be thought,
That does not make his Will, e're he go out.

If this you scape, twenty to one, you meet   405
Some of the drunken Scowrers of the Street,

374 A[rche]r] *Ed.* (*1854* subst.); *Arche* (*1722*); A——r *1683*   401 need] *Ed.*
(*1770*); need, *1683*

Flush'd with success of warlike Deeds perform'd,
Of Constables subdu'd, and Brothels storm'd:
These, if a Quarrel, or a Fray be mist,
Are ill at ease a nights, and want their Rest.   410
For mischief is a Lechery to some,
And serves to make them sleep like *Laudanum*.
Yet heated, as they are, with Youth and Wine,
If they discern a train of Flamboes shine,
If a Great Man with his gilt Coach appear,   415
And a strong Guard of Foot-boys in the rere,
The Rascals sneak, and shrink their Heads for fear.
Poor me, who use no Light to walk about,
Save what the Parish, or the Skies hang out,
They value not: 'tis worth your while to hear   420
The scuffle, if that be a scuffle, where
Another gives the Blows, I only bear:
He bids me stand: of force I must give way,
For 'twere a sensless thing to disobey
And struggle here, where I'd as good oppose   425
My self to P[reston] and his Mastiffs loose.
Who's there? he cries, and takes you by the Throat,
Dog! are you dumb? Speak quickly, else my Foot
Shall march about your Buttocks: whence d'ye come,
From what Bulk-ridden Strumpet reeking home?   430
Saving your reverend Pimpship, where d'ye ply?
How may one have a Job of Lechery?
If you say any thing, or hold your peace,
And silently go off; 'tis all a case:
Still he lays on: nay well, if you scape so: 435
Perhaps he'l clap an Action on you too
Of Battery: nor need he fear to meet
A Jury to his turn, shall do him right,
And bring him in large Damage for a Shooe
Worn out, besides the pains, in kicking you.   440
A Poor Man must expect nought of redress,
But Patience: his best in such a case
Is to be thankful for the Drubs, and beg

426 *P[reston]*]] *Ed. (1722); P— 1683*

That they would mercifully spare one leg
Or Arm unbroke, and let him go away   445
With Teeth enough to eat his Meat next day.
    Nor is this all, which you have cause to fear,
Oft we encounter midnight Padders here:
When the *Exchanges* and the Shops are close,   ⎫
And the rich Tradesman in his Counting-house   ⎬   450
To view the Profits of the day withdraws.   ⎭
Hither in flocks from *Shooters-Hill* they come,
To seek their Prize and Booty nearer home:
Your Purse! they cry; 'tis madness to resist,
Or strive with a cock'd Pistol at your Breast: 455
And these each day so strong and numerous grow,
The Town can scarce afford them Jail-room now.
Happy the times of the old *Heptarchy*,
E're *London* knew so much of Villany:
Then fatal Carts thro *Holborn* seldom went,   460
And *Tyburn* with few Pilgrims was content:
A less and single Prison then would do,
And serv'd the City, and the County too.
    These are the Reasons, Sir, which drive me hence,
To which I might add more, would Time dispense,   465
To hold you longer; but the Sun draws low,
The Coach is hard at hand, and I must go:
Therefore, dear Sir, farewel; and when the Town
From better Company can spare you down,
To make the Country with your Presence blest,   470
Then visit your old Friend amongst the rest:
There I'll find leisure to unlade my mind
Of what Remarques I now must leave behind:
The Fruits of dear Experience, which with these
Improv'd will serve for hints and notices;   475
    And when you write again, may be of use
    To furnish Satyr for your daring Muse.

A Dithyrambique on Drinking:
Suppos'd to be spoken by Rochester at the Guinny-Club.

Aug. 5. 1677.

Οὐκ ἐστὶ Διθύραμβος ἂν ὕδωρ πίνῃ.

(1)

Yes, you are mighty Wise, I warrant, mighty Wise!
  With all your godly Tricks, and Artifice,
Who think to chowse me of my dear and pleasant Vice:
  Hence holy Sham! in vain your fruitless Toile,
  Go! and some unexperienc'd Fop beguile,   5
To some raw ent'ring Sinner cant and whine,
Who never knew the worth of Drunkeness and Wine;
  I've tried and prov'd and found it all divine:
It is resolv'd; I will drink on and dy,
  I'le not one Minute loose, not I,   10
To hear your troublesom Divinity:
Fill me a topfull Glass, I'le drink it on the Knee,
Confusion to the next that spoils good Company.

(2)

  That gulp was worth a Soul, like it, it went,
  And thorowout new life and vigour sent;   15
  I feel it warm at once my head and heart;
I feel it all in all and all in every part:
  Let the vile Slaves of business toil and strive,
  Who want the leisure or the wit to live:
  Whil'est we life's taedious journy shorter make,   20
And reap those joys which they lack sence to take.
Thus live the Gods (if ought above our selves there be)

0.1 Dithyrambique on Drinking] *R*; Dithyrambick *1683*   0.2 *R*; The Drunkards Speech in a Mask. *1683*   0.3 *R*; *not in 1683*   0.4 *1683*; *not
in R*   7 Drunkeness] *R*; Drunkenness *1683*   10 not I,] *1683*; damme,
not I, *R*   21 lack] *1683*; want *R*   *Twelve lines, not in 1683, follow in
R (see Appendix II)*

They live so happy, unconcern'd and free:
Like us they sit and with a careless brow
Laugh at the petty jars of human kind below: 25
    Like us they spend their age in gentle ease,
Like us they drink; for what were all their Heav'n, alas!
If sober, and compell'd to want that happiness.

(3)

Assist Allmighty Wine, for thou alone hast Power,
    And other I'll Invoke no more,   30
    Assist, while with just Praise I thee Adore;
    Aided by thee I dare thy Worth Reherse
In Flights above the common Pitch of groveling Verse:
    Thou art the World's great Soul, that Heav'nly Fire,
    Which dost our dull half-kindled Mass Inspire;   35
We nothing gallant, and above our selves produce,
    Till thou dost Finish Man and Reinfuse:
Thou art the only Source of all the World calls Great,
Thou didst the Poets first and they the Gods Create;
    To Thee their Rage, their Heat and Flame they ow,   40
    Thou runst half share with Art and Nature too:
    They ow their Glory and Renown to Thee
    Thou givst their Verse and them Eternity:
    Great Alexander, that bigst Word of Fame,
    That fills her Throat and almost rends the same;   45
    Whose Valour found the World too strait a Stage
    For his wide Victories and Boundless Rage,
    Got not Repute by War alone but Thee,
He knew he ne're could Conquer by Sobriety,
And Drunk as well as Fought for universal Monarchy.   50

(4)

    Pox o' that lazy Claret! how it stays?
    Were it again to pass the Seas,

27, 28 they ... alas! | If sober] 1683; they'd drink, but Heav'n, alas! | Is
sober R   33 Pitch] R[1], 1683 (pitch); reach R[2]; strain R[2]   36 gallant]
1683; brave R[1]; high R[2]   and] 1683; or R   above] 1683, R[1]; more than R[2]
our selves] 1683; Brute R   40 Heat and] R; Heat, their 1683   41 runst]
R; must 1683   48 Repute] 1683; Renown R   50 Monarchy.] 1683; Monarchy:
R Six lines, not in 1683, follow in R (see Appendix II)   51 Claret!] 1683;
Wine! oh R

'Twould sooner be in Cargo here,
Tis now a long East-India Voyage half a Year:
  'Sdeath! here's a Minute lost, an Age I mean,   55
  Slipt by and ne're to be retriev'd agen:
  For pity suffer not the pretious Juice to die,
  Let us prevent our own and its Mortality:
Like it, our Life with standing and Sobriety is pal'd
  And like it too when dead can never be recal'd.   60
      Push on the Glass, let it measure out each Hour,
        For every Sand an Health let's pour;
      Swift as the rowling Orbs above,
    And let it too as regularly move,
  Swift as Heav'ns drunken red-fac'd Traveller the Sun,   65
    And never Rest, till his last Race be done,
    Till Time it self be all run out, and we
    Have drunk our selves into Eternity:

(5)

  Six in a Hand begin! we'll drink it twice apiece,
    A Health to all that love and Honour Vice: 70
  Six more as oft to the great Founder of the Vine
    (A God he was, I'm sure, or should have bin)
    The second Father of Mankind I meant;
    He, when the angry Pow'rs a Deluge sent,
    When for their Crimes our sinful Race was drownd,   75
    The only bold and vent'rous Man was found,
Who durst be Drunk agen, and with new Vice the World replant:
  The mighty Patriarch 'twas of blessed Memory,
  Who scap'd in the great Wreck of all Mortality,
And stock'd the Globe afresh with a brave drinking Progeny: 80
    In vain would spiteful Nature us Reclaim,
    Who to small Drink our Ile thought fit to damn,
    And set us out o'th' reach of Wine,

---

56 retriev'd] *1683*; restor'd *R*   57 For pity suffer] *1683*; Kill *R*
to] *1683*; better our selves should *R*   59 Like ... with] *1683*; our Life
like it by *R*   pal'd] *R* (= pall'd); pall'd *1683*   62 let's] *1683*; lets *R*
65 red-fac'd] *1683*; reeling *R*   77 World] *1683*; Θ *R*   78 Patriarch]
1683; Noah *R*   79 in the great] *1683*; i' th' general *R*   80 And ...
afresh] *1683*; and peopled th' empty Globe *R*   *Two lines, not in 1683, follow
in R; (see Appendix II)*

In hope strait Bounds could our vast Thirst confine;
He taught us first with Ships the Seas to roam,   85
Taught us from forreign Lands to fetch Supply,
Rare Art! that makes all the wide World our Home
Makes every Realm pay Tribute to our Luxury:

(6)

Adieu poor tottring Reason! tumble down!
This Glass shall all thy proud usurping Powers drown,   90
And Wit on thy cast Ruins shall Erect her Throne:
Adieu! thou fond Disturber of our Life,
That checkst our Joys, with all our Pleasure art at strife:
I've something brisker now to Govern me,
A more exalted noble Faculty,   95
Above thy Logick and vain boasted Pedantry:
Inform me (if you can) ye Reading Sots, what 'tis
That Guides th' unerring Deities,
They no base Reason to their Actions bring,
But move by some more high more heav'nly Thing   100
And are without Deliberation wise;
Ev'n such is this, at lest tis much the same,
For which dull Schoolmen never yet could find a Name.
Call ye this Madness? damn that sober Fool
(Twas sure some dull Philosopher, some reas'ning Tool)   105
Who the reproachful Term did first devise,
And brought a Scandal on the best of Vice:
Go! ask me what's the Rage young Prophets feel
When they with Holy Frenzy Reel,
Drunk with the Spirits of Infus'd Divinity,   110
They rave and stagger, and are mad like me:

(7)

Oh what an Ebb of Drink have we?
Bring, bring a Deluge, fill us up the Sea,
Let the vast Ocean be our mighty Cup,
We'll drink't and all its Fishes too like Loaches up: 115

84 strait] *1683*; strait narrow *R*   105 dull] *1683*; grave *R*   some
reas'ning] *1683*; or reas'ning *R*

264 A DITHYRAMBIQUE ON DRINKING

Bid the Canary Fleet land here, we'll pay
    The Fraight, and Custom too defray;
Set every man a Ship, and when the Store
Is emptied, let 'em strait dispatch and sail for more:
    Tis gone; and now have at the Rhine   120
    With all its petty Rivulets of Wine;
The Empire's Forces with the Spanish we'll combine,
We'll make their Drink too in Confederacy joyn:
    'Ware France the next; this Round Bordeaux shall swallow,
    Champagn, Langon, and Burgundy shall follow: 125
        Quick let's forestall Lorrain,
    We'll starve his Army, all their Quarters drain,
And without Treaty put an End to the Campagn:
Go! set the Universe a tilt, turn the Globe up,
    Squeez out the last, the slow unwilling drop: 130
A Pox of empty Nature! since the World's drawn dry,
        'Tis time we quit Mortality,
        'Tis time we now give out and dy,
Lest we are plagu'd with Dulnes and Sobriety:
    Beset with Linkboys we'll in Triumph go   135
A Troop of staggr'ing Ghosts down to the Shades below;
    Drunk we'll march off and reel into the Tomb,
    Nature's convenient dark Retiring Room;
And there, from Noise remov'd, and all tumultuous Strife
Sleep out the dull Fatigue, and long Debauch of Life.   140

Exit reeling

117 Fraight,] *1683*; Fraught *R*   119 'em] *R*; them *1683*   122 we'll]
1683; well *R*   126 let's] *1683*; lets *R*   136 down to] *1683*; down *R*
139 And ... remov'd] *1683*; There free from Noise *R*   140 the dull ... long]
1683; the long *R*   *Two lines, not in 1683, follow in R; (see Appendix II)*
140.1 *R; Tries to go off, but tumbles down, and falls asleep. 1683*

4

REMAINS

R E M A I N S

O F

Mr. *John Oldham*

IN

VERSE AND PROSE.

[ORNAMENT]

LONDON:

Printed for *Jo. Hindmarsh*, Bookseller to his Royal
Highness, at the Black Bull in *Cornhil*, 1684

Advertisement.

The Author of these following Poems being dead, the Publisher
thought fit to acquaint the World, that the reason why he exposed
them now in Print, was not so much for his own Interest (tho a
Bookseller that disclaims Interest for a pretence, will no more
be believed now adays, than a thorough paced Phanatick, that   5
pretends he makes a journey to New England *purely for conscience*
sake) but for securing the reputation of Mr. Oldham; *which might*
otherwise have suffered from worse hands, and out of a desire he
has to print the last Remains of his friend since he had the
good fortune to publish his first Pieces.   10

  He confesses that it is the greatest piece of injustice to pub-
lish the posthumous Works of Authors, especially such, that we
may suppose they had brought to the file and sent out with more
advantages into the World, had they not been prevented by un-
timely death; and therefore assures you he had never presumed to   15
print these following Miscellanies, had they not already been
countenanced by men of unquestionable repute and esteem.

  He is not of the same perswasion with several others of his
profession, that never care how much they lessen the reputation
of the Poet, if they can but inhance the value of the Book; that   20
ransack the Studies of the deceased, and print all that passed
under the Author's hands, from Fifteen to Forty, and upwards:
and (as the incomparable Mr. Cowley *has exprest it) think a rude*
heap of ill placed Stones a better Monument than a neat Tomb of
Marble.   25

25 There follows a paragraph concerning the 'Character of an Ugly Old
P[arson]', which, being prose, is not included in the present edition.

C O U N T E R P A R T

TO THE

S A T Y R against *V E R T U E.*

In Person of the Author.

I.

Pardon me, Vertue, whatsoe'er thou art,
  (For sure thou of the God-head art a part,
  And all that is of him must be
        The very Deity.)
Pardon, if I in ought did thee blaspheme,   5
  Or injure thy pure Sacred Name:
Accept unfeign'd Repentance, Prayers and Vows,
The best Atonement of my penitent humble Muse,
The best that Heav'n requires, or Mankind can produce.
All my Attempts hereafter shall at thy Devotion be,   10
Ready to consecrate my Ink and very Blood to thee.
  Forgive me, ye blest Souls that dwell above,
Where you by its reward the worth of Vertue prove.
Forgive (if you can do't) who know no Passion now but Love.
    And you unhappy happy few,   15
  Who strive with Life, and Humane Miseries below,
        Forgive me too,
If I ought disparag'd them, or else discourag'd you.

II.

  Blest Vertue! whose Almighty Power
  Does to our fallen Race restore   20
All that in Paradise we lost, and more,
  Lifts us to Heaven, and makes us be
  The Heirs and Image of the Deity.
Soft gentle Yoak! which none but resty Fools refuse,
  Which before Freedom I would ever chuse.   25
Easie are all the Bonds that are impos'd by thee;
    Easie as those of Lovers are,
  (If I with ought less pure may thee compare)

Nor do they force, but only guide our Liberty:
  By such soft Ties are Spirits above confin'd;   30
  So gentle is the Chain which them to Good does bind.
Sure Card, whereby this frail and tott'ring Bark we steer
      Thro' Life's tempestuous Ocean here;
      Thro' all the tossing Waves of Fear,
      And dangerous Rocks of black Despair.   35
Safe in thy Conduct unconcern'd we move,
  Secure from all the threatning Storms that blow,
      From all Attacks of Chance below,
And reach the certain Haven of Felicity above.

                              III.

Best Mistress of our Souls! whose Charms and Beauties last,   40
      And are by very Age encreast,
  By which all other Glories are defac'd.
  Thou'rt thy own Dowry, and a greater far
  Than All the Race of Woman-kind e'er brought,
  Tho' each of them like the first Wife were fraught,   45
  And half the Universe did for her Portion share.
That tawdry Sex, which giddy senseless we
  Thro' Ignorance so vainly Deifie,
Are all but glorious Brutes when un-endow'd with thee.
      'Tis Vice alone, the truer Jilt, and worse,   50
      In whose Enjoyment tho' we find
  A flitting Pleasure, yet it leaves behind
      A Pain and Torture in the Mind,
And claps the wounded Conscience with incurable Remorse,
Or else betrays us to the great Trepans of Humane Kind.   55

                              IV.

  'Tis Vice, the greater Thraldom, harder Drudgery,
  Whereby deposing Reason from its gentle Sway,
  (That rightful Sovereign which we should obey)
      We undergo a various Tyranny,
And to un-number'd servile Passions Homage pay.   60
  These with *Egyptian* Rigor us enslave,
  And govern with unlimited Command;
      They make us endless Toil pursue,

      And still their doubled Tasks renew,
To push on our too hasty Fate, and build our Grave,   65
Or which is worse, to keep us from the Promis'd Land.
      Nor may we think our Freedom to retrieve,
      We struggle with our heavy Yoak in vain:
        In vain we strive to break that Chain,
        Unless a Miracle relieve;   70
      Unless th' Almighty Wand enlargement give,
      We never must expect Delivery,
Till Death, the universal Writ of Ease, does set us free.

V.

Some sordid Avarice in Vassallage confines,
      Like *Roman* Slaves condemn'd to th' Mines;   75
    These are in its harsh *Bridewel* lash'd and punished,
    And with hard Labour scarce can earn their Bread.
    Others Ambition, that Imperious Dame,
    Exposes cruelly, like Gladiators, here
      Upon the World's Great Theatre.   80
Thro' Dangers and thro' Blood they wade to Fame,
To purchase grinning Honor and an empty Name.
    And some by Tyrant-Lust are Captive led,
      And with false Hopes of Pleasure fed;
    'Till tir'd with Slavery to their own Desires,   85
Life's o'er-charg'd Lamp goes out, and in a Snuff expires.

VI.

    Consider we the little Arts of Vice,
    The Stratagems and Artifice
Whereby she does attract her Votaries:
    All those Allurements and those Charms   90
      Which pimp Transgressors to her Arms,
    Are but foul Paint, and counterfeit Disguise,
    To palliate her own conceal'd Deformities,
And for false empty Joys betrays us to true solid Harms.
      In vain she would her Dowry boast,   95
    Which clog'd with Legacies we never gain,
      But with unvaluable Cost;
      Which got we never can retain;

But must the greatest part be lost,
  To the great Bubbles, Age or Chance, again.   100
'Tis vastly over-balanc'd by the Joynture which we make,
  In which our Lives, our Souls, our All is set at Stake.
      Like silly *Indians*, foolish we
  With a known Cheat, a losing Traffick hold,
    Whilst led by an ill-judging Eye,   105
    W'admire a trifling Pageantry,
  And merchandize our Jewels and our Gold,
For worthless Glass and Beads, or an *Exchange*'s Frippery.
  If we a while maintain th' expensive Trade,
    Such mighty Impost on the Cargo's laid,   110
      Such a vast Custom to be paid,
  We're forc'd at last like wretched Bankrupts to give out,
Clapt up by Death, and in Eternal Durance shut.

VII.

What art thou, Fame, for which so eagerly we strive?
    What art thou but an empty Shade   115
  By the Reflection of our Actions made?
Thou, unlike others, never follow'st us alive;
But, like a Ghost, walk'st only after we are dead.
  Posthumous Toy! vain after-Legacy!
    Which only ours can be,   120
  When we our selves no more are we!
Fickle as vain! who dost on vulgar Breath depend,
    Which we by dear Experience find
More changeable, more veering than th'unconstant Wind.
What art thou, Gold, that cheat'st the Miser's Eyes?   125
  Which he does so devoutly idolize;
For whom he all his Rest and Ease does sacrifice.
  'Tis Use alone can all thy Value give,
And he from that no Benefit can e'er receive.
Curst Mineral! near Neighb'ring Hell begot,   130
Which all th' Infection of thy damned Neighbourhood hast brought.
    Thou Bawd to Murthers, Rapes and Treachery,
    And every greater Name of Villany;
From thee they all derive their Stock and Pedigree.
Thou the lewd World with all its crying Crimes dost store,   135

And hardly wilt allow the Devil the cause of more.
  And what is Pleasure which does most beguile?
  That Syren which betrays us with a flattering Smile.
    We listen to the treacherous Harmony,
      Which sings but our own Obsequy,   140
  The Danger unperceiv'd till Death draw nigh;
Till drowning we want Pow'r to 'scape the fatal Enemy.

VIII.

  How frantick is the wanton Epicure!
  Who a perpetual Surfeit will endure?
  Who places all his chiefest Happiness   145
    In the Extravagancies of Excess,
  Which wise Sobriety esteems but a Disease?
  O mighty envied Happiness to eat!
  Which fond mistaken Sots call Great!
  Poor Frailty of our Flesh! which we each day   150
Must thus repair for fear of ruinous Decay!
  Degrading of our Nature, where vile Brutes are fain
      To make and keep up Man!
  Which, when the Paradise above we gain,
Heav'n thinks too great an Imperfection to retain!   155
  By each Disease the sickly Joy's destroy'd;
    At every Meal it's nauseous and cloy'd,
  Empty at best, as when in Dream enjoy'd;
  When, cheated by a slumbering Imposture, we
  Fancy a Feast, and great *Regalio's* by;   160
      And think we taste, and think we see,
  And riot on imaginary Luxury.

IX.

Grant me, O Vertue, thy more solid lasting Joy;
  Grant me the better Pleasures of the Mind,
Pleasures, which only in pursuit of thee we find,   165
  Which Fortune cannot marr, nor Chance destroy.
  One Moment in thy blest Enjoyment is
Worth an Eternity of that tumultuous Bliss,
    Which we derive from Sense,
Which often cloys, and must resign to Impotence.   170

140 Obsequy,] *Ed.* (*1854*); Obsequy. *1684*

Grant me but this, how will I triumph in my happy State?
   Above the Changes and Reverse of Fate;
        Above her Favors and her Hate.
   I'll scorn the worthless Treasures of *Peru*,
      And those of t' other *Indies* too.   175
I'll pity *Caesar*'s Self with all his Trophies and his Fame,
And the vile brutish Herd of Epicures contemn,
And all the Under-shrievalties of Life not worth a Name.
   Nor will I only owe my Bliss,
   Like others, to a Multitude,   180
Where Company keeps up a forced Happiness;
   Should all Mankind surcease to live,
   And none but individual I survive,
Alone I would be happy, and enjoy my Solitude.
   Thus shall my Life in pleasant Minutes wear,   185
   Calm as the Minutes of the Evening are,
   And gentle as the motions of the upper Air;
   Soft as my Muse, and unconfin'd as she,
When flowing in the Numbers of *Pindarique* Liberty.
   And when I see pale gastly Death appear,   190
 That grand inevitable Test which all must bear,
   Which best distinguishes the blest and wretched here;
   I'll smile at all its Horrors, court my welcome Destiny,
   And yield my willing Soul up in an easie Sigh;
   And Epicures that see shall envy and confess,   195
That I, and those who dare like me be good, the chiefest Good
                        [possess.

        193 its] *Ed.* (*1687*); it *1684*

        Virg[il,]   E C L O G U E   VIII.

              The Enchantment.

      Poet, *Damon*, *Alpheus*, Speakers.

   Damon and *Alpheus*, the two Shepherds Strains
   I mean to tell, and how they charm'd the Plains.
   I'll tell their charming Numbers which the Herd,

Unmindful of their Grass, in Throngs admir'd.
At which fierce Savages astonish'd stood,   5
And every River stopt its list'ning Flood.
    For you, Great *Sir*, whether with Cannons Roar
You spread your Terror to the *Holland* shore,
Or with a gentle and a steady Hand
In Peace and Plenty rule your Native Land,   10
Shall ever that auspicious Day appear,
When I your glorious Actions shall declare?
It shall, and I throughout the World rehearse
Their Fame, fit only for a *Spencer*'s Verse.
With you my Muse began, with you shall end: 15
Accept my Verse that waits on your Command;
And deign this Ivy Wreath a place may find
Amongst the Laurels which your Temples bind.
    'Twas at the time that Night's cool shades withdrew,
And left the Grass all hung with Pearly Dew;   20
When *Damon*, leaning on his Oaken Wand,
Thus to his Pipe in gentle Lays complain'd.
    D. Arise, thou Morning, and drive on the Day,
While wretched I with fruitless words inveigh
Against false *Nisa*, while the Gods I call   ⎫   25
With my last Breath, tho' hopeless to avail,   ⎬
Tho' they regard not my Complaints at all.   ⎭
    Strike up my Pipe, play me in tuneful Strains
    What I heard sung on the Mænalian *Plains.*
Mænalus ever has its warbling Groves,   30
And talking Pines, it ever hears the Loves
Of Shepherds, and the Notes of Mighty *Pan*,
The first that would not let the Reeds untun'd remain.
    Strike up my Pipe, play me in tuneful Strains
    What I heard sung on the Mænalian *Plains.*   35
Mopsus weds *Nisa*, Gods! what Lover e'er
Need after this have reason to despair?
Griffins shall now leap Mares, and the next Age
The Deer and Hounds in Friendship shall engage.
Go, *Mopsus*, get the Torches ready soon;   40

10 Land,] *Ed.*; Land. *1684*

Thou, happy Man, must have the Bride anon.
Go, Bridegroom, quickly, the Nut-scramble make,
The Evening-star quits *Oeta* for thy sake.

Strike up my Pipe, play me in tuneful Strains
What I heard sung on the Mænalian *Plains.*   45

How fitly art thou match'd who wast so nice!
Thou haughty Nymph who did'st all else despise!
Who slight'st so scornfully my Pipe, my Herd,
My rough-grown Eye-brows, and unshaven Beard,
And think'st no God does mortal things regard.   50

Strike up my Pipe, play me in tuneful Strains
What I heard sung on the Mænalian *Plains.*

I saw thee young, and in thy Beauty's Bloom,
To gather Apples with thy Mother, come,
'Twas in our Hedge-rows, I was there with Pride,   55
To shew you to the best, and be your Guide.
Then I just entring my twelfth Year was found,
I then could reach the tender Boughs from Ground.
Heav'ns! when I saw, how soon was I undone!
How to my Heart did the quick Poyson run!   60

Strike up my Pipe, play me in tuneful Strains
What I heard sung on the Mænalian *Plains.*

Now I'm convinc'd what Love is; the cold *North*
Sure in its craggy Mountains brought him forth,
Or *Africk*'s wildest Desarts gave him Birth,   65
Amongst the Cannibals and Savage Race;
He never of our Kind, or Countrey was.

Strike up my Pipe, play me in tuneful Strains
What I heard sung on the Mænalian *Plains.*

Dire Love did once a Mother's Hand embrue   70
In Childrens Blood; a cruel Mother, thou;
Hard 'tis to say of both which is the worst,
The cruel Mother, or the Boy accurst.
He a curst Boy, a cruel Mother thou;
The Devil a whit to chuse betwixt the two.   75

Strike up my Pipe, play me in tuneful Strains
What I heard sung on the Mænalian *Plains.*

Let Wolves by Nature shun the Sheep-folds now:
On the rough Oaks let Oranges now grow:

Let the coarse *Alders* bear the *Daffadill*,   80
And costly Amber from the Thorn distill:
Let Owls match Swans, let *Tyt'rus Orpheus* be,
In the Woods *Orpheus*, and *Arion* on the Sea.
   Strike up my Pipe, play me in tuneful Strains
   What I heard sung on the Mænalian *Plains.*   85
Let all the World turn Sea, ye Woods adieu!
To some high Mountain's top I'll get me now,
And thence my self into the Waters throw.
There quench my Flames, and let the cruel She
Accept this my last dying Will and Legacy.   90
   Cease now my Pipe, cease now those warbling Strains
   Which I heard sung on the Mænalian *Plains.*
   This *Damon*'s Song; relate ye Muses now
   Alpheus Reply: All cannot all things do.
 A. Bring Holy Water, sprinkle all around,   95
And see these Altars with soft Fillets bound:
Male-Frankincense, and juicy Vervain burn,
I'll try if I by Magick Force can turn
My stubborn Love: I'll try if I can fire
His frozen Breast: Nothing but Charms are wanting here. 100
   Bring Daphnis *from the Town, ye Magick Charms,*
   Bring home lov'd Daphnis *to my longing Arms.*
Charms in her wonted Course can stop the Moon,
And from her well-fix'd Orb can call her down.
By Charms the mighty *Circe* (we are told)   105
Ulysses fam'd Companions chang'd of old.
Snakes by the Vertue of Enchantment forc'd,
Oft in the Meads with their own Poyson burst.
   Bring Daphnis *from the Town, ye Magick Charms,*
   Bring home lov'd Daphnis *to my longing Arms.*   110
First, these three several Threads I compass round
Thy Image, thus in Magick Fetters bound:
Then round these Altars thrice thy Image bear:
Odd Numbers to the Gods delightful are.
   Bring Daphnis *from the Town, ye Magick Charms,*   115
   Bring home lov'd Daphnis *to my longing Arms.*
Go tie me in three knots three Ribands now,
And let the Ribands be of diffrent Hue:

Go, *Amaryllis*, tie them strait, and cry,
At the same time, "They're true-love-knots, I tie.   120
  Bring Daphnis *from the Town, ye Magick Charms,*
  Bring home lov'd Daphnis *to my longing Arms.*
Look how this Clay grows harder, and look how ⎫
With the same Fire this Wax doth softer grow; ⎬
So *Daphnis*, let him with my Love do so. ⎭   125
Strow Meal and Salt (for so these Rites require)
And set the crackling Laurel Boughs on fire:
This naughty *Daphnis* sets my Brest on flame,
And I this Laurel burn in *Daphnis'* Name.
  Bring Daphnis *from the Town, ye Magick Charms,*   130
  Bring home lov'd Daphnis *to my longing Arms.*
As a poor Heifer, wearied in the Chase,
Of seeking her lov'd Steer from place to place,
Through Woods, through Groves, through Arable, and Wast,
On some green River's bank lies down at last.   135
There Lows her Moan, despairing and forlorn,
And, tho' belated, minds not to return:
Let *Daphnis'* Case be such, and let not me
Take any care to give a Remedy.
  Bring Daphnis *from the Town, ye Magick Charms,*   140
  Bring home lov'd Daphnis *to my longing Arms.*
These Garments erst the faithless Traitour left,
Dear Pledges of his Love, of which I'me reft:
Beneath the Threshold these I bury now,
In thee, O Earth; these Pledges *Daphnis* owe.   145
  Bring Daphnis *from the Town, ye Magick Charms,*
  Bring home lov'd Daphnis *to my longing Arms.*
Of *Mæris* I these Herbs and Poysons had,
From *Pontus* brought: in *Pontus* store are bred:
With these I've oft seen *Mæris* Wonders do,   150
Turn himself Wolf, and to the Forest go:
I've often seen him Fields of Corn displace,
From whence they grew, and Ghosts in Church-yards raise.
  Bring Daphnis *from the Town, ye Magick Charms,*
  Bring home lov'd Daphnis *to my longing Arms.*   155

---

129 *Daphnis'*] *Ed.* (*Daphnis 1687*); *Daphnis's 1684*   133 place,] *Ed.*
(*1697*); place *1684*   138 *Daphnis'*] *Ed.* (*Daphnis 1687*); *Daphnis's 1684*

Go, Maid, go, bear the Ashes out at door,
And then forthwith into the neighb'ring current pour,
Over thy Head, and don't look back be sure:
I'll try, what these on *Daphnis* will prevail,
The Gods he minds not, nor my Charms at all.   160
    Bring Daphnis *from the Town, ye Magick Charms,*
    Bring home lov'd Daphnis *to my longing Arms.*
Behold! the Ashes while we lingring stay,
While we neglect to carry them away,
Have reach'd the Altar, and have fir'd the Wood,   165
That lyes upon't: Heav'n send it be for good!
Something I know not what's the matter: Hark!
I hear our *Lightfoot* in the Entry bark.
Shall I believe, or is it only Dream,
Which Lovers fancies are too apt to frame?   170
    Cease now ye Magick Charms, behold him come!
    Cease needless Charms, my Daphnis *is at home!*

Upon the Marriage of the Prince of Orange
with the Lady Mary.

November 5. 1677. at Bedington.

(1)

As when of old some bright and Heav'nly Dame
A God of equal Majesty did wed;
Strait thro' the Court above the Tydings spread,
Strait at the News th'immortal Offspring came,
And all the Deities did the high Nuptials grace;   5
With no less Pomp, no less of Grandeur we
        Behold this glad Solemnity,
        And all confess an equal Joy,
And all expect as God-like and as great a Race:
Hark how united Shouts our Joys proclaim,   10
Which rise in Gratitude to Heav'n from whence they came;
Gladsome next those, which brought our Royal Exile home,
When he resum'd his long usurped Throne:
        0.3] *R(9ber); not in 1677 (1687)*

Hark how the mighty Vollies rend the Air,
And shake at once the Earth and utmost Sphere;   15
   Hark how the Bell's harmonious Noise
   Bear Consort too with human Joys;
 Behold those many Fires, which up and down
Threaten almost new Conflagration to the Town;
Well do these Emblems, mighty *Orange*, speak thy Fame,   20
Whose Loudness, Musick, Brightness all express the same:
 Twas thus great Jove his Semele did wed,
In Thunder and in Lightning so approach'd her Bed.

(2)

Hail happy Pair! kind Heav'ns great Hostages!
Sure Pledges of a firm and lasting Peace!   25
Call't not a Match; we that low Stile disdain,
Nor will degrade it with a Term so mean;
   A League it must be said
Where Countries thus Espouse, and Nations Wed:
   Our Thanks, propitious Destinie!   30
   Never did yet thy Pow'r dispence
A more Plenipotentiary Influence,
Nor Heav'n more sure a Treaty ratify:
To *You*, our great and gracious Monarch, too
   An equal Share of Thanks is due,   35
Nought could this glorious Work produce, but Heav'n and You:
     Let others boast
   Of Leagues, which Wars and Slaughter cost;
 This Union by no Blood cemented is
Nor did its Harmony from Jars and Discords rise: 40
 Not more to your great Ancestor we ow,
 By whom two Realms into one Kingdom grow;
 He join'd but what Nature had join'd before,
 Lands disunited by no parting Shore;
 By you to forreign Countries we're Allied,   45
You make us Continent, whom Seas and Waves divide.

18 many] *R²*; num'rous *R¹*, *1677* (*1687*)   20 Fame,] *1677* (*1687*); Fame *R*
cropped   36 glorious] *R²*; mighty *R¹*, *1677* (*1687*)   43 had join'd before]
R (²before ¹had join'd)

(3)

How well, Brave Prince, do you by prudent Conduct prove
   What was denied to mighty Jove
   Together to be Wise and Love?
In this you highest Skill of Choice and Judgement shew,   50
 Tis here display'd, and here rewarded too;
Others move only by unbridled guideless Heat,
But you mix Love with Policy, Passion with State:
 You scorn'd the Painter's Hands your Hearts should ty,
Which oft (and here they must) th' Original bely,   55
 (For how should Art that Beauty undertake,
 Which Heav'n would strive in vain agen to make?)
Taught by Religion you did better Methods try,
And worship'd not the Image, but the Deity:
 Go, envied Prince, your glorious *Bride* receive,   60
 Too great for ought, but mighty *York* to give;
She, whom if none must Wed, but those who merit Her,
Monarchs might cease Pretence, and slighted Gods despair:
 Think You in her far greater Conquests gain,
Then all the Pow'rs of France have from your Country ta'ne, 65
In her soft Arms let Your Ambition bounded ly,
And fancy there an Universal Monarchy.

(4)

 And You; fair Princess, who could thus subdue,
 What France with all its Forces could not do;
    Enjoy Your glorious Prize,   70
 Enjoy the Triumphs of your conqu'ring Eys;
 From Him, and th' Height of your great Mind look down,
   And with Neglect despise a Throne,
And think't as great to merit, as to wear a Crown:
Nassaw is all, which your Desires, or Thoughts can frame, 75
 All Titles lodge within that single Name,
A Name, which Mars himself would with Ambition bear,
Prouder in that then to be call'd the God of War:
To You, great Madam, (if your Joys admit Increase,
If Heav'n has not already set your Happiness   80

58 better] R^2, *1677* (*1687*); wiser R^1 66 soft] *R*; fair *1677* (*1687*), R93

Above its Pow'r to raise)
To You the zealous humble Muse
These solemn Wishes consecrates and vows,
And begs you'll not her Offering refuse,
Which not Your Want, but her Devotion shows.   85

(5)

May Your great Consort still successfull prove
In all his high Attempts, as in your Love;
May he thro' all Attacks of Chance appear
As free from Danger, as he is from Fear;
May neither Sence of Grief or Trouble know,   90
But what you must to others in Compassion show:
May your bright self be fruitful in as num'rous Store
Of Princely Births, as she who your great Father bore;
May Heav'n, to your just Merits kind,
Repeal the ancient Curse on Womankind;   95
Easy and gentle as the Labours of the Brain,
May yours all prove, and just so free from Pain;
May no rude Noise of War approach your Bed,
But Peace her downy Wings about you spread,
Calm as the Season, when fair Halcyons breed: 100
May You, and the just Owner of your Brest,
Both in as full Content and Happiness be blest,
As the first sinless Pair of old enjoy'd,
Ere Guilt their Innocence and that destroy'd:
Till nothing but Continuance to your Bliss can add,   105
And you by Heav'n alone be happier made;
Till future Poets, who your Lives review,
When they'd their utmost Pitch of Flatt'ry shew,
Shall Pray their Patrons may become like you,
Nor know to frame a skilful Wish more great,   110
Nor think a higher Blessing in the Gift of Fate.

91 you must to others in Compassion] *R*; in Pity you to others *1677* (*1687*);
for others you in Pitty *R*92   92 your bright self] *R*3; your fair self *R*²;
You *R*¹, *1677* (*1687* subst.)   94-5 *Placed as in 1677* (*1687*), *R*92; *in R they
follow* 96, 97, *but with marginal note:* 'Hi 2 versus priores praecedere debent.'

AN

O D E

For an Anniversary of MUSICK
on S. Cecilia's *Day*

I.

Begin the SONG! your Instruments advance!
        Tune the Voice, and tune the Flute;
        Touch the silent, sleeping Lute,
And make the Strings to their own Measures dance.
Bring gentlest Thoughts, that into Language glide,   5
Bring softest Words, that into Numbers slide:
        Let every Hand, let every Tongue,
        To make the noble Consort, throng;
Let all in one harmonious Note agree,
        To frame the mighty Song,   10
For this is Music's sacred Jubilee.

II.

Hark! how the waken'd Strings resound,
  And sweetly break the yielding Air!
The ravish'd Sence, how pleasingly they wound,
  And call the list'ning Soul into the Ear!   15
Each Pulse beats Time, and every Heart
With Tongue and Fingers bears a part.
  By Harmony's entrancing Power,
When we are thus wound up to Extasy,
  Methinks we mount, methinks we tow'r,   20
    And seem to leave Mortality,
And seem to antedate our future Bliss on high!

III.

How dull were Life, how hardly worth our Care,
  But for the Charms which Music lends!

7 let] *1685*; and *1687*, R240   13 And sweetly] *1685*; And *1687*
21 *1685*; *not in 1687*   24 which] *1685*; that *1687*

How pall'd its Pleasures would appear,   25
    But for the Pleasure which our Art attends!
      Without the Sweets of Melody,
        To tune our Vital Breath,
      Who would not give it up to Death,
    And in the silent Grave contented lye?   30

                    IV.

Music's the Cordial of a troubled Breast,
    The softest Remedy that Grief can find;
The gentle Spell, that charms our Cares to rest,
    And calms the ruffling Passions of the Mind:
        Music does all our Joys refine,   35
          'Tis that gives Relish to our Wine,
            'Tis that gives Rapture to our Love;
          It wings Devotion to a pitch Divine,
    'Tis our chief Bliss on Earth, and half our Heav'n above.

          CHORUS
    Come then with tuneful Breath, and String,   40
    The Praises of our Art let's sing;
    Let's sing to blest CECILIA's *Fame,*
That grac'd this Art, and gave this Day its Name:
    While Music, Wine, and Mirth conspire
      To bear a Consort, and make up the Quire.   45

  25 pall'd] *1685*; faint *1687*   34 ruffling] *1685*; ruffled *1687*
35 Joys] *1685*; Joy *1687*   36 'Tis that gives] *1685*; It gives the *1687*
38 It] *1685*; And *1687*   40 *Breath*] *1685, R240*; Throat *1687*   44 *While*]
1685; With *1687*; Let *R240*

To Madam L. E. *upon her Recovery from a late Sickness.*

Madam,

Pardon, that with slow Gladness we so late
Your wish'd return of Health congratulate:
Our Joys at first so throng'd to get abroad,
They hinder'd one another in the crowd;

And now such haste to tell their Message make,   5
They only stammer what they meant to speak.
    You the fair Subject which I am to sing,
To whose kind Hands this humble joy I bring:
Aid me, I beg, while I this Theme pursue,
For I invoke no other Muse but you.   10
    Long time had you here brightly shone below
With all the Rays kind Heaven could bestow.
No envious Cloud e're offer'd to invade
Your Lustre, or compel it to a Shade:
Nor did it yet by any Sign appear,   15
But that you thoroughout Immortal were.
Till Heaven (if Heaven could prove so cruel) sent
To interrupt the Growth of your content.
As if it grudg'd those Gifts you did enjoy,
And would that Bounty which it gave, destroy: 20
'Twas since your Excellence did envy move
In those high Powers and made them jealous prove.
They thought these Glories should they still have shin'd
Unsullied, were too much for Woman-kind;
Which might they write as lasting, as they're Fair,   25
Too great for ought, but Deities appear:
But Heaven (it may be) was not yet compleat,
And lackt you there to fill your empty Seat.
And when it could not fairly woo you hence,
Turn'd Ravisher, and offer'd Violence.   30
    Sickness did first a formal siege begin,
And by sure slowness tryed your Life to win;
As if by lingring methods Heaven meant
To chase you hence and tire you to consent.
But, this in vain, Fate did to force resort,   35
And next by Storm strove to attack the fort.
A Sleep, dull as your last, did you Arrest,
And all the *Magazines* of life possest.
No more the Blood its circling course did run,
But in the veins, like Isicles, it hung.   40

24 Woman-kind;] *Ed.* (*1854*); Woman-kind. *1684*   32 win;] *Ed.* (*1854*); win.
1684   36 strove] *Ed.* (*1687*); shove *1684*   38 the] *Ed.* (*1854*); there
1684; their (*1687*)

No more the Heart (now void of quickning heat)
The tuneful March of vital Motion beat.
Stiffness did into all the Sinews climb,
And a short Death crept cold through every Limb.
All Signs of Life from sight so far withdrew,   45
'Twas now thought Popery to pray for you.
    There might you (were not that sense lost) have seen
How your true Death would have resented been:
A Lethargy, like yours, each breast did seize,
And all by Sympathy catcht your Disease.   50
Around you silent Imagery appears,
And nought in the Spectators moves, but Tears.
They pay what grief were to your Funeral due,
And yet dare hope Heaven would your Life renew.
    Mean while, all means, all drugs prescribed are,   55
Which the decays of Health, or Strength repair,
Medicines so powerful they new Souls would save,
And Life in long-dead Carcasses retrieve:
But these in vain, they rougher Methods try,
And now you're Martyr'd that you may not die;   60
Sad Scene of Fate! when Tortures were your gain:
And twas a kindness thought to wish you pain!
As if the slackned string of Life run down,
Could only by the Rack be screwed in tune.
    But Heav'n at last (grown conscious that its pow'r   65
Could scarce what was to die with you restore)
And loth to see such Glories over-come,
Sent a post Angel to repeal your doom;
Strait Fate obey'd the Charge which Heaven sent,
And gave this first dear Proof, it could Repent: 70
Triumphant Charms! what may not you subdue,
When Fate's your Slave, and thus submits to you!
It now again the new-broke Thread does knit,
And for another Clew her spindle fit:
And life's hid spark which did unquencht remain,   75
Caught the fled light and brought it back again:
Thus you reviv'd, and all our Joys with you

66 restore)] *Ed.* (restore, *1687*); restore. *1684*   77 Joys] *Ed.* (*1854*);
Joy *1684*   you] *Ed.* (*1695*); you, *1684*

Reviv'd and found their Resurrection too:
Some only griev'd, that what was Deathless thought
They saw so near to Fatal ruin brought: 80
Now crowds of Blessings on that happy hand,
Whose skill could eager Destiny withstand;
Whose learned Pow'r has rescu'd from the Grave,
That Life which 'twas a Miracle to save;
That Life which were it thus untimely lost,   85
Had been the fairest Spoil Death ere could boast:
May he henceforth be God of healing thought,
By whom such good to you and us was brought:
Altars and shrines to him are justly due,
Who shew'd himself a God by raising you.   90

    But say, fair Saint, for you alone can know,
Whither your Soul in this short flight did go;
Went it to antedate that Happiness,
You must at last (though late we hope) possess?
Inform us lest we should your Fate belye,   95
And call that Death which was but Extasie,
The Queen of Love (we're told) once let us see
That Goddesses from wounds could not be free;
And you by this unwish'd Occasion show
That they like Mortal us can Sickness know: 100
Pitty! that Heav'n should all its Titles give,
And yet not let you with them ever live.
You'd lack no point that makes a Deity,
If you could like it too Immortal be.

    And so you are; half boasts a Deathless State;   105
Although your frailer part must yield to Fate.
By every breach in that fair lodging made,
Its blest Inhabitant is more displaid:
In that white Snow which overspreads your skin,
We trace the whiter Soul which dwells within;   110
Which while you through this shining Hue display
Looks like a Star plac'd in the Milky way:
Such the bright Bodies of the Blessed are,
When they for Raiment cloath'd with Light appear,

90 you.] *Ed.* (*1687*); you: *1684*   97 see] *Ed.* (*1854*); see: *1684*
110 the] *Ed.* (*1687*); ye *1684*

And should you visit now the Seats of Bliss,   115
You need not wear another form but this.
Never did Sickness in such pomp appear, ⎤
As when it thus your Livery did wear, ⎬
Disease it self look'd amiable here.   ⎦
So Clouds which would obscure the Sun oft gilded be,   120
And Shades are taught to shine as bright as he.
    Grieve not fair *Nymph*, when in your Glass you trace
The marring footsteps of a pale Disease.
Regret not that your cheeks their Roses want,
Which a few Days shall in full store replant,   125
Which, whilst your Blood withdraws its guilty Red,
Tells that you own no faults that blushes need:
The Sun whose Bounty does each Spring restore
What Winter from the rifled Meadows tore,
Which every Morning with an early ray   130
Paints the young Blushing Cheeks of instant Day:
Whose skill (inimitable here below,)
Limns those gay Clouds which form Heaven's colour'd bow,
That Sun shall soon with Interest repay,
All the lost Beauty Sickness snatch'd away.   135
Your Beams like his shall hourly now advance,
And every minute their swift Growth enhance.
    Mean while (that you no helps of health refuse)
Accept these humble Wishes of the Muse:
Which shall not of their Just Petition fail,   140
If she (and she's a Goddess) ought prevail.
    May no profane Disease henceforth approach ⎤
This sacred Temple with unhallow'd touch, ⎬
Or with rude sacriledge its frame debauch. ⎦
May these fair Members always happy be   145
In as full Strength and well-set Harmony,
As the new Foundress of your sex could boast,
Ere she by Sin her first Perfection lost:
May Destiny, just to your Merits, twine,
All your smooth Fortunes in a Silken Line.   150

138 health] *Ed.* (*1703*); healths *1684*   142 approach] *Ed.* (*1722*); approach,
1684   148 Perfection] *Ed.* (*1687*); Persecution *1684*

And that you may at Heaven late arrive,
May it to you its largest Bottom give.
May Heaven with still repeated Favours bless,
Till it its Pow'r below its Will confess;
Till wishes can no more exalt your Fate,   155
Nor Poets fancy you more Fortunate.

On the Death of Mrs. Katharine
Kingscote *a Child of Excellent Parts and Piety.*

She did, She did—I saw her mount the Skie,
And with new Whiteness paint the Galaxy.
Heav'n her methought with all its Eyes did view,
And yet acknowledg'd all its Eyes too few.
Methought I saw in crowds blest Spirits meet,   5
And with loud Welcomes her arrival greet;
Which could they grieve, had gone with grief away
To see a Soul more white, more pure than they.
   Earth was unworthy such a prize as this,
Only a while Heaven let us share the Bliss: 10
In vain her stay with fruitless Tears we'd woo,
In vain we'd court, when that our Rival grew.
Thanks, ye kind Powers! who did so long dispense,
(Since you so wish'd her) with her absence thence:
We now resign, to you alone we grant   15
The sweet Monopoly of such a Saint;
So pure a Saint, I scarce dare call her so,
For fear to wrong her with a Name too low:
Such a Seraphick brightness in her shin'd,
I hardly can believe her Woman-kind.   20
'Twas sure some noble Being left the Sphere, ⎫
Which deign'd a little to inhabit here,   ⎬
And can't be said to die, but disappear.   ⎭
Or if she Mortal was and meant to show
The greater skill by being made below;   25

Sure Heav'n preserv'd her by the fall uncurst,
To tell how all the Sex were form'd at first:
Never did yet so much Divinity
In such a small Compendium crouded lye.
By her we credit what the Learned tell,   30
That many Angels in one point can dwell.
More damned Fiends did not in *Mary* rest,
Than lodg'd of Blessed Spirits in her Breast;
Religion dawn'd so early in her mind,
You'd think her Saint whilst in the Womb enshrin'd: 35
Nay, that bright ray which did her Temples paint,
Proclaim'd her clearly, while alive, a Saint.
Scarce had she learnt to lisp Religion's Name,
E'er she by her Example preach'd the same,
And taught her *Cradle* like the *Pulpit* to reclaim.   40
No Action did within her Practice fall
Which for th' Atonement of a Blush could call:
No word of hers e'er greeted any Ear,
But what a dying Saint confest might hear.
Her Thoughts had scarcely ever sully'd been   45
By the least Foot-steps of Original Sin.
Her Life did still as much Devotion breath
As others do at their last Gasp in Death.
Hence on her Tomb of her let not be said,
So long she liv'd; but thus, so long she pray'd.   50

40 *Cradle* like] *Ed.* (*1687*); *Cradle*-like *1684*

[Title-page in *Remains*, 1684]

TO THE

M E M O R Y

OF

Mr. *CHARLES MORWENT*.

A PINDARIQUE.

---

*Ignis utique quo clariùs effulsit, citiùs extinguitur,
eripit se aufertque ex oculis subitò perfecta virtus: quic-
quid est absoluti faciliùs transfluit, & optimi neutiquam
diurnant.*   Cambden. de Phil. Syd.

O celeres hominum bonorum dies.   Apul.

LONDON,
Printed in the Year, 1684.

To the Memory of my Dear Friend,
Mr. Charles Morwent:

A   P I N D A R I Q U E.

Ostendunt terris hunc tantùm fata, nec ultrà
Esse sinunt.——   Virg.

I.

Best Friend! could my unbounded Grief but rate
  With due proportion thy too cruel Fate;
  Could I some happy Miracle bring forth,
  Great as my Wishes and thy greater Worth,
    All *Helicon* should soon be thine,   5
    And pay a Tribute to thy Shrine.
The learned Sisters all transform'd should be,
No longer nine, but one *Melpomene:*
Each should into a *Niobe* relent,
At once thy Mourner and thy Monument.   10
      Each should become
    Like the fam'd *Memnon*'s speaking Tomb,
     To sing thy well-tun'd Praise;
    Nor should we fear their being dumb,
Thou still would'st make 'em vocal with thy Rays.   15

II.

O that I could distil my vital Juice in Tears!
  Or waste away my Soul in sobbing Airs!
     Were I all Eyes,
    To flow in liquid Elegies:
     That every Limb might grieve,   20
    And dying Sorrow still retrieve;
My Life should be but one long mourning day,
And like moist Vapors melt in Tears away.
    I'd soon dissolve in one great Sigh,
      And upwards fly,   25
Glad so to be exhal'd to Heav'n and thee:

26 thee:] *Ed.* (*1854*); thee. *1684*

A Sigh which might well-nigh reverse thy death,
And hope to animate thee with new Breath;
Pow'rful as that which heretofore did give
A Soul to well-form'd Clay, and made it live.   30

III.

Adieu, blest Soul! whose hasty Flight away
        Tells Heaven did ne'er display
Such Happiness to bless the World with stay.
Death in thy Fall betray'd her utmost spite,
And shew'd her shafts most times are levell'd at the white. 35
She saw thy blooming Ripeness time prevent;
She saw, and envious grew, and straight her arrow sent.
So Buds appearing e'er the Frosts are past,
        Nip'd by some unkind Blast,
Wither in Penance for their forward haste.   40
    Thus have I seen a Morn so bright,
    So deck'd with all the Robes of Light,
    As if it scorn'd to think of Night,
    Which a rude Storm e'er Noon did shroud,
And buried all its early Glories in a Cloud.   45
    The day in funeral Blackness mourn'd,
    And all to Sighs, and all to Tears it turn'd.

IV.

But why do we thy Death untimely deem;
        Or Fate blaspheme?
    We should thy full ripe Vertues wrong,   50
        To think thee young.
Fate, when she did thy vigorous Growth behold,
    And all thy forward Glories told,
Forgot thy tale of Years, and thought thee old.
    The brisk Endowments of thy Mind   55
    Scorning i'th' Bud to be confin'd,
Out-ran thy Age, and left slow Time behind;
Which made thee reach Maturity so soon,
And at first Dawn present a full-spread Noon.
So thy Perfections with thy Soul agree,   60
Both knew no Non-age, knew no Infancy.

Thus the first Patern of our Race began
His Life in middle-age, at's Birth a perfect Man.

V.

So well thou acted'st in thy Span of Days,
As calls at once for Wonder and for Praise.   65
Thy prudent Conduct had so learnt to measure
   The different whiles of Toil and Leasure,
No time did Action want, no Action wanted Pleasure.
Thy busie Industry could Time dilate,
          And stretch the Thread of Fate: 70
Thy careful Thrift could only boast the Power
To lengthen Minutes, and extend an Hour.
  No single Sand could e'er slip by
  Without its Wonder, sweet as high:
And every teeming Moment still brought forth   75
   A thousand Rarities of Worth.
While some no other Cause for Life can give,
  But a dull Habitude to live:
Thou scorn'dst such Laziness while here beneath,
And Liv'dst that time which others only Breath.   80

VI.

Next our just Wonder does commence,
How so small Room could hold such Excellence.
Nature was proud when she contriv'd thy Frame,
   In thee she labor'd for a Name:
Hence 'twas she lavish'd all her Store,   85
As if she meant hereafter to be poor,
   And, like a Bankrupt, run o'th' Score.
Her curious Hand here drew in Straights and joyn'd
All the Perfections lodge in Humane kind;
   Teaching her numerous Gifts to lie   90
   Crampt in a short Epitome.
So Stars contracted in a Diamond shine,
   And Jewels in a narrow Point confine
   The Riches of an *Indian* Mine.
       Thus subtle Artists can   95
Draw Nature's larger self within a Span:

A small Frame holds the World, Earth, Heav'ns and all
Shrunk to the scant Dimensions of a Ball.

VII.

Those Parts which never in one Subject dwell,
But some uncommon Excellence foretel,   100
   Like Stars did all constellate here,
   And met together in one Sphere.
Thy Judgment, Wit and Memory conspir'd
To make themselves and thee admir'd:
And could thy growing Height a longer Stay have known,   105
Thou hadst all other Glories, and thy self out-done.
   While some to Knowledge by Degrees arrive,
     Thro tedious Industry improv'd,
Thine scorn'd by such pedantick Rules to thrive;
     But swift as that of Angels mov'd,   110
And made us think it was intuitive.
Thy pregnant Mind ne'er struggl'd in its Birth,
But quick, and while it did conceive, brought forth;
The gentle Throes of thy prolifick Brain
   Were all unstrain'd, and without Pain.   115
   Thus when Great *Jove* the Queen of Wisdom bare
   So easie and so mild his Travels were.

VIII.

Nor were these Fruits in a rough Soil bestown
As Gemms are thick'st in rugged Quarries sown.
Good Nature and good parts so shar'd thy mind,   120
     A Muse and Grace were so combin'd,
'Twas hard to guess which with most Lustre shin'd.
   A Genius did thy whole Comportment act,
   Whose charming Complaisance did so attract,
     As every Heart attack'd.   125
Such a soft Air thy well-tun'd Sweetness sway'd,
As told thy Soul of Harmony was made;
All rude Affections that Disturbers be,
That mar or disunite Society,
     Were Foreiners to thee.   130
Love only in their stead took up its Rest;

Nature made that thy constant Guest,
And seem'd to form no other Passion for thy Breast.

IX.

This made thy Courteousness to all extend,
And thee to the whole Universe a Friend.   135
Those which were Strangers to thy native Soil and thee
    No Strangers to thy Love could be,
  Whose Bounds were wide as all Mortality.
    Thy Heart no Island was, disjoyn'd
(Like thy own Nation) from all human kind;   140
But 'twas a Continent to other Countreys fixt
As firm by Love, as they by Earth annext.
Thou scorn'dst the Map should thy Affection guide,
Like theirs who love by dull Geography,
Friends but to whom by Soil they are ally'd: 145
    Thine reacht to all beside,
To every member of the world's great Family.
Heav'ns Kindness only claims a Name more general,
    Which we the nobler call,
Because 'tis common, and vouchsaf'd to all.   150

X.

  Such thy Ambition of obliging was,
Thou seem'dst corrupted with the very Power to please.
    Only to let thee gratifie,
At once did bribe and pay thy Courtesie.
Thy Kindness by Acceptance might be bought,   155
  It for no other Wages sought,
      But would its own be thought.
  No Suiters went unsatisfy'd away,
  But left thee more unsatisfy'd than they.
Brave *Titus*! thou mightst here thy true Portraicture find, 160
And view thy Rival in a private mind.
  Thou heretofore deserv'dst such Praise,
When Acts of Goodness did compute thy days,
Measur'd not by the *Sun*'s, but thine own kinder Rays.
Thou thoughtst each hour out of Life's Journal lost,   165

158 away,] *Ed.* (away *1854*); away; *1684*

Which could not some fresh Favor boast,
And reckon'dst Bounties thy best *Clepsydras*.

XI.

Some Fools who the great Art of giving want,
Deflower their Largess with too slow a Grant;
Where the deluded Suitor dearly buys   170
          What hardly can defray
    The Expence of Importunities,
  Or the Suspense of torturing Delay.
Here was no need of tedious Pray'rs to sue,
    Or thy too backward Kindness woo.   175
      It moved with no formal State,
  Like theirs whose Pomp does for intreaty wait:
      But met the swift'st Desires half way;
    And Wishes did well-nigh anticipate;
    And then as modestly withdrew,   180
Nor for its due Reward of Thanks would stay.

XII.

Yet might this Goodness to the happy most accrue;
    Somewhat was to the miserable due,
      Which they might justly challenge too.
  Whate'er mishap did a known Heart oppress,   185
      The same did thine as wretched make;
  Like yielding Wax thine did th' Impressions take,
  And paint its Sadness in as lively Dress.
Thou could'st afflictions from another Breast translate,
    And forein Grief impropriate;   190
Oft-times our Sorrows thine so much have grown,
        They scarce were more our own;
  We seem'd exempt, thou suffer'dst all alone.

XIII.

Our small'st Misfortunes scarce could reach thy Ear,
        But made thee give in Alms a Tear;   195
    And when our Hearts breath'd their regret in sighs,
    As a just Tribute to their Miseries,
    Thine with their mournful Airs did symbolize.

Like throngs of sighs did from its Fibres crowd,
    And told thy Grief for our each Grief aloud: 200
        Such is the secret Sympathy
    We may betwixt two neighb'ring Lutes descry,
If either by unskilful hand too rudely bent
    Its soft Complaint in pensive murmurs vent,
        As if it did that Injury resent: 205
    Untoucht the other strait returns the Moan,
        And gives an Eccho to each Groan.
    From its sweet Bowels a sad Note's convey'd,
        Like those which to condole are made,
As if its Bowels too a kind Compassion had.   210

XIV.

Nor was thy goodness bounded with so small extent,
        Or in such narrow Limits pent.
    Let Female Frailty in fond Tears distill,
        Who think that Moisture which they spill
                Can yield Relief,   215
    Or shrink the Current of anothers Grief,
Who hope that Breath which they in sighs convey,
        Should blow Calamities away.
        Thine did a manlier Form express,
    And scorn'd to whine at an Unhappiness;   220
Thou thought'st it still the noblest Pity to redress.
    So friendly Angels their Relief bestow
           On the unfortunate below
    For whom those purer minds no Passion know:
    Such Nature in that generous Plant is found,   ⎫   225
    Whose every Breach does with a Salve abound, ⎬
    And wounds it self to cure another's Wound.   ⎭
    In pity to Mankind it sheds its Juice,
    Glad with expence of Blood to serve their Use:
    First with kind Tears our Maladies bewails,   230
              And after heals;
And makes those very Tears the remedy produce.

199-200 from ... for] *Ed.* (*1703*); for ... from *1684*   229 Use:] *Ed.*
(*1697*); Use. *1684*

XV.

Nor didst thou to thy Foes less generous appear,
    (If there were any durst that Title wear.)
        They could not offer Wrongs so fast,   235
        But what were pardon'd with like haste;
    And by thy acts of Amnesty defac't.
    Had he who wish'd the Art how to forget,
        Discover'd its new Worth in thee,
    He had a double Value on it set,   240
And justly scorn'd th'ignobler Art of Memory.
    No Wrongs could thy great Soul to Grief expose,
    'Twas plac't as much out of the reach of those,
            As of material Blows.
    No Injuries could thee provoke,   245
        Thy Softness always dampt the stroke:
    As Flints on Feather-beds are easiest broke.
    Affronts could ne'er thy cool Complexion heat,
    Or chase thy temper from its setled State:
        But still thou stoodst unshockt by all,   250
    As if thou hadst unlearnt the Power to hate,
    Or, like the Dove, wert born without a Gall.

XVI.

Vain *Stoicks* who disclaim all Human Sense,
And own no Passions to resent Offence,
May pass it by with unconcern'd Neglect, ⎫   255
And Vertue on those Principles erect,   ⎬
Where 'tis not a perfection, but Defect. ⎭
Let these themselves in a dull Patience please,
        Which their own Statues may possess,
        And they themselves when Carcasses.   260
Thou only couldst to that high pitch arrive,
To court Abuses, that thou mightst forgive:
Wrongs thus in thy Esteem seem'd Courtesie,
And thou the first was e'er oblig'd by Injury.

XVII.

Nor may we think these God-like Qualities   265
        Could stand in need of Votaries,
249 chase] *1684*; chafe *conj. Ed.*

Which heretofore had challeng'd Sacrifice.
      Each Assignation, each Converse
      Gain'd thee some new Idolaters.
Thy sweet Obligingness could supple Hate,   270
And out of it its Contrary create.
Its powerful Influence made Quarrels cease,
And Fewds dissolv'd into a calmer Peace.
Envy resign'd her Force, and vanquish'd Spite
      Became thy speedy Proselyte.   275
Malice could cherish Enmity no more;
  And those which were thy Foes before,
    Now wish'd they might adore.
Cæsar may tell of Nations took,
And Troops by Force subjected to his Yoke: 280
We read as great a Conqueror in thee,
Who couldst by milder ways all Hearts subdue,
      The nobler Conquest of the two;
Thus thou whole Legions mad'st thy Captives be,
And like him too couldst look, and speak thy Victory.   285

XVIII.

Hence may we Calculate the Tenderness
        Thou didst Express
To all, whom thou didst with thy Friendship bless:
To think of Passion by new Mothers bore
      To the young Offspring of their Womb,   290
Or that of Lovers to what they Adore,
        Ere Duty it become:
    We should too mean *Ideas* frame,
    Of that which thine might justly claim,
And injure it by a degrading Name: 295
        Conceive the tender Care,
Of guardian Angels to their Charge assign'd,
         Or think how dear
    To Heaven Expiring Martyrs are;
    These are the Emblems of thy mind,   300
The only *Types* to shew how thou wast kind.

284 thy] *Ed.* (*1687*); the *1684*

XIX.

On whom soe're thou didst confer this Tye
    'Twas lasting as Eternity,
And firm as the unbroken Chain of Destiny,
Embraces would faint shadows of your Union show,   305
    Unless you could together grow.
That Union which is from Alliance bred,
        Does not so fastly wed,
    Tho' it with Blood be cemented:
That Link wherewith the Soul and Body's joyn'd,   310
Which twists the double Nature in Mankind
    Only so close can bind.
That holy Fire which *Romans* to their *Vesta* paid,
    Which they immortal as the Goddess made,
    Thy noble Flames most fitly parallel;   315
For thine were just so pure, and just so durable.
Those feigned Pairs of Faithfulness which claim
      So high a place in ancient Fame,
      Had they thy better Patern seen,
      They'd made their Friendship more divine   320
And strove to mend their Characters by thine.

XX.

Yet had this Friendship no advantage been,
    Unless 'twere exercis'd within;
What did thy Love to other Objects tie,
    The same made thy own Pow'rs agree,   325
    And reconcil'd thy self to thee.
    No Discord in thy Soul did rest,
    Save what its Harmony increast.
Thy mind did with such regular Calmness move,
As held resemblance with the greater Mind above.   330
    Reason there fix'd its peaceful Throne,
        And reign'd alone.
The Will its easie Neck to Bondage gave,
And to the ruling Faculty became a Slave.
    The Passions rais'd no Civil Wars,   335
Nor discompos'd thee with intestine Jars:
        All did obey,

And paid Allegiance to its rightful Sway.
    All threw their resty Tempers by,
           And gentler Figures drew,   340
Gentle as Nature in its Infancy,
As when themselves in their first Beings grew.

XXI.

Thy Soul within such silent Pomp did keep,
As if Humanity were lull'd asleep.
So gentle was thy Pilgrimage beneath,   345
    Time's unheard Feet scarce make less Noise,
Or the soft Journey which a Planet goes.
    Life seem'd all calm as its last Breath.
A still Tranquillity so husht thy Breast,
    As if some *Halcyon* were its Guest,   350
        And there had built her Nest;
It hardly now enjoys a greater Rest.
As that smooth Sea which wears the Name of *Peace*,
    Still with one even Face appears,
And feels no Tides to change it from its place,   355
No Waves to alter the fair Form it bears:
        As that unspotted Sky,
    Where *Nile* does want of Rain supply,
Is free from Clouds, from Storms is ever free:
So thy unvary'd mind was always one,   360
And with such clear Serenity still shone,
As caus'd thy little World to seem all temp'rate Zone.

XXII.

Let Fools their high Extraction boast,
And Greatness, which no Travel, but their Mothers, cost.
    Let 'em extol a swelling Name,   365
Which theirs by Will and Testament became;
    At best but meer Inheritance,
    As oft the Spoils as Gift of Chance.
Let some ill-plac't Repute on Scutcheons rear
As fading as the Colors which those bear;   370
    And prize a painted Field,
    Which Wealth as soon as Fame can yield.

359 free:] *Ed.* (*1722;* free, *1710*); free. *1684*

Thou scorn'dst at such low rates to purchase worth,
Nor couldst thou owe it only to thy Birth.
Thy self-born Greatness was above the Power   375
Of Parents to entail, or Fortune to deflower.
Thy Soul, which like the Sun, Heaven molded bright,
    Disdain'd to shine with borrow'd Light.
Thus from himself th' Eternal Being grew,
And from no other Cause his Grandeur drew.   380

XXIII.

    Howe'er if true Nobility
Rather in Souls than in the Blood does lie:
If from thy better part we Measures take,
And that the Standard of our Value make,
Jewels and Stars become low Heraldry   385
    To blazon thee.
Thy Soul was big enough to pity Kings,
And lookt on Empires as poor humble things.
    Great as his boundless mind,
Who thought himself in one wide Globe confin'd,   390
    And for another pin'd.
Great as that Spirit whose large Powers rowl
Thro' the vast Fabrick of this spatious Bowl,
And tell the World as well as Man can boast a Soul.

XXIV.

Yet could not this an Haughtiness beget,   395
Or thee above the common Level set.
Pride, whose Alloy does best Endowments mar,
(As things most lofty smaller still appear)
    With thee did no Alliance bear.
Low Merits oft are by too high Esteem bely'd,   400
    Whose owners lessen while they raise their Price;
    Thine were above the very Guilt of Pride,
Above all others, and thy own *Hyperbole*:
    In thee the wid'st Extreams were joyn'd
    The loftiest, and the lowliest Mind.   405
    Thus tho some part of Heav'ns vast Round
Appear but low, and seem to touch the Ground.

Yet 'tis well known almost to bound the Spheres,
'Tis truly held to be above the Stars.

XXV.

While thy brave Mind preserv'd this noble Frame,   410
   Thou stoodst at once secure
From all the Flattery and Obloquy of Fame,
Its rough and gentler Breath were both to thee the same:
Nor this could thee exalt, nor that depress thee lower;
 But thou from thy great Soul on both look'dst down 415
Without the small concernment of a smile or frown.
 Heav'n less dreads that it should fir'd be
 By the weak flitting Sparks that upwards fly,
 Less the bright Goddess of the Night
 Fears those loud howlings that revile her Light   420
 Than thou malignant Tongues thy Worth should blast,
Which was too great for Envy's Cloud to overcast.
 'Twas thy brave Method to despise Contempt,
 And make what was the Fault the Punishment.
What more Assaults could weak Detraction raise,   425
   When thou couldst Saint disgrace,
   And turn Reproach to Praise.
So Clouds which would obscure the Sun, oft guilded be,
 And Shades are taught to shine as bright as he.
  So Diamonds, when envious Night   430
 Would shroud their Splendor, look most bright,
And from its Darkness seem to borrow Light.

XXVI.

 Had Heaven compos'd thy mortal Frame,
 Free from Contagion as thy Soul or Fame:
 Could Vertue been but Proof against Death's Arms,   435
  Th'adst stood unvanquisht by these Harms,
 Safe in a Circle made by thy own Charms.
 Fond Pleasure, whose soft Magick oft beguiles
   Raw unexperienc'd Souls,
   And with smooth Flattery cajoles,   440
   Could ne'er ensnare thee with her Wiles,
 Or make thee Captive to her soothing Smiles.

In vain that Pimp of Vice assay'd to please,
In hope to draw thee to its rude Embrace.
    Thy Prudence still that *Syren* past   445
    Without being pinion'd to the Mast:
All its Attempts were ineffectual found;
    Heaven fenc'd thy heart with its own Mound,
And forc'd the Tempter still from that forbidden Ground.

XXVII.

The mad *Capricio's* of the doating Age   450
Could ne'er in the same Frenzy thee engage;
But mov'd thee rather with a generous Rage.
    Gallants, who their high Breeding prize,
Known only by their Gallanture and Vice,
Whose Talent is to court a fashionable Sin,   455
And act some fine Transgression with a janty Meen,
    May by such Methods hope the Vogue to win.
    Let those gay Fops who deem
    Their Infamies Accomplishment,
Grow scandalous to get Esteem;   460
And by Disgrace strive to be eminent.
    Here thou disdain'dst the common Road,
      Nor wouldst by ought be woo'd
To wear the vain Iniquities o'th' Mode.
Vice with thy Practice did so disagree,   465
Thou scarce couldst bear it in thy Theory.
Thou didst such Ignorance 'bove Knowledge prize,
And here to be unskill'd, is to be wise.
    Such the first Founders of our Blood,
      While yet untempted, stood   470
    Contented only to know Good.

XXVIII.

Vertue alone did guide thy Actions here,
Thou by no other Card thy Life didst steer:
    No sly decoy would serve,
To make thee from its rigid Dictates swerve,   475

462 disdaind'st] *Ed.*; disdainst *1684*   463 woo'd] *Ed.* (*1687*); wood *1684*

      Thy Love ne'er thought her worse
Because thou hadst so few Competitors.
Thou couldst adore her when ador'd by none
Content to be her Votary alone:
      When 'twas proscrib'd the unkind World   480
      And to blind Cells and Grotto's hurld,
When thought the Fantom of some crazy Brain,
Fit for grave *Anchorets* to entertain,
A thin *Chimæra*, whom dull Gown-Men frame
To gull deluded Mortals with an empty Name.   485

XXIX.

      Thou own'dst no Crimes that shun'd the Light,
      Whose Horror might thy Blood affright,
      And force it to its known Retreat.
While the pale Cheeks do Penance in their White,
And tell that Blushes are too weak to expiate: 490
Thy Faults might all be on thy Forehead wore
      And the whole World thy Confessor.
      Conscience within still kept Assize,
    To punish and deter Impieties:
That inbred Judg, such strict Inspection bore,   495
      So travers'd all thy Actions ore;
      Th' Eternal Judge could scarce do more:
      Those little Escapades of Vice,
      Which pass the Cognizance of most
I'th' Crowd of following Sins forgot and lost,   500
Could ne're its Sentence or Arraignment miss:
Thou didst prevent the young desires of ill,
      And them in their first Motions kill:
The very thoughts in others unconfin'd
        And lawless as the Wind,   505
      Thou couldst to Rule and Order bind.
They durst not any stamp, but that of Vertue bear,
And free from stain as thy most publick Actions were.
Let wild Debauches hug their darling Vice
      And court no other Paradise,   510
        Till want of Power
      Bids 'em discard the stale Amour,

And when disabled strength shall force
A short Divorce,
Miscall that weak forbearance Abstinence,   515
Which wise Morality and better Sence
Stiles but at best a sneaking Impotence.
Thine far a Nobler Pitch did fly
'Twas all free choice, nought of Necessity..
Thou didst that puny Soul disdain   520
Whose half-strain Vertue only can restrain;
Nor wouldst that empty Being own
Which springs from Negatives alone,
But truly thoughtst it always Vertues Skeleton.

XXX.

Nor didst thou those mean Spirits more approve,   525
Who Vertue, only for its Dowry love,
Unbrib'd thou didst her sterling self espouse:
Nor wouldst a better Mistress choose.
Thou couldst Affection to her bare *Idæa* pay
The first that e'er caress'd her the Platonick way.   530
To see her in her own Attractions drest
Did all thy Love arrest,
Nor lack'd there new Efforts to storm thy Brest.
Thy generous Loyalty
Would ne'er a *Mercenary* be,   535
But chose to serve her still without a Livery.
Yet wast thou not of Recompense debarr'd,
But countedst Honesty its own Reward;
Thou didst not wish a greater Bliss t'accrue,
For to be good to thee was to be happy too,   540
That secret Triumph of thy mind,
Which always thou in doing well didst find,
Were Heaven enough, were there no other Heaven design'd.

XXXI.

What Vertues few possess but by Retail
In gross could thee their Owner call;   545

521 half-strain] *Ed.* (*1722*); half strain *1684*

They all did in thy single Circle fall.
Thou wast a living *System* where were wrote
All those high Morals which in Books are sought.
   Thy Practice did more Vertues share
Than heretofore the learned Porch e'er knew,   550
Or in the *Stagyrites* scant *Ethics* grew:
Devout thou wast as holy *Hermits* are,
Which share their time 'twixt Extasie and Prayer.
Modest as Infant Roses in their bloom,
  Which in a Blush their Lives consume,   555
  So Chast, the Dead are only more,
Who lie divorc'd from Objects, and from Power.
  So pure, that if blest Saints could be
Taught Innocence, they'd gladly learn of thee.
Thy Vertues height in Heaven alone could grow   560
Nor to ought else would for Accession owe:
It only now's more perfect than it was below.

XXXII.

Hence, tho' at once thy Soul liv'd here and there,
Yet Heaven alone its Thoughts did share;
It own'd no home, but in the active Sphere.   565
Its Motions always did to that bright Center rowl,
 And seem'd t'inform thee only on Parole.
Look how the Needle does to its dear *North* incline,
 As were't not fix't 'twould to that Region climb;
    Or mark what hidden force   570
  Bids the Flame upwards take its course,
  And makes it with that Swiftness rise,
 As if 'twere wing'd by th' Air thro' which it flies.
Such a strong Vertue did thy Inclinations bend,
 And made 'em still to the blest Mansions tend.   575
 That mighty Slave whom the proud Victor's Rage
  Shut Pris'ner in a golden Cage,
  Condemn'd to glorious Vassalage,
  Ne'er long'd for dear Enlargement more,
Nor his gay Bondage with less Patience bore,   580

569 were't] Ed. (1722); wer't 1684

Than this great Spirit brookt its tedious Stay,
  While fetter'd here in brittle Clay,
 And wish'd to disengage and fly away.
 It vext and chaf'd, and still desir'd to be
Relecas'd to the sweet Freedom of Eternity.   585

XXXIII.

  Nor were its Wishes long unheard,
  Fate soon at its desire appear'd,
  And strait for an Assault prepar'd.
  A suddain and a swift Disease
First on thy Heart Life's chiefest Fort does seize, 590
And then on all the Suburb-vitals preys:
 Next it corrupts thy tainted Blood,
And scatters Poyson thro' its purple Flood.
 Sharp Aches in thick Troops it sends,
And Pain, which like a Rack the Nerves extends. 595
  Anguish through every Member flies,
  And all those inward *Gemonies*
  Whereby frail Flesh in Torture dies.
  All the staid Glories of thy Face,
Where sprightly Youth lay checkt with manly Grace, 600
  Are now impair'd,
 And quite by the rude hand of Sickness mar'd.
  Thy Body where due Symmetry
  In just proportions once did lie,
  Now hardly could be known, 605
 Its very Figure out of Fashion grown;
 And should thy Soul to its old Seat return,
  And Life once more adjourn,
 'Twould stand amaz'd to see its alter'd Frame,
And doubt (almost) whether its own Carcass were the same. 610

XXXIV.

 And here thy Sickness does new matter raise
  Both for thy Vertue and our Praise;
  'Twas here thy Picture look'd most neat,

---

587 appear'd,] *Ed.* (*1722*); appear'd. *1684*

When deep'st in Shades 'twas set.
Thy Vertues only thus could fairer be   615
Advantag'd by the Foil of Misery.
Thy Soul which hasten'd now to be enlarg'd,
        And of its grosser Load discharg'd,
Began to act above its wonted rate,
And gave a Prælude of its next unbody'd State.   620
        So dying Tapers near their Fall,
When their own Lustre lights their Funeral,
Contract their Strength into one brighter Fire,
And in that Blaze triumphantly expire.
So the bright Globe that rules the Skies,   625
Tho' he guild Heav'n with a glorious Rise,
Reserves his choicest Beams to grace his Set;
            And then he looks most great,
        And then in greatest Splendor dies.

                                XXXVI.

Thou sharpest pains didst with that Courage bear,   630
And still thy Looks so unconcern'd didst wear:
Beholders seem'd more indispos'd than thee;
        For they were sick in Effigie.
Like some well-fashion'd Arch thy Patience stood,
And purchas'd Firmness from its greater Load.   635
Those Shapes of Torture, which to view in Paint
                Would make another faint;
Thou could'st endure in true Reality,
And feel what some could hardly bear to see.
Those Indians who their Kings by Torture chose,   640
Subjecting all the Royal Issue to that Test
                Could ne'er thy Sway refuse,
If he deserves to reign that suffers best.
Had those fierce Savages thy Patience view'd,
                Thou'dst claim'd their Choice alone;   645
They with a Crown had paid thy Fortitude,
                And turn'd thy Death-bed to a Throne.

                640 chose] *1684*; choose *conj. Ed.*

XXXVII.

All those Heroick Pieties,
  Whose Zeal to Truth made them its Sacrifice:
  Those nobler *Scaevola's*, whose holy Rage   650
  Did their whole selves in cruel Flames engage,
  Who did amidst their Force unmov'd appear,
      As if those Fires but lambent were;
  Or they had found their *Empyreum* there:
  Might these repeat again their Days beneath,   655
They'd seen their Fates out-acted by a natural Death,
  And each of them to thee resign his Wreath.
  In spite of Weakness and harsh Destiny,
To relish Torment, and enjoy a Misery:
          So to caress a Doom,   660
  As make its Sufferings Delights become:
  So to triumph o'er Sense and thy Disease,
  As amongst Pains to revel in soft Ease:
  These wonders did thy Vertues worth enhance,
And Sickness to dry Martyrdom advance.   665

XXXVIII.

Yet could not all these Miracles stern Fate avert,
          Or make't withold the Dart.
  Only she paus'd a while with Wonder strook,
A while she doubted if that Destiny was thine,
  And turned o'er again the dreadful Book,   670
      And hop'd she had mistook;
  And wish'd she might have cut another Line.
      But dire Necessity
      Soon cry'd 'twas thee,
  And bad her give the fatal Blow.   675
Strait she obeys, and strait the vital Powers grow
  Too weak to grapple with a stronger Foe,
  And now the feeble Strife forgo.
  Life's sap'd Foundation every Moment sinks,
  And every Breath to lesser compass shrinks;   680
  Last panting Gasps grow weaker each Rebound,

654 there:] *Ed.* (there; *1854*); there. *1684*

Like the faint Tremblings of a dying Sound:
And doubtful Twilight hovers o'er the Light,
Ready to usher in Eternal Night.

XXXIX.

Yet here thy Courage taught thee to out-brave   685
    All the slight Horrors of the Grave:
        Pale Death's Arrest
        Ne'er shock'd thy Breast;
  Nor could it in the dreadfulst Figure drest.
That ugly Skeleton may guilty Spirits daunt,   690
When the dire Ghosts of Crimes departed haunt,
Arm'd with bold Innocence thou couldst that *Mormo* dare,
    And on the bare-fac'd King of Terrors stare,
As free from all Effects as from the Cause of Fear.
Thy Soul so willing from thy Body went,   695
    As if both parted by Consent.
No Murmur, no Complaining, no Delay,
Only a Sigh, a Groan, and so away.
    Death seem'd to glide with Pleasure in,
  As if in this Sense too 't had lost her Sting.   700
Like some well-acted Comedy Life swiftly past,
  And ended just so still and sweet at last.
Thou, like its Actors, seem'dst in borrow'd Habit here beneath,
      And couldst, as easily
As they do that, put off Mortality.   705
Thou breathedst out thy Soul as free as common Breath,
As unconcern'd as they are in a feigned Death.

XL.

Go happy Soul, ascend the joyful Sky,
Joyful to shine with thy bright Company:
    Go mount the spangled Sphere,   710
And make it brighter by another Star:
Yet stop not there, till thou advance yet higher,
    Till thou art swallow'd quite
In the vast unexhausted Ocean of Delight:
Delight which there alone in its true Essence is,   715
Where Saints keep an eternal Carnival of Bliss:

Where the *Regalio*'s of refined Joys,
    Which fills, but never cloys.
Where Pleasure's ever growing, ever new,
Immortal as thy self, and boundless too.   720
There may'st thou learned by *Compendium* grow;
    For which in vain below   .
We so much time, and so much pains bestow.
There may'st thou all *Idæa's* see,
    All wonders which in Knowledge be   725
In that fair beatifick mirror of the Deity.

XLI.

Mean while thy Body mourns in its own Dust,
And puts on Sables for its tender Trust.
Tho' dead, it yet retains some untouch Grace,
Wherein we may thy Soul's fair Foot-steps trace;   730
Which no Disease can frighten from its wonted place:
    E'en its Deformities do thee become,
    And only serve to consecrate thy Doom.
Those marks of Death which did its Surface stain
    Now hallow, not profane.   735
    Each Spot does to a Ruby turn;
    What soil'd but now, would now adorn.
Those Asterisks plac'd in the Margin of thy Skin
    Point out the nobler Soul that dwelt within:
Thy lesser, like the greater World appears   740
All over bright, all over stuck with Stars.
So *Indian* Luxury when it would be trim,
    Hangs Pearls on every Limb.
Thus amongst ancient Picts Nobility
    In Blemishes did lie;   745
Each by his Spots more honourable grew,
And from their Store a greater Value drew:
Their Kings were known by th' Royal Stains they bore,
    And in their Skins their Ermin wore.

717-18 *Regalio*'s ... Joys, / ... fills, ... cloys;] *Ed.*; *Regalio's* ... Joy,
/ ...fill, ... cloy. *1684*   719 Pleasure's] *Ed. (1854)*; Pleasures *1684*

XLII.

Thy Blood where Death triumph'd in greatest State,   750
Whose Purple seem'd the Badge of Tyrant-Fate,
      And all thy Body o'er
       Its ruling Colours bore:
That which infected with the noxious Ill
       But lately help'd to kill,   755
    Whose Circulation fatal grew,
And thro' each part a swifter Ruin threw.
Now conscious, its own Murther would arraign,
And throngs to sally out at every Vein.
Each Drop a redder than its native Dye puts on,   760
As if in its own Blushes 'twould its Guilt atone.
  A sacred Rubric does thy Carcass paint,
  And Death in every Member writes thee Saint.
  So *Phœbus* cloaths his dying Rays each Night,
And blushes he can live no longer to give Light.   765

XLIII.

Let Fools, whose dying Fame requires to have
  Like their own Carcasses a Grave,
  Let them with vain Expence adorn
       Some costly Urn,
  Which shortly, like themselves, to Dust shall turn.   770
    Here lacks no *Carian* Sepulchre,
Which Ruin shall e'er long in its own Tomb interr;
    No fond *Egyptian* Fabric built so high
      As if 'twould climb the Sky,
    And thence reach Immortality.   775
    Thy Vertues shall embalm thy Name,
And make it lasting as the Breath of Fame.
        When frailer Brass
    Shall moulder by a quick Decrease;
    When brittle Marble shall decay,   780
    And to the Jaws of Time become a Prey.
Thy Praise shall live, when Graves shall buried lie,

756 grew,] *Ed.* (*1697*); grew. *1684*   772 interr;] *Ed.* (*1854*); interr.
1684

Till Time it self shall die,
And yield its triple Empire to Eternity.

*To the Memory of that worthy Gentle-
man, Mr.* Harman Atwood.

PINDARIQUE.

I.

No, I'll no more repine at Destiny,
Now we poor common Mortals are content to die,
    When thee, blest Saint, we cold and breathless see,
        Thee, who if ought that's great and brave,
    Ought that is excellent might save,   5
    Hadst justly claim'd Exemption from the Grave,
And cancell'd the black irreversible Decree.
    Thou didst alone such Worth, such Goodness share
    As well deserv'd to be immortal here;
Deserv'd a Life as lasting as the Fame thou art to wear. 10
    At least, why went thy Soul without its Mate?
Why did they not together undivided go?
    So went (we're told) the fam'd Illustrious Two.
        (Nor could they greater Merits shew,
        Altho' the best of Patriarchs that,   15
        And this the best of Prophets was)
    Heav'n did alive the blessed Pair translate;
Alive they launch'd into Life's boundless Happiness,
And never past Death's Straights and narrow Seas;
Ne'er enter'd the dark gloomy Thorowfare of Fate.   20

II.

Long time had the Profession under Scandal lain,
        And felt a general tho' unjust Disdain,
        An upright Lawyer Contradiction seem'd,
        And was at least a Prodigy esteem'd.

2 die,] *Ed.* (*1687*); die. *1684*   10 Deserv'd] *Ed.*; Deserve *1684*

If one perhaps did in an Age appear,   25
  He was recorded like some Blazing Star;
And Statues were erected to the wondrous Man,
As heretofore to the strange honest Publican.
To thee the numerous Calling all its thanks should give,
  To thee who couldst alone its lost Repute retrieve.   30
  Thou the vast wide extremes didst reconcile,
  The first, almost, e'er taught it was not to beguile.
To each thou didst distribute Right so equally,
Ev'n Justice might her self correct her Scales by thee.
      And none did now regret,   35
      Her once bewail'd Retreat,
  Since all enjoy'd her better Deputy.
Henceforth succeeding Time shall bear in mind,
And Chronicle the best of all the kind:
  The best e'er since the man that gave   40
      Our suffering God a Grave;
(That God who living no Abode could find,
Tho' he the World had made, and was to save)
Embalming him, he did embalm his Memory,
  And make it from Corruption free: 45
Those Odors kindly lent perfum'd the Breath of Fame,
And fixt a lasting Fragrancy upon his Name;
And rais'd it with his Saviour to an Immortality.

III.

Hence the stale musty Paradox of equal Souls,
  That ancient vulgar Error of the Schools,   50
Avow'd by dull Philosophers and thinking Fools.
  Here might they find their feeble Arguments o'er-thrown:
    Here might the grave Disputers find
    Themselves all baffl'd by a single Mind,
  And see one vastly larger than their own,   55
    Tho' all of theirs were mixt in one.
  A Soul as great as e'er vouchsaf'd to be
    Inhabiter in low Mortality;
  As e'er th'Almighty Artist labour'd to infuse.
    Thro' all his Mint he did the brightest chuse;   60
      With his own Image stampt it fair,
      59 infuse.] *Ed.*; infuse, *1684*

And bid it ever the Divine Impression wear;
  And so it did, so pure, so well,
We hardly could believe him of the Race that fell:
  So spotless still, and still so good,   65
 As if it never lodg'd in Flesh and Blood.
Hence conscious too, how high, how nobly born:
  It never did reproach its Birth,
By valuing ought of base or meaner worth,
But look'd on earthly Grandeur with Contempt and Scorn. 70

IV.

 Like his All-great Creator, who
Can only by diffusing greater grow:
He made his chiefest Glory to communicate,
 And chose the fairest Attribute to imitate.
  So kind, so generous, and so free,   75
As if he only liv'd in Courtesie.
To be unhappy did his Pity claim,
Only to want it did deserve the same:
Nor lack'd there other Rhetorick than Innocence and Misery.
  His unconfin'd unhoarded Store   80
Was still the vast Exchequer of the poor;
  And whatsoe'er in pious Acts went out
He did in his own Inventory put:
For well the wise and prudent Banker knew
His Gracious Sovereign above would all repay,   85
  And all th' expences of his Charity defray;
  And so he did, both Principal and Interest too,
And he by holy Prodigality more wealthy grew.
 Such, and so universal is the Influence
Which the kind bounteous Sun does here dispense: 90
With an unwearied indefatigable Race,
 He travels round the World each day,
And visits all Mankind, and every place,
And scatters Light and Blessings all the way.
 Tho' he each hour new Beams expend,   95
Yet does he not like wasting Tapers spend.
Tho' he ten thousand years disburse in Light,
The boundless Stock can never be exhausted quite.

V.

Nor was his Bounty stinted or design'd,
As theirs who only partially are kind;   100
Or give where they Return expect to find:
    But like his Soul, its fair Original:
            'Twas all in all,
        And all in every part,
Silent as his Devotion, open as his Heart.   105
Brib'd with the Pleasure to oblige and gratifie,
    As Air and Sunshine he dispos'd his Kindness free,
    Yet scorn'd Requitals, and worse hated Flattery,
    And all obsequious Pomp of vain formality.
        Thus the Almighty Bounty does bestow   110
    Its Favors on our undeserving Race below;
        Confer'd on all its loyal Votaries;
    Confer'd alike on its rebellious Enemies.
            To it alone our All we owe,
        All that we are and are to be,   115
        Each Art and Science to its Liberality,
    And this same trifling jingling thing call'd Poetry.
Yet the great Donor does no costly Gratitude require,
            No Charge of Sacrifice desire;
        Nor are w' expensive Hecatombs to raise,   120
                As heretofore,
    To make his Altars float with reeking Gore.
A small Return the mighty Debt and Duty pays,
Ev'n the cheap humble Off'ring of worthless Thanks and Praise.

                    VI.
But how, blest Saint, shall I thy numerous Vertues summ, 125
        If one or two take up this room?
    To what vast Bulk must the full *Audit* come?
As that bold Hand that drew the fairest Deity,
        Had many naked Beauties by,
And took from each a several Grace, and Air, and Line,   130
        And all in one Epitome did joyn
To paint his bright Immortal in a Form Divine:
        So must I do to frame thy Character.
I'll think whatever Men can good and lovely call,

And then abridge it all,   135
And crowd and mix the various *Idæa's* there;
And yet at last of a just Praise despair.
Whatever ancient Worthies boast,
Which made themselves and Poets their Describers great,
From whence old Zeal did Gods and Shrines create;   140
Thou hadst thy self alone engrost,
And all their scatter'd Glories in thy Soul did meet:
And future Ages, when they eminent Vertues see,
(If any after thee
Dare the Pretence of Vertue own,   145
Without the Fear of being far out-done)
Shall count 'em all but Legacy,
Which from the Strength of thy Example flow,
And thy fair Copy in a less correct Edition show.

VII.

Religion over all did a just Conduct claim,   150
No false Religion which from Custom came,
Which to its Font and Country only ow'd its Name:
No Issue of devout and zealous Ignorance,
Or the more dull Effect of Chance;
But 'twas a firm well-grounded Piety,   155
That knew all that it did believe, and why;
And for the glorious Cause durst die,
And durst out-suffer ancient Martyrology.
So knit and interwoven with its being so,
Most thought it did not from his Duty, but his Nature   160
Exalted far above the vain Attacks of Wit,   [flow.
And all that vile gay lewd Buffoons can bring,
Who try by little Railleries to ruin it,
And jeer't into an unreguarded poor defenceless thing.
The Men of Sence who in Confederacy join   165
To damn Religion, had they view'd but thine,
They'd have confest it pure, confest it all divine,
And free from all Pretences of Imposture or Design,

161 vain] *Ed.*; vain small *1684*   165 join] *Ed.* (*1687*); join, *1684*
166 Religion,] *Ed.* (*1687*); Religion *1684*

Pow'rful enough to counter-act lewd Poets and the Stage,
And Proselyte as fast as they debauch the Age;   170
So good, it might alone a guilty condemn'd World reprieve,
   Should a destroying Angel stand
   With brandish'd Thunder in his Hand,
   Ready the bidden Stroke to give;
Or a new Deluge threaten this and every Land.   175

VIII.

Religion once a quiet and a peaceful Name,
Which all the Epithets of Gentleness did claim,
 Late prov'd the Source of Faction and intestine Jars:
   Like the Fair teeming *Hebrew*, she
 Did travel with a wrangling Progeny,   180
And harbor'd in her Bowels Fewds and Civil Wars.
 Surly, uncomplaisant, and rough she grew,
 And of a soft and easie Mistress turn'd a Shrew.
 Passion and Anger went for marks of Grace,
And looks deform'd and sullen sanctifyed a Face.   185
 Thou first its meek and primitive Temper didst restore,
 First shew'dst how men were pious heretofore:
The gaul-less Dove, which otherwhere could find no Rest,
  Early retreated to its Ark, thy Breast,
  And straight the swelling Waves decreast   190
  And straight tempestuous Passions ceast,
Like Winds and Storms where some fair *Halcyon* builds her
  No overheating Zeal did thee inspire,   [Nest.
   But 'twas a kindly gentle Fire,
   To warm, but not devour,   195
And only did refine, and make more pure:
Such is that Fire that makes thy present blest Abode
  The Residence and Palace of our God.
 And such was that bright unconsuming Flame,
   So mild, so harmless and so tame,   200
  Which heretofore ith' Bush to *Moses* came:
At first the Vision did the wondring Prophet scare,
But when the voice had check'd his needless Fear
He bow'd and worshipp'd and confest the Deity was there.

   181 Wars.] *Ed. (1687)*; Wars, *1684*

IX.

Hail Saint Triumphant! hail Heav'ns happy Guest.   205
    Hail new Inhabitant amongst the blest!
Methinks I see kind Spirits in convoy meet,
    And with loud Welcomes thy Arrival greet.
    Who, could they grieve, would go with Grief away
    To see a Soul more white, more pure than they: 210
        By them thou'rt led on high
To the vast glorious Apartment of the Deity;
Where circulating Pleasures make an endless Round
To which scant Time or Measure sets no Bound,
    Perfect unmixt Delights without Alloy,   215
And whatsoe'er does earthly Bliss annoy,
Which oft does in Fruition Pall and oft'ner Cloy:
Where being is no longer Life but Extasi;
But one long Transport of unutterable Joy:
    A Joy above the boldest Flights of daring verse,   220
And all a Muse unglorifyed can fancy or rehearse:
        There happy Thou
    From Troubles and the bustling toil of Business free,
    From noise and *tracas* of tumultuous Life below,
Enjoy'st the still and calm Vacation of Eternity.   225

207 meet,] *Ed.* (*1687*); meet. *1684*   212 Deity;] *Ed.*; Deity. *1684*
219 Joy:] *Ed.*; Joy. *1684*

5

UNCOLLECTED POEMS AND FRAGMENTS

A Rant to his Mistress.

May the 15th [16]76

(1)

By Heav'n, and all its Gods I swear,
  Or if a greater Oath there be,
  There's not a God inhabits there
But what would Barter all his Heav'n for thee.
Ev'n Jove himself, their Father and their King,   5
  Would leave his Grandeur and his Throne
And turn a Bird, a Beast, or any thing;
  Might he possess but thee alone.

(2)

I swear there is no greater Happiness,
Or if there be, I can no greater guess,   10
    Then 'tis to sit and gaze
  On the rare Beauties of thy face:
Ev'n Heav'n it self would that fair Prospect prize
And look for ever with unwearied view,
  And tho it look'd with all its Eyes   15
  'Twould still confess 'em all too few.

(3)

They say, 'tis all the Heav'n the Blessed know
To view the Mirror of the Deity;
  I'm sure 'tis all my Heav'n below
    To look on thee,   20
That's here the Beatifick Sight to me,
And 'tis my Hell when I thy Presence must forgo.

(4)

  To read my Destinies,
I'll not consult the Planets of the Skies,
But those more radiant Stars thine Eyes;   25
  If these appear benign,
Let other Stars with any Aspect shine;

So we are in Conjunction,
I fear not theirs, nor what it can portend,
   My Fates on that, not this depend,   30
   They all depend on that alone.

October [16]78   The Desk.
                          An Heroique Poem.
                             First Canto.

   I sing of Battels and that sacred Wight,
Who by long contests and unconquer'd might
In Pourges, fam'd by his great acts, at last
A fatal Desk within a Chappel plac't:
In vain to cross his high designs the Chanter twice   5
Made the whole Chapter in rebellion rise,
This Dean by's Sexton's aid did all withstand,
And to the last his Churche's cause maintain'd:
   Tell me, o Muse, what spite, what baneful rage
Could holy men in such fierce broils engage;   10
What made so long the two fam'd rivals jar;
Can devout minds so much of malice bear?
   And You, great S^r, whose wise preventing pow'r
Gave this the Churche's growing Schism a cure,
Bless with your kind regards the great affair,   15
And from so grave a subject laughter bar:
   Long time had Pourges ancient Church enjoid
A constant peace, by nought of broils annoid;
Her healthful Canons in good plight and case,
Thriv'd and grew fat by long and holy ease: 20
Without one's stirring from his downy bed
These godly Sluggards had their Matins said,
Ne're wak'd but just to dine, and in their place
Left the deputed Chanters God to praise.
   When Discord, with foul Crimes all over staind,   25
And proud with late success of conquests gaind,
In chase of new, leaving the Cordeliers

Now her next course towards the Minims steers,
Dreadful her march, and wheresoe're she hies,
Peace stands amaz'd aloof, or trembling flies,   30
Meeting at length her Palace in her walk,
By some near tree she stops, and makes an halt;
There with glad eys her empire she surveys,
Pleas'd at the tumult she her self dos raise
There sees she, wheresoever she lets rome   35
A wandring view, her faithful Normans come,
There sees she in vast crowds each trice resort
The Laity, Clergy, Country, City, Court;
And all about Lawy'rs in thick squadrons stand,
And wave the standards of her high command: 40
One Church alone triumphs o're her designs,
And in soft peace amidst all tumult reigns,
This alone braves, alone her pow'r contemns,
And bars her entrance with a stout defence:
Discord, whom the loth'd sight of quiet alarms,   45
At this her self and snakes to vengeance arms,
Her mouth around a scatter'd poison throws,
And from her eys fire in long flashes glows:
    What? says she, with a voice was seen to make
The Chappel and its whole foundations shake,   50
Have I till now engag'd in mortal jars
The Carmelites, Celestins, Cordeliers?
Made the poor Austins my fierce anger know,
Much war and many sieges undergo?
Have I so oft by my own force alone   55
Amongst all Orders seeds of faction sown?
And shall this Church, a rebell only, dare
Spite of my arts in peace to persevere?
Am I a Goddes then? will any more
Mankind my pow'r with sacrifice adore?   60
    This said, she, her foul projects to disguise,
Takes an old Chanter's visage, meen and voice,
Thick flaming rubies paint his warlike face,
And grave Bamboo supports his reeling pace:
She, thus prepar'd, without all further stay   65
To find the Prelat out directs her way:

Far back in an apartment wisely made,
Where noise can ne're the privacy invade,
Within an alcove's close obscure retreat,
The scene of undisturbed ease and quiet,   70
A bed with well-stuff'd pride it self dos raise,
Rich with the spoils of all the feather'd race:
Four stately curtains drawn exclude the light,
And in the midst of day create a night:
There, free at once from noise and care and pains   75
Stretch'd wanton Sloth on downy empire reigns;
There tis, the Dean, with breakfast late refresht,
Waits dinner, and beguiles the time in rest:
Plump Youth sits smiling in his cheerful face
And ore his strutting cheeks her bloom displays: 80
Two stories down his brace of chins advance,
And strive to meet half way his rising paunch:
Vast bulk and compass his huge wast contains,
And the strait girdle's narrow bounds disdains:
The yielding Bed with weight of such a pack   85
Shrinks under, and its twisted bedcords crack:

    The Goddess entring finds the table spread,
With plates and napkins in just order laid;
Much she admires, and much discovers there
The conduct of the Church and decent care;   90
Then tow'rds the bed her soft approach she makes,
And with these terms the sleeping Dean bespeaks:
    Sleeps't thou? fond man, sleepst thou? while near the
Ev'n now the Chanter in full Quire displays   [place
His harden'd impudence and thy disgrace?   95
Sings the Te Deums, the Processions gos,
And show'rs of Blessings lavishly bestows?
Sleeps't thou? o sensless of approaching fate!
Whilst dangers thus surround thy tottring state?
Whilst in dispute thy threaten'd Miter stands,   100
The likely Spoil of bold usurping hands?
Up from this lazy bed, that holds thee now,
Bid Sleep, or els thy Bishoprick adieu:

85 yielding] R^2; loaded R^1 86 twisted] R^2; massy R^1, *cancelled*

She spoke; and from her cursed mouth a blast
Sent with her words infects his tainted brest;   105
Hate, Strife, and malice strait take up the place,
And peace with all its gentler forms deface:
The Dean awakes, rais'd by the dismal noise, ⎫
And with a look agast, and trembling voice,   ⎬
His blessing on the parting Fiend bestows: ⎭   110
As a fierce Bull, whom some ambitious Breeze
Dares sting, and with his life the glorie buys,
The haughty Beast with rage the wound resents,
And his high passion in loud bellow'ings vents;
The Prelat so, rising from's frightful dream,   115
Dos to his men his mighty grief proclaim,
With dauntless courage he resolves to meet
The full-charg'd Quire, and stem th' attacks of Fate,
Dinner it self, nor all its charms can make
From that resolve his firm intentions shake: 120
In vain his Almoner, wise Gilotin
Disswades with grave advice the rash design,
Shews him the danger, how 'tis allmost noon,
How dinner must be spoil'd, if it go on:
    What rage, says he, what unheard frenzy now   125
Makes you from dinner to dull service go?
You, whom the Fates for noble ease ordain,
Should better your great character maintain:
Leave this to meaner vassals of the trade;
Was it to pray that you were Prelat made?   130
At lest why now? why this untimely zeal,
When weightier matters your devotion call?
When reeking dainties your attendance wait,
With all that may the eye, or palat treat?
Is this a time for fasting? is it Lent,   135
Ember, or Vigil to be abstinent?
No, no, be wise, all present feuds forego,
Your rage dos now deserve a nobler Fo:
Nor let this prudent maxim be forgot,
"Dinner twice heated is not worth a groat: 140
    This said; he with a quick dispatchful care
Makes the Potage upon the board appear:

The Dean with holy reverence at the sight
Stands mute awhile, and lost in rapture quite:
This staggers all his late resolves at last;   145
Tis now decreed to stay till dinner's past;
Dull ceremony bar'd, he falls to eat,
Hast and his passion make him grace forget:
With such fierce rage the morsels down he throws,
As if he with his meat devour'd his Fos: 150
Thick crowding bits, by his tir'd jaws unbroke,
Are swallow'd, and allmost the passage choke:
The faithful Gilotin, who still dos bear
In all his just concerns a loyal share,
Flies thence amaz'd, and wing'd with fear and speed,   155
Thro' his whole party dos the terrour spread:
Quick as th' alarm the troops together fly,
Resolv'd to vanquish in his cause or dy:
So march'd of old upon the Thracian plains
The dreadful Squadrons of embattel'd Cranes,   160
When by their Chief the warlike Pygmies led,
Durst Hebre's banks their native realm invade:
The Dean, to see the wisht assembly met,
Takes heart, and rising dos their entrance greet;
His looks no more their former fury wear,   165
But recompos'd put on a gentler air;
The Gammon, such high Friends to entertain,
Tho' late remov'd, is now recall'd again:
Himself the first, the company to grace,
With brisk Pontack fills up a top-full glass;   170
He drinks it off, and all in order strait
Their Leader's great example imitate:
Another round succeeds, and out of hand
They find the large capacious vessel drain'd:
Soon as wine's generous heat their heads has warm'd,   175
Enflam'd their Spirits, and their courage arm'd;
The cloth's remov'd, and every man intent,
With eys and ears are on the Prelat bent;
Who to the wondring audience with a voice ⎫
And looks, that well befit his present woes, ⎬   180
Dos in these terms his mighty grief disclose: ⎭

   Ye great Associates of my toils and cares,
Of which each feels, and each a burthen shares;
You, by whose aid and friendship long sustain'd,
I ore a factious Chapter conquest gain'd,   185
And settled now in my establisht throne,
Am rais'd to sing Magnificat alone:
Will you ere let an haughty fool depose
Him, whom your high and open suffrage chose?
How long will you the Chanter's yoke endure?   190
How long submit your trampled necks and pow'r?
Shall he usurp my rights? shall he give laws,
And the great charter of your Desk dispose?
This very morning (tis no idle dream;
A God in sleep to me reveal'd the same)   195
He durst, bold man, in Quire my Blessings give,
He durst invade my great prerogative:
Thus his the fruits of all my pains he makes,
And my own arms to work my ruin takes:
   Did I ere think?—and more he would exprest,   200
But left his looks and sighs to say the rest:
In vain he would th' unfinisht speech pursue,
Vast floods of tears his gushing eys oreflow:
Still, as he'd try, grief spoils the weak efforts,
And crowding sobs rise up, and choke his words: 205
Kind Gilotin, with whom this most had wrought,
For cure has the restoring bottle brought:
When Sidrac, who by weight of years opprest,
That stay'd, and made him slower than the rest,
Arrives at last with reverend cane in hand,   210
And out of breath at th' entrance makes a stand:
This hoary Nestor had four ages bin
O'th' Quire, and all their different customs seen,
Whom high deserts from bare Churchwarden's place
Did by degrees to Vestry-keeper raise: 215
He to the Prelat cast in dolefull trance,
The cause conjectur'd, makes his slow advance:
Thrice does he cough, thrice stroke his formal beard,
And in grave words thus to advise is heard:
   Leave, worthy Dean, says he, vain tears and sighs, 220

Be they the lot of thy false enemies:
To save thy rights and empire only hear
What now propitious Heav'n does me inspire:
Within the Quire, where, at thy left hand set,
The Chanter dos display his pride and state,   225
Upon that frame of boards, we there behold,
Which books and leaning elbows dos uphold,
Stood heretofore (I well remember yet)
A large-built Desk of huger bulk and rate,
Whose vast extent, rais'd with prodigious height,   230
The place around orelook'd and shadow'd quite:
Behind its eaves, as some concealing Skreen,
The Chanter hid, was by the Quire unseen;
While on the other side the Dean in view
All the regards of the whole Chappell drew: 235
But some ill Genius, urg'd with fatal Spite
To th' holy Desk, to work its fate thought fit,
(Whether in night contriv'd by wicked hand
Or from all age by Destiny ordain'd)
One morning down it fell in pieces quite,   240
These very eys beheld the dismal sight:
I, who with Heav'n espous'd the Chanters side,
The ruins to the Vestry had convey'd,
Where thirty years lain buried and forgot
'Mongst dust and worms it dos inglorious rot: 245
Now this I counsel: When returning night
With its black veil drawn ore shuts out the light,
Three of us, whom the Fates by lot shall bid,
Silent, and by its fav'ring darkness hid,
Shall to the Vestry undescry'd repair,   250
And searching out the Desk with heedful care,
Shall reunite the loose ill-jointed mass,
And see't remov'd and fixt i'th' ancient place:
Which if next day the Chanter dare subvert,
What more can strengthen and make good thy part?   255
Expos'd to all attacks of thy just rage he lies,
A thousand dreadful Writs and Processes:
Rather then lose thy rights, which Heav'n maintains,
Let all be ruin'd; 'tis the Churche's Sence:

By these braue ways a Prelat should make known   260
His gallantry, his conduct and renown:
Let not your glories and your high-born mind
Be to a narrow Quire and Pray'rs confin'd;
In Aleth this may pass, where easy fools
Move by Religion and dull vertue's rules;   265
Pourges and we, who boast a nobler name,
From such poor ties a free exemption claim:
And while these troubles shall thy pow'r enhance,
Thou may'st thy Blessings uncontroul'd dispence;
Nay, to outbrave the Chanter and his pride,   270
Do't in his sight, and bless himself beside.
   Well this discours dos the whole audience move,
Who its great authour justly all approve,
But most the ravisht Dean, whose grateful zeal
In loud applause dos his high transport tell: 275
'Tis mov'd that strait thro' all the troop be chose
The three, to whom the Fates shall give their voice;
But all contend alike with rival strife,
Each in the service vows to stake his life:
Leave, says the Dean, this generous contest leave;   280
The lot alone must the decision give;
To end this feud we cuts resolve to draw,
Be chance our guide, and Destiny our law:
He says; they all obey; each would be first,
And pressing elbows writing elbows thrust: 285
Soon thirty names appear in paper writ,
Some by their marks and some by proxy set:
In equal pieces these with justness cut
After due shuffling in a cap are put;
For drawing which with more unbiast hand,   290
A Quirister is to the work ordain'd,
Young Guillaume, whom all marks of candour grace,
Whose blushes artless modesty confess:
Mean while the Dean dos all just reverence shew
Which to that great solemnity is due;   295
With head uncover'd, lifted hands and eys,
Thrice dos he bless the names, and shakes 'em thrice:
He turns the cap: The stripling draws: and strait

Brontin appears, the first mark'd out by Fate:
At this the Dean happy success dos bode   300
And joyful murmurs run thro' all the crowd:
All's husht: and now the name, the glorious name ⎤
Of great La Tour the Clock-keeper dos claim   ⎬
Next place in the high enterprise of fame: ⎦
This young Adonis, small of size and height,   305
Of Anne his consort is the sole delight:
Kindled with mutual flames this charming pair
Are both each others happiness and care:
And they were both (if not by fame belied)
Ere wedlock long in chast embraces tied;   310
But three years since, that tie faster to bind,
Th' Official had the knot of marriage join'd:
This sturdy Brave of cudgelling renown
In Wakes dire rights has his high valour shewn;
In his fierce looks and haughty port and meen,   315
A warlike air and face of action's seen:
One name is left to come, once more the Dean
Shuffles the pack and shakes 'em well again:
Each thinks his name will prove the last oth' three;
But what strange joys and transports ravish thee,   320
O mighty Sexton, brave Boirude, when thou, ⎤
Support o'th' Cross and of thy Master too, ⎬
Seest to the Dean thy name appear in view? ⎦
Tis said, thy tallow face and tawny brows
Did at the time their ancient paleness lose,   325
Thy lubber carcase too, crippled before
With age and gout, now warm'd with martial pow'r,
With active bounds cut capers on the floor:
    All bless the ruling Fate of human things,
Which their just cause to such good hands resigns: 330
With this th' assembly rise, and out of doors
All in disorder shape their hasty course:
    The Dean alone, with rage a while appeas'd,
    Till supper lulls himself and cares to rest.

In Praise of Poetry.

Peace then ye dull Blasphemers! who profane
    Our sacred and diviner Strains,
  Who cry tis all Chimerical and vain
  The meer Capricios of unsettled Brains:
  Wit is an Arbitrary Monarch, who   5
No Law, but what its self establishes, will know
Its Pow'r unlimited,—Dominion absolute
    At lest tis like our well-form'd State
Where subject Art may advise and counsell give
But not encroach upon the great Prerogative   10

    *   *   *   *   *   *

Stand off unhallow'd Rabble! these high Misteries
  Are seen only by clear enlighten'd Eys:
  All rude unknowing Readers they disdain,
  Such, who when they'd unskillfully explain,
Wrest with false Glosses and the sacred Text profane   15

    *   *   *   *   *   *

  Great Gift of Heaven! which it vouchsafes to few
And dos alone on its best Favorites bestow:
  To praise great Heros and thereby to raise
  Our Names as high as theirs we are to praise
Poet, th' expensive Wonder, Heav'n but seldom makes, 20
  Is what in Boast and Pride it undertakes,
    When it intends to shew
Its utmost Skill, and best of Workmanship below:

0.1 *R*100   1-4 *R*96   1 Peace ... Blasphemers!] *R*96; Peace dull Blasphemers! [*then a gap*] *R*100   5-10 *Text from R*96; *R*95 *runs* Wit is an Arbitrary
Monarch— | At lest tis like our Government | Art may advise & counsel give |
But not encroach on the Prerogative   7 Dominion] *Ed.*; —Jurisdiction
Dominion *R*96   11-15 *Text from R*85   11 high] *R*²; great *R*¹   12 Are
seen only by] *R*²; Admit no view of *R*¹   clear] *R*³; vulgar *R*¹; choice *R*²
enlighten'd Eys] *R*²; Eys *R*¹   13 Readers] *R*²; Judges *R*¹   16-19 *Text
from R*100   20-32 *Text from R*87; *R*100 *has* Poet! the Expensive Wonder
Heav'n but rarely makes | Rarely as Heros born seldomer than Kings: *then a
gap*   23 best of] *R*³; choicest *R*¹; chiefest *R*²

I mean not all Pretending Fools, who claim
And impudently dare usurp the Name;   25
A name to base and recreant Souls neer due,
But given and vouchsaf'd to the elected few
Who are predestinate to Glory and immortal Fame.
That high exalted Genius, if we now can find
                Thro the whole Race of human kind   30
That Man that's rais'd above the Rest of Men as far
As Seraphims above the Rank of meaner Angels are: ...

       *   *   *   *   *   *

What Homer, Virgil, Tasso were,
What lofty Pindar, and his Roman Heir,
What our great Cowley and immortal Ben,   35
What I would be, but tis to great a Bliss for Fate t'ordain.

       *   *   *   *   *   *

Am I deceiv'd? or dos my swelling Brest
Enlarge it self for some approching Guest?
'Tis so, tis surely so; I feel the entring God
Within me shed his Light and Rays abroad: 40
All vulgar Thoughts and what was human found
Are now in a diviner Fury drown'd:
                What dos the mighty Pow'r inspire?
What new and unattempted Task require?
Sing, sing (he says) the Worth and Glories of a Muse,   45
What Honours to her Votaries she brings,
Once sacred thought, and crown'd as well as Kings,
What Wonders she did heretofore produce

       *   *   *   *   *   *

Happy the Man! whom she thinks fit to save
                From Fate, Oblivion and the Grave.   50

       *   *   *   *   *   *

Nor are these all the Wonders thou, o Muse canst do. &c.

---

30 Race] R^3; Lists R^1; Dregs R^2 32 meaner] R^2; common R^1 33-6 *Text from* R100   36 What I would be,] R^1; What all would be, R^2 but tis to great a Bliss for Fate t'ordain.] R^3; but ah! poor I must wish in vain; R^1; but few (ah happy few!) must ere attain R^2 37-48 *Text from* R99   49-50 *Text from* R88   51 *Text from* R93

Satyr on Wit

I oft have thought—What is this thing call'd Wit?

[a] November [16]78   The Vision.
                              A Satyr.

   'Twas late, and now all Noise as well as Light
Lay dead and buried in black Shrowds of Night,
When Men, their Toils and very Vices sleep,
All, save whom Lust or Treason waking keep;
Whole Nature slept, as if its work were done,   5
Still, as of old ere Motion's self begun:
And I, by nought of Cares or Fears opprest,
Nought, that disturbs the Guilty or distrest,
Alike in depth of Night and Silence drownd,
By Sleep's soft magick had my Sences bound: 10
  A dreadful Vision strait, more dreadful far
Than those of dying Jesuits in despair,
Did to my scar'd and frighten'd Soul appear:
Led to the top of a steep Rock I came;
Thrown headlong thence I fell methought in dream.   15
Down, vastly down I fell or seem'd to fall
Deeper than thought can reach or fancy tell;
Thro the vast caverns of eternal night,
Dark as old Chaos ere the birth of light
Darkness thick-wove, without one mingling ray,   20
Compar'd to which our night it self were day.
Sure this, thought I, must be the dismal road
That leads the damned to their curst abode:
My headlong flight allow'd no time for fear,
Or stop; nor had I thought, but I was there: 25
  Thro all the Avenues of Hell I past,

26 Avenues] R^1; suburbs marches skirts precincts *Rm*

Where Rome has her feign'd Purgatory plac'd,
With fancied Limbos of the dreaming Schools,
By Knaves invented, and believ'd by Fools:
To tenfold Adamant, that circles in   30
The flaming Realms of the infernal King;
This too I past, quick as thro open air
Shot ey-beams dart, at once both here and there:

             *   *   *   *   *   *

Instead of Tapestry the walls to grace,
A well-wrought Imag'ry adorn'd the place: 35
Vulcan (of old renown'd) the skilful Fiend
Had all the mighty workmanship design'd:
Where lively portraitures in figure tell
The great Exploits of Lucifer and Hell:
How he of old against th' Almighty led   40
A rebel Host and durst his Heav'n invade:
Squadrons of Seraphims in march appear
Well-rang'd with van, main battle, wings and rear:
But not the Overthrow, nor how they fell
That foul disgrace the Artist dos conceal: 45
How he by subtle treachery did deceive
The Mother of mankind, unwary Eve:
In scaly foulds he hugs the fatal Tree
The root and stock of all our miserie.
    Next Hell's first Hero, Cain, with hands embrued   50
In early murder, stains of Brother's blood:
By at his feet the slaughter'd Abel lies
And looks forgiveness with his dying eys:
Here Sodom's lewdness, many a filthy scene,
Outdon by draughts of modern Aretine   55
Outdon by lust of Monks in Cloister walls
And fouler Jesuits in Confessionals.
There Corah's factious Crew with mutinies
Gainst faithful Moses in rebellion rise:
Hither they down thro the cleft Earth were sent;   60

28 fancied] R^2; all the R^1 dreaming] R^2; doating R^1 30 To] R^3;
Thro R^1; Thick R^2 33 dart] R^3; pass R^1; fly R^2 58 factious] R^2;
rebel R^1 *cancelled*

The figure now and very work seems rent:
Next canton dos the great Arch-Traitor hold
Who for vile coyn his God and heaven sold:
From his curst lips Hail Master! seems to fly,
And shapes of Jesuits stand absolving by: 65

[b]   Where streams
Of Blood threaten'd to quench the neighbouring flames,
There with grim Majesty high on [a] state
Of glowing flames th'Infernall Monarch sate

Rang'd in due order stood at his right hand   5
Great Loyola and all his faithfull Band
Who ready still with low submission wait
There, as on Earth his Ministers of State:

[c   The scene thus set, there was to be an ironical speech
      satirizing the Jesuits: there is a marginal note:]

      Lucifer giving thanks to Loyola, Great Pillar of our
      Realm.

   2 quench] *Ed.*; quench'd *R*   flames] *Ed.*; flame *R*   3 [a] state] *Ed.*;
state *R*   4 sate] *Ed.*; state *R*

                    Advice to a Painter.

      Come Painter, once again assume thy skill,
      Pencill and Colours, which have long layn still.

      Dash with bold strokes, bold [as] our fears are now,
      Bold as their Crimes, that help'd to make 'em so:

               3 [as] our] *Ed.*; our *R*

Next our State-Messalina represent,   5
Whose taile's the Rudder of our Government
In which a drained King and Kingdom's spent.
Damn'd Gulph of Lust!

                    Satyr on the times.   [a]

        I had no Action to be tried in Town,
No suit at Court to dance attendance on
The great Triumvirate: I'd no Address
To carry up; no Evidence's place
To get, nor to hunt News was my Intent   5
How forwardly the Quo Warranto went,
Nor how his Royal Highness got ashore
And who were sav'd or drown'd at Leman-ore.
But 'twas ordain'd it seems (the Lord knows how)
That I poor Wretch of late should thither go: 10
The fates three days of pennance did assign
To expiate some crying sin of mine:
Thus long with patience I the torture past
Like the 3 Children in the fiery furnace cast:
I only wanted Fox to have bin by   15
To tell my sufferings to Posterity:
I'd bin recorded then and found a Place
With the chief Martyrs in Q[ueen] Marie's days.

    4 carry up; no] R^2; carry; nor no R^1 5 get] R^2; seek R^1 9 Lord
knows] R^2; fates know R^1 11 assign] R^2; injoyn R^1 13 Thus long] R^2;
Three days R^1 18 Q[ueen]] $Ed.$; Q./ R

            A Satyr upon the Town and Times.   [b]

        Heaven knows for what great crying sin of mine,
(But sure it must be for some heynous sin)
The fates did so severe a Curse assign.

                3 assign] R^2; enjoin R^1

'Thank fate I had no Action to be tried
No suit at Court to Halifax, or Hide: 5
I carried no Abhorrence, or Adress   ⎫
Nor was I of the Irish Witnesses;   ⎬
That Warcup might assure me of a Place: ⎭
But (for what sin of mine I do not know
The fates ordain'd that I should thither go.   10

Nothing henceforth shall ever bring me there
But a Pursuivant or a Messenger:

        12 Pursuivant] R^2; sub-poena R^1

            Horace B[ook].4. Ode. 13. imitated

                To Lyce the Punk.

So, Lyce, now my Pray'rs are heard at last
The Fates, I thank 'em, have my wishes blest:
I pray'd thou mightst be old, and so thou art;
Age with a vengeance now has done its part:
Yet thou pretendst to charms, and spite of time,   5
Still keepst the Affectation of thy Prime:

        *   *   *   *   *   *

Whither (alas!) are now those Beauties fled
Which heretofore our sparks in triumph led
What is of that young lively blush become
Fresher than Infant Roses in their Bloom: 10

2 wishes] R^2; Prayers R^1 8 sparks] R^1; captive hearts Rm

340

Juvenal's 10 Satyr imitated.

Search thro the world, from London to Japan,
From thence round to Peru, and back again,
You'l find at last but few, a very few,
Who can discern 'twixt good that's truely so ...

[On the death of King Charles I.]

But mention not the horrid execrable cause
    That made our Nation wretched in his Loss;
        Let not the conscious Marble tell
What Crimes forc'd him to Heav'n, and those that forc'd him hence
        Lest proud Usurpers, who shall after be,   [to Hell
    Take hence their Patterns of successful Villany;   6
Lest Heav'n (who like our gracious Monarch to at last
    (We hope) an Act of Amnesty has past)
        By seeing it should mindful grow
        Of what Arrears it still dos ow,   10
            And send fresh Judgements down
    And make us in new Plagues our Guilt attone.

9 seeing] R^2; reading R^1

[Cadmus and the Dragon's Teeth,
Out of Ovid's Metamorphoses, Book III, Lines 106-115,
Imitated.]

The Clods, as if Inform'd with some new Soul,
Forthwith take motion, and begin to rowl;
First tops of Lances pierce the teeming Ground,
Whose very Birth tells they are made to Wound:
Then rising Casks their painted Crests display   5

Whose Form at once shews terrible and gay:
Next may he Shoulders, Breasts, and Arms descry,
Whose brandish'd Spears proclaim some Battle nigh:
Untill at length in perfect view appears
A growing Harvest of young Cuirassiers.   10
Thus we in Theaters, the Scenes withdrew,
When some more solemn Spectacle they shew,
See Images in slow Machines arise,
Still mounting by insensible degrees;
New-peeping Heads our longing View first greet,   15
And humble Faces leuell with our Feet:
Next gliding Trunks are in soft order shown,
And neather Limbs heaue upper gently on:
So still their Motion, their Ascent so slow,
You'd justly think they did not moue, but grow: 20
At last their sluggish Feet advanc'd in sight,
Present us Statues in full Bulk and Height:
Mean while we struck with fix'd Amazement stare,   ⎫
And mar'l what strange Conveyance brought 'em there, ⎬
Made by Surprize more Statues then they are: ⎭   25
No less astonish'd doubtfull Cadmus gaz'd,
Doubly, by Wonder, and by Fear amaz'd:

Upon the Author of the Play call'd Sodom

[Written on or before 20 January 1677/8]

    Tell me, abandon'd Miscreant, prethee tell,
What damned Pow'er, invok'd and sent from Hell
(If Hell were bad enough) did thee Inspire
To write what Fiends asham'd would blushing hear?
Hast thou of late embrac'd some Succubus,   5
And us'd the lewd Familiar for a Muse?

  1-3 *R*82, 83, *Y, 1680*   4 To write what] *R*83*m, Y, 1680*; What modest *R*83
Fiends asham'd ... hear] *Y, 1680*; Fiends would blush to hear *R*83
5-6 *R*83, *Y, 1680*

Or didst thy Soul by Inch oth' Candle sell,

To gain the glorious Name of Pimp to Hell?

If so; go, and its vow'd Allegiance swear,

Without Press-money, be its Voluntier: 10

May he who envies thee deserve thy Fate,

Deserve both Heav'ns and Mankinds scorn and hate.

Disgrace to Libels! Foil to very Shame!

Whom 'tis a scandal to vouchsafe to damn!

What foul Description's foul enough for thee,   15

Sunk quite below the reach of Infamy?

Thou covet'st to be lewd, but want'st the Might

And art all over Devil, but in Wit.

Weak feeble strainer at meer Ribaldry,

Whose Muse is impotent to that degree,   20

'T had need, like Age, be whipt to Lechery.

      Vile Sot! who clapt with Poetry art sick,

And voidst Corruption like a Shanker'd Prick,

Like Ulcers, thy Imposthum'd addle Brains

Drop out in Matter, which thy Paper stains: 25

Whence nauseous Rhymes by filthy Births proceed,

As Maggots in some Turd ingendring breed.

---

7 Or didst thy] *Y, 1680*; Who dost thy *R82*; Who would his *R82m*   Soul ...
sell] *R82, Y, 1680*   8 *R82 (omits Name), Y, 1680*   9 *Y, 1680*; Go and
allegiance to the Devil swear *R82*; Go Voluntier, be damn'd without Pretence
R92   10 Without Press-money] *R92, Y, 1680*; With [*sic*] Press-mony *R82*
be its Voluntier] *Y, 1680*; be his Voluntier *R82*; and [*sic* = at] the Devil's
Expence *R92*   11 May ... thee] *R82, Y, 1680*   deserve thy Fate,] *Y, 1680*;
thy Fate deserve. *R82*   12 *Y, 1680 (reading Heav'ns,)*   13 *R83, Y,
1680*; Thou Foyle *R91m*   14 Whom 'tis a scandal] *R83m, Y, 1680*; Honour'd
to much *R83*   to vouchsafe] *Y, 1680*; when we vouchsafe *R83*   to damn!] *R83²,
Y, 1680*; to name *R83¹*   15 What ... Description's] *R83, Y, 1680*   foul]
Y, 1680; vile *R83*; fit *R83m¹*; bad *R83m²*   enough for thee,] *R83, Y, 1680*
16 Sunk quite] *R84, 90, 92, Y, 1680*; Who'rt sunk *R83*   below ... Infamy?]
R83, 84, 90, 92, Y, 1680   17 Thou covets't] *R83, Y, 1680*; Who covet'st
R92; But coveting *R84*   to ... but] *R83, 92, Y, 1680*; to ... thou *R84*
wants't ... Might] *R83, 84, 92, Y, 1680*; wants't ... hit. *R90*   18 *R83, 84,
90, 92, Y, 1680*   19 Weak feeble] *Y, 1680*; Impotent *R98*; Thou arrant *R92*
strainer] *R98, Y, 1680*; Bungler *R92*   at meer Ribaldry] *R92, Y, 1680*; at
dull Ribaldry *R98*   20-1 *Y, 1680*; Whose Muse had need be whipt to Lechery:
R98   22-3 *R86, 98, Y, 1680*   24 Like Ulcers,] *R85, Y, 1680*; Lewd
Coxcomb! *R98*   thy ... Brains,] *R86, Y, 1680*; whose ... Brain [*sic*] *R98*
25 Drop ... which] *R86, Y, 1680*; Drops ... and *R98*   26-7 *Y, 1680*;
There nasty Births so naturally breed | As vermine from engendring Turds
proceed, *R83*

Thy Muse has got the Flowers, and they ascend
As in some greensick Girl, at upper End.
Sure Nature made, or meant at least 't have don't,   30
Thy Tongue a Clitoris, thy Mouth a Cunt.
How well a Dildoe would that place become,
To gag it up, and make 't for ever dumb!
At least it should be syring'd——
Or wear some stinking Merkin for a Beard,   35
That all from its base converse might be scar'd:
As they a Door shut up, and mark't beware,
That tells Infection, and the Plague is there.
    Thou Moorfields Author! fit for Bawds to quote
(If Bawds themselves with Honour safe may do't)   40
When Suburb-Prentice comes to hire Delight,
And wants Incentives to dull Appetite,
There Punk, perhaps, may thy brave works rehearse,
Frigging the senseless thing with Hand and Verse;
Which after shall (prefer'd to Dressing-Box)   45
Hold Turpentine, and Med'cines for the Pox:
Or (if I may ordain a Fate more fit
For such foul, nasty Excrements of Wit)
May they, condemn'd, to th' publick Jakes be lent,
(For me, I'd fear the Piles in Vengeance sent   50

28 Thy Muse] *R*86, 98, *Y, 1680*   has got] *R*86, *Y, 1680*; had sure *R*98
the ... ascend] *R*86, 98, *Y, 1680*   29 As ... greensick] *R*86, 98, *Y, 1680*
Girl,] *1680, Y*; Girls *R*86, 98   at ... End] *R*86, 98, *Y, 1680*   30 Sure
Nature] *R*86, 98, *Y, 1680*   made, or ... least] *R*86, *Y, 1680*; made (at lest
she meant *R*98   't have don't,] *R*86, *Y, 1680*; 't have don't) *R*98
31 *R*86, 98, *Y, 1680*   32-3 *Y, 1680*   34 *Y, 1680*; siring'd *R*83*m*
35 *Y, 1680*; Wear a Merkin for a Beard *R*83*m*; Wrap stinking Merkins *R*86
36-7 That ... and] *Y, 1680*   mark't] *Ed.*; mark'd *Y, 1680*   beware] *Y, 1680*
38 *Y, 1680*   39-40 *R*83, 86, *Y, 1680*; Thou Poet to Moorfields, whom Bawds
to name | Would fear, with [*sic* = and with] a Blush attone their shame *R*90
41 When ... comes] *Y, 1680*; When Fleetstreet Sinners come *R*86; To Fleetstreet
Sinners come *R*83; When *R*83*m*   to ... Delight,] *R*83, 86, *Y, 1680*   42 And
wants] *Y, 1680*; And want *R*86, 83*m*; Who lack *R*83   Incentives ... Appetite,]
*R*83, 86, *Y, 1680*   43 *R*83, 86, *Y, 1680*   44 Frigging ... thing] *Y,
1680*; Frigging some sensless Ass *R*86; Frigging some woful Tool *R*83; wretched
thing *R*83*m*   with ... Verse;] *R*83, 86, *Y, 1680*   45 *R*83, 86, *(hyphen
from Y, 1680)*; May they, prefer'd to clapt Whore's Dressing-box, *R*91, 98
46 *R*83, 86, 91, 98, *Y, 1680*   47 Or] *R*83, *Y, 1680*; But *R*86   47-8 (if
... Wit)] *R*83, 86 *(brackets from Y; misbracketed 1680 (if ... fit))*
49 May] *R*86, *Y, 1680*; Or may *R*98   they, condemn'd,] *Ed.*; they condemn'd
*R*86, *Y, 1680*; they *R*98   to th' ... Jakes] *R*86, *Y*; to th' ... Jakes, *1680*;
to some ... Jakes *R*98   be lent,] *R*86, 98, *Y, 1680*   50-3 *R*86, 98, *Y,
1680*

Should I with them profane my Fundament)
There bugger wiping Porters when they shite,
And so thy Book itself turn Sodomite.

53 R98, Y, 1680

Sardanapalus

Ode

1.

Happy, Great Prince! and so much happier thou
In that thou thine own Happiness did'st know!
Happy, who wast content with what thy wish Enjoy'd,
Nor valueds't this—what the whole World cou'd boast beside.
Restless Ambition ne'r Usurpt thy Mind,   5
To vex thy Pleasures, and disturb Mankind:
With gallant height of Soul, thou didst contemn
That Bauble Honor, and that Geugaw Fame,
And all the Undershrievalties of Life not worth a name!
With wiser choice, thy Judgment plac'd aright   10
In C-t its noble Innocent delight:
    C-t was the Star that rul'd thy Fate,
C-t thy sole Bus'ness, and Affair of State,
And C-t the only Field to make thee Great:
C-t thy whole life's fair Center was, whither did bend 15
All thy Designs, and all thy Lines of Empire tend:
    And C-t the sure unerring Card,
Which, plac'd at Helm, the mighty Vessel and its motion steer'd.

---

2 did'st] *MSS* –*Hv, S*; dost *Hv, S*   3 wast] *Hv, H2, H3, F, D, S, W, V*;
was *H1, P2, P3, T*   thy] *Hv, H1, H2, H3, P3, S, V*; they *F, P2, D, T, W*
4 valueds't this—] *MSS* –*H1, V*; valued'st *V*; valued *H1*   whole World] *MSS*
–*H1, V*; World *H1, V*   6 Pleasures] *MSS* –*S*; pleasure *S*   7 With] *MSS* –*S*;
thy *S*   11 its] *MSS* –*H1, V*; that *H1, V*   14 the] *MSS* –*H1, V*; thy *H1, V*
Field] *MSS* –*S*; Way *S*   15-18 As *MSS* –*P3*; *not in P3*   18 plac'd] *MSS* –*T*;
pleasd *T*   Helm] *MSS* –*P2, P3 absent*; th'Helm *P2*   motion] *MSS* – *H1, V*; *P3*
absent; Master *H1, V*

2.

Som Saucy Pedants, and Historians, idly Rail,
    And thee Effeminate unjustly call: 20
    How ill to him do they that Title give,
Who burnt himself, rather than be debar'd to swive?
    Much of thy Ancestors they fondly prate,
    By boasted Conquests, and rude War made Great:
Of *Nimrod*, *Ninus*, and *Semiramis* they tell;   25
Mean Heroes, who cou'd only Fight, and Vanquish well:
How to gain Empire did their Thoughts and Swords employ,
    Which 'twas thy nobler Talent to Enjoy.
        They now are Dust, as well as Thou,
        Of Life, and all its Joys, bereft,   30
    And nothing but their empty Mem'ries left,
    An happiness which thou enjoyest too:
For thine as lasting in the Register of Fame shall be:
    And where in Fame does the vast diff'rence lye,
T'have Fought, or F-k'd for Universal Monarchy?   35

3.

Methinks I see thee now in full Seraglio stand,
        With Love's great Scepter in thy hand,
And over all its Spacious Realm thy Power extend:
    Ten Thousand Maids lye prostrate at thy Feet,
    Ready thy Pintle's high Commands to meet;   40
    All C-ts of Honor, som of Queenly Breed,
That come to be Anointed with thy Royal Seed.
Here Eunuchs, thy wise Privy Counsellors, debate
    In close Cabals, affairs of greatest weight,

20 thee] *MSS* –*H1*; the *H1*   25 *Ninus*] *MSS* –*P1*; Nimus *P1*   27 How] *MSS*
–*H2*, *V*; They *H2*, *V*   gain] *MSS* –*F*, *T*; give *F*, *T*   Empire] *Hv*, *H1*, *H2*, *H3*,
F, *D*, *T*, *V*, *W*; Empires *P2*, *P3*, *S*   28 'twas] *MSS* –*P3*, *S*; was *P3*, *S*
nobler] *Hv*, *H2*, *H3*, *F*, *P3*, *D*, *S*, *V*; noble *H1*; Noblest *P2*, *T*, *W*   29 as well
as] *MSS* –*H2*, *S*; as *H2*, *S*   31 their] *MSS* –*P2*; Thin *P2*   Mem'ries] *Hv*, *H1*,
H2, *H3*, *F*, *V*, *W*; Mem'ry's *P3*, *T*; Memoryes *D*; Mem'ry *P2*; Members *S*   32 An]
H1, *H3*, *F*, *P2*, *P3 subst.*, *D*, *T*, *V*, *W*; A *Hv*, *H2*, *S subst.*   34 the] *MSS* –*S*;
that *S*   36 Seraglio] *MSS* –*H1*; salglio *H1*   38 its] *MSS* –*P2*; the *P2*
39 Maids lye] *MSS* –*H1*, *V*; fair ones *H1*, *V subst.*   40 thy] *MSS* –*P3*; y^r *P3*
Commands] *Hv*, *H2*, *H3*, *F*, *P2*, *P3*, *S*, *T*, *W*; command *H1*, *D*, *V subst.*   42 come]
MSS –*P2*; came *P2*   thy] *MSS* –*P3*; Y^r *P3*   43 Eunuchs] *Hv*, *H2*, *H3*, *F*, *P2*, *W*;
Evnuchs *V*; Eunvuchs *P3*; Enuchs *D*, *T*; Evenechs *H1*; Evnuch *S*   Privy] *MSS* –*V*;
not in V   44 greatest] *MSS* –*S*; greater *S*

Of *Pego*'s Conquests, and its deep Intrigues of State: 45
Plenipotentiaries of Great C-t, they here
    Ambassages of high Importance bear:
Each day of new Alliances they come to Treat,
    And for thy gracious Audience duly wait,
    From Eastern Ganges, to th' *Egyptian* Clime   50
    Where *Nile* its Courses has at certain time
And daubs the Fields with filthy Mud, and Menstruous Slime.
      Far as wide Nature spreads her Thighs,
      Thy Tarse's vast Dominion lyes:
    All Womankind acknowledge its great Sway,   55
And all to its large Treasury their Tribute pay,
Pay Custom of their unprohibited Commodities.
      No glorious Beauties, which profess the Trade,
      Here find their noble Services unpaid;
      Vast heaps of Gold, and piles of Gems lye by,   60
      To recompence industrious Lechery.
      One earns a Province with an artful Kiss;
      Another justly merits Subsidies,
At whose blest touch Imperial Pego does vouchsafe to rise:
    But happy she, and most of all rewarded is,   65
Who ever can invent new Motions to advance the Bliss.
    All this thou dost with such wise Manage'ry bestow,
    As does at once thy Bounty and Discretion show:
    Nor dost thou e'r withhold thy Liberality,
Nor ever drain the vast Exchequer of thy Lechery.   70

---

45 Conquests] *Hv, H2, H3, F, P2, D, S, T, W*; conquest *H1, P3, V*
Intrigues] *MSS -V*; intrigue *V*   46 they] *MSS -H1, V*; do *H1, V*
47 Ambassages] *Hv, H2, H3, F, P3, S, T, W*; Ambassyes *D*; Ambassy's *V*; Embas-
sys *H1*; Ambassadors *P2*   49 thy] *MSS -P3*; y^r *P3*   52 Fields] *MSS -H1,
P2*; field *H1, P2*   Mud] *MSS -P3*; Mad *P3*   Menstruous] *Hv, H2, H3, F,
P3, S, T, V, W*; menstrous *H1*; monstrous *P2*   53 Far] *MSS -V*; For *V*
wide] *Hv, H2, H3, F, P3, D, S, T, W*; wide open *H1, V*; wise *P2*   54 Tarse's]
MSS -P3, S; farses *P3, S subst.*   55 its] *MSS -H1, V*; the *H1, V*   great]
MSS -S; own *S*   56 Treasury] *MSS -S*; Treasure *S*   57 of] *MSS -H1, V*;
with *H1, V*   58 which] *MSS -H1, V*; who *H1, V*   61 industrious] *MSS -P2*;
Illustrious *P2*   64 blest] *Hv, H2, H3, F, P2, P3, S, T, W*; great *H1, D, V*
Pego] *MSS -P3*; Pegs *P3*   65 happy she] *MSS -P2*; Happiness *P2*   66 Who
ever] *MSS -H1, V*; who *H1, V*   Motions] *MSS -S*; Notions *S*   68 at once] *Hv,
H1, H2, H3, F, P2, S, T, V, W*; as once *P3*; once *D*   thy] *MSS -P3*; y^r *P3*
69-70 *As MSS -H1, V*; *not in H1, V*   70 ever drain] *MSS -P2*; overdrain *P2*

4.

Thus did'st thou spend thy Dayes in blest Retreat,
Free from the Trouble, and Impertinence of State;
Exempt from all the vain Anxiety and Fear
      Which other Sceptred Wretches wear:
    None of the Rabble's Mutinies and Jars,   75
    Or Senceless Grievances e'r reach'd thine Ears.
Still were they shut to all Complaints, but those of Love;
All, but the soft Remonstrances of the Alcove.
    In vain the Railing Satyrs of the Age
      Attack'd thee with Poetic Rage   80
    They spread their loose Lampoons in vain,
And with Leud Wit thy Sacred Pintle did Profane:
    With Kingly Gallantry they still were borne,
      And still despis'd with Gene'rous Scorn:
        Nor did it more avail   85
That babling Oracles thy Ruin did foretell,
And Boding Fools pretended Treachery reveal:
      Secure of Danger, Death, and Hell,
Pego within kept awful and Regardless State,
And smil'd at all the Terrors of approaching Fate.   90

5.

    Malicious Rebels idly did contrive
To stop thy course of Pleasure, idly did they strive
    T'abridge thy Soveraign Pr-k's Prerogative:
    In vain they did Essay
Unjustly to Depose it from its Rightful Sway: 95
    In vain they urg'd the Impudent pretence
    Of Laws, and Liberties, in their defence,
    When thou that Royal Standard did'st advance:

71 thy] *MSS* –*P3*; the *P3*   73 all the vain] *MSS* –*H1*, *V*; all *H1*, *V*
74 Which] *MSS* –*P3*; with *P3*   75 Rabble's] *MSS* –*S*; Rabble *S*   76 Grievances e'r] *MSS* –*H3*; Grievances *H3*   thine] *MSS* –*T*, *W*; thy *T*, *W*   83 borne]
Ed.; born *MSS*   84 despis'd with] *MSS* –*S*; not in *S*   87 Boding] *MSS* –*P3*,
S; boating *P3*; boaded *S*   89-90 As *MSS*; not in *S*   89 and Regardless]
Hv, *H1*, *H3*, *F*, *P2*, *P3*, *D*, *T*, *W*; high, regardless *V*; and regarded *H2*; *S absent*
90 at all] *MSS* –*P2*; as at *P2*   92 Pleasure] *MSS* –*P2*, *S*; Pleasures *P2*, *S*
they] *MSS* –*D*, *T*; thy *D*, *T*   strive] *MSS* –*P3*; stive *P3*   95 Unjustly] *MSS*
–*P3*, *S*; Injustly *P3*, *S*   97 their] *Hv*, *H2*, *H3*, *F*, *P2*, *P3*, *S*, *T*, *W*; this
H1, *D*, *V*

Thrice did'st thou Conquer in thy Pintle's Cause,
Thrice did'st thou put to flight thy Vanquish'd Foes; 100
Till Fate grew envious at thy Happiness,
        Revolted, and withdrew Success,
And did at last th'unjuster side Espouse.
        What Loyal Subject cou'd forbear
To curse the Partial Gods, and spiteful Stars,   105
When by their Treachery thou abandon'd were,
The bravest Cause, and bravest Prince, that ever drew a Tarse?
  Yet cou'd not all their Influence, or Malignant force,
        From thy great purpose thee Divorce:
        Fates, do your worst, said'st thou,   110
        Our Pr-k shall Reign in spite of you:
Not all your Heav'n shall bribe me from Delight,
Nor all your Thunder from my Pleasure fright.
Sink Nations, Kingdoms perish, Empire fall,
One thrust in Charming C-t shall over ballance all.   115
    If I must dye, Clasping my Joys I'll go,
And boldly Swive my Passage to the Shades below:
    And through all Ages, all Posterity,
    This my sole Glory shall Recorded be;
No Monarch ever F-kd, or Dy'd like Me.   120

                    6.

Great was the bold Resolve, and firm as Fate it stood;
And quick as Thought, thou did'st thy mighty Words make
        At thy Command, in Inner Palace-yard,   [good:
A pompous Pile was strait magnificently rear'd.
        Of costly Cedar were the Pillars made,   125
Their Shafts with Lust's Mosaic curiously inlaid:

  100 flight] *MSS* –*P3*; flightly *P3*   Foes] *Hv, H2, H3, P2, P3, S*; Foe *H1, F,
D, T, V, W*   101 Till ... thy] *MSS* –*P3*; Tell ... y^r *P3*   104 Subject]
MSS –*V*; Subjects *V*   105 the] *MSS* –*S; not in S*   106 were] *MSS* –*Hv*; wert *Hv*
107 ever drew a] *MSS* –*P2*; e're drew *P2*   109 From] *MSS* –*P3, S; not in P3, S*
Divorce] *MSS* –*P3*; diverse *P3*   110 your] *MSS* –*H1*; their *H1*   113 Plea-
sure] *Hv, H1, H2, H3, F, T*; Pleasures *P2, P3, D, S, V, W*   114 Nations] *MSS*
–*P2*; Nation *P2*   116 my] *MSS* –*S*; w^th *S*   ·   117 Shades] *MSS* –*P3, S*; Shade
P3, S   118 through] *MSS* –*W*; thou *W*   Ages, all] *Hv*; Ages, and all *H2, H3,
F, D, T*; ages and all *H1, P2, P3, S, V*; Ages and *W*   119 sole] *MSS* –*T*;
stole *T*   122 mighty] *MSS* –*H1; not in H1*   124 rear'd] *MSS* –*Hv*; read *Hv*
125 were] *Hv, H1, V*; was *H2, H3, F, P2, P3, D, S, T, W*   126 Lust's] *H1, H2,
H3, P3, S, T, V*; Lusts *Hv, P2, D, W*; Lust *F*   Mosaic] *MSS* –*H3*; [*blank*] *H3*

Their Chapiters, with well carv'd Freeze and Cornice
Bore gaping C——ts, with bossy Pintles interlac'd;   [grac'd,
          The Architraves were all of unctuous Pine,
          Whose Lecherous Trunk spends clammy Turpentine,   130
          Much fam'd of old, for use on *Hymen*'s night,
          That serv'd the Lover to his Joyes to light:
          In modern times more fam'd, and better known
          For Virtue of its Celebrated Gum,
          For cure of Amorous Hurts in high Renown,   135
And well approv'd by all experienc'd Pr-ks in Christendom.
          Atop, a Hundred Golden Beds were Spread;
          All conscious marks of thy great Prowess bore,
          All Dy'd a Thousand Times in Maiden gore,
Which thy victorious Lance in many a fierce Campaign had   140
          Around the walls, in distant Arches plac'd,   [shed.
          Stood Statues of thy glorious Punks deceas'd.
     In Picture by, the brave Atchievements of thy Tarse,
     Which Poets had Recorded in Immortal Verse:
          Lust's gaudy Pageants, whose each lively Scene   145
          Show'd the choice Artist's Mastery and Design
     And far surpast the Wit of modern *Aretine*.
     And over all, display'd, and waving to the Sun,
Thy Royal Arms, *Priapus* Rampant, was in Banner hung.

                              7.

          Thither, intent on thy great End,   150
          Thou did'st with awful Majesty ascend;
          Where in the midst, on glorious Bed of State,
          A Princely Maid for thy approach did wait:

127 Chapiters] *MSS -H1, V*; Capiters *H1, V*   well] *MSS -V; not in V*   Cor-
nice] *MSS -Hv, P2*; Cornish *Hv, P2*   129 all] *MSS -S; not in S*
130 spends] *MSS Hv, V*; spend *Hv, V*   131 Much] *MSS -H2*; Such *H2*   Hymen's]
MSS subst. -H1; hymens *H1*   135 cure] *MSS -P3*; curse *P3*   in] *MSS -H1*; of
H1   137 Atop] *Hv*; A top *H1, H3, F, P3, D, S, T, V, W*; O'top *H2*; At Top *P2*
Beds] *MSS -S, T*; [illegible] *S*; Heads *T*   140 *As MSS -H1, V; two lines,
divided* Lance/In *H1, V*   142 Stood Statues] *MSS -S*; good Statutes *S*   thy]
MSS -P3; y^r *P3*   Punks] *MSS -T*; Punk *T*   143 Picture by,] *Hv, D, T, V, W*;
Picture, by *H2, H3, F*; Picture by *P2, P3, S*; pictures by *H1*   thy] *MSS -P2,
P3*; y^r *P3*; the *P2*   144 *As MSS -H1; not in H1*   145 gaudy] *MSS -H1, V*;
gorgeous *H1, V*   Scene] *MSS -P2*; Scheme *P2*   148 Sun] *MSS -S*; Sum *S*
149 *As MSS -H1, V; two lines, divided* Arms/Priapus *H1, V*   Rampant] *MSS -S*;
not in S   Banner hung] *MSS -H3*; Triumph shown *H3*   152 on] *Hv, H2, H3,
F, P2, P3, S, T, W*; of *H1, D, V*

Stretch'd out the willing Virgin lay, unbound,
Ready from thy kind Stroke to meet the gentle Wound.   155
An hundred more on the Surrounding Beds lay by,
   All gallant Vent'rers in thy Destiny:
   And of thy Race as many Princes too,
T'attend thy Fate, their Loyalty and Duty show.
   By Order now, at the loud Trumpet's call,   160
   The starting Pr-ks at once strive for the Goal;
All press, all act, what ever mortal Strength can do,
   But none their mighty Soveraign outgo.
      When thus in State thou'dst F-k'd awhile,
   With dauntless Look, and a regardless Smile,   165
      Thou bad'st 'em fire the Sacred Pile:
      See, great *Priapus*, did'st thou cry,
      Behold thy Zealous Votary,
Behold the mighty Hecatombs he Offers thee!
Much more thou woud'st have said; but the ascending Smoke   170
   Broke off thy Pray'r and did its utt'rance choak.
      Devouring Flames did strait succeed,
      And now thy Lust's strange Fire-works play'd:
      Here, glowing C-t, with flaming Beard,
      Like blazing Meteor appear'd;   175
      There, Pintle, squirting fiery Streams,
      Like lighted Flambeau, spending Flames.
Thus Lechery's great Martyr, Revelling in Fire,
   At every Pore dripping out Scalding Lust,
   With all thy Strength collected in one Thrust   180

---

154 lay] *MSS* –P3, *S; not in* P3, *S*   155 *As MSS* –H1, *V; two lines, divided*
meet/The H1, *V*   kind] *MSS* –H3; great H3   156 *As MSS* –P3; *not in* P3
An] H1, H2, H3, *F, D, S, T, V, W;* A *Hv,* P2; P3 *absent*   159 T'attend] *MSS*
–H1; to attend H1   thy] *MSS* –S; their *S*   163 Soveraign] *Hv,* H1, H2, H3,
F, P3, *T, S, W;* Sovreign P2, *D, V*   164 thou'dst] *Hv,* P3, *D, S, T, V, W;*
th'hadst H1, H2, H3, *F,* P2   166 *As MSS* –P2; *not in* P2   Thou] *MSS* –P2, P3;
The P3; P2 *absent*   bad'st] H2, P3, *S, T, W;* bid'st *Hv,* H1, H2, H3, *F, D;* P2
absent   'em] *MSS* –S; *not in* S   168 Votary] *Hv,* H1, H2, H3, *F,* P2, *T, V,*
W; Notary *D;* [*blank*]tary P3, *S*   169 Hecatombs] *MSS* –H1; hecatomb H1
170 *As MSS* –H1, *V; two lines divided* said / But H1, *V*   171 off] *MSS of* H3,
W; –H1; oft H1   173 Lust's] *Hv,* H2, *W;* Lusts H1, H3, *F,* P2, P3, *D, S, T, V*
174 glowing] *MSS* –H1; glorious H1   177 lighted] *MSS* –H1; light lighted H1
Flambeau] *Hv,* H2, *F,* P3, *D;* Flamboy H3, *T, W;* Flambeaux P2; flambeaus H1, *S, V*
179 every] *Hv,* H1, H2; ev'ry *V;* e'ry H3, *F,* P2, P3, *D, T, S, W*   dripping]
MSS –V; dropping *V*   180 Thrust] H3, *T, V;* Thrust, *Hv, S;* thrust; H1, H2,
P2; Thrust: *W;* Thrust. *F,* P3, *D*

At gaping C-t, thou didst give up thy mighty Ghost,
And 'midst a Glorious heap of burning C-ts expire.

181 At] *MSS* —*S*; of *S*   gaping C-t] *Hv*, *P2*, *W*; Gasping c-t *F*; gasping
—— *H1*, *H2*, *H3*, *P3*, *D*, *S*, *T*, *V*

In Obitum optimae spej Juvenis
Johañis Frend ex Aulâ S^{tj}
Edmundj Febre occumbentis.
[20 March 1673]

Hĩc Phoebo dederas operam, jam Sydera scandis
    Numine per cupiens sic propiore fruj.
Eridanum mavis Helicona atq₃ Iside spreto,
    Coelestis solùm lympha placere potest.
Macte Beate! gradum tibj laeta Hierarchia praebet   5
    Et potes Angelicos nunc celebrare choros.
Nondum Agnina tegit Pellis, Coelestis at Agnus
    Te nunc Justitiâ vestiet ipse suâ.
Sic fieri Bustum et Febrem sensisse juvabit,
    Et vivum proprios anticipasse Rogos.   10
Purgatrix data (Papriolis jam credite) flama est.
    Igne hic lustratus purior Astra petit.

Epitaph on Dr Abia Qui,
    buried, Malmesbury Abbey churchyard,
    8 October 1675.

He by whose charter thousands held their breath,
Lies here, the captive of triumphant death;
If drugs, or matchless skill, could death reclaim,
His *life* had been immortal as his *fame*.

3 death *1805*; life *1805 E*

COMMENTARY

SATYRS UPON THE JESUITS AND SOME OTHER PIECES

Advertisement

4. *Casaubon, and several other Criticks.* Isaac Casaubon (1559-1614) published his *De satyrica Graecorum poesi et Romanorum satyra* at Paris in 1605. The other critics might include Scaliger, Heinsius, and Nicholas Rigault. See Dryden, *Essays*, i. lxvii, ii. 44, ll. 8-11 and n.

10. Oldham, like Marston and Hall, follows Persius in placing a prologue before his satires, but does not imitate him directly.

13. *Sylla's Ghost in the great Johnson.* The prologue of Ben Jonson's *Catiline.* See W.M. Williams's article on *Catiline*'s influence on 'Jesuits' in *ELH*, xi (1944), 38-62. Williams's one-sided view is qualified in C.H. Cable's 'Oldham's Borrowing from Buchanan', *MLN*, lxvi (1951), 527.

17. *the Franciscan of Buchanan*: *Franciscanus et Fratres* (1566), by George Buchanan (1506-82), famous Protestant reformer and Renaissance Latin poet. See 'Jesuits III', headnote.

19. *Padders in Wit*: plagiarists, compared to footpads, as by Dryden, Prologue to *Albumazar* (1668), ll. 15-26.

22. *Whence he had the hint of the fourth.* Horace, *Satires*, I. 8. Oldham wrote 'Horat. *l*. 1 Sat. 8' opposite the title in the draft opening of this satire (R 257).

25. Cf. Cowley, 'A Satyre. The Puritan And The Papist' (*Essays*, p. 154): 'They have made *Images* to *speake*, tis said'.

26 f. *Of Buffoonery.* A Gallicism.

28 ff. Minucius Felix was a Roman advocate of the 2nd century AD; his dialogue *Octavius* is one of the earliest apologies for Christianity. Arnobius major flourished in the 3rd century, and attacked pagan mythology in his *Adversus Gentes*; Lactantius Firmianus belongs to the 4th century. See Burton, *Anatomy*, pp. 666 f., with examples of their 'raillying'.

34. *the next Poem.* 'Aude aliquid. Ode'. See Introduction, pp. xxviii, xci.

40-6. See Introduction, pp. xxxiii, xli-v.

51. *the last Trifle*: 'Byblis', which ends, with 'Finis', the first issue of the volume, though the title-page envisages 'other *Pieces*', not just this one, to follow 'the *Satyr* against *Vertue*'. 'Upon a Woman' was added in the second issue. See my account of the three issues, in *SB*, xxvii (1974), 190-2.

53. *the late Translations of Ovid's Epistles. Ovid's Epistles, Translated by Several Hands* (1680), which Dryden edited for Jacob Tonson, was advertised in *The Protestant (Domestick) Intelligence*, 6 Feb. 1679/80; and see Macdonald 11a and b.

56. *Mr. Sandys his Translation. Ovids Metamorphoses. English'd by G. S.* (i.e. George Sandys, 1578-1644). Dryden refers to it in his Preface to *Ovid's Epistles*; Oldham evidently read it, partly perhaps on account of this

reference, after beginning his 'Byblis' in 1680, and before writing this
Advertisement, published c.Nov. He concurred in the current estimate; Dryden, in 1693, recollected the Ovid of 'the so-much admired Sandys' as not
deserving its reputation (*Essays*, ii. 10; but see also 247).

61. *the use of Mr. Jordan's Works.* On Jordan, see 'Spencer's Ghost', 11. 62-6
     and n. Allusions to the uses of waste paper were common in the classics and
     in Oldham's contemporaries; e.g. Persius, I. 43, Horace, *Epistles*, II. i.
     269, Catullus, XCV. 7 and Dryden, *MacFlecknoe*, 11. 100-1.

Satyrs upon the Jesuits: Prologue

According to the title-page of *Satyrs Upon The Jesuits*, which there is every
reason to believe, the whole series was 'Written in 1679'. The success of
Garnets Ghost in the pirated edition early that year evidently decided Oldham
to embark on more than one sequel, introduced, like the satires of Persius
(see Advertisement, 11. 14-17) by a Prologue. Though the evidence is not
decisive, it points strongly to this—following 'Garnet's Ghost' (?Jan.; begun
Dec. 1678)—as composed prior to 'Jesuits II' (datable after 16 Mar., probably
early July), with 'Jesuits III' and 'IV' (after 16 July) reasonably assignable
to c.Aug.–Sept. and c.Nov. (see headnotes). Late Mar. is the earliest date for
the Prologue, and April the most likely. Some lines of it were scribbled on
R187, which already contained a draft letter of 2 Mar.; and it borrows (see
11. 7 f., n.) from *Dr Wild's Poem ... Upon the ... New Parliament* that met on
the 6th. A discarded passage (R177) describes how every would-be author 'starts
... up in pamphlet or lampoon': one topic is what 'Made York and bankrupt
Danby run away'. James sailed for Brussels on 4 Mar., arousing many suspicions
(cf. e.g. a squib 'On His Royal Highness's Voyage beyond Sea, March 3d, 1678',
collected in *POAS*, 1702, ii. 216). Danby, faced with impeachment, went into
hiding in Whitehall from 24 Mar. to 14 Apr.: Oldham's line may have been written before he surrendered and was sent to the Tower, or at least while he was
remembered as recently a fugitive. If, as Sir Charles Firth encouraged me to
believe, the 'cashier'd resenting' statesman of 1. 54 is Shaftesbury, that
allusion predates his appointment, 21 Apr., as President of the Council (he
was not again dismissed till 15 Oct.). Mengel supposes (Yale *POAS*, ad loc.)
that Danby is meant. If he was resentful, however, nothing is heard of it;
whereas the King had given his opinion, at least to Sunderland, that Shaftesbury 'was only angry in revenge, because he was not employed' (Burnet, ii.
209). If the draft, and 11. 1-9 of the finished Prologue, refer to the flood
of pamphleteering released by the lapse of the Licensing Act (ibid. 220 f.),
they must be subsequent to 27 May; but there was no dearth earlier. As to the
peril (11. 8 f.) of holding aloof from the pack in full cry, it was on 21
Mar. that Sir Edward Sackville, brother of Dorset the poet, was charged by
Oates in the Commons with impugning his evidence; whereupon he was expelled
the House and sent to the Tower (Kenyon, pp. 150, 154).

1. In his abrupt openings Oldham follows Juvenal and Cowley (as Cowley fol-
    lowed Donne). Juvenal I opens with:
                Semper ego auditor tantum ? nunquamne reponam
                vexatus totiens rauci Theseide Cordi?
    An earlier draft (R183) begins: 'Shall I alone sit tamely by ?'

7 f. Cf. *Dr. Wild's Poem*: 'Each Protestant' should
                ... turn Poet; and who not
                Should be suspected guilty of the Plot....
Oldham is evidently the borrower: his *'Prologue'* was not published till 1681.
Wild died in 1679; and allusions in *Dr. Wild's Poem* to 'This Seventy-nine',
'this March-Brood', show that it refers to the Parliament which met 6 Mar.
1678/9.

8. As their initial excitement faded, the Tories began to complain bitterly
of the peril of taking a judicious view. Reresby tells us that when he
dined at Bishop Gunning's on 26 Nov. 1680, he was forced to undertake the
duty of checking Oates in his calumnies against the Queen, nobody else
'darring to contradict him (for fear of being made a party to the Plott)'
(Reresby, pp. 208 f.). Cf. Burnet (a Whig but no fanatic), ii. 195 f., and
171, 271 f.; Dryden, Pref. to *Religio Laici* (1682), ll. 167-70, 208 f. See
also Introduction, pp. xxix-xxxiii.

12. *Mistaken honest Men.* A reminiscence of Cowley's '*(Mistaken Honest men)*'
in his ode on Brutus (*Poems*, p. 195).

15. *sham upon.* 'Shamming, is telling you an insipid, dull Lye with a dull
Face, which the slie Wag the Author only laughs at himself' (Wycherley,
The Plain Dealer, 1677). *OED*, which dates the appearance of this slang term
about that year, quotes Oldham's 'Dithyrambique' for its earliest example
of 'sham' (hoaxer; see l. 4 n.) and 'Juvenal III' for 'shams' (hoaxing; see
ll. 38 f., n.).

16. *dull Old Fisher-men.* The apostles.

17. Franciscus Suarez (1548-1617), Spanish Jesuit and theologian. From his
Defensio catholicae fidei contra anglicanae sectae errores (1613), Foulis
(p. 98) quotes the proposition that a heretic king '*after the Decree of
Deposition gone out against him ... is altogether deprived of his Kingdom.
... and so he may be used as a Tyrant or Vsurper, and by consequence, MAY
BE SLAIN BY ANY PRIVATE MAN*'. Antonio Escobar Y Mendoza (1589-1669), Spanish
Jesuit and greatest of the casuists attacked by Pascal in *Les Provinçiales*
for justifying a relaxed morality. His *Theologia Moralis* (1643) went through
many later editions. (See Ogg, *Europe*, pp. 343 ff.) An earlier draft (R182)
has 'Bawny' for 'Suarez'. Étienne Bauny (1564-1649), Jesuit casuist, published his *Somme des péchés* in 1630 and his *Theologia Moralis* in 1640-7. His
moral writings were condemned at Rome in 1640.

22. *contradiction-bore.* born of contradictions.

26 f. 'Prize' signifies a prize-fight with swords, such as were staged at
the Bear-garden; cf. 'Art of Poetry', ll. 623 f. and n. In some of these
contests the weapons were buttoned or blunted, while in others they were
not. Cf. Shadwell, *Epsom Wells* (1672), I. i, p. 12: 'Since they were so
much too hard for us at Blunts, we were fools to go to sharps with them.'
Cf. R182: 'yᵉ blunt Foils of Wit'.

28-31. Imitating Juvenal, I. 79 f.

31. *Wild, or Withers.* See 'Spencer's Ghost', ll. 99 f., n.

35. *private daggers.* See the accounts of St. Germain forcing Luzancy to recant his Protestantism at the dagger's point in 1675: Marvell, *Poems* (3rd
edn.), ii. 171; Reresby, pp. 100 f. The eighth item in the Pope-burning
procession of 17 Nov. 1679 was 'Six Jesuits, with bloody daggers'. According to Oates, a Jesuit named Coniers had consecrated a knife a foot in
length to stab the king.

35. *Saint Omer's dose.* Jesuit poison. The Jesuit seminary at St Omer was
that from which Oates returned to England with his story of the Plot. There
may be an allusion to 'Jesuits' powder' or quinine, about the medicinal or
harmful properties of which a fierce controversy still raged: the thirteenth
item in the Pope-burning procession was 'The Pope's doctor, i.e. Wakeman,
with jesuits'-powder in one hand.' Wakeman had been accused of undertaking
to poison the king. On the Pope-burning processions of the period, see
articles by J.R. Jones and Sheila Williams, cited 'Juvenal XIII', ll. 50 f.,
n.

36. *Godfrey*. For Godfrey's murder, see 'Jesuits I', 0.1 n.

38 ff. This rhetorical figure of contradictions is a commonplace of satiric
tradition. Cf. Juvenal, ii. 24-8, and *'Ane vther Ballat of Vnpossibilities'*
(cit. Walker, *English Satire and Satirists*, p. 25). See also Oldham,
'Jesuits II', ll. 241-9.

42. *Bawds shall turn Nuns*. Oldham's draft (R186) has 'Cresswell' in the margin. For Mother Cresswell, see 'Spencer's Ghost', 1. 163 and n. Oldham was
familiar with Otway's *Don Carlos* (1676), in which the epilogue concludes
'I'le e'n forsake the Play-House, and turn Nun', though the allusion there
is to Dryden's reputed mistress Anne Reeve, who actually did retire to a
convent.

42. *Salt D[uchesse]s*: lustful duchesses. The draft (R186) has 'French salt
bitch' in the margin. This refers to Louise de Kéroualle ('Carwell'),
Duchess of Portsmouth and the King's mistress from 1672 till his death: cf.
'The Downfal of the French Bitch', in *POAS* (1704), iii. 211. It was quite
usual to couple with Portsmouth the Duchesses of Cleveland (Charles's mis-
tress until 1671) and of Mazarine, who won his favours on her arrival from
France, Nov. 1675. Cf. 'England's Court Strumpets', op. cit., p. 190, and
Rochester's 'Dialogue' (*Poems*, p. 129).

51 f. *The rage ... of Women's Pride*. Cf. Juvenal, X. 326 ff.

54. *cashier'd resenting statesmen*: a reference, probably, to Shaftesbury;
less probably, to Danby (see headnote).

55. Cf. 'Upon a Woman', ll. 36 f.

61 f. Cf. 'Upon a Woman', ll. 42 f., 44.

64 f. The draft (R178) has 'Till I [grow dreaded like ye Bar, & frighten
worse.' No doubt 'till I become' of 1681 was derived from this earlier version of the line. The reading of the 1681 errata, 'till it become', evidently embodies Oldham's final intention: it is found a few lines lower down
the same MS draft.

66. *Popes Anathema's*. Cf. *The Popes Dreadfull Curse. Being the Form of Excommunication of the Church of Rome* (1681), p. 2 n.: 'The Publication of
this is to shew what is to be Expected from the Pope, if he come to be
Supream Head of the Church in this Nation.'

Satyr I: Garnet's Ghost

'Garnet's Ghost' was begun before Oldham wrote the draft of his letter to
Spencer, dated Dec. 1678, announcing 'Novum quiddam jam parturit Musa. In
proditores stricturus sum calamum.... Ego Garnetti manes excivi; quid portent
novi, propediem scies; spirant (ni fallor) scelus & nequitiam Jesuitâ dignâ'
(R179). It was 'printed against the author's consent ... 1679' (Wood, iv.120).
Luttrell inscribed his copy '2^d 1679' (*Bibliography*, I.2). The heading states
that it is 'Written by the Author of the *Satyr against Virtue* (not yet Printed)'. That poem appeared and was followed by an answer, still in the same
year. The MS of 'Garnet's Ghost' which came to the pirate's hands gave it in
what was probably the original form; at least one later version also circulated in MS, and was copied by the lady who compiled H.M. Margoliouth's MS m
(see *Bibliography*, I.16, and Marvell, *Poems*, i.318). The authorized text published in 1681 had been revised still further.
    'Garnet's Ghost', 'Loyola's Will', and 'S. Ignatius his Image' are all three
cast in a traditional form which may be called the self-incriminatory monologue. It goes back to the Middle Ages; the Pardoner's Prologue in Chaucer is

an example of it. Sixteenth- and seventeenth-century ballad-writers, and, e.g.
Denham ('Mr Hampden's Speech against Peace', 1642/3), Quarles ('Know this my
Brethren', 1646), and Corbet ('The Distracted Puritane', 1648) used it too
(see my annotated index to *Rump Songs*, 1662, Oxford Bibliographical Society,
Proceedings, v.287 f., and nn. 13, 119, 133). In *Pym's Iuncto*. a poetical
broadsheet (BL Thomason, 669 f. 8, 8 May 1643; repr. in *Rump*, 1662), Pym, like
Garnet, rouses his followers to acts of unprecedented villainy. Striking self-
incriminatory orations, though these were not monologues nor the whole of the
poem, were familiar to Oldham in Lucifer's address to the assembled devils,
and the speeches of Æquivocus, Pope Paul V, and Loiol's eldest son in
Fletcher's *Locusts*, I.xxii ff., II.x ff., IV.vii ff. and xviii. Fletcher published with it the briefer *Locustae*, in Latin, out of which it grew; his
Locusts, or Apollyonists, are those of Revelation, IX.1-11. These anti-Jesuit
satires were a major source of Oldham's (see my 'Oldham and Fletcher').

   A further genre to which Oldham's poem belongs is the Fictitious Ghost. His
adoption of this form was inspired, he tells us in his 'Advertisement' (above,
l. 13), by the speech of Sylla's ghost in Jonson's *Catiline*, which follows
the precedent of Seneca's ghost-prologues to *Thyestes* and *Agamemnon*. In
another line the genre descends from *The Mirror for Magistrates* (1559; expanded edns. to 1587). Alternatively, it might be named the 'supposed Ghost',
after 'Leyland's supposed Ghost', printed at the end of Ralph Brooke's *Dis-
coverie of certaine Errours ... in the ... Britannia* (1595). Without exhaus-
tive research, I have enumerated (Brooks, 'Ghost') sixty-one pieces assignable
to the 'ghost' genre dating from the late 16th century to 1701. Of these
pieces 24 precede Oldham's; a dozen of its successors manifestly derive from
it, including such late examples as *Bishop Bonner's Ghost* (1798) by Hannah
More, and *Brissot's Ghost [appearing] ... to a Meeting of Those who call
themselves Friends of the People* (1794). Among the antecedents of 'Garnet's
Ghost' a number have particular relevance. The ghost is often a villain, as
in 'Mitchell, that designed to Murder Dr. Sharp ... his Ghost', 1678 (from
Robert Mylnes' MS, Ebsworth, IV.147), or politically obnoxious, as in *Colonel
Rainsborowes Ghost*, 1648 (BL Thomason 669 f. 13 (46)). Some are historical,
like Henry VIII and Wolsey, in *A Messenger from the Dead, or Conference Full
of stupendious horrour ... Between the Ghosts of Henry the 8. and Charls the
First of England, in Windsore Chappel*, 1658 (Bodl. Wood 364 (26), in prose)
and *Canterburies Dreame: in which The Apparition of Cardinall Wolsey did
present himselfe unto him* [viz. Laud; 1641] (BL Thomason E 158 (3)). Strafford
appears to Laud, as a proponent of the same policy, executed for it, in *The
Deputies Ghost : Or An Apparition to the Lord of Canterbury in the Tower*,
1641 (Bodl. Ashmole H23 XXXI). An assembly of confederates is exhorted in
'A Song by Pym's Ghost to the Parliament' (Bodl. MSS 84 f. 122 and 152 f. 8).
*Bradshaw's Ghost; a poem: or a dialogue between John Bradshaw, Ferry-man
Charon, Oliver Cromwell, Francis Ravilliack, and Ignatius Loyola, 1660*, n.d.
(P.J. Dobell, *Literature of the Restoration*, item 1136), links the Jesuits
and sectaries as regicides. Oldham was not alone *c*.Dec. 1678 in choosing the
'Ghost' form for polemic on the plot: Wood dates in that month *The Answer of
Coleman's Ghost to H. N.'s Poetick Offering*.

0.1. *Garnet's Ghost*. See 'The Life of Father Garnet', Foulis, pp. 696 ff.
   Henry Garnet (1555-1606), Jesuits' Provincial in England, in a show trial
   (see Salisbury's letter, Caraman, p. 376, cf. 395) was found guilty of high
   treason (by a jury whose foreman was Baptist Hickes, ancestor of Oldham's
   patron Sir William) for supporting the Gunpowder conspirators, and was
   executed 3 May 1606. From Catesby he had derived a general suspicion of the
   plot, and a full knowledge from Father Tesimond (alias Greenway) under the
   seal of confession; but his contemporary apologist, Gerard, acknowledges
   the seal void in English law. (Ibid., pp. 377-81, 391 f.) His failure *effectually* to discourage the plotters, or to inform the government, created the

general belief that he had 'committed treason enough for God's sake'.
Though he was not the villain that Oldham depicts, as the principal Jesuit
implicated in the last great Catholic conspiracy against an English sovereign he was the appropriate personage to speak Oldham's poem, and to exhort
the cabal. See *A True and Perfect Relation of the Whole proceedings against
... Garnet a Jesuite, and his Confederates* ... (1606); Taunton, pp. 162,
289-300, 314-20, 326-8, 330; S.R. Gardiner, *What Gunpowder Plot Was* (1897),
pp. 177-8, 192-9.

0.3. *the Murder of Godfrey*. Sir Edmund Berry Godfrey died a violent death
between 12 Oct. 1678, when he disappeared, and the 17th, when his body was
found in a ditch at the foot of Primrose Hill, where it had not been the
day before. He was J.P. for Middlesex and Westminster. Oates swore his
information on the plot before him, 6 Sept., and again, leaving a copy with
him, on the 28th. Though Godfrey was a staunch Anglican, 'few men of his
zeal lived on better terms with the papists' (Burnet); the same day, he
gave a warning to Coleman, the Catholic whose incriminating letters, while
James's secretary, were soon to be regarded, with Godfrey's fate, as positive confirmation of the plot. If, as Pollock concluded, he learned from
Coleman that the Jesuit consult of 24 Apr. had been held, not (as Oates
swore) at the White Horse Tavern, but in James's residence, that would
account for his realization that Oates was perjured, and for his foreboe-
ing that a dangerous secret (unspecified) would be his own death. The
secret's importance to the Catholics has been minimized; but 5 Jesuits went
to execution without trying to discredit Oates by revealing it. When Godfrey's body was found, his sword had been driven through it, evidently after
death; the neck was dislocated (but see Firth, loc. cit. below), showing
marks of strangulation. Murder by a common criminal was ruled out; his
valuables were untouched. Green, Berry, and Hill, servants in Somerset
House, were convicted, on the evidence of Prance and Bedloe, of having
there committed the murder; Bedloe had previously deposed that three Jesuits, Walsh, Prichard, and Lefevre, had directed the crime. Green, Berry,
and Hill were executed in Feb. 1678/9. They were undoubtedly innocent, but
it seems impossible to determine whether Godfrey was in fact murdered by
Catholics, or by Oates and his associates to give colour to their story, or
even whether he may not have committed suicide (but see Simpson in Kenyon,
p. 265). See Burnet, ii. 162-5, 167, 191-5; Pollock, pp. 83-105, 117-66,
and authorities there cited; C.H. Firth, *EHR*, xxi (1906), 169; Kenyon,
Append. A; Ogg, ii.579-84.

1. *By hell 'twas bravely done!* Cf. an impromptu formerly ascribed to
Rochester (see *Poems*, p. 224): 'By heavens! 'twas bravely done'.

2. Cf. Pseudo-Denham, *Second Advice to the Painter* (1667; Osborne, No. 10),
Yale *POAS*, i.9:
> What lesser Sacrifice than this was meet
> To offer for the Safety of the Fleet ?
See also Introduction, p. xlvii.

8 ff. Cf. Jonson, *Catiline*, I.483-7:
> ... I'haue kill'd a slaue,
> And of his bloud caus'd to be mixt with wine.
> Fill euery man his bowle. There cannot be
> A fitter drinke, to make this *sanction* in.
> Here I beginne the sacrament to all.

15 f. A draft (R248) has 'I thought' for 'we think', confining the allusion
to Garnet. In May 1605, the Gunpowder plotters did receive communion together to confirm their oaths. The officiating priest was not Garnet; but
in a letter to the Privy Council he states that he was *accused* of having

'given the most holy sacrament to six of the confederates at the very undertaking so bloody an enterprise' (Taunton, p. 303). The revision, 'we think',
refers to such receiving of communion as (so it was thought) was a regular
practice of Catholic (especially Jesuit) conspirators. Cf. Robert Bolron,
The Papists' Bloody Oath of Secrecy ... *With the Manner of Taking the Oath,
upon their Entring into any Grand Conspiracy against the Protestants*, 1680
(16 Nov.).

16. Cf. Fletcher, *Locusts*, V.iii: 'this Iesuite ... Binds them to hell in
sin, & makes heavens Lord the seale.'

23, 27 f. *Are you then Jesuits?* ... *And can you fail* ... *Shall* ...? Cf.
Fletcher, *Locusts*, II.xxxviii: 'And shall wee, (Spirits) shall we ... / ...
shall we, can we faile ?'

27. It was reported that the conspirators more than once bungled their attempts to shoot the king. See Burnet, ii.189, and Pollock, pp. 70, 72-3.

30. See Appendix III (R248).

31. *late Sect'ries*: the Independents, responsible for Charles I's execution,
1649.

35. *eas'd him of both Life and Crown*. Echoes Otway, *Don Carlos*: see (and
also for ll. 112-14 n., below) Appendix III (R250, 'Ease ...' and n.).

40, 45. See Appendix III (R249), 'usurp ...').

43. That the regicide sectaries were puppets of the Jesuits was a belief
popularized by William Prynne: see Miller, pp. 85 f. and nn. Cf. Henry
Care, *The History of the Damnable Popish Plot* (1680), pp. 69, 72: 'The
disloyal principles on which the fanatic rebels proceeded they wholly
learnt from the Jesuits', who were 'the prime authors of those damnable
courses which took away [the King's] life' (quoted Yale *POAS*, ii, ad loc.);
Duport's *Sermon on Fifth of November*, cit. J.N. Figgis, *The Divine Right
of Kings* (2nd edn., 1914), p. 380; and Figgis, op. cit., p. 179 and n.

48. *that matchless Assassin*. The murderer, in 1312, of the Emperor Henry VII.
He 'marcheth for *Italy*', and there 'dyeth, not without great suspition of
being poysoned (and that too at the receiving of the Sacrament) as many of
their Historians do confess' (Foulis, p. 302; cf. Fletcher, *Locusts*, III.
xxxix). Sir T. Browne, *Pseud. Ep.*, VII.§19, rejects the story as a vulgar
error. Latin lines quoted by Foulis denounce the sacrilegious poisoner as
'Jacobita secundus/Judas'—a Jacobite (Dominican) friar; hence Oldham's
draft couplet (R250) calling him
        ... that great Assassine (whose envied name
        Another Order must with glorie claim).

51 f. Quoted in *Truth and Honesty In Plain English* ... (1679), p. 22. The
passage refers also to ll. 271-3 below: 'In a quarter of an hour they will
Dissolve a Parliament, and Adjourn King, Lords and Commons into another
world, with the help of Gunpowder. They will stab you the greatest Monarch
in the twinckling of an Eye, and convey *Jesus Christ* into the Body of an
Emperor to take away his Life, according to that excellent saying of a late
admired Poet,
        To give his Poyson stronger Force and Power
        He'l mix a God with it to make it work more sure.'
The tract is later than 12 July, when Parliament was dissolved by proclamation.

55. *Clement* ... *Ravillac's name*. In 1589, Henry III of France, having been
excommunicated by the Pope, was murdered by Jacques Clément, a Dominican
friar. The Pope was said to have commended Clément's deed in a speech to

the Consistory (Foulis, pp. 547, 550 ff.). In 1610, François Ravaillac
assassinated Henry IV of France in the midst of his preparations for an
expedition in support of the German Protestants. Oldham read detailed accounts of both assassinations in Foulis, see pp. 550-60, 640 f.

59 f. The apostrophe echoes *Second Advice to the Painter* (Yale *POAS*, i.15):
'Heroick Act! and never heard till now!' See *The Terrible and Deserued
death of Francis Rauilliack, shewing the manner of his strange torments at
his Execution* (1610). Clément, however, was dispatched at once on the scene
of his crime, 'inadvertently', as Foulis grimly remarks. R247 refers, correctly, to Ravaillac's torture alone.

64-76. Gunpowder Plot, 1605. Cf. 'Aude aliquid. Ode', st. 10, on Fawkes.
There, as in ll. 66 f., the plot is compared with the revolt of Satan, whose
invention of gunpowder and use of it against the heavenly hosts, in *Paradise
Lost*, VI.571-95, was evidently in Oldham's mind. With ll. 73-6 cf. ll. 237 f.
of 'Aude aliquid', and the draft couplet quoted in the note to l. 45 of 'The
Vision'.

71. *that Pow'r, who, of himself afraid.* Cf. Fletcher, *Locusts*, V.xv: 'But
hellish Faux laught at blinde heaven's affright.'

71-4. Cf. Cowley, 'Davideis' (*Poems*, p. 246):
                Nay their *God* too—for fear *he* did, when *We*
                Took noble Arms against his *Tyrannie*...
Lines 73 f. are indebted to Dryden's *State of Innocence* (1677), I.i, p. 3,
where Lucifer aspires
                T'oerleap th' Etherial Fence, or if so high
                We cannot climb, to undermine his Sky,
                And blow him up....

79. *Had I bin Man.* A phrase from Otway's *Don Carlos* (1676), p. 56. Cf. Jonson, *Catiline*, I.22, 25 (Sylla):
                What now, had I a body againe, I could, ...
                Thinke thou, and practice.

81 f. Cf. Lee, *The Rival Queens* (1677), I.i, p. 9:
                ... though the Earth yawn'd ...
                I'd leap the burning Ditch to give him death,
                Or sink my self for ever.

93 f. Cf. 'Jesuits II', l. 177 and n.; also autograph nn. derived from Lee,
Sophonisba: see Appendix III (R180, 263) and below ll. 341-50 n.

95 f. Cf. Dryden, *Aureng-Zebe* (1676), IV, p. 51, and Cowley, 'Davideis'
(*Poems*, p. 245). See Appendix III, R249 ('Courage ...') and n.

97 f. *Or is't Religion* ? Cf. Jonson, *Catiline*, iii.515 ff., and Fletcher,
Locusts, I.xxx, II.xv.

98. *That frivolous pretence.* A reminiscence of 'Business! the frivolous
pretence', in Cowley, 'The Complaint' (*Poems*, p. 437).

99-101. These lines, with 73 ff., and 'Aude aliquid. Ode', ll. 60, 159 f.,
have parallels in 'Britannia and Rawleigh' (see Marvell, *Poems* (3rd edn.),
i.196, 400 f.), ll. 76, 80-4:
                Virtues a faint-green-sickness of the souls,
        with which the Gods infected princes,
                        Fearing the mighty Projects of the great
                        Should drive them from their proud Celestiall seat,
                        If not ore aw'd by new found holy cheat.
                        These pious frauds (too slight t'ensnare the brave)
                        Are proper arts, the long-eard rout t'enslave....

The poem is authoritatively dated *c*.Feb. 1674 by Godfrey Davies (*HLQ*, ix (1946), 311). Hence, contrary to my contention in *N & Q* (clxxix (1940), 146), Oldham must have been the borrower (see also Marvell, *Poems*, 2nd edn., 1952, i.xiv). 'Britannia and Rawleigh', though not printed till 1689, circulated in MS and might have been seen by Oldham among Whigs at Beddington, 1676.

103 ff.   See Appendix III (R249, 250, 261, 281). Oldham's nn. and quotations show the inspiration throughout ll. 95-128 (and cf. 'Jesuits II', ll. 239 ff.) of the heroic drama: Otway, *Don Carlos* (1676), Lee, *Sophonisba* (1676), *Mithridates* (1678), Dryden, *Tyrannick Love* (1670), 1 *Conquest of Granada* (1672), *Aurent-Zebe* (1676), and *All for Love* (1678).

108.   On R246 (see Appendix III) Oldham has a note from G. Hall, which refers to Luther's story of the Archbishop of Mainz, who having chanced upon a Bible, 'and for four hours ... read in it', when asked 'what he did with that book?' is said to have answered, 'I know not what Book it is; but sure I am, that what I find written in it is against us.'

112 f.   Cf. Dryden, 1 *Conquest of Granada* (1672), II.i, p. 19: 'Vertue intrudes with her lean holy face'.

114 f.   Cf. Satan in *Paradise Lost*, I.159 ff.

121.   *In steams of ... slaughter drown.* To 'drown' in 'steams' is a forced notion; but I believe the awkwardness to be Oldham's, overlooked in echoing from Lee, *Mithridates* (1678), V.ii, p. 61, 'drunk with Death, and steaming Slaughter', transcribed on R261 (see Appendix III). In the 1679 piracy, 'streams' is probably the 'correction' a copyist would naturally make.

136, 138-9.   *Then you're true Jesuits ... / ... worthy a Plot / Like this.* Cf. Fletcher, *Locusts*, IV.xxix: 'I have a plot worthy of Rome and us'.

138.   *undertake.* In the 17th century, the word is often used of *treacherous* enterprises. See *OED*, 'undertake' II, intr. †8.

142.   *Apostate Monk*: Luther. 'Apostate' is from G. Hall, p. 33, who, like Oldham, so terms Luther with ironical effect. Cf. Fletcher's 'that recreant frier' (*Locusts*, II.xxiii), 'that uncloister'd Frier' (IV.x). Cf. 'Jesuits III', l. 51.

149.   *a late reigning Witch.* Queen Elizabeth I.

154-9.   'Queen *Mary* whose Piety and Mercy is much commended by *Sanders* and other *Romanists*, Reigned about five years; yet in that short time were put to death for Religion above 260.' (Foulis, p. 418); 300 or scarcely fewer is A.F. Pollard's estimate (*History of England* [1547-1601], p. 155).

165.   Juvenal, I.155-6 and Tacitus, *Annals*, XV.xliv refer to the burning of the Christians. Oldham adopts Tacitus' grim comment on Nero's victims: 'ubi deficisset dies in usum nocturni luminis urerentur'.

179.   *reverend Bears.* Oldham knew the ironic application of the epithet to 'reverend *Owls*' in *MacFlecknoe*, which he had transcribed.

182.   *Sorbon dotards.* On the 'continual bickering' between the University and the Jesuits, see Foulis, p. 99.

186.   *Annalists.* One of Oldham's frequent references to Foxe and his *Acts and Monuments* or 'Book of Martyrs'. See 'Jesuits IV', l. 313 n.

195 f.   'the works of *Wickliffe* were brought into *Bohemia* ... which hapning into the hands of *John Husse*, and *Hierome* of *Prague*; ... wrought in their hearts a desire to reforme the Church.... [B]eing summoned to the Councell of *Constance*, they were there condemned for *Hereticks*, and burned *anno* 1414, yet had their doctrine such deep root in the hearts of the people,

that it could never be destroyed by the Tyrannies of war or persecutions (though both were used).' (Heylyn, ii.89.) But see Ranke, ii.226-8, 270, for the final rooting out of Hussite beliefs, from 1620-8.

197. Waldo (d. 1217) whose disciples were known as the Poor Men of Lyons. His movement became fused with earlier ones in a Waldensian church. As a result of persecution, by the 16th century Piedmont and the Italian valleys of the Cottian Alps, the Vaudois country, were their only stronghold. In 1655 the Vaudois suffered the massacre that Milton's noble anger has made famous; Jean Leger, their historian, enumerates 1,712 martyrs. After a further struggle in 1663-4, the Waldenses were left unmolested until after Oldham's death. See Heylyn, i.193.

198. *those of Wickliff*. Persecution under the statute *De Haeretico Comburendo* had all but extinguished Lollardy by the mid-15th century.

202. *the Church to heal*. In G. Hall, p. 139, the Archbishop of Spalata confesses that, but for 'fire' and 'axe' heretical sects would proliferate among 'the Romanists themselves'.

203 ff. Charles IX of France; the massacre of St Bartholomew's day, 1572. According to the account Oldham had read in Foulis, 'Charles iX, King of *France*, under the pretence of ... the King of *Navar's* Marriage, invited all the Grandees of the *Hugonots* of *France*, with *Leicester* and *Burghley* ... and the Sons of the *Palatine* Elector ..., intending ... to ruine the Protestant Religion. The French ... appear'd, [and] were, by order of the King, in one day, [(to the number of] several thousands] slain without respect to Sex, age, or quality.... [B]y the Kings Order was [this Massacre] also acted all *France* over, to the unthought-of slaughter of many thousand Protestants.... As for the *Romanists* in *France*, they celebrated these slaughters as one of the most glorious actions in the world; ... But the greatest joy of all, for this slaughter, was at *Rome*' (p. 416).

210. Cf. Settle, *The Empress of Morocco* (1673), p. 61:
> Let single Murthers Common Hands suffice
> I Scorn to kill less than whole Families.

211 f. *He scorn'd Retail*. Cf. cleveland's 'Smectymnuus', 11. 65-7:
> *Caligula*, whose pride was Mankinds Baile,
> As who disdain'd to murder by retaile,
> Wishing the world had but one generall Neck....

212. *by th' great*. En gros—by wholesale. After Dryden, 1 *Conquest of Granada* (1672), II.i, p. 14:
> Death did at length so many slain forget;
> And lost the tale, and took 'em by the great.

219. *Macguire*. The anomalous *Macquire* or *Mac-quire* of the substantive editions seems not to have been Oldham's form. Connor, Lord Macguire, Baron of Enniskillen, was executed for his share in the rising of 1641, dubbed by the Protestants the Irish Massacre. For details of Macguire's bloody deeds, see *The Whole Triall of Connor Lord Macguire* (1645); and *The last Speeches and Confession of the Lord Maguire* ... (Feb. 1644), sig. A3ᵛ.

233 ff. *Dare you beyond*, &c. Cf. Jonson, *Catiline*:
> These are too light. *Fate* will haue thee pursue
> Deedes, after which, no mischiefe can be new. (I.43-4)

> ... no rage, gone before, or comming after,
> May weigh with yours. (III.649-50)
And cf. 'Jesuits I', 1. 332 n.

235-40. Cf. Jonson, *Catiline*, III.746-9:
>   The cruelty, I meane to act, I wish
>   Should be call'd mine, and tarry in my name;
>   Whil'st after-ages doe toile out themselues
>   In thinking for the like, but doe it lesse.

Garnet exhorts the Jesuits to baffle this wish of Catiline's; whose 'madder
Poet' is of course Ben Jonson.

240. Joseph Hall, *Virgidemiarum*, IV.vii.9-12, had imagined Juvenal's ghost
making the same comparison.

243 ff. Cf. Jonson, *Catiline*, I.121: 'such an action, which the gods will
enuy', and Otway, *Don Carlos* (1676), I.i, p. 3:
>   What King, what God would not his pow'r forgo
>   T' enjoy so much Divinity below?

245. *A Complice*. Bell emended to 'Accomplice'. But Oldham had deliberately
preferred the present form, altering, on R293, 'Accomplice' into 'A Complice'.

247 f., 256.   *Nor let Delay (the bane of Enterprize)*
>   *Marr yours.... Break out upon your Foes.*

Cf. Fletcher, *Locusts*, II.xxxviii: 'Why sit we here ...? Kindle your ...
rage ... breake out upon the light.' Probably the 'breaking' of Otway's
grenade (see below, ll. 254 ff. n.) formed a hook-and-eye with Fletcher's
'breake out upon'. In *1682* the storm-imagery, such as Fletcher has in II.
xxxix f., takes over the function of the image from Otway. With Oldham's
first phrase, cf. Jonson, *Catiline*, III.ii.495 f.

252 f. *Forestall even wishes*. Cf. Jonson, *Catiline*, III.i.184-6:
>   Doe, and not wish; something, that wishes take not:
>   So sodaine, as the gods should not preuent,
>   Nor scarce haue time, to feare.

L. 253 reflects Otway, *Don Carlos* (1676), p. 58:
>   No, I will stay and ev'n thy prayr's prevent
>   I would not give thee leisure to repent.

254 ff. Oldham revised l. 257 away from his source in Otway's simile of the
'Granado' which 'breaking deals destruction all around' (*Don Carlos* (1676)).
See Appendix III (R250), and Introduction, p. lxxxii f.

258. In the speech of Sylla's Ghost (Jonson, *Catiline*, I.65 f.), Rome's
blinded walls are not to
>   ... recouer sight, till their owne flames
>   Doe light them to their ruines.

258 f. That the Catholics were responsible for the Great Fire was generally
believed: an inscription to that effect was placed on the Monument in 1681
(cf. Luttrell, i.115). Oates declared that they were preparing to repeat
their exploit. It was rumoured that Lord Ossory had discovered a hundred
thousand fireballs and hand-grenades concealed in Somerset House. See Marvell, *Poems* (3rd edn.), i.194 (l. 14 and n.); Pollock, pp. 11, 84, 171 f.

262 f. Cf. Jonson, *Catiline*, I.i:
>   I would haue seene *Rome* burn't,
>   By this time; and her ashes in an vrne.

264. *Divan*. The probability that this was suggested by 'our dark divan' (the
infernal council) in Dryden, *State of Innocence* (1677), I.i, p. 3, is increased by Oldham's having made a separate memorandum, 'Divan', as a usable
idea, on R267.

265. *that damn'd Committee*. Parliament. On the committees for investigating
the Plot, set up by the Commons (21 Oct. 1678), Lords (23 Oct.), and

Council (1st week of Dec.), see Kenyon, pp. 81, 129; but no 'prelates' (1. 269) sat on these.

271 ff. *Lop off the Lords / And Commons, &c.* Cf. Jonson, *Catiline*, IV.iii. 597 f.:

> Let me kill all the *Senate*, for my share
> Ile doe it at next sitting.

279 ff. See *Jesuits Assassins: All Extracted out of Dr Tong's Papers* (1680) for an account of the supposed extent of the massacre planned by the Jesuits.

279-303. Cf. Jonson's *Cataline*, I.240-4:

> Not infants, in the porch of life were free.
> The sick, the old, that could but hope a day
> Longer, by nature's bountie, not let stay.
> Virgins, and widdowes, matrons, pregnant wiues,
> All dyed.

and III.626-9:

> When husbands, wiues,
> Grandsires, and nephewes, seruants and their lords,
> Virgins, and priests, the infant, and the nurse
> Goe all to hell, together, in a fleet.

See also below, 11. 281 ff., 292 ff.; 'Jesuits II', 11. 98 ff.; 'Jesuits III', 11. 153, nn. The multiple sources in heroic drama are documented in Appendix III (R265, 'Triumph'd ...', 'I'th midst ...', and nn.). Cf. also Lucan, *Pharsalia*, II.99-110, 148-65 (Marius' and Sulla's proscriptions).

281 ff. ... *spare / No Age, Degree, or Sex.* Cf. Jonson, *Catiline*, I.239, 244:
[*Cethegus*]: No age was spar'd, no sexe.
[*Catiline*]: Nay no degree....
                 'Twas crime inough, that they had liues.

288 ff. *Spare not young Infants.* Cf. Lee, *Mithridates* (1678), V.i., p. 56:

> ... Lightning edge your Souls
> To mow off hoary Heads, hurl Infants puling
> From the lug'd breast, kill in very Womb:
> To Beauties cries be deaf....

In R265 1. 288 runs: 'Pitty not Infants lugging at ye Brest'.

299. *Age, just crawling on the verge of Life.* Cf. Dryden, *All for Love* (1678), II.i, p. 19: an 'old age' that would 'crawl upon the utmost verge of life'. On R265, besides this echo, Oldham has two nn. from the same play, for which and a n. on R162, see Appendix III.

303. Cf. the like hypocrisy in *Don Carlos* (1676), IV.i, p. 44.

306 f. Cf. Lee, *Sophonisba* (1676), III.ii, p. 38: 'not one shall dare / ... for his Soul whisper a dying Prayer.'

309. *witty handsome malice.* Cf. Lee's 'witty horrour' (*Mithridates* (1678), III.ii, p. 31).

312. The thought is from Jonson, *Sejanus*, II.198 f.

314. Cf. Otway, *Don Carlos* (1676), IV.i, p. 49: 'And childless Mothers curse your Memory'. See Appendix III (R286).

315-17. Cf. Jonson, *Catiline*, III.i.189 f.

317-20. Cf. Lee, *Mithridates* (1678), V.i, p. 66:

> ... make all *Synope*
> But one vast Grave, to hold the infinite bodies
> Which we must shovel in ...

and Settle, *The Empress of Morocco* (1673), p. 24:

> I'le send such throngs to the infernal shade,
> Betray, and kill, and damn to that degree,
> I'le crowd up Hell, till there's no Room for Me.

Cf. also Fletcher, *Locusts*, II.xx.

321-5. The 'Tyrants wish' is Caligula's in Suetonius, *De Vita Caesarum*, IV.xxx.2: 'Infensus turbae faventi adversus studium suum, exclamavit: *Utinam P. R. unam cervicem haberet*', alluded to also by Cleveland (see above, 11. 211 f., n.) and adapted by Fletcher, *Locusts*, IV. xxx:

> The Flowre of England in one houre I'le mow,
> And head all th'Isle with one unseen, unfenced blow.

Even closer to Fletcher than Oldham's 11. 321 ff. are his drafts on R252. L. 322 echoes from the same stanza 'To kill a King is stale, and I disdaine' —a draft (R261) picks up the word 'disdain'.

326-37. Cf. three passages in Jonson's *Catiline*:

> ... what the *Gaule*, or *Moore* could not effect,
> Nor emulous *Carthage*, with their length of spight ... (III.752 f.)
>
> ... what / ... HANNIBAL could not haue wish'd to see ...
> (Sylla, I.23-4)
>
> What all the seuerall ills, that visite earth,
> (Brought forth by night, with a sinister birth),
> Plagues, famine, fire could not reach vnto
> The sword, nor surfets; let thy furie doe. (Sylla, I.49-52.)

326 f. Cf. Cowley, '*Discourse* ... *Concerning* ... *Cromwell*' (*Essays*, p. 353):

> Let rather *Roman* come again,
> Or *Saxon*, *Norman*, or the *Dane*....

328-31. Cf. *A Satyrical Poem on the most Horrid and Execrable Jesuitish Plot in 1678 ... By ... W.M.* (1679):

> We ruminate on th' *past*, and *present* Age;
> Th' *Laments* of *BELGIA* under *D'ALVA*'S Rage ...
> Th' *INVINCIBLE-ARMADO*, and its Freight
> Of *SPANISH* VILLAINY in EIGHTY EIGHT.

329. *fraight of cruelties*. I take 'fraight' in the 1682 text to be Oldham's revision of his original 'fraught' (1681, R261, R293), though it may be a compositor's normalization. As a noun, 'fraught' was a Scotticism (*OED*). Oldham is likely to have caught the form from his source, Fletcher, *Locusts*, V.xxxv (where the word is not a noun), on the Armada, 'Full fraught with brands, whips, gyves for English slaves'. It looks as though by 1682 he had realized the correct noun was 'fraight'. For the allusion, see Thomas Deloney's ballad (repr. Ebsworth, vi.387): *A new Ballet of the straunge and most cruell Whippes which the Spanyards had prepared to Whippe and torment English men and women: which were found and taken at the ouerthrow of certain of the Spanish Shippes in July last past* (1588).

330 f. *Medina ... bloudier Alva*. The Duke of Medina Sidonia, commander of the Armada, and the Duke of Alva, who, whilst governor of the Netherlands (1567-73), erected and presided over the 'Council of Blood'. Alva is said to have boasted that he had executed 18,600 persons; his victims were not quite so numerous.

332 f. See Appendix III (R293) on Oldham's use of lines from Lee, *Rival Queens* (1677).

338 f. Cf. Envy's speech in Bk I of Cowley's 'Davideis' (*Poems*, p. 247):

> ...—but I lose time, methinks, and should
> Perform new acts whilst I relate the old....

341. *waste a pray'r*. 'Waste' is authentic: not to be emended to 'waft'. Both Settle (*The Empress of Morocco* (1673), p. 19) and Rochester (*Poems*, p. 50) have 'lose a prayer', though with them the phrase does not, like Garnet's, express scorn of prayer itself.

341-50. See Appendix III, R260 and 261 ('The Infernal Prayer').

342. *Hell be your aid*. Cf. Jonson, *Catiline*, I.16 (Sylla): 'PLUTO be at thy councells'.

Satyr II

Judging from what evidence there is, this satire was composed a little after the Prologue. It is subsequent to 14 Mar. 1678/9: R194 bears the heading (only) of a letter so dated, which has been scored through, prior, no doubt, to writing out a passage of the satire on the same sheet: some lines on R194 itself. Oldham alludes, in ll. 206-20, to Jesuits' sworn protestations of innocence at the very gallows. The great outburst of pamphlets on their 'dying Vows' came after the execution of 'the Five Jesuits' on 20 June. Ten may be seen in Bodley Ashmole 1684 (VI to XV): cf., e.g. one perhaps by John Williams, 'In which it is proved, that according to their Principles', the Five 'not only might, but also ought, to die ... with Solemn Protestations of their Innocency'; and Clarkson(?), *The True Speeches of* Thomas Whitebread ... William Harcourt ... John Fenwick ... John Gavan ... *and* Anthony Turner, ... *before their Execution at Tyburn June the 20th MDCLXXIX. With Animadversions ... Plainly discovering the fallacy of all their Asseverations of their Innocency* (1679). Hence the present satire may most likely have been written after 20 June. But the evidence is not watertight. As early as the epilogue to *Troilus and Cressida* (produced *c.*Apr.), Dryden could gibe at Catholics 'sure oth' Churches Blessing / By suffering for the Plot without confessing'. However, this final couplet might have been added before publication, subsequent to 20 June. Of those suffering for the Plot before Whitebread and his companions (see below, l. 277 n.) only Grove (24 Jan.) and Pickering (9 May) were Jesuits. Oldham's reference to Scotch Covenanters would have most point if he were writing in June or shortly after: the Conventiclers' rising (see l. 241 n.) was not defeated till the 22nd, and *c.*30 May Rochester told Savile that this war 'takes up all the discourse of politic persons' (*Letters*, p. 225).

1-4. Cf. Cowley's *Discourse ... Concerning ... Cromwell* (*Essays*, pp. 352-3):
> If by our sins the Divine Justice be
>   Call'd to this last extremity ...

and

> Come rather Pestilence and reap us down
>   Come Gods sword rather than our own.

Cromwell brings 'worse Plagues than *Egypt* knew' (cf. ll. 15-19 below). See also Appendix III, R292.

15-18. Cf. Marvell, 'The Loyall Scot', ll. 108 f.:
> Instead of all the Plagues had Bishops come,
> Pharaoh at first would have sent Israell home.

The lines occur in a passage interpolated by Marvell or another; see *Poems* (3rd edn.), i.385 f.

17. See ll. 262 f., n.

29. Raleigh's widow had meant to bury him at Beddington. Oldham's patron there, Sir Nicholas Carew, was his great-nephew. See Introduction, pp. li f. and n. 96.

31. *Biscain*. Aspatheia (Azpeitia) in Biscay (actually Guipúzcoa) was Loyola's birthplace: cf. L[ewis] O[wen], *Speculum Jesuiticum* (1629), pp. 1 f. See Appendix III (R166).

41 f. See 'Jesuits' IV.33 n. The 'brother Traytor' is Judas.

43 f. For the parallel with Paris in Hecuba's dream, see Appendix III (R178). With special aptness, Fletcher, *Locusts*, V.ix, had given Faux's mother dreams like that of Hecuba: 'Oft' she 'dream't she bore ... A brand of hell sweltring in fire and smoke'. At II.viii, Loyola is said to take 'his ominous name', Ignatius, 'from Strife and Fires'.

45 ff. According to Foulis, *History of the Wicked Plots and Conspiracies of Our Pretended Saints* (1674), 'The *French* besieging *Pamplona*', in 1521, he had 'both his leggs grievously hurt'. Ribadeneyra authoritatively states, however, that he was left merely halting 'a little of one lege'. (*Life of Ignatius*, p. 133.) His disablement was the occasion of his conversion.

50. *Janizaries of the Cause*. Cf. Burton, *Anatomy*, p. 648, where he refers to the Pope's 'Janisary Jesuits'.

51. *Life-Guard*. Cf. Cleveland, 'The Rebell Scot', l. 97: 'They are the Gospels Life-guard'. On the Life-Guards, first regularly constituted in 1661, see Clifford Walton, *History of the British Standing Army* (1894), p. 6.

57 f. For an account of the Jesuits' trading activity, see Varenius, pp. 189-90. In Protestant eyes, it was the worse for their casuistical defence of it: they maintained (cf. Ranke, ii.430) that it was no different in principle from the agriculture practised by earlier Orders.

58. For Indigo and Cochineal, see Heylyn, III.222, IV.129. The correction of 1682, 'truck't', is confirmed by the MS draft (R245).

59. *Factors*: mercantile agents.

59 f. Cf. J. Eachard, *Some Observations upon the Answer to an Enquiry into the Grounds ... of the Contempt of the Clergy* (1671), p. 129: 'others ... are very much for *trafficking* with *Christ*: And in the *late times* we may remember ... what a perfect *merchandize* they made of *Christ; and what abundance of eminent *holders* forth of *Christ* and his cause were sent into the Country* to sell *Christ* for *spoons, bodkins, and thimbles*.' Butler (*Hudibras*, I.ii.569 f.) had alluded to the contributions so gathered and used to finance anti-Royalist forces:
> A *Thimble, Bodkin*, and a *Spoon*
> Did start up living men ... [etc.].

The parallel of Puritan and Papist is drawn in *The Second Part of the Loyal Subjects Litany* (1680), praying deliverance 'From a Preacher with Reliques or Spoons in his hand', and is characteristic of the views of a Church-and-King man. (I owe the quotations from Eachard and the *Litany* to Miss K.M. Eidmans.) Cf. also Pepys, iv.93 and n.

63. *both Indies*: the East Indies with India, Japan, and China and the West Indies with Spanish America. In the East, Xavier and his companions were the pioneers, in the West, Nombrega and Anchieta, the evangelists of Brazil. L[ewis] O[wen], *Speculum Jesuiticum* (1629), mentions Brazil, Mexico, Peru, Paraguay, and Granada as Jesuit provinces in the West, and China, Japan, Malabar, and the Moluccas in the East. Cf. Ranke, i.182.

66. Cf. R. Fletcher, *Obsequies On ... John Prideaux* (1650):
> ... perhaps their *French* or *Spanish* Wine
> Had fill'd them full of Beads and *Bellarmine*.

Robert Bellarmine (1542-1621), the Italian cardinal, Jesuit, and theologian, was one of the foremost apologists of the temporal authority of the Pope, especially in his *Disputationes ... adversus hujus temporis haereticos* (1587-90). See Foulis, pp. 68 f.

67-73. The Papacy blessed the colonial and missionary enterprize of Spain and Portugal: in 1593 Alexander VI divided the colonizable world between them. To Bartolomé de las Casas, the conquests were motivated merely 'out of a ... blinde desire of heaping up Gold and riches, which is common to all that have gone into *America*'. See *The Tears of the Indians: being an ... Account of the Cruel Massacres ... of above Twenty Millions of Innocent People ... in ... the West Indies ... made English by J[ohn] P[hillips]* ... (1656), p. 103 (original Spanish, 1552); for other translations (1533, 1625) see Cleveland, *Poems*, ed. Morris and Withington, p. 122.

75 ff. Cf. Burton, *Anatomy*, p. 31: 'the *Spaniard* in the West *Indies*, that killed up in 42 years (if we may believe *Bartholomæus à Casa* their own bishop) 12 millions of men, with stupend & exquisite torments; neither should I ly (said he) if I said 50 millions'. See previous n.

80-2. For devil-worship, with human sacrifices, in Spanish America, see Burton, *Anatomy*, pp. 668-9. De las Casas relates 'the cruel and hard usage which the *Spaniards* afflict those innocent people withall which bred in them such a loathing of the *Spanish* name, that ... the *Indians* call them *Yaes*, which in their language signifies Devils' (*The Tears of the Indians* (1656), p. 73).

86. Cf. *The Tears of the Indians* (1656), A3^V: 'they kill'd up the poor Indians, not as if they had been their Fellow Mortals, but like Death it self; and invaded their Land, not like Men, but like the Pestilence'.

89 f. Cf. Marvell, 'The Loyall Scot', ll. 178 ff., referring to Blood's attempt to steal the crown, 9 May 1671:
>   He Chose the Cassock Circingle and Gown,
>   The fittest Mask for one that Robs a Crown.
See below, l. 110 n.

98 ff. *Your cool and sober murderer*. Echoing Dryden, *All for Love*; see Appendix III (R263 and R265).

101 ff. Cf. Butler, *Hudibras*, III.ii.111, 117-18:
>   The *Independents* ...
>   Were Free of ev'ry Spiritual Order,
>   To *Preach*, and *Fight*, and *Pray* and *Murther*;
and L'Estrange's story (quoted in Grey's n.) of the chief regicides '*seeking the Lord in Prayer*' as cover for hastening the King's execution.

105 ff. See Foulis, cit. below, l. 151 n.

110 f. Probably suggested by Cleveland's 'Had *Cain* been *Scot*', ('*The Rebell Scot*', l. 63), combined with Marvell, 'The Loyall Scot', 184-5: 'had he but put on / A Bishops cruelty, the Crown had gone'.

119. i.e. a deed which Hell cannot find flames enough to punish, and which the Schools can find no term bad enough to describe. (The Schoolmen were known for their refinement of terminology.) Cf. Donne, 'Satyre II', ll. 35-8:
>   ... for whose sinfull sake
>   Schoolemen new tenements in hell must make:
>   Whose strange sinnes, Canonists could hardly tell
>   In which Commandments large receit they dwell.
See below, ll. 227 f. and n. R191, which has 'For which Hell *flames*, ye schools a name must need', confirms the correction of the 1681 errata, 'Title', for 'little' of the 1681 text.

123 f. Cf. 'Death of Kings / In your opinion are but vulgar things'—*Second Advice to a Painter* ('Now Painter, try if thy skill'd hand can draw': No. 24 in Osborne). Luttrell dated his copy '1679'.

124 f. Indebted to G. Hall; see Appendix III (R188).

127-34. Cf. *The Black Box of Roome opened* (1641): '... putting the knife
into the intended Murtherers hand, they pronounce these words, saying ...
goe thus I say, thou magnanimous Champion of the chaire of *Rome*, and be
valiant and God strengthen thine arme for the great works now intended by
thee.... And thou oh dreadfull and terrible God, ... [he] being by us disposed to this meretorious Murther, vouchsafe to fortifie his senses, and
encrease his forces.' Cf. also *The Jesuits' Manner of Consecrating both the
Persons and Weapons imploy'd for the Murdering Kings and Princes by them
accounted Hereticks.... Translated out of Hospinian's History of the Jesuits*
(1678), p. 3: '... the Parricide is brought to the Altar, over which ...
hangs a picture containing the story of *James Clement*, a *Dominican Monk*,
with the figures of several Angels protecting and conducting him to Heaven.
This Picture, the Jesuites shew their bullie; and at the same time, presenting him with a celestial Coronet, rehearse these words, *Lord, look down, and
behold this Arm of thine, the Executioner of thy Justice. Let all thy Saints
arise and give place to him.*'

135. *S. Guy.* Guy Fawkes.

139. Both are notorious for their persecutions of the Christians. See R192
(Appendix III).

140. *Herostratus.* See 'Aude aliquid. Ode', ll. 185 ff. and n.

141. *And ... Tholouse.* Lucilio Vanini, b. 1585, an Italian free-thinker, was
arrested in Toulouse and executed on 9 Feb. 1619. See Burton, *Anatomy*,
p. 690, and cf. 'Juvenal XIII', ll. 188 f., and R189 (Appendix III).

141 ff. Imitating Juvenal, I.73-5. Oldham's l. 142 is adopted verbatim in
Thomas Wood's *Juvenalis Redivivus* ... (1683).

150. *Tyburn onely stocks the Calendar.* Veneration accorded to men executed
as agents of the Counter-Reformation campaign against the throne and reformed religion of England had long incensed Protestants, to whom it was a
glaring proof of the Roman Church's blessing on traitorous conspiracy. For
the 'Tyburn martyrs' of Elizabeth's and James's reigns, see, in *The Fierie
Tryall of Gods Saints ... as a Counter-poyze to I. W. Priest his English
Martyrologe* (1612), 'A Beadroll of all such traiterous Priests, Jesuits,
and Popish Recusants, as are [by I.W.] recorded for Martyrs in this Kingdome'. The Catholics who suffered for the Popish Plot were also at once
acclaimed as martyrs by their co-religionists abroad. According to *The True
Domestick Intelligence* of 18 Nov. 1679, a Holborn cellar yielded articles
kept as relics of the Five Jesuits and Coleman; cf. also *The Answer of
Coleman's Ghost* [1678], and *News from Heaven* (Bodl. Wood 424(5) and (28)).
Executions for the Plot in 1678-9, all at Tyburn, are listed at l. 277 n.
below.

151. *Unhappy Judas.* See Appendix III (R194) for a couplet forming a link
with what precedes, and a n. indicating the source: Foulis on the conspirators in Throckmorton's plot (1583): 'And besides ... rewards of riches and
favour ..., they were promised the highest of Spiritual Benefits, because
their Treasonable Actions could be no less than meritorious, by which they
would be certain to enjoy Heaven ... hereafter: For no less rewards did
these evil Counsellors impudently promise to these bloudy Traytors. As if
these Casuists were related to the old Hereticks the *Cainani*, who reverenced *Cain* for killing his brother *Abel*, and worshiped *Judas* for betraying
our Innocent *Saviour*. But why might they not promise as much, when they
knew that the Pope, who cannot err, had formerly bequeath'd such blessings
to the enemies of Queen *Elizabeth*.' Other possible reminiscences of this
passage are at 105 f., 133 f., above, and 'Jesuits III', ll. 570 ff., IV.250.

157-62. Cf. Jonson, *Catiline*, III, ll. 237-8, 241-2:
                   Hath IOVE no thunder? or is IOVE become
                   Stupide as thou art? ð neere wretched *Home* ...
                   What will awake thee, heauen? What can excite
                   Thine anger, if this practice be too light?
         Cf. also Juvenal, XIII.113 f.

165. *dispense*: exempt from penalty. The dispensing power was the sovereign's
prerogative of waiving the application of a law in particular instances.

165 f. Cf. Cleveland, 'The Rebell Scot', ll. 117 f.:
                   The Indian that heaven did foresweare,
                   Because he heard some Spaniards were there,
and the *The Tears of the Indians* (1656), p. 23, which describes the martyrdom in Cuba of the native prince, Hathvey, who being called upon by a Franciscan monk to turn Christian and secure salvation, asked 'if the door of
heaven was open to the Spaniards'. Being answered '*Yes, to the good Spaniards*. Then replyed the other, Let me go to Hell that I may not come where
they are.' Another version, cited by Morris and Withington (Cleveland, ad.
loc.), from Wm. Lightfoot, *The Complaint of England* (1587), has the monk
say that all Spaniards go to heaven, since they die in the Catholic faith.

167-72. Cf. Juvenal, VI.634-8. In imitating Juvenal's 'sed clamat Pontia,
feci' (l. 638), Oldham is led to imply that Garnet died vaunting his part
in Gunpowder Treason. This has no basis in fact, and Foulis correctly represents him as penitent. In two letters quoted by Taunton, pp. 317 f., and
Caraman, p. 422, Garnet declares that he 'always condemned the intention
of the Powder Plot' and that he had sinned in not revealing the general
knowledge he had of it from Catesby out of confession.

172-5. Cf. G. Hall's irony, pp. 116, 119: 'What though *Luther* profess that
he believes verily that Rome hath slain an hundred thousand Martyrs ...
grant that she hath been the death of so many heretiques, yet ... the meer
killing is not that which deserves either blame or approbation; all is in
the cause that merits it' ('Mother Church's sake').

177. For Oldham's use of Lee, *Sophonisba*, see Appendix III (R180, R261,
R263).

181 f. The well-worn Tarquin story comes from Livy, I.liv. Oldham had met,
among other allusions to it, Jonson's in *Catiline*, III.644 f. In R247, opposite a draft of ll. 63, 65, 91-100, he jotted 'The tally of devotion was
heads instead of beads Tarquins poppies': originally, then, he meant to
equate the decapitation of each poppy (signifying a human victim) with the
telling of a bead, as a measure of devotion, in the rosary. See also
'Jesuits IV', ll. 133-5 n.

184-7. Cf. Fletcher, *Locusts*, II.xxxvii:
                   Shall they spend, spill their dearest blood, to staine
                   Romes calendar, and paint their glorious name
                   In hers, and our Saint-Rubrick?
         Cf. 'Aude aliquid. Ode', ll. 93 f., which derives more closely from
         Fletcher:
                   Tame easy Fops! who could so prodigally bleed,
                   To be thought Saints, and dy a Calendar with Red!
         and cf. ll. 148-50 above. See also Foulis, pp. 699, 706.

187. *painted straws*. Alluding to Garnet (Fletcher's 'strawie Saint') and
what Foulis (pp. 704 f.) describes as the 'pretty Miracle' of his straw,
on which his 'Face miraculously appear[ed] as painted ... a Crown on his
Head', attesting him a martyr. The straw 'tainted with a little of *Garnet's*
blood' was carried from the scaffold by 'one *John Wilkinson* ... as an holy

Relique'. For its notoriety after the semblance supposedly formed by the
blood congealed on the wheaten ear had been discerned, see Robert Pricket,
The Jesuits Miracles [1607], with an engraving of the straw (illustrated
also in Caraman, p. 445); and H.L. Rogers, 'An English Tailor and Father
Garnet's Straw', *RES*, n.s. xvi (1965), 44-9. According to Foulis, 'though
at first there was but one *Straw* and Face, yet it seemeth that they had
afterwards an ambition to multiply them'.

188. *Mohatra*: a dodge, stigmatized by Pascal, *Lettres*, no. 8, pp. 115 f. to
avoid the guilt of usury. (The Jesuits did not deny that Mohatra was forbidden, but their theologians, Escobar and Lessius, found pretexts for the
evasion of the ban.) 'There's nothing strange in it but the name. Escobar
shall explain it to you. The *Contract Mohatra* is that whereby a man buies
some commodity ... at a very dear rate, and upon trust, for to sell it
again immediately to the same person for ready money, and at a verie easy
rate'. The man thus 'receives a sum of money in hand, yet is obliged for
a far greater'—*The Mystery of Jesuitism* (1679), p. 100. Instead of the
French, this translation of the *Lettres* may possibly have been Oldham's
source. It was no doubt published, postdated (imprimatur, A8^V, 13 Nov.
1678), just as he was beginning the *SJ*; and in the Argument on p. 95,
MOHATRA, alone in caps., may have leapt to his eye.

190-6. An imitation of Juvenal, XIII.76-83.

195. For the Virgin's milk, see 'Jesuits IV', 1. 187 n.; and for veneration
of the Magdalene's tears, cf. Crashaw's 'The Weeper', and Southwell's
'Marie Magdalens Funerall Teares'.

199. *Ladie's Psalter*: the full rosary of fifteen large beads for the Pater-
nosters, and 150 small ones for the Ave Marias. As the number of Aves corresponded with that of the Psalms, the devotion acquired the name of Our
Lady's Psalter.

208 f. Knights of the Post were professional false-witnesses, so nicknamed,
it is said, from their habit of waiting outside the sheriffs' doors, by the
posts on which proclamations were nailed. Cf. 'Upon a Woman', 11. 91 ff.;
'Juvenal XIII', 11. 221 ff. and n.; and *Hudibras*, III.iii.725-30. Donne,
in 'Satyre II', 1. 73, also alluded to the shamelessness of 'carted whores'.

210-20. Cf. Burnet, ii.227 f., on the Five Jesuits, who 'at their execution
... did, with ... the deepest imprecations possible, deny the whole evidence upon which they were condemned', and sought, by repudiating the doctrine that equivocation was permissible, to prevent their denials being
discounted (see their *True Speeches*, cit. above, headnote). Yet 'several
books were writ, to shew that lying for a good end was not only thought lawful among them, but had been often practised'. (A pamphlet to this effect
was recommended by Halifax to Henry Savile, 7 Aug. 1679; translated it
would help influence French opinion (Foxcroft, i.182).) To his honour, Burnet, when Anglican divines 'went far in this charge, against all regard to
their dying speeches', 'looked ... on this as ... the putting of them to a
second death'.

213, 216. See Appendix III (R197) for debt to Dryden, *Indian Emperour*.

217 f. Cf. *A Protestant Letter to the Lords in the Tower*, 14 Feb. 1680[/1],
by J.B., who had perhaps (see below 11. 270-3 n.) read this satire: 'Do
not imitate those who rather chuse to go to Hell with a Plot in their Hearts,
than divulge it.'

223 f. Acquiescence in Jesuit claims to religion would discredit religion
itself; cf. in Otway, *Don Carlos* (1676), V.i, p. 56, Heaven's apparent
acquiescence in the abuse of religion by oath-breakers as calculated to
'make us Infidels'.

227-30. Cf. Donne, 'Satyre II', l. 35 f.:
                    ... for whose sinfull sake,
                    Schoolemen new tenements in hell must make:
Cf. also Dryden, *All for Love* (1678), IV.i, p. 59, and below, ll. 278-85 n.

233 f. On R281, 'Can feeble Tests bind you?' shows Oldham thinking of the
Test Act, 1673, and that of Nov. 1678 for 'disabling Papists from sitting
in either House of Parliament'.

236. *the French Harries*: see 'Jesuits I', l. 55 nn.

238-40. The heads and quarters of traitors were set up on poles above Westminster Hall, on London Bridge, and at the city gates. These last, too,
were in Oldham's mind; cf. R186:
                    And those alone ye crowd of Martyrs throng
                    Who on our Gates and Bridge are Streamers hung....
Cf. Pepys, 20 Oct. 1660; *On the Six new Pinnacles upon Westminster Hall*,
1661 (Bodl. Wood 416 (90)); *6 State Trials* (1512); Kenyon, p. 99.

241. *Tories*: Irish outlaws. For the party use, established *c.*1681, see below,
'An Allusion to Martial', l. 20 n.

241. *Scotch Covenanters*. Trouble with the Covenanters, recurrent throughout
the reign, came to a head with the murder of the persecuting archbishop
Sharp (3 May 1679) and a minor insurgent victory at Drumclog (11 June);
the rebels were routed (22 June) by Monmouth at Bothwell Brigg. In England,
opposition leaders had considerable sympathy with the revolt (see Jones,
pp. 79 f., and Pollock, pp. 234-6); Oldham evidently had not.

244 f. i.e. 'Take goats and cloistered marmosites for chaste, and two-edged
parasites for plain and open.' On R285, 'chast as ... cloyster'd Marmasites
& Goats' and 'Take Goats for chast or cloister'd Marmasites' confirm this
sense. Donne, 'Elegie II', ll. 39 f., illustrates the reputation of marmo-
sets:
                    Here needs no spies, nor eunuches; her commit
                    Safe to thy foes; yea, to a Marmosit.

248. *in time*. So the 2nd edition, a revision no doubt. The 1st has 'in them':
viz. 'in these instances of Tories, &c.'.

252. *the Swedish Law*. Cf. W.M.'s *A Satyrical Poem* (1679), quoted 'Jesuits I',
ll. 328-31 n., p. 6:
                    Make th' POPISH *Priests* and *Jesuits*, stand in awe
                    Of *Execution* by the *SVEDISH* Law,
to prevent the engendering of 'PAPIST *Brats* or BASTARD *Protestants*'. The
Epilogue to Dryden's *Spanish Fryar* (1681) has an exhortation (ll. 39-41)
to 'unman the Friar' by Swedish example, but the alleged law has not been
traced.

254. Cf. Burton, *Anatomy*, p. 348: '*Vt vivat castor, sibi testes amputat ipse*;
Alciat. Embl.' See Browne, *Pseud. Ep.*, II.§4.

256 f. Oldham implies that in the Jesuits England is afflicted anew with
wolves: cf., with anarchists or Scots as the wolves, *2 Henry IV*, IV.v.136 f.,
and Cleveland, 'The Rebell Scot', l. 40, where Morris and Withington note
as originating with William of Malmesbury the legend that they were extir-
pated under Edgar. He was said, e.g. in Grafton's *Chronicle* (1809 repr.,
i.123), to have virtually completed the extermination by an annual tribute
of 300 exacted from Wales. Oldham's tax on 'every shire' is presumably
a variant version.

260 f. Cf. Prologue ('Gentle reproofs have oft been tried in vain'):
                    Hang up his mangled Carcass on the Stage
                    To fright away the Vermin of the Age.

The Prologue is by Edmund Ashton (see Vieth, *Attribution*, pp. 266-8).

262 f.   The Jesuits are compared to the seventh Plague of Egypt: 'And the
Lord turned a mighty strong west wind, which took away the locusts, and cast
them into the Red Sea' (Exodus 10:19). Oldham recalls the titles of Phineas
Fletcher's Latin poem against the Jesuits (written by 1623) and its English
expansion: *Locustae* and *The Locusts or Apollyonists* (both publ. 1627). A
ballad of 1624, *The Travels of Time: Loaden with Popish Trumperies* (Rollins,
p. 184), begins: 'O Happy winde those *Locusts* hence doth blow'. Dryden concludes the Prologue to *The Kind Keeper* (produced 1678) with an application
of the metaphor to critics who are to be driven away 'with such a wind /
That not one Locust may be left behind!'

266.   *Go foul Impostors*: indebted to Cleveland; see Appendix III (R191).

269.   *slur ... top ... bubbled*: cheat, impose upon, swindled. The dicers' cant
terms, 'slur and top', are associated in Shadwell, *The Virtuoso* (1676), I,
p. 8; 'top' and 'bubble' in Etherege, *The Comical Revenge* (1664), II.iii,
p. 26. To 'top' is to retain one die at the top of the dice-box (*OED*); to
'slur', having placed one on the top of the other, to make the undermost
slide without turning (*The Compleat Gamester*, 1680, quoted Farmer and Hen-
ley, *Slang and its Analogues*).

270-3.   Indebted to G. Hall; see Appendix III (R284); cf. 'Jesuits III',
ll. 491, 497 f.; 493 f., nn. J.B., the author of *A Protestant Letter to the
Lords in the Tower*, 14 Feb. 1680/1, probably remembered Oldham's lines when
he wrote, 'Let not the Priests Hoodwink you, or Blind-fold you, and then
lead you to Hell.'

275.   *Chastel*: Jean Chastel, a Jesuit who unsuccessfully attempted the life
of Henry IV of France in 1593; see Foulis, pp. 591-2. He was executed, and
the Jesuits banished for a time.

276.   Robert Catesby (1573-1605), originator of Gunpowder Plot; cornered and
shot at Holbeach House resisting arrest, 8 Nov. 1605. For 'Catesby', R197
has 'Campian' (Edmund Campion, SJ, 1540-81: zealous missionary, no con-
spirator).

277.   Those executed for the Plot or related offences in 1678-9 were Staley,
26 Nov., and Coleman, 3 Dec. 1678; Ireland and Grove, 24 Jan., Green and
Hill, 21 Feb., and Berry (who died a Protestant) 28 Feb. 1678/9; Pickering,
9 May, Whitebread, Fenwick, Harcourt, Gavan, and Turner—the Five Jesuits
—20 June, and Langhorn, 14 July 1679. See Kenyon, pp. 99, 115, 144, 146,
153, 167.

278-85.   Cf. Fletcher, *Locusts*, I.xxxviii: 'let / Our Iudge fall short ... /
Let heaven want vengeance, hell want punishment / To give our dues'.

282-5.   Cf. Sylla's speech, Jonson, *Catiline*, I.70-2:
           ... *Furies*, upon you, for *Furies* call.
           Whilst, what you doe, may strike them into feares,
           Or make them grieve, and wish your mischiefe theirs.
For ll. 282 f., see Appendix III (R197, 'a ghost ...'), quoting Settle,
Empress of Morocco, and with ll. 284 f. cf. ibid., IV.i, p. 36:
           ... search but my Soul
           There ye Infernal Furies read a scrowl
           Of Deeds which you want Courage to Invent
           Of which Hells Legends want a President [*sc*. Precedent].

Satyr III: Loyola's Will

This third satire was probably composed towards the end of the summer, 1679.
Notes on Ignatius Loyola, made in preparation for it, fill the margins of the
draft letter (R166) dated 'Rygate, June 3, 1679'. It was still no more than
half-written at some date after mid-July. A list of 'Heads yet untouch'd'
(R196: see Appendix III) contains a virtual quotation from *The Excommunicated
Prince* (1679), an unacted play which bears Bedloe's appointment, 16 July, of
four publishers to print it. Some of the 'Heads' are 'touch'd' in ll. 315,
321-4, 345, 428, 596 (see nn.); so these must be subsequent to the list. The
satire must have been completed in time for 'Ignatius His Image' to follow
before the end of the year.

1-4. For Oldham's n. on Loyola's career, see Appendix III (R166). At Loyola's
death the Society of Jesus 'numbered thirteen provinces, exclusive of the
Roman' (Ranke, i.182). Seven belonged to Spain, Portugal, and their colonies,
and three to Italy; hence l. 4.

2. *Fratermitie's*. 1682 mistakenly extrudes the 'e'; the drafts (R164, 184)
have 'Fraternity's'.

5. *Laden with Years, and Sins*: almost verbatim from Donne; see Appendix III
(R176).

17-19. Cf. Cowley, 'Davideis', Lucifer's council (*Poems*, p. 245):
              A Troop of gastly *Fiends* compass him round,
              And greedily catch at his lips fear'd sound.
The debt is clearer still on R184, which has 'catch' for 'wait', and 'Lucifer' for 'Monarch'.

20 f.; 27, 30. Cf. 'The Desk', ll. 163 ff., 48, 182.

21. *the Wish'd Assembly*. Apparently Oldham once intended to name individual
Jesuits; see Appendix III (R164). According to L[ewis] O[wen], *Speculum
Jesuiticum* (1629), p. 37, Loyola saw 'Hosius' ascend to heaven and believed that Codurius had been seen 'in company of many heauenly Angels'. See
also 'Jesuits IV', ll. 35 f., n.

24-9. Cf. Lucan, *Pharsalia*, v.165-96, esp. 190-3. R168 has 'Mithridates p. 3.'
The reference is to p. 2 of Lee's *Mithridates* (1678), I.i:
              And as at *Delphos*, when the glorious Fury
              Kindles the Blood of the Prophetick Maid....
Cf. also ibid., p. 8:
              A Prophesying Priest, with start-up Hair,
              With rolling Eyes, and Nostrils wide as Mouths ...
and Lucifer's council in Cowley's 'Davideis' (*Poems*, p. 245):
              Thrice did he knock his Iron teeth, thrice howl ...
              His eyes dart forth red flames....

32 f. In Fletcher, *Locusts* (IV.xviii) also, the cause of the Roman church is
declining and the Jesuits are its last support:
              Though Dominick, and Loiola now sustaine
              The Lateran Church, with age it stoopes, and noddes....
Cf. II.xxxiii; and for 'band' and 'I ... have chose', II.xxvii and V.iii.

36 f. *mad German ... Genevah's Rebel ... the ... Swiss*: Luther, Calvin, and
Zwingli.

42 f. According to Foulis (p. 36), Bellarmine told 'the Pope that *he had no
limits or bounds in the whole world, but those which the world it self had*'.

51. *Th'incestuous Monk*: Luther; he married a nun, his *sister* in Christ.

52 f. On 15 May, 1213, King John made over his kingdom to the Holy See to be held as a fief for a rent of 1,000 marks. Cf. Foulis, p. 278.

54 f. That Catholic rule, restored, would mean resumption of former abbey lands was reiterated in current polemic. Cf. 'Horace I.ix', 1. 19; Junius Brutus, pseud. [Charles Blount], *An Appeal from the Country to the City* (1679), p. 8; Burnet, ii.215; Dryden, Pref. to *Religio Laici*, ll. 161-4. Possible resumption had aroused great apprehension under Mary Tudor (Ranke, i.201, 203, 211-14).

65. *Universal Ghostly Monarchy*: world-hegemony, claimed by the speaker to rest on spiritual authority. 'Universal Monarchy', a favourite term with Oldham, was a recognized one. Cf. Jeremy Taylor, *XXVIII Sermons* (1651), p. 229: 'Suppose a man lord of all this world, an universal Monarchy, as some princes have lately designed'- E.[viz. I.] Tonge, *The Northern Star ... or the Northern the Fourth Universal Monarchy* (1680); and Oldham's Jonson ode, 1. 182, 'Dithyrambique', 1. 50, 'Upon the Marriage', 1. 66, 'Sardanapalus', 1. 35, and nn.

76-9. Cf. Buchanan, *Franciscanus*, p. 260:
      Cur ego vos ... amicis
      Non monitis horter? digressum & pauca sub ipsum
      Edoceam? ...
      Huc animos juvenes certatim advertite, & acri
      Mente Seraphinae mysteria discite sectae.

83. See 1. 130 n., below.

84 ff. Cf. Fletcher's baker's dozen of monstrous Popes, *Locusts*, III.xxxiv-ix and his nn.

84 f. Cf. Fletcher, *Locusts*, IV.iii:
      ... a chayre, farre fetch't from Dodon ground.
      Thence without feare of errour they define ...
and G. Hall, p. 76: 'But let them have been Devils incarnate elsewhere, yet if they be once set in the holy Chair no error in judgement of faith dare offer to fasten upon them.' The 'punk' is the legendary Pope Joan, who 'played her part as laudably as the greatest of their learned Doctors; and all because she sat in the same chair of Papal Office ... though she left some blurr upon her honesty' (p. 80).

85. *a Fiend*. Fletcher refers to 'Sylvester II and many others' 'Studied in ... black art' as 'incarnate fiends' (*Locusts*, III.xxxviii). Oldham may further have in mind the belief (Dante, *Inferno*, XXXIII.121-33) that before death the soul may be in hell, and the body animated by a demon.

88-96. Of these crimes which do not annul a Pope's character as His Holiness, Oldham drew the majority from G. Hall, Foulis, and Fletcher. Hall (p. 80) tells of Pope Marcellinus's idol-worship and (pp. 81 f.) quotes the 'blasphemous slander' repeated by Pico della Mirandola, about a Pope who confessed to a servant 'that even whiles he held the Papal See ... he believed there was no God at all', and another Pope who admitted 'that the immortality of the soul was not believed by him'. Cf. further ibid., pp. 75 f.: 'Yea, let [the Pope] be an arrant Conjuror.... Let him be as perjured an impostor and as shamelessly incestuous as Alexander VI'. In Fletcher (*Locusts*, III. xxxvi, xxxviii f. and nn.) Leo X is an atheist, John XXII and XXIII blasphemers, Sylvester II a black magician, and Alexander VI, Lucrezia Borgia's father, husband, and brother. Foulis (pp. 328 f.) refers to Alexander VI's poisonings, and declares 'all the *Roman* Historians themselves ... confess him to have been a Monster among men'. He discusses (pp. 144 ff.) the

simoniacal elections of Alexander VI and Sixtus V, comments upon the complicity of Sixtus IV in a sacrilegious murder, and quotes Cornelius Agrippa
as saying 'That he built at *Rome* a very famous Bawdy-house'. From these
sources Oldham derives 'Heathen', 'Atheist', 'Magician', 'Perjured', 'Blaspheamer', 'Pois'ner', 'Monster', 'Sacrilegious', 'Bawd', and 'Simony'.

99 f. Cf. Buchanan's account (p. 258) of the magical effect of becoming a
friar:

> ... erit subito doctus, sapiens, & honestus
> Et gravis, & prudens: jam de balatrone modestus
> De lenone pudens, & de latrone severus,
> Et frater superûm, & coeli pene insitus aulae.

103. f. Cf. Foulis, p. 33: '*Bernardus Justinianus*, Agent from the *Venetians*,
assured Pope *Paul* the Second that *he could damn and save whom he pleased*.'

105 ff. See Foulis (p. 251) for 'that fond Rule in Bellarmine, that ... whom
he [the Pope] declares a Saint, must of consequence be in Heaven, though he
were in Hell before'.

110. 'Rage' is evidently a verb. R197 has 'Whom when Gout or Stone afflicts,
shall curse', with 'fit of rage' in the margin.

114. *Pantofle*. Foulis, p. 162, has this proper term for the Pope's slipper.
OED cites Oldham's and Burnet's usage (the 'ceremony of the pantoufle') as
'somewhat alien or historical in tone'.

115 ff. The Pope's commands are 'esteem'd as authentick as the Word of God,
or Holy Scriptures themselves' (Foulis, c4^V).

116, 123. 'The Holy Scriptures ... must ... not be credited or trusted to.'
(Foulis, c4^V.)

118. Cf. G. Hall, p. 45: 'Have they any such ... faithful Records as the
golden legend, *John Capgrave* [&c.] which perhaps the Hereticks and some ill-
advised friends may slander as lyes, calling them *Miraculorum monstra*, as
Melchior Canus did'. The Italian, Jacobus de Voragine (*c.*1230-98) compiled
the *Legenda Aurea* (properly, *Historia lombardica, seu Legenda Sanctorum*).
Capgrave (1393-1464), Provincial of the Friars Hermits, was reputed author
of the *Nova Legenda Angliae*, though it was not even extensively revised by
him.

119. *Amadis de Gaul*: a Spanish romance, a favourite with Loyola.

120 f. Cf. Foulis, p. 33: 'the Papal *decretal Letters* ... they say are to be
numbered amongst the Canonical Scriptures'.

123 f. Cf. Foulis, p. 37: 'Albizzi ... told two Cordeliers, that the Gospel
would not be the Gospel, if the Pope had not approved of it'; and G. Hall,
p. 90 (citing Bishop Jewel): 'the Pope may dispense (saith one) against
Pauls Epistles; against the new Testament, saith another; against both Old
and New Testament, saith a third ... of wrong he can make right ... saith a
sixth'. On R195 the echo extends to a line which precedes 1. 123: 'Again
think Moses fable if he please'.

124. *Black White, and Vertue Vice*. Cf. Foulis d1^r, and pp. 33 f., 36. He
cites Loyola's 'Rule of Obedience': '*If the Church affirm that to be black,
which our own eyes judge to be white, we ought also then to declare that it
is black*'; and Bellarmine: 'If the Pope should err, in commanding Vices or
prohibiting Vertues, then is the Church obliged to believe that Vices are
good, and Vertues are evil.'

127. *Euclid*. Cf. Foulis, p. 36: '[The Pope] *is the Cause of Causes, and can
declare square things to be round*.'

128 f. Cf. (in Foulis, d1^V) Tindal's hard-pressed antagonist, who 'burst out
—*We had better be without Gods Laws then the Popes.*'

130. *Missions*. Cf. Heylyn, I, fol. 93^r: 'To the three vows of *Poverty, Obedience*, and *Chastitie* ... *Ignatius* ... added the Vow of *Mission*: whereby his
followers are bound to obey their *Generall*, or the Pope, without demanding
any reason, in all dangerous or hazardous attempts whatsoever, whether it
be undertaking some tedious voyage for the propagation of the *Romish* Religion,
or the massacring of any Prince whose life is a hindrance to their proceedings.' See Ranke, i.152: 'They superadded the special obligation "to perform
whatsoever the reigning pontiff should command them, to go forth into all
lands, wherever he might please to send them, without ... delay".'

130-42. Cf. Burton, *Anatomy*, p. 650: 'What makes them so freely venture their
lives, to leave their native countries, to go seek martyrdome in the *Indies*,
but superstition?' Cf. also 'Jesuits II', ll. 53 ff.

133. *Bantam*. In western Java. It was in Portuguese hands and therefore a
field for Jesuit missionaries at the time of Loyola's death. It fell to the
Dutch in 1595.

136 f., 141. Cf. Fletcher, *Locusts*, II.xxxvii: 'Venter life, limbe, through
earth, and water fly / To winne us Proselytes?'

137. *Like great Xavier's*. St Francis Xavier (1506-52), one of Loyola's first
two disciples, apostle of the East Indies. Oldham read the account of his
mission in Varenius: see Appendix III (R166, 196). For Xavier's belief that
the Japanese religion was similar in certain respects to the Catholic, see
Appendix III (R196, 'Comites Xaverii ...' and n.).

140. *Burning Line*. On Xavier's outward voyage he twice crossed the Equator.

142. See Appendix III (R197, 'Religion do you frown ...' and n.) for a link
with Dryden, *Indian Emperour*.

145. Cf. Fletcher, *Locusts*, III.xiv: 'some learne of th' Inquisition / To
finde new torments, and unused paines', echoed in 'Jesuits II', l. 282. Cf.
also G. Hall: see Appendix III (R196, 'Sanbenito ...' and n.).

147 f. Cf. Foulis, p. 416: 'Must *Campo Flori* in *Rome* smoak by the burnt
bodies of people by the Authority of the Pope, in this acting onely as a
Secular Prince' (not ecclesiastical).

150. Cf. Milton's famous sonnet, and the diplomatic appeals and protests
dispatched by Cromwell, which as Latin Secretary Milton composed. See further Appendix III (R169).

153 f. See Appendix III, R265 ('storms borrow ...' and 'Ill kill ...') for
use of Dryden and Lee.

155. Cf. Dryden, cited Appendix III (R197, 'burn, ravish ...' and n.).

157. *Mufty*: the head of the ecclesiastical order among the Muslims. Protestants were fond of coupling Rome with Islam as powers hostile to Christianity, each priest-ridden and under despotic leadership. Cf. 'Jesuits II',
ll. 50 f., and n.; and *A Second Consultation between the Pope and the Turk
concerning the propagation of the Catholick Faith* (1679; licensed Jan.
1678/79); the Pope makes overtures (which the Turk rejects) for an alliance
against his Protestant heretics: 'If *Universal Monarchy* / You do receive
from me / The *Universal Pastor* I / May be allow'd to be.'

182 ff. Cf. Buchanan, *Franciscanus*, p. 257:
           Adjice praeterea quos praeceps alea nudat,
           Quos Venus enervat, quos & potatio pernox
           Ejecit patriis laribus, quos urget egestas

> Et quibus haudquaquam res sunt in amore secundae, ...
> Quos scelus infamat ...
> Huc, velut ad tutum cunctis est cursus asylum.
> Hoc procerum è numero crescit generosa propago
> Funigeri gregis: hi patres ...
> Quos metus, ira, furor, mens tarda, ignavia, crimen,
> Ambitio, res adversae, fastidia vitae, ...
> Et mendax virtutis amor, collegit in unum.

Cf. G. Hall's quotation of Caesarius Branchidorus (p. 25).

185. Cf. Fletcher, *Locusts*, IV.xxi:
> Trade we with ...
> Those who disgrac't by some misgovernence
> (Their owne or others) swell with griefe or spight.

200 f. Alluding to Romulus and Mahomet. Cf. Livy's account of Romulus's courting of the mob (I.viii), and Heylyn, III.121-2, which describes how after Mahomet had produced 'some parts of his *Alcoran* ... he next proclaimed Liberty to all Slaves and Servants ... which drew unto him such a rabble of unruly people, that without fear or opposition, he dispersed his Doctrines'.

202 f. Cf. Buchanan, *Franciscanus*, p. 257:
> ... Francisci in syrmate fune
> Cingimur, & tanquam pariter cum vertice radi
> Mens etiam scelerata queat: de sacrilegis &
> De parricidis, de furibus, atque cinaedis,
> Nos faciat coeli subitos rasura colonos.

204-13. Cf. Buchanan, *Franciscanus*, p. 266:
> Primum iter ingressus tenerum de fronte pudorem
> Excute: nec vacuae est unquam pudor utilis alvo,
> Nec decet audacem nisi ficta modestia scurram.
> Quod si naturae vitio male firma ruborem
> Frons trahit, & subitas confundit purpura malas,
> Tum tibi vel frictus, vel Bacchi largior usus,
> Curaque & assiduae meditatio garrula rixae
> Durabit solidum rubicunda per ora cruorem.

220. Cf. Alexander Cooke, *Pope Joan* (1625), pp. 8-9: 'the chaires of Porphyry, wherein they say the Pope is tried whether he be a man or no man' to prevent a repetition of the imposture of Pope Joan.

223-36. Cf. Burton, *Anatomy*, pp. 645-7: 'Polititians, ... make Religion meer policie, a cloak, a humane invention; *nihil aeque valet ad regendos vulgi animos ac superstitio* ... they invent new religions, ceremonies, as so many stalking horses to their own ends.... Next to Polititians, if I may distinguish them, are some of our priests, (who make Religion Policy).'

231 f. Indebted to Settle; see Appendix III (R193).

242 f. Cf. Lee, *Mithridates* (1678), III.ii, p. 28:
> ... Oh, feeble Virtue! Hence,
> I blow thee from the Palace to the Cottage....

249 ff. Cf. Ranke, i.153, 177: '... the Society of Jesus ... was a company of clerks regular ... but the members were nevertheless broadly distinguished from those of other congregations.... the Jesuits ... dispensed entirely with the monastic habit, exempted themselves from all those devotional exercises in common, by which so much time is occupied in convents. ... The members severally were also enjoined to avoid excess in their religious exercises: they were not to weaken themselves by fastings, vigils or castigations, ... In labour, also, moderation was commanded.'

251. G. Hall (p. 67) refers to the 'self-afflicting Capuchine'. Heylyn (I,
fol. 92^v) refers to the Capuchins as being 'bound by their Rule to spend
their time in prayer; and ... generally thought to be the devoutest of all
the Orders *Monastical*'. The Carthusians 'eat no flesh, live by couples,
labour with their hands, watch, pray, and never meet together but on Sun-
daies'. The Cordeliers (or Franciscans) 'are bound to profess absolute
beggery, and are not permitted to carry any money about them, or more vic-
tuals than will for the present serve themselves and their Brethren'.

257. Cf. Heylyn, I, fol. 93^r: 'the severest kind of *Recluse* ... is the *Ana-
choret*, or *Anchoret*, so called ... because they use to live retired from
company. They are kept in a close place, where they must dig their graves
with their nails; badly clad, and worse dieted.'

261 ff. Ranke (ii.425, 428) describes the decline of the Jesuits' 'severe
practices of private devotion' during the 17th century. Oliva, the vicar
of the Society 'was a man who loved external tranquillity and the luxuries
of life', and whose 'apartments ... were arranged with the most refined
attention to comfort'. Oldham treats a later abuse as inherent in the first
principles of the Society.

268. Aulus Vitellius, emperor, Apr. —Dec. AD 69. See Suetonius, *De Vita
Caesarum* (VII-VIII, ed. G.W. Mooney, p. 107). Notorious glutton and gour-
met, in a vast platter he used to mingle flamingoes' tongues, scarfishes'
livers, lampreys' guts, and the brains of pheasants and peacocks.

275 f. Cf. Buchanan, *Franciscanus*, p. 268:
          Frigida tu Christi, & comitum praecepta severis
          Linque scholis.

280 ff. For the Cainani, who worshipped Judas, see 'Jesuits II', 1. 151 n.

284. Cf. *Rival Queens* (1677), IV.i, p. 43 [really 45]: Roxana (says Cassan-
dra) 'scorns to sin / Beneath a God'.

287-92. Cf. Buchanan, *Franciscanus*, p. 261:
          Nec tamen aetatis, nec te discrimina sexus
          Praetereant. Primae quoniam lanuginis aetas
          In Venerem est praeceps, lucris addicta senectus ...
          Vana superstitio mentes exercet aniles....

297. *Surius*. Cf. Cowley, *A Satyre. The Puritan and the Papist* (1643), *Essays*,
p. 151:
               Not all the *Legends* of the *Saints* of old
               Not vast *Baronius*, nor sly *Surius* hold
               Such plenty of apparent *Lies*....
Laurentius Surius (1522-78) was a German Carthusian and hagiographer, who
published in six folio volumes (Cologne, 1570-77) *De Probatis Sanctorum
Historiis ab A: Lipomano olim conscriptîs nunc primum a Laur. Surio emen-
datis et auctis.*

297 f. *Talmud ... Alcoran*. Cf. Burton, *Anatomy*, p. 663: 'such gross fictions'
as 'the *Turkes* Alcaron, the *Iewes* Talmud, and Papists Golden Legend', one
would swear 'could never proceed from any other spirit, than that of the
divell himself, which is the Author of confusion and lies'. St Francis'
Alcoran is *L'Alcoran des Cordeliers*; Foulis (p. 2, n.g.) cites a version
'*tant en Latin qu'en François*', 1556. If the English translation, *The
Alcoran of the Franciscans* (1679), appeared before the present lines were
written, they may refer to it specifically.

303 f. Cf. Foulis, p. 8 f.: ''Tis no great honour to her, that they tell us,
she was so familiar with some men, as to come down from Heaven to be

marryed to them.... But because there is few satisfied with a bare Marriage, they will have her to be much given to kissing too.' St Ignatius,
bishop of Antioch, was said to have exchanged letters with the Virgin, who
promised to visit him, with St John, in order to confirm him in the faith:
see *The Golden Legend* III.16, 19. And cf. *The Alcoran of the Franciscans*
(1679), p. 2: 'Whilst he was in prayer to the Virgin ... The Virgin her
self in a most beautiful manner appeared to him, and gave up her self to
be held and kist in the arms of St. *Francis* from the beginning of the night
till day.'

305 f. Cf. *The Golden Legend*, IV.242: 'When the Duke of Normandy had assieged
the city of Chartres, the bishop of the city took the coat of our Lady and
set it on the head of a spear like a banner and went out against the enemy
surely, and the people followed him. And anon all the host of the enemies
were turned into frenzy.

306. *twelve Score*: twelve score paces; long range for accurate archery. See
2 Henry IV, III.ii.41-5.

307 f. Cf. Foulis, p. 26: 'a great shoal of Fishes held their heads out of
the Water ... to hear Fryar *Anthonies* Sermon', after which 'some of them
open'd their mouths, others bow'd down their heads, whilst others hum'd
him; and then departed with a great deal of comfort'. Cf. *The Alcoran of
the Franciscans* (1679), p. 52. G. Hall, p. 41, yields a hint for fish
caught: 'if *St. Tony* had wheedled these devout animals into a net, and
pickled them up ... had [it] not been a breach of trust[?]'.

310, 311 f., 313 f. Cf. Foulis, p. 26: 'a Sheep bleated and kneel'd before
the Altar; And the story saith, that the stones answered *Amen*, to blind
Venerable *Bedes* Sermon'; and p. 27: 'A Womans Bees not thriving, ... she
steals a consecrated Wafer, and placeth it in one of her Hives, hoping it
would drive away the disease, and bless all their undertakings. The devout
Bees, in honour of such a sacred Guest, fall to Work, and with their Honey-
combs, make a pretty little *Church* with *Windows*, a Covering or *Roof*, with
a *Door*, a *Belfrey*, I and an *Altar* too, upon which they had laid the Hoast,
about which they continually flew, and by their Humming prais'd the Lord.
A pretty company of Catholicks, and a notable Argument for *Transubstantiation.*'

315 f. Cf. G. Hall, p. 38: 'The Abby of *Fusniack* was horribly infested with
flyes; *Excommunico eas*, said the holy Abbot of *Clarevall*; on the next morning those noysome guests are found all dead in the floor.' The story appears
in full in the Bollandist account of St Bernard (*Acta Sanctorum*, August,
iv.272). Oldham's 'Fly-Flap' comes from Joseph Hall (*Virgidemiarum*, IV.vii),
who gibes at a lazy acolyte defending the chalice from a devout fly 'With
a broad fly-flap of a peacock's tail'. For two other legends Oldham thought
of introducing here, see Appendix III (R173 and R196, 'St. Nicholas sucking' and n.).

317 f. Cf. Foulis, p. 23: 'But I believe the Turks are not so good at fly-
ing, as some of our Saints are; for *Antonius* got from *Padoa* in *Italy*, to
Lisborn in *Portugal* in one night, and the next night home again. And *Ignatius Loyola* in a moment whisk'd from Rome to Colen.'

318. *Lapland witch*. Cf. Butler, *Hudibras*, III.i.411 f.:
                      ... mounted on a Broom, the Nag
                      And Hackney of a Lapland Hag.

319 f. Cf. Foulis, p. 23: 'a *German Dominican* did but lay his Cowl upon the
waters, set his feet on it, and so slipt over a broad River very cleverly.
... Thus *Fransois de Paula* using his Coat or Cowl instead of a Ship, ...
passed gallantly over the *Sicilian* waves.'

321-4. On Xavier's 'Wonders' (miracles) see Appendix III (R196), and for the
crab, ibid., and *Joannis Eusebii Nierembergii* ... *Historia Naturae* (1635),
p. 14: 'S. Xauerio effigiem Christi crucifixi, quam in mare sedandum miserat,
cancer restituit.' Fausto Rodriguez testified (see Bouhours, *Life of Xavier*,
tr. Dryden, p. 223) that this miracle took place at Baranura in the Moluccas.
Stories abound of storms quelled by Xavier, but in none I have found does he
employ the sacred wafer.

327-42. Cf. Buchanan, *Franciscanus*, p. 270:
>   Illa tamen patribus seges olim uberrima nostris
>   Fingere nocturnos lemures, manesque vagantes
>   Lustrali composcere aqua, magicisque susurris,
>   Frigida nunc tota est: postquam nasuta juventus
>   Pectora crassorum male credula ridet avorum....

327-30. Cf. *The Last Sayings* ... *of Mr. Thomas Hobbes* ... (1680): 'For Fairies
and walking Ghosts, I think that opinion is taught only to keep in credit
the use of Exorcisms, Crosses, and Holy-Water, to lay those Spirits which
never were raised.'

330. Salenger is Sellinger's, or St Leger's, Round, an old English dance.

333 f. This story from Erasmus' *Epistolarum* ... *Libri XXXI* is translated by
Lewes Lavater, *Of Ghostes And Spirites Walking By Night* (1572), ed. Dover
Wilson and May Yardley, p. 43: '... this Priest vpon Ester eue, put lyue
crabs priuely into ye churchyard, hauing wax candles on light cleauing to
their sides: which when they crauled amongst the graues, seemed to be suche
a terrible sighte, that no man durst approch neere them. Hereof rose a fear-
full reporte, wherewith all men being amazed, the priest declareth to y^e
people in the pulpit, that they were ye soules of dead men which desired to
be deliuered out of their torments by Masses and almes deeds.' 'White Sheets'
in l. 331 probably alludes to another imposture related by Lavater, loc.
cit., from the same source.

340. *Hecla* ... *Mongibel*: the principal volcano of Iceland, and another name
of Etna. Cf. Heylyn, III.133 f.: 'Stranger things are not spoken of *Aetna*
... and here [Iceland] the superstitious people have the same opinion which
they have in *Sicil*: that underneath must needs be hell, and the habitations
of the damned. But to judicious men the naturall reason of these flames is
plain and obvious.'

340. *Patricks hole*. For the 'cheat of St Patrick's little hole', Foulis (c3^v)
refers to Bp. Henry Jones, *Saint Patricks Purgatory* (1647). According to
the legend (first recorded, apparently, by Henry of Saltry, *fl.* 1140), a
deep pit, in which the pains of purgatory were miraculously set forth to
view for the edification of the Irish, had opened at the intercession either
of the great St Patrick or of an abbot of the same name. It was situated on
an island near the source of the Liffey, and was enclosed in a vault 16½
feet long by 2 feet 1 inch wide. In 1497 Rome ordered it, though formerly
served by the clergy, to be demolished as superstitious; but it was revived.
It was again demolished by Order in Council in 1632.

341 f. Cf. Buchanan, *Franciscanus*, p. 271:
>   Sed tamen hoc aevo temere miracula fingi
>   Noluerim, nisi monticolas inter crassosque
>   Pastores.

Loyola died at Rome: to which l. 342 will thus refer.

343-50. Cf. Buchanan, *Franciscanus*, pp. 272 f.:
>   ... Quapropter moneo dehinc fingite parce
>   Somnia, nocturnos lemures, miracula, nî fors
>   Aut apud extremos fieri dicantur Iberos,

> Americosve, aut Aethiopias, calidove sub axe,
> Et caput ignotis ubi Nilus condit arenis
> Unde aderit nemo, qui testis dicta refutet.

and see Burton, *Anatomy*, p. 881: 'Now for visions, revelations, miracles, not only out of the Legend, out of purgatory, but every day comes news from the Indies, and at home, read the Jesuits' Letters.' See further Appendix III (R196, 'Jos. Anchieta' and n.).

345 f. Cf. *Life of Ignatius*, pp. 327 f.: 'in Brasil ... Goa ... Malucas ... and in the kingdomes of Mogor, and Pegù ... our Fathers are resident (to omit, as more known, the firme lād Perù ...)'.

351 ff. Cf. Buchanan, *Franciscanus*, p. 260:

> Sancta quidem certis fulcitur secta columnis,
> E quibus in primis locuples confessio largo
> Proventu est, gnavum non deceptura colonum:
> ... unica nunquam
> Artifici imponit Confessio callida docto.
> Hoc telo armatus noster se regibus ordo
> Terribilem ostendit....

358. An allusion to Pope Alexander III who 'set his foot upon the Emperours [Barbarossa's] neck' (Foulis, p. 261). Cf. Fletcher, *Locusts*, III.xxxiv: 'that monstrous Prelate, who / Trampled great Fredericks necke with his proud durty shooe', and IV.viii, which may have influenced Oldham's phrasing (italics mine): 'findes for's lordly *foot* no *stool*, but *necks* of Kings'.

360. If this is a reflection on James, Duke of York, it would be the only one in the published *Satyrs*; see Introduction, pp. xxx-xxxii. A rough draft for 'Jesuits I' has 'Let lazy Princes wait, / Till their slow Crowns be given by Fate': see Appendix III (R260). Cf. Henry Savile, 'Advice to a Painter to draw the Duke by' (Marvell, I.217, 421), admonishing Charles:

> Let not thy life and crowne togeather end,
> Destroyd by a false brother, and false friend ...
> See in all ages what examples are
> Of Monarchs murthered by th' Impatient heir.

On the other hand, the adage was commonplace; cf., e.g. Jonson, *Sejanus*, II, ll. 240 f.:

> And princes that will keepe olde dignitie,
> Must not admit too youthfull heires stand by....

367-76. Cf. Buchanan, *Franciscanus*, pp. 260 f.:

> Ergo ...
> ... matrona locum ditissima primus
> Vendicet, aut dulci assuetus danista lucello:
> Proxima mercator teneat loca: tertius ordo
> Nobilium est, quos aut ditat quaesita rapinis
> Praeda, vel innocuo manus oblita sanguine civis
> Reddidit insignes ...
> Sed neque lenonem, nec tu contemne latronem
> Spes modo sit lucri ...
> Det miles praedae partem, furtique latrones....

367. Cf. *Excommunicated Prince*, p. 32: 'Misers unlock their Darling Coffers now.' See 'Jesuits IV', ll. 124 ff., n.

376. *Gabelles*: taxes (not, at this date, the French salt tax).

378. *Becket's and Loretto's Shrine*: St Thomas à Becket's shrine at Canterbury, and Our Lady of Loretto near Ancona in Italy. Cf. Burton, *Anatomy*, p. 649: 'What a deal of mony by musty reliques, Images, Idolatry have their Mass-Priests engrossed ... Lauretum ... S. *Thomas Shrine*, &c. may witness.'

383 f., 390 ff. Buchanan (pp. 264 f.) relates an incident which left a Franciscan and his order discredited, 'Inter inhumani risum & ludibria vulgi',
and continues:
> Sed quid opus toties sese objectare periclis,
> Et non parsurae cuiquam committere famae
> Cum liceat tuto, liceat rumore secundo
> Undique securos Veneris decerpere fructus?

399. Cf. the Epilogue to Dryden's *Spanish Friar* (1681):
> This gains them their whore-converts, and may be
> One reason of the growth of Popery.

Loyola founded an establishment for converted courtesans. See *The Life of
St. Ignatius* (1686), tr. from Bouhours, pp. 182-3.

402-21. Cf. Buchanan, *Franciscanus*, pp. 261 f.:
> Segnior in Venerem siqua est, accende monendo,
> Pande voluptatisque modos, formasque latentes,
> Quaerendoque doce Veneris quem nesciat usum ...
> Interdum tanquam cupias reprehendere luxum
> Vestis, & accensum gemmis quod fulgurat aurum,
> Lacteolas furtim dextra constringe papillas ...
> Et pede tange pedem, dextram dextra, oribus ora:
> Sic, dices, rides, sic molliter oscula jungis;
> Oscula commissas inter luctantia linguas.
> Sic te tractandum praebes, tractataque gaudes,
> Sic pede, sic digito, sic tu promittis ocello
> Hoc loqueris nutu, tali noctem abnuis ore....

423. Pietro Aretino (1492-1556). Though he wrote pious works and five reputable comedies, the allusion to his indecent compositions, such as *Sonnetti
lussuriosi* and *Ragionamenti del Zoppin*, is a commonplace. Cf. 'The Vision',
1. 55.

425-7. Cf. Buchanan, *Franciscanus*, p. 261:
> Talia quaerenti facilem quae commodat aurem,
> Sit licet antiquis magis illa severa Sabinis
> Nosse volet, notum, quod posse juvare putabit.

428. *Carnaval*. Cf. G. Hall, p. 19: 'They have their Jovial (which some
sowre Cynick would call licentious) *Carneval* ... each man striving to out-
go other in strange prancks of humorous debauchednesse.' See Appendix III
(R196, 'Carnevals').

433. Caius Petronius (d. 66 BC), Nero's courtier, *arbiter elegantiae*, and
the author of the *Satyricon*.

435-41. Cf. Buchanan, *Franciscanus*, p. 262 f.:
> O mihi si calido ferveret corpore sanguis
> Integer ... !
> Nunc quoniam haec nobis invidit serior aetas
> Commoda, & effoetis membris ignava voluptas,
> Vestrum opus hoc, juvenes, vestra haec vindemia....

435 ff. In his youth, says Fr. Polanco, SJ, who later became his secretary,
'He was free in making love to women.'

443 f. Cf. Buchanan, *Franciscanus*, p. 266:
> Sed me praeteritae suavissima mentio vitae
> Longius ac volui tenuit.

447 f., 457 f. Cf. Buchanan, *Franciscanus*, p. 262:
> Grande scelus levibus contentus plectere poenis.
> Nec precibus longis lacrymisve piacula dele

>   Horrida, sed nummis loculos, non pectora fraude
>   Exhauri, vel templa jube, vel claustra, vel aras
>   Extruat, aut multis redimat jejunia Missis.

453. *Compostella*. The shrine of St James at Compostella in Galicia, like that of Our Lady at Monserrat, was a famous place of pilgrimage.

457. To expiate her murder of King Edward her stepson (AD 979), Elfrida 'built two Nunneries, *Almesbury* in *Wiltshire* and *Warwell* in Hampshire. An easie way of recompence for rich people, to ease themselves of the most crying sins' (Foulis, p. 207).

459-68. Cf. G. Hall, p. 73: 'I like not these severe & cruel Taskmasters, which make the way to Heaven more strait and difficult then it is ... and is not this a more easie and pleasing way to glory, trow we ...?' Buchanan's *Franciscanus* (p. 266) disclaims for the neophytes the route 'per Aristotelis spineta asperrima'; 'commodius patefiet iter', he assures them.

460-2. *make the paths ... Heavn's joys*. Pascal, *Lettres* (no. 9), pp. 133 f., has his Jesuit spokesman explain that 'les gens du monde sont ... détournés de la dévotion' because 'on lui a associé la douleur et le travail', and therefore 'nous avons cru qu'il étoit d'une extrême importance de détruire ce premier obstacle': hence Fr. Le Moine's *La Dévotion aisée* and its well-deserved success. Pascal (pp. 134-45) goes on to show how the Jesuits excuse vanity, ambition, avarice, sloth, gluttony, lying, etc. See also Ogg, *Europe*, p. 344.

466. *Purlieus*: a deafforested tract, no longer subject to most forest laws; hence 'a place where one has the right to range at large' (*OED*).

467. In the 1681 version, the syntax was awkward, and though the simplification is not beyond the powers of an unauthorized corrector, it is reasonable, given Oldham's undoubted revisions in 1682, to believe it his.

469-71. Cf. Pascal, *Lettres* (no. 7), pp. 92-4: his Jesuit spokesman dwells on 'l'importance ... dans notre morale' of 'ce principe merveilleux ... notre méthode de *diriger l'intention* [qui] consiste à se proposer pour fin de ses actions un objet permis ... nous corrigeons le vice du moyen par la pureté de la fin ... et vous avez vu ... que ceux qui donnent de l'argent pour des bénéfices seroient de véritables simoniaques sans un pareille diversion'. Cf. also pp. 80 f.

474. *Sooth up*. Cf. Etherege *The Man of Mode* (1676), III.ii.144 f.: 'Do not you fall on him, *Medley*, and snub him. Sooth him up in his extravagance!'

474 f. Cf. *A Truth known to very Few: vizt. That the Jesuites are down-right compleat Atheists* [i.e. Pelagians] ... (1680). Cf. also Juvenal, XIII.86-8.

476-85. Cf. Pascal, *Lettres* (nos. 7 and 8), pp. 94, 113 f.. 119, 121. His Jesuit spokesman complacently reports the means found by 'the casuists 'nos pères', especially Lessius, Éscobar, and Bauny,: to exonerate men and women guilty of theft, homicide, usury, and prostitution. 'L'usage de certaines paroles' renders a loan not usurious; 'une nécessité grave, quoique non pas extrême' excuses robbery; the 'désir de défendre son honneur', homicide, even though 'vengeance' be the unavowed motive (cf. 1. 477). The hired murderer and the prostitute may keep their gains, for 'les biens gagnés par des crimes peuvent être légitimement retenus'.

491-502. Cf. Dryden, *Religio Laici* (1681), 11. 370-97.

491, 497-500. Cf. Fletcher, *Locusts*, I.xxiv: 'that sacred word (Lockt up by Rome) breakes prison ... / Speakes every tongue'. G. Hall, p. 70, ironically praises the Catholic Church for not only discouraging 'Lay persons ... to read the Sacred Scripture, but absolutely forbidding the use of them in

their native Languages, upon no small penalty ... lest they should understand and trouble their heads about it.' Cf. below, ll. 519 f., nn., and
'Jesuits I', l. 108.

493 f. See 'Jesuits II', ll. 270-3, and Appendix III (R284). Introducing the
passage there quoted, G. Hall writes: 'it hath always been found dangerous
to let the Vulgar know too much; since knowledge is an edge tool, which
unskilfull hands ... are ... apt to wound themselves [with].'

496. *Bacon*: Roger Bacon (?1214-94), philosopher and mechanician. For his
popular reputation as a 'conjurer' (magician), even up to the 17th century,
cf. Foulis (p. 109), and besides Robert Greene's famous play, such chapbooks as *The History of Frier Bacon* (1683), and *The three Famous Conjurers,
Fryer Bacon, Bongey, and Vandermast* (n.d.), and also *Frier Bacon His Discovery Of The Miracles of Art, Nature, And Magick ... translated out of
D*[r]*. Dees own Copy by T. M.* (1659).

496. *Haly and Albumazar*. As with the Bacon of the chapbooks, it is to their
popular reputation Oldham alludes. They were household words, because
quoted as authorities in astrological almanacs; e.g. John Gadbury's for
1666, and William Lilly's for 1668 and 1669. Oldham has them also in the
'Character of an Ugly Old P---', where the third member of the trio is 'the
Spirit *Fircu* in the Fortune book'; popular literature—almanacs, chapbooks,
fortune-books—is the context in which he thinks of them. Astrology was
commonly associated with necromancy, but the association may have been
strengthened through an Albumazar who *was* depicted as a wizard, the 'hero'
of Tompkis's *Albumazar* (1615), revived Feb. 1668 with a prologue by Dryden
which mistakenly claimed it as the original of Jonson's *Alchemist*. Histori-
cally, Albumazar is Abou-Maschar Djafar ibn Mohammed (?776-884) the celebrated Arab astronomer: known in Christendom by a treatise attr. to him
and translated in the 15th century as *Flores astrologiae*. Among various
Halys, the great astrological authority is Haly Abenragel (early 11th century); Sir Christopher Heydon, for example, in *A Defence of Judiciall
Astrology* (1603), p. 165, quoted as from 'Haly' a passage found on p. 297
of *Albohazen Haly Filii Abenragel, Scriptoris Arabici, De Judiciis Astrorum
Libri Octo* (1571). Chaucer's Haly, says Phyllis Hodgson (*General Prologue
...* (1969), p. 218), is possibly Hali ibn el Abbas (d. 904), Persian physician.

502. *Sorbonne*. The theological faculty of the University of Paris; perti-
nently described on the title-page of *A Truth Known to very Few* (1680) as
*the Famous Faculty of Sorbonne, well-known to be the best Divines of all
the Roman Catholick Party*, between whom and the Jesuits there was no love
lost.

503. *Soveraign Prelate*: the Pope is 'Sovereign Priest' where in Dryden's
Indian Emperour the Spaniards assert his supremacy over kings: see Appendix
III (R183, 197).

504. Cf. Rochester, 'A Satyr against ... Mankind', l. 219: 'And, with the
rabble world, their laws obey.'

505-8. Cf. Foulis, p. 38, on what is laid down for an Emperor when being
crowned by a Pope: '*he is* ... *to kneel and worship him bare-headed; then
to approach nearer and kiss his feet*'; after coronation, '*to hold the
Stirrop till his Holiness mounts* ... and then like a Lackey' to lead the
horse '*some way by the Reins*'. But 'if there be *two Kings* present, then
... *one of them on his Right-side, the other on his Left, must lead his
Palfrey along by the Bridle*'. For instances, see ibid., pp. 181, 227, 253,
255, 259, 260, 299.

515. Peter Lombard (d. *c*.1160), Italian theologian, author of commentaries
on the Psalms, sometimes called *Magna Glossa*, and on the harmony of the
four Gospels. G. Hall (p. 55) calls him 'the great Master of Sentences' in
allusion to his *Sententiarum libri IV*.

512 f. Cf. Dryden, *Religio Laici* (1681), ll. 400 f., 407 f.

519-36. Cf. Buchanan, *Franciscanus*, pp. 269-70:

> Tarsensis fuge scripta senis, fuge toxica nostri
> Ordinis. O primis utinam periisset in annis!
> Aut mansisset adhuc hostis licet, ante renatus
> Vivisica quam lympha esset! tam multa dedisset
> Funera grassatus ferro, ingentique procella
> Afflixisset adhuc tenerum pietatis ovile:
> Plus tamen adscriptus nobis, plus factus amicus
> Obfuit ...
> ... vigilare decet, cunctosque monere
> Opportune, importune ne incauta juventus
> Occulta attingat prorsus mysteria Pauli,
> Neve in vulgares vesana audacia linguas
> Transferat, indocto non committenda popello.
> Quae quia non penitus fas est abolere ...
> ... saltem
> Efficite ut vulgus tenebris velut abdita caecis
> Sorbonae haec senibus lippis tractanda relinquat....

(With the last line, cf. l. 501 f. above.) Cf. also Edwin Sandys, *Europae
Speculum* (1629), p. 116: 'yea some parts of Scripture, as S. PAVLS Epistles,
they are so jealous of, and thinke so dangerous, that by report of divers,
... some of theyr Iesuites of late in Italy in solemne sermon ... haue
censured St PAVL for a hoteheaded person, ... yea he was dangerous to
reade as savouring of haeresie in some places, and better he had not written of those matters at all.'

519 f. The reading of the Bible is compared with the wearing of illegal
weapons. Cf. G. Hall, p. 138: 'to be sure to keep their people from fighting, they keep them always blindfold ...: *Andrew Carolstadius* was a doctor
of eight years standing ere he read the Bible: and what courses are taken
to restrain Layicks from reading of that perilous book, hath been in part
intimated already.'

531. Julian the Apostate, Roman emperor (360-3). Libanius, St Cyril, and St
Jerome mention a polemical work which he composed in 363 against the Christian Scriptures.

539-42. These lines strongly recall Dryden's *MacFlecknoe*, especially ll. 18,
134-6, 145 f.

553 f. Cf. Foulis, p. 100: 'This Principle [of King-killing] was by *Ledesma*
first publish'd in Spanish ... and ... had the priviledge of the King of
Spain. 'Tis strange ... that Kings should thus be persuaded to sign an
Order for their own execution.... The *Guisian* Faction in *France*, making a
firm League or *Covenant* pretending to maintain the *Roman* Religion ... at
last bandy'd against their King, Henry the Third ... and ... the King was
murdered by one of their Gang.'

555 ff. Cf. Foulis, d1^v: 'And if a Governour be not of the *Roman* Church, and
so by their consequence be an Heretick ... their *Bulla Coenae Domini* ...
will tell you how they are Curs'd and Excommunicated to the purpose. And
according to the Canon-law, he that kills an Excommunicated person, in
meer Zeal for the *Roman* Church, doth not incur the crime of Homicide.'

557. *Peter-pence*. According to Heylyn, I.98, 'their Peter-pence ... was an Annual rent upon every chimny in the Realm, first granted to the Pope by *Offa* King of the *Mercians*, An° 730, or thereabouts'. It was abolished by Henry VIII in 1534. The Pope's excommunication of Henry (11 July 1533), though it preceded the refusal of Peter-pence, followed directly upon the confirmation of the Act withholding Annates; so that there is point in Oldham's gibe. An abortive n. on R253—'King Henry & his woolpack Fools'—makes it the more likely that here he had Henry in mind. On 'Annats. Advowsons. Peterpence' see R196 (Appendix III).

558. *unquestion'd Pow'r*. Cf. Foulis, b1^V: 'For if you doubt ... the truth of this Assertion,—*According to the Church of* Rome, *Kings may justly and lawfully be deposed*—.... The true blew Romanists [e.g. Bellarmine] will positively assure you, that it is a truth so certain that not so much as *any one do make any doubt of it*.' Oldham (Appendix III, R197) refers to Dryden's *Indian Emperour* (1667), p. 11, in which the Spaniards tell Montezuma that the Pope 'Has this your Empire to our Monarch given', and 'His pow'r must needs unquestion'd be below.'

560, 568-70. Cf. Fletcher, *Locusts*, V.iii (italics mine):
> this Iesuite,
> Who (Loiol's Ensigne) thirsts for English blood.
> He *culs* choice soules (soules vow'd to th' Prince of night,
> And Priest of Rome) *sweares them* ...
> ... *close to conceale*,
> And execute what he should then reveale ...
> *Binds* them to hell in sin....

567. Cf. Settle, *Empress of Morocco* (1673), p. 40: 'More Fierce than Lust, more Valiant than Despair.'

571 f. Of the assassins alleged to have been enlisted to kill King Charles, Grove was supposed to have chosen a temporal reward (£1500) and Pickering a spiritual one, thirty thousand masses (Burnet, ii.189).

573 f. Cf. Foulis's account (p. 547) of the promises made by the Jacobin Friars to Jacques Clément: '*he shall be well recompenced for the fact; if he die, he shall surely fly to Heaven as a Saint, and be enrolled amongst the* Roman *Martyrs on Earth; but if he live, he and his shall be provided for, that he shall have a Bishoprick if not a Cardinalship.*'

579. *to know the sundry ways to kill*. According to Foulis, p. 103, 'Johannes Mariana', the most famous Jesuit apologist of tyrannicide, 'is as particular as any in the way of King-killing, laying down the several Methods and means of that wicked art'. Mariana's doctrine of tyrannicide in his *De Rege* is discussed by J.N. Figgis in *Studies of Political Thought from Gerson to Grotius*, 1907 (1916), p. 148. Mariana decides, for example, that a tyrant may legitimately be poisoned 'through clothes or cushions'.

581 f. Cf. Scroggs' remarks at the trial of Green, Berry, and Hill (7 State Trials 218, quoted in Pollock, p. 357): 'Such courses as these we have not known in England till it was brought out of their Catholic countries; what belongs to secret stranglings and poisonings are strange to us, though common in Italy.'

586. *Steals ... unseen*. Indebted to Dryden, *All for Love* (1678), V.i, p. 77, where the 'best of Thieves' opens 'life, and, unperceiv'd by us, [does] steal us from our selves'.

589. *Gloves*. Albreta, Queen of Navarre, was said to have been poisoned with a pair of gloves. See *The Cabal of Several Notorious Priests and Jesuits, Discovered* (1679).

589. *Saddle Pomel*. Foulis (p. 465) tells of Queen Elizabeth's providential escape when Edward Squire, an underservant in her stables (incited, says Foulis, by one Walpole, SJ), put poison on the pommel of her saddle.

592. *Pontick Mountebank*. Mithridates VI, King of Pontus (d. *c*.63 BC), celebrated not only for having immunized himself, by repeated small doses, against all poisons, but for his knowledge of antidotes, whence mithridate, a supposedly universal one, took its name.

595. *great Borgia or his Sire*. Caesar Borgia (d. 1507) was the second son of Rodriguez Borgia (1431-1503), who became Pope Alexander VI in 1492. Both were suspected of dispatching their enemies by poison. See Ranke, vi.39-41 and nn., and Lee's play, *Caesar Borgia* (Sept. 1679).

596. Oldham's list of 'Heads yet untouch'd' (R196) includes the note 'Conclave' from G. Hall, p. 8, where the costly magnificence of the conclave of cardinals is described.

599. *the slurr'd guilt*: the guilt of the Jesuit assassin is slid on to an innocent man. *OED* gives no exact parallel. For the literal sense of 'slur' in dicing jargon, see 'Jesuits II', 1. 269 n.

609. *Cog*: cheat; literally, controlling the fall of the dice by sleight of hand, or (occasionally) substituting a false die for a true one (*OED*).

609. *equivocate*. See Pascal, *Lettres*, p. 140: his Jesuit spokesman extols 'notre doctrine des équivoques, par laquelle "il est permis d'user de termes ambigus, en les faisant entendre en un autre sens qu'on ne les entend soimême," comme dit Sanchez, *Op. mor.* p. 2 liv. III. ch. VI, n. 13'.

611 f. 'It was his [Lysander's] policy "to cheat boys with knuckle-bones, but men with oaths".' (Plutarch, *Lives*, VIII. §4.)

617-24. Cf. Buchanan, *Franciscanus*, pp. 267-8:
          Haec qui sacrilegis ausit convellere verbis
          Schismaticus sit, & Haereticus, sit torris Avernae
          Ollae, opifex scelerum, Furiarum filius, Orci
          Germen, & in mentem quicquid tibi splendidabilis
          Suggeret....

617 ff. Pascal heads no. 15 of his *Lettres*, 'Que les jésuites ôtent la calomnie du nombre des crimes, et qu'ils ne font point de scrupule de s'en servir pour décrier leurs ennemis.' He cites as a Jesuit 'thèse publique' the precept: 'Ce n'est qu'un péché veniel de calomnier et d'imposer de faux crimes pour ruiner de créance ceux qui parlent mal de nous'.

621. Cf. Foulis, e2^r, for the like list of names with which Protestants are pelted.

626. A proverb: Tilley, W929 (cf. S522); his examples are predated by Wyatt's application of it to his accusers, in 1541: slanderers 'use for a general rule "Whom thou lovest not accuse; for though he heal the wound, yet the scar shall remain"'.

629 f. Cf. G. Hall, p. 33: and Zachary Grey's n. to *Hudibras*, II.iii.155: 'some Popish writers' (he indicates examples) 'affirm, that Luther was begot by an Incubus, and strangled by the devil.... Mr. Oldham alludes to this aspersion'. Cf. also Foulis, b1^r.

640. The three Sibylline books, purchased by Tarquinius Superbus, were consulted only at the express command of the senate, and were entrusted to a small body of custodians and interpreters, who made known to the public not the actual oracle found in the books, but only its interpretation.

647-52. Cf. Buchanan, *Franciscanus*, p. 273:
> Si quis erit fratrum qui suasu daemonis ausit
> Effere in vulgus mysteria condita ...
> ... haec prodere si quis
> Audeat, extemplo scelerato sanguine poenas
> Solvat, & aeterna compostus pace quiescat.

653. Cf. Otway, *Don Carlos* (1676), p. 63: 'But one thing more, and then Vain World adieu!'

657-63, 665. Cf. Dryden, *MacFlecknoe*, 11. 12, 112-15. On R171 Oldham names Hannibal, as Dryden does.

666 f. In Statius' version of the Theban legend (*Thebaid*, XII.429 ff.), the hate of Eteocles and Polynices, sons of Oedipus, was not quenched even in death; for when their bodies were placed together on the pyre, the flame parted into two. Cf. Ovid, *Ibis*, 11. 35 f.

676 f. Cf. Settle, *The Empress of Morocco* (1673), p. 52:
> A Train of Devils ...
> Shall ... with loud ecchoes houle;
> As if they watcht to seize her flying Soul.

Satyr IV: S. Ignatius his Image

Before the end of 1679 (see 'Prologue', headnote) this satire completed the series. It is subsequent to the sketch for an Advertisement, R166 (but that may have been drafted either between Satyrs III and IV, or between II and III: see Appendix III and n.). Its composition following on Satyr III scarcely needs confirming: one may note, however, that it contrasts in tone with its predecessors (see Introduction, pp. 23, 29); that it leading topic of Romish 'lies and legends' had a contributory role at III.301-50; and that it continues to draw upon what till III.315 were 'Heads yet untouch't (Appendix III, R197), and upon *The Excommunicated Prince*, 16 July. Two allusions inconclusively suggest a date *c*.Nov. Pope-burnings on the 5th (11. 320-2) would be most recently topical after those (very numerous: Luttrell, i.29) in 1679, though they attracted attention also in 1678 and 1677. Again, Madam Cellier (11. 295-7) was not altogether unknown earlier: in the spring James employed her in 'obscure negotiations' with Shaftesbury (Jones, pp. 75, 110): moreover, she must already have had some reputation as a Popish midwife (and it is with sex, as a bawd, not politics, that Oldham connects her). But it was from 29 Oct., over the Meal Tub plot, that she became notorious. Previously, I have not traced her, in prologue, epilogue, pamphlet, or lampoon, sufficiently a public figure for Oldham's allusion.

Priapus' image, Horace's mouthpiece (Satire I.viii), gave classical precedent, as Oldham claims, for Ignatius's image as his. But this established genre, though less familiar than the 'Ghost' or 'Legacy', was, like them, not without popular antecedents. Written in popular style for the political-ballad audience, there was Marvell's 'Dialogue between the Two Horses', exchanged by the brass and marble mounts of the equestrian 'Charles I' and 'Charles II', subjects of his 'Statue at Charing-Cross' and 'Statue in Stocks-Market'. Two satires in *Rump*, 1662 (I.140, 340) are given to inanimate speakers: 'A Vindication of Cheapside-Crosse', where it complains against its demolition, 2-4 May 1643; and (dated 1660 by Firth) 'A Quarrel betwixt Tower-Hill and Tyburn'.

1-6. Cf. Horace, *Satires*, I.viii.1-3: 'Olim truncus eram' &c.; and Fletcher, *Locustae*, p. 11:
> Hic truncum, hic saxum (saxo contemptior ipso)
> Propitium implorat supplex.

7 f. A draft (Appendix III, R257) establishes the sources in Fletcher and G. Hall.

9 f. See 'Jesuits II', ll. 45 ff., n. Fletcher too refers to him as 'that lame souldier Saint' (*Locusts*, II.viii).

11-15. Cf. *Life of Ignatius*, pp. 13-15: 'He ... caused his sword, and dagger ... to be hanged vp at our B. Ladies Altar [at Monserrat], seeking other ... weapons to serue our Lord with all.' At her altar, throughout the night of 25 Mar. 1522, he watched 'like a new knight of Christ those his new and in appearance ... weake weapons'.

16 ff. The 'well-hung *God*' is Priapus, god of gardens and procreation; his statue was used as a scarecrow. Cf. Horace, *Satires*, I.viii.6 f. and Jonson, *Catiline*, III.159-61:
> ... were I set vp, for that woodden god,
> That keeps our gardens, could not fright the crowes,
> Or the least bird from muiting on my head.

With ll. 20, 24 ff., cf. Horace, ibid., ll. 37-9; Juvenal, I.129 ff.; Persius, I.112 ff.

28. *Fox his Lists*: the *Acts and Monuments*, or 'Book of Martyrs'.

33 f. See *Life of Ignatius*, pp. 41-50. He left Venice 4 July 1523, reaching Jerusalem 4 Sept., but was dissuaded from his project of spending the rest of his life there by the Provincial of the Franciscans. Christ appeared to him on the Mount of Olives. He arrived back at Venice in mid-Jan., 1524.

35 f. L[ewis] O[wen], *Speculum Jesuiticum* (1629), tells how Loyola, recruiting three new disciples, brought the number of his company to ten, '*vt iam ... patrum δεκὰς fieret: qui numerus olim vocatus Atlas, in quo etiam mysticum latet. Sic enim fulciunt papatum Jesuitae, vt vertice supposito sydera fulcit Atlas.*' The decemvirate were Xavier, Faber, Laynes, Salmeron, Rodricus, Bobadilla, Iaius, Codurius, Braetus, and himself. In 1537 he offered their services to Paul III, who confirmed the Order of Jesuits in 1540.

37 f. Cf. Butler, *Hudibras*, III (1678), ii.605 f.:
> To hang, like *Mahomet*, in th' Air,
> Or St. *Ignatius*, at his Prayer;

and with Zachary Grey's n., citing Maffei, *Vita Ignatii* (1590); and *Life of Ignatius*, p. 201: 'in Barcelona John Paschall often beheld him in prayer eleuated in the ayre, a foote & more aboue the ground, speaking with God'. Oldham may have linked Butler's 'Mahomet' with what Foulis (p. 156) writes of Pope Gregory: 'I can easily persuade my self, that he had not (as the Turks story of their great Prophet) the Pigeon or Holy Ghost, at the writing of these Letters, directing him at his ear, as they say he sometimes had; *and so they always paint him.*' [italics mine; Oldham is imagining a picture of Loyola].

39. *Galesh*: a light carriage, calèche.

40. Cf. *Life of Ignatius*, p. 10: 'In this his change of life he greatly feared the weakenes of his flesh, but the ... Virgin ... appeared vnto him one night ..., with her most pretious Sonne in her arms' so that 'from that instant to the end of his life, he remayned pure and chast'.

41 ff. See *Life of Ignatius*, pp. 256 ff., chap. 21, 'Of the miraculous Cures of diseases, done by the intercession of B.F. Ignatius'; and chaps. 22 and 23.

45 f. The College of Physicians was founded by Thomas Linacre in 1518, under letters patent from Henry VIII. The Bills of Mortality, recording deaths in London parishes, seem to have begun in 1592. The deaths were enumerated

according to their causes; in, for example, *The Diseases and Casualties this Week ... 15-22 April 1690* (preserved in a vol. of broadsides, Bodl. Firth, b.16), the list is sufficiently long and diverse: they are classified under forty-four heads, ranging from Abortive and Apoplexy, to Grief, Rising of the Lights, Suddenly, Worms, and Plague. See also the Bill reproduced in Pepys, vi, between pp. 234 and 235. The sometimes amateurish designations came from the 'Searchers of the Dead', usually old women (ibid., p. 283, n. 4).

47. Cf. Cleveland, 'To P. Rupert', l. 157: 'S. *Peters* shadow heal'd'. See Acts 5:15.

48. *my all powr'ful Name.* Cf. Foulis, p. 5: '*Valderama* saith, Though *Moses* did great wonders with his Rod, that was onely by the vertue of the name of God written on it; and also what the *Apostles* acted, were onely by the power of the name of God: But as for *Loyola* ... he onely by his own name writ in a piece of Paper, did more Miracles than *Moses* and all the Apostles; which was admirable.'

54. *juggling Feat.* A phrase from *The Excommunicated Prince*, p. 39; this page also furnished a jotting on R196 (Appendix III, 'Holy Medals ...' and n.).

55 ff. *Joannis Eusebii Nierembergii ... Historia Naturae* (1635), p. 418, alleges cures from the miraculous sweat of S. Ignatius's image. Oldham echoes *Excommunicated Prince*:

> We have anointed its Face, and set behind it
> A Chaffin-dish of Coals, to make it seem
> To sweat, and weep, by melting of the Liquor
> Our Springs, our Wheels, and such like Engines
> Are of great Use to make it move, and speak.

57. *Spitchcock'd*: the image is from eels made into a spitchcock: cut into short pieces, dressed with breadcrumbs and chopped herbs, and broiled or fried. R. Wild, *Letters* (1672), p. 9 applied it similarly: 'more souls ... than all the Popes ... have saved from being made Spitchcocks in that Kitchin of Holiness' (*OED*).

60 ff. Cf. Cleveland, 'Upon Sir Thomas Martin', ll. 4-6: not
> ... *Bartlemew* Fare
> Can match him; Natures whimsey, that out-vyes
> *Tredeskin* and his ark of Novelties.

See *Musaeum Tradescantianum: or, a Collection of Rarities. Preserved at South-Lambeth near London by John Tradescant* (1656). The collection, begun by the elder John Tradescant (d. 1637?) and handed down to the younger (1608-62), was assigned by deed of gift to Elias Ashmole. Following his intention (announced 1677) in 1683 it was bestowed on the University of Oxford, and became the nucleus of the Ashmolean Museum.

61. *Sands Waterworks.* Perhaps the nine-mouthed fountain illustrated in *The Loyal Protestant* for 9 Mar. 1680/81, with the advertisement: 'Next door to the *Popes Head Tavern* in *Moor-fields* is to be seen that ... Rarity ... the Indian Water-works.' These were certainly exhibited at Bartholomew Fair in 1682: see *The Loyal Protestant* 15 Aug. onward, and Morley, p. 286. William Sandys's waterworks of 1635-7, suggested by Mengel (Yale *POAS*, ad loc.) were not a 'rarity', but sluices, locks, &c. to make the Avon navigable (Thomas Habington, *Survey of Worcestershire*, ed. John Amphlett (1893), i.24, ii.468 f.).

61. *German Clockwork.* Cf. Pepys, 4 Sept. 1663: 'to Bartholomew Fayre ... and saw some German Clocke works, the Salutation of the Virgin Mary, and several Scriptural stories; but above all there was at last represented the sea, with Neptune, Venus, mermaids, and Ayrid [i.e. Arion] on a dolphin,

the sea rocking, so well done that had it been in a gaudy manner and place, and at a little distance, it had been admirable'. Cf. an advertisement in *The Loyal London Mercury* for 23-6 Aug. 1682.

63 ff.   Cf. Marvell, 'Dialogue between the Two Horses', ll. 15-20:
          All Popish believers think something divine,
          When Images speak, possesses the shrine:
          But they that faith Catholick ne're understood,
          When Shrines give Answers, say a knave's in the Roode;
          Those Idolls ne're speak, but the miracle's done
          By the Devill, a Priest, a Fryar, or Nun.
Evelyn, 13 July 1654, describes a hollow statue contrived by Dr Wilkins, 'which ... uttered words by a long concealed pipe ... whilst one speaks through it at a good distance'.

67.   *Hocus Tricks*. Hocus Pocus was a meaningless juggler's incantation like Hey Presto! or Hiccius Doccius. The derivation of hocus pocus from 'Hoc est Corpus' is unsupported by early evidence: *OED* attributes it to Tillotson, *ante* 1694, but see also Anthony Wood, *History and Antiquities Of The University Of Oxford*, published from his MS in 1796, ii.94.

74.   Cf. (in reverse) G. Hall, p. 10: 'sumptuously ... built', 'richly furnisht', 'gorgeously decked' as Catholic edifices are, 'the *Chinoese* and *Indian* Temples erected to their hellish *Pagodi* are yet much fairer and wealthier than they'.

80 f.   See Pliny's well-known story of Cleopatra's wager with Mark Antony (*Natural History*, IX.lviii.§§119-21).

82 f.   Cf. G. Hall, p. 10: 'Look to their Images, and see how trimly they are dressed with variety of Robes ...'; and Fletcher, *Locusts*, III.xxxvii.2; priests 'trimme their puppet god with costly gauds'.

85.   The Lord Mayor's Show was an object of ridicule to those who were not 'cits'. See 'Spencer's Ghost', ll. 62-6 n. The ceremony of riding Skimmington, as Marvell explains ('Last Instructions to a Painter', l. 377 ff.) is designed to shame the husband-beating virago: the next-door couple are mounted 'on lean Jade',
          The Distaff knocks, the grains from Kettle fly
          And Boys and Girls in troops run houting by....
Butler's depiction, *Hudibras*, II.ii.609-58, 695-712, is more elaborate, and has the husband and wife on separate steeds.

86.   See Horace, *Epistles*, I.vi.41-4. Lucius Licinius Lucullus (*c*.109-57 BC) was asked for a hundred purple cloaks. Ignorant at first whether he had any, he found himself able to furnish five thousand.

87.   Cf. G. Hall, pp. 7 f.: 'the state of his Holiness at the Feast of his Coronation', 'with the glorious Robes of his Pontificality on his back', 'is enough to dazzle your eyes'.

88.   *Sicily's Tyrant*. Cf. Foulis, *History of the Wicked Plots ... of our Pretended Saints* (1662), p. 2 (citing Valerius Maximus): '*Dionysius* of *Sicily* ... took away a Golden Cloak from *Jupiter*, saying, that *Cloth was warmer for winter, and Lighter for Summer*; And so having cut off Aesculapius his Golden Beard, excused it, by affirming, That *it was not fit for him to have a long Beard, since his father* Apollo *had none.*'

100 f.   The most notorious universal medicines of the day are described in Dr Christopher Merett's *Short View Of The Frauds, and Abuses Committed by Apothecaries* (2nd edn., 1670), p. 56: 'The last of any Fame with us, were Dr. *Goddard*'s Drops, a good Medicine, but not so universal ... as he would have made the World believe', nor in fact a new one: that it was 'Spirit

of Harts-horn, some relations plainly argue.' The proprietor is wrongly
identified by *Biographia Britannica* and the *DNB* with Jonathan Goddard
(1617?-1675) Warden of Merton College, 1651-60, and Fellow of the Royal
Society and of the College of Physicians. Merett, in *Self-Conviction* (1670),
p. 10, quoting and answering a calumniator of the physicians, writes: '*One
of your selves*, Dr. Goddard *with his Drops*.... Whom you might have distinguished from my learned Colleague, Dr. *Jonathan Goddard*, had you not a
mind to have asperst him, ... but the other *Goddard* was none of our selves.'

102. *Morphew*: a leprous or scurfy eruption (*OED*).

106. *Wiltshire Drum*. See Appendix IV.

107. Cf. Butler, *Hudibras*, II.iii.155, 161 f. See *The Devill of Mascon. Or,
a true Relation of the chief things which an Vncleane Spirit did, and said
at Mascon in Burgundy, in the House of Mr. Francis Perreaud Minister of the
Reformed Church* ... (2nd, enlarged edn., 1658). The first (trans. from
Perreaud's French) was of 1653; another was published in 1679. This demon
'upon the twentieth of September' 1612 'began to whistle ... and presently
to frame an articulate and intelligible voice, though somewhat hoarse'. He
'continued speaking & provoking us to speak till the 25 of November when he
spake these last words Ha ha je ne parleray plus'. On one occasion he
'desired us ... that we should send for Mr. *Du Chassin* the Popish Parson
... & that he should not faile to bring holy water along with him, for that
(said he) would send me away packing presently'.

108 f. Cf. Heylyn, I.158; and *The Golden legend*, ii.311: 'Clodovius the king
of France ... came to Rheims to S. Remigius and prayed him that he would
christen him. And when S. Remigius baptized him he had no chrism ready,
then a dove descended from heaven which brought the chrisom in an ampull
of which the king was anointed and this ampull is kept in the church of
S. Remigius at Rheims, of which the kings of France be anointed when they
are crowned.'

116 f. Cf. Butler's couplet, *Hudibras*, III (1678), i.411 f. (given above,
'Jesuits III', l. 318 n.), and Zachary Grey's n. quoting Reginald Scot,
The Discovery of Witchcraft, III.i.40: 'He (the devil) teacheth them to
make ointments of the bowels and members of children, whereby they ride in
the air.'

118-23. *Altar-Pix*: the vessel in which the consecrated Host is kept. Cf.
Burton, *Anatomy*, p. 655: '[† Lege Hossman. Mus exenteratus.] Hunc Deum
muscae et vermes irrident, quum ipse polluunt & devorant, subditus est igni,
aquae, & latrones furantur, pixidem auream humi prosternunt, & se tamen non
defendit hic Deus.'

122 f. Cf. G. Hall, p. 55: 'If some villainous heretical Mouse shall have
unhappily light upon a consecrated host; let *Peter Lombard* be ask't, *Quid
sumit Mus*? He will answer you *Deus novit*:... For, if he shall say, A Wafer,
it is Heresie; for consecration is past; the bread is substantiate into the
body of Christ. If he shall say, The body of Christ, how odious it sounds
to seek a Saviour in a Mouses belly?'

124 f. Cf. Butler, *Hudibras*, III (1678), ii.329 f.:
            ... with Spels,
        For Hallowing Carriers Packs, and Bells.

124-37. See Appendix III (R196) for items from *Excommunicated Prince*, some
of which appear also in a discarded draft for 'Jesuits III', ll. 285 ff.
(R172). For ll. 124-7, 130-2, cf. G. Hall, pp. 53 f.: he banters the 'See
Apostolique' for its 'exorcization of Devils', its consecrations in the
'Canonization of Saints, hallowing of Bells', and benediction of the Agnus
Dei with holy water; and the Roman Church 'for the blessing of Clouts in
the ... cure of Diseases', and of 'Beads, Grains'. On p. 57, he ironically

objects to the forbidden practice of hanging the Host on the church door to
bless the air against hailstones, as encroaching upon the 'well-allowed use'
of the Agnus Dei, whose wax is 'burnt for a suffumigation against Storms and
Tempests'. For the hallowing of salt, and of balms ('Bawms'), and for the
efficacy of hallowed objects against pestilence, disease, and sin, see Titus
Oates, *The Witch of Endor ... an account of the ... Conjurations of the
Papists* (1679), pp. 1, 17; 5, 21, 24: he also describes the christening of
bells, and sanctification of crosses, beads, and holy candles, pp. 6, 20,
40, 43.

127. *Waxen Lambs*: Agnus Dei's.

133-5. Cf. G. Hall, p. 49, mocking the 'thraves and lasts of private Oraisons' in the Roman Church, 'which without the well-devised help of stringed
calculation, could never keep even reckoning?' Cf. ibid., p. 51. See Appendix III, R196 ('thraves ...'), R247, and 'Jesuits II', ll. 181 f., n. A
thrave is two shocks of corn, generally of twelve sheaves each; a last,
twelve (now ten) quarters of grain, twelve sacks of wool, or the like.

138-41. Irish Emma has eluded me. See Brooks, 'Oldham: Some Problems', pp.
572 f. Cf., however, Sir John Temple, *The Irish Rebellion* (1646), p. 105:
'*Elizabeth Champion* ... saith, that she heard the Rebels say, that they had
killed so many *English* men, that the grease or fat which remained upon their
swords and skeines, might serve to make an *Irish* candle, *jurat April 14,
1642*'; and on p. 101: '*Elizabeth Baskerville* deposeth, that she heard the
wife of *Florence FitzPatrick* find much fault with her husbands souldiers,
because they did not bring along with them the grease of Mistresse Nichol-
son, whom they had slaine, for her to make candles withall, *jurat April 26.
1643.*' Temple's book was republished in 1679. His second atrocity story had
been improved on: according to *Popish Politics Unmasked*, 1680 (cf. *Commons
Journals*, 15 Jan. 1673), quoted Yale *POAS*, ii.384-99 n., Colonel Fitzpatrick's
mother 'was hanged ... for murdering several English, and making candles of
their fat'. Another instance of the atrocity being actually committed, the
victim a 'young fat Scotsman' in Co. Tyrone, is alleged in Dr Edmund Bor-
lase's *History of the Execrable Irish Rebellion* (republ. 1680), p. 124.

142 f. Cf. G. Hall, p. 53, on the Papal blessing of flags or banners 'with
the sure promises of victory, as in 88'.

144 f. See *The Jesuit's Manner of Consecrating both the Persons and Weapons
imploy'd for the Murdering Kings and Princes* ... (1678); and *The Black Box
of Roome opened* (1641), p. 4, with another description of the alleged ritual.

145. *resty Kings*. This irony is from G. Hall, p. 92: 'the great Kings of the
earth grow resty, ... having got the bit between their teeth'.

148, 156. According well with Varenius's narrative (for the reference, see
Appendix III, R196). Three Japanese Kings were brought by the Jesuits to
Europe, leaving Japan in 1582: 'Tandum relictâ Italia reversi sunt ...
ferentes secum literas Papae Sixti, & reliquias quasdam, fragmentúmque
sanctæ crucis, tradenda Christianos Regibus Japoniae pro sacro donativo et
honorario.... Verum enimvero praecipua causa, quae Jesuitas ad hoc impulit,
fuit ... ut non parvum thesaurum indé reportarent vel lucrarentur.'

151. *by Candles Inch are sold*: a method of auction vividly described by
Pepys, 8 Nov. 1660 and 3 Sept. 1662. The successful bidder was he who cried
last before the inch of candle burnt itself out.

157. Cf. Lee, epilogue to *Caesar Borgia* (acted *c.*Sept. 1679, printed 1680):
        Old Emissaries shall their Trade forbear,
        Spread no more *Savoy* Reliques, Bones and Hair,
        Shall sell no more like Baubles in a Fair.

The Benedictines' lodgings in the Savoy were searched by Sir William Waller in Jan. 1678/9, and 'many Popish Trinkets and Reliques, and bones of Saints, or such presumed' were found. See *An Impartial and Exact Accompt of the divers Popish Books, Beads, Crucifixes, and Images taken at the Savoy, by Sir William Waller ... and burnt by order, in the New Palace-yard Westminster: the 11 of February, ... 1678*; and the town-talk recorded in *CSPD*, 1679-80, p. 40.

167. For St Catherine's hair, see Foulis, pp. 24 f.

170. See Oldham's n. from Varenius, Appendix III (R166, 'Xavier ...') and 'Jesuits III', l. 137 n.

173 f. The lanthorn borne before Judas at the Betrayal is mentioned as a relic by G. Hall, p. 61; and, as exhibited at St Denys, in Sir Andrew Balfour's *Letters ... Containing Excellent Directions ... For Travelling thro' France and Italy*, 1700 (written *c*.1668). That which Fawkes was carrying when arrested was preserved by his Protestant captors, and passed into the Ashmolean collection, where it may still be seen. It was constantly associated with him, much as associated with the saints: cf. for example, Cleveland, 'The King's Disguise', ll. 57 f. and Samuel Ward's print, *The Destruction of the Spanish Armada 1588, and the Detection of the Gunpowder Plot 1605* (BL, *Catalogue of Prints and Drawings*, I.i. no. 41).

175. *Garnet's Straws*. See 'Jesuits II', l. 187 n.

175. *Becket's Bones and Hair*. See Foulis, pp. 249-51 on spurious relics of Becket. Becket is coupled with Garnet as a traitor and no martyr.

176-8. 'Kentish long-tails' were proverbial: cf. Marvell, 'The Loyall Scot', l. 95. G. Hall, p. 45, assigns the alleged punishment to 'all the persecutors of St. *Thomas Becket*' whose descendants 'fools abroad believe ... are at this day born with long hairy tales'. William Lambarde, *A Perambulation of Kent* (1576) cites the same authorities as Oldham: Polydore Vergil, *Anglicana Historia* ('British Histories') and 'the new Legend' (*Nova Legenda Angliae*, which passed under the name of John Capgrave). From Polydore, Lambarde represents the miraculous punishment as inflicted upon the men of Stroud, who in contempt of Becket had cut off the tail of his horse. 'Capgrave' (*Nova Legenda*, Rolls Series, ii.392) relates a different judgement suffered by the Brocs for the same mutilation. Since Robert de Broc was accessory to the murder, this may help to explain how Oldham came to attach the legendary punishment of the insult to the greater crime. The 1656 edn. of Lambarde (pp. 431-9) gives a critical account of contradictory versions of the story: his own copy of the 1576 edn. (Bodl. 4°. Rawl. 263) has the revision in MS.

179. *S. Lawrence Coals*: those which heated the gridiron on which he was martyred.

181. *Wildefortis wondrous Beard*. St Wilgefortis ('Wildefortis' is Oldham's form of the name in R196, Appendix III) was said to have been the Christian daughter of a pagan king of Portugal. Destined for marriage to a pagan prince, to preserve her vow of chastity she prayed God to disfigure her, and a miraculous beard grew upon her face; whereupon her father had her crucified. The legend cannot be traced earlier than the 15th century. Oldham may have known that a chapel had been dedicated to her at the church of S Mary-le-Port, Bristol. See further *Catholic Encyclopaedia*, xv.622-3; Richard Stanton, *A Menology of England and Wales* (1887) p. 670.

183 f. Cf. G. Hall, p. 62: 'whereas *John Baptist* lost but one head, now there are two sensibly to be seen; one at *Amiens* in *France* (as our Rhemists) the other in St. *Sylvesters* Abby in *Rome*; besides the scattered parcels of it

in several places'; and Foulis, p. 15: 'those of *Rome* [assure] us that his whole head is in the Cloister of St. *Sylvester*; those of *Malta* say, they have the hinder part of it; *Amiens* and St. *John Angelique* brag of the forepart'.

185 f. Cf. Cleveland, 'The Rebell Scot', ll. 79 f.: 'Tooth-drawers ... use to hang their Teeth upon their Belt.' Foulis, p. 15, refers to St Apollonia's teeth as relics; and Titus Oates, in *The Pope's Ware-house* (1679), p. 39, declared, 'I have seen as many of St. *Stephen*'s Teeth as would fill a Peck.'

187 ff. Cf. Foulis, p. 15: 'What might I say of the Milk of the Blessed Virgin, now so plentifully brag'd of in many places, that the famous *Erasmus* is of opinion, that it is impossible for one teeming Woman, though the Childe had suck'd nothing, to afford so much.' Cf. Erasmus's 'The Religious Pilgrimage' (in R. L'Estrange, *Twenty Select Colloquies out of Erasmus*, 1680).

188. (*like Ass's*): esteemed a remedy for the pox.

190 f. Apparently the Virgin's relief of Poitiers is here assimilated to the relief of Chartres (see 'Jesuits III', l. 305 n.), in which her mantle was decisive. At Poitiers, a mantle played little or no part until it became the centrepiece of the annual thanksgiving ceremony. In 1202 the mayor's clerk promised the English to betray the town, but could not lay hands on the keys: the Virgin's image was found holding them. Meanwhile, the Virgin herself, richly clad, and a heavenly host at her back, appeared to the besiegers, whereupon they fell upon one another. The 'Miracle des Clés' was commemorated each Easter day with an offering of many candles; latterly these were replaced by a sumptuous mantle, carried in the procession; a ritual 'toilette de la bonne Vierge' similarly being invested in it by the wife of the Mayor. See A.R.H. Thibaudeau, *Histoire de Poitou* (1839), i.248, and Ch. de Chergé, *Le Guide du Voyageur à Poitiers* (1851), pp. 172-5.

194-6, 198. For satire on false relics in Fletcher's *Locusts*, III.xxxi and xxxvii, see Brooks, 'Oldham and Fletcher', p. 29.

194. *Souldiers Spear*. For the Invention of the Holy Spear, see *Anonymi Gesta Francorum et Aliorum Hierosolymitanorum*. The legend is ridiculed by Oates, *The Pope's Ware-house* (1679), p. 17.

194. *Passion Nails*. Cf. Fletcher, *Locusts*, III.xxxi: 'Cartloads of Crosse, and straunge-engendring nayles'. S. Baring Gould, *Lives of the Saints* (1872-89), November, 136, enumerates some 25 churches claiming to possess nails of the true cross. Cf. Oates, *The Pope's Ware-house* (1679), pp. 10, 16, 18.

195. New St Paul's was begun in 1675 and took 35 years to build.

196. Cf. Foulis, p. 15: Erasmus declared 'that if the pieces of the Cross now brag'd of and shew'd about, were gathered together, they would fill or load a great Ship'. See above, ll. 187 ff., n.

199. *Tabor*: Sir Richard Tabor, 1642?-1681, as Mengel (Yale *POAS*, ad loc.) points out. He perfected a method of administering quinine ('Jesuits' bark') to cure fever, and was credited with saving Charles II's life in his illness of Aug. 1678; in consequence, he became court physician.

200 f. See 'Upon a Bookseller', l. 88 and n. Cf. 'Juvenal III', ll. 228 f.

204. Cf. *Excommunicated Prince*, p. 39: 'These are their Tools and Impliments'; viz. the Catholics' hallowed objects and substances.

205. *Trangums*: trumpery ornaments; objects of contempt (*OED*). Cf. Wycherley, *The Plain Dealer* (1676), III.i, p. 47.

207. Luttrell, i.187 [May 1682] records the trial of John Wilmore, 'The 23^d', indicted 'for spiriting or kidnapping away a young boy under the age of 13 years, called Richard Siviter, and sending him to Jamaica.' Witnesses testified that 'there was in generall such a trade as kidnapping or spiriting away children', and that 'there had been above 500 sent away in two years at Christmas last',

210-16. A rhetorical formula exemplified in Juvenal, X.219-26.

212. *Jubilee*. See Appendix III (R196; and R164 'A Jubilee in 25 Year'). In *Room for a Ballad: Or, A Ballad for Rome* (1674), the Jubilee is annotated as 'A Time when the POPE useth to grant general Pardons', now held every 25 years (instead of 50); the next being in 1675.

213. The Datary is an officer of the Papal Court: his functions relating to grants and dispensations gave wide scope for venality.

214. In his voluminous *Theologia Moralis*. See 'Jesuits, Prologue', l. 17 n.

215. Cf. G. Hall, p. 27: 'in that City alone in the year 1565 ... there were reckoned no fewer than 2800. Curtisans.'

217 ff. Cf. Cowley, 'Davideis', I, n. 11 (*Poems*, p. 268), citing Jesuit authors: if we presume 'Hell to be in the *Center* of the Earth, it is far from infinitely large ...; yet, ... where e'er it be, it is not so strait, as that *Crowding* and sweating should be one of the *Torments* of it, as is pleasantly fancied by *Bellarmin*. *Lessius* in his Book *de Morib. Divinis*, as if he had been there to *survey* it, determines the *Diameter* to be just a *Dutch* mile. But *Ribera*, upon (and out of the *Apocalypse*) allows *Pluto* a little more elbow-room, and extends it to 1600 furlongs'.

227-35. Cf. Buchanan, *Franciscanus*, p. 267:
> Nec minus horrendos purgatrix flamma vapores
> Evomat ...
> Ista relegatos coelesti à limine manes
> Contineat sedes, donec mercede soluta
> Extrahat è calida exactos fornace sacerdos:
> Is musset Missas, veniis venetur, & undis
> Irrorans, magicis findat cava busta susurris:
> Sed tantum dîtes cruciatu liberet umbras.

Cf. also Fletcher, *Locusts*, II.xxx: 'With gold buy out all Purgatory feares.'

235. The Fleet and King's Bench Prisons were especially used for debtors.

236 ff. Cf. Foulis, cl^V, referring to 'Indulgentiæ Ecclesiarum urbis *Romanæ* Impressum *Romæ* 1509', and other works 'publish'd by their Authority, to procure the greater ... belief for such like pardons as these.... And their ... Prerogative is so great forsooth, that they cannot only pardon past sins, but sins to come.... And ... their prices are cheap enough.' He then prints a list for absolutions as 'set down in their Taxa S. Cancellariae Apostolicae' (Oldham's 'holy Chamber') including Sacrilege, 7 grossos; Simony, 7 grossos; Rape, 6 grossos; Incest, 5 grossos; keeping a Concubine, 7 or 8 grossos; 'And if one Kill his Father, Mother, Brother or Wife, he must pay for his Absolution 1 *Ducat*, and 5 *Carlins*.' G. Hall (pp. 87 f.) likewise refers to the *Taxa*, and to the Pope's '*Diplomata confessionalia*': a man bent on committing a sin, say of lust or revenge, upon purchasing one of these Bulls may choose his confessor, who is empowered to grant him a plenary indulgence 'in what case soever shall be propounded'. This accords with 'the old Doctrine that *Tetzel* ... taught, ... that the Pope's Indulgences could ... pardon those sins which a man intended to commit in time to come'.

238-40. Cf. *The Second Advice to the Painter* (dated by Luttrell '1679'; no.
24 in Osborne): 'the Book of Rates' (viz. the *Taxa*)
>   Will be convenient too, that of every Sin
>   The Value may be known....

246. *Ingle*: catamite.

250 ff. Cf. *Excommunicated Prince*, p. 39: merely approaching 'our Churches
and Altars' 'forgives some Sins', and 'the Sound ... of Bells' 'christen'd
after our way' has 'much Virtue'.

251 f., 256. Cf. G. Hall, p. 122: 'How favourable is that determination,
that as for venial sins, we need not trouble our selves in confession with
them.' For 'a venial sin ... a little aspersion of holy water is sufficient'. Cf. 'Jesuits II', 1. 124 f. and R188.

257 f. Cf. Browne, *Pseud. Ep.*, III.xxviii: 'Some doubt many have of the
Tarantula ... of *Calabria*, and that magical cure of the bite thereof by
Musick ... the learned *Kircherius* hath positively averred it, and set down
the songs and tunes solemnly used for it.'

259-72. Cf. Buchanan, *Franciscanus*, p. 269:
>   Tum licet adjicias magnae primordia Missae;
>   Quoque sacerdotum gentem decorârit honore
>   Coelituum pater: ut soli sibi fingere numen
>   Murmure verborum possint, tenuique farinae
>   E massa generare Deum, genitumque repente
>   Frangere, sacrato fractum mersare falerno,
>   Visceraque, & carnes, cumque albis ossa medullis,
>   Semianimesque artus avidum demergere in alvum:
>   Tanta sacerdoti cum sit permissa potestas ...
>   De pane ut numen faciant, de numine φ φ:
>   Unde homini fragili haec projecta audacia, ut ausit
>   Christophorum vel Christivorum violare nefando
>   Sacrificum verbo, aut sceleratam impingere dextram.

265 ff. Cf. Fletcher, *Locusts*, III.xxxvii.8 f.: some, not
>   ... using any help, but of the Baker;
>   (Oh more then power divine!) make, chew, and voide their Maker.

(See further my 'Oldham and Fletcher', pp. 418 ff.). Scroggs's sneer, 'They
eat their God, they kill their King, and saint the murderer' (*7 State
Trials*, 134) was notorious (see Kenyon, p. 128), and the gibe, from the
Reformation to *Absalom and Achitophel* (ll. 118-21) was traditional. Cf.
Barnabe Googe, *The Popish Kingdome*, 1570 (1880 reprint, pp. 31 f.), and
Marston, *Scourge of Villanie* (1599), 'Satyre II', ll. 84-91.

273 f., 281-4. Cf. Buchanan, *Franciscanus*, p. 269:
>   ... citiusque parentis
>   Invalidi jugulum ferro, reclude, profana
>   Quam violes dextra rasi male sanus honorem
>   Verticis; uxorem quamvis manifestus adulter,
>   Et natos, natasque tuas compresserit, & te:
>   Sed nube, atque tace potius, nullumque recuses
>   Flagitium, quam traducas quos unctio sanctos
>   Et rasura facit....

276. Cf. G. Hall, p. 38, deriding the 'power which every Priest ... dares
challenge to exercise, even ... to create his maker'.

295. *great Cellier*. The notorious Catholic midwife, bawd, and political
agent; nicknamed by her enemies the 'Lady Errant'. She was deep in the
intrigues to discredit Oates by perjuries and sham plot-discoveries.

The most famous of these, the Meal-Tub Plot, takes its name from Sir William Waller's discovery of papers in her meal-tub, 29 Oct. 1679. For the sequel see below, 'Upon a Bookseller', l. 81 and n.

304 f. For the debt to G. Hall, see Appendix III, R196 ('Rochets ...'). The rochet is a kind of short surplice; the chimer, the upper robe to which the lawn sleeves of a bishop are attached. Maniples, stoles, albs, and 'ammits' (*recte* amices) are described in *The Popish Mass Display'd: Or, The Superstitions and Fopperies of the Romish Church Discovered*, No. 1, 20 Apr. 1681: 'The *Maniple* is ... like a Childs Dading Sleeve, having in one end ... an Eye ... wherein the Priest, putting his left hand, letteth it hang upon his Arm.... The *Stole* is a ... Robe, Embroidered, the length and breadth thereof, both before and behind, with a large Gold or Silver Cross; its all in one entire Piece, and hath a back part and a fore-part each reaching below the knees, but hath no sides ... it is to be ... Red upon a Martyrs day, White upon a Virgins day, Black upon those days in which they say Masses for the Dead, and upon all other days Green.... The *Alb* is the Surplice', somewhat shorter than the Anglican one. The amice represents the cloth with which Jesus was blindfolded: the priest first puts it over his eyes, then 'layeth it strait behind upon his Head, and afterward plucketh it over his Face, letting it fall about his Neck'.

306 f. Cf. G. Hall, pp. 49 f., on the Catholics' 'world of new-multiply'd Rosaries', 'the setled course of their Canonical hours', and their swarm of 'Masses and Dirges and Funeral Obsequies'. See further, Appendix III (R172, and R196, 'Trentals ...', 'Offices ...').

307. *Trentals*. Trental, a Roman Catholic office of 30 masses for the dead.

308 f. *their Pageants ... Their holy Masques*. See Appendix III, R196 ('Carnevals | Pageantry Jubilee'). Cf. G. Hall's condemnation (pp. 19 f.) of 'too scenical' Popish representations of the Nativity, Passion, and Resurrection.

313 f. Cf. Cowley, 'The Chronicle' (*Poems*, p. 42):
                    I more voluminous should grow ...
                    Then *Holinshead* or *Stow*.
Pierre Crabbe (1470-1553) was author of an unfinished *Concilia omnia* in 2 folio vols. (1538), extended to 3 (1551). Surius (see 'Jesuits III', l. 297 n.) added a 4th vol. to Crabbe's work. John Stow (1525-1605), wrote, among other works, *The Annales* (at first *The Chronicles*) *of England* (1592), a quarto of more than 1300 pp. John Foxe (1516-87) is the martyrologist, whose famous *Actes and Monuments* appeared in Mar. 1562/3. It is a great folio of over 1700 pp. In the epithet 'lying', the Image must be speaking (unexpectedly) from the Romanist point of view. It is slanderous: Foxe, says A.F. Pollard (*History of England, 1547-1603*, p. 153), has few serious errors of fact, though his animus affects his deductions.

322. 'for the *Powder-plot*' points the allusion to Pope-burnings on 5 Nov., though they were being eclipsed by those on the 17th, Queen Elizabeth's 'birthday' (actually, accession day). They had been revived 5 Nov. 1673: on this and its sequels, 5 Nov. 1677, 1678, 1679, and 17 Nov. 1676, 1677, 1679, see Miller, pp. 183-5; that of 17 Nov. 1679 was the first to be elaborately stage-managed, and financed in part by the Whig Green Ribbon Club. Cf. Luttrell, i.29, 1679: 'The 5th ... being gunpowder treason, there were many bonefires and burning of popes as has ever been seen on the like occasion.... On the 17th ... were severall bonefires'; 'at Temple gate ... was a pope burnt in pontificalibus that cost above 100 *l*.'

Aude Aliquid. Ode [alias A Satyr Against Vertue]

This piece is best known by the title under which it was piratically published
in 1679: *A Satyr Against Vertue*. Oldham repudiates the name (above, 'Advertisement', ll. 35-43) and is justified by the autograph fair copy (R2), headed
with the quotation from Juvenal (I.73 f.) and 'Pindarique'. The title in the
1682 edn., the only good text of the poem printed in his lifetime, no doubt
represents his final choice.
   On the likelihood that this was the poem which prompted Rochester to seek
his acquaintance, see Introduction, pp. xxviii f. and nn. 17, 18. The autograph revision of the sub-title (R2) reveals Oldham's conception, and is
therefore made part of the heading in the present text; the Court-Hector was
Rochester himself. A news-letter of 26 June 1675 reported that 'My Lord
Rochester in a frolick after a rant did yesterday beat doune the dyill which
stood in the middle of the Privie [Gard]ing, which was esteemed the rarest in
Europ' (Marvell, *Poems* (3rd edn.), I.409). Aubrey's notes (ii.34) on Franciscus Linus, maker of the set of chronometrical dials, adds detail: they
'were ... broken all to pieces (for they were of glasse spheres) by the earl
of Rochester, lord Buckhurst, Fleetwood Shephard, etc., comeing in from their
revells. "What!" said the earl of Rochester, "doest thou stand here to [fuck]
time?" Dash they fell to worke.' Oldham's 'Ode' purports to be Rochester's
rant on the occasion. The fancy is not too extravagant: Rochester told Robert
Parsons that *'One day at an Atheistical Meeting, at a person of Qualitie's,
I undertook to manage the Cause, and was the principal Disputant against God
and Piety, and for my performances received the applause of the whole company'* (Parsons, *A Sermon Preached at the Funeral of ... John Earl of Rochester* (1680), p. 23). On Oldham's other poems associated with Rochester, and
the drafts terming him 'our witty bawdy peer', see Introduction, pp. xli-xlv,
and nn. 58, 62, 69, 70, 73. Cf. also the odes on Morwent, st. xxvii, and
Atwood, ll. 161-8.
   On the libertinage attacked in those passages, the doctrine assumed in
'Sardanapalus', and preached by the spokesmen of the 'Dithyrambique' and
'Boileau VIII', as well as here by the Court Hector, see Dale Underwood,
Etherege and the Seventeenth Century Comedy of Manners (1957), pp. 10-15, and
D.H. Griffin, *Satires against Man: The Poems of Rochester* (1973), ch. 2. Dwelling on man's mortifying characteristics, the libertine is sceptical of all
that man prides himself upon, especially his creed of absolute values and his
reason; man's true rationality is to test actuality by the senses, and to
accept the guidance of pleasure and natural instinct, in rejecting which he
is inferior to the animals.
   The 'Ode' had something of a *succès de scandale*. Wood (iv.121) doubtless
reckoned it among 'the mad ranting and debauched specimens of poetry of this
author Oldham' which Rochester 'seemed much delighted in'; and in 1679 the
pirated edition provoked an anonymous *Pindarique Ode, Describing the Excell-
ency of True Virtue*.
   Yet the ironical mode of the poem ought not to have been a stumbling block.
It belongs to an established genre, the Paradoxical Encomium (see H.K. Miller's article, *MP*, liii, 1956, 145-78) of which it is the inverse form (see
Introduction, p. xli).

0.1. *Court-Hector*. Properly, the Hectors were 'a set of disorderly young men
   who infested the streets of London' (*OED*). Cf. Shadwell, *The Scowrers* (1691),
   p. 3: 'I knew the Hectors, and before them the Muns and Titire Tus' (see
   OED). Cf. 'Juvenal III', ll. 405 ff. and n.

1. Imitated from Cowley's 'Now *Blessings* on you all, ye peaceful *Starrs*' ('Ode Upon His Majesties Restoration and Return', *Poems*, p. 420) and 'Now, Blessings on ye all, ye Heroick Race' ('Ode. Upon Liberty', *Essays*, p. 390).

4. *The Stagyrite*: Aristotle.

7. Though it 'was the assertion of Procopius, Nazianzen, Justin Martyr, and is generally believed among us', Browne, *Pseud. Ep.*, VII.13, rightly refuses to credit that 'Aristotle drowned himself in Euripus, as despairing to resolve the cause of its reciprocation, or ebb and flow seven times a day, with this determination, *Si quidem ego non capio te, tu capies me.*'

8-10. In *Plus Ultra* (1668), Glanvill revived the apocryphal story that Aristotle, 'to procure more *Fame* for his *own* Performances', and '*conceal* his *thefts*', destroyed 'the most considerable *Remains* of the *Ancients*'. See further, J.I. Cope, *Joseph Glanvill* (1956), p. 115 and n.

13-19. Cf. Almanzor's rant, 1 *Conquest of Granada* (1672), I.i, p. 7:
>   I am as free as Nature first made man,
>   'Ere the base Laws of Servitude began,
>   When wild in woods the noble Savage ran.
Hobbes believed that the state of nature was one of anarchic war and was superseded by civil society in which private power is subjected to a sovereign (*Leviathan*, chs. 13 and 17).

20-5. Cf. Denham, 'Of Prudence', ll. 149 f.:
>   Why should we fondly please our Sense, wherein
>   Beasts us exceed, nor feel the Stings of Sin ...
and Randolph, 'Upon Love fondly refus'd for Conscience sake', ll. 1, 29 f.:
>   Nature, Creations law, is judg'd by sense, ...
>   Man is the Lord of Creatures, yet we see
>   That all his Vassals Loves are free.

26 ff. Cf. 'Consideratus, Considerandus', ll. 19, 27-8 (formerly attr. to Rochester, *Poems* (Pinto), p. 126, but see Vieth's edn., p. 235):
>   Vertue's ...
>   Shun'd by the Great, and worthless thought by most,
>   Urg'd to be gone, or wish'd for ever lost....

30. Cf., in Dryden, *Aureng-Zebe* (1676), p. 29, the hero's apostrophe to 'Virtue ... / With thy lean Train, the Pious and the Wise'.

38. *Excise*. The Excise was introduced by Pym in 1643, and after 1660 became the biggest item in the hereditary revenue of the crown.

43 ff. *that nice Goddess*: Astraea, or Justice, the last immortal to forsake the earth when the wicked iron age succeeded the brazen (Ovid, *Metamorphoses*, I.149 f. Cf. Atwood ode, ll. 34-7.

53 f. *Too difficult for Flesh and Blood*. Cf. Burnet, *Some Passages*, p. 115. To the argument that salvation being so high a reward, it is not unreasonable the terms should be difficult, Rochester replied 'We are sure the terms are difficult, but are not so sure of the Rewards'.

55. Cf. Cowley, 'Answer to the Platonicks' (*Poems*, p. 80):
>   So Angels love; so let them love for me;
>   When I'am *all soul*, such shall *my Love* too be....

56. Cf. Cowley, 'The Complaint' (*Poems*, p. 437): 'Business! the grave impertinence'.

60-3. Cf. Cleveland, 'The Antiplatonick', ll. 25 f.:
>   Vertue's no more in Woman-kind
>   But the green-sicknesse of the mind,

and 'To P. Rupert', ll. 49 f.:
> But why, my Muse, like a Green-sicknesse-Girle,
> Feed'st thou on coales and dirt?

64. *Jilt*: harlot. The modern sense (first recorded 1674) does not apply here.

66. *Chows'd by a Dowry in Reversion*: cheated (see 'Dithyrambique', l. 3 n.) by a dowry conditional on the expiry of the right of the present possessor. Cf. Cleveland's 'Square-Cap', ll. 13-14, in which the heroine has 'a Dowry in Reversion'. The present passage, and ll. 119-21 of the 'Counterpart', are no doubt indebted to Cowley's remarks on fame in the preface to his *Works* (1668): '*Fame* ... is an *Estate* (if it be any, for men are not oftner deceived in their hopes of *Widows*, ...) that hardly ever comes in whilst we are *Living* to enjoy it, but is a *fantastical kind of Reversion to our own selves*.'

67 ff. *The greatest Votarie*: Brutus, as depicted in Cowley's ode upon him (*Poems*, pp. 195, 197); the best of pre-Christian mankind, who made 'Virtue' his 'Life's Center', till final defeat wrung from him the '*Tragick Word*', that Virtue had proved 'An *Idol* only and a *Name*'. Brutus's dying exclamation (quoted from a Greek tragedy) is said to have been 'Te colui (Virtus) ut rem; ast tu nomen inane es' (Dio Cassius, XLVII.49). Cf. Bacon, *Advancement of Learning*, II.xxiii.46.

75 ff. Cf. Waller, 'To the Mutable Fair', ll. 33-6: Juno 'did once escape' the 'bold Ixion's rape':
> She, with her own resemblance, graced
> A shining cloud, which he embraced.

91. *obstinately Good*: from Lee, *Sophonisba* (1676), I.i, p. 3.

93 f. Oldham, in 1676, is already taking a hint from Fletcher, *Locusts*, II. xxxvii, in which the same gibe is directed at the Gunpowder plotters. See my 'Oldham and Fletcher', and 'Jesuits I', ll. 204 f., II.150, II.185-7 nn.

97. Cf. Denham, 'The Progress of Learning', l. 36: '*Socrates* whom th'Oracle call'd Wise'.

98. In Christian belief, the real author of the heathen oracles was the devil. See Milton, *Paradise Lost*, I.517 f., *Paradise Regained*, I.455 ff. Cf. 'Jesuits IV', ll. 63 f.

102 f. Alluding primarily to Aristophanes' ridicule in the *Clouds*, but also to the attacks of Eupolis, Callias, Ameipsias. (See Diogenes Laërtius's life of Socrates).

108-18. Cf. Ovid, *Metamorphoses*, IX.551 ff., and Oldham's version in 'Byblis', ll. 197 ff. Cf. also Rochester's epilogue to Dr Davenant's *Circe* (1677):
> 'Twas impotence did first this vice begin:
> Fools censure wit as old men rail of sin,
> Who envy pleasure which they cannot taste,
> And, good for nothing, would be wise at last.

and the last stanza of his 'Disabled Debauchee'.

119. Cf. Dryden 1 *Conquest of Granada* (1672), I.i, p. 8: 'Stand off; I have not leisure yet to dye.'

120-8. Cf. the ode on Morwent, ll. 509-17.

130. *the Bill of Maladies*. See 'Jesuits IV', l. 45 f. and n.

143-6. Cf. 'Jesuits II', ll. 213-16 and n.; and Randolph, p. 129 'Upon Love fondly refus'd for Conscience sake':

> What's Conscience but a Beldams midnight theme?
> Or nodding nurses idle dreame?

145 f. 'though [Rochester] thought the Soul did not dissolve at death; Yet he doubted much of Rewards or Punishments' (Burnet, *Some Passages*, pp. 53 f.).

147 ff. Cf. 'Jesuits III', ll. 223 ff. and n.

150. *Wheadle*! A piece of cajolery. Cf. Etherege, *She wou'd if she cou'd* (1668), I.i: 'Dos't think to pass these gross wheadles on me too?', and his cheating character Wheadle, in *The Comical Revenge* (1664).

154-7. That 'those who pretended to believe lived so that they could not be thought to be in earnest when they said it' was, affirmed Rochester, a chief cause of his religious scepticism: making him doubt their full conviction of what they urged upon others. (Burnet, *Some Passages*, p. 120); cf. 'Spencer's Ghost', ll. 259 f., n.

161-9. Cf. Rochester's satire upon the fops in his 'Letter from Artemisia', ll. 152 f., 160 f. (which Oldham at some time transcribed):
> ... foppery, without the help of sense,
> Could ne'er have rose to such an excellence....
> We owe that name to industry and arts:
> An eminent fool must be a fool of parts.

Cf. the ode on Morwent, ll. 453 ff.

167 f. Cf. Settle, Prologue to *Cambyses King of Persia* (1667): 'Poets ought To write with the same spirit Caesar fought.'

170. *Debauches*: debauchees.

172. Cain and Judas, reverenced by the Cainani; see 'Jesuits II', l. 151 n.

173-84. Cf. Ovid, *Metamorphoses*, IX.497 ff., and Oldham's version of the passage, 'Byblis', ll. 89 ff.

173 f. *move ... to the Seats above*. In Burton, *Anatomy*, p. 665, Saturn and Jupiter are represented as monstrous human kings, subsequently mythologized into gods.

185 ff. *that Wretch*: cf. 'Jesuits II', l. 140; Herostratus, having set fire to the temple of Diana at Ephesus (356 BC) confessed he had done so to immortalize himself. 'The Ephesians passed a decree condemning his name to oblivion, but Theopompus embalmed him in his history, like a fly in amber.' See Strabo XIV.22; Valerius Maximus, VIII.14.5; Aulus Gellius, II.6; E. Elder, 'Herostratus', in W. Smith's dictionary of classical biography. 'We are his Rivals' declares Shadwell's Don Antonio in *The Libertine* (1674), V.i, p. 75.

188. *the no-great Fault of Sacriledge*. Cf. Cowley, 'The Request' (*Poems*, p. 66): 'the no-great privilege of Captivity'.

193. *the vain-glorious Carian*: Mausolus, king of Caria 377-333 BC. The monument erected to his memory by his sister and widow Artemisia, and known as the Mausoleum, was one of the seven wonders of the ancient world.

196. *a Tomb*: a Pyramid. Cf. Cowley, 'The Thraldome' (*Poems*, p. 68):
> Like an *Egyptian Tyrant*, some
> Thou weariest out, in building but a *Tomb*.

205. *Boutefeu*: an incendiary. From French, but common in English literature of this period.

206. *the inglorious Founder*: Chersiphron of Cnossus (Strabo, *Geography*, XIV.i.22). Cf. Browne, *Urne-Buriall*, ch. 5: 'Herostratus lives that burnt the Temple of *Diana*, he is almost lost that built it.'

207. *that mighty Emperour*: Nero; see Suetonius' life, ch. 38.

211 f. Tacitus mentions the story as a rumour only: *Annals*, XV.39.

213 f., 219. From Cowley's lines on Cain, *Discourse ... concerning ... Cromwell* (*Essays*, pp. 373 f.):

> 'Twas a beginning generous and high ...
> So well advanc'd, 'twas pity there he staid;
> One step of Glory more he should have made,
> And to the utmost bounds of Greatness gone;
> Had *Adam* too been kill'd, he might have Reign'd Alone.

216 f. Cf. Fletcher, *Locusts*, IV.xxxv: 'Ile ... fire the shaking towne and quench't with royal blood.'

223 ff. Cf. 'Jesuits I', ll. 64-76 and n.

239 f., 248. Echoing Fletcher, *Locusts*, I.xx.7 f., on Satan:

> To be in heaven the second he disdaines:
> So now the first in hell, and flames he raignes....

Cf. also I.xviii.9, II.xv.9. So Milton's Satan (*Paradise Lost*, I.262 f.):

> To reign is worth ambition though in Hell:
> Better to reign in Hell, then serve in Heav'n.

245 f. Cf. Cleveland, 'To P. Rupert', ll. 99 f.: 'Such a foe / Can make them victors in their overthrow'.

249 f. Cf. Cowley, 'The Motto' (*Poems*, p. 16):

> Tell me, ye mighty *Three*, what shall I do
> To be like one of you.

253 f. Cf. [R. Fletcher], 'An Epitaph' (*Rump Songs*, I.285):

> To puny the records of time,
> By one grand *Gygantick* crime.

257 f. Cf. Otway, *Alcibiades* (1675), III.i:

> My fury had begot so vast a Birth,
> Fate wanted strength enough to bring it forth.

260. Cf. an interpolated line in Flatman's 'Translated out of Part of Petronius Arbiter's *Satyricon*', l. 88: 'And stock the large plantations of the Dead.'

265. *Privative of Good*. Cf. 'privative of beauty' in John Hall, 'To the Deformed X.R.', l. 31.

272 f. Cf. Cowley, 'The Prophet' (*Poems*, p. 102):

> Tis I who *Love*'s *Columbus* am; 'tis I
> Who must new *Worlds* in it descry....

274. *the Pillars*. Hercules' Pillars marked the limit of possible travel to the West.

281-3. Cf. Cowley's verses in the *Discourse ... concerning ... Cromwell*, in which 'the first-born Man', 'the mighty Heir, the noble *Cain*' is ironically celebrated.

289. *The Stoicks dull Equality*. 'They also maintain that all sins are equal' since 'he who commits a greater and he who commits a less sin are both equally not in the right path' (Diogenes Laërtius, VII.64, 65, tr. W.L. Davidson).

An Apology for the foregoing Ode

6. *to Flatter Vice*. Dryden's phrase, dedication to *Aureng-Zebe* (1676), A2^V.

7 f. Cf. Spencer's verse-letter to Oldham (see Appendix I, 1. 168).

9 f. Cf. Dryden, Prologue to *Tyrannick Love* (1670):
>   But when a Tyrant for his Theme he had
>   He loos'd the Reins, and bid his Muse run mad....

16. Cf. Dryden, Prologue to *Aureng-Zebe* (1676): 'But he has now another taste of wit.'

18 f. Rochester, 'A Satyr against ... Mankind', 11. 198 f., writes of 'that sensual tribe whose talents lie / In avarice' etc.

22. *Profaness*. See *SJ*, 'Advertisement', 1. 42 and n.

27. *Licence*. The Licensing Act (1662-79) provided a statutory basis for Roger L'Estrange's rigorous censorship of the Press. (See Ogg, ii.514-16.) Political satires were often circulated in MS.

39. *our Nobles*. Evidently a hit at Rochester. Cf. Appendix II, fragments from R95, 220.

44-6. Cf. Cowley, 'Ode of Wit' (*Poems*, p. 18): ''tis just / The *Author blush*, there where the *Reader* must'.

49. Cf. *The Car-man's Poem: Or, Advice to a Nest of Scriblers* (Bodl. Wood 417, 10): 'Car-men turn Poets now, why may not I?'

57 f. Dryden stepped up his hero's wildness for the revival of *The Wild Gallant* (1667), but still apologizes, in the Prologue, for 'his want of wickedness', for which the play was 'damned' when first produced.

69-71. Cf. Joseph Hall, *Virgidemiarum*, V.iii:
>   The satire should be like the porcupine,
>   That shoots sharp quills out in each angry line,
>   And wounds the blushing cheek....

The Passion of Byblis

This translation of Ovid, *Metamorphoses*, IX.454-632, was written after the appearance of *Ovid's Epistles Translated*, ed. Dryden (1680), announced 23-6 Mar. (Macdonald 11a); see Oldham's 'Advertisement' (above, 1. 52). It was published in the 1st issue of *SJ* (1681), really *c*.Nov. 1680.

John Dennis criticized it, to justify bringing out his own, in the preface and nn. to his quarto, *The Passion of Byblis Made English* (1692). Along with much carping, he has a censure or two worth noting. The original required in its translator, he observes, not the 'Force' or 'Genius' characteristic of Oldham, but 'Tenderness of Soul' alien to him. Reluctant to admit this limitation as Oldham was, he himself concluded from his 'Byblis' that his 'vein' lay 'another way' (see Advertisement, 1. 64). Dennis further objects, with reason, to the imperfect rhymes: 'a thing must be much more tender in perfect Rimes.... For ... jarring sounds must render that harsh, which agreeing sounds would render easie.'

26 f. Cf. Dryden, tr. of 'Canace to Macareus', *Ovid's Epistles* (1680):
>   I knew not from my Love these Griefs did grow
>   Yet was, alas, the thing I did not know.

30. *sooths*: indulges, flatters. Cf. Shakespeare, *Venus and Adonis*, 1. 850, and 'sooth up', 'Jesuits III', 1. 474 and n.

77 f. In l. 78 Oldham invents a reason for the wish he translates in l. 77. Dennis finds it inept, but substitutes another, equally needless. The wish simply expresses the girl's idolizing of her brother: if they *were* of different lineages, in her fondness she would want him to have the advantage.

186. *thought*: thought capable of having borne.

212-17. The tone of Ovid's 'tamen ut sit causa timendi' no doubt suggested Oldham's expansion into a characteristic rant.

217. Echoing Dryden, tr. of 'Canace to Macareus', *Ovid's Epistles* (1680): 'And Guilt that made them [sc. tumultuous Joys] anxious made them great.'

267. Cf. 'To Madam L.E.', 1. 44 and n.

276. *hung*. Hooked: having firmly taken the bait. Oldham's term of art is up-to-date: *OED*'s earliest example is from 1674.
strook. The angler 'strikes' when in order to pierce the fish's mouth with the hook, he gives a jerk to the tackle: 'a patient Angler', as in Dryden, *Astraea Redux* (ll. 171 f.) 'ere he strooke, Would let' his fish 'play a while upon the hook'.

310 f. Cf. Waller, 'To the Servant of a Fair Lady', ll. 21 f.:
              You the soft season know when best her mind
              May be to pity, or to love, inclined....

319. *rebate*. Cf. 'Jesuits III', 1. 59 and n.

335. *efforts of Love*: manifestations of its powers and properties (*OED*, effort † 1); stressed 'effórt'. Cf. Thomas Shipman, *Carolina: Or, Loyal Poems* (1683), p. 117: '*French Wines* work small efforts; as may be known.'

350. Oldham stopped short of Byblis' metamorphosis no doubt for the same reason as Dennis inflicted on her a different fate. In 'the time of Augustus', Dennis writes, 'those Transformations were a part of the Roman Religion'. Now that they are incredible, they are no longer moving.

A Satyr Upon a Woman

Written at Whitsuntide 1678, this was first published in the second issue, Christmas 1680, of *SJ* (1681). It had evidently been meant to appear in the first issue, of which the title-page announces 'other Pieces' to follow *The Satyr against Vertue*, whereas only 'Byblis' was then included.
The jilt here attacked was an actual person: on R99 a rough draft of ll. 1-10 is headed 'To L. G.' Neither she nor the 'friend' has been identified. Whether she might be Lady Grey, wife of Forde, Baron Grey of Werk, a target of lampoons *c*.1679-81, is discussed in my 'John Oldham: Some Problems', pp. 569 f.

0.1. The title is given in what is presumably its revised shape, from the 1682 edn. In the autograph fair copy (R54) it began 'On a Woman ...'. This was already changed to 'A Satyr Upon a Woman ...' in the edn. of 1681. Then in 1682, 'my Friend' became 'his Friend'. The date is from the MS; none appears in the 2nd edn., and a less precise one, 'Written in the Year 1678', on the internal title-page of the 1st.

4. *quit the partial Skies*: acquit heaven of being partial; unjustly indulgent. 'The partial Skies' is from Waller's 'The Country to my Lady of Carlisle', 1. 15.

23 f. Cf. Jonson, *Volpone*, I.i:
> ... It is true, they [i.e. physicians] kill
> With as much license as a judge.

34 f. If a murderer touched or even sometimes only approached the corpse of his victim, it was supposed to accuse him by bleeding afresh. This belief is fully described in James I's *Daemonologie*, and, from Holinshed, is put to dramatic use in Shakespeare's *Richard III* (I.ii.55-9). Scott made it the basis of a great scene in *The Fair Maid of Perth*.

36 f. Cf. 'Jesuits, Prologue', l. 55.

52 f. Cf. Dryden, *Aureng-Zebe* (1676), p. 62: 'Ah Sex, invented first to damn Mankind!' and Otway, *Don Carlos* (1676), p. 49:
> Th'art Woman, a true Copy of the first,
> In whom the race of all Mankind was curst.

54. *Woman! nay worse!* Cf. Dryden, *Indian Emperour* (1667), p. 65: 'Woman! that's too good, / Too mild for thee.'

58 f. In marrying her, one would become a witch by entering into a contract and carnal intercourse with a fiend. This sense of 'compact' is not noted in *OED*, but is frequent: e.g. Alexander Roberts, *A Treatise of Witchcraft* (1616), p. 34: 'there passeth betweene the Witch and her Diuell, a compact ...'; R. Scot, *The Discovery of Witchcraft: Proving, That the Compacts and Contracts of Witches with Devils ... are but Erroneous Novelties*; Browne, *Pseud. Ep.*, I.x.41.

62 ff. Based on Dryden, *Amboyna* (1673), IV, p. 50: 'Sure the Devil has lent thee all his stock of falshood, and must be forc'd hereafter to tell truth.'

64-73. Cf. Dryden, *Aureng-Zebe* (1676), p. 62:
> Nature took care to dress you up for sin:
> Adorn'd, without; unfinish'd left, within ...
> Heav'n did, by me, the outward model build:
> Its inward work, the Soul, with rubbish fill'd.

And see *Paradise Lost*, VIII.537-39.

73. The comparison is from G. Hall, p. 28.

76 f. Cf. Cowley, 'The Change' (*Poems*, p. 77):
> So the Earths face ... [has] beauties numberless:
> But at the *Center*, *Darkness* is, and *Hell*;
> There wicked *Spirits*, and there the *Damned* dwell.

80. Champions of the Pope's temporal authority as Jesuits were, it was believed that some took the oath of allegiance with the aid of mental reservation or of dispensations from Rome.

81. Dryden's *The Kind Keeper*, which satirized this 'crying sin of keeping', had been performed—and very coldly received—Mar. 1677/8.

91-3. See 'Jesuits II', l. 208 n. Westminster is Westminster Hall, where sat the four courts of justice: Common Pleas, King's Bench, Chancery, and Exchequer (see De-Laune, *The Present State of London* (1681), pp. 124-32).

114. Cf. Dryden, 1 *Conquest of Granada* (1672), V.ii, p. 64:
> Your power, like Heav'n upon the damn'd, you use ...
> To ... keep me fresh for pain.

Cf. *Paradise Lost*, II.155-9.

124. Cf. Donne, 'The Curse', l. 6: 'May he be scorn'd by one, whom all else scorne.'

127 f. Cf. Donne, 'The Expostulation', l. 42: 'In plaguing him, let misery be witty.'

135 f. Cf. Rochester, 'Song' (*Poems*, p. 32):
>Die with the scandal of a whore
>And never know the joy.

141 ff. Cf. 'Jesuits, Prologue', ll. 51 ff.

153-6. She is to continue to sin as it were on credit—beyond the limit of what she pays for in present suffering,—with her soul as security. For 'run o'th'Score' (let a credit account mount up) cf. Pepys, 30 Dec. 1667.

156. Cf. Donne, 'The Expostulation', ll. 45 f.: 'May he ... not be trusted more on his Soules price.'

157-9. Cf. Otway, *Don Carlos* (1676), p. 48: 'She unrepenting dies, and so she's damnd.'

SOME NEW PIECES

Advertisement

3. *as I did*: in the Advertisement to *SJ*.

8 f. *Johnson ... Roscommon*: in *Q. Horatius Flaccus: his Art of Poetry, Englished by Ben Jonson* (1640); *Horace's Art of Poetry. Made English By ... The Earl of Roscommon* (1680), advertized in *The London Gazette*, 24-7 Nov. 1679 (Wood dated his copy 'Nov').

14. *a Task impos'd upon me*. See Introduction, pp. xxxiii, liv.

22-35. Oldham's doctrine of Imitation derives from the theory of Denham and Cowley in their prefaces to *The Destruction of Troy* and *Pindarique Odes* in 1656; the practice of Sprat, Boileau, and Rochester; and Dryden's discussion in the preface to *Ovid's Epistles Translated* (1680). He recalls Dryden's phrases, brings out what Dryden had implied, and frames his own theory and practice to meet Dryden's objections. See Brooks, 'Imitation'.

24 f. Cf. Dryden, op. cit. (*Essays*, i.239): 'I take the imitation of an author ... to be an endeavour of a later poet ... to write, as he supposes that author would have done, had he lived in our age, and in our country.'

32-6. Oldham is accepting, for his variety of Imitation, the principle which Dryden (*Essays*, i.242) had intended to rule out literalism and Imitation alike: 'There is ... a liberty to be allowed for the expression'; 'words and lines' need not 'be confined to the measure of the original', but 'the sense of an author, generally speaking, is to be sacred and inviolable'. Oldham's plea differentiates Imitation, as he is practising it, from Cowley's or Rochester's concept of it: except when actually replacing the original allusions with topical ones, he translates faithfully; see Brooks, 'Imitation', pp. 135-7 and nn., but also 'Juvenal XIII', 'Juvenal III', headnotes, for his freer method there.

33. *a Rule*. Dryden, in the same preface, had quoted this; Horace's ll. 133 f.; Oldham's ll. 227 f.

36. *Where I ... have varied from it*: notably at l. 403, leaving untranslated a dozen lines scarcely conformable to his modernized version.

42 f. Cowley (*Essays*, p. 438) speaks of 'Horace's ... own familiar stile' in 'his Epistles'.

53. *a Scene*: Act III, Scene i.

55-7. *by Dr Sprat ... Horace's Works*. This is the anonymous version of Satire I.ix in *The Poems of Horace ... Rendred in English and Paraphrased*

by Several Persons, ed. Alexander Brome (1666; 2nd edn., 1671; 3rd, 1680).
Despite Oldham's disclaimer, he had not 'finish'd his Imitation' before
becoming acquainted with it. Paul Hammond (pp. 115, 121, 123 f.) adduces
many convincing debts in his first 86 lines, and there is another in l. 130.
Oldham's attribution helps us to add a new piece, indeed two, to the Sprat
canon; in the same vol. the opening of Satire II.vi, leading up to Cowley's
paraphrase of the famous fable, is clearly also Sprat's: see Brooks, 'Contributors', and Brooks, 'Imitation', pp. 129 f. Oldham may have owed his
information to one of the contributors: either Flatman, whom he probably
knew, or Robert Thompson, who handled the affairs of Whitgift Hospital on
behalf of Sheldon and Sancroft (see Bodl. MS Tanner 162, *passim*).

57. *The Odes are there done too*: by Sir Richard Fanshawe; I.xxxi also by Sir
Thomas Hawkins, and II.xiv by 'S. W.', but as Samuel Woodforde tells us in
his *Paraphrase Upon the Canticles* (1679), p. 161, really by his father,
Robert. See Brooks, 'Contributors', and E.N. Hooker, 'The Early Poetical
Career of Samuel Woodforde' (*Essays ... Dedicated to Lily B. Campbell*,
1950, esp. pp. 91-3).

62. *Sternhold and Hopkins*: whose metrical version of the Psalms, completed
in 1562, was a stock target. Cleveland, *Character of a London Diurnal* (1647)
remarks how 'Sternhold and Hopkins murder the Psalms'; cf. e.g. Rochester's
amusing extempore st. (*Poems*, p. 22), *Absalom and Achitophel*, *Pt. II*, l. 403,
and *Religio Laici*, l. 456.

68. *other Pieces*. The relevant piracies are *Garnets Ghost, Father Whitebread's
Walking Ghost*, and *A Satyr Against Vertue* (all 1679). Publication of 'Upon
the Author of ... *Sodom*' (in Rochester's pirated *Poems*, 1680) was, and of
The Clarret Drinker's Song (1680) may have been, unauthorized: but the texts
are sound. Jordan's garbled *Claret-Drinkers Song* (n.d., ?1685) is after
Oldham's death. See Introduction, pp. xc f.

72-5. The pieces afterwards grouped as 'Divine Poems' were scattered throughout in the first, 1633, edn. of Donne's verse. In Cowley's *Works* (1668) the
poems on 'Reason ... in Divine Matters' and 'Christs Passion' are printed
among secular ones in 'Miscellanies' and 'Verses written on several occasions'.

78-91. For the probability that Oldham is primarily answering Sir William
Soame, and the possibility that in *An Essay Upon Poetry* (1682) Mulgrave retorts to this apologia, see Introduction, pp. xxxiii, liii f., nn. 36, 104,
105; and ibid., pp. xlvi, lv, nn. 76, 108, 109, with R. Selden's article
there cited, for the harking-back to what was now very much a minority view
of the decorum of satire.

86. *tuant*: cutting, deadly; see 'Boileau VIII', l. 49 and n.

97. René Rapin (1621-87) was pronounced by Dryden (in 1677) as, among French
critics, along with Boileau 'the greatest of this age' (*Essays*, i.181). Oldham is citing the *Eclogae Cum Dissertatione De Carmine Pastorali* (1659),
p. 171. After enquiring 'Quid enim epitaphio Bionis ... [suaviús] fingi
potest?' Rapin declares that Bion, 'scriptor tam delicatus támque suavis,
... omnésque sermonis delicias congessit in Adonidis epitaphium'. Both
authors, however, are censurable, he concludes, for a perpetual elegance
which contravenes the simplicity proper to pastoral.

104. *Vulcanius*: Bonaventura Vulcanius (De Smet) of Bruges (1538-1614), professor of Greek at Leyden. His translation into Latin verse of the *Idyllia*
of Bion and Moschus was published in 1584.
      Douza: Janus Dousa (Van der Does) the elder (1545-1604), Dutch classical
scholar and Latin poet. His 'Epitaphium Adonidis ex Graeco Bionis totidem
numeris redditum' appeared in his first collection of poems, 1569.

105. *le Fevre*: Tanneguy Lefèvre (Tanaquillus Faber, 1615-72) taught at Sau-
mur, and was father and preceptor of Mme Dacier. His 'Veneris lamentatio ad
Adonin e Bione Smyrnaeo', first published in his Terence (1671), pp. 448 ff.,
was reprinted in his *Epistolae. Pars Prima*, a corrected edn., 1674. It expands and seeks to embellish the idyll, and omits the passage rendered by
Oldham's ll. 166-91.

128. *Resveries*: fanciful notions. The word, in this spelling, had been recently re-borrowed from French in this new sense (*OED*).

Horace His Art of Poetry, Imitated

For Oldham's important account of his Imitation, see Advertisement (above)
ll. 5-54. It was composed not long before its publication, in *Some New Pieces*,
towards the end of 1681 (Bibliography, II.7), and after that of Roscommon's
translation, Nov. 1679 (on which, and Jonson's, see Advertisement, ll. 8 f.,
and n.). The probability that it was occasioned by Soame's attack 'upon the
Author of "Sardanapalus"', is suggested in the Introduction, pp. xxxiii, liv,
and nn. 36, 105.

19. *Dove*. So Jonson and Roscommon; Horace has simply 'avibus'.

37 f. Cf. *The Escurial, or A Description of that wonder of the world for
... magnificence of structure: built by [Philip II] of Spain and lately
consumed by fire*, 1671 (see Pepys, ix.353, n. 1). Cowley contrasts Evan-
der's royal cottage with the Escurial in 'Of Agriculture' (*Essays*, p. 407).

41-3. Cf. Roscommon:
> Most Poets fall into the grossest faults
> Deluded by a seeming Excellence.

80-3. Horace's 'hoc amet, hoc spernat' seems to have suggested these lines,
which have no equivalent in the Latin, or in Jonson, Roscommon, or Boileau.
The doctrine is from Aristotle, *Poetics*, IX.1-4. Cf. Sidney, *Defence of
Poetrie* (ed. Feuillerat, iii.15).

113. Tangier came to Charles II as part of his wife's dowry. The mole was
begun in 1663; work upon it ceased in 1680. Though unfinished, it had
reached a length of 1436 ft. It was demolished preparatory to the evacuation
of Tangier in 1684. A full account of it, from the contemporary evidence, is
in Routh, Ch. 17.

116 f. In 1663 a corporation was set up to further the work of fen-drainage
which Bedford and his fellow-adventurers, with Vermuyden as engineer, had
started under Charles I. In Lincolnshire alone, 25,000 acres of arable were
reclaimed. Cf. Evelyn, 22 July 1670; see also Ogg, i.55-7.

118. *Middleton*: Sir Hugh Middleton, goldsmith, 1560?-1631. He constructed
the New River at Islington, completing it in 1613. It played an important
part in the water-supply of 17th-century London.

121-7. Cf. Jonson:
> ... so farre off it is, the state,
> Or grace of speech, should hope a lasting date,
> Much phrase that now is dead, shall be reviv'd ...
> If Custome please....

145. *Keen Iambicks*. Horace has 'proprio iambo'; and in *Odes*, I.xvi.24,
'celeres iambos'. Oldham echoes Cleveland's 'Come keen *Iambicks*' ('Rebell
Scot', l. 27) and Dryden's *MacFlecknoe*, l. 204. See R. Merton, *N & Q*, ccii
(1956), 55.

156-9. Volpone and Morose are leading characters in Jonson's comedies of *Volpone* and *Epicoene*; Catiline and Sejanus give their names to his Roman tragedies.

162 ff. Cf. Roscommon:
> Yet Comedy sometimes may raise her voice
> Tragedians too, lay by their state to grieve:

194. *Jodelet*: 'Todelet' (in all edns.) originated from the easy misreading of T for J. The reference is evidently to Davenant's *The Man's The Master* (seen by Pepys, 26 Mar. 1668, publ. 1669), in which Scarron's masquerading valet, Jodelet (who reappears in so brilliant a guise in *Les Précieuses Ridicules*) is naturalized in England. You must not, says Oldham, make a pretended aristocrat talk exactly like a true one. This is a sufficiently skilful imitation of Horace's 'intererit multum, divusne loquatur an heros'; a hero (who may be godlike) should not talk like an actual god.

200. *Bore*. i.e. Boor. See *Remarks upon Remarques* (1673), p. 99: 'a Country *Hero* among a company of poor ignorant brutish Boors (that word is Teutonick) ...', i.e. the same word as modern Boer. Cf. Thomas Shipman, *Carolina* (1683), p. 118: 'These *Holland Boars* are worse than other Swine', which unites the meanings Boar, Boer, and Boor.

236 f. Cf. Roscommon's 'How far is this from the *Maeonian* Stile?', Boileau's 'O! que j'aime bien mieux cet Auteur plein d'adresse' (*L'Art poétique*, Chant III, p. 128), and Jonson's 'Who nought assaies unaptly, or amisse'.

290 f. From Boileau, ibid., Chant III, p. 132:
> Inhabile aux plaisirs dont la jeunesse abuse,
> Blâme en eux les douceurs, que l'Age lui refuse.
There is no direct equivalent in the Latin.

292. Verbatim from Roscommon.

296 f. Cf. Roscommon:
> Thus all the treasure of our flowing Years,
> Our ebb of life for ever takes away.

312. The allusion to Oedipus (added by Oldham) is probably topical: Dryden and Lee's *Oedipus* had been produced so recently as the beginning of 1679; they kept the blinding of the hero off-stage, as in Sophocles.

319. *an handsome Third days share*. The profits of the third performance, the dramatist's return from the theatre, were crucial to his emolument, because they were more precarious yet might be much higher than what patron or bookseller contributed. A usual fee for a dedication was 20 guineas, minor authors receiving less; the copy money might be from £10 to £20; but 50 or 60 guineas would be a fair average for the third day's share of plays which were well received. A great popular success might produce more; Shadwell got £130 from the third day of *The Squire of Alsatia*. On the other hand many plays were damned on the first night. (See Johnson's *Lives of the Poets*, ed. Cunningham, i.299 and ii.390.)

337. Blackfriars, the Cockpit or Phoenix, and Salisbury Court, were the most important Caroline playhouses. The second Blackfriars dated from 1596 and was pulled down 6 Aug. 1655. The Cockpit in Drury Lane became a theatre about 1617. It was reopened after the Restoration, but very shortly closed again.

336 ff. Cf. Killegrew's well-known boast to Pepys, 12 Feb. 1666/7, that by his pains the theatre was now 'a thousand times ... more glorious than ever herétofore'—in fiddlers, candles, and appointments generally.

339. Cf. Roscommon: 'And pleas'd the thin and bashfull Audience'.

340. *Bussy d'Ambois*: Chapman's play (1607), seen in about 1675 and admired sufficiently by D'Urfey, 'in spight of the obsolete Phrases and intolerable Fustian', for him to revive it in 1691. Oldham may well have been reading Dryden's dedication of his *Spanish Friar* (1681) in which *Bussy* is condemned as 'a hideous mingle of false poetry, and true nonsense' (*Essays*, i.246).

341. *Gorboduc, or Ferrex and Porrex*, by Sackville and Norton, appeared in 1562: Gorboduc was a legendary king of Britain. Oldham blindly follows Dryden, who alludes to 'the tragedy of Queen *Gorboduc*' in his dedication to *The Rival Ladies* (*Essays*, i.5). Pope wrote to Robert Digby, 2 June 1717, 'Mr. Warton forced me to take Gorboduc, which ... has done Dryden and Oldham some diskindness.... It is truly a scandal, that men should write with contempt of a piece which they never once saw, [being] ignorant even of the sex, as well as sense, of Gorboduc.'

342-6. Charles was the first English king who frequently attended the public playhouse: he intervened in the actors' business disputes, had his favourites among them, lent state robes for coronation-scenes, and once or twice suggested subjects to playwrights. (Nicoll, i.8 f.; Hume, pp. 27 f., 300, 329, 371, 487; James Sutherland, 'The Impact of Charles II on Restoration Literature', *Restoration and Eighteenth Century Literature*, ed. Caroll Camden (A.D. McKillop festschrift), 1963.)

346 ff. For the elaboration in this period of stage-scenery, costume, dancing, and music, see Nicoll, i.28-63.

350. Davenant's *Siege of Rhodes* (1656) is reckoned the first English dramatic opera. *The Tempest* of 1667 has operatic features, and in Shadwell's version became essentially an opera: *Macbeth* followed suit in the same year. Then came Shadwell's *Psyche* and Davenant's *Circe* in 1675 and 1677.

358. *the Poets day*. See l. 319 above, and n.

362. Cf. Roscommon's line on 'Satyrs' (which suggests the topical allusions in ll. 363, 367 f.: '(Whose motion, words, and shape were all a Farce)'.

362-8. Cf. Dryden, 'Epilogue to the University of Oxford', 1673:
      Th'*Italian* Merry-Andrews took their place
      And quite debauch'd the Stage with lewd Grimace; [etc.]
In 1677 Ravenscroft produced his 'Comedy after the Italian Manner', *Scaramouch a Philosopher, Harlequin a School-Boy* ... for which the 'inspiration probably came from Fiorilli's second visit (summer 1675)'. See Hume, p. 302 (cf. p. 283 n. 1) and Sybil Rosenfeld, *Foreign Theatrical Companies in Great Britain in the Seventeenth and Eighteenth Centuries* (1955).

367 f. A broadside entitled *Roger in Amaze; Or, The Countryman's Ramble Through Bartholomew Fair* tells how
      ... one in blew jacket came in, which some do Andrew call,
      Ad's heart talked woundy wittily to them all.
In Harleian MS 5961 is preserved the title-page only of a pamphlet relating to one of the most celebrated of these performers, *A new Fairing for the Merrily Disposed: or the Comical History of the Famous Merry Andrew W. Phill*[ips] (Morley, pp. 249, 293 f.). Cf. also *A Description of Bartholomew Fair* (*c*.1680; *Pepys Ballads*, ed. Rollins, iii.78) st. 10; and Pepys, 29 Aug. 1668.

376. The coarse repartee of the famous fish-market was already a proverb (Tilley, B 350), and the watermen of Thames had a like reputation. Tom Brown has a specimen of this ribaldry in 'A Walk round London and Westminster' (*Works*, 1707-8, iii.58 ff.), but he has clearly given it a literary dress.

378. The 1722 editor supposed an allusion to Charles Saunders's *Tamerlane the Great*, produced Mar. 1681. But Oldham took his illustration straight from Cowley's 'Ode of Wit' (*Poems*, p. 18):

> 'Tis not such Lines as almost crack the Stage
> When Bajazet begins to rage,

a reference to Thomas Goffe's *The Raging Turke, or Baiazet the Second* (1631). Saunders's piece may, however, have encouraged the borrowing.

387. *invent*: to treat in the way of literary composition (*OED* v.2.b.).

388, 391 f. Cf. Roscommon:

> And if your Stile be natural and smooth ...
> So much good Method and Connexion may
> Improve the common and the plainest things.

395. Hyde Park, and the Mall in St. James's Park. In Etherege's *Man of Mode* (III.iii.41 ff.) Young Bellair remarks to Harriet, as they walk in the Mall, 'Most people prefer *High Park* to this place', and she replies 'It has the better Reputation I confess: but I abominate the dull diversions there, the formal bows, the Affected smiles, the silly by-Words, and amorous Tweers, in passing; here one meets with a little conversation now and then.'

402. Oldham omits Horace's technical discussion of classical metres, ll. 251-62 of the Latin.

405, 418, 421 f., 424 f. Cf. Dryden's verdict, in *Of Dramatick Poesie*: 'The sweetness of English verse was never understood or practised by our fathers', and in the dedication of *The Rival Ladies*: the excellence of rhyme was 'never fully known till Mr. Waller taught it; he first made writing easily an art; first showed us to conclude the sense most commonly in distichs, which, in the verse of those before him, runs on for so many lines together, that the reader is out of breath to overtake it' (*Essays*, i.7, 35).

417. Cf. Roscommon: 'Read them by day, and think of them by night.'

418 ff. A clench is a pun or play on words. Cf. Dryden, 'Defence of the Epilogue' (1672): Jonson 'was not free from the lowest and most grovelling kind of wit, which we call clenches'. Giving examples, he continues: 'This was then the mode of wit ... the vice of the age, and not Ben Johnson's.' In *Of Dramatick Poesie* he condemns the same addiction in Shakespeare (*Essays*, i.80, 173).

420. Verbatim from Roscommon.

439 ff. The expansion of Horace's ll. 282 f. was suggested by Boileau, *L'Art poétique*, Chant III, p. 130:

> Aux accez insolens d'une bouffonne joie,
> La sagesse, l'esprit, l'honneur furent en proye.
> On vid, par le public un Poëte avoué
> S'enrichir aux dépens du mérite joué,
> Et Socrate, par lui, dans *un choeur de Nuées*,
> D'un vil amas de peuple attirer les huées.
> Enfin de la licence on arresta le cours.
> Le Magistrat, des loix emprunta le secours....

456. The plaint is especially significant as being Oldham's own.

457. *to file, and finish*. Dryden's phrase, in his epilogue to Etherege's *Man of Mode* (1676).

459 ff. Oldham's free version follows Roscommon's:

> Remember of what weight your Judgment is,
> And never venture to commend a Book,
> That has not pass'd all Judges and all Tests.

465 ff. The 'furor poeticus', formerly glorified, had fallen under suspicion: see Spingarn, i.x-xi, and G. Williamson, *Seventeenth Century Contexts* (1960), 'The Restoration Revolt against Enthusiasm'. The reaction went hand in hand in literature and in religious politics: Méric Casaubon's *Treatise concerning Enthusiasme* (1655), in which inspiration and ecstasy were analysed and shown to be not supernatural, but merely the working of nature and subject to illusion, was directed in part against the claims to private revelation advanced by certain of the sectaries. See 'Ode on Jonson', ll. 54 ff. and n., and 'Praise of Poetry' (R96, R99).

476. *Cromwel's Porter*: a religious maniac, confined in Bedlam. Cf. D'Urfey, Prologue to *Sir Barnaby Whigg* (1681):
> Like Lunaticks ye roar and range about ...
> Like Oliver's Porter but not so devout.

He is portrayed in Marcellus Laroon's *London Cries* (?1688). See also Etherege (ed. Brett-Smith, p. 199, l. 337 and n.).

477 f. Cf. Roscommon: 'Lunacy beyond the Cure of art'.

478. *Allen*: Thomas Allen MD (Fellow of Caius College, Cambridge 1651-60; of the Royal Society 1667; and of the College of Physicians 1671) was physician to Bedlam. He died 1684. See Pepys's *Diary*, ed. Wheatley, iii.327 n.

512. *Some one well humor'd Character*. Horace has 'speciosa locis morataque recte'; Oldham follows Roscommon:
> ... such a lucky Character
> As being humor'd right and well persu'd....

519. Cf. Roscommon: 'Our *Roman* youth is bred another way'.

521. *Wingate*: *Of Natural and Artificial Arithmetic* (1630) by Edmund Wingate (1596-1656): a standard textbook.

547-50. The Latin is 'neu pransae Lamiae vivum puerum extrahat alvo'. Ll. 550 f. follow Roscommon:
> Or venture to bring in a Child alive
> That Canibals have murther'd and devour'd.

Downes (*Roscius Anglicanus*, 1708, pp. 33, 38) remembered the use of 'machines, as flyings for the Witches' both in *Macbeth*, revived 18 Feb. 1673, and in Shadwell's *Lancashire Witches*, produced *c*.Sept. 1681; and ll. 548 ff. are aimed at one or both of these. Cf.
> *MacFleckno*, for the Mirth of Mankind fram'd
> For Magic Broomsticks and for Witches fam'd,

in a satire ('Wretch, whosoe're thou art that long'st for praise') among the Welbeck MSS deposited in the University of Nottingham library (it was printed in the apocryphal *Posthumous Works ... by Samuel Butler*, iii.1717); and for the *Macbeth*, cf. Dryden, 'Epilogue to the University of Oxford' (1673), ll. 22, 29-30.

560. *Paul's Church-yard*. In his list of booksellers' signs here, F.G. Hilton Price, *The Signs of Old London, London Topographical Record*, iii.110 ff., gives many of the Restoration period.

564 f. Cf. Roscommon: 'A string may jarr in the best Masters hand'.

572 ff. Cf. Roscommon:
> But he that hath been often told his fault,
> And still persists, is as impertinent,
> As a Musician that will always play,
> And yet is always out at the same Note.

576. *bubble*: a dupe or gull (*OED* sb. 5). Cf. 'Jesuits II', l. 269 n.

577. 'To hit a blot', at backgammon, meant to take an exposed piece or man. See *OED* blot, sb.[2].

578-81. The Latin is:

> Sic mihi, qui multum cessat, fit Choerilus ille,
> quem bis terve bonum cum risu miror;

Oldham follows Roscommon:

> When such a positive abandon'd Fopp,
> (Among his numerous Absurdities)
> Stumbles upon some tolerable Lines,
> I fret to see them in such company,
> And wonder by what Magick they came there.

with a final touch from *Hudibras*, II.iii.563 ff.:

> Quoth *Hudibras*, you'r in the right,
> But how the *Devil* you come by't,
> I can't imagine....

579. *Lucks*: happens. An obsolete usage (*OED* cites this example and one from Eachard, *Contempt of the Clergy*, a work Oldham knew).

589. Cf. Roscommon: 'Some love the dark, some chuse the clearest light'.

595. *Indifference allow*. The 1681 text had 'do difference allow'; 'Indifference' (meaning mediocrity) is the reading of the errata. Originally Oldham formed the line on Boileau's version (*L'Art poétique*, Chant IV, p. 135): 'Il est dans tout autre Art des degrés differens'. To clarify the sense, and avoid the duplication of 'do', he revised it on a hint from Jonson's (ll. 555 f.):

> ... neither, Men, nor Gods, nor Pillars meant,
> Poëts should ever be indifferent. [sc. mediocre].

598. *Willis*: Dr Thomas Willis (1621-1675), buried in Westminster Abbey. *A Pindarique Elegy On the most Famous and Learned Physitian D[r]. Willis* (Wood 429 (34)) was 'Printed', according to Wood's note, 'at Oxon by L. Lichfeild 22 Nov. 1675'. A portrait is reproduced in Abraham Wolf, *A History of Science ... in the 16th and 17th Centuries*, 1935 (illustn. 225). Willis is remembered for his work on the anatomy of the brain, on nervous disorders, and above all on saccharine diabetes. Oldham's friend, Dr Richard Lower, was Willis's disciple and successor. Cf. *An Elegy On The Death of ... Dr. Richard Lower* (1691):

> When the learn'd *WILLIS* dy'd, he did impart
> His utmost Skill to thy capacious Heart....

The extent and pre-eminent fame of Willis's practice, as of Lower's, is illustrated in Sir William Petty's references to them in his correspondence with Southwell (ed. Lansdowne, 1928, pp. 214, 222).

600. *Sprat*: Thomas Sprat, 1635-1713; Bishop of Rochester from 1684. On 23 Nov. 1680 Evelyn 'went to St Paul's, to hear that great wit, Dr Sprat.... His talent was, a great memory, never making use of notes, a readiness of expression in a most pure and plain style of words, full of matter, easily delivered.' Burnet is unfavourable: 'Sprat had studied a polite style much, but there was little strength in it'; upon which Dartmouth comments: 'He was highly valued by men of wit, and little by those of his own profession' (i.261 and n.).

Tillotson: John Tillotson (1630-94), Archbishop of Canterbury from 1691. He was a disciple of the Cambridge Platonists; and according to his friend Burnet (i.335) 'had the brightest thoughts and the most correct style of all our divines, and was esteemed the best preacher of the age'. He abandoned all ostentation of learning, directing his appeal to the reason of a lay audience assumed to be capable of judging for itself without special professional training. See Leslie Stephen, *English Literature and Society in the Eighteenth Century* (1904), p. 50; Spingarn, introduction §IV, especially p. xliv; and Mackay's introduction to James Arderne, *Directions Concerning the Matter and Stile of Sermons*, 1671 (Luttrell Society, 1952). Dryden himself professed to have learnt prose style from Tillotson.

603. *Finch*: Sir Heneage Finch, created Earl of Nottingham, 1681, and at this time Lord Chancellor. He is characterized under the name of Amri in *The Second Part of Absalom And Achitophel* (11. 1019 ff.), where he is praised for his exposition of the laws, 'with such Charms of Eloquence'. Pepys 'seems always to have admired his style' (v.140, n. 2), 3 May 1664, 13 Oct. 1666. Burnet (ii.43) is critical: 'He was long much admired for his eloquence, but it was laboured and affected: and he saw it as much despised before he died.' Thomas Shipman has 'eloquent as *Finch*' in *Carolina*, 1683 ('The Pick-Packet', 1665).

604. *Selden's Learning*. Cf. Jonson's 'Epistle to John Selden'. Clarendon says of Selden (1584-1654): 'He was of so stupendious learninge in all kindes, and in all languages, (as may appeare in his excellent and transcendent writings) that a man would have thought, he had bene intirely conversant amongst bookes, and had never spent an howre, but in readinge and writinge' (Nichol Smith, p. 167).

604. *Vauhan*: Sir John Vaughan (1603-74), friend of Selden, MP for Cardiganshire, and from 1668 Chief Justice of Common Pleas. His 'sense' may be assessed from his *Reports and Arguments* [in] *Common Pleas* (1677): of constitutional importance were his judgements in *Bushell's Case*, 1671, which established the immunity of juries from prosecution for their verdicts, and the rules he laid down in *Thomas* v. *Sorrell*, 1674, defining the royal dispensing power. Pepys was told by Finch that he was 'of excellent judgement and learning, but most passionate and opiniastre'; refers to him as 'the great speaker', and valued proportionately his high praise of the masterly speech Pepys himself made, 5 Mar. 1668, in defence of the Navy Office (3 July 1666, 28 Mar. 1664, 6 Mar., 6 Apr., 18 May 1668). See also Clarendon, *Life* (1857), i.30.

607. *Fleckno*: Richard Flecknoe (d. 1678?), whom Marvell had satirized in 'Fleckno, an English Priest at Rome'. Oldham had already transcribed the lines in which Dryden immortalized him as 'Through all the realms of nonsense, absolute'.

608. *second Rate*. See 1. 672 n.

615. *entertain*: 'entertainment ... a feast or banquet' (*OED*).

622 f. Cf. Pepys, 12 Apr. 1669: '... thence by water to the Bear-Garden.... Here we saw a prize fought between a soldier and country fellow, one Warrell.... He did soundly beat the soldier, and cut him over the head.' Cf. ibid., 27 May 1667. Bear-Garden was on the south side of the river, near the present site of Southwark Bridge. Cf. 'Jesuits, Prologue', 11. 26 f.

624-7. The *Spectator* (V.ii, No. 161) describes a wake; the sport of throwing the bar is mentioned. Sir Thomas Parkyns (*The Inn-Play*, 2nd edn., 1714) refers to 'country rings for wrestlings at wakes and other festivals'. According to Carew's *Survey of Cornwall* (1602), p. 75, it was a rule in west-country wrestling that a girdle to take hold by should be worn. See Joseph Strutt's *Sports and Pastimes of The People of England* (1903), ed. J. Charles Cox, p. 71, etc.

630 f. Cf. Colonel Edmund Ashton's 'Prologue against the Disturbers of the Pit':

> ... every one with Insolence enjoys
> His Liberty and Property of Noise.

(text, Rochester, ed. Pinto, p. 54; authorship, Vieth, *Attribution*, pp. 266-8).

635 f. Cf. R. Fletcher, 'A Survey of the World', *Ex Otio Negotium* (1656):
> ... the *Dallying Gallant* ...
> Thinks there's no Heaven like a Bale of Dice,
> Six Horses and a Coach with a device:
> A cast of Lackeys....

From the technical meanings it bore in certain sports and crafts, 'cast' was occasionally used for a set or suit of other things (*OED*, sb. III, 13-17).

637. *Flanders*: Flanders-horses. For the prestige they conferred cf. *HMC*, Finch, II.81, 19 July 1680: 'My brother ... will be to morrow at Tunbridge with his chariott and six Flanders horses ... so that he will be the chief spark there.'

638-42. Cf. Roscommon:
> ... you are of too quick a sight
> Not to discern which way your Talent lies
> Or vainly struggle with your Genius.

656. The expansion follows Boileau (*L'Art poétique*, Chant IV, p. 139): 'Les Tygres amollis dépouilloient leur audace'.

659 f. Cf. Cowley, 'Ode. Of Wit' (*Poems*, p. 17):
> Such were the *Numbers* which could call
> The *Stones* into the *Theban* wall.

667. Cf. Boileau, op. cit., p. 138: 'Enferma les Cites de murs et de rem-pars'. The Latin is 'oppida moliri'.

670. Cf. Boileau, op. cit.: 'Et sous l'appuis des lois mit la foible inno-cence'.

671 f. See Appendix II, ll. 70 f.

672. The classification of warships from first-rates down to sixth-rates, according to their force, was introduced, apparently, in 1653 (Pepys, iii. 128, n. 1). Oldham's is the *OED*'s earliest instance of the generalized sense of the noun: 'a person or thing of the highest class'.

673, 676 f. Oldham leaves out Tyrtaeus (whom Horace couples with Homer), and, like Boileau (loc. cit., p. 139), inserts Hesiod:
> Hésiode à son tour, par d'utiles leçons,
> Des champs trop paresseux vint haster les moissons.

678 f. Cf. Boileau, op. cit.:
> Depuis le Ciel en vers fit parler les Oracles ...
> Apollon par des vers exhala sa fureur.

Horace has merely 'dictae per carmina sortes'.

696 ff. Foot- as well as horse-races were held at Newmarket. 'Letters from New-market inform us', says *The True Domestick Intelligence* for Mar. 16-19, 1679/80, that 'on the 18 instant are to be Run several Foot-Races, to a considerable value'.

697. *Airings*. Used of the exercising of horses, 'to bring them to a perfect wind'; see *OED*, which has no instance of the word as applied to a man in this sense.

701. *Of good repute in either Chappel*. Cf. Pepys, 8 Sept. 1667: 'to the King's Chapel ... and there I hear Cresset sing a Tenor part along with

the Church music.... [M]eeting Creed, I with him ... to the Queen's Chapel
and hear their music.' Cf. Chamberlayne, *Angliae Notitia* (1682), i.172:
'There are Nine and Twenty Gentlemen of His Majesties Chappel-Royal, ...
all of the most eminent of England in their Profession'; and see *The King's
Musick*, ed. H.T.C. De Lafontaine (1909), pp. 297-364 (on 1676-83), *passim*.

717. *hire the House*: this appears to mean that they pay the actors to produce their plays. The theatres were known as 'the King's House' (Drury Lane)
and 'the Duke's House' (Dorset Gardens).

725 ff. Oldham consulted Boileau (*L'Art poétique*, Chant I, p. 110) as well
as the Latin:
> Chaque vers qu'il entend, le fait extazier.
> Tout est charmant, divin, aucun mot ne le blesse,
> Il trépigne de joye....

735. Cf. Roscommon: 'As men that truly grieve at Funerals'.

742. *sound*: supported both by the Latin (*perspexisse*) and by Roscommon's
version: 'seen the bottom of his deepest thoughts'; 'found' of the 2nd and
subsequent edns. originates in a misreading of the long s.

745. *learned Ben*: Jonson; cf. Oldham's ode on him, ll. 196 f. and n. Drum-
mond records his characteristic advice to read Quintilian, 'who, he said,
would tell me the faults of my Verses as if he lived with me' (Spingarn,
i.210).

776. A red cross and the words 'Lord have mercy upon us' were set on the
doors of plague-stricken households. A pamphlet, *The Shutting Up Infected
Houses As it is practised in England Soberly Debated* (1665), protests
against the inhumanity of the measure and urges its unsoundness.

779. Cf. Roscommon: 'Than Poetasters in their raging fits'.

780 f. Oldham adds the simile of the dog.

785. Like lesser ditches, Fleet-Ditch was not railed off.

791. Empedocles of Agrigentum.

810. *Bedlam or Hogsdon*: so Marvell, *The Rehearsal Transprosed* (1672), quoted
Wheatley, ii.246, who comments: 'Hoxton was synonymous with Bedlam as a
place for lunatics, for whom there were three distinct asylums.' Bedlam or
Bethlehem Hospital, which before the Great Fire had stood in Bishopsgate,
was rebuilt in 1676 in Moorfields.

812. The Tower menagerie was one of the sights of London: see 'Juvenal III',
l. 286 n. There were four lions in 1681, but three of them died that year.
See *Grimalkin, Or, The Rebel-Cat* (1681), *The Lions Elegy Or Verses on the
Death of the three Lions in the Tower* (1681), and *A Pleasant Funeral-
Oration, at the Interment of the Three (lately Deceased) Tower-Lyons* (1681).

813 ff. Cf. Boileau, *L'Art poétique*, Chant IV, p. 136:
> ... ce Rimeur furieux
> Qui ...
> Aborde en recitant quiconque le saluë,
> Et poursuit de ses vers les Passans dans la rue.

An Imitation of Horace: Book I, Satyr IX

Donne was inspired by the same original in his 'Satyr IV' (the insufferable
courtier) and perhaps in 'Satyr I' (W. Milgate (ed.), *The Satires ... of John*

Donne (1967), pp. 116, 148 f.). Jonson's and Sprat's versions are noted in Oldham's 'Advertisement': on Paul F. Hammond's demonstration of his debts to Sprat, from which I derive the nn. on them, below, see ibid., ll. 55-7 n.

1 f. Cf. Sprat, 'Of late ... I musing walkt'. For the Mall, see 'Art of Poetry', l. 396 n.; it is where, notes Hammond, the narrator is 'Seized' (cf. l. 4) by his victimizer in Rochester's 'Timon'.

3 f. Cf. Sprat, 'with familiar freedom' and 'Whom scarce I knew, save onely by his name'. In 'Timon' the victimizer 'just my name had got'. But all three poets are translating 'quidam notus mihi nomine tantum'.

14. Cf. Sprat, 'The more I honour you', for 'pluris ... mihi eris'.

16 f. Cf. Sprat, 'And still all ways to shake him off I tri'd, / Sometimes I walk'd apace'.

19. *Bagnio*: the Turkish bath, 'lately erected in *London*' was 'as near the *Turkish*-Fashion as may be'; see *A True Account of the Royal Bagnio, with a Discourse of its Vertues* (1680: 'March 31', Luttrell, *Catalogues* No. 2, p. 10, item 69), printed by Oldham's publisher, Hindmarsh.

22. Sprat (as narrator) 'whisper'd' his footboy; Oldham, to himself. He has other small debts at l. 25, where Sprat has 'an impertinent man'; 45, 'trouble'; 79, 'My last hour's come'; 84, 'fatal tongue'; 86, 'Talkers'.

24. *Manly*: the hero of Wycherley's *Plain Dealer* (1676): cf. II.i, where, after threatening Novel with kicking, he puts him and Lord Plausible out of the room.

26-35. Oldham expands Horace's half-dozen words, and in ll. 107-24 adds more of the impertinent's talk. Both passages owe something to the impertinent in Donne's 'Satyr IV' (cf. especially his ll. 101-5, 108 f., 111-14, 127), who retails court scandal and trite politics.

27 f. See Luttrell, i.91, May 1681, on two months of widespread drought, not broken in and about London till late June (i.104), when 'seasonable showers for this week past ... brought the price of hay, corn and provisions to a moderate rate again'. Cf. Evelyn, 29 Apr., 12 June 1681.

29. On 12 Dec. 1680 Evelyn records how the comet, visible all over Europe, troubled his mind. The bore repeats a rumour of a new one.

31-3. In Etherege's *Man of Mode* (1676; II.ii.57-8) Belinda pretends she has had to entertain 'Welch acquaintance' at the play with just such conversation: 'that is sparkish Mr. such a one who keeps reverend Mrs. such a one, and there sits fine Mrs. such a one who was lately cast off by my Lord such a one'. It was fit only for the hearing of country cousins, or the mouth of a brisk bore.

34. *the Groom-Porters*. Pepys went as a spectator to the Groom-Porter's, 1 Jan. 1667/8: see his full description. The gamesters 'began ... at about eight at night', though 'their heat of play' he learnt, 'begins not till about eleven or twelve'. He marvels 'how easily here, where they play nothing but guinnies, a £100 is won or lost'; how 'old gamesters', without money, 'come ... and look on'; 'how persons of the best quality ... play with people of ... meaner'; and 'lastly ... the formality of the groome-porter, who is their judge of all disputes in play and all quarrels'.

36. Cf. Sprat: 'I minded not a word'.

39. Cf. Sprat: 'fain be rid of me'.

41. *in a Course*: 'under the doctor'; for 'a course of physick', cf. Pepys, 1 Apr. 1666; 'a course of diet', Wood, *Life and Times*, iii.13.

52. Lambeth Palace, 'my Lord's', is the residence of the Archbishop of
Canterbury, 'his Grace' of l. 126 (see n.). Whitgift School was under his
jurisdiction. From Lambeth, on Archbishop Sancroft's behalf, Dr Thompson
corresponded with Oldham's former headmaster, Shepheard, who also made business journeys thither (Bodl. MS Tanner 162 ff. 64, 69, 97).

55. *wheadle*. See 'Aude aliquid. Ode', l. 150 n., and cf. 'A Letter', ll. 80 f.

59 f. Cf. Sprat: 'If once you knew me, Sir'.

68. Rochester had died 26 July 1680.

70. The Anglicization, 'Andrew', can hardly be Oldham's. Cf. *MacFlecknoe*,
l. 53: 'St. Andrés feet ne'er kept more equal time'. The famous Frenchman
arranged the dances in Shadwell's *Psyche* (1674-5) and was the leading dancer
in the court masque, *Calisto* (1675). See Etherege, *Man of Mode* (1676) and
Brett-Smith's n. (p. 253, l. 311, p. 321).

72. *Humphreys*. Pelham Humfrey (1647-74) entered the Chapel Royal as a choris-
ter, 1660. He studied composition under Lully in Paris from 1664. Returning
in 1667 he became a gentleman of the Chapel Royal, and Master of the Children in 1672. Flatman wrote a pastoral song on his death.
     Blow. Dr John Blow (1649-1708) succeeded Humfrey as Master of the Chil-
dren, 1674, and was organist of Westminster Abbey, 1668-79, and again from
1695. Next to his pupil Henry Purcell, he was the greatest English composer
of his time. He was to write the music to Oldham's St. Cecilia Ode (see
headnote, below), performed the year after the poet's death.

73 f. Cf. Sprat: 'Here it was time to interpose: Have you / No mother, Sir,
nor other kindred'.

91-3. Cf. Jonson, *Poetaster*, III.i.214, 217:
               Now, let me dye, sir, if I know your lawes ...
               Besides, you know, sir, where I am to goe.

94. Horace has only 'Dubius sum quid faciat, inquit', without stage-
direction. Cf. Sprat, 'Here he perplext stood still' [with an appropriate,
though different, gesture].

107-24. Without equivalent in the Latin: see n. to ll. 26-35; and with ll.
123 f., cf. Donne, 'Satyre IV', ll. 1-3; more of Donne's opening is echoed
in 'On the Times' (R222 f.).

110. *Doway ... St. Omers*: the colleges at which priests were trained for the
English mission. Oates entered St. Omers 10 Dec. 1677; expelled 23 June
1678, he came forward with his story of the Popish Plot on his return to
England.

111-13. Edward Fitzharris, an Irish Catholic, was arrested in Mar. 1681 for
a treasonable libel. Hoping to save himself, he pretended he could make
great discoveries concerning the Plot. Lest the King and his ministers
should stifle this evidence, the Commons decided to take the matter out of
their hands by impeaching Fitzharris before the Lords; who, however, rejected the impeachment. The Commons then voted that all who concurred in
trying Fitzharris in any other court were betrayers of the liberties of
their country. He was nevertheless prosecuted for the libel; on 11 May three
judges to one pronounced that the impeachment would not bar a trial; and he
was finally tried and found guilty 9 June, sentenced 15 June, and executed,
after a vain attempt to obtain a pardon, 1 July. See Burnet, ii.283-5;
Luttrell, i.68, 82, 96, 98 f., 104 f.; *The Examination of Edw. Fitzharris,
relating to the Popish Plot*, Mar. 10 1680/1; *The tryal and condemnation of
Edw. Fitz-harris Esq* (1681); *An Elegie Upon Edward Fitz-Harris, Executed
at Tyburn for High-Treason upon Friday July 1, 1681*; and Jones, pp. 174-6.

115. Louis XIV's confessor was the Jesuit Père de la Chaise; his mistresses at this time were Mme de Montespan and Mme de Maintenon—probably the latter is meant.

116-18, 120. Cf. E. Settle, *The Character of a Popish Successor and What England may Expect from Such a One* (1681)—including (p. 13) 'Fire and Faggot'. The pamphlet preceded the Oxford Parliament (21 Mar.); a series of answers and counter-answers denied and reasserted that a Popish successor would be bound to crusade against English Protestantism.

119. Cf. *An Appeal from the Country to the City* (1679), by Charles Blount (pseudonymously), p. 8 ad fin.: 'More Romish Canons fitting to be considered by all Abby-Landed Men.... So that if any men (who have Estates in Abbey-Lands) desire to beg their Bread, and relinquish their Habitations and Fortunes to some old greasie bald-pated Abbot, Monk, or Friar, then let him Vote for a Popish Successor.' See also 'Jesuits III', l. 54 and n.

126. *his Grace*: a title reserved for Archbishops and Dukes. Here (see l. 52 n.) it is the Archbishop; in Sprat's 'I pray Sir get his Graces hand to this' it fits himself and the Duke of Buckingham, whose chaplain he was. The title in Sprat may have put the Archbishop and Lambeth (connected with Whitgift School) into Oldham's head.

136-42. Hammond cfs. Jonson, *Poetaster*, III.i.248-59. Oldham's 'no Family / Throughout the whole three Kingdoms is more free', as an expansion of 'domus hac nec purior ulla est' is evidently indebted to Jonson's 'That place is not in *Rome* ... / More pure or free'. Cf. also ll. 140-2 ('none ... Place') with Jonson's

> There's no man greev'd, that this is thought more rich
> Or this more learned; each man hath his place, ...

but each is close to the Latin; Oldham the closer.

151-6. Hammond draws attention to Jonson's version of the Horatian passage (ll. 56-9), *Poetaster*, III.ii.271-7. Oldham owes to it 'Hang on his coach' (cf. 'run by his coach') and the reference to the 'Groom', without equivalent in the Latin.

160. The doctor friend is Richard Lower, for whom see Introduction, p. xxiv and n. 38; 'Juvenal XIII', l. 197 n.

Paraphrase upon Horace: Book I, Ode XXXI

3. *Esham*'s: Evesham's, pronounced Eezham's; cf. 'Lords of fat E'sham' (Pope, *Imitations of Horace*, ed. J. Butt, p. 181, Epistle II.ii.240) and 'Worcestershire, and the Vale of Esam' (Duke of Newcastle, *A New Method ... to Dress Horses*, 1667, p. 60). In 1938, Strickland Gibson told me that 'Evesam' still survived as a local pronunciation. For 'Eves' as 'Ease' cf. Shakespeare, *Richard III*, V.iii.22, Q1, F1: 'Ease-dropper' (subst.).

5. Cf. Randolph, 'A Pastoral Courtship' (*Poems*, p. 112): 'More white and soft then *Cotsall wooll*.'

6. *Lemster*: the Leominster district, Herefordshire: 'The excellencie of Lemster wooll' is celebrated in the seventh song of Drayton's *Polyolbion*. Cf. *CSPD*, 1675-1676, p. 374.

11. For Lombard-street and its banker-goldsmiths, Vyner, Backwell (till 1672), Duncombe, and Kent among the chief, see F.G. Hilton Price, *A Handbook of London Bankers* (1876), and his *Signs of Old Lombard Street* (1887). Cf. 'Boileau VIII', ll. 311 f. and n.

15-18. An exceptionally 'plenteous vintage' in the Canaries is reported by *The True News: Or, Mercurius Anglicus*, Mar. 3-6, 1679/80: 'there was a greater scarcity of Casks, than of Wine'; duties on the Spanish wines just arrived were forecast at 'above 80000 *l.*'.

21. *Florence* ... *Mont-Alchine*: wines from those places (Montalcino is a town near Siena). Neither is in *OED*; for the second, see Evelyn, 2 Nov. 1644 (quoted Hammond): 'Mount Alcini famous for the rare Muscatello'. A version of John Philips, *Ad Henricum St John*, entitled *A Modern Latin Ode Attempted in English* (1707; repr. Philips, *Works*, 1714), claiming a taste for the 'finest Tea, and best *Virginia*', adds 'Hermitage, or *Mont'Alcino*'.

22. French wines follow the Italian. 'Mant' is not in *OED*: but is characterized as 'a very good Claret' in W. Hughes, *Compleat Vineyard* (1665), p. 65 (quoted Hammond). Robert Hooke, 22 Apr. 1678 (*Diary*, ed. Robinson and Adams) 'told Wild of Mant wine'. Cf. *Covent Garden Drollery* (1672; ed. G. Thorn Drury, p. 79): 'In *Burgundy* and *Mant* the great ones rayle': Mant, notes the editor (p. 141), 'is probably a shortened form of "Vin d'Amant", mentioned in a list of wines by Henry Bold, *Poems*, 1664, p. 170.' Bold has 'Wines of *Nantz*' in the same list, distinct from his 'vin ... d'*Amant*'; clearly in the present passage 'Mants' is not an error for 'Nantz'. 'Frontignac' is an erroneous form of Frontignan, and signifies a muscat wine made there. Chablis, a celebrated white wine, was named from a small town in the department of Yonne. For Oldham's spelling, cf. Shadwell, *The Sullen Lovers* (1668; V.92): 'You must have your cellars full of Champaign, Chablee.' Champagne, like Chablis, was a new luxury in Restoration England: see G. Scott Thomson, *Life in a Noble Household* (1940 edn.), pp. 191-4, quoting Woburn Abbey accounts.

23. German wines. According to Phillips's dictionary (1696 edn., see *OED*) an '*Auln* or Aum of Renish Wine' contains 40 gallons, 40 pints. Hock, from Hockamore, is properly the wine produced at Hochheim on the Main; Backrag is from Bacharach on the Rhine; Moselle is a dry white wine from near the Moselle river.

27 f. Cf. Cowley, *Cutter of Coleman-Street*, Prologue (*Essays*, p. 266), on the 'dreadful Fleets of *Tunis* and *Argier*', which make 'The Merchand Ships so much their passage doubt.' The newspapers record many hairsbreadth escapes, like the *Leopard*'s, homeward bound from Zant to Plymouth (*The Currant Intelligence*, 14 and 24-28 Feb., 1679[/80]. 'In November last', reports *The Protestant (Domestick) Intelligence*, 24 Feb. 1679[/80]: 'there were in *Argiers* about 1600 English slaves': the same month Charles granted a brief to collect ransom. Cf. William Okeley, *Eben-Ezer* (1676), relating 'the Miserable Slavery of Algiers' and his 'Miraculous Deliverance'. See also Routh, ch. 8.

29. *Cyprus Birds*: unknown to *OED*; but see *The Ornithology of Francis Willughby*, tr. John Ray, 1678, p. 227: 'Beccafigo's abound ... in the Island of *Cyprus*'. Salted, 'great numbers' are exported; 'in *England* they are called ... *Cyprus birds*. [Our merchants, no less than the Italians of classic times and ours, esteem them] for the delicacy of their taste'; 'deservedly', since they feed 'upon two of the choicest fruits, *viz.* Figs and Grapes.... *Beccafigo*'s are ... most in season in the Autumn, ... being then fattest.'
      Ortolans. Cf. Cowley, 'Of Agriculture' (*Essays*, p. 413):
> Nor *Ortolans* nor *Godwits* nor the rest
> Of costly names that glorify a Feast....

Pepys, 10 July 1668, was shown a treat for the King, 'birds ... from Bordeaux ... almost all fat. Their name is Ortolans.'

Paraphrase upon Horace: Book II, Ode XIV

4. Not in the Latin; Clark (p. 122) derives it from Boileau, 'Epistre III': 'Le moment où je parle est déjà loin de moi.' Cf. also Horace, *Odes*, I.xi, 'dum loquimur, fugerit invidia / aetas'.

20. Cf. Thomas Flatman, 'A Dooms-Day Thought. Anno 1659', ll. 27 f.:
Go to the dull church-yard and see
Those hillocks of mortality.

25 ff. Aimed at Louis XIV. See the discarded variant of this passage, 'A Dithyrambique', l. 21 (Appendix II); and cf. 'The Careless Good Fellow', ll. 31 ff., and n.

32. Poor prisoners in the gaols depended for their food largely upon the alms-basket; cf. *OED*, basket, 1.c., quoting *Trials of White* etc. (1679).

38. For disorders of the lungs, Montpellier, says Steele (*Tatler*, No. 125, 26 Jan. 1710) is as much the place of resort as in classical times Anticyra for distempered brains. Clarendon, partly no doubt for its salubrity, made it his residence in exile from July 1668 to 1679. When Rochester was ill in 1678, Henry Savile (13 July) urged him to winter there (Rochester, *Letters*, p. 204).

45. *Bedrols*: bead-rolls, long list of names; originally, of persons especially to be prayed for.

The Praise of Homer. Ode

The title—and topic—were no doubt suggested by Cowley's ode 'The Praise of Pindar' (see 'Dithyrambique', headnote). There is no certain indication of date. But ll. 1-4, 137 (see nn.) have antecedents in a draft for the ode on Jonson, material which may have had a place in the stanzas excised from it in Dec. 1678 (see the ode, headnote), and perhaps Oldham is here drawing on what he had discarded. For another possible link with the Jonson ode, see ll. 42-4 n., below.

1-4. Cf. the draft (R224) for the 'Ode on Jonson'; Appendix II, ll. 105-8.

13-15. Metaphors such as this reflect the growth of finance which marked the 17th century. Advocating a national bank in emulation of the great Bank of Amsterdam, Petty wrote in his *Quantulumcumque concerning Money* (1682): 'We have in England Materials for a Bank which shall furnish Stock enough to drive the Trade of the whole Commercial World' (R.D. Richards, *Early History of Banking in England*, 1929, p. 103). Oldham echoes Cowley's elegy on Katherine Philips (*Poems*, p. 442):
Orinda on the Female coasts of Fame,
Ingrosses all the Goods of a Poetique Name ...
Does all the business there alone, which we
Are forc'd to carry on by a whole Company.

17-21. Cf. Denham, 'Progress of Learning', ll. 61 ff.:
I can no more believe Old *Homer* blind
Then those, who say the Sun hath never shin'd;
The age wherein he liv'd, was dark, but he
Could not want sight, who taught the world to see.

37. *Purliews*: suburbs. Cf. *Paradise Lost*, II.832.

42-4. Cf. Randolph, 'An Eglogue' to Jonson, *Poems* 1638 (*Jonson*, xi.395, ll. 145 f.): Aristotle

> Knows all the Heavens, as if he had been there,
> And helpt each Angell turn about her spheare.

Perhaps it was when composing his ode on Jonson that Oldham's attention was directed to this. Cf. the like conceit in Cowley (*Poems*, p. 417): as physiologist, Harvey

> ... so exactly does the work survey,
> As if he hir'd the workers by the day.

62-92. The drafts of this stanza in R88, 92, 258 f. were not written originally for the present ode. Homer is not addressed: he is 'ye Grecian', 'He', 'That Poet'. The five-line fragment on R92 looks as though it belonged to Oldham's projected ode 'In Praise of Poetry' (R100 etc.).

62. *Macedonian Youth*: Alexander.

65. *Budg*: stiff, formal, pompous.
Philosophers: Originally the allusion was to Aristotle alone: 'ye awful Stagyrite' (R88), and 'Philosopher' (R258), with corresponding singulars below, in ll. 66, 70, 78, 79. He became Alexander's tutor in 342 BC, remaining so till his pupil's accession in 335, when he retired to Athens. According to Plutarch (*Lives*, VIII.3, tr. B. Perrin) Alexander 'admired [Aristotle] at the first, and loved him', but cooled off later.

70 f. Rhetoric, logic, and ethics. R88 has: 'He might ye Art of Speaking & of Thinking teach.'

77 f. Cf. Dryden, Epilogue to *Marriage à la Mode* (1673):

> Not with dull Morals, gravely writ, like those,
> Which men of easie Phlegme, with care compose.

80. Cf. Plutarch, op. cit., VIII.2: since Alexander 'thought ... the Iliad a viaticum of the military art, he took with him Aristotle's recension of the poem, called the Iliad of the Casket, and always kept it ... under his pillow, as Onesicritus informs us.'

89 f. Cf. Juvenal, X.168 f. Cowley has this commonplace in 'Against Fruition' (*Poems*, p. 99). Cf. 'Boileau VIII', ll. 142 ff.

93 ff. Cf. Denham, 'Cooper's Hill', l. 70: 'for *Homer*'s Birth seven Cities strove'.

100. The deification of Homer is the subject of a relief now in the British Museum (see Gilbert Norwood, *Writers of Greece* (1925), frontispiece).

105. *fabulous Arthur*. So Milton thought him (*Works*, x.127 f.): '... who *Arthur* was, and whether ever any such reign'd in *Britain*, hath bin doubted heretofore, and may again with good reason'.

105. *boasted Constantine*: his father Constantius having died at York, he was saluted Emperor. Milton (*Works*, x.92 f.) notes the 'fame ... seconded by most of our own Historians, though not ... the ancientest' that he was born in Britain, son of a British princess; but rightly rejects it on the testimony of Roman authors, 'neerest to those times'.

110-22. Milton, making choice of the vernacular, was conscious of a sacrifice: 'not caring to be once nam'd abroad, though perhaps I could attaine to that, but content with these British Ilands as my world' (*Reason of Church Government*, Works, iii.i.236).

131. *God of Wit*: Apollo.

132-72. Indebted to the opening of Cowley's Pindarique 'The Resurrection', which describes how Verse, when Virtue dies,

> ... with comely pride
> *Embalms* it, and erects a *Pyramide*
> That never will decay
> Till *Heaven* it self shall melt away,
> And nought behind it stay.

and how then

> ... *Virgils* sacred *work* shall dy.
> And he himself shall see in one *Fire* shine
> Rich *Natures* ancient *Troy*, though built by *Hands Divine*.

Cf. the last stanza of the ode on Morwent.

137. Cf. the draft (R225) for the 'Ode on Jonson' (Appendix II, 1. 129).

144. *proudest Louvres, and Escurials*: coupled in Cowley, 'The Garden', (*Essays*, p. 423), and see 'Art of Poetry', 1. 37 and n.

152 ff. Caligula, according to Suetonius (Cal., XXXIV.2), 'Cogitavit etiam de Homeri carminibus abolendis, cur enim sibi non licere, dicens, quod Platoni licuisset, qui eum e civitate quam constituebat eiecerit'. 'His damned *Successor*' is Nero.

Bion, A Pastoral ... bewailing the Death of ... Rochester

The Greek original is the third idyll of Moschus of Syracuse, fl., with Bion of Smyrna, late in the third century BC. Nothing suggests that Oldham knew Thomas Stanley's verse translation of their idylls, 1651.

John Wilmot, 2nd Earl of Rochester, d. 26 July 1680, aged thirty-three. On Oldham in Rochester's circle, see Introduction, pp. xxviii f., xlii-v and nn. 17, 57-67, 69, 71-5; on the elegy, Advertisement pp. 89 f., especially ll. 111-23: in ll. 1-15, Oldham is revising an anonymous stanza. Other elegies on Rochester were written by Thomas Flatman (*Poems and Songs*, 1682; Latin versions by himself, edn. of 1686, and by Nathaniel Hanbury, *State-Poems, Continued*, 1702, p. 253); Anne Wharton (*Examen Miscellaneum*, ed. Gildon, 1702, with Waller's and Jack Howe's poetical compliments on it); Aphra Behn (*Miscellany*, 1685); Samuel, Thomas, and Mary Woodforde (Bodl. MS Rawl. Poet. 25, f. 146), Samuel Holland (s. sh. fol., 1680) and anon., 'Alas! what dark benighting Clouds or shade' (BL Lutt., I.124, 'Aug. 5', 1680).

39. Cf. 'S. Cecilia Ode', 1. 15.

65. 'Fall' is transitive: cf. 'Shrubs which fall their leaves', Ray, *Flora*, 1665-76 (*OED*).

83 f. A variant of the legend of the Memnonides—birds which sprang from Memnon's ashes, flew three times about his pyre with cries of grief, and then slew one another. (Ovid, *Metamorphoses*, XIII.576 ff.) In mentioning only one bird, Oldham follows his original.

141-7. The Thames suggests Spenser, both because of his referring to it as his birthplace and of the refrain of *Prothalamion*.

152. Spenser matriculated as sizar of Pembroke Hall, Cambridge, 20 May 1569, and studied there till he took his MA in 1576. He speaks of 'my Mother Cambridge' in *The Faerie Queene*, IV.xi.34.

153. Rochester matriculated at Wadham College, Oxford, 18 Jan. 1660, aged twelve; he went down in 1661, the MA being specially conferred upon him, 9 Sept., by Chancellor Hyde. See V. de Sola Pinto, *Enthusiast in Wit* (1962), pp. 5 ff., 10-12.

156 f. Oldham perhaps recalled Rochester's line 'With war I've nought to do' ('Upon Drinking in a Bowl'; see 'The Cup', introductory n.), and his

Strephon dialogues, from which several of his elegists evidently adopted
their pastoral name for him (*Poems*, ed. Pinto, pp. 9, 12; and n., p. 165).

159. Among Rochester's poems, some forty treat of love. A handful are the
finest Restoration love-lyrics we have; but Rochester's value lies quite as
much in his poetical metaphysics and satire.

167 f. See below, 'The Vision', l. 42 n. Book VI of *Paradise Lost* would not
now be chosen as a supreme example of Milton's excellence; but Roscommon
made it the subject of his unrhymed tribute to Milton in *An Essay on Translated Verse*, and Addison gave it disproportionate praise. The early estimate is probably an unconscious reflection of the view, combated by Milton
in the opening of Book IX and expressed by Dryden in the 'Discourse ...
concerning ... Satire' (*Essays*, ii.31), that 'an heroic poem requires to
its necessary design, and as its last perfection, some great action of war'.
See Johnson's unfavourable criticism of Book VI (*Lives of the Poets*, ed.
Birkbeck Hill, i.185).

169 f. Cowley entered Trinity College, Cambridge, as a Westminster scholar,
14 June 1637. He became a minor Fellow in 1640, took his MA in 1643, and
was ejected next year by the Parliamentarians. His *Naufragium Joculare* was
produced at Cambridge 2 Feb. 1638 and *The Guardian* in 1641: 'Davideis' was
also chiefly written there. L. 170 seems to refer to *The Mistress* (1647),
the first collection of his love-verses.

171 f. *Cooper's Hill*, Sir John Denham's most celebrated poem, appeared in
1642. Oldham has the opening passage in mind:
>   ... where the Muses & their train resort,
>   *Parnassus* stands; if I can be to thee
>   A Poet, thou *Parnassus* art to me.

173 f. Mrs Katherine Philips, the Matchless Orinda (1631/2-1664), whose
poems were published in 1664 (surreptitiously) and in 1667. Cowley wrote
lines 'On Orinda's Poems' and 'On the death of Mrs. Katherine Philips'
(*Poems*, pp. 404, 441). He declares in the latter that Apollo, if he should
crown a woman laureate, would choose Orinda before Sappho or the Muses
themselves.

181, 187 f. At least two elegies were printed 1680, and others, e.g. Flatman's, were probably known to Oldham. As Thorn Drury observed, ll. 187 f.
refer to Waller's 'Of an Elegy made by Mrs. Wharton on the E. of Rochester'.
See headnote.

191-6. On Oldham's debt to Rochester, see Introduction pp. xlv f.

210 f. Echoing *Othello*, V.ii.12 f.

217 f. *Maevius*: the type of a bad poet; Virgil *Ecl*. III.90.

The Lamentation for Adonis

'June 2. 81' is appended to an autograph fair copy of the last twenty-six
lines (R217). On Oldham's use of Lefèvre's Latin version, see Advertisement
(above), ll. 105-10 and n.

9. *and tear thy locks*. From Lefèvre, p. 253, 'Scissa genas, & scissa comas';
not in the Greek.

27. Cf. Lefèvre, p. 253:
>   ... non ille dolores,
>   Non tristes aestus animi, non sentit amorem.

35 f. Cf. Lefèvre, p. 253:
             Accendunt luctus & Oreades; & iuga montis,
             Et nemora, & fontes acri plangere resultant.

37-50. The expansion of the original seems to be mainly Oldham's own.

60 f. Cf. Lefèvre, p. 254:
             Et quà luce perît Veneri formosus Adonis,
             Illâ ipsâ periit Veneri praestantia formae.

77. *clips*: embraces.

79. Cf. Lefèvre, p. 254: 'Quo fugis, ô miserande puer?'

95-110. Bion's Venus exclaims simply 'but wretched I live and am a goddess,
and cannot follow thee'. Oldham copies Lefèvre, pp. 254 f.:
             Moreris, puer, at mihi vita est,
      Vita mihi in luctu, posthac, lacrymisque trahenda,
      Heu dolet, heu! dolet esse Deam: finire labores
      Possem, si Stygias possem descendere ad undas,
      Me potius iuvat esse Nihil, quàm sidera plantis
      Tangere, & ingratam producere Nectare vitam,
      In vacuum qui mersus abit vastumque Profundum,
      Praeteriti non ille memor, non ille futuri
      Sollicitus, vitae & mortis discrimina nescit;
      At quem destituit rerum regina Voluptas,
      Si vivit, miser est, rabido data praeda dolori,
      Cum nequeat memores animo depellere sensus.

111. Cf. Lefèvre, p. 255:
             Clade mea felix, & nostro laeta dolore
             Ac spoliis ditata meis:

124. See 'Bion', l. 138 n.

163-191. From the Greek alone; Lefèvre omits the passage.

193-5. The lamentation was a yearly rite; cf. *Paradise Lost*, I.446 ff., on
Thammuz, the Syrian Adonis.

Paraphrase upon the 137 Psalm

Oldham knew Donne's *Poems*, 1633 (Advertisement (above), ll. 72-4, and n.), so
the paraphrase there, probably by Francis Davison, may have suggested his (see
Grierson's Donne, i.424). But he does not echo Davison's version, nor Crashaw's, Sidney Godolphin's, nor those in Bodl. MSS Ashmole 38, p. 98 c, attributed without sufficient grounds to Carew. In this and the next poem, and in
'David's Lamentation', his style of paraphrase is modelled on Cowley's in
'The 34 Chapter of the Prophet Isaiah' and 'The Plagues of Egypt' (*Poems*,
pp. 211 ff., 219 ff.).

35 f. Judges, XXI.19, 21.

57. See Introduction, pp. lxxxvii f.

80 f. Cf. 'Jesuits I', ll. 262 f.

103-7, 114 f. Cf. ibid., ll. 281-92, and Jonson, *Catiline*, I.i.

Paraphrase upon the Hymn of St. Ambrose

In Wither's *Hymnes and Songs of the Church* (1623), the *Te Deum* is entitled
'The Song of St. Ambrose'. It was supposed to have been extemporized by

Ambrose and Augustine, reciting alternately, immediately after Augustine's baptism, AD 387. The legend rests on a spurious passage of the *Chronicon* of Dacius (Bishop of Milan, AD 550).

11. Cf. Cowley, 'Davideis' (*Poems*, p. 251):
>   Only he spoke, and every thing that *Is*
>   From out the womb of *fertile Nothing* ris.

17. Cf. Cowley, loc. cit.: 'They sing loud anthems of his endless praise'.

21 f. Cf. Cowley, loc. cit.:
>   Where *Heaven*, as if it left it self behind,
>   Is stretcht out far, nor its own *bounds* can find ...
>   Nor can the glory contain it self in th' endless space.

23-5. Cf. Cowley ['In the Drake Chair'] (*Poems*, p. 413):
>   The straights of time too narrow are for thee,
>   Lanch forth into an indiscovered Sea,
>   And steer the endless course of vast Eternitie....

26-9. Cf. Cowley, 'Davideis' (*Poems*, p. 251):
>   Not absent from these meaner *Worlds* below;
>   No, if thou wert, the *Elements League* would cease, ...
>   And this vast work all ravel out again
>   To its first *Nothing*; for his *spirit* contains
>   The well-knit *Mass*, ...

34 f. Cf. Cowley, loc. cit.:
>   For there no twilight of the *Suns* dull ray,
>   Glimmers upon the pure and native day.
>   and in his 'Plagues of Egypt' (*Poems*, p. 227):
>   When (Lo!) from the high Countreys of *refined Day*,
>   The *Golden Heaven* without *allay*,
>   Whose *dross* in the Creation purg'ed away,
>   Made up the *Suns* adulterate ray.

38 f. Cf. 'Aude aliquid. Ode', 1. 260.

45. *the rebel World*: from Cowley, 'Isaiah 34' (*Poems*, p. 211).

53. Cf. Cowley, 'The Extasie' (*Poems*, p. 206): 'And mount *herself*, like *Him*, to' *Eternitie* in *Fire*', and perhaps linking with this to suggest l. 52,
>   All the young *Branches* of this Royal Line
>   Did in their *fire* without *consuming shine*,
>   ... through a *rough Red sea* they had been led ...
>   in the 'Ode. Upon his Majesties Restoration' (*Poems*, p. 425).

60. Identical with 1. 221 of the ode on Atwood.

68. Cowley, 'Davideis' (*Poems*, p. 251), has 'Thou Great *Three-One*'.

76-9. Cf. Donne, 'A Litanie', 11. 28 ff.:
>   O Blessed glorious Trinity,
>   Bones to Philosophy, but milke to faith,
>   ... let all mee elemented bee,
>   Of power, to love, to know, you'unnumbered three.

80. Cf. Cowley, 'Christs Passion' (*Poems*, p. 402): 'Mountainous heap of wonders!'

91. Identical with 1. 58 of the ode on Atwood.

95. Cf. Cowley, 'The Muse' (*Poems*, p. 186):
>   Nay thy *Immortal Rhyme*
>   Makes this one short *Point* of *Time*,
>   To fill up half the *Orb* of *Round Eternity*.

98. Cf. Rochester's phrase, 'making of his priest a sacrifice' (*Poems*, p. 3, l. 15), and Donne, 'The Calme', ll. 25 f.:
> ... as on Altars lyes
> Each one, his owne Priest, and owne Sacrifice.

100. Cf. the ode on Morwent, ll. 687 f.; *Hamlet*, V.ii.347 f.; and Rochester's 'everlasting fiery jails' in his translation (l. 14) from Seneca's *Troades*.

104 f. Cf. Cowley, 'Christs Passion' (*Poems*, p. 402):
> How Hell was by its Pris'ner Captive led,
> And the great slayer Death slain by the Dead.

117-19. Cf. Cowley, 'Isaiah 34' (*Poems*, p. 212): '*Nature* and *Time* shall both be *Slain*'.

131-6. Cf. 'Counterpart', ll. 32-6, 39, a variant of this passage.

153 f. Cf. *Paradise Lost*, XI.99 ff., where Michael is commanded to set 'Cherubic watch' at the East of deserted Eden, lest the Fiend 'new trouble raise' and 'Paradise a receptacle prove / To Spirits foul'.

A Letter from the Country to a Friend in Town

The friend in town is John Spencer, barrister of the Inner Temple since 28 Nov. 1675 (F.A. Inderwick, ed., *Calendar of the Inner Temple Records* (1896), iii.105, see also 325, 332). He was half-cousin of Sir Nicholas Carew, Oldham's Beddington patron (Manning and Bray, *History ... of ... Surrey*, facing p. 523; R. Clutterbuck, *History ... of ... Hertford* (1815-27), iii.97; *GEC Baronetage*, ii. 200). The Carews and Spencers were and remained on familiar terms: three of John's elder brothers and sisters were christened at Beddington (Parish Register, ed. W. Bruce Bannerman, *Publications of the Surrey Parish Register Soc.*, x (1912), 17 f.) and in 1703 he was to be joint trustee for the Carew heir (Manning and Bray, p. 533). In the draft of a Latin letter (R279) addressed to him as 'mi amicissime!', Dec. 1678, Oldham expects soon to have his company: no doubt as in 1676, when he wrote at Beddington (R21) the paraphrase of the 137th Psalm, the poet will be spending the Christmas season there, and knows that so will his friend. Just possibly their acquaintance may have begun at Oxford: Spencer (aged 17) matriculated at Magdalen Hall, 12 July 1667, where a contemporary was William Hickes of the Wickwar family with whom the Oldhams had links (Joseph Foster, *Alumni Oxonienses* (1891); see Introduction, pp. xxvii, xxxii-iv and nn. 16, 23, 37). But Spencer took no degree, and may have gone down before, in June 1670, Oldham came up. In later life he succeeded (1699) to the Spencer baronetcy, and became MP for Hertfordshire (1705); he died 16 Nov. 1712 (Clutterbuck, op. cit.; *GEC Baronetage*, loc. cit.; *Victoria County History, Hertfordshire*, genealogical vol., p. 291. See also Introduction, p. xxviii, nn. 15, 16).

Spencer's autograph verse-epistle, dated 18 Mar. 1677/8, to which Oldham was replying, is now MS R198-204; the text is printed as Appendix I. The 'Letter', a draft towards which (R87) is headed 'In Answer to Mr. Spencer', was evidently on the anvil from Mar. till Oldham could date the final form of it as 'Written in July 1678'. Drafts (R85, 87-9, 93-6, 103) show something of its evolution; for these, see Appendix II. Oldham meant to make even more than he eventually did of Spencer's wisely prudent choice of profession and of his happy lot in the metropolis contrasted with his own exile in anti-cultural rusticity; to pursue Spencer's topic of wit; and to answer his attack on satire—witness a heading (R94) 'The Poet addressing himself to Satyr', and passages on R95, 103. Others (R94 f.) were designed for the speech where the poet swears never to write again ('Letter', ll. 84 ff., 113-32), or for one by his dissuading friends; some were utilized in 'Spencer's [sc. Spenser's] Ghost', ll. 74-84, 116 f., 224-6.

1-12. Ovid's exile is described in his *Tristia* and *Ex Ponto*. He was relegated to Tomis (modern Constanta in Romania) by Augustus in AD 8. With ll. 9 f. cf. *Ex Ponto*, II.vii.71 f., IV.ii.25 ff., and Cowley (*Poems*, p. 7): 'One may see through the stile of *Ovid de Trist.* the humbled and dejected condition of *Spirit* with which he wrote it; ... The *cold* of the Countrey had strucken through all his faculties, and benummed the very *feet* of his *Verses*.' *Ex Ponto*, I.iii depicts Ovid's partial revival on receipt of a letter from Rufinus; IV.viii welcomes and answers one from Suillius.

7 f. Cf. Cowley, '[On Verses from Broghill]', (*Poems*, p. 408), where he calls the praise of such men as Broghill
              A Cordial, that restores our fainting Breath,
              And keeps up Life even after Death.
    Cf. also Dryden, 'To the Lady Castlemaine', ll. 51 f.:
              ... your Applause and Favour did infuse
              New Life to my condemn'd and dying Muse.
    and 'Jesuits III', ll. 271 f.

13. Cf. Cowley, 'Answer to ... Verses sent me to Jersey' (*Poems*, p. 43): 'Such comfort to us here your *Letter* gives'.

13 f. At Croydon; Oldham is chafing at his life as usher of the Free School.

19 f. A variant of 'To Madam L.E.', ll. 3 f.; cf. Cowley, 'To the Bishop of Lincoln' (*Poems*, pp. 28 f.):
              Great *Joys* as well as *Sorrows* make a *Stay*;
              They hinder one another in the Crowd
    and more remotely, Shakespeare, *King John*, V.vii.19 f.

23 ff. Cf. Cowley, ['On Verses from Broghill'] st. 4 (*Poems*, p. 408).

41. Spencer discussed wit in his letter (Appendix I, ll. 64 ff., etc.).

42 f. 'Verse' is plural, as in 'Boileau VIII', ll. 334 f.

53-8. Originally Oldham intended to refer directly to Spencer's livelihood at the bar: see Appendix II.

79 f. Cf. Rochester, 'A Satyr against ... Mankind', ll. 31 f.:
              Pride drew him in, as cheats their bubbles catch,
              And made him venture to be made a wretch.

80 f. '*Cully*, a Fool or silly Creature that is easily drawn in and Cheated by Whores or Rogues'.—*A New Dictionary of the Terms ... of the Canting Crew*, by B.E. Gent., quoted, to illustrate the name of Sir Nicholas Cully, in Brett-Smith's Etherege, p. 304; q.v. also for R H[ead], *Proteus Redivivus; or the Art of Wheadling, or Insinuation* (1675); to wheadle someone was to cajole in order to swindle him. A rook is a cheat or sharper (*OED*).

83. *Hit*: win the game. At backgammon there are three kinds of wins: the hit, the gammon, and the backgammon. A saving-share is one 'Not turning to loss, though not gainful' (Johnson). Cf. Lee, *Sophonisba* (1676), IV.i, p. 45.

96 f. *That ... wretch*: Midas.

105. *ill-pack'd*. Shuffled badly, or disadvantageously to the player who is complaining (*OED*).

108. Both as critic, in the *Poetics*, and poet, in the ode on Hermias which Oldham translated.

112. *resent*: repent, regret (*OED* v. I 2 b).

119-24. Cf. Boileau, *Satires*, p. 15, Satire II:
              Maudit soit le premier, dont la verve insensée
              Dans les bornes d'un vers renferma sa pensée,

Et donnant à ses mots une étroite prison,
Voulut avec la Rime enchaîner la Raison.

127 ff. Cf. Cowley ['On Verses from Broghill'], *Poems*, p. 407:
Then in a rage I took
And out at window threw
Ovid and *Horace*, all the chiming Crew,
Homer himself went with them too,
Hardly escap'd the sacred *Mantuan* Book.

131-8. Cf. Boileau, *Satires*, p. 13, Satire II:
De rage quelquefois ne pouvant la trouver,
Triste, las, & confus, je cesse d'y rêver:
Et maudissant vingt fois le Demon qui m'inspire,
Je fais mille sermens de ne jamais écrire:
Mais quand j'ai bien maudit & Muses & Phebus,
Je la voi qui paroist quand je n'y pense plus.
Aussitost, malgré moi, tout mon feu se rallume;
Je reprens sur le champ le papier & la plume,
Et de mes vains sermens perdant le souvenir,
J'attens de vers en vers qu'elle daigne venir.

149. Cf. Cleveland, 'The Hecatomb to his Mistress', l. 73: '(what Divines
hunt with so cold a sent)'.

158 f. Cf. Dryden, 'Prologue to *The Wild Gallant*, revived', 1667:
(Pleas'd with some Sport, which he alone does find
And thinks a Secret to all Humane Kind,).

162-81. The high point of the *Letter*. The thought and some phrases were suggested by the opening of Dryden's dedication of *The Rival Ladies*, 1664
(*Essays*, i.1): 'This worthless present was designed you, long before it was
a play; when it was only a confused mass of thoughts, tumbling over one
another in the dark; when the fancy was yet in its first work, moving the
sleeping images of things towards the light, there to be distinguished, and
then either chosen or rejected by the judgement.' In *The Road to Xanadu*
(1927), J.L. Lowes takes Dryden's account of the creative process for one
of his texts; and Oldham's could be illustrated at length from Lowes's book.
Oldham's description is not merely derivative; it is a true representation
of his own mental habit, as the notes and rough drafts in R bear witness.

169-71, 192-5. Cf. Cowley, 'Davideis' (*Poems*, p. 253):
As first a various unform'd *Hint* we find
Rise in some god-like *Poets* fertile *Mind*,
Till all the parts and words their places take,
And with just marches *verse* and *musick* make.

178 f. Cowley (*Poems*, p. 5) refers to an imperfect version of his play, *The
Guardian*, as 'only the hasty *first-sitting* of a *Picture*'.

199 f. Cf. Cowley, ['In the Drake Chair'] (*Poems*, p. 412):
As well upon a staff may Witches ride
Their fancy'd Journies in the Ayr....
Cf. Cleveland, 'A Letter to a Friend disswading him from his Attempt to
marry a Nun', *Poems* (1653): 'as if their Travel (like Witches in the Air)
were nothing but the Waftage of a deluded Phantasie, perswading themselves
that they circle the Globe, when the Card they sail by, is nothing else but
a slumbring Imposture.'

201. Cf. Denham, 'Natura Naturata'; we are 'led astray / From Nature, both
her Guide and way.'

204. Cf. Etherege, *The Man of Mode* (1676), III.ii.265 ff.: 'Nature has her
cheats, stum's a brain, and puts sophisticate dulness often on the tastless
multitude for true wit and good humour.' See Brett-Smith's n.: to stum is
to raise a new fermentation in wine by adding stum or must to it: this
produces a false sparkle.

224-7. Cf. Boileau, *Satires*, p. 69, Satire VII (imitating Horace, *Satires*,
II.i.57-60):

> À Rome, ou dans Paris, aux Champs ou dans la Ville,
> Deust ma Muse par là choquer tout l'Univers
> Riche, gueux, ou content, je veux faire des Vers.

229. *Feebles*. Cf. *OED*, sb. 3 = Foible 1. [i.e. a weak point; a failing or
weakness of character]. Its earliest instance is from Mrs Behn, *Sir Patient
Fancy*, this same year (1678). But cf. the *Third Advice to the Painter*
('Sandwich in Spain'), 1667 (no. 11 in Osborne): 'We'll find they're feeble,
like *Achilles* Heel', where 'their feeble' is obviously the true reading.

234. Only one of Oldham's poems had yet been printed: *Upon the Marriage of
the Prince of Orange with the Lady Mary*, in the anonymous single-sheet
folio edn. of Nov. 1677 (*Bibliography* II.1).

Upon a Bookseller

The context of this onslaught becomes clear when its date, Christmas 1680
(R61), is correlated with the three issues of *Satyrs Upon The Jesuits*, 1681
(but first issued *c*.Nov. 1680). In the 'Advertisement', Oldham justified his
including the so-called 'Satyr Against Vertue' by the need to supersede current bad texts, but was furious to find that the new text, with minimal correction, had been printed from the corrupt piracy of 1679, and so published.
Holding Hindmarsh, his publisher, responsible, he wrote 'Upon a Bookseller'
and had an errata-list added to a third issue (see my article *SB*, xxvii (1974),
190-2, and Introduction, pp. xxxiii, lxxix, and nn. 34, 198-200). The satire,
now entitled 'Upon a Printer', was published, of course by Hindmarsh, in *Some
New Pieces* (1681), but not in the first issue. It is squeezed, unleaded, into
two leaves inserted between the original I2 and I3. The first issue, its text
ending with 'Finis' on I2^V (I3 is an advertisement leaf) is so rare as to be
known only from a cutting in G. Thorn Drury's interleaved Jacob, *The Poetical
Register*, in the Bodleian (see *Bibliography*, II.8); I have never seen a copy.
Of the alternative titles, which is an editor to adopt? 'Upon a Printer' is
a revision presumably approved by the author; it might even reflect acceptance
of an assurance from Hindmarsh that responsibility for the outrage lay with
Mary Clark and her printing-house. But the belated inclusion of the piece may
indicate the bookseller's reluctance to be pilloried in his own publication;
a reluctance the change of title was perhaps conceded in order to overcome.
Compared with the autographs, in the authorized version of the 'Aude aliquid.
Ode', published in 1682, a change of title, and the 'Dithyrambique', when
published in 1683, of title and conclusion, was made to veil the application
to Rochester, unsuited for the general reader. As there, so here I have chosen,
while acknowledging the authenticity of the revision, to keep the autograph
title, which matches the poem as written and originally conceived.

5 f. Cf. Dryden, Epilogue to *Troilus and Cressida* (1679):

> But I want curses for those mighty shoales
> Of scribling *Chlorisses*, and *Phillis* fools.

Cf. also the title-poem, by Dorset (see N. Ault (ed.), *Seventeenth-Century
Lyrics*, 1928, pp. 347 f., and n., pp. 487 f.), of *Methinks the Poor Town*
(1673):

> Methinks the poor town has been troubled too long
> With Phyllis and Chloris in every song.

18. Clark, p. 121, compares Boileau, 'Satire IX', l. 283: 'C'est pour elle, en un mot, que j'ai fait voeu d'écrire.'

27 f. The second Exclusion Parliament, summoned for 7 Oct. 1679, was prorogued by stages until 21 Oct. 1680, Whigs meanwhile petitioning that it might meet, and Tories addressing the crown in abhorrence of the petitions (see 'The Careless Good Fellow', ll. 13 f., n.). Assembled, it resolved that 'abhorring' was a breach of parliamentary privilege; and, almost daily, directed the Serjeant-at-Arms, John Topham, to arrest offenders. Hence, says Roger North, it became 'proverbial on all Discourse of peremptory Commitments, to say, *take him Topham*.... [T]he Dread was almost universal.... For, being named in the House for an *Abhorrer, take him Topham*.' Topham died Dec. 1692 (Wood, *Life and Times*, iii.410). See *A List of Abhorrers: or The Names of such Persons as were lately under the Custody of the Serjeant at Arms for Abhorring* (1681); North, *Examen*, pp. 549, 560; Luttrell, i.187, 257, 557; *CSPD*, 1679-80, pp. 76, 101.

27-35, 42-4. Oldham is imitating Horace, *Satires*, II.i.47-9, and 39-46 which he transposes into a fiercer key.

28. *Messenger*: 'an officer, that ... waits upon the Sergeant at Arms, to apprehend Prisoners of State' (so defined, in this sense, by Edward Phillips in the augmented 5th edn., 1696, of *The New World of Words: Or, Universal English Dictionary*).

29. Sir William Scroggs (1623?-1683), Lord Chief Justice since 1678, had presided at principal trials arising out of the Popish Plot. His reputation has suffered from Roger North's portrayal of him (quoted Kenyon, p. 117): whatever the violence of his tirades on popery and the Plot, his treatment of Oates's and Bedloe's evidence (ibid., pp. 121 f., 159, 164, 168, 170 f., 175 f.) show him less unfair and more independent than he has been given credit for. For his part in the acquittal of Wakeman, he was unsuccessfully impeached by the Whigs, 22 Dec. 1680. Now too unpopular to be useful, he was dismissed by the King in Apr. 1681.
    the coif: the white cap formerly worn by lawyers, and especially by serjeants-at-law, as a distinctive mark of their profession (*OED*, sb. 3).

31 f. Cf. 'Art of Poetry', l. 377 and n.

47. The enemy (unidentified by scholars) against whom Ovid, during his Scythian exile, wrote his elaborate maledictory poem, *Ibis*.

48-51. Cf. Jonson, *Poetaster*, 'Apologetical Dialogue', ll. 161 f., and A.B. 'On Mr Cleveland' before Cleveland's *Works*, 1687:
             Cleveland again his sacred Head doth raise ...
             Again with Verses arm'd, that once did fright
             Lycambes's Daughters from the hated Light....
The story runs that Archilochus (*fl.* 700 BC) was promised Lycambes' daughter Neobule in marriage; when the promise was broken he revenged himself by satire so biting that Lycambes and his daughters hanged themselves. See Horace, *Epodes*, VI.13, *Epistles*, I.xix.23 ff.

65. Few of the broadsheets of bellmen's verses survive; but see *The Poor Gift of John Wood, Bell-Man: Presented To his Worthy Masters in the Parish of St. George's—Southwark* (1675), and Thomas Ouldman's for 1684, '5, '6, '8, and '9 (Bodl. Wood 416 (130), G. 15 (CXCIII-CXCVII)). Ouldman's for 1684 concludes with an epilogue preventing censure such as Oldham's:
             When these poor Lines do to some Scholars come
             Perhaps they may be Laughed at ...
but trusts that some perhaps will make due allowances. Strickland Gibson told me in 1937 that lamplighter's addresses, an interesting parallel to the bellmen's broadsheets, had survived at Oxford until recent times. Cf. further 'Juvenal III', l. 369; and one of Oldham's drafts for his lines on

the author of *Sodom* (R82):

> Go write what Belmen may at Midnight whine,
> When they charm Trading Fools in wretched Rhime....

66. The singing of crickets, presumably in cages, was evidently one of the diversions of Bartholomew Fair, held in Smithfield. The modern Japanese still carry them in little cages, to enjoy their chirping.

67. *Howard.* Cf. 'Boileau VIII', ll. 328 ff., and 'Spencer's Ghost', l. 98. The Hon. Edward Howard, b. 1624, published *The Brittish Princes: an Heroick Poem* (1669); and four plays, *The Usurper* (1668), *Six Days' Adventure* (1671), *The Womens Conquest* (1671), and *The Man of Newmarket* (1678). Shadwell satirized him in the person of Ninny, 'a conceited Poet', in *The Sullen Lovers* (1668); and *The United Kingdom*, an unpublished play of his, was ridiculed in *The Rehearsal*. A collection of satirical verses upon him is printed in Dryden's 'Miscellany' (*Sylvae*, 1693, pp. 68-74); this includes pieces by Buckingham, Lord Vaughan, Mr Mat. Clifford, and Dr Sprat, and two by Dorset. The majority are mock-eulogies upon *The Brittish Princes*, on which Samuel Butler also wrote two pieces in the same strain (one of which appears in *Sylvae* erroneously attributed to Waller; see Butler, *Satires* ..., ed. Lamar, pp. 115 ff. and nn.).

68. *Jordan.* See 'Spencer's Ghost', ll. 62-6, 65 f. and nn.

68. *Dutch Hudibrass*: the anonymous *Hogan-Moganides: or the Dutch Hudibras* (1674).

73-6. Dryden writes of 'grave penny Chroniclers' in his prologue to Southern's *Loyal Brother* (1682). These hacks, for whom Grub-street was already famous, wrote the popular ballads and pamphlets describing the execution of malefactors and recounting their careers. One such pamphlet, *The Behaviour of the five Prisoners in Newgate ... Together with their Last Dying Words at Tyburn*, quoted by Rollins (*Pepys Ballads*, iii.138) gives details of a 'Holborn Cavalcade' (Holborn was the road from Newgate and the Tower to Tyburn gallows): on 19 Dec. 1684, Richard Jones and Jenny Voss, a notorious thief, were carried to Tyburn in one cart, and 'with each of them their Mourning Coffins, Jenny Voss's being cover'd with black Cloath; they both appear'd very sorrowful, crying out and ringing their hands as they went along'; another criminal preceded them on a sledge, and two more followed in a second cart, accompanied by Gilbert Burnet and Samuel Smith the ordinary of Newgate.

81. *Reading.* Cf. *Letters of Algernon Sidney* (1742), p. 48: 'Reading was this morning [28 Apr. 1679] in the Pillory, and is condemned to a year's imprisonment and 1000 pounds fine, for having endeavoured to corrupt Bedloe'. According to Burnet (ii.198), 'Reading, a lawyer of some subtilty but no virtue, was employed by the [Catholic] lords in the Tower. He ... offered [Bedloe] much money if he would turn his evidence against [them] only into a hearsay.' The proposition, alleged Reading, originated with Bedloe. He, however, had acquainted Rupert and Essex with the negotiation from the first, and drew Reading, in the presence of hidden witnesses, into 'discourses which discovered the whole practice of that corruption'.

81. *Christian.* Edward Christian, servant to the Earl of Danby, was tried 25 June 1680, along with Thomas Blood, Thomas Curtis, Arthur Obrian, and Jane Bradley, for conspiracy against the Duke of Buckingham. The four men were found guilty, and Christian was sentenced to the pillory. (See Luttrell, i.34, 48; and *The Narrative of Col. Tho. Blood*, 1680). From *The Hypocritical Christian* (1682) we learn that 'Poor Mr. *Christian*'s dead'.

81. *Cellier.* See 'Jesuits IV', ll. 295 ff. and n. Mrs Cellier, 'the Popish midwife', acquitted of high treason 11 June 1680, thereupon published

Malice Defeated; or a Brief Relation of the Accusation and Deliverance of Elizabeth Cellier ('Sept. 1. 1680', Luttrell, *Catalogues*), for which she was found guilty of libel 11 Sept. She was sentenced, among other penalties, 'to stand on the pillory at these three places, the Maypole in the Strand, in Covent Garden, and at Charingcrosse; the libells being at the same time to be burnt in her sight by the common hangman'. 'The 23d, [Oct.] Mrs. Cellier stood the third and last time on the pillory at Charingcrosse ... for printing that scandalous narrative of hers.' (Luttrell, i.55, 57.) Cf. *The Popes Letter to Madam Cellier*, 1680 ('Sept. 22', Luttrell, *Catalogues*; with verses entitled 'Maddam Celliers Lamentation Standing on the Pillory'); also *To the Praise of Mrs Cellier The Popish Midwife: on her incomparable book*, and *The Devil pursued ... A Satyr upon Madam Celliers standing in the Pillory* ('Sept. 14. 1680' and 'Oct. 4. 1680', Luttrell, *Catalogues*). *A Weekly Advertisement of Books. Begun Thursday, October 7. 1680*, advertises 'Mr. *Prance*'s Answer to Mrs. Cellier's Libel, ... To which is added, The Adventure of the Bloody Bladder, a Tragi Comical Farce, acted with much applause at *Newgate*, by the said Madam *Cellier* on *September* 18 instant.' Cf. Luttrell, *Catalogues*, 'Second Continuation', p. 4, No. 17, 'October 1': and pp. 3-4, Nos. 8-15, 18, 20, 21.

88. Cf. 'Jesuits IV', ll. 200 f.; and 'Juvenal III', ll. 228 f. Thorn Drury, in his interleaved Oldham, annotated the present passage: '... people in the Debtors Prisons ... let down a shoe by a string from a grate to the street applying pathetically to the passers-by to pity the poor debtors:
> Or else poor D.   to the Goal must go
> Angling for money in a shoe.
>   Poeta de Tristibus: Or, The Poets Complaint, 1682.
4° p. 24. The second line, which should be 'Angling for single money in a shoe' is from Shadwell's Libertine'. The receptacle was not always a shoe: cf. Congreve, *The Way of the World*, ed. Kathleen M. Lynch, III.122: 'I hope to see him lodge in Ludgate first, and angle into Blackfriars for brass farthings, with an old mitten'.

93 f. Cf. Horace, *Satires*, II.ii.98 f.

POEMS, AND TRANSLATIONS

Advertisement

2 f. As the printed dates would show, this could only be meant of certain poems; particularly, perhaps, of 'Nobility', 'To a Friend', and 'Spencer's Ghost', which may belong to 1683 or late 1682. 'Boileau VIII' was the most recent of the dated pieces.

3-5. The Cosmelia poems, clearly, and perhaps 'Dithyrambique'; he had kept them six or seven years, and not published them in either of his earlier volumes. If, like 'Dithyrambique', 'Upon a Lady' was written for the Rochester circle, it is doubtless included.

11-14. Presents in return for dedications formed a considerable part of an author's gains; see 'Art of Poetry', 1. 320 n., and Beljame, *Le Public et les Hommes de Lettres* (1881), pp. 127 ff. The art of dedication was carried to great lengths, as, e.g. by Thomas Fuller (see Strickland Gibson, Oxford Bibliographical Society's *Proceedings* (1936), iv.81, 93, 134). For Oldham's scorn of the practice, cf. 'Spencer's Ghost', ll. 143 ff.

17-21. Butler (*Hudibras*, I.i.647-50) sneers at
> The praises of the Author, penn'd
> By himself or wit-ensuring friend,

> The Itch of Picture in the Front,
> With Bays, and wicked Rhyme upon't....

Cf. 'Spencer's Ghost, ll. 69 f. and n.; and Henry Higden's 'address' before his *Modern Essay On the Thirteenth Satyr of Juvenal* (1686).

The Eighth Satyr of Monsieur Boileau, Imitated

Nicholas Boileau-Despreaux (1636-1711) wrote his 8th satire in 1667 (published 1668). Rochester imitated, or rather 'alluded to' it in his 'Satyr against ... Mankind', written before 23 Mar. 1675/6, and printed June 1679. (*HMC* 7th Report, Appendix, p. 467; Wood, iii.1229). Oldham's much closer Imitation shows here and there the influence of Rochester's, which he had transcribed (the transcript, up to l. 165, 8 lines from the end of the version without the palinode, is preserved in R110-15). See below, ll. 43, 70, 218, 245, 358, nn.

This Imitation was reprinted, with infelicitous changes by Ozell, in *The Works of Monsieur Boileau. Made English ... By Several Hands* (1712), i.209. (*Bibliography*, II.40).

For Oldham as a pioneer in Imitation and in the translating of Boileau, see Brooks, 'Imitation', and Clark pp. 117-22, 134-6, 143 f., 186, and Appendix E, where he prints (from R124-35) Oldham's translation (the first in English; Oct. 1678) of *Le Lutrin*, Chant I.

7. *Perspective*: a magnifying-glass or microscope; though often a telescope or spy-glass.

11-15. Cf. Rochester, 'Satyr', ll. 60 f., 64. The *adversarius* apostrophizes
> Blest, glorious man! to whom alone kind heaven
> An everlasting soul has freely given ...
> And this fair frame, in shining reason dressed....

31. The yearly ritual dance seems to have been performed for the last time at the Revels in the Inner Temple hall, 2 Feb. 1733; a description from two eyewitnesses is printed in Edward Wynne's *Eunomus* (1772), iv.87: '[A] large ring was formed round the [empty] fire-place.... Then the master of the revels ... took the Lord Chancellor by the right hand; and he, with his left, took Mr. J. Page, who joined to the other Judges, Serjeants, and Benchers present, *danced*, or rather walked, *round about the coal fire* ..., three times; during which, they were aided in the figure of the dance by Mr George Cooke, the prothonotary, then upwards of 60: and all the time of the dance, the *antient song*, accompanied with music, was sung by one Toby Aston, dressed in a bar gown.'

43-5. Reason misleading men into doubt is from Rochester's 'Satyr', ll. 12-19, not the French:
> ... Reason, an *ignis fatuus* in the mind ...
> Pathless and dangerous wandering ways it takes ...
> Whilst the misguided follower ...
> Stumbling from thought to thought, falls headlong down
> Into doubts boundless sea....

49. *tuant*: trenchant (from Fr. *tuer*, to kill); used also in *Some New Pieces*, Advertisement, ll. 55 f. The borrowing never caught on: with one exception, *OED*'s instances all belong to 1672-3. When Oldham wrote 'tuant' in the 'Apology' for the 'Satyr Against Vertue', it proved unintelligible to transcribers (the 1679 edn. left a blank; the 1680 Rochester, Portland MS PwV40, and Princeton MS AM. 14401 read 'angry'). Oldham revised it to 'pointed'.

69. The soldiers' buff-coat; the crape gown of the divine.

70. Cf. Rochester, 'Satyr', pp. 16 f.:
     ... the misguided follower [of Reason] climbs with pain,
     Mountains of whimseys, heaped in his own brain.

71-5. The added touch of the turnspit angels was suggested by Cowley's
     'Davideis', IV, n. 25: 'the old senseless opinion, that the Heavens were
     divided into several *Orbes* or *Spheres*, and that a particular *Intelligence*
     or *Angel* was assigned to each of them, to turn it round (like a *Mill-horse*,
     as *Scaliger* says) to all eternity'.

76 f. Oldham's addition. Cf. the contrast in *Absalom and Achitophel*, ll. 329-
     32, of Charles II's moderation with the 'Arbitrary Sway' of Louis.

83-6. The author of the *Travels of the Grand Duke Cosmo III in England* (1669)
     declares that in Ireland wolves are common. Cromwell, by Order in Council,
     had set a price upon their heads; and in 1662 there had been talk of a bill
     'to encourage the killing of Wolves ... in Ireland'. See J.E. Harting,
     British Animals Extinct Within Historic Times (1880), pp. 195-7.

97. *Th'Exchange*. The second Royal Exchange stood in Cornhill, on the site of
     that founded by Gresham and destroyed in the Great Fire. Chamberlayne
     (II.191) describes it. Cf. ibid. (1683), IV.33: 'As for Merchandise imported
     from other Countries, the Royal Exchange is the place most proper for Bar-
     gains, where ... between the Hours of 11. and 1. Merchants of all Nations
     meet and discourse of their affairs.' Presumably these were the hours of
     most business, not of opening and closing. Cf. *Great Britains Glory, Or A
     brief Description of the ... Royal Exchange ... by Theophilus Philalethes*,
     1672 (in verse).

99. *double the Cape*: of Good Hope.

101. *Bantam*. The kingdom and the port of Bantam were in Java, on the Sunda
     Straits. The East India Company traded thither for spices, especially
     pepper. A few months before the present poem was written, ambassadors from
     the king of Bantam had visited Charles II: arriving in London 9 May 1682,
     and re-embarking 12 July (see Luttrell, i.182, 205; Evelyn, 19 June 1682;
     and *An Heroick Poem to the King upon the Arrival of the Morocco and Bantam
     Embassadors*, 1682). But by 23 Sept. it was known in England that civil war
     was endangering the Bantam pepper factory. The Dutch espoused the rebel
     cause, seized the port on 2 Dec. and instituted a monopoly in their own
     favour. The trade to which Oldham alludes was thus destroyed before his
     poem appeared in print. See Luttrell, i.253; *A True Account Of the Burning
     and sad Condition of Bantam ... in a Letter ... which arrived ... the 23th
     of ... September 1682*, and *A short Account Of the Siege Of Bantam* (1683).

101. *Japan*. For the Restoration merchant, trade with Japan was a project,
     never realized. The East India Company had had a factory at Firando (Hirado)
     from 1613 to 1623. There was a determined attempt to reopen the trade in
     1669 to 1673. The 'Return' actually reached Nagasaki 29 June 1673, but
     failed to persuade the Japanese to lift their ban on commerce with all Euro-
     peans save the Dutch. By 1677, according to John Bruce's *Annals of the
     Honourable East India Company* (1810), ii.412, 'an intercourse with Japan'
     was despaired of.

102. *Sugars from Barbadoes*. From 1640 to 1650 onward, sugar had superseded
     tobacco as the principal product of Barbados, which was now 'little more
     than one large sugar factory'. The sugar export was a declared monopoly of
     the mother-country. See further, Ogg, ii.665; V.T. Harlow, *A History Of
     Barbados 1625-1685* (1926), pp. 44, 259-65 etc.

102. *Wines from Spain*. e.g. from Malaga and Alicant. See the account of
     Spanish trade in *The Fourth Part Of The Present State Of England. Relating
     To its Trade and Commerce ...* (1683) [by J. S.], pp. 183-94.

109. Buckingham told the king that in 1650 his estate had been worth £30,000
a year (Letter of 1674, printed in Lady Burghclere, *George Villiers Second
Duke of Buckingham*, 1903, p. 301). By 1669 he was being described to Pepys
(14 Feb. 1668/9) as one of 'a broken sort of people'; 'the Duke of Buckingham's condition is shortly this: that he hath about 19600 l a year, of
which he pays away about 7000 l a year in interest, about 2000 l in Fee-
farm rents to the King, about 6000 l in wages and pensions, and the rest to
live upon, and pay taxes for the whole'. Characterizing him as Zimri (*Absalom and Achitophel*, ll. 544 ff.), 'In squandring Wealth', says Dryden, 'was
his peculiar Art'. Cf. *The Litany of the D. of B.*:

> From selling Land, twice ten Thousand a Year
> All spent, no Mortal can tell how or where ...
> From being still cheated by the same Undertakers,
> By Levellers, Bawds, Saints, Chymists, and Quakers
> Who make us Gold-finders, and themselves Gold-makers ...
> From selling six Palaces for less than they rent for,
> And buying* three Hillocks for the three kings of *Brentford*
> Libera nos, &c.

*Sion-Hill, College-Hill, and Clifton [i.e. Clifden] Hill.

110. *C[layto]n*: Sir Robert Clayton (1629-1707), not 'Alderman Cuddon' as the
1722 editor supposed. Clayton had 'got' a good deal of what Buckingham had
spent; cf. Evelyn, 18 Nov. 1679: 'some believ'd him gilty of hard-dealing,
especially with the Duke of *Buckingham*, much of whose estate he had swallow'd'. *The Litany of the D. of B.* ends with a petition against 'making our
Heirs to be *Morris* and *Clayton*'. His vast wealth was all the more topical
in 1682 from having, in Feb., been augmented by the bequest of his partner
Morris's estate. As a prominent Whig, he is appropriately pilloried with
Buckingham and Bethel. Thomas Cuddon, knighted 1697, but (according to A.B.
Bevan's lists) never Alderman, was not in the public eye before 1696, when
he became chamberlain of London. (For him, see J.A. Venn, *Alumni Canta-
brigienses* (1922); W.A. Shaw, *Knights of England* (1906); A.I. Suckling,
History ... of Suffolk (1846-8), i.73 ff.; Luttrell, iv.132, v.251; Le Neve,
Monumenta Anglicana, 1717, p. 53.) Coming to London a poor boy, Clayton was
enabled by a bequest from his uncle to make his fortune as a money-lender.
He was Alderman from 1670, Sheriff in 1671, Lord Mayor in 1679-80, and an
MP for London in the three Exclusion Parliaments of 1679-81; as Evelyn says
(loc. cit.), he was reckoned one of the wealthiest citizens. He is Tate's
'extorting Ishban' in *The Second Part of Absalom and Achitophel* (11 Nov.
1682); but Evelyn 'never saw any ill by him, considering the trade he was of'.

110. *stingy B[eth]el*: Slingsby Bethel, Whig sheriff of London, 1680-1; Dryden's Shimei, whose 'Shrieval Board / The Grossness of a City Feast abhorr'd'.
He 'kept no house, but lived upon chops: whence it is proverbial, for not
feasting, *to Bethel the city*' (North, *Examen*, p. 93; cf. Burnet, ii.254).
Cf. *News from Guildhall, Or the Combate of the Gyants*, n.d., 'To Beth—
being as Signal for Hospitality as Loyalty, I leave a bended Nine-pence to
entertain the ... Free-Men on the next Election of Whig Sheriffs'; and *Iter
Boreale: Or Esq; Spare-Penny's Departure to the North, July the Third* (1682),
which refers to Bethel's flight from royal vengeance to Hamburg, where he
remained till the Revolution.

119. *to fine for Shrieve*. A fine was exacted from a sheriff of London elect
if he chose to decline the office. At this time it was £400, the sum Luttrell
(i.217) notes as paid by Box, Sept. 1682. Box was a Tory candidate at the
disputed election of July: the Tory Lord Mayor declared him chosen, but he
fined off (exercised the above option). Cf. 'Spencer's Ghost', l. 165, and
'Juvenal III', l. 215.

121. The news-sheets often refer to the commerce on this route: see, for example, *The London Gazette*, Oct. 7-11, 1680: 'The *Streights* Convoy has been long detained in the *Downs* by contrary Winds.'

128-31. Oldham amplifies the French. The plight of disabled soldiers was topical in 1682: Charles II had laid the first stone of Chelsea Hospital in the spring. Planned by Evelyn and Sir Stephen Fox, the Hospital was badly needed. According to articles of 1673, a wounded soldier's pay ceased when he was pronounced unfit for further service. Compensation ('Blood money'), or else a pension, for disablement by wounds was not made an established allowance until 1685. See Clifford Walton, *History of the British Standing Army 1660-1700* (1894), pp. 592, 594-6, 600. Soldiers' pay was continually in arrear (cf. ibid., p. 588); Sir James Turner, in *Pallas Armata* (1683), p. 198, comes to much the same satirical conclusion as Oldham: 'if you will consider how their wages are paid, I suppose, you will rather think them Voluntaries', than Mercenaries 'for doing the greatest part of their service for nothing'.

130 f. Cf. Dryden, Prologue to *Marriage-A-La-Mode*, l. 16: 'In Wars abroad, they grinning Honour gain', and 'Counterpart', l. 82. Falstaff's phrase was a Restoration favourite, suiting the reaction against Civil War heroisms; cf. Pepys, 2 Nov. 1667; Dryden, 1678 (*Essays*, i.198); *Merry Drolleries*, ed. Ebsworth, p. 36. The official Gazette, published twice a week, had been started at Oxford in 1665: it became *The London Gazette* with its 24th number, when the court had returned to the capital after the plague.

139. *Huff*. In John Tatham's *The Scots Figgaries* (1652), Trapheir is admitted into the fraternity of the Huffs—a set of tityre tus (see *OED*), hectors, scourers, or Mohocks, as they called themselves at different periods of the 17th and early 18th centuries. Huff, 'an impudent cowardly Hector' is a character in Shadwell's *Sullen Lovers* (1668).

142 ff. See Juvenal, X.168 f. and cf. 'Homer', ll. 89 ff. and n. The phrasing is indebted to Lee's *Rival Queens* (1677), IV.i, p. 40: 'My Soul is pent, and has not elbow room.'

151. *Bedlam*. See 'Art of Poetry', l. 811, n.

155. *Rainolds*: Edward Reynolds (1599-1676), *A Treatise Of The Passions and Faculties of the Soule of Man. With the severall Dignities and Corruptions thereunto belonging* (1640), a quarto of 553 pages. Reynolds was Bishop of Norwich from 1661 till his death. The *Treatise* had been recently reprinted (1679) among his collected works.

159. Unlike Boileau's La Chambre and Coëffeteau, Henry More (1614-87) and Ralph Cudworth (1617-88) had not written specific treatises upon the passions; but they were two of the most distinguished religious and moral philosophers of the day. Cudworth's *True Intellectual System of the University* had appeared in 1678, and More's *Opera Omnia* in 1679. See Burnet's famous account of the Cambridge Platonists (i.331 ff.).

171 ff. Boileau is imitating Juvenal, XV.159 ff. Cf. Butler, *Hudibras*, I.i. 759-70; and Denham, 'Friendship and Single Life'.

171-3. Claude Duval (1643-70), John Nevison (1639-85), William Davis the Golden Farmer (1627-90), and Thomas Simpson, alias Old Mob (executed in 1690), were all on the road in Charles II's reign. The King issued repeated proclamations 'For the Apprehending of Robbers or High-way-men'; thus £10 for a conviction was offered from 20 June 1677 to 1 Feb. 1678, from 5 Mar. 1680 to 2 Mar. 1681, and from 14 May 1681 to 5 May 1682. The proclamation renewing the offer on 31 Jan. 1683 names eleven known offenders, including the notorious Nevison. See also Joan Parkes, *Travel In England In The Seventeenth Century* (1925), chap. 6.

174 f. Cf. Luttrell (i.124), Sept. 1681: 'Ever since the dissolution of the
last parliament [28 Mar. 1681], the presse has abounded with pamphlets ...
some ... branding the two late parliaments, and standing very highly for
the church; the other side defending the parliament, and cryeing up ... the
true protestant religion, and opposing a popish successor: whence the
latter party have been called by the former, whigs, fanaticks, covenanteers,
bromigham protestants, &c.; and the former are called by the latter, tories,
tantivies, Yorkists, high flown church men, &c.; whereby ... there is a
great ... animosity between [the self-styled] church of England men and ...
dissenters.'

176 f. Exactly translated; but the almost inevitable application to Shaftesbury may not be unintended.

180. *Whig and Tory Lions*. Disgust at the violence of both factions is expressed in *The Condemnation of Whig and Tory* (1681):
> Sirs, What's the matter? 's all the World grown mad? ...
> To two Extreams we all do madly run;
> And Moderation (which should heal us) shun, etc.

180 f. The function of the two London sheriffs in selecting juries, and the
Mayor's influence on the choice of sheriffs, were crucial to the royal
counter-attack upon the Whigs. The indictment against Shaftesbury was thrown
out by a grand jury the Whigs had packed. In Sept. 1681 a Tory, Sir John
Moore, though strongly opposed, was elected Lord Mayor. Conflict became
violent from June 1682, when he claimed to nominate one sheriff, naming the
Tory, Dudley North. On the 24th, the Whig sheriffs, Pilkington and Shute,
conducted the poll for two successors, continuing it when Moore, insisting
that North was already chosen, adjourned it. Their attempt at the Common
Council, 5 July, to declare the Whig candidates elected was quashed. At a
new poll, 14 July, Moore accepted votes for only one vacancy: Box, a Tory,
was said to be chosen. When he 'fined off', his place was supplied, Moore
refusing a poll, by another Tory, Peter Rich (father, interestingly enough,
of Elias, a Whitgift pupil of Oldham's). The sheriffs proceeded with the
poll, but on 28 Sept. North and Rich were sworn into office. After a lesser
struggle, which turned on a disputed scrutiny of illegal votes cast at the
poll of 4 Oct. (when the Whigs had a majority), the Tory Sir William
Pritchard was sworn, 28 Oct., as the next Lord Mayor. See R.R. Sharpe, *London and the Kingdom* (1894) ii.468-94; Luttrell, i.196, 203-10, 217-32 *passim*; North, *Examen*, pp. 595 ff., North, *Lives*, i.219-24, ii.181-4. Pamphlets
flew; twenty-six are extant in the Ashmole collection in Bodley (G.16, and
1674), and five more listed in P.J. Dobell's catalogue, *The Popish Plot*
(1919).

186 f. The statute *De scandalis magnatum* gave peers a special remedy at law
against any who aspersed them. An action of scandalum magnatum had just been
brought against Hindmarsh, Oldham's publisher, and the Revd Adam Elliot, by
Lord North and Grey; see a news-letter of 7 Oct., in *CSPD*, 1682, p. 461;
cf. p. 453, and Luttrell, i.231. The statute (of Richard II) had been first
resuscitated in 1676; Shaftesbury sued Lord Digby under it and obtained
£1,000 damages. Actions grew common: seven are chronicled by Luttrell in
the first ten months of 1682. The majority were political; many were vindic-
tive. The excessive damages habitually granted by the jury made them an
effective method of ruining an opponent or an enemy. A clause to abolish
the privilege had been inserted in the Commons' abortive bill of 1680 for
regulating the trial of peers; and Aphra Behn alludes to it tartly in an
epilogue of 1682 (Wiley, p. 98, ll. 6 f.). See Luttrell, i.150, 170, 171,
183, 186, 188, 190, 192, 197-8, 231, 236, 240; Ogg, ii.463-6, 605; also
i.136-7.

190-3. The Court of Arches with its presiding judge, the Dean of the Arches, took the name from the arches of Bow-Church, Cheapside, where it was once held. It is 'the highest Court belonging to the Archbishop of *Canterbury*. ... Hither are all Appeals directed in Ecclesiastical Matters within the province of Canterbury.' (Strype's Stow, edn. of 1754, i.171.) From the Arches appeals lay to the highest tribunal for ecclesiastical causes, the Court of Delegates. From the 13th century, impotence was a good cause in ecclesiastical law for declaring a marriage null. On 13 Feb. 1731/2, the Arches tried such a suit, Weld alias Aston *v*. Weld; I have traced none in Oldham's time. He may not have had a particular one in mind: the stroke is Boileau's, merely turned by Oldham against the Arches, which was worth a gibe in 1682. It was an organ of the matrimonial jurisdiction at Doctors Commons, which the case of Emerton and Mrs Hyde had brought into disrepute. *Mr. Emerton's Cause Now Depending before the Delegates* ... (1682) and *Mr. Emmerton's Marriage With Mrs. Bridget Hyde Considered* (1682), both raise the question of its curtailment. See also Luttrell, i.52, 191, 199, 205 f., 230, 233, 251, 255.

194 f. In Jan. 1682 the crown had instituted quo warranto proceedings against the body corporate of London, in order that the ancient charter should be either surrendered or declared forfeit, to be replaced by a new one subjecting the choice of City officers to royal approval. Thus there would be no Whig sheriffs in London for the future. Service of the writ was notified to the Common Council of London on 18 Jan.; their plea was put in on 13 June; printed copies of it, and of the Attorney-General's replication, were advertised that month. With their rejoinder, 19 Oct., we reach the month in which Oldham is writing. Pamphlets had argued the case, cited precedents, or pointed a moral; *The Forfeitures of London's Charter*, advertised in May, for example. Judgement against the charter was finally entered 4 Oct. 1683. See pamphlets in the Bodleian (Ashmole 1674, LX-LXXVI; Ashmole 734, I-III; Gough Lond. 1.12, 1.15); *Term Catalogues*, I.487, 495; Luttrell, i.158-283 *passim*; Evelyn, 18 June 1683; R.R. Sharpe, *London and the Kingdom* (1894), ii.476-8, 494-504; T.B. Howell's *State Trials* (1809-), viii.1039-1358.

205 f. For the invention of gunpowder by Satan, cf. *Paradise Lost*, VI.470-91, Spenser, *Faerie Queene*, I.vii.13, and Ariosto, *Orlando Furioso*, IX.91, XI.23.

208. The Pandects were originally the fifty books of Justinian's compendium of the Roman Civil Law: thence, a complete body of the laws of any country or of any system of law.

218 f. Without direct equivalent in the French: suggested by Rochester 'Satyr', 1. 85 ('The limits of the boundless universe') and 11. 68 f.:
          [We] soaring pierce
     The flaming limits of the universe,
where the source is Lucretius, I.73.

227 f. By the charter of the Royal College of Physicians, none but Fellows, Candidates, or Licentiates of the College might practise medicine within seven miles of London (elsewhere, authorization extended to Extra Licentiates, and University graduates). 'Licentiates' says Chamberlayne (ii.280) 'judged unfit to be Fellows' yet thought able to 'do good ... in some Kind of Diseases ... are [therefore] after due Examination, ... Licensed to Practice'. The licentiate has a bad name: in *The Character of a Quack Astrologer* the Quack is said to differ 'from an honest, able Artist, as a Licentiate from a Doctor'. In *Lex Talionis* (1670), a retort to Dr Christopher Merett's attack, and others, upon the apothecaries, many are claimed to have a better knowledge of the elements of medicine 'than some Licentiate *Doctors*'. Merett replied that 'licentiate' was a term oftener used than understood. Is Oldham attacking a real abuse, or merely concurring in a

widespread prejudice? The licentiates recorded in *The Roll Of The Royal College of Physicians* (1861, ed. W. Munk) include none of the known quacks of the period: if the record is complete, Thomas Suffold, who combined medicine with astrology, lied in advertising himself as a 'Licensed Physician'. A good proportion of licentiates had medical degrees, though several had had them conferred 'per Literas Regias' after being licensed without them; some had arts degrees only, and one is described as 'no graduate, at least in medicine'.

229-31. Oldham particularizes the 'argument frivole' of Boileau's doctor: basing his version on Mosaic Law. Cf. *The Triall of a Black-Pudding; or, The unlawfulness of Eating Blood proved by Scriptures* (1652); and *Hudibras*, III.ii.321 f.

232 f. Without equivalent in the French. Cf. the *New Pneumatical Experiments about Respiration ... communicated by ... Robert Boyle*, in the *Philosophical Transactions* of the Royal Society, Nos. 62 and 63, 8 Aug. and 12 Sept. 1670. Title XIX is headed 'Of the Phaenomena suggested by Winged Insects in our Vacuum', and describes the asphyxiation under Boyle's air-pump of half-a-dozen varieties of insect. The Royal Society's experiments with the air were much ridiculed: see Pepys, 1 Feb. 1663/4, and No. 122 of the *Transactions*, 21 Feb. 1675/6, p. 538.

245 f. Cf. Rochester's phrase in 'A Satyr', 1. 82 f.:
            Filling with frantic crowds of thinking fools
            Those reverend bedlams, colleges and schools.

252. *Hodder*. *Hodder's Arithmetick: Or, That necessary Art made most easie*, by James Hodder the writing-master; a thirteenth edition had appeared in the preceding year, 1681. Education for commerce and trades, alternative to liberal education in the classics, was a current topic. Hodder includes 'Merchants Accompts', and Kersey's prospectus in the 1650 edn. of Wingate (cf. 'Art of Poetry', 1. 521 n.) offers 'Merchants accompts in the Italique methode of debtor and creditor, according to the modern practice'. The statutes (1662) of Woodbridge (Suffolk) Grammar School provide that the ten free boys should learn Latin and Greek, but if parents or guardians 'desire that they be taught only Arithmetic and to write, to be fitted for trades', the schoolmaster is to comply. Private writing-masters sometimes launched out into arithmetic and other commercial subjects, and among the unofficially tolerated schools which arose after the Act of Uniformity (1662), some specialized in commercial education. Merchant Taylors had a Mathematical School from 1673. Sir William Petty, in his *Advice of W.P. to Mr. Samuel Hartlib for the Advance of Some Particular Parts of Learning* (1648) had advocated turning ordinary schools into trade schools. See Foster Watson, *The Beginnings of the Teaching of Modern Subjects in England* (1909), pp. xliv-vi, 225, 324, 327 f., 330; William Boyd, *History of Western Education* (1950: 5th edn., enlarged), pp. 270 f., 273.

255 f. Customs and Excise, with Hearth-money, were at this time the chief items in the hereditary revenue of the crown. They were farmed out to speculators who in return for advancing a lump sum and paying an agreed rent, enjoyed the proceeds of the tax. There was much misappropriation and withholding of revenue by the farmers, and even by sub-commissioners of Excise (1. 256). See Ogg, ii.424-31, 446; G.N. Clark, *The Later Stuarts* (1934), p. 7; and for Excise, 'Aude aliquid. Ode', 1. 38.

257. Cf. Oldham's other allusions to the notorious 'Irish witnesses': 'Juvenal III', 11. 109 f. and 'On the Times', R222, 11. 7 f. During the Popish Terror, according to Burnet (ii.291), certain Irishmen 'hearing that England was ... disposed to hearken to good swearers, ... came over to swear that there was a great plot in Ireland.... The witnesses were brutal and profligate men:

yet the earl of Shaftesbury cherished them much.' 'David Fitzgerald', wrote
Luttrell, 'has been often heard to say that he could have as many witnesses
as he pleased from Ireland to forswear themselves for 2s.6d. each.' By 1681
the 'Irish-evidence' had come 'under another management' and were laying
a Presbyterian plot to the charge of their former employers. On 29 Oct.
'severall of the Irish witnesses of the presbyterian plott were together at
the Rose tavern' and 'upbraided one another with money they had received'
in bribes. They testified against College at his trial in Aug. 1681, and
against Shaftesbury at his indictment in Nov. See Burnet, ii.295; Luttrell,
i.89; 140; 108, 117; 105, 121, 146; see also 126. Their venality was still
topical in 1682: *The Irish-Evidence convicted by their own Oaths: Or, Their
Swearing and Counter-Swearing Plainly Demonstrated* (1682) gives the fullest
'*Account Of Their Past and Present Practices*'. Dryden alludes to them in the
preface to *The Medall* (Mar. 1682). Cf. e.g. *Satyr To His Muse, c.*24 July
1682 (Macdonald 212), p. 17.

257. *Case-harden'd*: *OED* first records 'case-harden' in 1677. The present passage antedates its earliest instances of the figurative use (1713), and of
'case-hardened' as an adjective, literal (1691) and figurative (1769).

259. *Algerine.* See 'Horace, I.xxxi', ll. 27 f. and n.

267. *When*: whereupon.

267-74. Cf. Advertisement to *Poems* (1683), ll. 11 ff.

271. Oldham echoes *MacFlecknoe*, l. 170.

275 ff. A commonplace in which Boileau follows Horace's *Satire* II.iii.96-8;
cf. Cowley, 'The Given Love' (*Poems*, p. 68).

283. *Bovey.* Oldham takes his allusion from Rochester's 'Letter to Artemisia',
ll. 70 ff. (see R118):

> Bovey's a beauty, if some few agree
> To call him so; the rest to that degree
> Affected are, that with their ears they see.

Vieth notes that Rochester's Bovey is identified by marginal glosses in
several early texts as Sir Ralph Bovey, baronet (d. 1679). Alternatively, he
has been identified with James Bovy (or Boeve) 'a solicitor, and lawyer, and
merchant all together' (Pepys, 20 May 1668). Looks might be thought likelier
to draw comment in the milieu of a baronet than of a bourgeois: yet the merchant was gentleman enough to boast a coat of arms. It may be significant
that Aubrey particularizes his appearance: 'As to his person he is about
5 foot high, slender [*cancelling* spare body], strait, haire exceeding black
and curling at the end, a dark hazell eie [*cancelling* a very black eie] of
a midling size, but the most sprightly that I have beheld. Browes and beard
of the colour as his haire' (i.113, 115). He suits Oldham's allusion by his
wealth (a point not derived from Rochester). He had been cashier to a banker
from *c.*1641-9, 'his dealing being altogether in money-matters'; he married
the daughter of William de Visscher, a merchant reputed to be worth
£120,000; and retired from business aged 32. (Aubrey, i.112-15, ii.271). Yet
though short, thin, and getting elderly (b. 1622), evidently he was not repulsive. If he is the right Bovey, Rochester might simply mean that his good
looks were ordinary enough and now rather *passé*, yet enjoyed an absurd vogue.
If so, Oldham was ignorant of Bovy's appearance, or was forcing the parallel
with 'the loathsom'st object'.

295 f. Edward Stillingfleet (1635-99), Dean of St Paul's from 1678 and afterwards Bishop of Worcester, wrote 'against popery ... with such an exactness
and liveliness, that no books of controversy were so much read and valued as
his'. (Burnet, i.336.) These 14 anti-Romanist writings occupy vols. iv-vi of
his *Works* (1710); the most famous was perhaps the *Discourse concerning the*

Idolatry practised in the Church of Rome (1671). Bellarmine (d. 1621; cf. 'Jesuits II', l. 66 n.) is here mentioned, I believe, simply as outstanding among Catholic controversialists.

298. *Father Simon*. Richard Simon (1638-1712), author of the celebrated *Histoire Critique du Vieux Testament*. This was published in 1678 but almost at once suppressed, chiefly because it denied Moses' authorship of the Pentateuch. In 1682 it was a live topic in England. Henry Dickenson's English translation came out early in that year; Evelyn wrote to Dr Fell 19 Mar. 1681/2 begging him to have it answered. An answer—W. L[orimer]'s *Excellent Discourse Proving the Divine* ... *Authority of the Five Books Of Moses* [translated from Du Bois de la Cour, with] *An Examination Of a considerable part of Pere Simon's Critical History of the Old Testament* (1682), was advertised in the *Term Catalogues* in Nov. Dryden's *Religio Laici*, addressed to Dickenson upon his translation, was published Nov. 30. Like Oldham, Dryden (in ll. 234-8) stresses Simon's industry and Rabbinical learning.

311 f. See 'Horace, I.xxxi', l. 11 and n. Of 44 houses of 'Goldsmiths keeping Running cashes' listed in *A Collection Of The Names Of The Merchants Living in and about The City of London* (1677), 27 were in Lombard Street. Cf. 'The Creditors Complaint against the Bankers' in Thompson, p. 219:

> *Bankers* now are brittle Ware ...
> An Iron Chest *is still the best,*
> *'Twill keep your* Coyn *more safe than they;*
> *For when they've feather'd well their Nest,*
> *Then the* Rooks *will flee away.*

313. Duns Scotus and William of Ockham, types of the schoolman, coupled in Dryden's Prologue at Oxford, *c.*1681, l. 19.

316. *your self*: 'Speak for yourself!'—Boileau's 'parlez de vous, poëte'.

328-37. Edward Howard was lampooned for his heroic poem, *The Brittish Princes* (1669), and hissed for his plays, of which four appeared in print from 1668 to 1678 while at least three others remained unpublished. See 'Upon a Bookseller', l. 67 and n.; and 'Spencer's Ghost', l. 98 and n.

334 f. 'Put' in l. 335 is correct, 'Verse' being plural.

358-61. This turn of thought is independent of Boileau, and epitomizes a phase of Rochester's philosophy. It was probably suggested by the complaint against false Reason in 'A Satyr', ll. 104-9: 'Your reason hinders, mine helps to enjoy', etc. and cf. Randolph, 'Upon Love Fondly Refus'd for Conscience Sake':

> Nature, Creations law, is judg'd by sense,
> Not by the Tyrant conscience,
> Then our commission gives us leave to doe
> What youth and pleasure prompts us to....

359.   Alas! I do not ravenously pursue
>   What opportunity might prompt us to
—Brome's *Horace*, 2nd edn. (1671), Odes, I.23, translated R.T.—no doubt Dr Robert Thompson (see Brooks, 'Contributors'). Oldham had seen Brome's Horace in 1681 (Advertisement, *Some New Pieces*, ll. 55 ff.). Thompson echoes Randolph, and perhaps Charles Cotton, 'Sonnet' (*Poems*, ed. J. Beresford, p. 160):

> Tis not too late to love, and do
> What Love and Nature prompt thee to....

362-76. Cf. Butler, *Hudibras*, I.i.771-84.

373-6. The opening of Juvenal XV was the origin of many 17th-century allusions, including Boileau's here, to the bestial gods of Egypt. Of those

Oldham certainly knew, cf. Cowley, 'The Plagues of Egypt', St. 19, n. 2 (*Poems*, p. 238), and Dryden, 'Epilogue to the University of Oxford', 1673, ll. 26-8.

377. With ll. 380 f., this gibe at the Host carried in procession is of course not from Boileau. Cf. 'Jesuits IV', ll. 265 ff., and Thomas Tuke's verses *Concerning The Holy Eucharist and the Popish Breaden-God* (1625).

393 f. Oldham adds the reference to Balaam's ass.

400. *The two-leg'd Herd*. Without equivalent in the French. The phrase, like Dryden's 'unfeather'd two-legg'd thing' in *Absalom*, l. 170, alludes to Plato's definition of man.

401. *old*: exceedingly strange.

403 f. The phrasing is indebted to Donne, 'Satyre I', ll. 17 f., 21:
> Not though a Captaine do come in thy way
> Bright parcell gilt, with forty dead mens pay ...
> Nor come a velvet Justice....

405 f. Cf. the harangue of 'Scoto Mantuanus', and 'Alexander Bendo's' bill; 'Scoto' (*Volpone*, II.i) being Jonson's protagonist masquerading as a mountebank, and 'Bendo', Rochester, in a real-life escapade, following suit (see V. de Sola Pinto, ed., *The Famous Pathologist, or The Noble Mountebank, by ... Alcock and ... Rochester*, 1961). *Hudibras*, III.ii.971 f., has charlatans '*Mounted* in a *Crowd*'; in *The Character Of A Quack Doctor* (1676), the Quack, as a mountebank, sells drugs fit '*only to treat rats with*' (parallels italicized). See 'Spencer's Ghost', ll. 78-81, 229-32 and nn.

407 f. Cf. 'Jesuits IV', l. 85, and 'Spencer's Ghost', ll. 63 f. and n. Full accounts of the celebrations in this and the previous year are given in *London's Joy, Or, The Lord Mayor's Show ... Perform'd On ... October XXIX. 1681 ... Devised ... by Tho. Jordan, Gent.*, and *The Lord Mayor's Show ... Perform'd on ... September XXX. 1682*. The corresponding pamphlets for 1671 and 1678 are reprinted in *Lord Mayors' Pageants* (1842-3) by F.W. Fairholt, ii.109-76 (Percy Society, vol. 10). The Show was commonly mentioned with contempt, as a spectacle suited to the tastes of the gaping Cockney populace. Cf. Pepys, 29 Oct. 1660.

412 f. Westminster is Westminster Hall, where sat the courts of Common Pleas, King's Bench, Chancery and Exchequer; see De-Laune, pp. 124-32. With the complaint of lawyer's din and jargon cf. Milton, 'Ad Patrem', l. 72, and Cowley, 'Claudian's Old Man of Verona' (*Essays*, p. 447).

414 f. Sir George Jeffreys was currently seconding the Attorney-General in the proceedings against London's charter. He is caricatured under his nickname of 'Mouth' in Tho. Thompson's *Midsummer Moon: Or the Livery Man's Complaint* (1682): 'Room for the Chap-faln *Mouth* ... he's chiefly Devil about the Mouth';
> Oft with success this Mighty Blast did bawl ... [etc.]
> This demy Fiend, this Hurricane of Man
> Must shatter *London*'s Glory (if he can?)
> And him our prudent Praetor wisely chose
> To splutter Law, and the dinn'd Rabble pose;
> They have a thousand Tongues, yet he can roar
> Far louder, tho' they had a thousand more.
Cf. North (*Lives*, i.288) on his scolding from the bench 'in ... Billingsgate language.... He called it "giving a lick with the rough side of his tongue". It was ordinary to hear him say "Go, you are a filthy, lousy, knitty rascal."' Cf. 'Juvenal XIII', l. 179; and for Billingsgate, 'Art of Poetry', l. 377 and n.

419. Cf. *Hudibras*, III.iii.456:
>   Lawyers have more sober sense
>   Than to argue at their own expence.
To let oneself be 'treated', or (*a fortiori*) injured, at one's own expense,
was to be the most absurd of dupes. Cf. Rochester, 'A Letter from Artemisia',
1. 225, 'Satyr', 11. 35 f., and Dryden, Prologues to *The Assignation*, 11.
5 f., and *The Disappointment*, 1. 4.

The Thirteenth Satyr of Juvenal, Imitated

Like 'Boileau VIII', this is one of a group of 6 major poems (see Introduction, pp. lx f.) which, it appears from the 'Advertisement' (11. 2 f.) above,
had been recently composed when published in *Poems, And Translations*, *c*.mid-
July 1683. Among them, 'Juvenal III' was written in May, and 'Boileau VIII'
in Oct. 1682. By three of its allusions, 'Juvenal XIII' is placed between
late Mar. 1682 and 22 Jan. 1683. On the latter date, Lord Chief Justice
Pemberton was demoted from the King's Bench to Common Pleas, and was no
longer, as 1. 255 implies, at the head of the twelve Judges. Executed 10 Mar.
1682, Boroskie was then hung in chains; 'Thames his double tide' was on the
22nd (cf. 11. 102, 417, and nn.). The present Imitation does not furnish, as
Oldham claimed reasonably enough for the 'Art of Poetry', a continuously
faithful version of the original. Though Juvenal's sequence of topics is maintained, almost fifty lines, even disregarding expansions, have no equivalent
in the Latin; and not all the modern allusions replace Roman ones.

26. i.e. under James I.

36. *red Letter*: holy day; cf. 'Aude aliquid. Ode', 11. 93 f.; 'Jesuits II',
1. 187.

39. *Padding*: the footpad's vocation; *OED*, Padder sb^1, 1610.

42 f. Cf. Edmund Ashton, 'Prologue against the Disturbers of the Pit':
>   Should true Sense, with revengeful Fire, come down,
>   Our *Sodom* wants Ten Men to save the Town.
For authorship, see Vieth, *Attribution*, pp. 266-8.

50 f. Pope-burnings on Queen Elizabeth's accession-day took place each year
from 1676 to 1681, except apparently in 1678, when those on 5 Nov. (see
'Jesuits IV', 11. 320 ff., n.) were expensively elaborate (see J.R. Jones,
'The Green Ribbon Club', *DUJ*, Dec. 1956; and Miller, pp. 184-7; Sheila
Williams, 'The Pope-Burning Processions of 1679, 1680, and 1681', Warburg
Institute, *Journal*, xxi (1958), 104 ff.). In 1679, 1680, and 1681, the
effigy was carried in a grand procession organized by the Whig Green Ribbon
Club (Miller, p. 185). Engravings and descriptions were published: cf. *The
Solemn Mock Procession of the Pope ... &c. through ye City of London, Novem-
ber ye 17th, 1679*, which acclaims 'the prodigious shout' when the effigy was
cast into the bonfire; *Englands Misery* (1680) in which the Pope is called
'Antichrist'; and *The Procession: Or, the Burning of the Pope in Effigie,
In Smithfield Rounds ... 17th of November 1681. Being Queen Elizabeth's
Birthday*; Luttrell too (i.144), records this occasion: the route; and the
spectacle: in effigy, 'Godfrey on horseback and held up by a Jesuite; ...
the observator' L'Estrange, 'severell fryers, Jesuites, popish bishops and
cardinalls, in their proper habits; then ... suborned persons; and lastly
the pope, whose pageant was fastned on a sledge and drawn by four horses,
in all his pontificalibus.' Cf. Dryden, Prologue to *The Loyall Brother*
(1682), 11. 18-47.

57-60. Hobbes's reputation for atheism and irreligion was general; cf. the
examinations of his doctrine printed by Clarendon in 1670, Tenison in the

same year, and Eachard in 1673; and such poetical pamphlets as 'Mr. Cowley's Verses in Praise of Mr Hobbes, Oppos'd' (1680), and 'An Elegie Upon Mr. Thomas Hobbes' (1680). It misrepresented his stated doctrines and conscious creed (cf. Aubrey, i.353), but was perhaps not altogether unfair to the tendency of his materialism. *The Last Sayings ... of Mr. Thomas Hobbes ... Who departed this Life ... December. 4. 1679* (1680), saddled him with a dictum 'That God is Almighty Matter'. For his rejection of the orthodox belief in hell, a part, in his view, of the 'Spirituall Darknesse' created by ecclesiastics to further their spiritual sovereignty, see *Leviathan*, chs. 44, 47.

58. *shams*. See 'Jesuits, Prologue', 1. 15 n.

61-79. An equivalent for ll. 38-52 of the original, not a version of them. Juvenal contrasts the vices of the Olympians and the torments of Hades with Saturn's age of innocence. In an Imitation, he is to speak 'as if he were living and writing now': it would have been improper to introduce a direct version of a passage which implied real belief in the Roman mythology. For the same reason the story of Glaucus (ll. 329 ff. and n., below) is told as a story merely, and not (as in the original) for a positive fact.

76 f. To enforce trusts and uses belonged especially to Chancery. Its equitable jurisdiction had sprung originally from the special remedies it granted for special hardships of which poverty in the litigant was one. It seems doubtful whether in Oldham's day proceedings in equity were any less costly than at common law.

78 f. i.e. pillories. Cf. 'Upon a Woman', ll. 94 f.

82. *Blazing-Star*: a comet; regarded as a prodigy in nature, portending calamity. Cf. *The Petitioning-Comet ...* (1681), and its reference to 'the *Blazing-Star* before the late *Civil Wars*'.

85 f. It was as grave, almost, as an unclergyable felony. From the 16th century felonies had come to be divided into the clergyable, in which benefit of clergy might be claimed, and the unclergyable, in which it might not. By Oldham's time, benefit of clergy meant simply remission of the sentence to first offenders who could read a verse of a Latin psalm; they were branded in the thumb and released. For its rise and curtailment, see Maitland, pp. 229 f.; Tanner, p. 14.

93 f. John Stow (1525-1605) compiled *The Chronicles of England* (to 1580) and republished it with continuations, as *The Annales of England*, in 1592 and 1605. Cf. 'Jesuits IV', ll. 313 f. There is a list of prodigies very similar to Oldham's in Jonson's *Volpone*, II.i.37-49, the items of which are to be found in Stow: a new star, three porpoises above London Bridge, and a whale 'As high as *Woolwich*'.

96. The Monument was begun in 1671. An early print of it, which gives the height, 202 feet, is reproduced in Firth's edition of Macaulay, i.176. Cf. 'Juvenal III', 1. 121 n.

99. Cf. Rochester, 'My Lord All-Pride', ll. 23, 24 f.:
>   So have I seen, at Smithfield's wondrous fair ...
>   A lubbard elephant divert the town
>   With making legs, and shooting off a gun.

William Blaythwaite wrote to Sir Robert Southwell, 4 Sept. 1679, of visiting 'the Elephant' at Bartholomew Fair (Morley, p. 248). *The City Mercury* No. 3, Nov. 11-18, 1675, has an advertisement headed The Elephant: 'That Wonderful Beast lately sent from *East-India* to ... Lord Berkley, And since sold for Two thousand pounds Sterling: Is now to be seen at the *White Horse* Inn over against *Salisbury* Court in Fleet-*street*'.

100 f. A whale had appeared at Gravesend in 1658, but none, that one knows of, so far up the river since. Was not Oldham's 'Whale At Bridge' suggested by the 'three porcpisces seene, aboue the bridge' and the 'whale ... As high as *Woolwich*', in *Volpone* (above, ll. 93 f., n.)?

101. *the last great Comet, or the Hail*. Luttrell (i.45) describes the hail: 'On the 18th [of May 1680], between ten and 11 of the clock in the morning, was a most violent storm of hail ... the hailstones many of them as big as pidgeons eggs, and did great mischief to the glasse-windowes in London, and killed severall Birds.' See [An] *Account Of A Strange and Prodigious Storm of Thunder, Lightning & Hail*, ... *in and about London, on the Eighteenth of ... May* (1680). (Cf. Luttrell, *Catalogues*, first catalogue, p. 15, item 60: 'May 21'.) John Hill, in *An Allarm To Europe; By a Late Prodigious Comet seen November and December 1680*, couples the comet and the hail as a twofold portent of disaster. From the precedent of high mortality following the like hailstorm at Nottingham in 1558, and from 'pretty smart effects' of the recent storm, already observable, Hill concludes that 'this Prodigious *Comet* ... concurring in Nature with that Haile, must of necessity have extream Effects upon the Bodies of Man-Kind'. Cf. *The Petitioning-Comet* (1681) and Evelyn, 12 Dec. 1680. No further comet is recorded until Sept. 1682.

102. *Thames his double Tide*. On Wednesday 22 Mar. 1681/2 the tide flowed at London Bridge thrice in twelve hours. The phenomenon is chronicled by Luttrell (i.173); and reported by *The True Protestant Mercury* of 22-5 Mar. 1682 as 'a thing not known in many years, which occasions various Discourses'.

102 f. Cf. e.g. the *Very Strange Relation of the Raining Shower of Blood at Shewall, Hereford* (1679), and the 'Blood that rained in the Isle of Wight, attested by Sir Jo: Oglander', among Tradescant's Rarities (*Museaum Tradescantianum*, reprinted 1925, p. 44). The 'Streams of Milk' are in Juvenal.

118 f. See 'Dithyrambique', l. 54 and n.

120-2. Precisely these oaths were used by Jennison, one of the witnesses of the Popish Plot, in a letter printed in 1679: 'he protested, as he desired the forgiveness of his sins and the salvation of his soul, that he knew no more, and wished he might never see the face of God if he knew any more'; and yet subsequently he did not scruple to publish a long additional narrative (Burnet, ii.197).

129-34. Epicureans: see 'Ode on Jonson', ll. 41-3 and n. 'Epicure' in the 17th century most often signifies not a man of refined pleasures, but an anti-christian ranking next to the atheist, as in Burton, *Anatomy*, heading of Pt. 3, Sect. 4, Memb. 2, Subsect. 1.

137 f. See l. 78 f., and the passages there cited.

145. *both the Spittles*: the hospitals of St Thomas in Southwark, and St Bartholomew in West Smithfield. See De-Laune, p. 85.

145-7. Cf. *Hudibras*, III.i.1237-40:

> What made thee break thy plighted Vows?
> That which makes others break a house,
> And hang, and scorn you all, before
> Endure the plague of being poor.

130. *Bedlam*. See 'Art of Poetry', l. 811 n.

152. *what tho?* What then? what if it is so? See *OED* under *What* A.4.c.

159 f. Wittily bringing out the implication of replies made by Captain Vrats, condemned for Thynne's murder, Feb. 1681/2 (see l. 249 n.): they are recorded by Evelyn, 10 Mar., as told by 'a friend of mine' who accompanied Vrats to his execution, and by Dr Anthony Horneck, *The Last Confession* ...

of ... John Stern (1682), who reports the Captain's confidence that 'God would consider a Gentleman, and deal with him suitably to the condition and profession he had placed him in', and that 'God he believed had a greater favour for Gentlemen, than to require all these *punctilioes* at their hands'. A God who is sure to treat a gentleman as a gentleman, is evidently one himself: Vrats told Horneck 'he had far other apprehensions of God than I had'; Oldham spells such a presumption out. Vrats' unconcern is confirmed by his bearing at his execution: see *A Complete Collection of State Trials* (fol.), 1730, iii.500.

176. *sham*: see 'Jesuits, Prologue', 1. 15 n. Cf. 'Dithyrambique', 1. 4, and 'Juvenal III', 1. 145 nn.

179. Cf. 'Boileau VIII', ll. 414 f. and n.

188 f. *Vaninus*. Lucilio Vanini (b. 1585) wrote a treatise against Providence, *Æternae Providentiae Amphitheatrum* (1615), and he is ironically called 'Bless'd Saint' as having been burned for atheism, at Toulouse, 1619. Cf. 'Jesuits II', 1. 141.

190 f. Cf. Raleigh, *The Historie of the World* (1614), preface: 'Certainly, these wise worldlings have either found out a new God; or made One: and in all likelihood such a Leaden One, as *Lewis* the eleventh ware in his Cappe; which, when he had caused any that he feared, or hated, to be killed, hee would take it from his head and kisse it: beseeching it to pardon him this one evill act more, and it should be the last'. Philippe de Commynes, an eyewitness (*Mémoires*, ed. B. de Mandrot (1901-3), i.142), testifies to the leaden image itself, worn on 'ung maulvais chapeau'. For the monarch's superstitious regard for the collection of images borne on his hat, see Claude de Seyssel, *Histoire de Louys XII* (1615), p. 93: 'Lesquelles à tous propos ... il baisoit, se ruant à genouils ... si soudainement quelques fois, qu'il sembloit plus blessé d'entendement, que saige homme'. In various versions, his behaviour is remarked by Voltaire (*Œuvres*, 1756, xii.260); Pope, *Moral Essays*, I.89 and n., and Scott, in *Quentin Durward* (*passim*).

197. *Scarborough*. Sir Charles Scarburgh (1616-94), principal physician to Charles II, friend of Sir Thomas Browne, and an original Fellow of the Royal Society. He was a skilled anatomist, succeeding Harvey as anatomy lecturer at Surgeons' Hall, and publishing in 1676 (in W. Molins's Μυοτομια) a guide to human dissection entitled *Syllabus Musculorum*. His ability and success as a practitioner had been celebrated by Cowley in a Pindarique ode.

197. *Lower*: Oldham's friend, Dr Richard Lower (see Introduction, p. xxxiv and n. 38; 'Art of Poetry' 1. 599 n.). From Willis's death in 1675, he 'was esteemed', as Wood informs us (iv.297), 'the most noted physician in West-minster and London, and no man's name was more cried up at court than his' until his Whiggism during the Popish Terror cost him the majority of his patients there. Sir William Petty (whom Lower was to attend on his death-bed in 1687) reckoned that his own former practice of £280 per annum, though not bad for hard times, was 'not like' Lower's (*Petty—Southwell Correspondence*, ed. Lansdowne (1928), p. 223). His genuine greatness in the practice and study of medicine is confirmed by modern authorities: see Intro-duction, loc. cit.

216. *Westminster*. See 'Boileau VIII', ll. 412 f. and n.

221. *Temple-Walks*. Where the professional witnesses hung about for hire. Cf. *Hudibras*, III.iii.759, and Otway, *The Souldiers Fortune* (1681), I.i, p. 1: 'the worthy Knight[s] of the ... Post: your Peripatetick Philosophers of the Temple walks.... Villains that ... will forswear themselves for a Din-ner, and hang their Fathers for half a crown.' Cf. also 'Jesuits II', ll. 208; 'Upon a Woman', ll. 91 ff.

221. *Smithfield*: at the notorious horse-fair. To hinder the sale of stolen horses, a statute of 31 Eliz. provided that every seller of a horse in any fair or market must, unless personally known to the toll-taker, establish his ownership by the oath of a credible witness. In *The Second ... Part of Conny-catching* (1592), ed. G.B. Harrison, pp. 15 ff., Robert Greene describes how the horse-thief evaded the statute by the use of false witnesses, 'commonly old Knights of the post'. In Oldham's time, to enforce the statute was still an important part of the toller's duty (see George Meriton, *A Guide for Constables... Toll-takers in Fairs &c.*, 6th edn., 1681; 1st, 1668); a new generation of perjurers evidently continued the practices of their Elizabethan forebears.

233-5. Pepys relates the trial of Gabriel Holmes and others, 4 July 1667, 'for making it their business to set houses on fire merely to get plunder'. The previous day Sir Richard Ford had told him that by the evidence at the Sessions-house it was plain there was a combination of rogues organizing this type of crime, and that 'a great number' were likely to be convicted. Two boys testified they had been placed by a gang 'to take up what goods were flung into the streets out of the windows, when the houses were on fire'. From l. 235 it appears that Oldham no longer held the Papists responsible for the Great Fire. But because he accepted the 'evidence' (few realized how flimsy it was) that the Fire had been started and spread by design, he now attributed it to fire-raising criminals like Gabriel Holmes. (See *A True ... Account Of The ... Informations Exhibited To The ... Committee appointed by the Parliament To Inquire into the ... Burning Of ... London*, 1667.)

240 f. Cf. Camden's *Britannia* (1586), translated (edn. of 1789, i.338): 'The abbey church' of St Alban's 'has a most beautiful brass font, in which the children of the Kings of Scotland used to be baptised. Sir Richard Lee ... placed it here as part of the spoils of Scotland', with a vainglorious inscription, which Camden gives. The font was 'made money of by the Parliament soldiers' (see N. Salmon, *History of Hertfordshire* (1728), p. 89), to whom, as in the next couplet, Oldham alludes.

242 f. See Bruno Ryves, *Mercurius Rusticus: Or, The Countries Complaint of the barbarous Out-rages Committed by the Sectaries of this late flourishing Kingdome* (1646), pp. 201-6. '... the Rebells under the Conduct of Sir *William Waller*, entering the City of *Chichester* on *Innocents day*, 1642. the next day their first businesse was to Plunder the Cathedral Church; the Marshall therefore and some other Officers ... seize upon the Consecrated Plate ... they left not so much as ... a Chalice for the Blessed Sacrament ... they rush out thence and break open a Parish Church, ... called the *Subdeanery* ... and finding no more Plate but the *Chalice*, they steale that too.' I discuss my failure to trace the authority for l. 243 in 'Some Problems', pp. 571 f.

244 f. See *An Elegy on Colonel Blood, Notorious for Stealing the Crown, &c. Who Dyed the Twenty-Sixth of August 1680* (BL Lutt. i.16, dated by Luttrell '30 Aug.'); *A Second Elegy to the Memory of ... Collonel Thomas Blood* (1680); and *Remarks On The Life and Death Of The Fam'd Mr. Blood*, 2nd edn. (1680) (advertised in *The City Mercury*, 18 Nov. 1680). John Strype, in his continuation of Stow's *Survey* (see 1754 edn., i.97), gives a full account of the exploit (but wrongly dated) from the information of the keeper, Edwards, whom Blood and his accomplices assaulted. It took place 9 May 1671; see *The London Gazette*, No. 572. Marvell's lines upon it had furnished Oldham with hints for 'Jesuits II', ll. 89 f., 110; see also John Freke, 'The History of Insipids' (Rochester, *Poems* (Pinto), no. LVIII, ll. 43-6; but see Rochester, *Poems* (Vieth), p. 225, citing Frank H. Ellis, 'John Freke and *The History of Insipids*', *PQ*, xliv (1965), 472-83).

246-8. From Oates's sworn information of 5 Sept. 1678 to the evidence at
Plunket's trial on 3 May 1681, the Plot was affirmed by an enormous mass
of false testimony on the part of Oates, Bedloe, Prance, Dangerfield, Dugdale, Turberville, Bolron, Arnold, the Irish witnesses, and many smaller fry.
Dugdale, Turberville, and the Irish changed sides in 1681, and perjured
themselves against Shaftesbury and Stephen College. Before this, however,
there had been several attempts to tamper with the witnesses or to discredit
them by evidence as false as their own. The most famous, the Meal Tub Plot,
was discovered in Oct. 1679; and Reading was condemned 24 Apr. 1679, Knox
and Lane 25 Nov. 1679, Tasborough and Price in Jan. 1680, and Simpson
Tonge committed to Newgate, Sept. 1680, all for intrigues of the same sort.
The Several Informations of Mr. Simeon Wright (1681) gives a resumé of the
witnesses and counter-witnesses; for the Irish, see 'Boileau VIII', 1. 257
n., 'On the Times', ll. 7 f., n. See 'Jesuits II', ll. 210 ff., 'Juvenal
III', ll. 38 f.; Jones, pp. 187 f., Kenyon, pp. 60, 91, 100, 132, 138, 152,
189-92, 197-204, 214, 241, 244.

249. *Thinne's ... Murderers*. Thomas Thynne of Longleat, 'Tom of Ten Thousand', the wealthy Whig and friend of Monmouth gibed at by Rochester and
Dryden, was shot in his coach, at Charing Cross, on 12 Feb. 1682. Oldham's
friend Dr Lower actually had the extracted bullets in his possession for
a day or two, borrowing them from Thynne's chirurgeon. (*The Tryal ... Of
George Boroski*, 1682, p. 13.) The assassins, Borosky, Stern, and Vrats,
were instigated by a Swedish nobleman, Count Königsmark, who had 'had some
pretensions to the lady Ogle, whom Mr. Thin had since married'. The Count,
thanks chiefly to the venality of the jury, was acquitted; his bravos were
condemned, and executed 10 Mar. See Luttrell, i.164-8, 170, 174; Evelyn,
15 Nov. 1681, 10 Mar. 1682, Reresby, pp. 249-55. Settle (prologue to his
Heir of Morocco, 11 Mar. 1682: Wiley, pp. 84 f.) devoted twenty lines to
the crime, and it provoked numerous ballads and elegies, e.g. *The Matchless
Murder*, printed for J. Conyers; J.M.'s *Murther Unparalel'd* (1682), and *Capt.
Vrats's Ghost to Count Coningsmark, By A Western Gentleman*; also two, dated
by Luttrell 15 and 28 Feb. 1681/2: *A Hew and Cry after Blood & Murther* and
An Elegy On the Famous Tom Thinn Esq ... By Geo. Gittos (BL, Lutt. I.151,
150.)

249. *Godfrey's Murderers*: Green, Berry, and Hill, as Oldham and very many
others still believed. They were certainly innocent. See 'Jesuits I', 0.2 n.
and ll. 1-7.

255. Sir Francis Pemberton (1625-97) had succeeded Scroggs as Lord Chief
Justice of the King's Bench 11 Apr. 1681. He was transferred to the Common
Pleas 22 Jan. 1682/3 to make way for Edmund Saunders, and was removed from
the bench altogether in the following Sept. See Luttrell, i.74, 76, 247;
and *DNB*.

260. Of the hundreds of Essex, two were particularly designated 'the Hundreds' by local usage. They were Rochford and Dengey, lying on the coast
between the Thames and the Blackwater. Their unhealthiness is noted by
Philip Morant in his history of the county (1768), i.iii.268. *The Essex
Ballad* (1680, 'Aprill 10', Luttrell, *Catalogues*) lists 'Agues' among the
things for which the county is 'much renowned', and Waller writes of 'the
malignant air' of 'those already cursed Essexian plains' ('Upon the Death
of My Lady Rich', ll. 7, 1). The similar notoriety of 'Sheppey Island' is
illustrated in Shadwell's *Sullen Lovers* (1668), p. 28: 'this is worse then
a *Sheerness* Ague'.

269. *entertain*. See 'Art of Poetry', l. 616 n.

285-93. Cf. Dryden, Prologue to *All For Love* (1678), ll. 21 f.:
            A brave Man scorns to quarrel once a day;
            Like Hectors, in at evr'y petty fray.

For the 'hectr'ing Blades' see 'Boileau VIII', l. 139 n.; 'Juvenal III',
ll. 405 ff., and n.

294 ff. Juvenal's allusion to Socrates is modernized by the addition of
ll. 295 f.

300-4. Cf. Charles's speech on the scaffold as rendered by George Bate in
Elenchus Motuum nuperorum in Anglia; ... Paris (1649), p. 205: '*Qua Chari-*
taté saevientes in me Hostes amplector, testem habeo Virum hunc probum
(Digito in Episcopum Londinensem intento) *veniam hisce omnibus intimis ex*
praecordiis indulgeo; Deúmque Misericordiarum obnixè veneror, ut seriam iis
resipiscentiam largiri dignetur, & remittat hoc facinus'; and also the medi-
tation upon death put into his mouth in Εἰκὼν Βασιλικὴ (1681), esp. p. 247.
In calling Charles 'the great'st of *mortal* sufferers' Oldham implies a
comparison with the Passion; cf. the Bishop of Downe's sermon, *The Martyr-*
dom of King Charls I or His Conformity with Christ in his Sufferings (1649,
reprinted 1660); see Nichol Smith, p. 48, l. 15 and n.

326. In the 'Book of Martyrs' (viz. *Actes and Monuments*, 1563); cf. 'Jesuits
IV', ll. 313 f. and n.

327. *Bradshaw, and Ravilliac*. François Ravaillac, assassin of Henry IV in
1610; and John Bradshaw (1602-59), Lord President of the commission which
condemned Charles I. They seem ill-chosen to illustrate the sure punishment
of remorse, since both were unrepentant. Ravaillac was executed with torture and when Bradshaw died the royalists lamented (e.g. in *The Arraign-*
ment Of the Divel, for stealing away President Bradshaw [1659]) that he had
escaped the hangman; at the Restoration they suspended his corpse with Cromwell's and Ireton's at Tyburn. For Ravaillac, cf. 'Jesuits I', ll. 55, 59 nn.

329. Juvenal took the story from Herodotus, VI.86, where Leutychides relates
it to the Athenians as a warning. The would-be knave was Glaucus son of
Epicydes. Oldham added ll. 329 f. for the reason explained in ll. 61-79 n.

330. *Hackwel*: *An Apologie Or Declaration Of The Power And Providence Of God*
In The Government Of The World, ... [a] *Censure Of The Common Errour Touch-*
ing Natures Perpetuall ... Decay (1627, 3rd enlarged edn. 1635) by George
Hakewill DD (1578-1649). For its vogue, cf. Pepys, 3 Feb. 1666/7, and Johnson, *Lives of the Poets*, ed. Birkbeck Hill, i.137 and n. 5.

330. *Beard's Theatre*: *The Theatre of Gods Judgements: Or, A Collection Of*
Histories ... concerning the admirable Iudgements of God vpon the trans-
gressours of his commandements. Translated Out Of French, And Augmented by
more than three hundred Examples (1597), by Thomas Beard, DD (d. 1632), who
was Cromwell's schoolmaster. It was several times reprinted in the 17th
century. Chs. XXIX and XXX are devoted to judgements upon perjurers, of the
same type as that related here.

340. *remotest*. Scansion requires 'remot'st'.

354. *by Lumly drest*: not with his own hands, but as connoisseur, and patron
of the feast. He is the Lord Lumley (1589-*c*.1662) to whom, with three
others, 'known for their Admired Hospitalities', Robert May dedicated *The*
Accomplisht Cook, Or The Art and Mystery of Cookery (1660). The foundation
of his art he owed, he declares, to their 'inimitable Expences' which they
'never weighed ... so that they might arrive to the high esteem they had of
their *Gustos*'. He pays tribute to those 'magnificent Trophies of Cookery
that have adorned your Tables', and to Lumley as 'that great lover ... of
Art, who wanted no knowledg in the discerning this mistery' (3rd edn., 1671,
A3^r-A4^r, A6^v). This Lumley's successor, Baron Richard Lumley, was an acquaintance of Rochester's: see J.H. Wilson, ed., *The Rochester—Savile Correspon-*
dence (1941), p. 58.

356. Oldham introduces the reference to Damocles. Cf. Rochester's 'A Very Heroical Epistle ... to Ephelia', ll. 55 f.:
> ... here with aching hearts our joys we taste,
> Disturbed by swords, like Damocles his feast.

372. See F.W. Fairholt, *Gog and Magog. The Giants in Guildhall* (1859). The Gog and Magog of this period replaced the pair burnt in the Great Fire. In *London Triumphant*, depicting the Lord Mayor's Show of 1672 (see Percy Society publications, x.76) Thomas Jordan describes them as two giants, each 'at least fifteen foot high, that do sit and are drawn by horses in two several chariots, moving, talking, and taking tobacco as they ride along'. At Guildhall, they were to be seen all the year round. According to the *Gigantick History of the Two famous Giants of Guildhall* (1741), they were 'made only of wicker work and pasteboard put together with great ... ingenuity'.

413. The prisoner at the bar had to hold up his hand in answer to his name before the indictment was read; again before the jury delivered their verdict; and yet again if they pronounced him guilty. Cf. *Hudibras* II.iii.1167 ff.; III.i.1456.

414 f. Under statutes passed since 1660, persons convicted of certain crimes might choose transportation instead of the death penalty. Luttrell (i.157, 13 Jan. 1681/2) refers to 'an order of the [Council] for transporting severall condemned popish preists in Newgate to the isles of Scilly'. The *Caribbes* are the Lesser Antilles (Barbados and the Leeward Is.): there is some account of transportation thither at this period in V.T. Harlow, *A History Of Barbados, 1625-1685* (1926), pp. 295-9, and C.S.S. Higham, *The Development Of The Leeward Islands Under The Restoration, 1660-1688* (1921), pp. 166, 170-4.

417. Cf. Luttrell, i.171: 'The body of Boraskie the Polander, who shott Mr. Thinn, is hang'd up in chains at Mile end, being the road from the sea-ports where most of the northern nations do land.' Cf. also *Capt. Vrats' Ghost* (1682):
> Poor Ignorant *Borisky's* angry Ghost,
> See with what Rage it comes thee to accost?
> Must He that Fatal Shot for ever rue,
> His Corps in Chains be hung to all Men's view
> And Spect'cle made to Forreigners for you?

Borosky suffered, with Vratz and Stern, 10 Mar. 1681/2; see further l. 249 n. and *The Loyal Protestant*, 11 Mar., and *The True Protestant Mercury*, 8-11 Mar. 1681/2.

David's Lamentation ... Paraphras'd

This paraphrase was doubtless inspired by Cowley's unfulfilled intention, recorded in the preface to his 1656 Folio, of concluding 'Davideis' with 'that most Poetical and excellent *Elegie* of *Davids* on the death of *Saul* and *Jonathan*' (*Poems*, p. 11). In it Oldham borrows from 'Davideis', which he makes his model for use of the Scripture narratives.

20 f. Cf. Cowley, 'Davideis' (*Poems*, p. 296):
> Slaughter the wearied *Riphaims* bosom fills,
> Dead corps *imboss* the *vail* with little *hills*.

32-6 and ff. In founding upon the Scriptural text an extended Pindarique ode, Oldham drew chiefly upon I Samuel. For Ashdod's idol and the vile Fish (both Dagon), see ch. v (also *Paradise Lost*, I.457 ff.); and for other allusions: Mount Gilboa, the fatal battlefield (l. 47), xiii and II.i.6, 21; Jabesh

and Ammon's proud tyrant, Nahash (11. 80-2), xi; Amalek and Agag (11. 84 f.),
xv; Micmash (1. 89), xiv.5 ff.; Helah (1. 91), Saul's encampment when at
Dammin (1. 90) David slew Goliath, xvii.1 f.; Saul's triumphant reception
(11. 91-5), xviii.6-8; Seir (Edom, dwelling about Mt. Seir), Moab, and
Zobah (1. 96), xiv.47; Seneh (11. 108-11), xiv.4, 15; Gibeah (11. 178-82),
Judges xx. For 11. 202, 208, the authority is I Samuel xviii:1-4, 27; xx:31.

80-2. Cf. Cowley, 'Davideis' (Poems, pp. 378 ff.).

108. *Seneh.* Cf. Cowley, 'Davideis' (Poems, p. 387).

108 f. Cf. Cowley, 'Davideis' (Poems, p. 387): he calls Jonathan 'an *Host*'.

110 f. It is Cowley ('Davideis', Poems, p. 387) who adds paralytic terror
to the 'very great trembling' of Scripture.

116. Cf. the 'Vision', R271, 11. 9 f.; 'Promising a Visit', 11. 31 f. and n.

118. Cf. Lee, *Sophonisba* (1676), III.i, p. 25:
      Where'er our General turn'd, death mark'd his look,
      And whom he ey'd with his cold Arrow strook....

125. Cf. Dryden, 1 *Conquest of Granada* (1672), II, p. 13:
      His Victories we scarce could keep in view,
      Or polish 'em so fast as he rough drew.

137-42. The epic simile closely resembles Dryden's in sts. 107 f. of *Annus
Mirabilis* (1667) from which poem Oldham undoubtedly borrows in 11. 169-71.

145. Cf. Cowley, 'Davideis' (Poems, p. 380):
      His amaz'd Troops strait cast their arms away;
      Scarce fled his *Soul* from thence more swift then *they*.

167-71. Borrowing from Dryden and Cowley. Cf. *Annus Mirabilis*, sts. 3 f. for
the anaphora with isocolon; 'the blest *Arabia's* spices' correspond to the
'Idumean Balm' and 'Ceilon['s] Spicy Forrests'; 1. 171 echoes 'The Sun but
seem'd the Lab'ror of their Year', and 1. 171 links with it 'the Heavn's
... kindly heat / In Eastern Quarries ripening precious Dew', and Dryden's
n.: 'Precious Stones at first are dew, condens'd, and harden'd by the
warmth of the Sun, or subterranean Fires'. With 167 f. cf. in 'Davideis'
(Poems, p. 263) 'The *Silk-worm*'s pretious death' and '*Tyrian Dy*'—from the
shell-fish, the murex.

178-82. At Gibeah in their civil war, Israel lost on the first day 22,000
men, 18,000 on the second; Benjamin 25,000 on the third. This gives threescore thousand on Cowley's principle of taking 'the next whole number'
because '*Poetry* will not admit of *broken ones*': ('Davideis', I. n. 23, Poems,
p. 272).

210 f. Cf. ode to Morwent, 11. 307-9.

212 f. Cf. Dryden, 2 *Conquest of Granada* (1672), III, p. 102:
      Not new-made Mothers greater love express
      Than he; when with first looks their babes they bless.
Cf. ode to Morwent, 11. 286-90.

216, 219; 221 f.; 223, 225. Cf. the ode to Morwent, 11. 222-4, and the
description of David and Jonathan's friendship in Cowley, 'Davideis' (Poems,
pp. 286 f.).

The Ode of Aristotle in Athenaeus, Paraphras'd

Aristotle's ode to Hermias, tyrant of Atarneus and Assos, whose guest he had
been for many years, is preserved in Athenaeus, *Deipnosophistes*, XV.696.

Werner Jaeger, *Aristotle* (tr. Richard Robinson, 1934, p. 118) has an English version and a discussion of it; for Hermias, see pp. 112-19. His honourable, but misplaced confidence in a safe-conduct enabled Mentor, sent against him by the Persians, to decoy him to an interview, seize him, and send him to Artaxerxes, who put him to death.

33 f. He staked his life on the principle of honour: but not in battle.

Upon the Works of Ben. Johnson

In the heading of the autograph fair copy, '1677/8' places the composition between 1 Jan. and 24 Mar. 1678, and 'reprinted' indicates Oldham's hope of getting his ode prefixed to a new edition of Jonson's *Works*. In Dec. 1678 he tells John Spencer (R279 f.) he has sent it to the bookseller—deducibly Herringman, who had brought out Oldham's first published poem in Nov. 1677, and with Martyn and Marriot had meditated a new Jonson at least since their edition of *The Wild Goose Chase* (1652). In their one-volume Beaumont and Fletcher (advertised in *The London Gazette*, 3-6 Feb. 1678/9) they announced that if that were a success, they would follow it with a Jonson. Evidently Oldham had wind of the renewed project two months before, and probably when he began the Ode. Jonson's works were not in fact reprinted till 1692, and the Ode, with 'reprinted' dropped from the title, first appeared in *Poems, And Translations* (1683). On submitting it to the bookseller, so Oldham told Spencer, he did not make it more polished, but retrenched five stanzas. The fair copy and first edition, in which the stanzas correspond, most likely preserve the full version. Rejected material, however (a few lines of which were used for the 'Homer' q.v. ll. 1-4, 137 nn.) is extant in a draft on R224 f. (see Appendix II); a former and longer version including it cannot be entirely ruled out.

1. Cf. Barten Holyday's ''Tis dangerous to praise' which opens his 'Epode' before Jonson's version (1640) of *Ars Poetica*, familiar to Oldham (*Jonson* xi.352, and 'Art of Poetry' headnote).

4. Cf. Jo. Rutter, in *Jonsonus Virbius*, 1638 (*Jonson*, xi.459, ll. 1, 3 f.):
    ... *thy* ... *name* ...
    Which none can *lessen*, nor we bring enough
    To raise it *higher*, through our want of *stuffe*....

5. Cf. Falkland, in *Jonsonus Virbius* (*Jonson*, xi.435, ll. 233 f., 237 f.):
    Let *Digby, Carew, Killigrew*, and *Maine,*
    Godolphin, Waller, that inspired *Traine* ...
    Answer thy *wish*, for none so fit appeares
    To raise his *Tombe*, as who are left his *Heires*....

6 ff. Cf. Dryden, *Of Dramatick Poesie* (*Essays*, i.81): 'Wit, and language, and humour also in some measure, we had before him; but something of art was wanting to the Drama, till he came.' Jonson himself, in his lines to Richard Brome (*Jonson*, viii.409, ll. 7 f.) speaks of 'those Comick Lawes / Which I, your *Master*, first did teach the Age'. See, to the same purpose, Heylyn, I.268; and in *Jonsonus Virbius*, King, Clayton, and Feltham (*Jonson*, xi.504, ll. 10-13; 320, ll. 12-16; 441, ll. 25 f.; 450, l. 1; 461, ll. 33-5).

9. Cf. Cartwright, in *Jonsonus Virbius* (*Jonson*, xi.458, l. 126): Ben's hasty competitors 'Are not *wits*, but materialls of *wit*'.

14-26. Oldham adapts Cowley's extended metaphor from the ode 'To Mr. Hobs' (*Poems*, p. 189), who is apostrophized as 'Thou great *Columbus* of the ... *Lands* of *new Philosophies*'. Cf. with ll. 15, 22, the account of Hobbes's vessel, unlike the '*Fisher-boats* of *Wit*', entering upon 'the vast *Ocean*' devoid of landmarks (nothing to be seen 'but *Seas* and *Skies*') 'Till unknown Regions it descries'. In ll. 22-6 Oldham recollects Cowley's n. (p. 91):

'the Ancients ... seldom ventured into the *Ocean*; and when they did, did only *Littus legere*, coast about near the shore'.

32.   Dryden speaks of 'this Anarchy of Wit' in the Prologue to *Albumazar* (1668), 1. 17.

38-49.   *Chaos ... harmony*. Richard West (*Jonsonus Virbius, Jonson*, xi.470, 11. 79 ff.) writes that, thanks to Ben,
> ... our ... ENGLISH ...
> (I had almost said a *Confusion*)
> Is now all *harmony*....

38.   'The Vision' (R270), 1. 19, is a variant of this.

41-3.   The allusion is a commonplace. Cf., e.g. Dryden, 'Prologue to the University of Oxford', 1673:
> Such build their Poems the *Lucretian* way,
> So many Huddled Atoms make a Play,
> And if they hit in Order by some Chance,
> They call that Nature which is Ignorance.

See 'Juvenal XIII', 11. 129 ff. and n.

52 f.   Cf. Jonson himself, in *Discoveries* (*Jonson*, viii.586); and prefacing *The Alchemist* (v.291): 'But how out of purpose, and place, do I name Art? when the Professors are growne so obstinate contemners of it, and presumers on their own Naturalls, as they are deriders of all diligence that way, and, by simple mocking at the termes, when they vnderstand not the things, thinke to get of[f] wittily with their Ignorance.'

54-8.   Cf. Thomas Rymer, *The Tragedies of the Last Age Consider'd* (1678), published Nov. 1677, p. 8: 'Say others, ... Poetry is the *Child* of *Fancy*, and is never to be school'd and *disciplin'd* by *Reason*; Poetry, say they, is *blind* inspiration, is pure *enthusiasm*, is *rapture* and *rage* all over.... Those who object against reason are the *Fanaticks* in Poetry, and are never to be sav'd by their good works.' Cf. Thomas Shipman, 'Belvoir', 1679 (*Carolina*, 1683, p. 235): 'I must not be / A *Schismatick* in *Poetry*'; Dryden, Prologue to *Oedipus* (1679), 11. 29-31; and Spencer's verse-letter to Oldham (Appendix I, 11. 78 ff.). See 'Art of Poetry', 11. 466 ff. and n.; and contrast 'Praise of Poetry' (R99, 96, 87) where Oldham treats 'furor poeticus' with much more favour. Randolph, pp. 96 f., had three renderings of the crucial text in Aristotle (*Poetics: Works* (Oxford) 1455.a.32); Dryden, in 1679, following Rapin and Castelvetro, whittles it away (*Essays*, i.221 f.); but contrast i.152, 11. 3 ff., i.186, 11. 23 ff., after Petronius and Longinus, and especially i.152, 11. 32 ff. Cf. Shadwell, Preface to *The Humorists*, 1671 (Spingarn, ii.159): 'In fancy mad men equal if not excel all others; and one may as well say that [such a man] is as good ... as a temperate wiseman, as that one of the very fancyful Plays ... can be so good ... as one of *Johnson*'s correct and well-govern'd Comedies.'

66.   Cf. Cowley, 'The Constant' (*Poems*, p. 135): 'Which does not *force*, but *guide* our *Liberty*!' Cf. 'Counterpart', 1. 31.

67-75.   For the hawking terms, 'haggard', 'at random', 'reclaim'd', 'brought to lure', 'Quarry', 'towring', 'lessen'd' (to fly to lessen), and 'turn'd', see *OED* and *Shakespeare's England*, ii.xxvii §2.

67-75.   Clarendon's view (MS 'Life' of himself), though not available to Oldham, is representative: Jonson's 'naturall aduantages were judgement to order and gouerne fancy, rather then excesse of fancy, his productions beinge slow and upon deliberaćon, yett then aboundinge with greate witte and fancy' (*Jonson*, xi.512; cf., e.g. 534, No. xxv, 11. 3 f.).

67-71.   Cf. Shadwell, Preface to *The Humorists*, 1671 (Spingarn, ii.159): '... nature ... subjected wit to the government of judgment, which is the noblest faculty of the mind. Fancy rough-draws, but judgement smooths and finishes; nay, judgment does in deed comprehend wit.' He is rejecting Dryden's endeavour to distinguish Jonson's excellence by a more critical use of the terms.

71-5. In asserting that Jonson possessed wit as well as judgement in perfection, Oldham appears to agree with Shadwell in the controversy between him and Dryden; cf. Dryden (*Essays*, i.81, 138, 172) and Spingarn (ii.150, 158 ff., 339-41). Dryden withdrew from the argument in his 'Defence of the Epilogue' (1672); but Shadwell could not let it alone: besides the dedication, prologue, and epilogue of his *Virtuoso* (1676), cf. *The Triumphant Widow* (by him and Newcastle), 1677, p. 61, where he makes Crambo expostulate: 'Oh, I hate Johnson, oh oh, dull dull oh oh no Wit'. It may be wrong, however, to stress the present passage, for in Pindarique eulogy the more idolatrous was almost of necessity the better opinion.

76 f. Cf. I.C. (loc. cit., n. on 140 f., 143 below): 'Art, and Nature strive / Thy banquets to contrive'.

78 f. Oldham adopts Cowley's image (for the conjunction of Scripture and Reason) from 'Reason. The Use of it in Divine Matters' (*Poems*, p. 47).

81 f. See this commonplace in Cowley, quoted in 'Boileau VIII', ll. 71 ff., n.

91 f. Cf. W. Cartwright, in *Jonsonus Virbius* (*Jonson*, xi.456, ll. 41, 43 f.):
> That *life*, that *Venus* of all things,
> Is not found scattred in *thee* here and there,
> But, like the *soule*, is wholly every where.

For the diffusion of the soul, see 'Dithyrambique', ll. 14-17 n., ode on Atwood, l. 102.

102 f. In R90 Oldham notes: 'Poetry till Ben like ye terms and notions of ye Schools he first refin'd it from pedantry & jargon, animated with Sence.'

104-7. *c.*14 Mar. 1677/8 (*HMC*, Le Fleming, p. 143) the Council was 'considering how to discourage the wearing of French stuffs and druggets to the neglect of the English'. Certain imports from France, cloth among them, were prohibited by the Poll Bill debated in Feb. and 'perfected' 4 Mar. 1678. Dryden, satirizing hack dramatists' French borrowing (Prologue, 1 *Conquest of Granada*, 1670, ll. 34-9) had used the same metaphor as Oldham. On the prevailing view of French imports as effeminate and economically disadvantageous, see further, e.g., J.B., *An Account Of The French Usurpation Upon The Trade of England* (1679); and Ogg, i.221, 225.

113-16. Cf. John Spencer's verse-letter to Oldham (Appendix I), ll. 159-62.

119-21. Cf. Shadwell, Epilogue to *The Humorists* (1671): 'learned Ben'
> ... alone div'd into the Minds of Men ...
> And all their vain fantastick Passions drew.

122-9. Cf. Waller in *Jonsonus Virbius* (*Jonson*, xi.447 f., ll. 5-12):
> Thou not alone those various inclinations,
> Which *Nature* gives to *Ages, Sexes, Nations,*
> Has traced with thy All-resembling *Pen*,
> But all that custome hath impos'd on *Men*,
> Or ill-got Habits, which distort them so,
> That scarce the Brother can the Brother know,
> Is represented to the wondring Eyes,
> Of all that see or read thy Comedies.

But Oldham's 'Whatere' and 'transform' suggest he used the slightly altered text of Waller's *Poems* (1645), which has 'That whate'er' for 'But all that' and 'habit ... deforms' for 'Habits ... distort'.

132 f.   Cf. Shadwell, Epilogue to *The Humorists* (1671):
>   A Humor is the Byas of the Mind,
>   By which with violence 'tis one way inclin'd
>   It makes our Actions lean on one side still
>   And in all Changes that way bends the Will.

He is paraphrasing Jonson's induction to *Every Man Out.* Dryden parodied
Shadwell's lines in *MacFlecknoe.*

134-7.   Cf. Waller (*Jonson*, xi.448, ll. 13 f., 28 f., 31 f.):
>   Whoever in those Glasses lookes, may finde
>   The spots return'ed, or graces, of his minde ...
>   For as thou couldst all *characters* impart,
>   So none can render thine ...
>   Who was nor this nor that, but all we finde,
>   And all we can imagine in mankind.

138-53.   This is the Restoration ideal of comedy, as expressed in the prologues; cf. especially Dryden's to *Sir Martin Mar-All* (1667):
>   Fools, which each man meets in his Dish each Day
>   Are yet the great Regalio's of a Play, etc.

140 f., 143.   Oldham had read the lines by I. C. before Jonson's *Quintus Horatius Flaccus: His Art of Poetry* (1640); the third st. and the n. there on
Menander's cook (*Jonson*, xi.337) helped to suggest the topics of variety
and of catering for the best-qualified tastes. Cf. esp.:
>   But if thou make thy feasts
>   For the high-relish'd guests ...
>   It were almost a sinne
>   To think that thou shouldst equally delight
>   Each severall appetite....

154-67.   Cf. Richard West, in *Jonsonus Virbius* (*Jonson* xi. 469, ll. 63 f.):
>   ... their poore Cobweb-stuffe finds as quick *Fate*
>   As *Birth*, and sells like Almanacks out of date....

157-63.   Cf. John Beaumont, in *Jonsonus Virbius* (*Jonson*, xi.438, ll. 48-51):
>   ... 'twas farre more strange
>   To see (how ever times, and fashions frame)
>   His wit and language still remaine the same
>   In all mens mouths....

With the phrasing of ll. 157 f., cf. the prologue to *The Doubtful Heir*, in
Shirley's *Poems* (1646) ('Narcissus', p. '154', really 54): 'Our Author did
not calculate his Play, / For this Meridian'.

168-70.   Marston, in *Sophonisba*, decries Jonson's transcriptions from the
classics; Tom May in his lines to John Ford (1629) and Denham in his 'On
Mr. Abraham Cowley' (1667) both refer to him as a plunderer. The notorious
denigration was Owen Feltham's in 'An Answer to ... Come leave the loathed
Stage' (*Jonson*, xi.339, ll. 11 ff.): ''Tis known' he does 'excell'
>   As a Translator: But when things require
>   A *genius* and fire,
>   Not kindled heretofore by others pains;

he has 'wanted brains / And art' to hit the target, as often as he has succeeded. Mayne and Cartwright reply to the charge (*Jonsonus Virbius*; *Jonson*,
xi.454, ll. 122-8; 458, ll. 129-42); Edward Howard, in the Preface to *The
Womens Conquest* (1671), wonders at it.

180-7.   Cf. Dryden, *Of Dramatick Poesie* (1668) (*Essays*, i.82): 'He was deeply
conversant in the Ancients, both Greek and Latin, and he borrowed boldly
from them: there is scarce a poet or historian among the Roman authors of
those times whom he has not translated in *Sejanus* and *Catiline*.... He in-
vades authors like a monarch; and what would be theft in other poets, is

only victory in him.'; cf. his Prologue to *Albumazar*, the same year, 11. 11-
14. Carew had justified Jonson by the same figure; see *Jonson*, xi.336,
11. 39 ff.

182. *Universal Monarchy*: world-empire, like Alexander's; applied metaphori-
cally to empire in poetry, as by Cowley to empire in love: see below, 'Upon
the Marriage', 1. 66 and n.

188-91. Jonson replied to gibes at his lack of facility in the apologetical
dialogue appended to *Poetaster* (*Jonson*, iv.323, 11. 193 ff.):
>   ... they say you are slow,
>   And scarse bring forth a play a yeere. AUT. 'Tis true.
>   I would, they could not say that I did that! [etc.]
The attack was continued by Dekker in *Satiromastix* (*Dramatic Works*, ed.
F. Bowers, 1953, e.g. i.326; cf. also *2 Return from Parnassus* (*The Three
Parnassus Plays*, ed. J.B. Leishman, 1949), 11. 296 f. It is rebutted by
Carew (in the poem cited above, 11. 180 ff., n.), by John Davies of Here-
ford, and, in *Jonsonus Virbius*, by Jasper Mayne, Feltham, West, and Cart-
wright, who declares
>   We do imbrace their slander: *thou* has *writ*
>   Not for *dispatch* but *fame*. (99-100)
(*Jonson*, xi.380, 11. 3-9; 452, 11. 49-66; 461 f., 11. 49-64; 469, 11. 53-66;
457, 11. 97-112.) Fuller, finally, in the celebrated comparison with Shakespeare (ibid. xi.510) pronounces Jonson '*Solid*, but *Slow* in his performances.'

192-4. He remembers with complacency the laborious habits of composition and
diligence in revision which (as his drafts testify) were indeed his.

196. Cf. Dryden, *Of Dramatick Poesie* (*Essays*, i.81): 'He was a most severe
judge of himself, as well as others.' He is depicted as judge at the sessions
of wit in Holyday's 'Epode' (see n. to 1. 1, and *Jonson*, xi.353, 11. 43 ff.).

205 f. Cf. Cowley, 'Friendship in Absence' (*Poems*, p. 28):
>   *Friendship* is less apparent when too nigh,
>   Like *Objects*, if they *touch* the *Eye*.

225 f. Cf. Dryden's verses prefixed to Lee's *Rival Queens* (1677), which we
know Oldham read (R293; cf. 264, 289):
>   But how shou'd any Sign-post-dawber know
>   The worth of *Titian* or of *Angelo*? ...
>   To draw true Beauty shews a Masters Hand.

230 f. Jonson's own dictum: 'Indeed, things, wrote with labour, deserve to be
so read, and will last their Age' (*Discoveries*, *Jonson*, viii.638).

234-6. Cf. Richard West, in *Jonsonus Virbius* (*Jonson*, xi.469, 11. 58 ff.):
>   ... 'twas the wisedom of *thy Muse* to sit
>   And weigh each *syllable*; suffering nought to passe
>   But what could be no better then it was.
'Nought ... But what ... could write exactly best' means 'nothing which
could not *subscribe itself* "exactest and best"'. In 'Aude aliquid. Ode',
1. 205, Oldham has: 'The *Boutefeu* can now Immortal write'; and cf. Milton's
'he ... must subscribe slave' (*Works*, iii.i.242).

235. *had gone full time*: were not premature births. Ben's 'fancies ... went
full time' affirms Nicholas Downey (before Samuel Harding's *Sicily and
Naples*, 1640; *Jonson*, xi.497, 1. 9).

237-9. Cowley calls the new-created world '*Gods Poem*', in 'Davideis', Book I
(see n., *Poems*, p. 253). Oldham is indebted to the passage in 'A Letter'
and probably here.

253-6. Cf. *Paradise Lost*, VII.548-57, esp. where God views 'this new created
World ... how good, how faire / Answering his great Idea'. Cf. his echo of
Milton's 1. 631 f. in 'Sardanapalus' (11. 1 f. and n.).

260-9. Jonson was lectured for his scorn of unfavourable audiences by Marston in the Induction to *What You Will* and by Dekker in *Satiromastix*, V.ii;
and Owen Feltham took him to task for his ode of defiance on the failure of
The New Inn. So, more mildly, did Carew; while Clayton and Cartwright in
Jonsonus Virbius praised the dramatist's independence and justifiable self-
confidence. Cf. with ll. 266-9 Cartwright on the ephemeral repute of those
> Who thought the peoples breath good ayre: styl'd name
> What was but *noise*; and getting Briefes for *fame*
> Gathered the many's *suffrages* ...

(*Jonson*, ix, pp. 408 f., xi, p. 369, ll. 31-3; pp. 339 f.; pp. 335 f., ll.
23 ff.; p. 450, ll. 3-6, p. 458, ll. 149-51, 153-5).

281 f. Cf. on this commonplace, Cowley, 'The Second Olympique Ode of Pindar'
(*Poems*, p. 168): 'Nothing but the Eagle is said to be able to look full
right into the *Sun*, and to make that tryal of her young ones, breeding up
none but those that can do so'; and with Oldham's lines, Richard West's
reference, in *Jonsonus Virbius*, p. '55' [i.e. 53] to
> Those shallow Sirs, who want sharpe sight to look
> On the Majestique splendour of *thy* Booke.

(*Jonson*, xi.468, ll. 13 f.).

283 f. Oldham no doubt recalled Richard West's
> Give Glo-wormes leave to *peepe*, who till *thy* Night
> Could not be seene, *we* darkened were with Light.

in *Jonsonus Virbius* (*Jonson*, ix.468, ll. 3 f.); but perhaps also *Paradise
Lost*, III.380 f.:
> Dark with excessive bright thy skirts appeer
> Yet dazle Heav'n....

289. Echoing Thomas Sprat, 'Upon the Poems of the English Ovid, Anacreon,
Pindar, and Virgil, ABRAHAM COWLEY, in Imitation of his own Pindarick Odes':
'As round, and full as the great circle of eternity'. The ode was circulat-
ing in MS by *c.*1680 (see Bodl. MS Eng. Poet. e. 4, pp. 49-67, with space
left for sts. 1 and 2). It appeared in *A Supplement to the Works of the
Most celebrated Minor Poets* (1750), p. 64.

The Ninth Ode Of the Third Book of Horace, Imitated

This ode was a favourite with 17th-century translators; cf., e.g. the versions
by Jonson, Herrick, Francis Davison, John Ashmore, and Patrick Hannay (see
Jonson, viii.293, xi.109). In Oldham's time there is Thomas Flatman's. *Reli-
quiae Wottonianae* (1651) has an imitation, as 'A Dialogue Betwixt God And The
Soul', and Bodl. MS Firth. e.6, 150^r, a burlesque. Oldham will almost certainly have known Jonson's translation. He paraphrases two other pieces which
Jonson picked upon, though his versions are not demonstrably indebted to Jonson's: Catullus, epigram VII (*The Forest*, VI) and a fragment attributed to
Petronius (*The Underwood*, LXXVIII, next after the Horace).

Upon a Lady, &c. Out of Voiture

The works of Vincent de Voiture (1598-1648) were first collected in 1650. In
the more recent edn. of 1665, Oldham's original is in Part II, at p. 32.
Thorn Drury noted another translation, in the six-line stanza of the original,
beginning 'I yield, I yield, fair *Phillis*, now' in *A New Collection Of Poems
and Songs, Written by several Persons ... Collected by John Bulteel*, 1674
(A.E. Case 157), p. 117.

Catullus Epigr. VII, Imitated

Burton, *Anatomy*, p. 506, notes that Ben Jonson's 'Kiss me, Sweet' (*Jonson*, viii.103) is inspired by Catullus's epigram.

4-10, 17 f. Cf. Cowley, 'The Account' (*Poems*, pp. 53 f.):
> When all the *Stars* are by thee told
> (The endless Sums of heav'nly Gold) ...
> Or when the drops that make the *Sea*,
> Whilst all her *Sands* thy *Counters* be;
> Thou then, and Thou alone maist prove
> Th'*Arithmetician* of my *Love*.

9. Cf. Waller, 'Of the Queen', ll. 35 f.:
> Thus, in a starry night, fond children cry
> For the rich spangles that adorn the sky.

10. Cf. Cowley, 'To the New Year' (*Poems*, p. 206):
> Great *Janus*, who dost sure my *Mistris* view
> With all thine eyes, yet thinks't them all too *few*....
Cf. 'Katharine Kingscote', ll. 3 f.; 'Rant' (R228), ll. 13-16.

20. Characteristically, Oldham alters to a hyperbole Catullus' reckoning of all these as 'enough and more than enough'.

Some Elegies Out Of Ovid's Amours, Imitated

Rochester translated *Amores*, II.ix (*Poems*, p. 35); of the three Oldham imitates, Henry Bold (*Poems* (1664), p. 194) rendered II.iv, and Sedley II.v (printed, with nineteen versions of others among the 'Elegies', by other authors, in Dryden's 'Miscellany', 1684). See Introduction, p. xxxvi.

Book II, Elegy IV

Cowley is indebted to the original in 'The Inconstant': cf. Oldham's ll. 11 f. and 52 with Cowley (*Poems*, p. 133):
> I never yet could see that face
> Which had no dart for me
and: 'If *Low*, her *Prettiness* does please ...'.

Book II, Elegy V

54 f. Like 'To Madam L. E.', ll. 130-3, this echoes Waller, 'Of the Misreport of her being painted' (ll. 19 f.)—'heaven'
> Paints her, 'tis true, and does her cheek adorn
> With the same art wherewith she paints the morn.

60. *sweet Disorder*. Herrick's phrase.

Book II, Elegy X

In what is otherwise a fairly close paraphrase, Oldham interpolates lines without equivalent in the Latin: 26, 28, 30 (second half), 39-41.

A Fragment of Petronius, Paraphras'd

The original was attributed to Petronius in Linocerius's edition (1585) where it follows some undoubted fragments: but it is not by him. See *Jonson*, xi.109: the n. to Ben's translation in *The Underwood*. He gives the Latin, for which see also *Anthologia Latina*, ed. F. Buecheler *et al.* (Teubner, 1964), i.ii.171.

1, 3, 7. Cf. Sir John Suckling's 'Against Fruition' (from *Fragmenta Aurea*, 1648, p. 19, as printed with Waller's answer in Waller, where Oldham would certainly see them):

> Fruition adds no new wealth, but destroys,
> And while it pleaseth much, yet still it cloys.
> ... this once passed
> What relishes? ...
> Urge not 'tis necessary; alas! we know
> The homeliest thing that mankind does is so.

13 f. For this elaboration of the Latin, cf. Rochester, 'A Dialogue Between Strephon And Daphne', ll. 39 f.

An Ode of Anacreon, Paraphras'd

The ode is from the *Anacreontea*, accepted in the 17th century as the work of Anacreon himself, but now assigned to imitators. This particular ode (No. 4 in J.M. Edwards's Loeb edn.) is cited, and attributed to Anacreon, in the *Attic Nights* of Aulus Gellius. On the inclusion of Oldham's rendering, probably taken from *Poems, And Translations* (1683), in T. Wood and F. Willis (eds), *Anacreon Done into English* (Oxford, 1683), see Introduction, p. xxxv and n. 32. There are three (indecisive) variants; at l. 39, Oxford's seems inferior. The derivation from, the Greek, of the poem, 'Vulcan! En faveur de moy ...', and, from that poem, of Rochester's 'imitation', 'Upon His Drinking a Bowl', was traced by Kurt A. Zimansky, who attributed 'Vulcan' to Ronsard (*The Critical Works of Thomas Rymer* (1956), p. 226): see Vieth's *Rochester*, p. 52. Oldham seems to have taken a touch or two from Rochester; but his treatment is modelled on Cowley's 'Anacreontiques: Or ... Copies of Verses Translated Paraphrastically out of Anacreon' (*Poems*, pp. 50 ff.).
'Fill me a Boul'—'The Words by Mr. Oldham. Set by Dr. Blow', which appears in Henry Playford's *Theater of Music*, Book IV (1687), p. 52 (*Bibliography*, II 36), is taken from these lines.

10 ff., 30. *Constellations*: Crater, the Cup, between Leo and Hydra; and Canis Major or Minor.

31 f. Cf. Cowley on 'all the *radiant Monsters*' in the heavens: 'First Nemean Ode of Pindar' (*Poems*, p. 174).

42-5. Cf. Rochester's version from Ronsard, ll. 17-20:

> But carve thereon a spreading vine,
>   Then add two lovely boys;
> Their limbs in amorous folds entwine,
>   The type of future joys.

50. *toping*. 'Tope' was still a new and fashionable word. *OED*'s earliest example is from 1651. See Brett-Smith's Etherege, 24.48, 198.309, and nn.

An Allusion to Martial. Book I. Epig. 118

The original is numbered I.117 in modern editions, but I.118 in those of
Schrevelius (1656, 1661, 1670) and Collesso (1680).
The 'Allusion' cannot be earlier than late 1680, when Hindmarsh published
the first issue of Oldham's first volume. Much the most likely time for Oldham to have lived in a London garret (11. 9-12) is after he left Reigate in
1681 and before he entered the household of Sir William Hickes; though a
second residence in London after leaving Sir William is not an absolute impossibility. See Introduction, p. xxxiii and n. 35.
The leaf containing 11. 11-26 is a cancel in every copy of the original
edition that I have been able to examine. See n. on 11. 19 f. below.

10. Clerkenwell extended northwards from Holborn and Smithfield to Islington.

12. The 5 flights of stairs are probably factual: they are 3 in the Latin.

15-19. Joseph Hindmarsh was Oldham's authorized publisher from the end of
    1680 onward. (See *Bibliography* and my 'Chief Substantive Editions of Old-
    ham's Poems, 1679-1684', *SB* xxvii (1974), 188-226). His shop was at the
    sign of the Black Bull in Cornhill over against the Royal Exchange. The
    year his patron James became King he either moved, or changed his sign, to
    the Golden Ball, still opposite the Exchange. (The Golden Ball was burnt
    down in 1748; a map of that date, reproduced facing p. 124 of E.F. Robin-
    son's *Early History of Coffee-Houses in England*, shows its exact
    position at the corner of Three Tuns Lane.) Hindmarsh's first entry in the
    Term Catalogues was in 1678; from this time until 1695/6 over 120 volumes
    are put down to him, including some by Dryden, Otway, Crowne, Ravenscroft,
    Aphra Behn, Nahum Tate, and many of D'Urfey's. In 1696 he was succeeded by
    Hannah Hindmarsh. This may be the date of his death, which in any event
    occurred before 1705 when John Dunton refers to him as 'deceased'. If the
    Thomas Hindmarsh whose sermon he printed was a relative, he himself may also
    have been originally a Lincolnshire man. See Plomer, *Dictionary of Book-
    sellers and Printers 1668-1725* (1922); MS Rawlinson C. 146 f. 77^V; Wing,
    index; for Thomas Hindmarsh, Plomer, i.437, J. Venn, *Alumni Cantabrigienses*
    (1922). See also n. on 11. 19-20.

18. The door-posts etc. were covered with title-pages of poetical volumes,
    fixed there as advertisements of the stock within. See 'Spencer's Ghost',
    11. 78 f. and n. The practice was ancient: indeed, Oldham is following the
    Latin closely here.

19 f. Hindmarsh was 'Bookseller to his Royal Highness' James Duke of York,
    and published numerous attacks on James's enemies, the Whigs and Trimmers,
    the most notable perhaps being D'Urfey's *Progress of Honesty* (1681). He was
    prosecuted in Oct. 1682 for the Revd Adam Eliot's *Modest Vindication of
    Titus Oates ... To Demonstrate Him only Forsworn in several Instances*. An
    earlier prosecution, Feb. 1681, for the Revd Thomas Ashington's *Presbyterian
    Pater Noster, Creed, and Ten Commandments* may be said to have made him for
    a time 'the noted'st Tory in the Town' (Luttrell, i.68, 98; 231, 249; *The
    True Protestant Mercury*, Apr. 13-16, 1681). The *Pater Noster*, according to
    a satirical advertisement in *Mercurius Bifrons*, 'May be had ... in *Cornhil*,
    at the sign of the *Popes Bull*, bellowing forth his *Roman Loyalty*, with the
    Progress of Honesty between his Horns, and furious Parson *Thom* astride on
    him ... crying out *Tantivy, Tantivy*, Hey for *Rome*.' Cf. the onslaughts in
    The Weekly Discoverer Strip'd Naked, Feb. 23, Mar. 2, 16, and the Whig
    Heraclitus Ridens, Mar. 8, 1681; a Tory defence, DM's *Letter ... concerning*

a late Prophane Pamphlet; and by Ashington himself, published by Hindmarsh, the more apologetic *Some Reflections Upon a Late Pamphlet, In a Letter to J. H.* Not improbably Oldham at first referred to this paper war more specifically. In a cancelled leaf, ll. 19 f. were represented by four, beginning Th To Th Th, as may be seen from the stub in Bodl. Antiq. e. E $\frac{1883}{1}$, I.5. The cancellation was no doubt to remove or soften a dangerous allusion.

24. *half a Crown*: *denaris quinque* in the original. The price was good but not uncommon for a poetical octavo, bound. Pepys paid it for *Hudibras* (Part I), 26 Dec. 1662. For similar volumes at 2/6 see *Term Catalogues*, ed. Arber, i.151, 188; ii.73, and at 2/-, 1/6 or 1/-, i.127, 170, 266, 350.

The Dream

Pastorals of unchartered love are not uncommon in Restoration and Caroline verse. 'The Dream' resembles several which were fathered on Rochester: Randolph's 'A Pastoral Courtship', for example, and Aphra Behn's 'The Disappointment', whose second and third stanzas can be compared with Oldham's ll. 39-68 and 63 f. The similarity between Chloris's 'I cannot—must not give' and Cosmelia's 'I cannot, will not yield' may not be accidental. But if not, one cannot say which poet was the borrower. 'The Disappointment' is in the 1680 Rochester, and so must have circulated in MS, but from how long before is uncertain. Since it was in 1676 and 1677, and as an attendant on Princess Mary, that Cosmelia is known to have been in touch with Oldham, it is likely that she accompanied Mary to Holland that Nov. (if she was Mary Langford, she certainly did), and that 'The Dream' is earlier. See 'Rant', 15 May 1676, 'Some Verses', Sept. 1676, and Introduction, p. xxix and nn. 19, 20.

19 f. Cf. Waller, 'The Fall', ll. 15 f.:
>   Thus the first lovers on the clay,
>   Of which they were composed, lay....

33. Cf. Otway, *Don Carlos* (1676), p. 3: 'Oh! the Impetuous sallyes of my Blood!'

66. The emendation in 1684 is clearly right; 1683, the sole authority, reads: 'In sleep we seem, and only sleep to make', but evidently the compositor repeated 'sleep' when he should have repeated 'seem'.

73 f. Settle has 'we'd antidate our Bliss' in *The Empress of Morocco* (1673) p. 18, a play from which Oldham made notes (including a page-reference) in R193, R197 etc. (Cf. also Marvell, 'Dialogue between Thyrsis and Dorinda' ll. 27 f.). See 'To Madam L. E.', l. 93; 'S. Cecilia Ode', l. 22.

75 f. Cf. Dryden, *Aureng-Zebe* (1676), p. 12:
>   If love be vision, mine has all the fire
>   Which, in first dreams, young prophets does inspire.

A Satyr Touching Nobility

Boileau's Satire V, of which (but for the omission of the last fourteen lines) this is a close imitation, was founded on Juvenal VIII, and published in 1666. The Juvenal is also the groundwork of Hall, *Virgidemiarum*, IV.iii. A date for Oldham's satire cannot be fixed more precisely than by the allusion to Dragon (see l. 43 and n.) which points to 1680-2. But all the similar satires for which he gives dates were written after *Some New Pieces* came out (late in 1681); it is natural to take it fairly closely with 'Boileau VIII' (Oct.

1682); and it is probably one of the pieces printed as Oldham 'finished them off' (Advertisement, 11. 3-5, n.).

13 f. Holinshed's chronicle appeared in 1578. Cf. Hall, *Virgidemiarum*, IV. iii.16 f.:
> Or cyte olde *Oclands* verse, how they did weild
> The wars in *Turwin*, or in *Turney* field?

33-54. Cf. Juvenal, VIII.56-70 and Hall, *Virgidemiarum*, IV.iii, 50 ff.

41 f. Horse-races at Newmarket are recorded in early Stuart times; e.g. in 1619 (19 Mar.) and 1634. Racing recommenced there in 1663, and from 1665, when the King instituted a twelve-stone plate, regular spring and autumn meetings were held. From 1666 Charles and his court seldom missed a meeting, and large sums were staked; 'Sir Robert Carr', on one occasion, 'lost £5000 or £6000 upon several matches at Newmarket'. See J.P. Hore, *The History of Newmarket* (1885), i.296, ii.118, 239, 246, iii.13; O. Airy, *Charles II* (1904), pp. 203-6.

43. *Dragon*: the most famous of English racehorses from about 1680 to 1682. We first hear of him, owned by Baptist May, running (with others) against 'Red Rose' 'the Topping Horse of *Newmarket*' in the Plate of 17 Mar. 1680. Matched with 'Red Rose', 22 Mar., he ran again 28 Apr. He was sold to the King, and his beating 'Why not' is reported in the *London Mercury* 13-17 Oct. 1682. But on 7 Oct. 1682 a letter from Newmarket informs Secretary Jenkins: 'His Majesty's horse Dragon, which carried 7 stone was beaten yesterday by a little horse called Postboy carrying 4 stone and the masters of that art conclude this top horse of England is spoiled for ever.' (*CSPD*, 1682, p. 456.) A story of Dragon's ruin by brutal castration, told in the *Adventurer*, no. xxxvii (1753), has implausibilities which discredit it. Indeed, his defeat did not end his career: on 10 Mar. 1684 the news was that 'on Wednesday the two famous horses, *Dragon* and *Why not*, are to run'. See J.P. Hore, *History of Newmarket*, ii.371, 373; iii.11, 44, 46-9; and *A List of the Horse Races ... to be run ... at New-Market*. Feb. 1679[/80] ('March 4', Luttrell, *Catalogues*).

43. *cast*: defeated in competition (*OED*, v.II.15).

65 f. Cf. Juvenal, VIII.121 f.:
> Curandum in primis ne magna iniuria fiat
> fortibus et miseris.

Oldham keeps nearer the original than Boileau ('fuiez-vous l'injustice'), but like him ennobles it.

75 f. Cf. Juvenal, VIII.131 ff., and Denham, *Cooper's Hill*, 11. 67 f.:
> Whether to *Caesar, Albanact*, or *Brute*,
> The Brittish *Arthur*, or the Danish *Knute*....

As Geoffrey of Monmouth relates, Brutus, grandson of Aeneas, was the founder of London (or Troynovant) and the kingdom of Albion. His sons succeeded him: Albanact in Scotland, Locrine in England, Camber in Wales.

92. *selves*: 'self' is what Oldham should have written: as the original shows, the poet is still addressing the 'Hero' (1. 33). But with 11. 104, 106, 'you' definitely becomes plural: I therefore retain 'selves' as a mistake of Oldham's.

99. *Bedlam*. See 'Art of Poetry', 1. 811 n.

136. The College of Heralds was incorporated by Richard III in 1484; see Mark Noble, *A History Of The College Of Arms* (1804).

138-41. John Gwillim (1565-1621), Pursuivant-at-arms, published *A Display of Heraldrie* in 1610. It had reached a 5th edn. (in which the author's name is

spelled Guillim, as Oldham has it) in 1679. The terms quoted are names of
'ordinaries' (the earliest, and commonest, heraldic charges) such as Gwillim describes in his second section.

155 f.   By privilege of his rank, 'the person of a peer was [exempt] from
arrest for debt or any claim arising out of property' (Tanner, p. 578). By
his privilege as a Lord of Parliament he might exempt his servants also by
granting them 'protections', often in writing. In the 17th century this last
privilege, says Maitland, 'grew to huge dimensions; it became almost impossible to get any justice out of a member of Parliament'. The creditor could
attach neither the lord nor his agents. (See Maitland, pp. 243 f., 322, 377;
A.S. Turberville, *The House of Lords in the Eighteenth Century* (1927),
pp. 26 f.) Votes of the House of Commons against protections were printed
19 Dec. 1670 (Steele, No. 3542). Cf. Timothy in Shadwell's *Miser* (1672),
II.i, p. 20: 'I have been all this morning dunning for money, at this end of
the Town ... but (a deus take 'em) they do fob me off with Protections here-
abouts.'

164.   *the Company*: one of the great City Companies of London merchants. According to *The Grand Concernments of England Ensured* (1659), p. 34, intermarriage
with the families of rich tradesmen was more and more coming to be considered
a good investment: 'the best Gentry of *England* are very desirous and do daily
match their Daughters into the City, and give three times the portions that
twenty years ago would have been given to a Citizen.' Such matches were still
looked at somewhat askance: cf. Pepys, 20 Oct. 1660: 'my Lady saying that she
could get a good merchant for her daughter Jem, [my Lord] answered, that he
would rather see her with a pedlar's pack at her back, so she married a
gentleman, than she should marry a citizen'. But like city bridegrooms, city
brides were sought after by the well-born: cf. Sir William Morrice's letter
(cit. Mary Coate, *Social Life in Stuart England* (1924), p. 90): 'There are
so many merchants' daughters that weigh so many thousands, that ours are
commodityes lying on our hands.'

174.   'In the Pepysian library are two very ancient sets of cries cut in wood,
with inscriptions: among others ... small coal a penny a peke' (R. Gough,
British Topography (1780), i.689). Addison mentions the hawkers of small
coal in his paper on the London cries, No. 251 of the *Spectator*. Cf. 'Spencer's Ghost', ll. 39 ff. and n.

175 f.   Cf. 'Spencer's Ghost', ll. 43 f.

177 f.   Sir William Dugdale (1605-86) was first Norroy and then from 1677
Garter King-of-arms. He published, in two volumes, *The Baronage of England*
(1675, 1676). His *Antiquities of Warwickshire* (1656) also abounds in
genealogies. For the fabrication of pedigrees, cf. *Hudibras*, II.iii.669-72:
                    ... a *Herauld*
          Can make a *Gentleman*, scarce a year old,
          To be descended of a Race,
          Of ancient *Kings* in a small space ...
and Zachary Grey's n. But Dugdale is maligned in the present allusion; he
was scrupulous in eschewing such fabrications.

                    A Satyr: Address'd to a Friend

Though evidence is lacking to date its composition, this satire belongs in
style and merit to Oldham's maturest work. It is not Imitated from any one
original. Like 'Spencer's Ghost' it might be regarded as 'alluding', distantly,
to Juvenal VII (the later part, as 'Spencer's Ghost' to the earlier). Materials
no less important, however, come from the opening of Juvenal V; Hall's *Virgidemiarum*, II.vi; Cowley's Essay and Ode on Liberty; Eachard's *Grounds*;

and Burton on the miseries of scholars. The concluding apologue, a device
learned from Horace Sat. II.vi (the Town and Country Mouse) and Cowley and
Sprat's Imitation of it, is taken primarily, as Hammond has shown (pp. 202-7)
from Romulus's 'Canis et Lupus' (see L. Hervieux, ed., *Les Fabulistes Latins*
(1884-99) II.242, f.) whose form of the fable 'Oldham chiefly follows', with
supplementation from Phaedrus (id., II.28 f.), La Fontaine, *Fables* (1668),
I.5, a version in the anonymous *Æsop Improved* (1673), pp. 37 f., and another,
apparently by Pierre de Boissat, in Baudoin, *Les Fables d'Esope* (1631; often
reprinted), pp. 238-40. Outside the fable, everything from the sources is
stamped with the impress of Oldham's personal experience. Like his 'Friend',
he had left college with his way to make; he had endured the life of a schoolmaster (11. 50 ff.) in Gloucestershire and at Croydon; as tutor at Thurland's
and at Rookholt his dependent position would be not unlike that of the private
chaplain he describes (11. 70 ff.). And throughout, the multiple source-
material is fused into a poetic whole by the emotion with which personal experience has fired him.

1 ff. Cf. the scholar imagined in Burton, *Anatomy*, p. 131. He 'is now con-
summate and ripe, he hath profited in his studies ..., he is fit for preferment, where shall he have it? he is as far to seek it as he was ... at the
first day of his coming to the University. For what course shall he take,
being now capable and ready? The most parable and easie ... is to teach a
School, turn Lecturer or Curate....' Or he may become 'a trencher Chaplain
in a Gentlemans house'.

7 f. Cf. Eachard, p. 18: 'most of those University youngsters', he antici-
pates, 'must fall to the Parish, and become a Town Charge' until they
become 23 (the earliest age for ordination, if the canon is not disregarded).
'For Philosophy is a very idle thing, when one is cold: And a small system
of *Divinity* ... is sufficient when one is hungry.' Oldham had read Eachard;
see 11. 41 ff., 80 ff., nn., below.

9. *Cartes*: René Descartes (1596-1650), inventor of co-ordinate geometry and
founder of the Cartesian philosophy. His *Discours sur la Méthode* appeared
in 1637, and his *Meditationes* in 1641. His system was studied in the English universities; Pepys is pleased that his brother Edward has acquired
a good knowledge of 'Des Cartes' at Cambridge, though vexed to find that it
has been at the price of neglecting Aristotle (5 and 8 Aug. 1663, and nn.;
cf. J.B. Mullinger, *Cambridge Characteristics in the Seventeenth Century*
(1867), pp. 108-22, there cited).

9. Antoine Le Grand (d. 1699), Franciscan missionary in England, where he
was to become Provincial in 1698. His abbreviation of Descartes, *Institutio
Philosophiae, secundum principia Renati Descartes ... ad usum juventutis
academicae* (1672) was, according to Wood, much read at Cambridge.

23. Echoing *Paradise Lost*, XII.646.

27-30. This miser and his heir are from Horace, *Odes*, II.xiv.25 ff.; *Satires*,
II.iii.122 f. Cf. 'Horace, II.xiv', 11. 53 ff.; and 'Boileau VIII',
11. 115 ff.

41-7. Cf. Eachard, p. 115: 'In short, Sir, we are perfectly overstock'd with
Professors of Divinity: There being scarce employment for half of those who
undertake that Office'; and p. 111: 'I am confident, that in a very little
time I could procure hundreds, that should ride both Sun and Moon down, and
be everlastingly yours, if you could help them but to a Living of Twenty-
five or Thirty pounds a year.'

52 f. Persons committed to Bridewell were flogged and set to beat hemp. Cf.
'Counterpart', 11. 76 f.

54 f. Dr Gill is Alexander Gill the younger, DD (1597-1642), from 1621 to
1630, usher under his father at St Paul's School; High Master 1635-9, when
he was dismissed for excessive severity to a boy named Bennett. He took
after his father who had 'his whipping fits' (Aubrey, i.262). 'Gill upon
Gill', dialogue-wise between father and son, and another lampoon, 'On Dr
Gill [the son] master of S. Pauls School' were printed in *The Loves of Hero
and Leander* (1651). Richard Busby, DD (1606-95) was master of Westminster
School 1638-91. J.H. Overton in the *DNB* complains of a lack of contemporary
evidence to confirm the tradition of his severity, but certainly it represents his reputation in his own day; cf., e.g. Rochester, 'Allusion to
Horace', ll. 39 f.:

> I laugh, and wish the hot-brained fustian fool
> In Busby's hands, to be well lashed at school.

and Shadwell, *The Virtuoso* (1676), III.ii, p. 46, in which Snarl attributes
his taste for flogging to Westminster School.

56 ff. Cf. Juvenal, VII, 215 f., 240 ff., 175 ff.

64 f. Cf. Juvenal, VII.186-8.

70-102. As Shadwell's depiction of Mr Smerk (*The Lancashire Witches*, 1681,
*c.*Sept.) also bears witness, the status of a private chaplain had improved
but little since Hall made it the subject of *Virgidemiarum*, II.vi. For
parallel discommodities see below ll. 72, 80-9, nn. Placing Hall's 16 lines
beside the present passage, one can compare him and Oldham at their best,
and treating an identical theme.

72, 79, 90. Cf. Hall, ibid., ll. 15 f. All his conditions observed, the
employer

> ... could contented bee,
> To giue fiue markes, and winter liuery.

the point being (notes Davenport) that 'the common serving-man's wage in
1598 ... was "foure Markes and a Lyuerie"'.

72. *thirty pounds a year*. A better salary than the schoolmaster's—Shepheard
had £20 per annum at Croydon—but still a meagre one. Cf. Earle's character
of 'a young raw preacher' in *Microcosmographie* (ed. Arber, p. 23): 'His
friends and much painefulnesse may preferre him to thirtie pounds a yeere.'

78 f. Suggested by Cowley's 'Of Liberty' (*Essays*, p. 381), where the
hierarchy of subservience, 'Groom' to 'Gentleman', 'Gentleman' to 'Lord',
and 'Lord' to 'Prince', is allowed no more substance than 'the difference
between a plaine, a rich and gaudy Livery'.

80-9. Cf. three 'conditions' of the Trencher-Chaplaincy in Hall, ibid.,
ll. 7 ff.:

> Secondly, that he doe, on no default,
> Euer presume to sit aboue the salt.
> Third, that he neuer change his Trencher twise.
> Fourth, that he vse all cumely courtesies:
> Sit bare at meales, and one haulfe rise and waite.

80-108, 128. Cf. Eachard, p. 19: '... shall we trust them [*sc.* those University Youngsters] in some good Gentlemens Houses, there to perform holy
Things? Withal my heart, so that ... he may not be sent from Table picking
his Teeth, and sighing with his Hat under his Arm, whilst the *Knight* and
my Lady eat up the Tarts and Chickens: It might also be convenient, if he
were suffered to speak now and then in the Parlour, besides at Grace and
Prayer time: And that my cousin *Abigail* and he sit not too near one another
at Meals. Nor be presented together to the little Vicarage.' Better, Eachard
continues, he should embrace poverty '(so that he may have the command of
his thoughts and time) than to ... obey the unreasonable humours of some

Families'. Cf. Macaulay, *History Of England*, ed. C.H. Firth (1913), i.315-18, and the contemporary illustrations there collected.

84 f.   See the two previous nn. The chaplain is nicknamed 'Sir Crape', a little derisively, from the crape gown of his calling: cf. *The Hypocritical Christian* (*c*.1682): 'And every Parson Dr. *Crape* he'l call'; and John Phillips's pamphlet *Speculum Crape-Gownorum* (1682).

87.   *Cistern*: a large vessel used at the dinner-table. Cf. Pepys, 7 Sept. 1667 and 14 Mar. 1667/8; according to Dr Mynors Bright's n. the plates were rinsed in it when necessary during the meal. But though the Latham and Matthews edn. repeats this, evidence is wanting.

89.   *Voider*. The name given both to the servant who clears away the remnants of a meal, and to the basket in which he collects them. In l. 147 the receptacle is meant; here probably the servant. Both senses are found in Cleveland: see 'Upon Sir Thomas Martin', ll. 15 f.:
> ... thou that art able
> To be a *Voider* to king *Arthurs* Table ...

and *The Character of a Country-Committee-man* (1649): 'it is ... broken meat ... only ... as in the Miracle of Loaves, the Voyder exceeds the Bill of Fare'.

90 f.   Cf. Cowley, 'Ode. Upon Liberty' (*Essays*, p. 391):
> Unhappy Slave, and Pupil to a Bell!
> Which his hours work as well as hours does tell!

and in the same essay 'Of Liberty', see, for 'Board-Wages', p. 384.

92 f.   Cf. Cowley, 'Ode. Upon Liberty' (*Essays*, p. 389):
> To thy bent mind some relaxation give
> And steal one day out of thy Life to Live.

Cowley uses the metaphor of a prisoner in the lines immediately preceding; but Oldham gives it a completely different turn.

95.   Cf. *Hudibras*, II.iii.68-70, on the dog who 'breaks loose'
> And quits his *Clog*; but all in vain,
> He still draws after him his Chain.

96-102.   Cf. Burton, *Anatomy*, p. 131. 'If he be a trencher-Chaplain in a Gentleman's house, as it befel *Euphormio*',—Barclay's *Euphormionis Satyricon* was a work Oldham knew, as a n. on R87 testifies—'after some seven years service, he may perchance have a Living to the halves (*sc.* a half-share in one), or some small Rectory with the mo[t]her of the maids at length, a poor Kindswoman, or a crackt Chamber-maid, to have and to hold during ... life'. Cf. above, ll. 80 ff. n.; 'Spencer's Ghost', ll. 255-8; John Earle, *Microcosmographie*, loc. cit. in l. 72, n.; and Beaumont and Fletcher, *The Women Hater*, III.iii.

98-101.   Cf. Shadwell, *The Lancashire Witches* (1682), p. 2:
> ... some cast Chamber-Maid shall smile upon you
> Charm'd with a Viccaridge of forty pound
> A year, the greatest you can ever look for.

103-6.   Cf. Juvenal, V.1-4. Hall, in *Virgidemiarum*, I.i.11 ff., trumpets his independence in the same spirit as Oldham:
> Nor can I crouch, and writhe my fauning tayle
> To some great Patron, for my best auaile.
> Such hunger-staruen, trencher Poetry,
> Or let it neuer liue, or timely die....

107 f.   Cf. Horace, *Epistles*, I.vii.35 f.

109 ff.   Cf. Juvenal, V.6-11.

111 f. In a ballad entitled *The Merry Beggars of Lincolns-Inn-Fields. Or, The Beggars Art to get Money, Shewing all the Pranks and Tricks they use* (licensed by R.P. and printed for C. Dennisson within Aldgate), the narrator confesses: 'I've got good store of Silver ... by my wooden Leg; ... for I tye up my Leg ...' and 'Sometimes my arm is wrapped up in a Linnen clout'. He relates the exposure of Harry, who 'tyed up his leg', but 'cut his string' and 'quickly found his feet' when a bystander suspected the trick and made to beat him.

115-22. These lines belong to the tradition studied in M.÷S. Røstvig's *The Happy Man*, 2 vols. (1954). Oldham's wish is Cowley's, as that was Horace's (*Satires*, II.vi.1-3, 60-2, 65 f.). Cf. Cowley, 'The Wish' (*Poems*, p. 88):
> Ah, yet, e're I descend to th'Grave
> May I a small House, and *large Garden* have!
> And a *few Friends* and *many Books*, both true....

129 f. Tactful, since Oldham's version is eclectic: see headnote for Hammond's identification of the sources.

131. *e're break of day*. Cf. *Æsop Improved*: 'Ere it were day'; Baudoin: 'environ le poinct du jour' (quoted Hammond).

134. *cast*: discarded, cast off: probably by confusion with cassed, broken or cashiered (*OED*, ppl. a. 3).

137. *With Complements*. Cf. La Fontaine: 'et lui fait compliment'; *Æsop Improved*: 'With usual ceremonies' (quoted Hammond).

139. *Towzer*. He was a mastiff (1. 199); mastiffs were often called Towzer. Pepys, 17 Feb. 1663/4, was sent 'an excellent mastiffe his name Towser'. In Whig caricatures, Roger L'Estrange appears as Towzer, a mastiff.

140-2. Cf. Phaedrus: Unde sic, quaeso nites?
> Aut quo cibo fecisti tantum corporis?
> Ego, qui sum longe fortior, pereo fame ...
> Romulus: Unde, frater, sic nitidus et pinguis es?
and *Æsop Improved*: 'so sleek' (quoted Hammond).

147-70. Unlike Phaedrus, Romulus (Hammond observes) has the dog begin with the delights he enjoys. Cf. especially with 11. 155, 170, 'amat me tota familia' and 'sic otiosus vitam gero'.

147. *Voider*. See 1. 89 n.

149 f. Cf. Rochester, 'Timon' (*c*.May 1674), 11. 73 f.:
> As for French kickshaws, sillery and champagne,
> Ragouts and fricassees, in troth w'have none.

151 f. The broken meat of a Lord Mayor's Feast would be the waiters' perquisite. When Pepys dined (29 Oct.) at the Feast of 1663, the Merchant Strangers' table had 'ten good dishes to a messe'.

156. 'The shock or shough was a kind of lap-dog thought to have been brought to England from Iceland' (Geoffrey Tillotson's n., Pope, *Rape of the Lock*, Twickenham edn., I.115).

171 f. *I envy ... good Fate*. Cf. Romulus: 'Bene ... vellem michi ista contingerent' (quoted Hammond).

179. *You need not doubt*. Cf. Romulus: 'noli timere' (quoted Hammond).

180, 185. Cf. *Æsop Improved*: 'Lay down thy fierceness, and I shall prevail' (quoted Hammond).

186. *to practise Complaisance*. Cf. La Fontaine: 'à son Maître complaire' (quoted Hammond).

188. *top my part*: play it to perfection (theatre-phraseology); the earliest in *OED* (V¹ IV.15) is of 1672.

194. *upper hand*: place of honour or precedence (*OED*, II. sv. ⱶ b).

202-11. *Sir ... you see.* Cf. in Baudoin, 'Tu dois sçavoir ... qu'au commencement ie soulois abouer aux Estrangers, & mesme à ceux de cognoissance, sans que ma dent espargnast non plus les uns que les autres. Mais ... mon Maistre ... joua si bien du bâton sur moy [que je] me suis corrigé ... et suis devenu plus doux que de coutûme, à force d'estre battu; neantmoins ceste cicatrice que tu me vois au col m'est toujours restée ...' (quoted Hammond).

215. Cf. Romulus (quoted Hammond):
> Non est, ait, opus michi istis frui quae laudasti
> Vivere volo liber, quodcumque venerit michi....

216. Cf. Hammond's quotations from Romulus and, for 'golden' chains, the 'Discours' (p. 244) in Baudoin: 'In eo quod placet nulla cathena / me tenet', and 'aymer ses chaisnes, pourveue quelles soient dorées', as inseparable from servitude.

217. Cf. Phaedrus' 'splendid clinching line' (Hammond): 'Regnare nolo, liber ut non sim mihi'.

Some Verses Written in Septemb. 1676

The date refers to all four pieces which follow. Cosmelia was a tire-woman or 'dresser' to Princess Mary; the fashionable pastoral-sounding name is bestowed on her as having charge, the poet insinuates, of her mistress's cosmetics as well as tresses (see Introduction, p. xxix and n. 19). His other Cosmelia poems are 'A Rant to his Mistress' (May 1676) and 'The Dream' (Mar. 1677).

Presenting a Book to Cosmelia

1-6, 11 f., 23-6. The general ideas resemble some in Cowley's 'On the Death of Mr. William Hervey', sts 14 f. Ll. 5 and 23-6 are variants of 11. 544 f., 547-50 of the Morwent ode.

18-20. Almost identical with the 'Counterpart', 11. 29-31. Cf. Cowley, 'The Constant' (*Poems*, p. 135):
> Close, narrow *Chain*, yet soft and kind,
> As that which *Spi'rits* above to *good* does bind,
> Gentle and sweet Necessity....

21 f. Cf. Dryden, 'Upon the Death of the Lord Hastings', 11. 33 ff.:
> Heav'ns Gifts, which do, like falling Stars, appear
> Scatter'd in Others, all, as in their Sphear
> Were fix'd and conglobate in's Soul ...
> Letting their Glories so on each Limb fall....

25 f. Cf. Donne, 'A Funeral Elegy. To L.C.', 11. 19 f.:
> ... in whose practise grew
> All vertues, whose names subtile Schoolmen knew.

27-32. Almost identical with 'Katharine Kingscote', 11. 41-6:

29-32. Cf. Cowley, 'The Innocent Ill' (*Poems*, p. 145):
> Though from thy *Tongue* ne're slipt away
> One word which *Nuns* at th'Altar might not say ...
> Though in thy thoughts scarce any Tracks have bin
> So much as of *Original Sin*....

33-8. A variant of ll. 552-7 of the ode on Morwent. L. 35 is a variant of
'Horace IV.xiii' (R218 f.), l. 10.

39 f. Cf. Cowley, 'Verses lost upon a Wager' (*Poems*, p. 149):
>   If *Truth* it self (as other *Angels* do
>   When they descend to humane view)
>   In a *Material Form* would daign to shine
>   'Twould *imitate* or *borrow* *Thine*.

41-51. Almost identical with 'Katharine Kingscote', ll. 17-27.

45-7. Cf. Waller, 'Upon the Death of my Lady Rich', ll. 86 f.:
>   We should suppose that some propitious spirit
>   In that celestial form frequented here,
>   And is not dead, but ceases to appear.

50 f. Cf. Waller, *The Battle of the Summer Islands*, I.46 f.:
>   Heaven sure has kept this spot of earth uncursed
>   To show how all things were created first.

The Parting

7 f. Cf. Cowley, 'Reason ... in Divine Matters' (*Poems*, p. 47):
>   Though it, like *Moses*, by a sad command
>   Must not come in to th'*Holy Land*
>   Yet ...
>   ... from afar 'tis all *Descry'd*.

9 f. Cf. Cowley, 'Looking on ... his Mistress' (*Poems*, p. 123):
>   To look on *Heav'n* with *mighty Gulfs* between
>   Was the great *Misers* [*sc*. Dives'] greatest pain....

12-15. Cf. Oldham's draft 'To Mrs Kingscot on the Death of her Daughter'
(R238), ll. 7 f.; and Cowley, 'On the Death of Mr. William Hervey' (*Poems*,
p. 33):
>   Thy *Soul* and *Body* when *Deaths Agonie*
>   Besieg'd around thy noble heart
>   Did not with more reluctance part
>   Than *I*, my dearest *Friend*, do part from *Thee*.

29. Cf. Dryden, *The Rival Ladies* (1664), I.i, p. 5:
>   ... me-thinks she should have left
>   A Track so bright I might have follow'd her;
>   Like setting Suns that Vanish in a Glory.

Complaining of Absence

19. Cowley has 'the *Poets Militant* Below!' in 'On the Death of Mr. Crashaw'
(*Poems*, p. 49).

26. Cf. Dryden, 2 *Conquest of Granada* (1672), IV.iii, p. 132: 'This minute
should begin my happiness'.

30 f. Cf. Cowley, 'The Given Love' (*Poems*, p. 68):
>   I'll on; for what should hinder me
>   From *Loving*, and *Enjoying* Thee?

Promising a Visit

5 f. Cf. Waller, 'Upon the Death of my Lady Rich', ll. 41 f.:
        ... bold hand as soon might hope to force
        The rolling lights of Heaven as change her course....

9-12. Cf. Cowley, 'My Fate' (*Poems*, p. 125):
        Go bid the *Needle* his dear *North* forsake,
        To which with trembling rev'erence it does bend ...
        Go bid th' ambitious *Flame* no more ascend....
Only when these abandon their '*old Motions*' will his love cease.

25 f. Cf. the ode on Atwood, ll. 172 f., and Otway, *Don Carlos* (1676, lic. 15 June), p. 19: '... Ile ... stand / Brandishing all my Thunder in my hand.'

31 f. Cf. Denham, *Cooper's Hill*, ll. 13 f.:
        My eye, which swift as thought contracts the space
        That lies between.

The Careless Good Fellow

Luttrell's copy (formerly *apud* ·C.H. Wilkinson) is inscribed '1^{d} 14 July 1680'; his identical note of date and price is in his *Catalogues*, Second Continuation, p. 13, No. 2, which gives the publisher, R. Harford. The 1680 edition; the garbled version, with five spurious stanzas, published (? *c.*1685) as a black-letter ballad by J. Jordan; and the inclusion in Tom Browne's *Remains* (1720), are described and discussed in *Bibliography*, II.4, 5, and the corrective n., pp. 38 d-f.
The title had plenty of precedents among drinking and anti-drinking ballads: for example, *The Good Fellows Frolick, The good Fellowes best Beloved*, and *The Good-Fellowes Advice*, recorded *c.*1641 (*BM Cat. of Prints and Drawings*, Div. I, vol. i, Nos. 276, 277, 282; cf. No. 1105); and so had the sentiment: cf. Alexander Brome, *Poems* (1668), p. 58: 'We that tipple ha' no *leisure* for *plotting* or *thinking*'. The stanza is that of Rochester's 'On the Women about Town' (*Poems*, p. 46; dated by Vieth 'shortly before 20 March 1672/3') which begins:
        Too long the wise Commons have been in debate
        About money and conscience, those trifles of state....
The tune of Jordan's ballad was 'Let Caesar live long'. It is clear from Ebsworth, iv.388 f., that it is not the tune to D'Urfey's 'Let the Traytors plot on' in *The Virtuous Wife* (1680: see John Playford, *Choice Ayres*, 1681, p. 7), but the other so named, to 'The Kings Health' (1680: see Thompson), which fits Oldham's poem.

1. Another drinking-ballad of the period (in MS Douce 357, f. 77) begins: 'A pox of the Troubles men make in the world'. There are further resemblances between a passage near the end of the ballad, and Oldham's concluding stanza: see ll. 37 n.

1-6. The detachment of this allusion to the Popish Terror, though partly dramatic (since it is the essence of the Good Fellow to slight all politics), is nevertheless noteworthy at so early a date. The mad violence of the agitation was disillusioning Oldham even while he continued, as st. 2 implies, to believe unreservedly in the guilt of the executed Catholics. For a full account of the changes in his (and England's) attitude, see Brooks, *Life*, the final fifth of ch. VI; cf. above, Introduction pp. xxix-xxxiii, 1-lii, and nn. 22-32.
    Cf. with the present stanza, 'The Pot-Companions, or Drinking and Smoaking

prefer'd before Caballing and Plotting', printed in 'Popish Nat' Thompson, p. 310:

> And here let us sit, like honest brave Fellows
> That neither are *Tories* nor *Whigs* in an Ale-house.

> We'll raise no disputes of the Church or the State
> To waken the *Plot*, which has slept out its date; ...
> For better it is to be honestly sotting,
> Than to live to be hang'd for Caballing and Plotting.

But this was written later, and despite the disclaimer, is built quite directly on the partisan contrast of loyal beer-drinking Tory with disaffected (and coffee-drinking) Whig.

5 f. The rhyme is monstrous, prompting the 1722 emendation, 'in state' (which inadmissibly repeats the rhyme-word of l. 2). But cf. the autograph ll. 69 f. of 'The Desk' (R126): 'quiet' rhymed with 'retreat'.

7-10. Up to this time, ten Catholics had suffered at Tyburn for the Plot, two for Godfrey's murder, and Staley for treasonous words; cf. 'Jesuits II', l. 277 n.

13 f. Cf. Ranke, *England*, iv.98: 'The power of the prerogative now centred in the right to summon Parliament or not.' Hoping to obtain a House of Commons less bent upon Exclusion, Charles had dissolved his third Parliament and summoned another for 7 Oct. 1679. But when the Whigs were again returned in overwhelming strength, he postponed it till the 17th, and prorogued it before it met to the 30th and thence by successive stages to 26 Jan. 1679/80, 11 Nov. 1680 (by an abortive proclamation of 11 Dec. 1679), 15 Apr., 17 May, 1 July, 22 July, 23 Aug., and finally to 21 Oct. 1680, when the session was allowed to begin. Oldham is writing after the fourth prorogation. (Luttrell, i.18, 21, 23, 24, 27, 32, 39, 44, 50, 53, 57; Steele, nos. 3691, 3696, 3702, 3717). The Whigs organized numerous petitions that the Parliament might meet; Charles, on 12 Dec., issued a proclamation against the petitions; and the Tories began to address the crown in abhorrence of them. (Luttrell, i.27 f., 30-4, 36, 41; Steele, no. 3703; Burnet, ii.248 f.) The Whig view of Charles's policy is well expressed in 'The Fancy' (*POAS*, iii, 1704, p. 199):

> To shake off Parliaments may be too great ...
> To baffle therefore, but not cast them off,
> Must be your work.
>   When January comes, Cold and ill way
> Will call it Love to put 'em off till May. (etc.).

15. Acts for burying in woollen were passed in 1668 and 1678; Dryden, also, makes topical reference to the second (Prologue to *Oedipus*, 1678, printed 1679, ll. 35 ff.). See further 'Juvenal III', ll. 270 f. and n.

17. The importation of claret and other French wines had been prohibited by Parliament early in 1678 (see 'Ode on Jonson', ll. 104 ff., n.). Cf. Dryden, Prologue to Lee's *Caesar Borgia* (1679):

> So big you look, tho' Claret you retrench,
> That arm'd with bottled Ale, you huff the French.

There was widespread smuggling: a proclamation of 19 Jan. 1679/80 complains that the prohibitions were 'daily disregarded' (Steele, no. 3706); and their effect was therefore the same as on a previous occasion, *c*.1650: cf. Denham, 'Natura Naturata':

> Forbidden Wares sell twice as dear;
> Even Sack prohibited last year,
> A most abominable rate did bear.

See also 'Juvenal III', ll. 125 f. and n.

19 f. Cf. Rochester, 'On the Women about Town', ll. 1 f., for which see head-note above.

19-22. The exclusion of James from the throne and the recognition of Monmouth as the heir was now the great object of the Shaftesbury Whigs, while Temple, Sidney, and Essex, with the sympathy of Halifax, did their best to safeguard the interests of the alternative Protestant candidate, William of Orange. The struggle, starting in Nov. 1678 in the last session of Charles's second Parliament, had been raging furiously ever since the third assembled in Mar. 1679. For its course, see Ogg, ii.584 ff., and Jones. Landmarks so far had been the Exclusion Bill, read twice in May 1679, then frustrated by the prorogation on the 27th, and subsequent dissolution; the exiles of James (to Brussels, from Mar. to Aug., and Scotland, from Oct.), and Monmouth (from Sept.); Monmouth's contumacious return, 27 Nov.; and James's recall, Feb. 1680. He reached London on the 24th, a fortnight before Old-ham's poem was written. Meanwhile the principles of exclusion, limitation, and indefeasible hereditary right were debated on every side: Burnet has a good summary of the controversy (ii.211-19; see also 232 f., 241-3, 247 f., 251). Cf. *A Poem Upon the Right of Succession of the Crown of England*, dated 1679 in Luttrell's hand, and reprinted by Ebsworth (v.54).

23 f. The loyal outburst ends inevitably with a toast. The 'good fellow' in *Poor Robins Character Of an Honest Drunken Cur* (1686), is likewise attached 'to Monarchical Government: he would not be without a King, if it were for no other Reason than meerly Drinking his Health'.

25 f. Henry Sidney (1641-1704) was afterwards Secretary of State, Lord Lieut. of Ireland, and Earl of Romney. His diplomatic struggle with D'Avaux is recorded in his *Diary* (ed. Blencowe, 1843, i.195 ff.). It was public know-ledge: see *The True Domestick Intelligence*, no. 66, Feb. 17-20 (1680), and especially no. 70, Mar. 2-5: 'From Holland we have advice, that Monsieur *de Vaux*, the *French* Ambassador pays visits to the particular Members of the States, and is very assiduous in his endeavours to obtain of them to con-tinue Newters for a certain time. On the contrary, Mr. Sidney is continually pressing them to a strict Alliance with his Majesties [*sic*] of *Great Britain*. The States onely wait the resolution of *Groninghen* and *Friezland*, and then they will give the *French* Ambassador a Catagorical Answer.' See also *The Two Memorials delivered by Mr. Sydney, to the States General* (1680), and *All the Letters, &c. concerning the offered Alliance of the Kings of England and France, to the States of the United Netherlands* (1680); and Luttrell, i.17, 34.

27 f. See *The True News: Or, Mercurius Anglicus*, no. 20, Feb. 28-Mar. 3, 1679/80: '*Paris, Feb.* 26 ... many Troops are marching towards *Dauphine* and *Provence*, which its presumed are the Forces designed for *Cassel* [*sc.* Casale], an important place under the Duke of *Mantua* and the very Key of *Italy*; and by all circumstances sold to *France*, though a force must formally seem to take it'; and ibid. no. 28, Feb. 21-5: '*Rome Feb.* 3. We expect other *French* Gallies ... with 500000 crowns, which it is said, the King of *France* sends hither to be deposited for the purchase of *Casall*.' Louis's designs on it are repeatedly discussed in the news-sheets of Feb. and Mar. 1679/80—e.g. *The True News*, Feb. 11-14; *The London Gazette*, Feb. 12-16; Mar. 29-Apr. 1; *The Current Intelligence*, Mar. 9-13; *Smith's Current Intelligence*, Mar. 13-16. They had got abroad through the treachery of his intermediary, Matthioli, who had divulged them to Spain, Savoy, and Venice. He did not actually take possession until Sept. 1681. See Ogg, *Europe*, p. 249.

29 f. For the Bordeaux fleet, and its dependence on fair winds, cf. *The London Gazette*, 25-9 Nov. 1680: '*Falmouth* ... The 20th Instant came in here the *Providence* of Southampton, bound for Holland from Bordeau', but '40 Sail

more ... were by contrary Winds forced back again', and ibid., 6-9 Dec.
1680: '*Falmouth, Decemb.* 2. The *Bourdeaux* Fleet and other Ships in this
Port homeward bound put to Sea on Tuesday morning last, the wind at S.W.'
In 1631 Marmaduke Rawdon, with a cargo of Bordeaux wine aboard the *Elizabeth* of Alborow, lay wind-bound about three weeks in the Garonne: the wind
then coming fair, they reached the Isle of Wight in a few days. (*The Life
of Marmaduke Rawdon Of York*, ed. Robert Davies, Camden Society, lxxxv, 1863,
pp. 10, 11, 15.)

31. *The Bully of France*: Louis XIV. Rochester, in 'A Satyr on Charles II'
     (his 'Sceptre' lampoon) had called Louis 'the hector of France', and said
     of Charles:
                    Him no ambition moves to get renown
                    Like the French fool, that wanders up and down
                    Starving his people, hazarding his crown.

33. See *The True News*, no. 33, Mar. 10-13, 1679/80, for the Dauphin's marriage
     to Maria Anna Christiana Vittoria of Bavaria. She and the French court had
     been journeying to meet one another; the news-sheets of Feb. and Mar. were
     full of their progress, and it was rumoured that when the marriage was con-
     summated, Louis would again declare war. See *The Haerlem Courant. Truly
     rendred into English*, no. 11, Feb. 1679/80.

34. Like Poor Robin's 'Honest Drunken Cur' (see ll. 23 f., n.), your Good
     Fellow 'hates Coffee, as *Mahomatizm*, and all the more because
                    Especially the *sober Party*
                    And News-mongers do drink't most hearty.
     (*The Character Of A Coffee-House ... By an Eye and Ear witness*, 1665.) The
     coffee-house was 'a mint of intelligence': 'He that comes often, saves two-
     pence a week in Gazettes, and has his news and his coffee for the same
     charge, as ... it is an exchange where haberdashers of political small-wares
     meet, and mutually abuse each other, and the publick, with bottomless
     stories, and headless notions' (*The Character of a Coffee-House, with the
     Symptoms of a Town-Wit*, 1673). Cf. also, in verse, *The Coffee House or
     Newsmongers Hall* (1672), a reprint of *News from the Coffee House* (1667).

37 ff. Cf. the ballad already cited from MS Douce 357 (above, l. 1 n.):
     hard-drinking parsons can mockingly tell 'the Stories of ffox', for
                    ... ag^t Popish ffaggot
                    They'r soe sopt in Clarret
                    And those that cant reach to't in Strong ale and bragget
                    That by a long wetting they hardly will burn
                    A cunning contrivance as good as to turn
                    ffor Smithfield and Westminster never knew yet
                    A Martyr to fflame that was th[o]rough wett....

39 ff. 'Mr. Fox' is the martyrologist, as in the ballad just quoted. Oldham
     remembers Scroggs's sardonic quip at Staley's trial: 'It is better to be
     warm here than in Smithfield' (Kenyon, p. 99), and imagines the Marian
     persecution revived, with the street-porters warming themselves at the
     fires in which new Smithfield martyrs are perishing. Cf. a n. for 'Jesuits
     I', ll. 153 ff. (R264): 'And a single blazing Heretick scarce serv'd to
     warm our hands.' The Good Fellow has no mind to be burnt for the difference
     between the Protestant and the Catholic Profession; he professes unalter-
     able faith only in his bottle.

A Satyr: The Person of Spencer is brought in &c.
[Spencer's Ghost]

The arguments from maturity of style, and from the analogy of dated poems in the same volume, favouring 1682 or 1683 as the dates of 'Nobility' and 'To a Friend', apply equally to this satire. It cannot be earlier than Samuel Butler's death, 25 Sept. 1680, and echoes the epilogue to Otway, *The Souldiers Fortune* (1681; but acted Mar. 1679/80), cf. 1. 247 and n. Oates is mentioned (1. 74) as though the days when he drew all eyes are over.
    Like 'To a Friend', it has no one original, but might be considered a distant 'allusion' to a part (this time, the earlier) of Juvenal VII. As a dissuasion addressed to the poet it has precedent in Propertius, III.iii, where Phoebus and then Calliope warn him from his aspiration to heroic poetry; and a source in Oldham's own design, discarded from 'A Letter', of a speech in which 'wise friends' were to 'dissuade' him from his profitless addiction (see Appendix II, 1, 11. 62-6). He has also drawn upon Boileau (*Satires*, I and IX) for the groundwork of nearly sixty lines in all. Spenser is an apt choice for the interlocutor. He complains of his 'long fruitlesse stay in Princes Court', and 'expectation vayne of idle hopes' (*Prothalamion*, 11. 6-8; cf. 'Mother Hubberds Tale', 11. 881-904). Drummond was told by Jonson that he 'died for lake of bread in King street and refused 20 pieces sent to him by my Lord of Essex & said he was sorrie he had no time to spend them'. Jonson exaggerated no doubt, and the conversations were unpublished, but the tradition current in Oldham's time was in line with his story. Cf. the life prefixed to the third edn. of Spenser's works, published Dec. 1678; and the prologue to Lee's *Theodosius* (1680):
            Think what penurious Masters you have serv'd,
            Tasso run mad, and noble *Spenser* starv'd,
where he is made the type of the ill-used poet, a role in which Butler seems to have coupled him, as Oldham does here, with Cowley and himself (see 11. 175-90 and n.).

5-7. Cf. Boileau, *Satires*, pp. 1, 2, Satire I:
            la mine affamée ... plus défait & plus blême
            Que n'est un Penitent sur la fin d'un Caresme.

10. Cf. Cleveland's *Character of a Diurnal Maker* (1654): [the title of 'scribbler'] hangs about him like an old wife's skin when the flesh hath forsaken her, lank and loose'.

29 f. 'Prosopopoia Or Mother Hubberds Tale', Spenser's satirical fable on contemporary politics and court life, first printed in his *Complaints* (1591).

36. *tumultuous*. The first edition has 'tumultous', probably a misprint; this form is not recognized by the *OED*. In the 'Counterpart', 1. 168, the word is normal.

39-42. The 'Brooms, Old Shoes and Boots' of 1. 41 is a reminiscence of *Hudibras*, I.ii.547, among the references to the London cries:
            And some for *Brooms, old Boots and Shoes,*
            Baul'd out to *purge the Common's House.*
The Cryes of the City of London, engraved by Tempest after Laroon, 1711, include 'Any Card matches or Save alls', 'Small Coale', 'Old Shooe's for some Broomes', '4 Paire for a Shilling Holland Socks', and 'Londons Gazette here'. Addison, in the 251st *Spectator*, confirms what Oldham says of the 'dismal Scream and Tone' in which some of the cries were delivered.

44. *the Register*: the parish register. Cf. 'Nobility', 11. 175 f.

47. Cf. 'all its slighted Immortality' (R288), originally intended for a place in 'Jesuits I', ll. 343 ff.

48-51. Homer, and Pindar in his Olympic and Nemaean odes. This burlesque kind of humour was popular. Pepys (2 Mar. 1661) relished in Thomas Heywood's play, *Love's Mistress*, 'a good jeere to the old story of the Siege of Troy, making it to be a common country tale'. Scarron, and Charles Cotton's *Scarronides, or Virgil Travestie* (1664-5) owed their vogue to the same taste. For Newmarket, see 'Nobility', ll. 41 f., n.

57. *clapt, and often rhim'd*. In the first and only authoritative edition the line runs: 'But who has kill'd, been often clapt, and oft has rhim'd'. Here 'often' is evidently a marginal revision which has been inserted in the line instead of being substituted, as Oldham meant, for 'oft has'. Cf. the like error in the ode on Atwood, 1. 161 and n.

58 f. Cf. 'The Author of *Sodom*', ll. 24 f.

62-6. As city poet, Thomas Jordan (1612?-1685) had described the Lord Mayor's Show each year from 1671 in pamphlets written partly in verse: see F.W. Fairholt, *Lord Mayor's Pageants* (Percy Society, x, 1843, pt. i, pp. 74-98, pt. ii, pp. 109-76). All, up to 1681 (except 1676, recorded in J.G. Nichols, *London Pageants*, 1831), may be seen in Bodley (Gough, Lond. 122, 15-24, Malone 126). In 1682 and 1683, owing to the civic broils, no pageant took place, but Jordan published the customary pamphlets, abbreviated to 4 leaves. Cf. 'Boileau VIII', ll. 407 f. and n., and 'Jesuits IV', l. 85.

65 f. Oldham had gibed at the fate of Jordan's works in *SJ* (1681), Advertisement, 1. 61. With the allusion to uses of waste paper (see also ll. 101, 105-8) cf. *MacFlecknoe*, ll. 100 f.; they were commonplace, and classical (cf. Persius, I.43; Horace, *Epistles*, II.i.269; Catullus, XCV.7).

69 f. One may instance Loggan's portrait of Alexander Brome, before his poems (1664), and White's of Herbert and of Flatman, before theirs (1674 and 1682). David Loggan (1635-1700?) and his pupil, Robert White (1645-1703), were the leading portrait-engravers of their day: long lists of their portraits will be found in Horace Walpole's *Catalogue Of Engravers, With ... Additions By ... James Dallaway* (1828), pp. 185-90, 208-20. Cf. the couplet, presumably Dryden's, in Soame's *Art of Poetry* (1683):
> And in the Front of all his Senseless Plays,
> Makes *David Loggan* Crown his Head with Bays.

74. *Oats*. From the end of 1678 to the early part of 1681, Titus Oates had made a great figure. He was pensioned, and lodged in Whitehall; guards were assigned for his protection; he consulted with the Whig lords at the Green Ribbon Club, or drove with them in their coaches. They promised him a bishopric; he put on, as Roger North relates (*Examen*, 1740, p. 205), 'Episcopal Garb (except the Lawn Sleeves)'; and even laid claim to gentle blood by engraving on his plate the arms of the 14th-century Sir Otes Swinford.

74. *Bedloe*. William Bedloe came forward in Oct. 1678 to earn the £500 reward for the discovery of Godfrey's murderers, and added his false testimony to that of Oates in all the principal trials for the Plot up to Sir George Wakeman's acquittal. The rash of pamphlets on his death, 20 Aug. 1680, gives some notion of his fame; e.g. *A Faithfull Account of the Sickness, Death, and Burial of Capt. William Bedlow*, from J.S., in Bristol, Aug. 23. 1680 (Luttrell, *Catalogues* 'Aug. 26'); *An Elegy Upon the Unfortunate Death of Captain William Bedloe*, and *An Elegie Upon the ... ever-to-be-remembred ..., Captain Will. Bedlow, Englad's [sic] Deliverer, and the Scourge of Rome* (BL, Lutt., I.9, 12; dated 25 and 27 Aug. 1680; 'Aug. 25', 'Aug. 27' in Luttrell, *Catalogues*: cf. *Funeral Tears on the Death of Captain William Bedloe*, '27 Aug. 1680', *The Epitaph of Captain William Bedlow*, 'Sept. 30,

1680') and *Tears, Tears, Tears ... upon notice of the Death of Captain Bedlow*, 5 Nov. 1680.

77 f.   Criminals passed up Holborn Hill on their way from Newgate to execution at Tyburn: cf. 'Juvenal III', ll. 460 f. and 'Upon a Bookseller', ll. 73 ff. and n. In his Prologue to *Circe* (1677, earlier form, ll. 13 ff.) Dryden imagines the commiseration of the ladies as 'some young lusty Thief' passes to his death.

78-84.   For an early version of these lines see Appendix II.1, ll. 71-6; cf. next n. Behind them lies Horace, *Satires*, I.iv.71 f.; his allusion, immediately above, to the informers Sulcius and Caprius probably suggested Oldham's, in l. 74, to Oates and Bedloe.

78-81.   Title-pages were posted up as advertisements: see 'An Allusion to Martial', l. 18 and n., and the numerous references to the practice cited by R.B. McKerrow, *Introduction To Bibliography* (1928), p. 90, n. 2. For the bills of quacks, cf. *The Character Of A Quack-Doctor* (1676): 'his *Draw-Net* is a *Printed Bill*, which Catches the Gudgeons in Shoals' [etc.]. *Medice Cura Teipsum.' Or The Apothecaries Plea* (1671) describes the printing and posting up of bills which signify the mountebank's 'name, ... his lodging, ... when he may be spoke with, and the diseases that he cures'. Three such bills, printed for 'Thomas Suffold, an Approved and Licensed Physician, and Student in Astrology' and 'J. Russell, Professor of Physick, and Oculist', may be seen in the Firth collection (Bodl. Firth b. 16). For 'Sham', see 'Juvenal XIII', l. 176, and n.

83.   *bilk'd Owner*: the bookseller (cf. the 'Bilk't Stationers' in *MacFlecknoe*), who is left with nothing but an unsaleable book in return for the copy-money. In a despairing attempt to attract customers, he advertises it in the *Gazette*; cf. Dryden's ironic comment on *A Key (with the Whip)* 1682 ('13 Jan.', Luttrell): 'I am afraid it is not read so much as the Piece deserves, because the bookseller is every week crying help at the end of his Gazette, to get it off' (Epistle, before *The Medall*, 15 or 16 Mar. 1682); Macdonald, pp. 27, 225 f.

84.   *'Mongst Spaniels lost*. Cf. e.g. *The London Gazette*, no. 1509, 3-6 May, 1680, where beside an advertisement for *The Wits Paraphras'd*, with the bookseller's address, there appears 'Lost or stolen out of *Warwick-Street* ... a very small Spaniell Bitch, liver coloured and white, ... Whosoever shall bring her to Mr. *Kunbolt*'s, a Bookseller near *Charing-Cross*, shall be very well Rewarded.'

85-111.   Cf. Boileau, *Satires*, p. 59, Satire IX:
     Vous vous flattez peut-estre en vostre vanité;
     D'aller comme un Horace à l'immortalité ...
     Mais combiens d'Écrivains d'abord si bien receus,
     Sont de ce fol espoir honteusement deceus?
     Combiens, pour quelques mois, ont veu fleurir leur livre,
     Dont les vers en paquet se vendent à la livre?
     Vous pourrez voir un temps vos Escrits estimez,
     Courir de main en main par la ville semez;
     Puis delà tout poudreux, ignorez sur la terre,
     Suivre chez l'Epicier Neuf-Germain & la Serre:
     Ou de trente feuillets reduit peut-estre a neuf,
     Parer demi-rongez les rebords du Pont-neuf.
(Cf. particularly Oldham's ll. 85-8, 93 f., 97-101, 103-6). Remembering that Oldham had transcribed *MacFlecknoe*, the resemblances between the latter part of the passage and ll. 95-106 of that poem are also significant. Heywood, Shirley, and Ogilby are pilloried in both; both allude to the bilked or broken stationers whom the bad poets have ruined, and to the uses

of waste paper. Compare also Oldham's reference to *'Duck-lane* Shops' with
Dryden's to 'dusty shops' and the neighbourhood of *'Bun-Hill* and distant
Watling-street'.

85. *soothst*: flatterest; see *OED*.

89-92. Marine insurance was described in 1601 (43 Eliz. cap. XII) as 'tyme
out of mynde an usage amongste merchantes'. It was a growing one in Oldham's
day. Facilities were publicly advertised: *The City Mercury* of 20 Jan. 1680
informs 'Merchants or Masters of Ships' that at 'the Office at the Royal
Exchange' they 'may be supplied with Money upon Bottomare ... and have
Polities, Charter-parties, or other Writing made'. See F. Martin, *The History Of Lloyd's And Of Marine Insurance In Great Britain* (1876), and Ogg,
i.233, n. 2.

96. *News-Books*: the small newspapers of the day; the term was in regular
use from 1650 to 1700. Wood (iv.381) speaks of 'the common news-book called
Mercurius Politicus'.

98. *Pordidg*. Samuel Pordage (1633-1691?), author of two rhymed heroic plays,
Herod and Marianne (1673), and *The Siege of Babylon* (1678); and probably
(Macdonald, 205, 207) two replies to Dryden, *Azaria and Hushai* and *The
Medal Revers'd*, both 1682, dated by Luttrell 17 Jan. and 31 Mar. L'Estrange
attacked him in the *Observator* of 5 Apr. 1682 as 'limping *Pordage* ... the
author of several libels'; and Dryden satirized him in Nov. in *Absalom* Pt.
II as 'lame *Mephibosheth*', one of the
      Poor Slaves in metre, dull and addle-pated,
      Who Rhime below ev'n *David's* Psalms translated.
But as Macdonald remarks (p. 325), his *Poems on Several Occasions* (1660)
'contain some good verse' and Aubrey, who 'knew [him] very well', calls him
'a civil courteous person, and a handsome man'. (ii.160 f.). See also
'Juvenal III', ll. 312-24.

98. *Fleckno*. See 'Art of Poetry', l. 608, and n.

98. *the British Prince?*: *The Brittish Princes: An Heroick Poem. Written by
the Honourable Edward Howard, Esq*; (1669). A laudatory epistle from Thomas
Hobbes, and commendatory verses by Orrery, Denham, and H. D., were prefixed.
These uncritical eulogies provoked a series of mock ones, by Butler, Dorset,
Buckingham, and others, which overwhelmed the piece in merited derision: see
'Upon a Bookseller', l. 67 and n. Cf. Rochester, 'An Epistolary Essay from
M. G. to O. B.', ll. 10 f., where Oldham's misquotation of the title is
paralleled:
      T'obtain one line of your well-worded sense,
      I'd be content t'have writ the *British Prince*.

99. *Quarles*: Francis Quarles (1592-1644), author of the celebrated *Emblemes*
(1635). For his early reputation cf. Benlowes' Latin panegyric, *Quarleis*,
in *Lusus Poeticus Poetis* (1634); and S. Sheppard's *Epigrams* (1651), p. 161.
Oldham would be familiar with Cowley's slighting reference to him and Heywood (preface to *Poems*, 1656): by versifying Scripture or other godly
matter, far from elevating poesy they abased divinity. Quarles's *Divine
Poems* and *Argalus and Parthenia* were reprinted in the 1670s, but according
to Phillips (*Theatrum Poetarum*) in 1676, 'his verses have been ever, and
still are, in wonderful admiration among the vulgar', and Wood (iii.684)
later describes him as 'an old puritanical poet ... the sometime darling of
our plebeian judgement'. Headley's critique in the *Gentleman's Magazine*,
1786 (lvi.666, 926; cf. 1106 and lxiii.211) foreshadowed his rehabilitation
by Lamb and others.

99. *Chapman*. Contemporary praise of Chapman may be found, e.g. in Jonson's
verses prefixed to his Hesiod (*Jonson*, viii.388), Drayton's 'Epistle to

Henry Reynolds' (*Works*, ed. J.W. Hebel, B.H. Newdigate and K. Constable,
iii.229, ll. 144 ff.), and Meres, *Palladis Tamia (Elizabethan Critical
Essays*, ed. Gregory Smith, ii.315, 318 etc.). Dryden, commenting on Waller's
and Mulgrave's admiration (in Restoration times) of Chapman's Homer, credits
it to Homer, not the translation, which clothes him in 'harsh numbers, improper English, and a monstrous length of verse' (dedication, *Examen Poeticum*, 1693, *Essays*, ii.14). Dryden's condemnation of Chapman's *Bussy
D'Ambois* in the dedication of *The Spanish Friar* (1681) (*Essays*, i.246),
was very likely in Oldham's thoughts here as well as in the 'Art of Poetry'
(see l. 341 and n.), where he himself mentions *Bussy* with contempt.

99. *Heywood*: Thomas Heywood (1575?-1648), the Elizabethan dramatist. As
early as 1651, 'Heywood's old Iron' was contrasted with 'Shakespeare's
Alchemy' in verses by Wil. Bell prefixed to Cartwright's poems. His *Hierar-
chie of the Blessed Angels* is censured along with Quarles's sacred narratives in the preface to Cowley's *Poems* (1656), and Oldham also knew the
passage of *MacFlecknoe* (ll. 100-3) in which he is linked with Shirley and
Ogleby as an unsaleable author. See above, nn. on ll. 85-111 and on Quarles
(l. 99).

99 f. *Withers ... And Wild.* Cf. 'Jesuits, Prologue', l. 31. Robert Wild
(1609-79), Puritan divine and Presbyterian Royalist, was the author of
Iter Boreale (1660) and other pieces, a number of which appeared as popular
broadsheets. Some of his verse was collected in 1668; the Revd John Hunt
edited it in 1870. *Iter Boreale* had considerable success; Pepys, 23 Aug.
1663, liked it 'pretty well, but not so as it was cried up'. In Dryden's
essay *Of Dramatick Poesie* (1668) (*Essays*, i.31 and nn.) Wild is condemned
by Lisideius for his 'clenches' and 'clownish kind of raillery', his Cleve-
landisms and his satirical malice that spares no man though it can hurt
none: and Eugenius calls him 'the very Withers of the city'.
    George Wither (1588-1667) was a Puritan pamphleteer, and a lyric and
satirical poet of a higher order than Wild. His best-known volume of satires
is *Abuses Stript and Whipt* (1613). Lamb and Coleridge praise his lyrical
gifts, displayed in *The Shepherds Hunting* (1615), *Fidelia* (1617), and *Faire-
Virtue* (1622), and especially in the famous 'Shall I, wasting in despair?'.
But from 1622 he became 'a garrulous preacher in platitudinous verse and
prose of the political and religious creeds of the commonplace middle-class
Puritan' (*DNB*). Restoration scorn of him was therefore natural. Butler sets
the tone in *Hudibras*, I.i.645 ff. (quoted below, 'Juvenal III', ll. 142 f.,
n.); cf. the anecdote in *Heraclitus Ridens*, no. 42, 15 Nov. 1681, of a
'Gentleman' (viz. Denham, see Aubrey, i.221, quoted Banks, p. 10) 'who
pleaded to his Majesty for a pardon for *George Withers* upon this modest
Topick, that if *George* were hang'd, he the Gentleman should be the worst
Poet in Christendom'. Yet Wither was not entirely neglected: a single sheet
folio, entitled *Mr George Wither Revived* ... and containing a long extract
from *Britains Remembrancer* (1628), appeared in 1680, being advertised in
The True News: Or Mercurius Anglicus, 18-21 Feb. 1679/80.

100. *Ogilby*. John Ogilby (1600-76) attempted heroic poetry in *The Ephesian
Matron, The Roman Slave*, and *Caroleis* (destroyed in the Great Fire); and
published versions of the *Æneid* (1649), *Æsop's Fables* (1651), the *Iliad*
(1660), and the *Odyssey* (1665). The *Aesop* has congratulatory verses by
Davenant and Shirley prefixed; and cf. the praise of his 'sparkling Genius'
in 'To Mr. John Ogilbie' (Pecke's *Parnassi Puerperium*, 1659, p. 81):
            Were *Maro* now alive, he must you prise:
            And by you, *Homer* shall regain his Eyes....
With this, contrast Prior's comparison between Ogilby and Creech, *c*.1685,
in 'A Satyr on the Modern Translators', ll. 140-4:
            Both writ so much, so ill, a doubt might rise,
            Which with most Justice might deserve the Prize;

>   Had not the first the Town with Cutts appeas'd,
>   And where the Poem fail'd the Picture pleas'd.

Cf. also Dryden (*Essays*, i.253, ii.271).

105. *Duck-lane*: the principal centre of the second-hand book trade (between Smithfield and Little Britain). Cf. Howell's *Familiar Letters* (edn. of 1737, p. 484): 'touching your Poet Laureate Skelton, I found him at last skulking in Duck Lane, pitifully tattered and torn'.

106. *Silvester*: Joshua Sylvester (1563-1618), whose translation of the Huguenot poet, Du Bartas—*Du Bartas His Divine Weekes and Works* (1592-1598) —was so popular in late Elizabethan times, and even afterward in homes like the youthful Milton's. In making him a typical victim of progress in taste, Oldham perhaps recalled Dryden's confession that when a boy he thought 'inimitable Spenser a mean poet in comparison of Sylvester's *Dubartas*', but in his mature judgement finds such a purple passage as he then admired, 'abominable fustian' (*The Spanish Friar* (1681); see 1. 99 n., on Chapman).

106. *Shirley*: James Shirley (1596-1666), the Caroline dramatist. He appears as one of the unsaleable authors in *MacFlecknoe*. Though his best social comedies were comparatively neglected, some of his plays were popular in the sixties and early seventies; *The Traytor* was revived as late as 1692 (Hume, pp. 237, 399; Nicoll, i.184, 427). He was censured in 'The Session of the Poets' (*c*.1665) (Macdonald, pp. 221 f. No. IV.). Phillips and Langbaine did him justice, however.

107. *Stourbridge*-Fair: held annually for three weeks from 18 Sept., half a mile east of Barnwell, near Cambridge; see William Addison, *English Fairs and Markets* (1953), ch. 3. Ned Ward, in *A Step to Stir-Bitch-Fair* (1700), mentions 'the great Number of Booksellers that are now crept into Possession' of what was 'originally *Cooks-Row*', where 'the most famous Auctioneer of all Great as well as Little *Britain*, sells Books by the Hammer'.

109. *vile Mundungus*: cheap, stinking tobacco.

112-18. Cf. Boileau, *Satires*, pp. 59 f., Satire IX:

>   Mais je veux que le Sort, par un hereux caprice,
>   Fasse de vos Escrits prosperer la malice ...
>   Que vous sert-il qu'un jour l'avenir vous estime,
>   Si vos vers aujourd'hui ...
>   Ne produisent rien, pour fruit de leurs bon mots,
>   Que l'effroi du Public & la haine des Sots.

But instead of this last thought, Oldham then (ll. 116-18) introduces one from Juvenal VII, 22-31: if Telesinus expects patronage for his lofty verses, he may as well burn them: he is toiling to win a miserable bust.

121-8. On the Renaissance ideal of the Heroic Poem, see W.L. Renwick, *Edmund Spenser* (1925), pp. 41-55, and W.P. Ker, *Essays Of John Dryden*, i.xv-xix. Dryden meditated a heroic poem on the subject (as we know from the 'Discourse ... concerning ... Satire', 1693; *Essays*, ii.38; cf. 32, 1. 1 n.) either of Arthur or of the Black Prince. In the dedication to *Aureng-Zebe* (1676)—a play well known to Oldham—he addresses Mulgrave on his projected heroic poem 'the subject of which you know is great, the story English', such that by it he might have 'done honour' to his 'Country'. Mulgrave had enabled him to speak of it to the King and the Duke, who commanded him to proceed. He asked Mulgrave to stir the King's memory; only if freed from material anxieties could he go forward: 'As I am no successor to *Homer* in his Wit, so neither do I desire to be in his Poverty'. Arthur was Spenser's hero, and was designed at one time to be Milton's. Henry V and the Black Prince inspired two of Roger Boyle's heroic plays, printed in 1667 and 1668.

123. *great Edward's greater Son*: Edward III and the Black Prince. Cf. Denham, *Cooper's Hill* (1642), 1. 77: 'But thee (great *Edward*) and thy greater Son'.

125 f. Cf. *Paradise Lost*, IX.14 ff.:
           ... more Heroic than the wrauth
           Of stern *Achilles* on his Foe pursu'd
           ... about *Troy* Wall; or rage
           Of *Turnus* for *Lavinia* disespous'd.
Sidney was Spenser's Maecenas, who made him known to the Queen, and as Spenser himself tells us in the sonnet to Sidney's sister, encouraged him in poetry. Spenser's 'great project', *The Faerie Queene*, the first great attempt to achieve the Heroic Poem in English, was begun about the time that he entered the household of Sidney's uncle, Leicester. Oldham had probably in mind a story, picturesque but unauthoritative, told in the 1679 edition of Spenser's Works. It depicts him visiting Leicester-House 'furnisht only with ... the Ninth *Canto* of the First Book of his *Faëry Queen*': Sidney, starting with £50 on reading st. 28, of Despair, at st. 29 doubled and at st. 30 redoubled the amount, bidding his expostulating steward to make haste to pay over the money, 'least advancing his Reward proportionably to ... his Pleasure in reading, he should hold himself obliged to give him more than he had'.

129. As first printed, the line perhaps lacks a syllable, which the misdated '1683' edition (found in *Works* 1686 and 1692) supplies by reading 'his Genius'. In view of 1. 63 of 'Aude aliquid. Ode', 'Had he a Genius and Poetique Rage' and 1. 123 of the ode on Morwent, 'A Genius did thy whole Comportment act', 'a Genius' seems a preferable emendation. The phrase would still signify 'How great a genius he has', not 'How great a genius he is'.

136. *Brief*: letters patent issued by the sovereign as Head of the Church, licensing a collection in the churches throughout England for a specified object of charity (*OED*). In Shipton Moyne parish register, and signed by Oldham's grandfather, is an entry of 51s. 5d. collected upon a brief to relieve the distressed inhabitants of Marlborough: it is undated, but the corresponding collection at Wotton-under-Edge was made 9 Aug. 1653. Pepys, 30 June 1661, observes that 'the trade of briefs is come now up to so constant a course every Sunday, that we resolve to give no more to them'; this was the fifteenth collection levied at his parish church in as many weeks.

139-42. Cf. Juvenal, VII.74 f., 77 f.

155. *the Company*: one of the City Companies. Cf. 'Nobility', 11. 177 f. and n.

157. *The blind old Bard*: Homer.

163. *Creswel's*. The notorious establishment, 'in *Moor-Fields*', of '*Mother Cresswell of Famous Memory*' is referred to in *The Observator*, 2 June 1684. Some twenty earlier allusions to her, the first being in 1660, are quoted in Montague Summers's n. on the prologue to Otway's *Venice Preserv'd* (1682), 1. 33. For the well-worn anecdote of her funeral-sermon, see Wheatley, under Bridewell. Two satirical pamphlets were written in her person: *The Poor-Whores Petition to ... the Countess of Castlemaine*, which is subscribed 'Madam Cresswell and Damaris Page', '25 March 1668'; and *A Letter From The Lady Cresswell to Madam C[ellier] the Midwife, on Publishing her late Vindication* ('Sept. 11. 1680', Luttrell, *Catalogues*).

165 f. This couplet appears in an earlier form in a rough draft for 'A Letter'. See Appendix II, 11. 65 f. (R94). Cf. Alexander Brome, 'To the High Sheriff of S.', *Songs and other Poems* (1668), p. 235:

> And here's the reason, which our *Muses* grieves,
> *Sheriffs* are made *Poets*, but ne'r *Poets Sheriffs*.

On fining for Shrieve, see 'Boileau VIII', l. 119 and n., and cf. 'Juvenal III', l. 215.

167. *My own hard Usage*. See headnote.

170-2. Cowley had been promised the mastership of the Savoy by both Charles I and Charles II; but in 1660 it was given to Sheldon and in 1663 to Henry Killegrew. A statement of his case in *CSPD*, 1661-2, p. 210 (quoted Nichol Smith, p. 307), represents 'that Cowley ... having seen all preferments given away, and his old University companions advanced before him, is put to great shame by missing this place'. In the 'Session of the Poets', *c*.1665 (Macdonald, pp. 221 f., no. IV) he is called '*Savoy* missing *Cowley*', and charged with a 'notable Folly', in printing 'his pitiful Melancholy'. This, like the present passage, alludes to his poem 'The Complaint', in which he styles himself 'The Melancholy *Cowley*'

> ... to whose share so little bread did fall,
> In the miraculous year, when *Manna* rain'd on all.

(*Poems*, p. 438 and see 'Of Myself', *Essays*, pp. 458 f.). 'The Complaint' is also referred to in Sprat's life of Cowley before his *Works*, 1668 (Spingarn, ii.141); and in Nahum Tate's *Poems* (1677), p. 18: 'Th'Ill-treated *Cowley* did his Muse upbraid'.

173 f. Cf. Thorn Drury in his edn. of Waller (i.xxi): 'The fortune which Waller inherited from his father' (Robert, who had estates in Hertfordshire and Buckinghamshire), 'which must have been largely increased during his long minority, has been variously estimated at from £2,000 to £3,500 a year; adding to this the amount which he received with [Anne] Bankes', his first wife, 'said to have been about £8,000, and allowing for the difference in the value of money, it appears probable that, with the exception of Rogers, the history of English literature can show no richer poet.'

175-90. Samuel Butler died 25 Sept. 1680, aged 68. He seems to have linked himself with Spenser and Cowley in a couplet,

> To think how Spencer died, how Cowley mourn'd
> How Butler's faith and service were returnd,

which was found in his commonplace book (*Hudibras*, ed. Nash (1793), I.x. facsimile, p. xxxix), and which may have gone about, since in the prologue to Lee's *Constantine the Great* (*c*.Dec. 1683) Otway has one virtually identical, with 'Tell 'em ... starv'd' for 'To think ... died' (see E.S. de Beer, *RES*, iv (1928), 165). A satire ascribed to 1679, 'Julian in verse to ease thy wants I write' (Macdonald, p. 214 nn.) complains that '*Hudibras* does starve among the Throng'. Dryden's lines on 'Unpitty'd *Hudibrass*' in *The Hind and the Panther* (1687: iii.247-50) are well known, with his reproach written to Laurence Hyde (?Aug. 1683), ''Tis enough for one age to have neglected Mr. Cowley, and starv'd Mr. Butler'. The conjecture (?Aug. 1683) dates this not many weeks after Oldham's poem was published. Yet Butler had not gone entirely unrewarded. On 30 Nov. 1674 Sir Stephen Fox was ordered to give him £200. *Hudibras* Part III, published just before 6 Nov. 1677, brought him £100, and a pension of £100 a year (12 and 17 Nov.): quarterly payment, with arrears from 29 Sept. 1677, was directed 25 Sept. 1678 (de Beer, loc. cit., pp. 164 f., citing W.A. Shaw, *Calendar of Treasury Books*, iv.267, v.478 f., 1116). Finally, between 27 Mar. and 3 May, a few months only before his death, he had £20 from the secret service funds 'as of free guift and royal bounty' (*Secret Services of Charles II and James II*, ed. J.Y. Akerman, Camd. Soc. lii (1851), p. 13; cf. my n. on it, *TLS*, 6 July, 1940, p. 327, and Norma Bentley's, *MLN*, lix (1944), 281). There may, however, be truth in the tradition (see Zachary Grey's *Hudibras*, I.x., n.) that much of what Butler received went to discharge his debts; and his pension, if paid no more regularly than Dryden's, might not always secure him from want.

177-80. When *Hudibras* Pt. I came out, it 'was not only taken into his majesty's hands and read by him with great delight, but also by all courtiers, loyal scholars and gentlemen, to the great profit of the author and bookseller' (Wood, iii.875). Charles gave inscribed copies to several people, and Clarendon had the author's portrait painted and hung in his dining-hall (*DNB*).

179-90. In reality, Butler died of a consumption (Wood, iii.876). Oldham imitates Boileau, *Satires*, pp. 7 f., Satire I:
>   Conduit d'un vain espoir, il parut à la Cour.
>   Qu'arrive-t-il enfin de sa Muse abusée ? ...
>   ... la fièvre ... / terminant son destin,
>   Fit par avance en lui, ce qu'auroit fait la faim.

185. *Flannel*: a flannel shroud, as enjoined by the Woollen Acts which Shadwell's Justice Clodpate (*Epsom Wells* (1673), I.i, p. 7) congratulated himself upon enforcing: 'I ... make people bury in Flannel, to encourage the Woollen Manufacture'. See 'Juvenal III', ll. 270 f. and n.

188. Butler's friend Longueville bore the charges of his burial at St. Paul's, Covent Garden, after a vain attempt to secure him a grave in the Abbey.

196 f. The playwright's livelihood was speculative because it depended on the 'third day's share'—see l. 205, n. The government, from which the right of promoting lotteries had to be purchased, did its best to popularize them. They were in ill-repute; the Royal Oak lottery, in particular, was alleged to be a swindle. See further Dryden, Epilogue to *The Unhappy Favourite* (*c*.1681), l. 5; John Ashton, *History of English Lotteries* (1893), pp. 32-48; Ogg, i.111 f., 163 f.

199 f. Cf. Sedley's Prologue to Shadwell's *Epsom Wells* (1673): 'You'll say you pay, and so may be severe', but
>   'Tis not fair Play, that one for his Half Crown
>   Shou'd judge, and rail, and damn for half the Town.
Half-a-crown was the price of admission to the pit: see Pepys, 1 Jan. 1667/8.

201-11. Based on Juvenal, VII.59-92. Ll. 201 ff. imitate ll. 79-81 in Juvenal; and ll. 207 f. epitomize his ll. 59-61 and 71-3. The references to Settle's pecuniary dependence on the stage are the counterpart of those made by Juvenal to the similar dependence of Statius.

201 f. The Prologue to Sedley's third play, *Bellamira* (1687), concludes:
>   Our Author try'd his own and cou'd not hit:
>   He now presents you with some Forraign Wit.
This, and Oldham's couplet, probably refer to the first production of *The Mulberry Garden*, 18 May 1668, of which Pepys says 'the whole of the play had nothing extraordinary in it ... insomuch that the King I did not see laugh nor pleased ...; insomuch that I have not been less pleased at a new play in my life I think'. Yet both *The Mulberry Garden* and *Antony and Cleopatra*, 1677, enjoyed a fair measure of success. See V. de Sola Pinto, *Sir Charles Sedley* (1927), pp. 133, 247 ff., and his edn. of Sedley, i.190.

203. *Settle*. Elkanah Settle (1648-1724); Dryden's Doeg. He was the author of *The Empress of Morocco* (from which Oldham had not disdained to borrow) and of eight other plays between 1671 and the spring of 1682, after which he produced nothing more for the theatre until 1691. See also n. on ll. 284 f.

205. The remuneration assigned to the author was the proceeds of the third
      night's performance: see 'Art of Poetry', 1. 320 and n. Cf. Dryden, Epi-
      logue to *The Unhappy Favourite* (1682): 'The Comet / Foreshews our ... thin
      Third-days'.

212 f., 216. After Juvenal, VII.96 f., which Hall had already imitated in
      Virgidemiarum, VI.i.205 f.:
                  Who had but liued in Augustus' daies
                  T' had beene some honour to be crown'd with Bayes.

218. *write Hackney*: to write as a hireling; a hackney being a horse kept for
      hire. Probably one more reminiscence of *Don Carlos* (1676), where Otway
      remarks in the preface: ''tis almost as poor a Trade with Poets, as it is
      with those that write Hackney under *Attorneys*'.

224-6. Once intended for 'A Letter': see Appendix II.1, 11. 69-71 (R94),
      where they are followed by early versions of 11. 78-84, 116 f., above. See
      also 11. 165 f., n.

224. George Farquhar, in *Love and Business [with] A Discourse ... Upon
      Comedy* (1702), p. 147, makes a gallant exclaim: '"I'll e'en write a Play
      my self; by which means ... I shall enjoy the Freedom of the House".' As
      Farquhar comments, it will secure free admission 'to him and his Friends
      for ever after'.

229-32. Cf. Boileau, *Satires*, p. 5, Satire I:
                  Tel aujourd'hui triomphe ...
                  Qu'on verroit, de couleurs bizarrement orné,
                  Conduire le carosse où l'on le voit trainé,
                  Si dans les droits du Roi sa funeste science,
                  Par deux ou trois avis n'eust ravagé la France.

229. An empyric is a quack doctor; for 'licence' see 'Boileau VIII', 11.
      227 f., n.

230. Cf. verses (possibly by Rochester) on the death of the Princess of
      Orange (1660), where physicians are called
                  Arts' basilisks, that kill whome'er they see,
                  And truly write bills of mortality,
      and Dryden, 'To ... John Driden, of Chesterton' (publ. 1700), 11. 71 f. The
      weekly Bills of Mortality, recording deaths in London parishes, seem to
      have begun in 1592. Cf. 'Jesuits IV', 11. 45 f.n.

231. *Wears Velvet, keeps his Coach*. On these attributes of a 17th-century
      physician: cf. *Lex Talionis ... Or A Short Reply To Dr. Merett's Book;
      And Others, written against the Apothecaries* (1670), p. 3: 'yet there is
      more in the business than a Velvet Jump, a pair of Silk Stockings, and a
      Cane with a Silver Head', and p. 17: 'I could tell him a way to ... com-
      mence *Doctor*, and easier learned, ... I believe some of them have come in
      that way, and equipage. For now there must be the little Coach, and two
      Horses, which in these days are very usual appendices to the *Doctor* in
      Physick.' The 'Emp'rick' in *The Character Of A Quack Doctor* (1676) 'grows
      Famous and Rich, and buyes him the worshipful Jacket ... and at last pur-
      chases a Title, and arrives at his Coach'.

241. The Levant, East India, and Royal African (originally the Barbary) Com-
      panies, founded in 1592, 1603, and 1663. With the Eastland Company and the
      Merchant Adventurers, they formed the chief channels of English export.
      Oldham's allusion must not be pressed too far: the Levant Company was suf-
      fering from French competition; the Barbary brought to perilous straits by
      the hostility of the Dutch, had had to be reorganized as the Royal African
      in 1672; and even the East India Company, despite its flourishing reputa-

tion, its dividends of 50 per cent in 1680 and 25 per cent on the average in succeeding years, and its loans to the king of £324,000 between 1660 and 1684, was less prosperous than it appeared, owing over half a million in 1681. See Pepys, iv.153, n. 1, ix.350, n. 3; Ogg, i.226-30, and authorities there cited; and K.G. Davies, *The Royal African Company* (1957).

243 f. Virginia represents the colonial trade with America under the Navigation Acts; Greenland the whale fisheries of the Greenland Adventurers, though these were declining; Bantam the easternmost enterprises of the East India Company; Seville, Alicante, Zante, and Smyrna the Straits, Mediterranean, and Levant trades. See 'Boileau VIII', ll. 101, 102, 121 and nn., for Bantam, Alicante, and the Straits; Ogg, i.219 f., 223, 233, for Smyrna and Greenland; and for Zante, *The Present State of the Morea, ... Described by Bernard Randolph, who resided in those parts from 1671 to 1679*, London, 1686, p. 24.

245. The contraband trade with France in luxuries and even less reputable articles; see 'Juvenal III', ll. 125 f.. 'The Careless Good Fellow', ll. 17 f. and 'Ode on Jonson', ll. 104 ff. and nn.

247 f. Improving on a couplet in the Epilogue to Otway, *The Souldiers Fortune*, produced March 1679/80, published 1681:
> So whoe'er ventures on the ragged coast
> Of starving poets, certainly is lost.

249-54. Cf. Boileau, *Satires*, p. 6, Satire I:
> Faut il donc désormais jouër un nouveau rôle?
> Dois-je, las d'Apollon, recourir à Barthole,
> Et feuillerant Loüet alongé par Brodeau,
> D'une robe à longs plis balayer les Barreau?
> Mais à ce seul penser, je sens que je m'égare,
> Moi, que j'aille crier dans ce païs barbare ...
> Où Patru gagne moins qu'Huot et le Mazier ...?

250. *Cook*: the *Institutes* (and perhaps also the *Reports*) of Lord Chief Justice Coke (1552-1634), the great common lawyer. Of the *Institutes* (1628-44) the 1st part, 'Coke upon Littleton', reached a 7th edn. in 1670, the last three a 6th in 1680 and 1681. Coke's name was pronounced 'Cook' by his contemporaries, and often spelt accordingly.

250. *Dalton*: Michael Dalton's *The Countrey Iustice, Conteyning The practice of the Iustices of the Peace out of their Sessions* (1618), which was frequently reprinted. Cleveland, in *The Character of a Country-Committee-Man* (1647) speaks of 'his *Dalton*'.

253. *Where M[aynar]d thrives*. Sir John Maynard (1602-90); 'This great man, as I must call him, since his natural and acquired abilities and the immense gains he had by practice entitle his name to that epithet, was an ante-Restoration lawyer, and king's serjeant from 1660' (North, *Lives*, i.149). The large fortune he made enabled him to purchase the manor of Gunnersbury, and to build a palatial mansion there, in 1663, from designs of Inigo Jones or his pupil Webbe.

257 f. See 'To a Friend', ll. 96-102 and n.

259. *sooth*. Cf. l. 85 and n.

259 f. Benjamin Calamy, in his *Sermon ... before the Lord Mayor ... on the 29th of May 1682*, insisting 'That Sovereign Princes are accountable to God alone, ... and, That in no Case by force we may resist them', declares: 'I know the very naming of this will offend some men ... By this test, they tell you, you shall know those amongst us that have a mind to be soonest prefer'd, or who are Friends to Arbitrary Power, or strive to please the

Court, by Preaching up such strict Obedience to the King ... This is the
common objection and clamour against *Clergymen* this day.' High Tory zeal for
Passive Obedience and Divine Right of Kings, originating in a defensible abhorrence of Calvinistic as well as Catholic theories of lawful resistance,
reached a bigoted climax in the Oxford decree of 21 July 1683 (Feiling,
p. 201). Even earlier, numerous sermons marked this Tory reaction: e.g.
Hickes's 'Discourse of the Sovereign Power', 28 Nov. 1682; Freeman's, 8 Oct.,
Sprat's, 20 Apr., two by Goulde and Dove, that year; and Sclater's, 24 Apr.
1681.

264. *Jack-pudding, Juggler ... or Rope-dancer.* A Jack-pudding: a low buffoon,
the staple of whose performance was to devour some sloppy dish with much
grimacing and slobbering. Cf. Shadwell, *The Sullen Lovers* (1668), II.iii,
p. 25, 'I had as live stand among the rabble, to see a Jack-pudding eate a
Custard'. Dryden in his prologue to Tate's *Loyal General* (1679), 1. 10, bids
the ill-judging members of the audience: 'Go back to your dear Dancing on
the Rope'. Pepys conversed with Jacob Hall, the most famous rope-dancer of
the day, after watching him at Southwark Fair, 21 Sept. 1668; and on 24 May
1667, when the diarist was entertained by the Lowthers at 'the old house'
in Islington, he was delighted with the juggler who came in after dinner.

269 f. Chosen divines preached at Court on Wednesdays and Fridays, as well as
Sundays, during Lent. See *Lent-Preachers Appointed to Preach before His
Majesty, For the Year 1684/5*, in the Firth collection (Bodl. Firth, b. 17),
and cf. *The London Gazette*, 22-6 Dec. 1681; similar lists appeared each year.
Pepys observed, when Morley preached at Court on Christmas day, 1662, 'how
far they are from taking the reprehensions of a bishop seriously, that they
all laugh in the chapel when he reflected on their ill actions and courses'.
Lenten doctrine no doubt met with the same reception.

276. *possess'd with Muse.* From Donne, 'Satyr II, 1. 61: 'sicke with Poëtrie,
and possest with muse'.

284 f. Settle may be in Oldham's mind, though he was not the only butt of
such shafts; Stapylton, in the 'Session of the Poets', *c.*1665 (Macdonald,
pp. 221 f., no. IV) is commanded
        ... once more to write a new Play,
        To be danc'd by the Puppets at *Barthol'mew Fair*.
Settle's connection with the Fair had evidently begun by the early 1680s.
He certainly wrote drolls after the Revolution for Elizabeth Leigh, and her
mother, Mrs Mynn, who had booths at Bartholomew and Southwark Fairs; and he
was in touch with the daughter as early as 1681, when he agreed to write a
play for her. Dryden, *Absalom*, Pt. II, Nov. 1682, 11. 453 ff., says that
        The height of his ambition is we know
        But to be Master of a Puppet-show;
        On that one Stage his works may yet appear,
        And a months Harvest keeps him all the Year.
Cf. *Reflexions upon a Late Pamphlet* (1683), a reply to Settle: 'A Dedication
to a *Pope Joan* or a *Fairy Queen* at a Bartholmew Fair bring in but rare and
uncertain profit'. See F.C. Brown, *Elkanah Settle* (1910), p. 35; J.L. Hot-
son, *Commonwealth and Restoration Stage* (1928), pp. 274-7.

286. *the very Nursery*: the Nursery in Golden Lane, Barbican, 'Where unfledg'd
Actors learn to laugh and cry', scene of the action in *MacFlecknoe*. Theatres
in Hatton Gardens and Vere St. were also used as Nurseries. Shadwell, in
The Sullen Lovers (May 1668), I, p. 4, has the gibing phrase 'Cast [viz.
sacked] Poet of the Nursery'. For a view slightly more favourable, but
damagingly qualified, cf. Pepys, 24 Feb. 1668.

287. *forc'd to starve, like me.* See headnote.

A Satyr, in Imitation of the Third of Juvenal

Boileau had already imitated Juvenal's grand indictment of Rome, applying it
to Paris; he then divided the Imitation into his Satires I and VI. Oldham
wrote with the French at hand (see below, ll. 18 ff., 46 f., 54 f., 303 ff.,
361 ff., 385 ff., 449 f., 454 and nn.). The Imitation is freer than in the
'Art of Poetry'. Whereas there the method adopted could fairly be said to provide a translation too, that is no truer of 'Juvenal III' than of 'Juvenal
XIII', though it is chiefly by interpolations that 'Juvenal XIII' parts company with the original; here it is chiefly by omissions. For his straight
translation of Satire III in the 1693 Juvenal, Dryden evidently consulted
Oldham's version. Boswell has comments comparing *London*, Johnson's famous
Imitation (1738), with Oldham's, in the *Life*, i.118-20. For possibilities of
comparison also in Swift's poems and Gay's, see Introduction, p. xxvi.

1. Boswell comments (*Life*, i.119 f.): '... his poem sets out with a strange
    inadvertent blunder: "Tho' much concern'd to *leave* my dear old friend"....
    It is plain he was not going to leave his *friend*; his friend was going to
    leave *him*. A young lady at once corrected this with good critical sagacity,
    to "Tho' much concern'd to *lose* my dear old friend."' Reading 'leave',
    R226 confirms the text.

5. *the Hundreds*: the Essex Hundreds: see 'Juvenal XIII', ll. 260 f. and n.

14-17. Substituted for Juvenal's 11-line description of the Porta Capena
    and Valley of Egeria.

16 f. 'The faction' was one of the opprobrious names bestowed upon the Whigs:
    (see Thomas Papillon's trial, 1689, p. 4). Shaftesbury, declares *The Loyal
    Scot: An Excellent New Song* (1682), 'with *Treats* and *Treason* daily crams
    his *City-Friends*'. The Whigs had planned a great feast at Haberdasher's
    Hall for 21 Apr. 1682: it was forbidden by proclamation on the 19th; where-
    upon some of them dined at separate places with part of the provisions. See
    The London Mercury, 17-20 Apr. 1682, and Luttrell, i.179 f. One of these
    places was probably Mile-end, where a Whig entertainment had been held in
    1681, no doubt because it lay handy for the brisk boys of Wapping. Cf. Ot-
    way's prologue to *Venice Preserv'd* for James's visit, 21 Apr. 1682; bidding
    the Whigs, 'Renounce ... Your Wapping Feasts and your Mile-End High-places',
    and *The Observator*, 27 Apr. 1682: 'I hear mine Host of *Wapping* is like now
    to be paid the Remnant of the Reckoning that was left at the Gun when the
    Whigs treated their Friends there last Summer.' Is not this the Gun at Mile-
    end (cf. Pepys, 2 June 1668)? The 1681 entertainment was scarcely 'fam'd ...
    in Prose, and Verse': the disappointment of 1682 emphatically was: cf. the
    satirical comments in the *Loyal Protestant* and *Heraclitus Ridens* on 25 Apr.
    1682; Otway's Prologue to *The City Heiress* (1682) by Aphra Behn, and her
    Prologue to *Romulus and Hersilia* (1682), anon. (Wiley, pp. 78, ll. 35 f.,
    p. 132, l. 25; cf. p. 74, n. 1, quoting *The Tory Poets* (1682), and p. 130,
    n. 1); *Absalom*, Pt. II (Nov. 1682), ll. 913-30; and such ballads as *The
    Loyal Feast ... and how it was Defeated* (1682); *An Answer to Thomson's Bal-
    lad call'd The Loyal Feast*, [1682]; *The Whigg-Feast* (1682); *Hemp for the
    Flaxman: Or, A Friday Feast Kid-Napped* [1682]; *A Congratulatory Poem on the
    Whiggs Entertainment* (1682); *An Answer To the Pamphlet called, The Loyal
    Feast* (1682).

18-23. Oldham expands the original, introducing the satiric monologue less
    abruptly. In ll. 22 f. he follows Boileau, *Satires*, p. 2, Satire I: the
    Latin is simply 'Hic tunc Vmbricius'; the French:

La colère dans l'âme, & le feu dans les yeux,
Il distila sa rage, en ces tristes adieux.

23. *Timon*. Rochester had used the name eight years earlier for the spokesman in his satirical sketch from London life, beginning: 'What *Timon*! does
old age begin t'approach ...?'

29 f. Substituted for an allusion to Daedalus, and no doubt suggested by
Cowley's fifth Anacreontique (*Poems*, p. 53) where the aging poet resolves
to 'manage *wisely* the *last stake*'.

35. *nauseous*. R227 reads 'plotting'.

36. *Morecraft*. The usurer in Beaumont and Fletcher's *Scornful Lady* (1616),
who tries to possess himself of the land to which the younger Loveless is
supposed heir. At the end of the play he turns swaggerer 'and is now called
Cutting Moorecraft'. Dryden refers to him by this title in the prologue to
Marriage A-La-Mode (1673).

38 f. According to the Tories, the Popish Plot was a sham: the Whigs had
conspired to fit the Catholics with a forged crime. The Whigs retorted that
this supposed conspiracy of theirs was the sham, with which they were being
saddled by the Papists. Minor plots were set on foot to plant evidence that
the other side was really conspiring (see 'Juvenal XIII', ll. 246-8 and n.).
These were 'The little Shamms', the issue of 'old Mother-Plot', to which
An Elegy On The Death Of The Plot makes reference in 1681. A Tory ballad
of 1683, on the Rye House conspiracy, is entitled *The Old New True Blew
Protestant Plot. Or Five Years Sham Plots Discovered in one True One*. Cf.
*A Just Narrative Of The Hellish New Counter-Plots Of The Papists, To cast
the Odium of their Horrid Treasons Upon The Presbyterians* (1679); *The Dis-
covery Of Captain Bury and Alderman Brooks. Of a new Design of the Papists
... to charge the late Plott upon the Protestants* (1679); Andrew Yarran-
ton's *Full Discovery of the First Presbyterian Sham Plot* (1681); E[dmund?]
H[ickeringill?]'s *Character Of A Sham-Plotter* (1681); R. L'Estrange's *The
Shammer Shammed* (1681); Thomas Dangerfield's *More Shams Still* (1681), and
Robert Ferguson's *No Protestant Plot* (1681), with 2nd and 3rd parts published in 1682.

43. *Guard*. i.e. in the professional army, which consisted of a few regiments
of Guards.

46 f. The Latin precluded close imitation: Oldham follows Boileau, *Satires*,
p. 3, Satire I:
          Que George vive ici ...
          Qu'un million comptant par ses fourbes acquis
          De clerc, jadis Laquais, a fait Comte et Marquis.

54 f. The original is: 'Quid Romae faciam? mentiri nescio'; Oldham follows
Boileau, *Satires*, p. 3, Satire I:
          Mais moi, vivre à Paris! eh, qu'y voudrois-je faire?
          Je ne sçai ni tromper, ni feindre, ni mentir....

58-60. Cf. Rochester, 'Upon His Drinking a Bowl', ll. 15 f.:
                    For I am no Sir Sidrophel,
                    Nor none of his relations.
See 'Ode Of Anacreon', headnote. Sidrophel is the astrologer, drawn from
William Lilly, in *Hudibras*, II.iii. Hudibras says of him and his fellows
(ll. 937 f.):
               Some take a measure of the lives
               Of Fathers, Mothers, Husbands, Wives.

60-2. See *Observations upon the Strange & Wonderful Prophecies Of Mr. John
Gadbury* (1680), quoting from Gadbury's almanac on 'an Eclipse of the *Sun*

in *Aries*', 20 Mar. 1680, 'these Insolent Words: *The Famous* Cambden ... *hath* TRULY *minded us of the danger attending* ENGLAND, *from Eclipses in* Aries,— *Si quando fuerit Eclipsis* in γ ant [sic] Ω *significat Mortem Regis*.' Cf. *The Northern Star: The British Monarchy*, 1680 ('May 10', Luttrell, *Catalogues*) A1^{r}: '*Their friend* Gadbury *hath* ... *let* [the Papists] *understand that this Blow is to be struck now or never*'. Examined at Mrs Cellier's first trial, June 1680, Gadbury admitted that during the King's illness the previous Aug. she had asked him to consult the stars to know whether it would end fatally: but he denied that he had done so. (*The Case of Tho. Dangerfield*, 1680, ('Octob^{r} 16', Luttrell, *Catalogues*), pp. 7-9). The accusations were still alive in 1682 (see *Animadversions Upon Mr. John Gadbury's Almanack ... For ... 1682. By Thomas Dangerfield* (1682), p. 6); and are referred to in other satires: e.g. 'An Ironical Encomium on ... the Incomparable Couple of Whiggish Walloons', *POAS*, iii, 2nd edn. (1716), p. 151:

> The Ides of *March* are past, and *Gadbury*
> Proclaims a downfal of our Monarchy; &c.

and 'Staffords Ghost Feb. 1682', *POAS*, i, 2nd edn. (1716):

> *York*'s most belov'd and boldest Friend is he,
> Who knows he must succeed by *Gadbury*.

80. th'*Exchange*: the Royal Exchange: see 'Boileau VIII', l. 97, n.

80. *that Pauls will cost*. New St. Paul's had been building since 1675, and was not completed until 1710; the eventual cost was £747,661. 10*s*.

81. By the wreck, 6 May 1682, of the *Gloucester* frigate, in which the Duke of York was sailing for Edinburgh; cf. 'On the Times', R223, ll. 7 f.; Burnet, ii.326 f. and nn; and Nat. Lee, *To the Duke On His Return*, 1682 ('May 29', Luttrell's copy; Wiley, p. 112, p. 113, ll. 4 ff.). There went down with her 'the dukes furniture and plate &c., to the losse of 30,000 *l*.' (Luttrell, I.185).

90. *Those, who were Slaves at home*. Cf. 'Boileau VIII', l. 76 and n.

91 f. Sir Fopling Flutter, the Man of Mode in Etherege's play, 'wears nothing but what are Originals of the most Famous hands in *Paris*'. Medley, in the same piece, satirizes the affected ladies who, like Melantha in Dryden's *Marriage-A-La-Mode*, use 'all the Foolish French Words' they can acquire (Brett-Smith, ii.231, 221; 209, 153 and n.): and Dryden in the dedication of *The Rival Ladies* (*Essays*, i.5) expresses the wish that both in conversation and literature, 'we might at length leave to borrow words from other nations, which is now a wantonness in us, not a necessity'. The leading dancing-master of the day, St. André, was a Frenchman: so was Grabut, the master of the king's music. Pelham Humphrey was sent to complete his musical education under Lully at Paris; Bannister is said to have been dismissed the king's service for asserting that the English violins were better than the French; and Pepys tells, 20 Nov. 1660, of the king putting 'a great affront upon Singleton's musique, he bidding them stop, and made the French musique play, which, my Lord says, do much outdo all ours'. As for French cooking, Pepys dined *à la française* at Lord Brouncker's house, and at Chatelin's, Monsieur Robins', and the Bear, Drury Lane, 'an excellent ordinary, after the French manner but of Englishmen' (2 Jan. 1665, 12 May, 1667, 18 Feb., 13 Mar. 1668). It is a boorish host in Rochester's 'Timon', ll. 73 f., who declares complacently:

> As for French kickshaws, sillery and champagne,
> Ragouts and fricassees, in troth w'have none.

93 f. Cf. Dryden, *The Spanish Fryar* (acted Mar. 1679/80, printed 1681), Prologue, ll. 45 ff.:

> When Murther's out, what Vice can we advance?
> Unless the new found Pois'ning Trick of *France*....

From 1679 to 1682 the Chambre Ardente was investigating the La Voisin and other poisonings.

95. *great Harry*: Henry V, victor of Agincourt.

97. *Pulvilio*: a perfumed powder.

98. *Chedreux Perruques*. Periwigs by the celebrated Chedreux, of Paris. Sir Fopling Flutter's periwig was a Chedreux. In the preface to *All for Love* (1678; *Essays*, i.195), Dryden dubs those who make French poetry their standard of judgement 'Chedreux critics'.

103. *Goals*: gaols; the spelling is common at this period.

104 f. St James's Square was planned by the Earl of St. Albans about 1663, and a warrant for its erection was issued to Bab May and Abraham Cowley 24 Sept. 1664. Among the 'great men' residing there about this time were St. Albans himself, Ormond, Essex, Dorset the satirist, and Halifax. See Wheatley, ii.298 ff.; A.J. Dasent, *The History of St. James's Square* (1895); Ogg, i.94 f.

109 f. Jo. Haynes (d. 1701) had been a popular low comedian since 1668, when Pepys notes that he was lately come from the Nursery. Actors joining the King's or the Duke's company were reckoned royal servants. Haynes's livery was granted 2 Oct. 1669; he was further certified His Majesty's servant, 14 Apr. 1679 and 10 July 1682. Famed for his fluent gags, and impudent assurance, he was suspended 4 Nov. 1675 because he had with 'scandalous language & insolent carriage abused Sir Edmund Windham', and was arrested, 18 June 1677, 'for reciteinge ... a Scurrilous and obscoene Epilogue'. See Nicoll, i.298 and n. 8, 313 n. 3, 319 n. 4, 326 n. 1, 328, 367; Wiley, pp. 195-9; and, in the Bodleian, MS Firth e. 6. f. 65[V] and Thorn Drury's MS collection on Restoration Players.

   Bryan Haynes, 'Aged thirty years and upward' in 1681, was one of the Irish witnesses whose brazen venality and brutality have been illustrated above ('Boileau VIII', 1. 257, n.). He was king's evidence first against the Papists, and then, turning his coat like his fellows, against College and Shaftesbury, 17 Aug. and 24 Nov. 1681. (See Luttrell, i.108, 117, 121, 137, 146; *The Irish-Evidence Convicted by their Own Oaths*, 1682, p. 11, and the trials of College and Shaftesbury).

111 f. 'Well-hung' means 'having pendent organs'—e.g. a long tongue; cf. Dryden's 'well hung Balaam' in *Absalom*, 1. 574.

117 f. This figure, a favourite with Oldham, is in the Latin. For 'Jack-pudding', see 'Spencer's Ghost', 1. 264 n. 'Operator' is either, as in 'Jesuits IV', 1. 186, a tooth-drawer, or a quack manufacturer of drugs (*OED*, 3 or 3b). 'Mr. Elmer, Operator' advertizes in *The Protestant (Domestick) Intelligence*, 17 Feb. 1679/80.

119 f. Oldham attempts no direct version of 'in caelum iusseris ibit' such as Johnson achieved with his famous 'And bid him go to Hell, to Hell he goes', itself a happy modification of Dryden's more literal 'And bid him go to Heav'n, to Heav'n he goes'.

120. The 'well-educated ape' in the induction to Jonson's *Bartholomew Fair* (1. 17) will 'come over the chain for a king of England, and back again for the prince, and sit still ... for the pope and the king of Spain'. Similarly with Rupert's dog, 'Boy' (Cleveland, 'To P. Rupert', 11. 125 f.).

121 f. *fly ... tried*. This combines, if my conjectures, fully discussed in 'Oldham: Some Problems', pp. 573-5, are accepted, allusions to the London Monument and to the Royal Society. Extensive search has failed to find in the pre-history of aeronautics a *Johnston*, or even a metrically possible

J--n (see Apparatus). Nor is an attempt to fly over the Great Pyramid in Egypt, or any other, upon record. The clue to Oldham's equivalent for 'in caelum iusseris ibit' lies, it seems, in his accommodation of Juvenal to Restoration London, where the Monument, commemorating the Great Fire, was sometimes known as the Pyramid: e.g. in 'Hodge's Vision from the Monument', which moreover Algernon Sidney reported to Henry Savile (Marvell, *Poems*, 3rd edn., i.237) as 'the speech of *Hodge* ... from the top of the *Pyramid*'. The Monument was closely associated with the Royal Society. Wren was consulted about it; Hooke designed it, supervized its erection, and (to confirm its stability) surveyed it in 1679. Its height suggested the Society's using it for barometry and astronomy, though for the latter it proved unsuitable (see Margaret 'Espinasse, *Robert Hooke* (1956), pp. 96 f.; James Elmes, *Memoirs ... of ... Wren* (1823), p. 289; Thomas Birch, *History of the Royal Society, 1660-87* (1856, 1857), iii.463; R.W.T. Gunther, *Early Science in Oxford* (1923-45), vi.526 f.). A corporate body and someone representative of it would be aptly referred to by Oldham's named individual 'and the rest'. I believe he wrote *A---n*. Francis Aston became one of the two Secretaries of the Royal Society on 30 Nov. 1681, and though it was not until Dec. 1682 that he became senior Secretary, from the first he was active in correspondence on its behalf, and seems soon to have taken an increasing share in its business (Birch, op. cit., iii.442, iv.58, 106, 108 f., 112-36 *passim*, 168, 226).

Aeronautical speculation among the Society's parent group is quipped at in Henry Stubbes's *Plus Ultra reduced to a Non Plus* (1670), p. 42: 'the contrivance of *wings* for *mankind*', he recalls, was 'projecting at *Wadham College*'. Hooke continued prolific in theories, designs, and models, and discussed the subject with other Fellows of the Society, Wilkins, Crowne, Moore, Henshaw, Walter Pope, Aubrey, Tompion, and especially Wren (whose 'way of kites' he mentions in his *Diary*, 11 Feb. 1675/6); on 8 May 1679 he initiated a consideration of it at the Royal Society meeting itself (Birch, op. cit., iii.481 f.; Gunther, op. cit., vi.5, 9, 427, vii.517 f., 523; 'Espinasse, op. cit., p. 117; H.W. Robinson and W. Adams (eds.), *The Diary of Robert Hooke 1672-80* (1935), pp. xvii, 70, 107, 109, 129, 273, 359 f., 411). No attempt is known, however, to proceed at the Monument from barometric experiment to aeronautics. Oldham's 'oer the Pyramid' seems to be simply an image for soaring into the heavens. The height both of the London and the Egyptian Pyramids was rhetorically exaggerated. In his ode on Morwent (ll. 773 f.) Oldham had written of the 'fond Aegyptian Fabrick, built so high / As if 'twould climb the Sky', recollecting Propertius' 'Pyramidum sumptus ad sidera ducti' (III.ii.19), whose 'ad sidera' would spring back to mind at Juvenal's 'in caelum' here. 'Th' Aegyptian Pyramids', according to *London's Index, Or Some Reflexions on the New Built Monument* (1676), are now put to shame and 'shrink in their heads', for

> Here's *Pelian* and *Ossa* too:
> *Typhon* had laid a Siege with less a do
> To Heav'n and scal'd the Sky
> Durst he have ventur'd half so high.

125 f. Trade with France was viewed with disfavour, as involving an adverse balance, and introducing effeminate luxuries. It was discouraged, notably by the prohibitions imposed in 1678. These stimulated smuggling. See 'Ode on Jonson', ll. 104 ff., and 'The Careless Good Fellow', ll. 17 f., and nn. The contraband sometimes included the leather goods mentioned by Oldham; a consignment was seized and burnt by the Customs in 1670. Savile writes to Rochester on 26 Jan., facetiously suggesting that as General of the Ballers he ought to take revenge. (Rochester, *Letters*, p. 63.)

131. *the Statute*: the private Act by which (alternatively to letters patent) an alien could become naturalized. There was as yet no general one. See D.C. Agnew, *French Protestant Refugees* (1886), ii.13, 43, etc.

135 f. The observations of a flea and a louse described and illustrated in
Hooke's *Micrographia* (1665), had already furnished Butler and Marvell with
a jest apiece (*Hudibras*, II.iii.305 ff.; 'Last Instructions to a Painter',
11. 16-18); and cf. Etherege's comparison in *The Man of Mode* (1676), II.i.
100: 'a Flea or a Maggot is not made more monstrous by a magnifying Glass'.

137 f. Cf. the simile in Donne's 4th satire, 11. 225 f.:
         ... though his face be as ill
         As theirs which in old hangings whip Christ....

140 f. Sir Martin Mar-all, in Dryden's play of that name (1667, printed
1668), 'sings like a Scritch-Owle', and therefore serenades his mistress in
dumb-show, his man Warner supplying the music from concealment. Unfortunately, he continues the dumb-show after Warner has finished the song. Shadwell alludes to this famous scene in the prologue to *The Humorists* (1671);
and Wycherley in *The Country Wife* (1675), I.i.

143. William Prynne (1600-69) and his fellow-Puritan, John Vicars (1580?-
1652) were versifiers as well as controversialists. Cf. *Hudibras*, I.i.639-
42 (and Wilder's n.):
              Thou that with Ale or viler Liquors
              Didst inspire *Withers*, *Pryn*, and *Vickars*,
              And force them, though it were in spight
              Of nature and their stars, to write ...
and on Prynne, A. B.'s verses before Cleveland's poems:
              When sage George Withers, and grave William Pryn
              Himself, might for a poet's share put in,
and Cowley's scornful references to him, in 'An Answer' (*Poems*, p. 44) as
'the *Homer* of the *Isle*'.

145. The earliest instance in *OED* of 'sham' in the generalized sense of
trickery, hoaxing.

154. *Frize-Campaign*: a campaign coat, such as soldiers wore, made of coarse
woollen cloth. Sedley, preface to *Bellamira* (1687), writes of 'our English
weather, where in the same day a man shall Sweat in Crape, and wish for a
Campagn Coat three hours after'.

155. *beyond Eighty*: degrees of north latitude. Oldham echoes Cowley's 'The
Parting' (*Poems*, p. 117), in which the first stanza begins 'As Men in
Groen-land left' and the third ends ''Tis beyond *eighty* at least, if you're
not here'.

169. Alluding to the 'Italian lock, Custos pudicitiae'. One was preserved
among Tradescant's Rarities. See 'Jesuits IV', 11. 60 ff., n.

176 f. Echoing *MacFlecknoe*, 11. 5 f.

182 f. Cf. Dryden, Epilogue to *Aureng-Zebe* (1676), 11. 20 f.:
              True *English* hate your Mounsieur's paltry Arts,
              For you are all Silk-weavers, in your hearts.
This refers to the riots of the previous August. See *CSPD*, 1675-6, p. 253,
10 Aug. 1675, R. M. to Sir Francis Radcliffe: 'today a great company' of
the London weavers 'fell upon the French weavers, broke all their materials,
and defaced several of their houses'. The Government should 'encourage our
natives more than foreigners'. With intensified persecution in France from
1680, immigration of the Huguenot weavers was increasing rapidly, and the
English government had affirmed a liberal policy toward the refugees by a
proclamation of 28 June 1681.

200 f. The Bankside, Southwark, once the site of the Stews, was still of
evil fame. The fiddler's song in Shadwell's *Epsom Wells* (1673), III.i,
makes reference to 'Suburb debauches': 'Suburbian' was a cant name for a
prostitute.

206-10. Noah and Lot.

215. See 'Boileau VIII', l. 119, and n. Cf. also 'Spencer's Ghost', l. 165.

228 f. See 'Upon a Bookseller', l. 88 and n.

231. *Point*: rich lace.

233. The fashionable cocking of a hat was of moment in the eyes of the town: cf. Etherege, *She wou'd if she cou'd* (1668), III.iii.145: 'never Hat took the fore-cock and the hind-cock at one motion so naturally', and Brett-Smith's n.

235. *grinning scorn*: the mockery of the rabble, so described also in a draft of 'Jesuits III', l. 339 (R185).

238-49. The building and appropriation of pews, beginning apparently in the 16th century, went on rapidly in the 17th, so that in 1714 we read: 'there is one great Fault in the Churches here, which we no where meet with abroad, and that is, that a Stranger cannot have a convenient Seat without paying for it'. (*A Journey through England in Familiar Letters*, i.202, quoted by J. Wickham Legg, *English Church Life* (1914), p. 35.) See also A.C. Heales, *History and Law of Church Seats or Pews* (1872), *passim*. The emphasis thus given to social precedence in church is exemplified in Pepys, 11 Nov. 1660, 30 Mar. and 24 Aug. 1662. The alley (l. 247) is the aisle.

241. *on Bulks begot*: in the street; bulk (*OED*, sb^2), a stall-like projection from the front of a shop.

242 f. Both prosperity and pride are traditionally ascribed to bastards: the superstition 'that Bastards have an unusual share of prosperity and happiness' is recorded by V.S. Lean (*Collectanea* (1902-4), ii.609; cf. Shakespeare, *King John*, I.i.180 f.); and Bailey (*Dictionary*, s.v. Bastard) quotes the proverb 'Bastard brood is always proud'.

243. Cf. R.W., *The English Rechabite* (n.d.), p. 15:
        Pharaoh's chief Butler had by th' Neck been ti'd.
        Had he not had a Proverb on his side....

244 f. Conventional names. An Alderman Gripe is a covetous old usurer in Wycherley's *Love in a Wood* (1672). Traverse's clerk in Shirley's *Honoria and Mammon* (1659), and Justice Trifle's in Davenant, *News from Plymouth* (1635), are each called Dash, since the true scrivener, 'for feare of writing false Latin ... abbreviates the ending ... of his word with a dash, and so leaves it doubtfull' (Wye Saltonstall, 'A Lawyer's Clearke', *Picturae Loquentes*, ed. C.H. Wilkinson, Luttrell Society, 1946, p. 34); moreover, he makes 'the wordes in his declaration spread', to enhance the price, so that 'a Clarke of a swooping *Dash* is [especially] commendable' ('A Puny-Clarke', *The Overburian Characters*, ed. W.J. Paylor (1936), p. 52).

256. Cf. Cleveland, 'The Rebell Scot', ll. 5-7:
        Ring the bells backward; I am all on fire,
        Not all the buckets in a Countrey Quire
        Shall quench my rage.
In the Great Fire, Dryden, in *Annus Mirabilis*, 229.2, depicts how some ran 'for Buckets to the hallow'd Quire'. After the Fire, the Common Council made provision for extra buckets in each ward. See *An Act For Preventing and Suppressing of Fires Within The City of London* (1667).

263-5. Davenant, *The Witts* (1635/6), V, 13^v, refers to this tradition concerning 'the dayes of *Edgar*', when 'they Coyn'd Leather'.

267. *Frize*: coarse woollen cloth, with a nap, usually on one side only.

268-71. Acts for burying in woollen shrouds were passed in 1666, 1678, and 1680. If *Oedipus* (produced Sept. 1678) is damned, it will be, Dryden con-

cludes his Prologue, 'The first Play bury'd since the Wollen Act'. The wool
trade was so important, declares 'Prince Butler's Tale' (1691), *POAS* (1707),
iv.422:

> That since the Living would not bear it,
> They should, when dead, be forc'd to wear it.

See 'Spencer's Ghost', l. 186 and n.

286. The Westminster tombs and the Tower with its menagerie were two of the
sights of London. Cf. Pepys, 3 May 1662, and 23 Feb. 1669. For the Tower,
see 'Art of Poetry', l. 812 n. Dr Walter Pope, in his *Life* of Seth Ward
(1697), p. 147, describes the 'custom for the Servants at the Church upon
all Holidays, *Sundays* excepted, betwixt the Sermon and Evening Prayers, to
shew the Tombs, and Effigies of the Kings and Queens in Wax, to the meaner
sort of People, who flock thither ... and pay their Twopence to see *The Play
of the Dead Volks*, as I have heard a *Devonshire* Clown not improperly call
it'. The price was the same as early as 1651 (Henry Vaughan, 'Upon a Cloke',
ll. 78 ff.). Camden furnished a guide-book: *Reges Reginae, Nobiles et alii
in ecclesia collegiata B. Petri Westmonasterii sepulti*, 1600 (see M. St.
Clare Byrne, *Elizabethan Life in Town and Country* (1925), p. 73 and n. 4).
Cf. also Donne, 'Satyre IV', ll. 75-7, Luttrell, i.368, and Brett-Smith's
n. in his Etherege, p. 317.

291 f. Cf. Butler, *Hudibras*, III.ii.215 f.:

> Toss'd in a furious hurricane
> Did Oliver give up his reign,

and *Flagellum* etc. (1663), p. 206 (n. in Marvell, *Poems*, i.258): 'He dyed
on *Fryday* the said 3d. of *September* at 3 of the clock in the afternoon,
though divers rumours were spread, that he was carried away in the Tempest
the day before.'

293-6. In Davenant, *The First Days Entertainment At Rutland House* (1657),
p. 50, the Parisian critic of London satirically declares that the newer
houses 'are enclosed with Pasteboard wals, ... so slight, and so pretily
gaudy, that if they could move, they would pass for Pageants'. Before the
Great Fire, most of the houses were of timber and plaster; after it, those
which had been burnt, about a fifth of the whole, were rebuilt of brick
with party-walls (P. Cunningham, *Handbook for London* (1849), i.xxvi). Pepys
describes the sudden collapse of a house 'from top to bottom', 14 Mar. 1664,
and reports others blown down 18 Feb. 1662 and 24 Jan. 1666; but on the former occasion the wind was 'such as hath not been in memory before, unless
at the death of the late Protector' (cf. ll. 291 f.).

296. *ensur'd from ... Fire*. Schemes of fire-insurance canvassed from 1660
led up to A. Newbold's of 1 Jan. 1679, published as *London's Improvement
And The Builder's Security Asserted* (1680)—see *A Second Letter to his
Honoured Friend Mr. M.T.* (?Matthew Taubman) [*c.*1682]. This the Common Council took up, but were forestalled by a private company, whose office, advertized in *The True News: Or, Mercurius Anglicus*, 5-8 May, 1680, was 'At the
House late the Ship Tavern, behind the Royal Exchange', the insurance being
'6d in the pound Rent for Brick Houses, and 12d for Timber', less the allowance for ground value. Cf. their *Propositions* (Bodl. Ashmole 1674, LVIII):
see further *Mercurius Civicus, Or, The City Mercury*, for 12, 20, 28 May,
11 June, 1680. The Common Council adopted their own proposals 16 Nov. 1681,
and recriminations kept the subject seething. On the side of the company,
see *Observations on the Proposals of the City to Insure Houses in Case of
Fire* (1681), and on the other, *To my Honoured Friend Mr. M.T. one of the
Committee chosen by the Common Council of London for the Insuring of Houses
from Fire* (1682). The company published *A Table of the Insurance Office* in
1682.

301. Cf. D.H. Lawrence, *Sons and Lovers*: '"... they used to ring the bells
backward for alarm". "How?" said Annie. "A bell sounds the same whether it's
rung backwards or forwards." "But," he said, "if you start with the deep
bell and ring up to thehigh one ...".' Among many 17th-century allusions cf.
Cleveland's in 'To P. Rupert', 1. 18: 'Bels which ring backward in this
great Combustion'.

303-5. Cf. Boileau, *Satires*, pp. 63 f., Satire VI:
              J'entens crier par tout ...
              ... 'Le feu vient de prendre à la maison voisine.'
              Tremblant & demi mort, je me leve à ce bruit....

307-9. One such incident had been reported in the previous few weeks. See
The Loyal Protestant, 28 Mar. 1682: '*Westminster March* 26. This morning
about Two of the Clock happened a dreadful Fire in *Channel-Row*.... Three
or Four persons are reported to be burnt in their beds, and one Maid leaping out of a window to save her self, dyed soon after.'

312. P[orda]ge. See 'Spencer's Ghost', 1. 98 and n.

318. *his Vatican*: his vast library. Cf. Thomas Fuller's reference to a hypothetical library 'exceeding ... many Vaticans, for choicenesse, and rarity'
(*Church History of Britain* (1655), VI. §iv).

326. *interessed*: the old (ME) form of the word, fairly common in the 17th
century.

328. The ceremony at which full degrees (those of Master and Doctor) were
conferred was called at Oxford the Act, at Cambridge the Commencement.

330. Fast days were proclaimed for the Great Fire itself and other great public calamities and crises: the martyrdom of Charles I, the Plague, the wars
with Holland, and the Popish Plot. (Steele, nos. 3410, 3426, 3474, 3558,
3649, 3659, 3683.)

331. *Brief*. See 'Spencer's Ghost', 1. 135 n.; and the briefs for fires at
Newport, Salop, 15 Oct. 1666, and Bicester, 26 Nov. 1667, recorded in Steele,
nos. 3478, 3509.

335 f. Cf. what Evelyn told Pepys about Clarendon's collection of portraits:
'when his designe was once made known, every body who either had them of
their owne or could purchase them at any price, strove to make their court
by these presents; by which meanes he got many excellent pieces of Vandyke
... & the best of our modern masters hands'. (Spingarn, ii.322.) Evelyn
refers to the Van Dykes at Suffolk House, Beaufort House, Lord Sunderland's,
and Sir William Temple's, and to Lord Milford's collection both of Van Dyke
and Rubens (*Diary, passim*); and cf. Dryden, *Essays*, ii.115.

337. Cf. Cowley's 'a hanging ... (The richest work of *Mortclake's* noble
loom)' in his paraphrase upon Horace, Sat. II.vi (*Essays*, p. 415). According to *The Present State Of England. Part III.* (1683), p. '86' [really 93]:
'Our Tapistry-work ... was brought ... by Sir *Francis Crane*', James I giving £2000 towards a building for it at 'Moreclacke'; 'Francis Clein [?Crane]
was the first Designer.'

339. *Scritore*: scrutoire (escritoire); *OED*'s first example is 1678.

351-4. A memorandum of Aubrey's (ii.60) gives an idea of the limited water-
supply of London at this time: 'now (1681/2) London is growne so populous
and so big that the New River of Middleton can serve the pipes to private
houses but twice a weeke'.

356. *Summer*. An authentic idiom: cf. the still current 'to winter'.

358. *Far as S. Michaels Mount.* So Cowley, *Discourse ... Concerning ... Cromwell (Essays,* p. 342): 'as far as from the Mount in *Cornwall'.*

361-74. Oldham owes two instances to Boileau, *Satires,* p. 59, Satire VI:
> Tandis que dans les airs mille cloches émuës
> D'un funebre concert font retenir les nuës;
> Et se mélant au bruit de la gresle et des vents
> Pour honnorer les Morts, font mourir les vivants.

and 'J'entens déja ... / les boutiques s'ouvrir'. Cf. 11. 367 f., 370.

361. The College of Physicians, and the weekly Bills of Mortality. See 'Spencer's Ghost', 1. 230 and n.

365 f. The Middle Region of the air was that in which storms were engendered: Cowley passes through it in st. 3 of his ode 'The Extasie' (*Poems,* p. 204). The air was theoretically divided into a Lower, a Middle, and an Upper Region: see Appendix D in A.W. Verity's 1910 edn. of *Paradise Lost.*

369. *Bell-mens midnight-Rhimes.* The 'bellman's drowsy charm' of 'Il Penseroso' wears a less romantic aspect here. On bellmen's verses, see 'Upon a Bookseller', 1. 65, n.

371 f. Cf. Pepys, 27 Nov. 1660: 'To Westminster Hall, and in King Street there being a great stop of coaches, there was a falling out between a drayman and my Lord Chesterfield's coachman, and one of his footmen killed'; and 22 Dec. 1663: 'I heard of a great fray lately between Sir H. Finch's coachman, who struck with his whip a coachman of the King's, to the loss of one of his eyes.'

373. 'It is very pleasant' says Pepys of W. Stankes the Brampton bailiff, 29 Apr. 1663, 'to hear how he rails at the rumbling and ado that is in London over it is in the country, that he cannot endure it'.

374. *A[rche]r.* The identification, by the 1722 editor, with John Archer (1598-1682), justice of Cammon Pleas, is not wholly satisfactory, for Archer died 8 Feb., before this satire was written, and, since 1672, had been banned from exercising his judicial functions. North (*Lives,* i.63) refers to him, however, as disliking a long cause: and his son had been at St. Edmund Hall at the same time as Oldham.

375 ff. Cf. Pepys, 30 Apr. 1663: 'But Lord! what a stir Stankes makes with his being crowded in the streets and wearied in walking in London.'

385-7. Cf. Boileau, *Satires,* p. 60, Satire VI:
> Là d'un Enterrement le funebre ordonnance,
> D'un pas lugubre & lent vers l'Eglise s'avance;
> Et plus loin, des laquais....

391. See 1. 80 n. The conveyance of Portland stone for the building of St. Paul's is mentioned by Evelyn, 2 Feb. 1695/6.

398 f. The custom persisted in London well into the 18th century; it figures in Hogarth's picture of a London night. Cf. Boswell on the present passage, *Life,* i.119, n. 1.

405 ff. The Scourers had succeeded the Hectors (for whom see 'Juvenal XIII', 11. 285 ff. and n.). In Shadwell's comedy, *The Scowrers* (1691), an assault on the watch is staged, V.i, and Whachum boasts 'I ... demolish Bawdy-houses ... scower the Streets, and the like, as well as any he that swaggers in the Town', and again, 'this morning I ... scower'd like Lightning, and kick'd fellows like Thunder, ha, ha, ha'. Cf. *The Character Of A Town Gallant,* 1680 ('July 28', Luttrell, *Catalogues;* 1st edn. 1675). History records the exploits of 'some young gentlemen of the Temple' at the King's Head in Chancery Lane, 13 Jan. 1681/2 (Luttrell, i.158); and of Philip,

Earl of Pembroke, who, having already had one victim in 1678, killed a Mr
Smith in a midnight scuffle in 1680; see *Great and Bloody News, from Turn-
ham Green, or a Relation of a sharp Encounter between the Earl of Pembrook,
and his Company, with the Constable and Watch belonging to the Parish of
Chiswick*, 1680 ('Aug. 25', Luttrell, *Catalogues*); *Great News from Saxony*
('Aug. 30. 1680.', op. cit.).

418. A proclamation by the Lord Mayor, 29 Nov. 1679 (Bodl. Nichols Newspapers, I.b) complains of 'The neglect of the Inhabitants of this City, in
hanging and keeping out their Lights at the accustomed hours, according to
the good and Antient usage of this City, and Acts of Common Council in that
behalf.'

426. *P[reston]*. Christopher Preston (1628 or 1629-1709), keeper of the
Hockley-Hole Bear Garden. I saw in Sir Charles Firth's collection a broadside, undated but belonging to 1709 (see Luttrell, vi.491), entitled *The
Bear-Garden in Mourning. Or, An Elegy On The Death of Mr. Christopher
Preston, Master of Her Majesties Bear-Garden at Hockley in the Hole, who
was torn to pieces last Night, being Sunday, the 18th of September, by one
of his own Bears, in the 81st Year of his Age*.

448. *Padders*: footpads; see 'Juvenal XIII', l. 39 and n.

449. *the Exchanges*: the Royal Exchange (see 'Boileau VIII', l. 97 n.) and
the New Exchange, with its two long double galleries of shops, frequented
by people of fashion. Etherege's *She wou'd if she cou'd* (1668), III.i, is
laid here (see further, Brett-Smith's n., p. 130; cf. 'Counterpart', l. 108).

449-51. An expansion of Juvenal's
            ... postquam omnis ubique
            fixa catenatae siluit compago tabernae ...
after Boileau, *Satires*, p. 62, Satire VI:
            Car si-tost que du soir les ombres pacifiques
            D'un double cadenas font fermer les boutiques,
            Que, retiré chez lui, le paisible Marchand
            Va revoir ses billets, & compter son argent,
            Que dans le Marché-neuf tout est calme et tranquille....

452. Shooters Hill had long been famed for robberies (see *The Enterlude of
Hyck-scorner*, in *Six Anonymous Plays, First Series*, ed. J.S. Farmer, pp.
139, 144, 153), and was so still: on 11 Apr. 1661 Pepys rode under a thief
hanging in chains there, *in terrorem*.

454. Cf. Boileau, *Satires*, p. 63, Satire VI:
            La bourse: Il faut se rendre: ou bien non, resistez;
            Afin que votre mort, de tragique memoire,
            Des massacres fameux aille grossir l'Histoire.
Juvenal has only 'interdum et ferro subitus grassator agit rem'.

458. *Heptarchy*. The seven Saxon kingdoms into which Britain, according to
16th- and 17th-century historians, was long divided. Milton, in his *History
of England*, reckons the Heptarchy as lasting from the 6th century until
about 800.

460. See 'Upon a Bookseller', ll. 73 ff., and 'Spencer's Ghost', ll. 77 f.,
and nn.

476 f. Oldham's Latin text evidently read:
            ... saturarum ego, ni pudet illas
            adiutor gelidos veniam caligatus in agros.
The better reading is now acknowledged to be 'auditor'.

A Dithyrambique on Drinking

The change in the published heading as compared with the autograph (see Apparatus) is without doubt an authentic revision, made, however, to conceal the original spokesman, a dramatization of Rochester. As in the parallel case of the 'Aude aliquid. Ode', the autograph title, because it preserves the conception which governed the writing of the poem, has been preferred. In the print, the final stage-direction, 'Tries to go off, but tumbles down, and falls asleep', belongs to the afterthought of 'The Drunkards Speech in a Mask' and must accompany it to the Apparatus. That sub-title is imitated from Waller (i.111) 'The Miser's Speech. In a Masque'. The stage-direction was suggested by a note of Cowley's to his 'Praise of Pindar' (st. 2, n. 1) seminal, evidently, for the 'Dithyrambique' from the start. Oldham's Greek epigraph comes from it (and as witnessing to his Cowleian inspiration, and not clashing with the autograph title, is here retained from the print). Dithyrambic, says Cowley, 'was a bold free *enthusiastical* kind of Poetry, as of men inspired by *Bacchus*, that is, Half-Drunk, from whence came the *Greek Proverb*,

Διθυραμβοποιῶν νουν ἔχεις ἐλαττονα—
You are as mad as a *Dithyrambique Poet.*

And another,

Οὐκ ἐστὶ Διθυραμβος ἄν ὕδωρ πίνῃ—
There are no *Dithyrambiques* made by drinking water.

Something like this kind (but I believe with less *Liberty*) is *Horace* his 19 Ode of the 2 B.... And nearer yet to it comes his 25 Ode of the 4 [i.e. 3] B. *Quo me Bacche rapis tui plenum?* ... For he is presently *half-mad*, and promises I know not what, ... and then he ends like a man ranting in his drink, that falls suddenly asleep.' The first Greek proverb was evidently taken by Cowley from Erasmus' *Adagia*. Erasmus' comment is close in spirit to Oldham's poem:

Id est, Haud Dithyrambus est acquam si potitet.
Non est hilaritas cum deest vinum. Excitat enim
Vini calor inveniendi vim, quae torpet nonnumquam
in jejunis: movet phantasias, addit impetus,
subministrat fiduciam. (*Adagia*, 1666, p. 466).

Oldham's 'Dithyrambique' combines the concept of the genre as Cowley describes it, and his personal knowledge of Rochester, 'extravagantly pleasant' (so Burnet depicts him) when the 'heat of his fancy' was 'inflamed by Wine'. For this, and the place of the poem among those Oldham devoted to the cults of Rochester's circle, see Introduction, pp. xliii f., and nn. 66, 67, 69.

Three passages of the autograph, absent from the published text, are given in Appendix II.3 (R206-211, 213). It was certainly Oldham's intention (and no doubt on critical grounds) to omit them. He used an altered version of the first in 'Horace II.xiv' written, apparently, later than the 'Dithyrambique', but published before it.

1 f. Cf. Cowley, 'Wisdom' (*Poems*, p. 86):
'Tis mighty *Wise* that you would now be thought
With your grave *Rules* from musty *Morals* brought.

3. *chowse*: to cheat; for the derivation, from cha͞ush, a Turkish official
messenger, in consequence of an incident of 1607, see *Jonson*, x.61 (citing
Sir William Foster's edn. of *The Travels of John Sanderson*; Foster's account
supersedes that in *OED*). Cf. 'Aude aliquid. Ode', l. 66.

4. The earliest instance in *OED* of 'Sham' meaning 'one who tries to delude'.

9. *It is resolv'd.* Cf. 'Jesuits, Prologue', l. 32.

12. For this drinking custom cf. *King William's Welcome To Ireland* (1690,

Pepys Ballads, ed. Rollins, v.170): 'Boys, let Healths go round, with Knees to the Ground', and Pepys, 23 Apr. 1661 (Coronation day).

14-17. See the ode on Atwood, ll. 102-4, and n., quoting Cowley and Burton for 'all in all and all in every part'; cf. Tilley A133, and A. Williams, 'A Note on Samson Agonistes, Ll. 90-4', *MLN*, lxiii (1948), 537. The localization or otherwise of the soul was much canvassed: cf. *Samson Agonistes*, ed. A.W. Verity, ll. 91-3 and n., citing Milton's *De Doctrina Christiana* and St. Augustine; and cf. Cleveland, 'On P. Rupert', ll. 103 ff., and 'Upon the King's return from Scotland', ll. 3-5. 'All ev'ry where, like *Mans*, must be the Soul', asserts Cowley ('Ode of Wit', *Poems*, p. 17).

21. There follow in R207 twelve lines on Louis XIV as 'Th'ambitious busling Monarch of the times', for which see Appendix II. A variant, shorter form of them had appeared in 'Horace II.xiv', included by Oldham in *Some New Pieces* (1681); no doubt one of his reasons, for dropping them from the final text of the 'Dithyrambique'. Cf. also 'The Careless Good Fellow', ll. 31 ff.

22-8. Epicurean philosophy, from its axiom that the gods dwell in eternal and perfect felicity, concluded that they were free of all care for the world and its sorrows (ll. 34-7), and were beings wholly contemplative (l. 38) since 'beatam vitam in animi securitate et in omnium vacatione munerum ponimus' (Cicero, *De Natura Deorum*, I.xx). Oldham's proof that they drink (ll. 39 f.) is parallel with Philodemus' argument, from the same axiom, that they must have the power of speech, since otherwise they would lack the highest bliss (of converse with their equals).

32 f. Cf. 'St. Ambrose', ll. 58, 60; 'The Dream', ll. 71 f.; and the ode on Atwood, ll. 220 f.

34 f. Alluding to the Stoic doctrine of the anima mundi: cf. Seneca, *Naturales Quaestiones*, VI.16, and Cicero *De Natura Deorum*, II.xii. Cf. the Morwent ode, ll. 392-4.

39. A variation on Cowley's address to Love, in 'The Request' (*Poems*, p. 65):
        I'le think Thee else no *God* to be;
        But *Poets* rather *Gods*, who first *created Thee*.

41. *runst half share*. So the autograph, rightly; in the first edition 'runst' has been misread 'must', an easy error of minims as Oldham writes initial r. In the phrase 'to run ... fortunes' (*OED*), as here, 'run' has somewhat the sense of 'partake'.

46 f. Cf. 'Homer', ll. 89 f., 'Boileau VIII', ll. 142 ff., and nn.

50. A variant of 'Sardanapalus', l. 35. For 'Universal Monarchy', cf. 'Jesuits III', l. 65 and n.; and *A Representation of the Present Affairs ... of Europe* (1676/7), p. 14: Charlemagne's division of his kingdom made 'an Eclyps in the Universal Monarchy, which the French at this day endeavour with so much zeal to retrieve'.

50. For six lines of the fair copy (R208) dropped at this point, see Appendix II.

54. Cf. 'Juvenal XIII', ll. 118 f. India was distant just about half a year's sailing. The *Court Minutes Etc. Of The East India Company* (1907), calendared by E.B. Sainsbury, show that the East Indiamen of Charles II's reign took over a year for the round voyage; the *Mary*, for example, dispatched to Surat in Apr. 1674, was back shortly before 12 July 1675. The passage itself used to take six or seven months; William Basse's fleet made the longer voyage to the Coromandel Coast from Dec. 1672 to July 1673. (See Sainsbury, op. cit.; Edward Terry, *A Voyage to East India* (1655); E. Keble Chatterton, *The Old East Indiamen*, 1914.)

57-60. Cf. Alexander Radcliffe's burlesque of 'Tell me dearest prythee do' in *The Ramble* (1682), p. 28:

Tell me *Jack*, I pry'thee do
Why the Glass still sticks with you:
What does Bus'ness signifie
If you let your Claret die?...
                    If it stand
                    In your hand
            It will then disband
        All its Spirits in a trice.

65. Cf. Cowley, 'Anacreontiques: II. Drinking' (*Poems*, p. 51).
        The busie *Sun* (and one would guess
        By's drunken fiery face no less)
        Drinks up the *Sea*....

69. *Six in a Hand*: a toper's idiom unknown to the *OED*. Its currency is con-
    firmed by John Dennis (*The Impartial Critick* (1693), Spingarn, iii.167):
    'He who Drinks five Brimmers in a hand' is drinking hard. The meaning has
    to be conjectured from Oldham's use, and from 'A Letter sent from a gentle-
    man to his friend', in *A Collection Of Poems Written upon Several Occasions
    by several Persons* (1673), p. 131:
            Seven Brimmers in a Hand went round
            In which seven worthy Wights were drown'd.
    Occurrences in Robert Gould's 'Satyr Upon Man' (*Poems*, 1689, p. 187) and
    Ambrose Philips (*Poems*, ed. M.G. Segar (1937), p. 105, reported by Anthony
    W. Shipps, *N & Q*, Dec. 1975, p. 562), palpably derive from Oldham. In the
    'Letter', there are seven successive toasts; but in Oldham 'Six' cannot
    refer to the number of toasts, nor, in view of 'Six more', to the number of
    drinkers. His lines can be reconciled with the 'Letter' if both the 'Six'
    and the 'Seven' 'in a hand' refer to the measures of wine ordered for each
    drinker, ready for filling and re-filling his glass. In the 'Dithyrambique',
    where all is hyperbole, the glasses would be outsize ones holding three
    measures, and filled twice for each toast, making twelve measures quaffed in
    all—the Roman *sextarius*. Martial often mentions the measures to be mixed or
    poured out; and potations of eleven (Epigram VI.lxxviii) are frequently and
    disastrously drunk by Phryx, his arch-tippler. The possibility (it is no
    more) that Oldham is thinking in these terms is discussed in Brooks, 'Old-
    ham: Some Problems', pp. 570 f.

71-80. Oldham gives a different turn to ideas expressed in the *Second Advice
    To A Painter*, 1667 (No. 10 of Osborne's bibliography; cf. Yale *POAS*, i. 42),
    where the author damns Noah for inventing ships:
            What tho he planted Vines, he Pines cut down;
            He taught us how to drink, and how to drown....

80. For two lines of the fair copy (R210) dropped at this point, see Appen-
    dix II.

81-3. Cf. the opening of Cowley's 'Answer to ... Verses' (*Poems*, p. 43): 'to
    a *Northern People*' to whom 'the Sun' assigns no wines, 'A rich *Canary Fleet*
    welcome arrives'.

103. *Schoolmen*: definition by distinctions and nomenclature being their
    special talent; cf. 'Jesuits II', l. 119 (with erratum, 'Title') and n.

104-6. Oldham's note opposite this passage (R211), 'Ebrietas e̅ voluntaria
    insania. Senec.', is from Seneca's *Epistulae Morales* LXXXIII.18. Seneca is
    thus the 'sober Fool' etc. of ll. 124 f.

105. *reas'ning Tool*. In Rochester's 'Satyr against ... Mankind', which Old-
    ham transcribed, Man is scornfully termed 'the reasoning engine' (l. 29).

108. *young Prophets*. Cf. 'The Dream', l. 75 f. and n.

110. Like the Apostles at Pentecost: Acts 2:13-18.

115. Thorn Drury, in his copy of Oldham in the Bodleian, illustrates this
bravado by a quotation from D'Urfey, *The Campaign* (1698), p. 11: 'drink 'em
alive in Plantain Wine like de Losh', and continues: 'In an interleaved copy
of Ray's Proverbs 2^d. ed^n p. 72 opposite "He hath swallowed a Gudgeon" there
is this MS note: "taken from the custom of swallowing Loaches in wine once
a fashion amongst Gentlemen afterwards descended to the vulgar—see Memoirs
of P.P. in Swifts Works at the latter end: a gudgeon being larger would take
a larger gulp".'

116 f. Cowley alludes to the arrival of rich Canary fleets in the passage
cited above, ll. 101 ff., n. Oldham's hyperbole stretches the revellers'
pockets as extravagantly as their throats: the custom alone, in an exceptionally good year, might be £80,000 or more; see *The True News* quoted in
'Horace, I.xxxi', ll. 15-18 n.

120-3. Rhenish follows Canary: the Rhineland was part of the Holy Roman Empire and the Canaries belonged to Spain. From Aug. 1673 to the peace of
Nijmegen in 1678, Charles II of Spain and the Emperor Leopold I, with Holland and the Duke of Lorraine, were confederates in the Grand Alliance of
the Hague against Louis XIV. Both Spanish and Imperial forces were operating
against Louis in Aug. 1677.

125. *Langon*: a white wine, named from Langon on the Garonne. The *OED*'s earliest example, under Langoon, is dated 1674.

126-8. Charles V, Duke of Lorraine (1643-90) joined the confederation against
Louis XIV primarily to recover the duchy which his father had sold to Louis
by the treaty of Montmartre. This poem was written at the moment of his
maximum success as generalissimo of the imperial forces. He had taken
Philippsburg in 1676; in 1677, to co-ordinate his efforts with those of
William of Orange, he moved westward to the Meuse. The *London Gazette*s of
late July and early Aug. report his burning of Mousson; Champagne, it is
supposed, lies at his mercy. Hence the rosy estimate of his military (and
bibulous?) chances by our rhetorical toper.
  'Without treaty' signifies 'by forcing an unconditional surrender'; but
there may be a specific allusion to the negotiations for peace at the con-
gress of Nijmegen opened in Mar. 1677.

135 f. Cf. Etherege, *Comical Revenge* (1664), I.ii.118: in a drunken revel
Sir Frederick Frollick, Jenny tells, 'march'd bravely at the rere of an
Army of Link-boys'; and Dryden's depiction of Shadwell (not published till
c.10 Nov. 1682: Macdonald, p. 31) in *Absalom*, Pt. II, ll. 458-60.

137 f. From Flatman, 'To the Memory of the Incomparable Orinda' (1667),
ll. 25 f.:
> Sooner or later must we come
> To Nature's dark retiring room.
The Cambridge History of English Literature, viii.84, inadvertently de-
prives Flatman of his due credit by praising Oldham's line without indicating its indebtedness.

Stage direction. See headnote.

REMAINS

Advertisement (anon., in Hindmarsh's edn.)

The Advertisement was written either by or for Hindmarsh. He is entitled to
claim that he has deserved well of Oldham and his readers. For the *Remains*,
in an age when many posthumous collections were thoroughly untrustworthy,
includes none but genuine pieces; for their authenticity, see Introduction,

pp. lxxv ff. With two exceptions, our texts are from *Remains* (1684); for 'Upon the Marriage' and the St. Cecilia ode, see headnotes.

10. *his first Pieces*. Hindmarsh did not yet know of the lines on William and Mary: four years before he brought out *SJ* (1681) they had been printed by Herringman. They do not appear in the *Remains* till the second edn. (1687).

18-20, 23-5. In posthumous editions, writers, so Cowley complains (*Works*, 1656, preface: see *Poems*, p. 5) commonly suffer either by 'the indiscretion of their *Friends*, who think a vast *heap* of Stones or Rubbish a better Monument, than a little *Tomb* of *Marble*, or by the unworthy avarice of some *Stationers*, who are content to diminish the value of the *Author*, so they may encrease the price of the *Book*.'

Counterpart to The Satyr against Vertue

It is pretended in the sub-heading that the 'Counterpart' is not by the real author of the original 'Satyr'. Oldham may have meant to circulate it under this fiction. It was no doubt written before (as author of *SJ*, 1681) he had acknowledged the 'Satyr', and belongs to 1679 or 1680.

29-31. Cf. Cowley, 'The Constant', *Poems*, p. 135:
   Close, narrow *Chain*, yet soft and kind,
  As that which *Spi'rits* above to *good* does bind, ...
  Which does not *force*, but *guide* our *Liberty*!
and 'Presenting a Book to Cosmelia', ll. 18-20.

32-6, 39. Cf. 'St. Ambrose', ll. 131-6.

55. *Trepans*: snares; see *OED*, 1671.

56-60. Indebted, with st. 5, to Cowley's discourse 'Of Liberty': the 'true Freeman ... [is] Not he who blindly follows all his pleasures ... but he who rationally guides them' (*Essays*, p. 384).

61-3. Cf. Cowley, 'The Plagues of Egypt', *Poems*, p. 219:
   In black *Egyptian Slavery* we lie;
   And sweat and toil in the vile Drudgerie
     Of *Tyrant Sin*....

71. *th' Almighty Wand*. Moses' rod is so termed three times in st. 3 of Cowley's 'Plagues of Egypt': '*Almighty*', he explains in n. 4, 'as it was the *Instrument* of the *Almighty* in doing wonders; for which it is called the *Rod* of the *Lord*.'

73. *Writ of Ease*: a certificate of discharge from employment. Cf. Dryden, *All for Love* (1678), Epilogue, ll. 18 f.

74-86. Cf. Cowley, 'Of Liberty' (*Essays*, pp. 377 f.): 'The great dealers in this world may be divided into the Ambitious, the Covetous, and the Voluptuous, and ... all these men sell themselves to be slaves.'

75. Cf. ibid., p. 384: 'The Covetous Man is ... *ad Metalla damnatus*, a man condemned to work in Mines, which is the lowest and hardest condition of servitude.'

76 f., 78, 83. Cf. Cowley, 'Ode. Upon Liberty' (*Essays*, p. 388):
   And they'r in Fortunes Bridewell whipt,
   To the laborious task of Bread;
  These are by various Tyrants Captive lead.
  ... Ambition with imperious force [rides them].
See R.S. Mylne, *Old Bridewell* (1905). It was, as described in Strype's Stow (1755), p. 644, a house of correction for 'idle and loose Livers ... taken up' in the 'Liberty of Westminster': besides whipping, they were condemned to 'Beating of Hemp, a Punishment very well suited to Idleness'.

82. 'I like not such grinning honour as Sir Walter hath. Give me life',
Falstaff's speech (1 *Henry IV*, V.iii.58 f.), a Restoration favourite. Cf.
Pepys, 2 Nov. 1667; Dryden, Prologue to *Marriage-A-La-Mode*, l. 18, and
Preface to *All for Love* (*Essays*, i.198); *Merry Drolleries*, ed. Ebsworth,
p. 36. See 'Boileau VIII', ll. 130 f. and n.

95 f. Cf. Cowley, 'Against Hope' (*Poems*, p. 109):
> Thou bringst us an *Estate*, yet leav'st us *Poor*,
> By clogging it with *Legacies* before!

103-8. Cf. Cowley, 'The Bargain' (*Poems*, p. 92):
> The foolish *Indian* that sells
> His precious Gold for Beads and Bells,
> Does a more wise and gainful traffick hold,
though the allusion, from *Othello* onwards, was a commonplace: Rochester has
it ('The Advice'), and Dryden (*The Maiden Queen* (1667), V.i, p. 56), and
the anonymous 'Consideratus, Considerandus' (for which see 'Aude aliquid.
Ode', ll. 26 ff., n.).

108. *an Exchange's Frippery*. Cf. Pepys, 10 Apr. 1663, and Etherege, *She wou'd
if she cou'd* (1668), III.i, laid in the New Exchange, 'a building on the
south side of the Strand ... with ... galleries of shops, one above the
other. All fashionable London frequented these shops to buy the newest expensive trifles.' (Brett-Smith's n., p. 310.)

109-13. Cf. Cowley, 'Against Hope' (*Poems*, p. 110):
> Good fortunes without gain imported be
> Such mighty *Custom*'s paid to Thee.

114-18. Cf. Cowley, 'Of Obscurity' (*Essays*, p. 309): 'I love ... a true good
Fame, because it is the shadow of Virtue.... The best kinde of Glory, no
doubt, is that which is reflected from Honesty ... but it ... is seldom
beneficial to any man whilst he lives, what it is to him after his death,
I cannot say.'

119-22. Cf. Cowley, 'The Complaint' (*Poems*, p. 440):
> Thou who rewardest but *with popular breath*,
> And that too after death,
and the preface to his works (*Poems*, p. 6), where fame is called 'this
posthumous and imaginary happiness' (italics mine).

130 f. Cf. *Paradise Lost*, I.690-3.

131 f. Cf. Settle, *Empress of Morocco* (1673), p. 34:
> Oh Prophane Gold, which from infectious Earth,
> From Sulph'rous and Contagious Mines takes Birth....
> Rapes, Murders, Treasons, what has Gold not Don?

138-42. Cf. Settle, ibid., p. 59:
> Guilt onely thus to guilty Minds appeares:
> As Syrens do to drowning Mariners:
> Seen onely by their Eyes whose Deaths are Nigh.
> We rarely see our Crimes before we Die....
and Oldham's 'Sunday Thought in Sickness', ll. 105 ff.

160. *Regalio*. Properly 'regalo', a choice repast or entertainment; 'regalio'
was common in Oldham's time: cf. e.g. Dryden, Prologue to *Sir Martin Mar-
all* (1667), ll. 1 f.

178. Identical with 'Sardanapalus', l. 9. For explication, see Introduction,
pp. lxxiv f., and nn. 176, 177.

187. Alluding to the supposed three regions of the air: cf. Dryden, *The Rival
Ladies* (1664), I.iii, p. 17: 'His Voice is soft as is the upper Air.'

188 f. Cowley speaks of 'my own Pindarick Liberty' in his 'Ode. Mr. *Cowley*'s
Book presenting it self to the [Bodleian]'; cf. his description of 'the
Pindarique way' in the 'Ode. Upon Liberty' (*Poems*, p. 410, *Essays*, p. 391).
Cf. Horace, 'Odes', IV.ii.7 f.

193 f. *its Horrors*. The original edition has 'it', at this date almost certainly an oversight; see Marvell, *Poems*, 'Eyes and Tears', 1. 38 n. Oldham
has 'it' for 'its' in MS R, but that also is probably a slip.

196. *dare ... be good*. Cf. 'I dare be good' in Settle, *Empress of Morocco*
(1673), V.i, p. 57; and Donne, 'To the Countesse of Salisbury, August 1614',
1. 31: 'now you durst be good'.

Virg[il], Eclogue VIII

See Introduction, p. lxxvi.

7 f. Alluding to the naval battles of the second and third Dutch wars, 1665-
7 and 1672-4.

42. *the Nut-scramble*: for 'sparge nuces'. As the bride approached, the bridegroom flung nuts among the boys carrying the torches. Cf. Catullus, LXI,
11. 128 ff.

70-4. The allusion is to Medea at Corinth.

82 f. i.e. Let Tityrus be the Orpheus of the woods and the Arion of the
waves. As a pentameter 1. 83 is highly irregular: 'Ĭn thĕ Wŏods / Ŏrphĕus /
aňd Ar/ĭŏn ŏn / thĕ Sĕa'.

120. *true-love-Knots*: felicitously rendering 'Veneris vincula'.

168. *our Lightfoot*. Marvell had used the name in 'A Dialogue between Thyrsis
and Dorinda', 11. 23 f.:
> No need of Dog to fetch our stray,
> Our Lightfoot we may give away....

In *The Shepherds Week, Thursday Or, the Spell*, which partly imitates Virgil's eighth eclogue, Gay in the corresponding passage has: 'But hold—our
Lightfoot barks, and cocks his ears'.

Upon the Marriage of the Prince of Orange with the Lady Mary

Princess Mary's marriage to William of Orange, negotiated mainly by Temple and
Danby, 'gave great content to the nation, and abated the fears of popery that
she was married to a Protestant prince'. (Reresby, p. 129.) William landed
at Harwich 9 Oct. 1677; the match was announced to the council 21 Oct., and
the marriage solemnized at 9 p.m. on Nov. 4; (see *The Diary of Dr. Edward
Lake*, ed. G.P. Elliott, *Camden Miscellany*, i (1847)). Oldham's poem was written
next morning, and a copy conveyed to Mary: see his Latin draft letter (Introduction, p. xxix and nn. 19, 20). It was the first of his pieces to be printed:
Herringman's s. sh. fol. was licensed by L'Estrange Nov. 8, 1677 (*Bibliography*,
II.1). Our text is from the autograph fair copy; see Introduction, pp. lxxxviii,
xciii.

The occasion inspired numerous panegyrics. Herringman printed Waller's *Of the
Lady Mary* in a s. sh. edn., licensed Nov. 2. (Cf. also Waller's *To the Prince
of Orange 1677*; Nat Lee's *To the Prince and Princess of Orange, Upon their
Marriage* (*Examen Poeticum* (1693), p. 168; *POAS* (1704), iii, p. 114); *A Congratulatory Poem On Occasion of His Highness the Prince of Orange His Marriage*
(anonymous, s. sh., BL, Luttrell, i.115); and a MS copy of verses addressed on
the same subject by A. B. to Secretary Williamson (*CSPD*, 1677-8, p. 480).

0.1. The date of composition is given from Oldham's fair copy, R27, confirmed by his draft letter (ibid., p. 106).

10 ff. Prior to the marriage, the betrothal had occasioned great rejoicing. William Temple says of its announcement in council, 'it was ... received there and every where else in the Kingdom with the most universal joy that I ever saw any thing in the King's reign'. (*Memoirs*, 1692, p. 296.) Dr Edward Lake, who performed the ceremony, records in his *Diary* 'Nov. 5. The lord mayor and aldermen came to congratulate the marriage, and there was a generall joy throughout the city, testifyed by ringing of bells, bonfires etc.'

12 f. For the wild rejoicings at the Restoration see Evelyn, 29 May 1660, and Cowley's 'Ode. Upon His Majesties Restoration and Return', st. 16 (*Poems*, p. 430).

15. A draft of this single line (R103) reads 'That shakes ... ye Town'.

19. Alluding to the Great Fire, 1666.

26-9. Cf. in *J. Cleaveland Revived* (1659), p. 51, 'Upon the Marriage of the young Prince of Orange [William II] with the Lady Marie' [daughter of Charles I], by Richard West (see Cleveland, *Poems*, ed. Morris and Withington, p. xxx):

> ... wedding's a too private stile, for this
> Not a plain ... match, but a league is,
> A league that shall incorporate these two
> Nations....

31 f. Cf. Cowley, 'Ode. Upon His Majesties Restoration and Return' (*Poems*, pp. 420-1):

> ... ye peaceful *Starrs*,
> Which meet at last so kindly, and dispence
> Your universal gentle Influence ...
> *Plenipotentiary Beams* ye sent....

34-6. Cf. Cowley, 'On his Majesties Return out of Scotland' (*Poems*, p. 23):

> 'Twas only *Heav'n* could work this wondrous thing,
> And onely work't by such a *King*.

37-9. Cf. ibid., p. 22:

> Others by *War* their *Conquests* gain ...
> This happy *Concord* in no *Blood* is writ....

41. *Ancestor*: James VI of Scotland and I of England.

53. Cf. 'Another upon the Same' (as Paynter's poem; see above, 11. 26-9 n.):

> Here Faith and Reason courts, this Match doth prove
> Wisdom in Youth, and Policy in Love.   '

54, 58 f. Cf. ibid.:

> Nor were their Hearts link'd by the Painters Hand,
> Or Legates Voice, such Bonds are Ropes of Sand;
> They their own Counsel, happier steps have trod,
> Who not salute the Image but the God.

57. The same compliment is in 'To Madam L. E.', 1. 65 f.

61. According to Burnet (ii.130), Mary's father James, Duke of York, 'with a seeming heartiness gave his consent in very obliging terms', though when the match was proposed he had 'seemed much concerned; but the king said to him, Brother, I desire it of you for my sake as well as your own: and upon that the duke consented to it'.

64 f. In 1676 Louis had taken Condé and Bouchain; in 1677 he took Valenciennes, 17 Mar., and Cambrai, 5 Apr.; William was obliged to raise the sieges of Maestricht and Charleroi, and on 11 Apr. was defeated at Mont-Cassel while endeavouring to relieve St. Omer which subsequently capitulated. With the exception of Maestricht, however, these towns were not Dutch; they belonged to the Spanish Netherlands.

66 f. Cf. Cowley, 'Leaving me ...' (*Poems*, p. 79): 'The *Universal Monarch* of her *All*'. Louis XIV's conquests, which William is to discount, were seen as a bid for Universal Monarchy; cf. 'Dithyrambique', l. 50 and n., and *The Petty-Southwell Correspondence* (ed. Lansdowne, p. 93), 20 Aug. 1681: anciently 'to conquer the [sparsely populated] World' was easy, but '(whatever the King of France may think) the Universall or Great Monarchy doth ... grow every Century ... more difficult'.

69. Despite their recent successes in Flanders (ll. 64 f. and n.), the French had failed to subjugate William. Called to the Stadtholderate to repel their invasion of the United Provinces in 1672, by the end of 1673 he had cleared Dutch territory of their troops.

72-6. As Stadtholder, William of Nassau was not a crowned head.

91. The line as Oldham revised it; see Introduction, p. lxxxviii. A draft, R92, reads 'for others you in Pitty'.

92. *your bright self*. The phrase as finally revised; see Textual Apparatus and Introduction, p. lxxxviii f.

92 f. The compliment is skilful: Queen Henrietta Maria was William's grandmother as well as Mary's. Her children were Charles II, 1630-85; Mary, Princess of Orange, 1631-60; James, Duke of York (James II), 1633-1701; Princess Elizabeth, 1636-50; Henry, Duke of Gloucester, 1640-60; and Henrietta, Duchess of Orleans, 1644-70.

94-7. Cf. Cowley, 'On Orinda's Poems' (*Poems*, p. 405):
            And in their Birth thou no one touch dost find,
          Of th' ancient curse to Woman-kind,
            Thou bringst not forth with pain,
      It neither Travel is, nor labour of the brain.

98 f. It was hoped that the marriage would hasten peace between France and the States General. 'Nephew,' said Charles II to William, 'remember that love and war do not agree well together.' Very shortly after the marriage, fresh terms were offered to Louis (Burnet, ii.130, 132 n.). The Franco-Dutch peace was signed 10 Aug. 1678.

100. Cf. 'Bion', ll. 79 ff., ode on Morwent, ll. 350 ff.; ode on Atwood, l. 192, and nn.

105. Cf. Dryden's *State of Innocence* (1677), III.i, p. 15: Eve to Adam: 'Heaven ... / Can give no more, but still to be the same.'

107, 110 f. Cf. 'To Madam L.E.', l. 155 f.

An Ode For ... S. Cecilia's Day

The first edition (*Bibliography*, II.13) was *A Second Musical Entertainment Perform'd on St Cecilia's day. November XXII. 1684. The Words by the late ingenious Mr. John Oldham*, set ... *by Dr John Blow, Master of the Children and Organist of His Majesty's Chappel-Royal* (1685). Published by John Playford, it is announced in an advertisement in his *Theater of Musick* (1685), A2ᵛ, as 'now in the Press' and 'to be performed at the Musical Feast on St

Cecilia's day next, Nov. 22. 1684'. The entertainments were inaugurated in
1683 when the ode was set by Purcell to Christopher Fishbourn's words. Oldham's ode is reprinted (p. 143) and discussed (pp. 16-19) in W.H. Husk, *An
Account of the Musical Celebrations of St. Cecilia's Day* (1857). If Husk is
right in supposing it commissioned after the success of its predecessor, it
must have been written between 22 Nov. and Oldham's death in the first week
of Dec. 1683. In Dec. 1949 the first modern revival of the ode was conducted
by my old friend Dr H. Watkins Shaw, the authority on Blow, in a Blow ter-
centenary concert at St Martin's in the Fields. He has an edition, John Blow,
Begin the Song (1950), and tells me that the work is of some importance in
the evolution of secular choral style in England, and includes an exceedingly
fine ground bass to the tenor and alto duet.

1-11, 40-5. A draft of the Chorus and 1st st. (R240) reads: [*Chorus, 4 ll
... without 42 f.*] Let Musick 44; [*Stanza 1, whole*] Awake ye silent Lute
[sparkling *margin*] 2; Joyn ye Voice & joyn ye Flute 3; let 4; gentle
Thoughts yt easy glide [*margin*] 5; Numbers smoothly slide [*margin*; slide
altered from glide] 6; Hand & 7.

1, 4. Cf. Cowley, 'The Resurrection' (*Poems*, p. 182): 'Begin the Song, and
strike the *Living Lyre*', to which 'the *Years to come*' with 'equal measures
dance'.

15. Cf. 'Bion', 1. 39.

19. See 'To Madam L.E.', 1. 63 f., n.

22. Cf. Settle, *Empress of Morocco* (1673), p. 18: 'We'd antidate our Bliss',
and Marvell, 'Dialogue between Thyrsis and Dorinda', ll. 27 f.; cf. 'The
Dream', 1. 74; 'To Madam L.E.', 1. 93.

25. *pall'd*. See 'A Dithyrambique', ll. 57-60 and n.

31 f., 34. Cf. Rochester, 'A Letter from Artemisia', which Oldham had transcribed:
    Love, the most generous passion of the mind,
    The softest refuge innocence can find ...
    That cordial drop heaven in our cup has thrown ... (ll. 40 f., 44).

To Madam L. E.

Resemblance to the consolatory poem for Joan Kingscote strongly suggests that
this too was addressed, in 1675 (the year Oldham spent, after Oxford, at
Shipton Moyne), to a local patron. An Estcourt seems likely. I have found
none with the initial L; but it might well stand for 'Lady'. If the autograph,
Hindmarsh's copy, was headed with a bare 'To L.E.' (cf. 'To L.G.' heading a
draft, R99, for 'Upon a Woman') he might be expected to add 'Madam'.

1-4. Ll. 3 f. were adapted in ll. 19 f. of 'A Letter'. Cf. Cowley, 'To the
Bishop of Lincoln' (*Poems*, pp. 28 f.):
                Pardon, my Lord, that I am come so late
                T'express my joy for your return of Fate ...
                Great *Joys* as well as *Sorrows* make a *Stay*;
                They hinder one another in the Crowd....

10. So in Waller's 'Thyrsis, Galatea' (1. 12), Thyrsis would 'to my aid invoke no muse but you'.

23 f. Cf. 'Katharine Kingscote', ll. 19 f.

31 ff. Cf. Cowley's metaphor in 'To Dr. Scarborough' (*Poems*, p. 198):
                The subtle Ague, that for *sureness* sake
                Takes its own times th'*assault* to make,
                And at each *battery* the whole *Fort* does shake....

33 f. Cf. Waller, 'À la Malade', ll. 7-9:
                    Hence, to this pining sickness (meant
                    To weary thee to a consent
                    Of leaving us)....

39 f. Cf. Dryden, 2 *Conquest of Granada* (1672), IV.iii, p. 129: 'My Blood, like Ysicles, hangs in my veins'.

41 f. Cf. Cowley, 'Ode. Upon Dr. Harvey' (*Poems*, p. 417): the 'Heart began to beat ... The tuneful March to vital Heat'.

44. Reversing Dryden, 1 *Conquest of Granada* (1672), I.i, p. 2: 'And a short youth runs warm through every Vein'. Cf. 'Byblis', l. 267.

46. Because it would be praying for the dead.

49-52. Cf. Donne, 'Funeral Elegy. To L.C.', ll. 23-6.

57 f. Cf. 'A Letter', l. 7 n.

63 f. Combining Waller, 'Chloris and Hylas', l. 3: 'Wind up the slack'ned strings of thy lute', and Settle, *Empress of Morocco* (1673), p. 19:
                    Tortures weak Engines that can run us down,
                    Or skrew us up till we are out of tune.

65 f. Cf. 'Upon the Marriage', ll. 56 f.

68. *A post-Angel*. From Cowley, 'Hymn. To light' (*Poems*, p. 444). Cf. Oldham's 'Sunday-Thought in Sickness', *Remains* (1684), p. 45.

70, 73, 74. *it ... It ... her*.... The lapse is probably Oldham's. The same confusion occurs in the ode on Morwent (ll. 475-80; see n.); and there it does not seem possible that it was produced by corruption.

75 f. Cf. Dryden, 2 *Conquest of Granada* (1672), IV.i, p. 118:
                    Like tapers new blown out, the fumes remain,
                    To catch the light, and bring it back again.

79 f. Cf. Waller, 'To the Queen ... After her happy recovery from a dangerous sickness', ll. 17 f.:
                    When that which we immortal thought,
                    We saw so near destruction brought.

81 ff. I have found no clue to this physician.

93. See 'S. Cecilia Ode', l. 22 and n.; and 'The Dream', l. 74.

97-100. Cf. Waller, 'Upon the death of my Lady Rich', ll. 21 ff.: the fellow-immortals of 'The Paphian queen' were 'Taught by her wound that goddesses may bleed'. The allusion is to Aphrodite wounded by Diomede, *Iliad*, V.330 ff.

101. Cf. Settle, *Empress of Morocco* (1673), p. 26:
                    ... Princess, to whom Heav'n
                    Has all its Titles but its Knowledge givn.

103 f. Cf. Denham, 'An Elegie upon ... Lord Hastings', *Poetical Works*, p. 146:
                                        ... He,
                    That onely wanted Immortality
                    To make him perfect....

106-8. Cf. Waller, 'À la Malade', ll. 22 ff.:
                    ... as ... sickness does invade
                    Your frailer part, the breaches made
                    In that fair lodging, still more clear
                    Make the bright guest, your soul, appear.

109 f. Cf. Cowley, 'My Heart Discovered' (*Poems*, p. 79):
> ... through her flesh, methinks, is seen
> The brighter *Soul* that dwells within:

and with the same rhyme as Oldham's, Dryden, 'Upon the Death of the Lord Hastings', ll. 63 f.

111-14. Cf. Cowley, 'Clad all in White' (*Poems*, p. 78):
> Thy *soul*, which does it self display,
> Like a *star* plac'd i'th' *Milkie* way.
>
> 4.
>
> Such robes the *Saints* departed wear,
> Woven all with *Light* divine;
> Such their exalted *Bodies* are....

L. 109 was clearly suggested by the first st. of the same poem.

117-19. Cf. the thought in Cowley's 'To the Bishop of Lincoln' (*Poems*, p. 29):
> Your very sufferings did so graceful shew,
> That some straight *envy'd* your *Affliction* too.

120 f. Cf. Cowley, 'Clad all in White' (*Poems*, p. 78):
> So *clouds* themselves like *Suns* appear,
> When the *Sun* pierces them with Light ...

and the Morwent ode, ll. 428 f.

122-5, 128 f., 134 f. Cf. Waller, 'To the Queen ... After her happy recovery from a dangerous sickness', ll. 3 ff.:
> ... every day,
> Restoring what was snatched away
> By pining sickness from the fair,
> That matchless beauty does repair
> So fast, that the approaching spring,
> (Which does to flowery meadows bring
> What the rude winter from them tore)
> Shall give her all she had before.

130-3. Cf. Waller, 'Of the Misreport of her being painted', ll. 19 ff.:
'heaven'
> Paints her, tis true, and does her cheek adorn
> With the same art wherewith she paints the morn;
> With the same art wherewith she gildeth so
> Those painted clouds which form Thaumantias' [sc. Iris'] bow.

131. *instant Day*. 'Instant' may mean 'oncoming' (Lat. 'instans'); see *OED*, and is therefore retained. But it may be a misprint for 'infant': cf. Oldham's favourite image of the blush of infant roses: 'To Cosmelia', ll. 35 f.; ode on Morwent, ll. 554 f.; and 'Horace, IV.13', ll. 9 f.

152. *Bottom*: the skein from which the thread was drawn (hence the apt name of Bottom the Weaver).

155 f. Cf. 'Upon the Marriage', ll. 107, 110 f.

On the Death of Mrs. Katharine Kingscote

The parish register of Kingscote, near Shipton Moyne, records: 'Katherin Kingscote the daughter of Abraham Kingscot. Gent. and Joane his Wife and borne the 20th day of July and was Baptised the 28th day of July 1664'; and 'Mistris Katherin Kingscote the daughter of Mrs. Joane Kingscote died the second day of December and she was buried the sixt day of December ... 1675.' See Introduction, p. xxvii; and for the Kingscotes, T.D. Fosbroke, *Berkeley Manuscripts* (1821), pedigree facing p. 218; his *Abstracts of Records* ...

respecting the County of Gloucester (1807), i.420 f.; also the *Visitation of
... Gloucester*, 1682 and 1683, ed. Fenwick and Metcalf (1884), p. 103. Oldham
had contemplated a poem of consolation directly addressed 'To Mrs Kingscot on
the Death of her Daughter': R238 has a draft opening:

> Madam,
>
>   when late your Tenderness resign'd
>   The dearest Pledge Fate here had left behind;

—Joan was widowed in 1670—

>   When she and all your Joy with her withdrew, .
>   Gone to make Heaven rich by robbing you:
>   Ah! by what Griefe were both your Hearts opprest
>   What just Concerns divided either Brest!
>   Her Soule with more Regret did not desert
>   Its happy Mate, then you from both did part:
>   And twas for her much easier to subdue
>   The Pow'rs of Death then to relinquish you.

1 f., 5 f. Cf. Robert Wild, 'In Memory of Mrs. E. T., who died April 7,
   1659':

>   Meantime, methought I saw at Heaven's fair gate
>   The glorious virgins meet and kiss their mate ...
>   The Milky Way too (since she passed it o'er)
>   Methinks looks whiter than it was before....

3 f. Cf. Cowley, 'To the New Year' (*Poems*, p. 206):
>   Great *Janus*, who dost sure my *Mistris* view
>   With *all thine eyes*, yet think'st them all too *few*....
   Cf. 'Rant', 1. 15 f. and 'Catullus VII', 1. 10.

5-8. Oldham makes use of these 11. in the ode to Atwood, 11. 207-10.

12. Cf. Waller, 'À la Malade', 1. 3: 'Is heaven become our rival too?'

17-27. Used again in 'To Cosmelia', 11. 41-51.

21-3. Cf. Waller, 'Upon the Death of my Lady Rich', 11. 86 ff.:
>   We should suppose that some propitious spirit
>   In that celestial form frequented here,
>   And is not dead, but ceases to appear.

26 f. Imitated from Waller; see 'To Cosmelia', 11. 50 f., n.

28 f. Cf. Cowley, 'On the Death of Mr. William Hervey' (*Poems*, p. 35):
>   Nor did more *Learning* ever crowded lie
>   In such a short *Mortalitie*.

32. Mary Magdalene, out of whom went seven devils.

41-6. Adapted in 'To Cosmelia', 11. 27-32.

43-6. Cf. Cowley, 'The Innocent Ill' (*Poems*, p. 145):
>   Though in thy thoughts scarce any Tracks have bin
>   So much as of *Original* Sin,
>   Such charms thy Beauty wears as might
>   Desires in dying confest *Saints* excite.

47 f. Cf. Cowley, 'On the Death of Mr. William Hervey' (*Poems*, p. 36):
>   With as much Zeal, Devotion, Pietie,
>   He always *Liv'd*, as other Saints do *Dye*.

To The Memory of Mr. Charles Morwent

The bosom friend of Oldham's young manhood had his grammar-school education at Wotton-under-Edge, under Thomas Byrton, MA, of Lincoln College, Oxford. At 15 he matriculated at St. Edmund Hall; he was, writes Anthony Wood, a 'handsome, genteel and good-natur'd man, very well belov'd' at the Hall. After taking his BA in 1674, he 'retir'd to Gloucester', where, still only twenty, he died of smallpox, 25 Aug. 1675 (monumental inscription, Gloucester Cathedral). He was b. at Tetbury, where his father Joseph was an attorney. Through his mother, Mary, née Savage, he was nephew (by marriage) to William Shepheard of Horsley (the next village to Kingscote), an active Oliverian lawyer and commissioner, whose last book came out in 1675; Mary's sister Elizabeth m. William's brother John of Tetbury. Elizabeth left a small legacy to 'my Kinsman Charles Morwent' (Will, 27 Dec. 1669, in Gloucestershire Record Office, proved 24 Aug. 1671). For the possible importance in Oldham's career of this Morwent—Shepheard connection, see Introduction, pp. xxvii f. and n. 13. Cf. Wood, iv.121; Tetbury parish register; *Visitation of the County of Gloucester ... 1682 ... 1683* (1884), ed. Fenwick and Metcalf, p. 159 (pedigree of Savage); T.D. Fosbroke, *Abstracts ... respecting the County of Gloucester* (1807), i.374, and *An Original History of the City of Gloucester* (1819), p. 136; A.T. Lee, *History of ... Tetbury* (1857), pp. 234, 240; Ralph Bigland, *Historical ... Collections, relative to the County of Gloucester* (monumental inscriptions at Tetbury and Hempstead); Joseph Foster, *Alumni Oxonienses*, Memoir, 1722, pp. iv f.

Only a preference for metaphysical over Augustan writing can have led A.W. Ward (*DNB*, Oldham) to regard this as the author's best performance. A similar overestimate no doubt prompted Previté-Orton's belief (*CHEL*, viii.84), echoed to me by Oliver Elton, that he must have elaborated it in his maturer years. It no longer seems beyond his early powers when its dependence on antecedent elegies and eulogies is recognized. Even the opening of st. 21, with its genuinely metaphysical overtones, is in a style from which he and the age moved away. Among the numerous borrowings, none is from a work later than 1675. Many of the lines appear almost verbatim in other poems of his; surely because (as in other instances) he cannibalizes freely from a piece which, far from embellishing, he has no intention of bringing out. During 1675, the year he spent chafing at home, he would have the leisure, and not improbably the inclination, to dwell on the death of the friend who might have made Gloucestershire more congenial to him, and to elaborate a long poem upon it.

1 f.   Cf. James Graham, Marquis of Montrose, lines on Charles I (*Poems*, ed. J.L. Weir (1938), p. 33):

> Great, Good and Just, could I but rate
> My Grief and Thy too Rigid Fate....

5-8.   The other eight Muses should change their own strains to that of Melpomene, Muse of tragedy. Oldham had probably a hint from the conclusion of Cowley's elegy on Lord Carleton (*Essays*, p. 40) where Calliope (though Muse of epic poetry) 'would sing a Tragicke Verse', and the tears of the Nine would have been sufficient to create their sacred spring.

12-15.   The statue of Memnon in Egyptian Thebes gave a mournful note when struck by the rays of the rising sun.

35.   i.e. aimed at the bull's eye; cf. 'Art of Poetry', l. 568, and Cowley, 'Ode. Upon Liberty', st. 6 (*Essays*, p. 391).

38-40, 55-63.   Cf. Waller, 'Epitaph ... Upon ... the only son of the Lord Andover', ll. 15-20:

> Like buds appearing ere the frosts are passed,
> To become man he made such fatal haste,
> And to perfection laboured so to climb,
> Preventing slow experience and time,
> That 'tis no wonder Death our hopes beguiled;
> He's seldom old that will not be a child.

52-4. Cf. Donne, 'Elegie on the Lady Marckham', 1. 60: 'Lest they that heare her vertues, thinke her old.'

64. Cf. Waller, on the death of Lady Hamilton, 'Thyrsis, Galatea', 1. 26: 'So well she acted in this span of life'.

73-80. Cf. R. Fletcher, 'An Epitaph on his deceased Friend', printed as Cleaveland's in *J. Cleaveland Revived* (1659):

> Each minute had its Weight of Worth,
> Each pregnant Hour some *Star* brought forth
> So whiles he travell'd here beneath,
> He liv'd, when others only breath.
> For not a Sand of time slip'd by
> Without its Action sweet as high.

85 f. See 'Upon a Woman', 11. 62 f. and n.

87. *run o'th' Score.* See 'Upon a Woman', 1. 155 n.

90 f. Cf. Cowley, 'The Soul' (*Poems*, p. 83):

> If all things that in *Nature* are ...
> Be not in Thee so' *Epitomiz'd* ...

and Donne, 'Obsequies to the Lord Harrington', 11. 77 f.

92. Cf. J.M.'s elegy, before *J. Cleaveland Revived* (2nd edn., 1660), p. 3:

> What in other petty Sparks was found
> In him's contracted as one Diamond.

95-8. Cf. Donne, 'A Valediction: Of Weeping', 11. 10-13:

> On a round ball
> A workeman that hath copies by, can lay
> An Europe, Afrique, and an Asia,
> And quickly make that, which was nothing, *All*....

Donne's terrestrial becomes in Oldham a celestial globe.

101 f. Cf. Cleveland, 'To P. Rupert', 11. 61 f.:

> ... all that were
> The wonders of their Age, constellate here,

and Dryden, 'Upon the Death of the Lord Hastings', 11. 33-5. In the Ptolemaic astronomy, the fixed stars were assigned to a sphere outside those of the seven planets but within the crystalline and primum mobile; cf. *Paradise Lost*, III.481-3, and Cowley's 'Reason. The use of it in Divine Matters', st. 5.

110 f. Oldham will have in mind Donne's 'Obsequies to the Lord Harrington', 11. 87-92, where with a fine audacity he describes the intuitive power of angels.

114 f. Cf. 'Upon the Marriage', 11. 96 f.

116 f. Athene sprang fully armed from the head of Zeus. Oldham's simile is consonant with the legend as given in Stesichorus and the Homeric Hymns. It is Pindar who relates that Hephaestus assisted the birth by cleaving his father's head with an axe.

127. Aristoxenus 'thought soules made / Of Harmony' (Donne, 'An Anatomy of the World', *Poems*, p. 240; see Grierson's n. citing Burton, *Anatomy*). Cf., once more, Donne's 'Obsequies to the Lord Harrington' (11. 1-3).

134-210. Cf. sts. IV and V of the ode on Atwood.

143-5. On Morwent as both of Oldham's neighbourhood and a general favourite at college, see headnote.

148-50. Cf. Dryden, 1 *Conquest of Granada* (1672), III.i, p. 24:
> This Godlike pity in you I extoll;
> And more, because, like heav'ns, 'tis general ...
and the ode on Atwood, 11. 110 ff.

152. Cf. ibid., III.i, p. 29: 'And I'm corrupted with the pow'r to please', and the ode on Atwood, 1. 106.

160-7. For the anecdote of the Emperor Titus (AD 41-81) to which Oldham alludes, see Suetonius, *De Vita Caesarum VIII*, Titus, viii: 'atque etiam recordatus quondam super cenam, quod nihil cuiquam toto die praestitisset, memorabilem illam meritoque laudatam vocem edidit: "Amici, diem perdidi".'

167. The ancients 'measured the hours ... by ... water in glasses called Clepsydrae'. (Browne, *Pseud. Ep.*, V.xviii.259.)

176 f. Cf. the ode on Atwood, 11. 108 f.

198. *symbolize.*Originally a technical term of early physics, used of elements or other substances having qualities in common. Hence to symbolize with something meant to partake of its qualities or nature (*OED*).

201 ff. Cf. Cowley, 'Davideis',
> Thus when two *Brethren strings* are set alike,
> To *move* them *both*, but *one* of them we *strike* ...
[*Poems*, p. 254.]
> The common Experiment of Sympathy in two Unisons ...
[*Poems*, p. 276 n. 39.]

213-18. Cf. Cowley, 'Ode (Here's to thee *Dick*)', *Poems*, p. 26:
> Neither their *Sighs* nor *Tears* are true;
> Those idely blow, these idlely fall....

222-4. Cf. 'David's Lamentation', 11. 221 f., where the debt to Cowley is apparent.

225-32. Balsam. See Pliny, *Natural History*, XII.54, and cf. Vaughan, 'An Epitaph Upon The Lady Elizabeth', 11. 23-5:
> And yet as *Balm-trees* gently spend
> Their tears for those, that doe them rend,
> So mild and pious thou wert seen....
On similar passages, see J.B. Leishman, *The Art of Marvell's Poetry* (2nd edn., 1968), pp. 159 f.

237. *acts of Amnesty.* Cf. the fragment on the death of Charles I, 11. 7 f. The Act of Indemnity and Oblivion, pardoning all (save the individuals excepted by name) who had taken part in the Rebellion or the Commonwealth governments, received the royal assent 29 Aug. 1660.

238-41. Cf. Cicero, *De Finibus*, II.xxxii.104: 'Themistocles quidem, cum ei Simonides an quis alius artem memoriae polliceretur, "Oblivionis", inquit, "mallem; nam memini etiam quae nolo, oblivisci non possum quae volo".'

247. Cf. Cleveland, 'The Antiplatonick', 1. 16: 'A Flint will break upon a Feather-bed'.

252. Cf. the ode on Atwood, 1. 188 and n.

256 f. Cf. 11. 520 ff. below, and 'Aude aliquid. Ode', 11. 265-7.

265-9. Cf. Cowley, 'To the Duchesse of Buckingham' (*Essays*, p. 52): if she had lived in primitive times, she would have had her apotheosis, and been idolatrously worshipped. Cf. the ode on Atwood, 11. 138 ff.

289 f., 298 f. Cf. Dryden, 2 *Conquest of Granada* (1672), III.i, p. 102:
> Not new-made Mothers greater love express
> ... when with first looks their babes they bless.
> Not Heav'n is more to dying Martyrs Kind;
> Nor guardian Angels to their charge assign'd ...
and 'David's Lamentation', 11. 212 f.

304. Cf. Cowley, 'My Fate' (*Poems*, p. 126):
> The fast-link'd *Chain* of everlasting *Fate*
> Does nothing tye more strong than *Me* to *You*,
and Donne, 'The Second Anniversary', 11. 143 ff.

307-9. Cf. 'David's Lamentation', 11. 210 f.

313 f. There was no image of Vesta, goddess of the hearth, in her temple in the Forum; an undying fire, tended by the Vestal Virgins, was the symbol of her presence.

317 f. e.g. the legendary Orestes and Pylades, Achilles and Patroclus, Theseus and Pirithous, Aeneas and 'fidus' Achates, Nisus and Euryalus.

327 f. Cf. 1. 127 and n.

331-8. Cf. 'Counterpart', 11. 56-60.

341. A line from Settle's *Empress of Morocco* (1673), I.i, p. 4.

344. Cf. R. Fletcher, 'On the death of ... Charles late King of England', printed as Cleveland's in *J. Cleaveland Revived* (1659):
> But an Eternal Hush, a quiet Peace ...
> Shall lull Humanity asleep....

346. *Time's ... feet.* Used in a simile for gentleness by Henry Vaughan, 'To ... Mrs. K. Philips', 11. 5 f.

350 ff. Cf. Marvell, 'The Character of Holland', 11. 129 f.:
> As the obsequious Air and Waters rest,
> Till the dear *Halcyon* hatch out all its nest.
and n. (*Poems*, 3rd edn., i.313): 'According to the ancients a fortnight's calm was created at about the winter solstice while the halcyon brooded on her floating nest.'

353-6. The Pacific: see *OED*. Whence did Oldham derive the notion that it was tideless (an epithet, normally, of the Mediterranean)?

357-61. A mind where Waller finds 'No cloud in so serene a mansion', 'holds resemblance', he declares, 'with those spotless skies, / Where flowing Nilus want of rain supplies' ('The Apology of Sleep', 11. 23-6). The simile was a commonplace: cf., e.g. Waller, 'A Panegyric to my Lord Protector', 11. 53 f.; Dryden, 2 *Conquest of Granada*, III.i, p. 102. On the belief cf. Browne, *Pseud. Ep.*, VI.§8.

385 f. Cf. Cleveland, 'The Hecatomb to his Mistresse', 11. 29 f.:
> Mettals may blazon common beauties, she
> Makes pearls and planets humble herauldry.

389-91. Alexander; cf. 'Homer', 11. 89 f. and n.

392-4. The Stoics supported their doctrine of the anima mundi by an argument from the soul in man. See Cicero, *De Natura Deorum*, II.xi, vii. Cf. 'A Dithyrambique', 11. 34 f. and n.

398. Cf. Jonson's chorus, *Catiline*, III.868 f., moralizing not on pride, but ambition: 'the eye / To which things farre seem smaller than they are'.

401, 403. Unrhymed, by oversight.

415 f. Cf. Waller, 'Of the Misreport of her being painted', ll. 9 ff.:
        ... unconcerned, she [Sacharissa] seems moved no more,
        With this new malice than our loves before;
        But from the height of her great mind looks down
        On both our passions without smile or frown.
See 'Upon the Marriage', l. 72 and n.

417. Cf. Dryden, *The Rival Ladies* (1664), I.ii, p. 13:
        I am no more afraid of flying Censures,
        Than Heav'n of being Fir'd with mounting Sparkles.

419 f. Cf. Waller, 'Of the Misreport of her being painted', ll. 1 ff.:
        As when a sort of wolves infest the night
        With their wild howlings at fair Cynthia's light,
        The noise may chase sweet slumber from our eyes,
        But never reach the mistress of the skies....

426. *Saint disgrace*: sanctify disgrace. For the verb, see *OED*.

428 f. Imitated from Cowley: see 'To Madam L. E.', 120 f. and n.

430-2. Cf. Cowley, 'To the Bishop of Lincoln' (*Poems*, p. 29):
        So though less worthy stones are drown'd in *night*,
        The faithful *Diamond* keeps his native *Light*,
        And is oblig'd to *Darkness* for a ray
        That would be more *opprest* than *helpt* by Day,
and Dryden, *The Maiden Queen* (1667), V.i, p. 56: 'So Stars in Night, and
Diamonds shine in Jet.'

433 f. Cf. the last line of the epitaph on Abia Qui.

442. *soothing Smiles*. Cf. 'Byblis', l. 30 and n.; 'Jesuits III', l. 474 and
n. For the bad sense of 'soothe' at this period cf. Otway's *The Orphan*
(1680), II.i, p. 20: 'Trust not a man ... / I charge thee let no more
Castalio sooth thee'.

443-6. Cf. 'Counterpart', ll. 87-94, 137-42; and pseudo-Denham, *Second Advice
to a Painter* ('Nay Painter, if thou dar'st'), 1667 (Osborne, No. 10):
        Ulysses so, till Syrens he had past
        Would by his Mates be pinion'd to the Mast.

449. Adapted in 'St. Ambrose', l. 154.

450. Capricio: an obsolete form of capriccio; a freak, prank, or caprice, in
which sense Oldham employs it in l. 4 of the fragments 'In Praise of Poetry'.

450 ff. See 'Aude aliquid. Ode', headnote; and the ode on Atwood, ll. 161-8.
Cf. also *The Character Of A Town Gallant*, 1680 (first published 1675): 'He
defies *Heaven*, worse than *Maximine*; ... and calls the *Devil*, the Parsons
Bugbear.... He denies there is any Essential Difference betwixt *Good* and
Evil, deems *Conscience* a thing only fit for *Children*, and ascribes all
Honesty to *simplicity*, and an unpractisness in the *Ways* and *Methods* of the
Town.'

462. Cf. 'Jesuits III', l. 283.

472 f. Cf. 'Counterpart', ll. 32 f.

475-80. The confusion of 'its' and 'her' in this stanza cannot be cured by
emendation, and is presumably due to the author: the same fault occurs
below, l. 700, and in the poem 'To Madam L. E.', ll. 70, 73, 74.

482-5. Cf. 'Aude aliquid. Ode', ll. 142-4 (143 n.), 150, 74; 'Jesuits I',
ll. 104 ff. and n., III.242 and n.

509. *Debauches*. See 'Aude aliquid. Ode', l. 170 n.

509-17. Cf. ibid., 11. 120-8, and the citations from Rochester, ibid.,
11. 108 ff., n.

518. Adapted in 'To Cosmelia', 1. 17 f. (see n.).

521. *half-strain*: deriving only on one side from a good stock. Cf. Dryden,
Amboyna (1673), V.i, p. 57: 'Sure you think my Father got me of some *Dutch*
Woman, and that I am but of a half straine courage'.

533. *Efforts*. See 'Byblis', 1. 335 and n.

536. Cf. Browne, *Religio Medici*, I.xlvii: 'I found upon a naturall inclination, and inbred loyalty unto vertue, that I could serve her without a
livery.' Livery meant originally an allowance of food, provisions, or cloth-
ing dispensed to retainers or servants.

544 f., 547-50, 552-7. Adapted in 'To Cosmelia', 11. 23 f., 5 f., 25 f., and
33-8. 'Horace, IV.13', 1. 10, adapts 1. 554.

550. *the learned Porch*: the Stoic school of philosophers (from the Painted
Porch, the public ambulatory at Athens frequented by Zeno and his disciples).

560-2. Combining Waller, 'On the Picture of a Fair Youth taken after he was
dead', 11. 15 f.:
>   [Her] mutual love advanced the youth so high
>   That, but to heaven, he could no higher fly.
and Donne, 'The Second Anniversary', 11. 501-3:
>   Shee, who left such a bodie, as even shee
>   Only in Heaven could learne, how it can bee
>   Made better....

565. *the active Sphere*: the primum mobile; cf. Cowley, 'On the Death of Mr.
William Hervey' (*Poems*, p. 36):
>   ... the First and *Highest Sphere*
>   Which wheels about, and turns all *Heav'n* one way.

568-71. Suggested by Cowley: see 'Promising a Visit', 11. 9-12, and n.

576-80. Bajazet, emperor of the Turks, was enslaved by Tamburlaine, and at
last dashed out his brains against the bars of the cage in which he was
kept. The usual version of the story makes the cage an iron one, but relates
that Bajazet on his first capture was thrown into golden chains. See Mar-
lowe, *Tamburlaine*, ed. Una M. Ellis-Fermor, pp. 28 f.

594. Aches is a dissyllable, ache being then pronounced as the name of the
letter 'h' now is.

597. The Gemonies were steps on the Aventine at Rome, to which the bodies of
executed criminals were dragged to be thrown into the river. Here the word
is given the figurative sense of 'tortures', a misapplication for which
OED quotes, besides the present passage, R. Fletcher's 'A Survey of the
World' (1656, printed as Cleveland's in *J. Cleaveland Revived*, 1659).
Fletcher and Oldham were drawing upon what they had been taught. In d'As-
signy's *Treatise of the Roman Antiquities*, for example, appended to P. Gaut-
ruche, *The Poetical Histories* (1671), a textbook used at St. Edmund Hall in
Oldham's time (it is listed among John Freind's books, MS Top. Oxon. f. 31),
we are told that some describe gemonies thus: 'The Executioner did fasten
a Hook in the mouth of the poor wretch, and did dragg him through the streets
from his Prison to this infamous place, and then he did cast him down headlong into the River, or did burn him, as some do relate' (p. 131).

613-16. Cf. Waller, 'The Countess of Carlisle in Mourning', 11. 5 ff.:
>   A spark of virtue by the deepest shade
>   Of sad adversity is fairer made;
>   Nor less advantage does thy beauty get ...

and 'The Night Piece; Or, a picture drawn in the dark', ll. 21 f.:
>   Like jewels to advantage set
>   Her beauty by the shade does get....

Cf. also Dryden, *The Maiden Queen* (1667), V.i, p. 56: 'Deep shades are thus to heighten colours set'.

621-4. Cf. Waller, 'Instructions to a Painter ... 1665', ll. 95 f.: 'Thus flourish they ... / As dying tapers give a blazing light'.

634 f. Cf. Thomas Shipman, 'The Old English Gentleman' (written 1665), *Carolina: Or, Loyal Poems* (1683): 'A *well-built-Arch* is stronger by its weight'. Cf. Marvell, 'The First Anniversary', ll. 95 f.:
>   ... the resistance of opposed Minds
>   The Fabric, as with Arches stronger binds....

640 ff. Cf. Waller, 'To the King, Upon His Majesty's Happy Return', ll. 95-8:
>   Rude Indians, torturing all the royal race,
>   Him with the throne and dear-bought sceptre grace
>   That suffers best. What region could be found,
>   Where your heroic head had not been crowned?

650 f. In *Tyrannick Love* (1670), I.i, p. 6, Dryden writes of the Christian martyrs:
>   Not *Mucius* made more hast his hand t'expose
>   To greedy flames, than their whole bodies those.

651. Cf. 'Aude aliquid. Ode', l. 7.

653. Cf. Cowley, 'Davideis' (*Poems*, pp. 331, 359): '*Lambent* fire is, A thin unctuous exhalation made out of the Spirits of Animals, kindled by Motion, and burning without consuming any thing but it self. Called *Lambent*, from *Licking* over, as it were, the place it touches. It was counted a *Good Omen*.'

654. *Empyreum*: the fiery sphere, the Heaven of Heavens in which dwells God Himself. Cf. Cowley, 'Davideis' (*Poems*, p. 251): 'Here peaceful Flames swell up the sacred place', and the ode on Atwood, ll. 197 ff.

665. *dry Martyrdom*. There is no satisfactory parallel to this use of 'dry' in *OED*. It may be merely intensive, signifying 'actual, or very Martyrdom': perhaps it is allied to sense 19: 'Of money, rent, or fees, paid in hard cash, in actual coin ... 1656. J. Harrington *Oceana* (1700) 36. Worth a matter of four million dry rents', i.e. actual income.

687 f. Cf. 'St. Ambrose', l. 100 and n.

692. *Mormo*: Bugbear; the word was originally Greek and meant a hideous she-monster. See *OED*.

700. For the confusion between 'it' and 'her', see above, ll. 475-80 n. Since it is perhaps the author's, I have not removed it.

710, 714. Cf. Cowley, 'The Extasie' (*Poems*, p. 265):
>   I touch at last the spangled *Sphære* ...
>   An unexhausted *Ocean* of *delight*
>   Swallows my senses quite....

715-20. Cf. the ode on Atwood, ll. 213 ff.

717 f. *Regalio's ... Joys ... fills ... cloys*. A conjectural emendation of the reading of 1684: '*Regalio's* ... Joy, ... fill, ... cloy.' *Regalio's*, one suggests, was taken for a plural (nominative plurals in 's were neither uncommon nor etymologically incorrect); the verbs 'fills' and 'cloys' were made plural to agree with it, and the noun 'Joys' singular to preserve the rhyme. For Regalio, see 'Counterpart', l. 160 and n.

721 ff.   For this idea, cf. Donne, 'The Second Anniversarie', ll. 299 ff.:
'In heaven thou straight knowst all, concerning it', etc.

724-6.   Cf. 'Rant', ll. 18, 21; Donne, 'Obsequies to the Lord Harrington',
ll. 35 f.:
        Though God be our true glasse, through which we see
        All, since the beeing of all things is hee ...
and Cowley, 'Ode. Of Wit' (*Poems*, p. 18):
        ... the *Primitive Forms* of all
        Which without *Discord* or *Confusion* lie,
        In that strange *Mirror* of the *Deitie*.

736 ff.   These extravagant lines recall Dryden's 'Upon the Death of the Lord
Hastings' (ll. 55-66), especially
        So many Spots, like *næves*, our *Venus* soil?
        One Jewel set off with so many a foil? ...
        Or were these Gems sent to adorn his Skin,
        The Cab'net of a richer Soul within?
        No Comet need foretel his Change drew on,
        Whose Corps might seem a *Constellation*.

758 f.   Cf. 'Upon a Woman', ll. 34 f. and n.

766-84.   Cf. 'Homer', ll. 132-72 and the passage there cited from Cowley.
With ll. 769, 778-81, cf. the opening of Cowley's 'Ode I. On the praise of
Poetry', *Essays*, p. 59.

771-4.   Propertius couples the Mausoleum and the Pyramid in similar terms in
Elegies, III.ii.19, 21-2. See 'Aude aliquid. Ode', ll. 193 ff. and nn.

To the Memory of ... Mr Harman Atwood

Harman Atwood, lord of the manor of Sanderstead and patron of the living, d.
16 Feb. 1676/7, aged about 69, and was buried on the 22nd. He improved the
family estate, acquiring Chesham Court in 1668, and in 1676 building a manor-
house at Sanderstead, which was about 3 miles from Croydon and a little further from Beddington. Like John Spencer, and the three uncles of Sir Nicholas
Carew, he was of the Inner Temple. His niece, Joan Atwood, m. John Shepheard,
the Whitgift schoolmaster, 23 Sept. 1675; their son, Atwood Shepheard, was b.
16 Nov. 1678; she d. 25 Nov. 1679. (Her d. is misdated 1769 in Manning and
Bray, II.573.) See further *Parish Registers of Sanderstead*, ed. W. Bruce Banner
man (1908); John Aubrey, *Surrey*, ii.62, monumental inscriptions; *Surrey Archaeological Collections*, xiv.26-9; *Calendar of the Inner Temple Records*, ed. F.A.
Inderwick (1896), iii.117; Joseph Foster, *Al. Oxon.* Even before Shepheard became schoolmaster, Harman took a benevolent interest in the Hospital: under
Christmas, 1674, the account book records his sending 'this q^{ter} 20^s to the
Box, a bounteous Benefactor Dei Gratias'. For his numerous major pious chari-
ties, and good standing in his profession, see below, ll. 21 ff. and 71-124,
150-204 nn. 'His reputation can never die', affirms Aubrey (op. cit., ii.60)
'while any respect is due to so singular Virtue, or while the celebrated Oldham bears any Vogue in the World.'

4 ff.   Cf. Cowley, 'Upon the Death of the Earl of Balcarres' (*Poems*, p. 414):
        Few persons upon Earth
        Did more then he, deserve to have
        A life exempt from fortune and the grave....

11 f.   The mate of Atwood's soul is his dead body.

13-18.   Suggested by Cowley, 'The Extasie' (*Poems*, p. 205):
        The mighty ' *Elijah* mounted so on high,
        That second Man, who *leapt* the *Ditch* where all

> The rest of Mankind *fall*,
> And went not *downwards* to the *skie*.

Elijah is called the second, because Enoch was the first; they are Oldham's Prophet and Patriarch.

19. Cf. 'St. Ambrose', 11. 23 f. and n.

21 ff. For Atwood as Inner Templar, Councillor at law, and, apparently, Principal of Clifford's Inn, see F.A. Inderwick, loc. cit., headnote. A notable series of diatribes against the legal profession, culled from Plato, Livy, and later authors, will be found in Burton's *Anatomy*, pp. 49 f. Apart from abuses, advocacy itself was suspect: to say the most that might be said on one side of a question today, and on theother in a similar cause tomorrow, seemed dishonest to those who did not grasp the adversative method embodied in the judicial process.

25 f. Adapted in 'Juvenal XIII', 11. 81 f.

34-7. See 'Aude aliquid. Ode', 11. 43 ff. and n.

40-8. Alluding to Joseph of Arimathea. As a member of the Sanhedrin he was no doubt learned in the Jewish law.

51. Cf. 'A Dithyrambique', 1. 105. 'Thinking Fools' is Rochester's phrase in 'A Satyr against ... Mankind', which Oldham had transcribed.

57 f. Cf. Cowley, 'On the Death of Mr. William Hervey' (*Poems*, p. 35):
> ... As large a *Soul* as ere
> Submitted to *inform* a *Body* here.

L. 58 is identical with 'St. Ambrose', 1. 91.

60-2. Cf. 'Homer', 11. 123 ff. and n.

71-124, 150-204. Despite the hyperbole, not mere conventional panegyric. 'He was', says Aubrey with ample evidence (*Surrey*, ii.60, iii.6), 'a singular Benefactor to the Church and Clergy as well as to the poor.' Besides benefactions at Sanderstead, at Warlingham (13 Nov. 1675) he ensured to the vicar and his curate the proceeds of the great tithes of Warlingham and Chesham. He rebuilt the vicarage (1674); and building almshouses for the aged widows or widowers, included accommodation for the curate, who was charged with teaching the poor children of the parish, and reading prayers, specified as those of the established Church.

71 ff. With sts. IV and V cf. the ode on Morwent, sts. IX-XIII.

102-4. Cf. Cowley, 'All-over, Love' (*Poems*, p. 91): 'Twas *all* in *all*, and *all* in *every Part*.' The diffusion of the soul was a question canvassed by St. Augustine; and cf. Burton, *Anatomy*, p. 20: 'Others make a doubt, whether it be all in all, and all in every part'. Cf. also 'A Dithyrambique', 11. 14 ff. and n.

106. Cf. the ode on Morwent, 1. 152 and n.

108 ff. Cf. the ode on Morwent, 1. 176 f.

117. Cf. Rochester, 'A Satyr against ... Mankind', 1. 49: 'this gibing, jingling knack, call'd wit'; see above, 1. 51 n.

128 ff. Cf. Cowley, 'Ode. Upon occasion of a Copy of Verses of my Lord Broghills' (*Poems*, p. 409):
> Tis said *Apelles*, when he *Venus* drew,
> Did naked Women for his pattern view,
> And with his powerful fancy did refine
> Their humane shapes into a form Divine....

Cleveland alludes to the story (from Pliny's *Natural History*) in 'To P. Rupert', 1. 77.

138-40. Cf. the ode on Morwent, ll. 265 ff. and n.

142. Cf. 'To Cosmelia', ll. 21 f. and n.

143-8. Cf. Donne, 'A Funerall Elegie', ll. 97 f., 103 f.:
                    if after her
        Any shall live, which dare true good prefer,
        Every such person is her deligate ...
        For future vertuous deeds are Legacies,
        Which from the gift of her example rise....

149. Cf. Donne, 'The Second Anniversary', ll. 308-10:
        ... the vertuous Actions they expresse,
        Are but a new, and worse edition
        Of her some one thought, or one action ...
    and 'An Anatomie of the World', ll. 227 f.:
        Shee that was best, and first originall
        Of all faire copies....

150-204. See l. 71 n., above.

151 f. Cf. Browne, *Religio Medici*, I.i: 'Not that I meerly owe this Title
    [of Christian] to the Font, my Education, or the clime wherein I was born,
    as being bred up either to confirm those Principles my Parents instilled
    unto my unwary Understanding, or by a general consent proceed in the Reli-
    gion of my Country.' Earle's sceptic (*Microcosmography*, XXXV) 'is troubled
    at this naturalness of religion to countries, that protestantism should be
    born so in England and popery abroad ...'.

161. In the unmetrical printed line 'Exalted far above the vain small Attacks
    of Wit', 'vain' was evidently Oldham's revision in the margin of his MS. The
    compositor inserted it, instead of substituting it for 'small', which was to
    be removed because it was virtually repeated in 'little' in l. 163.

161-8. See 'Aude aliquid. Ode', headnote, and the ode on Morwent, ll. 450 ff.

172 f. A variant of 'Promising a Visit', ll. 25 f.; cf. Otway, *Don Carlos*
    (1678), III.i, p. 19: 'Ile ... stand / Brandishing all my Thunder in my
    hand'.

176-81. Cf. Waller, 'To my Lord of Falkland' (*Poems*, i.76):
        In a late dream, the Genius of this land,
        Amazed, I saw, like the fair Hebrew stand,
        When first she felt the twins begin to jar,
        And found her womb the seat of civil war ...
    and *Religio Stoici. With a friendly Addresse To the Phanaticks Of all Sects
    and Sorts* (1665), A.4ʳ: 'It grieves me sore to see my Mother the Church
    tortur'd like *Rebecca*, by carrying strugling twins in her pained bowels.'

188-92. Cf. Cowley, 'Ode. Upon His Majesties Restoration and Return' (*Poems*,
    p. 422):
        Will Peace her Halcyon Nest venture to build ...
        And trust that *Sea*, where she can hardly say
        Sh'has known these twenty years one *calmy day*,
        Ah! mild and gaulless *Dove* ...
        Cans't thou in Albion still delight?
    The belief in the gall-less dove is refuted by Browne, *Pseud. Ep.*, III.§3.
    Like the halcyon, it was a commonplace of allusion: cf. the ode on Morwent,
    ll. 252, 350 ff. and n.; 'Bion', ll. 79 ff.; 'Upon the Marriage', l. 100;
    and Cowley, *Poems*, p. 286, *Essays*, p. 44.

193-5, 199-201. Cf. Donne, 'Elegie upon the Death of Mistress Boulstred',
    ll. 45 f.:
        Her heart was that strange bush, where, sacred fire,
        Religion, did not consume, but'inspire.

197 f. See the Morwent ode, 1. 654 and n. Cf. Cowley, 'On the Death of Mr.
William Hervey' (*Poems*, p. 35): 'the *Stars*, to which he now is gone ...
shine ... like *Flame* / Yet burn not.'

207-10. Adapted from 11. 5-8 of 'Katharine Kingscote'.

213-19. Cf. the ode on Morwent, 11. 715 ff.

221. Identical with 'St. Ambrose', 1. 60.

224. *tracas*: trouble, turmoil; from French *tracasserie*. *OED*'s latest example
is of 1673.

UNCOLLECTED POEMS AND FRAGMENTS

These consist in the first place of gleanings from the autograph MS: a complete lyric; the translation, complete so far as it goes, of Boileau, *Le
Lutrin*, Canto I; and fragments belonging to identifiable projects—no drafts
towards poems extant in finished form. There follow two obscene poems Oldham
would never have published: 'The Author of *Sodom*', given here from the complete professional transcript in Yale MS b. 105, compared with the extensive
autograph drafts; and 'Sardanapalus', from the best scribal copy, Harvard MS
Eng. 585, collated with eleven others (see Introduction, pp. xcii, xcvi, and
nn. 216-18). Finally, the Latin elegy on John Freind is from the transcript by
John's father, MS Top. Oxon. f. 31, pp. 287 f.; and the epitaph on Abia Qui,
not certainly but probably authentic, from J.M. Moffatt's report of the memorial
inscription (see Introduction, pp. xxv, xxvii, and nn. 4, 11).

A Rant to his Mistress

Oldham's autograph fair copy is on R228, 230. It is certainly his: the borrowings from Cowley are characteristic, and one of them is repeated from the
verses on Katharine Kingscote not published in Oldham's lifetime.
    The 'Rant' is to be grouped with the four poems which Oldham addressed to
'Cosmelia' a few months later, and with 'The Dream', of which she is the
heroine: on her identity, see headnote to that poem, and Introduction, p.
xxix, and nn. 19, 20.

3-7. Cf. Dryden, *Tyrannick Love* (1670), II.iii, p. 19:
            ... there's not a God inhabits there,
        But for this Christian would all Heaven forswear.
        Even *Jove* would try more shapes her Love to win....

13-16. Imitated from Cowley; see 'Katharine Kingscote', 1. 3 and n.

18. *the Mirror of the Deity*. Cf. the Morwent ode, 11. 724-6, and n.

23-31. Cf. Cowley, 'My Fate' (*Poems*, p. 126):
            But mark *her Face* ...
                For only there is writ my *Destiny*.
            Or if Stars shew it, gaze not on the Skies;
            But study the Astrol'ogy of her Eyes.
            If thou find there kind and propitious rays,
                What *Mars* or *Saturn* threaten I'll not fear ...
    and his 'Impossibilities' (p. 130):
            As *stars* (not powerful else) when they *conjoin*
                Change, as they please, the Worlds estate;
            So thy *Heart* in *Conjunction* with mine,
                Shall our own fortunes regulate;
            And to our *Stars themselves* prescribe a *Fate*.

The Desk: First Canto

From the autograph fair copy on R124-35, translated from Boileau, *Le Lutrin*. Page 136 is headed 'Second Canto' and 15 blank pages follow; but there is no evidence that canto II was ever begun, though a translation of canto IV, ll. 65 f., marked 'Lutr. p. 183', occurs in the margin of R66. With this exception, the rough drafts in the MS are all for passages of canto I. There are drafts for ll. 1-52 on R70-2; ll. 87-158 on R72, R74, R76; ll. 163-76 on R69; ll. 177-85 on R77^c, R79; ll. 188-210 on R79; ll. 212-49 on R80, R77^a; and ll. 258-301 on R66, R68; besides others for ll. 153, 155 f.; 180, 194 f., 214 f.; and 228 f., on R76, R69, R77^c, and R77^b.

The first four cantos of Boileau's *Lutrin* were published in the 1674 edn. of his works (he added V and VI in 1683). Oldham's is the earliest English translation of canto I. The first to be printed was *Le Lutrin: An Heroic Poem, Written Originally in French, by Monsieur Boileau* (1682), by N.O. Clark reprinted Oldham's 'The Desk. First Canto' in his Appendix E.

3. *Pourges*. The quarrel caricatured in *Le Lutrin* occurred at the Sainte-Chapelle in Paris; but Boileau did not admit this until 1683. In 1674, he began by laying the scene at Bourges; then, after printing but before publication, he changed this to the fictitious 'Pourges' by having the lower loop of the Bs erased.

48. Cf. 'Jesuits III', l. 27.

163 f. Adapted as 'Jesuits III', l. 20 f.

170. *Pontack*. It is Oldham who specifies the wine, which was at least as famous in England as in France, since *'Monsieur Pontaque'*, the 'owner of that excellent *Vignoble* of *Pontaque* & *Obrien*, whence the choicest of our *Burdeaux*-Wines come' kept a celebrated ordinary in London (Evelyn, 13 July 1683; see de Beer's n.).

In Praise of Poetry

Rather than reprint overlapping drafts, and several others without relating them to the rest, the editor has taken some liberties in assembling and arranging them. A rough draft on R100 has the title, followed by three fragments with spaces left between them: at the foot of the facing page, R99, is what appears to be a fourth of the series. The first of these fragments is expanded by a draft on R96: this gives us ll. 1-10 of the text. The second is overlapped and continued by another draft on R87; this gives ll. 16-32. The third and fourth furnish ll. 33-6 and 37-48. On R85, R98 and R88 are three other drafts which belong, apparently, to the same piece. I have placed them where they seem most naturally to fall, one between the first and second of the original fragments (ll. 11-15), and the others after the fourth (ll. 49 f. and 51). See the Textual Apparatus.

The position of the fragments in MS R dates them as not before summer 1678. Those on R87, R88 and R96 are evidently later than the drafts on the same pages for 'A Letter'; and that on R99 is almost as certainly later than the draft opening of the 'Satyr Upon a Woman'. The 'Satyr' was written at Whitsuntide 1678; the 'Letter' cannot have been begun before Mar. 1677/8 and in its final form was written in June.

1-10, 37-42. These lines counterbalance the 'Ode on Jonson', ll. 54 ff., and 'Art of Poetry', ll. 466 ff. Favourable to *furor poeticus* ('a diviner Fury'), they reflect, as Oldham's note 'Longin' (R96: see Appendix III) testifies, his response, like Dryden's (*Essays*, i.179-80), to Longinus, *On the Sublime*, brought into new prominence by Boileau's translation in 1674.

4. *Capricios*. See the ode on Morwent, 1. 450, and n.

15. Cf. Lee, *Rival Queens* (1677), Prologue, by Sir Carr Scroope:
    Now each Fanatick Fool presumes t'explain
    The Text, and does the sacred Writ profane....

20 f. Opposite these lines, R87m has 'Plin. Ep. i.14. Euphorm. p. 69. Actually it is in No. 13, Book I of the *Epistles* (at least in edns. I have seen) that Pliny describes how recitals of poetry were received in his day, and the greater encouragement it formerly met with. In *Euphormionis Lusinini sive Ioannis Barclaii Satyricon*, pp. 69-71 of the 1655 Elzevir edn., Barclay declares poetry a dangerous study for young scholars: they mistake their enthusiasm for inspiration, earn contempt by their ill success, and cannot combine with poetizing the profitable study of law. Great poetry, rarely achieved, brings fame, but is accompanied as a rule by poverty. Were it not that poetry unbends the mind, and, when great, kindles the spirit, it would be better banished from the Schools. Cf. central topics of 'A Letter' and 'Spencer's Ghost'.

26. A Renaissance commonplace; but here reminiscent of Longinus IX.3. Cf. J. Pulteney's trans. (assisted by Dryden; from the French version), *A Treatise of the Loftiness or Elegancy of Speech ... by Longin* (1680), p. 28: 'for is it possible that a man, whose thoughts are employed about base and servile matters, should ever be Author of any thing worthy to be committed to Posterity?'

32. The Seraphim were the highest of the nine angelic orders. Below them ranked Cherubim, Thrones, Dominations, Virtues, Powers, Principalities, Archangels, and Angels.

34. *his Roman Heir*: Horace, whose *Odes*, IV.ii, was in praise of Pindar, in fact considered himself the heir of Sappho and Alcaeus, and not of Pindar.

47. *Once sacred thought*. Cf. Lee, *The Rival Queens* (1677), Carr Scroope's Prologue: 'Wit, like Religion, once Divine was thought'.

Satyr on Wit

This project survives only as a title and opening line on R284, which echoes the first line of Cowley's 'Ode. Of Wit' (*Poems*, p. 16): 'Tell me, O tell, what kind of thing is Wit'. These are followed by drafts for the conclusion of 'Jesuits II' (*c.*June 1679) and a couplet of 'Jesuits I' (*c.*Dec. 1678). The project was perhaps inspired by Spencer's discussion of wit in the verse letter of 18 Mar. 1677/8 (see Appendix I). Spencer borrows from Cowley's 'Ode'; once where he postulates that 'Witt shou'd be durable', and again in 11. 229 f.:
    Most know what wit is not, none what it is;
    This it has of divine, that it receives
    No true portraiture but by negatives.

The Vision: A Satyr

Fragment [a] is from R270-3. This is the longest and most consecutive, and almost certainly the latest, of the extant drafts. A rougher one on R266 has two passages which carry the description a stage further, and a marginal note which indicates that an ironical monologue on the Jesuits was to have followed.

(See Introduction, pp. xxx, xlvii.) These are here printed as fragments [b] and [c].

The other two drafts are on R66 and R268. The former is dated, like that on R270, '9ʳ 78'. The satire was thus conceived soon after the finding of Godfrey's body (17 Oct.); no doubt it was abandoned when Oldham hit on the idea of 'Garnet's Ghost' (*c*.Dec.).

Dream-visions and visions of hell were forms that Reformation and 17th-century polemicists inherited from medieval times. Oldham's fragment belongs to the same tradition as Sir David Lyndsay's *The Dreme* (1528), Thomas Dekker's *Newes from Hell* (1606), and such pieces as *Archy's Dream, sometimes Iester to his Maiestie* (1641), *Hugh Peter's Dreame* (1659), *News from Hell; Or the Relation of a Vision* (1660), and *Saint Bernard's Vision* (?1670-1690). The tradition already included a famous attack upon the Jesuits: Donne's elaborate satire in Latin prose, translated as *Ignatius His Conclave, Or His Inthronisation In A Late Election In Hell* (1611).

Oldham's immediate inspiration was evidently Phineas Fletcher's *Locustae* and *The Locusts*, 1627 (see Introduction, pp. xxx, xlvii, and nn. 22, 83). Already he designed to have his villains condemned, as Fletcher's repeatedly are, by their own utterances or those of their patrons. Fletcher has a night-scene leading to an infernal council, where Æquivocus, devil-General of the Jesuits, brings hope, by his oration, to the loftily-enthroned Lucifer. As Oldham's Lucifer is to entitle Loyola 'Great Pillar of our Realm', so in a Papal council, when Æquivocus, 'Loiol's eldest son', has expounded his Gunpowder Plot, Paul III hails him 'Salve praesidium fidei columenque Latinae'; his upholding the 'Realm' is further emphasized when he is called 'Patronum Romae', and said to bring to *moenia Romae* a new lease of life (Cf. *Locustae*, p. 117; *Locusts*, I.v, xxi, II.v ff.; for other debts, see below, ll. 2, 7 f., 34, [b] 1 f. and nn.). Fletcher is linked, moreover, with Oldham's two other main sources. In the night-piece, Fletcher's 'deadly sleep' (I.vii.2) forms a verbal association with Cowley's '*Dead in this sleep*' (Saul's Hell-inspired dream, 'Davideis', *Poems*, p. 248) and both are picked up in Oldham's 'dead and buried' noise. He has Lucifer's throne-room adorned, 'instead of Tapestry' by narrative bas-reliefs. Saul's palace-hall, in Cowley (pp. 290-2) *is* hung with narrative tapestries; in Fletcher's papal hall (III.xxxii ff.) images, wrought by 'the workman with his Dedal hand', depict evil Popes and their evil doings. Oldham's artificer is the fiend Vulcan; that same Mulciber who in *Paradise Lost* (I.710 ff.), architect of Pandaemonium, embellished it 'with bossy Sculptures'.

The indebtedness of 'The Vision' to heroic models—*The Indian Emperour* and *Mithridates*, as well as the *Locust* poems, 'Davideis', and above all *Paradise Lost*—is significant: see Introduction, p. xlvii. It must be one of the earliest pieces in which so strong a Miltonic influence appears.

1 ff. Cf. Cowley, 'Davideis' (*Poems*, p. 247), Envy's appearance to Saul:
            It was the time when silent night began
            T'enchain with *sleep* the busie *spirits* of Man....
Oldham's opening lines may be compared with those of *The Vision* (?1682; repr. *State-Poems Continued*, 1697, p. 119): since neither can have influenced the other, the similarity bears witness to the common tradition behind them.

2-5. Cf. Dryden, *The Indian Emperour* (1667), III.ii, p. 29:
            All things are hush'd, as Natures self lay dead ...
            Ev'n Lust and Envy Sleep,
from the lines taken by Rymer (preface to Rapin, 1674: Spingarn, ii.174-81) to surpass all the descriptions of night by poets who had vied in the topos: he compares Apollonius, Virgil, Ariosto, Tasso, Marino, Chapelain, and Le Moyne.

2, 7 f. Cf. headnote, and Fletcher, *Locusts*, I.vii.5 f.: 'And now ... Onely sad Guilt ... and care, no rest can tast.'

14-23. Cf. the protagonist's dream (influenced by Clarence's, *Richard III*, I.iv.9 ff.) in Lee, *Mithridates*, IV.i, p. 48:

> Streight, like a Feather, I was borne by Winds,
> To a steep Promontory's top, from whence
> I saw the very Mouth of opning Hell;
> Shooting so fast through the void Caves of Night,
> I had not time to ponder of my passage ...
> Then was I thrown down the Infernal Courts
> Infinite fathom....

18 ff. Oldham adumbrates Hell's topography and history as represented in Milton: Chaos, Limbo, the imprisoning roof, the palace designed by Vulcan, the war in Heaven, and the temptation of Eve. The realm of '*Chaos* and ancient Night' is described in *Paradise Lost*, II.890 ff.

20 f. Cf. Cowley, 'Davideis' (*Poems*, p. 244):

> Here no dear glimpse of the *Suns* lovely face
> Strikes through the *Solid* darkness of the place;
> No dawning *Morn* does her kind reds display;
> One slight weak beam would here be thought the *Day*.

22 f. The draft on R266 has:

> Sure this, thought I, must be ye Place call'd Hell
> Of which Divines so much in Pulpits tell;
> The Place ye Men of Wit so railly here
> The Atheists Mockery & ye Atheists Fear....

28. *Limbos*. Cf. *Paradise Lost*, III.444-97.

30. Cf. *Paradise Lost*, II.434 ff., where the 'ninefold' 'convex of Fire' immuring the fallen angels is barred over them by 'gates of burning Adamant'.

32 f. Cf. 'David's Lamentation', 1. 116; 'Promising a Visit', 11. 31 f., and n.

34 ff. On the indebtedness to Fletcher and Cowley, see headnote.

35 f. Cf. *Paradise Lost*, I.731-51 on Mulciber or Vulcan as the architect of Pandæmonium, where 'Cornice' and 'Freeze' were 'with bossy Sculptures grav'n' (I.716).

42. *Squadrons of Seraphims*. Cf. *Paradise Lost*, VI.246 ff., where among the 'fighting Seraphim' Michael felled 'Squadrons at once'; 'tenfold Adamant' (cf. 1. 30) occurs just below. Satan's army is 'the rebel Host' at VI.647; and both the infernal and the heavenly troops perform regular military evolutions; cf. VI.558, and the whole passage.

45. R266 adds:

> A Faux was plac'd at entrance of ye Cell
> And shew'd in looks he durst even blow up Hell.

Cf. 'Jesuits I', 11. 64 ff. and n., and 'Aude aliquid. Ode', 11. 237 f.

46-8. Cf. *Paradise Lost*, IX.643 ff., where 'the Tree' is 'root of all our woe'. Eve is 'Mother of Mankind' (V.388 and elsewhere), and 'unwarie' (IX. 614). Milton makes the Serpent *pretend* to have climbed the tree (IX.589); describes his 'foulds' (IX.498 ff.; 'scaly fould' occurs in the portrayal of Sin, II.651); and repeatedly emphasizes his 'suttlety'.

50 ff., 58 ff. *Cain ... Corah*. Envy boasts of their exploits in similar fashion in 'Davideis' (*Poems*, p. 247).

55. *Aretine*: see 'Jesuits III', 1. 423 and n.

[b] 1 f. Cf. Fletcher, *The Locusts*, IV.xxxv.9: Æquivocus announces he will 'fire the shaking towne, and quench't with royall blood'; cf. 'Aude aliquid. Ode', 11. 216 f. and n.

Advice to a Painter

From R289. The space left between the second and third fragments was subsequently filled with drafts for 'Jesuits II' (c.June 1679). For other indications of date, see the notes on ll. 2-4 below. On R269 is a single line, 'Dear Sovereign! much our Care but Heaven's more', which seems designed as the first of an envoy, perhaps to the projected 'Advice'. The only other draft on the page is of a phrase for 'The Vision' (Nov. 1678). The 'Advice' was no doubt conceived as a satire on the Jesuits and the Plot, but soon abandoned; and therefore may be assigned to Oct. or Nov. 1678.

1. Marvell's 'Further Advice to a Painter' (like two 'Advices' later than Oldham's) begins: 'Painter, once more thy Pencil re-assume'; it circulated in MS, 1670/1.

2. *long layn still.* The series which Waller provoked seems to have temporarily halted by 1674. Osborne records thirteen 'advices' from 1666 to 1673, and only three minor ones from 1673 until the end of 1678, when *The Second Advice to a Painter* ('Now Painter try if thy skil'd hand can draw') appears to have begun the new series on the Popish Plot. It is evidently subsequent to Coleman's execution, 3 Dec. 1678; Oldham is presumably writing before its appearance.
   Oldham seems to have had a MS copy of the pseudo-Denham's *Third Advice*, and the envoy to the *Second* (R105, not recognizably in Oldham's hand), and he was possibly familiar with Marvell's 'Further Advice' (see previous note).

3. *Dash with bold strokes.* Cf. Lee's *Rival Queens* (1677), III.i, p. 27:
      Touch not, but dash, with stroaks so bravely bold,
      Till you have form'd a face of so much horrour,
      That gaping Furies may run frighted back.
   It is to 'R.Q. p. 27' that Oldham refers on R293, opposite a draft for 'Jesuits I' (Dec. 1678) to which the projected 'Advice' may thus be close in date.

3 f. *our fears ... their Crimes*: the Popish Terror, and the Popish Plot with the murder of Godfrey.

5. Referring, no doubt, to Louise de Kéroualle, Duchess of Portsmouth, though Cleveland and Mazarine were both compared to Messalina (see the pseudo-Rochesterian 'Satyr which the King took out of his pocket', probably by Lacy, Yale *POAS*, i.425, and 'Rochester's Farewell', possibly by Dorset, text in Rochester, *Poems* (Pinto), pp. 149 ff.; cf. Rochester, *Poems* (Vieth), pp. 231, 234). Cf. the complaint in Marvell's 'Britannia and Rawleigh', l. 122: 'Resigns his Crown to Angell Carwells trust.'

Satyr on the times [a], and A Satyr upon the Town and Times [b]

From R222 f.; the leaf is congruent with that containing the draft of 'Horace IV.13'. In the margin of [a] there are the following notes: opposite l. 1, To sell an Evidence to W---; 3, H or H; 10-12, faith To try my patience punish; 13-14, Scotch Boots; 15-18, record my Martyrdom Maccabees Bonner. Since [b] incorporates the references to Warcup and to Halifax or Hyde, it must be the later of the two drafts.
The fragment belongs to the summer of 1682; see [a] ll. 7 f., [b] l. 5 and notes. It strongly recalls the opening of Donne's fourth satire:

> Well; I may now receive, and die; My sinne
> Indeed is great, but I have beene in
> A Purgatorie ...
> I had no suit there, nor new suite to shew,
> Yet went to Court; ...
> ... So'it pleas'd my destinie
> (Guilty of my sin of going) ... etc.

3. *Triumvirate*: Halifax and Hyde (see [b] l. 5 n.), with Seymour, who was
    eliminated Oct. 1682 (Feiling, p. 190). This fragment must predate his fall.
    Address. See [b] l. 6 and n.

6. *Quo Warranto*: the writ impugning London's charter, issued Jan. 1682;
    judgement was pronounced 12 June 1683. See 'Boileau VIII', ll. 194 f. and n.

7 f. On the night of 5/6 May the *Gloucester* frigate, taking James to Scot-
    land, was wrecked on the Lemmon and Ore sand 16 leagues from the Humber,
    with about 130 lives lost. Sir Charles Scarborough, the famous physician,
    had a narrow escape; Pepys 'was numbered among the dead by all the City al-
    most'. There were sinister rumours that the heavy death-roll was due to the
    'cruel neglect' of the duke, 'who took care of his dogs, and of some un-
    known persons who were taken from that earnest care of his to be his priests'.
    Hence, probably, Oldham's gibe. (Burnet, ii.326 f. and nn.; Luttrell, i.184
    f.; J.R. Tanner, *Mr. Pepys* (1925), pp. 251 f.). There is a satirical refer-
    ence to the disaster in Tho. Thompson's *Midsummer Moon: Or, The Livery-Man's
    Complaint* (1682).
      On the other side were *A Pindarique Ode, On Their Royal Highnesses Happy
    Return From Scotland After His Escape at Sea* (1682), and *An Anniversary Poem
    On The Sixth of May* (1683) (BL, Luttrell, I.166: dated '11 June'), both
    printed for Hindmarsh. Cf. 'Juvenal III', l. 81 and n.

15. *Fox*: The martyrologist: see 'Jesuits IV', ll. 313 f., n.

[b]

5. *Halifax, or Hide*. Lawrence Hyde (1641-1711), created Earl of Rochester
    29 Nov. 1681; First Lord of the Treasury, 1679-84: and George Savile (1633-
    95), successively Viscount, Earl, and (17 Aug. 1682) Marquis of Halifax,
    Lord Privy Seal 1682-85. From June 1681 'an uneasy equilibrium of the
    Hyde and Halifax forces lasted till the end of the reign.... The elimina-
    tion of Seymour in 1682 left the two great rivals supreme.' (Feiling,
    p. 188).

6. *Abhorrence, or Adress*. After the refusal of the grand jury to find a true
    bill against Shaftesbury 24 Nov. 1681, 'a new run of addresses went round
    the kingdom', in which the Tories 'expressed their abhorrence of that asso-
    ciation found in lord Shaftesbury's cabinet, and complained that justice was
    denied the king: which was set off with all the fulsome rhetoric that the
    penners could varnish them with'. They continued throughout the spring and
    summer of 1682 (Burnet, ii.301 and n. 4; Luttrell, i.164-219, passim).

7 f. For the Irish witnesses, see 'Boileau VIII', l. 257 n. 'Eustace Cominus
    the Irish Evidence, his Farewell to England' (in Thompson) refers to their
    pensions: 'Then I was put in pay ... / Had five, six Groat a day'. Edmund
    Warcup (1627-1712), of Northmoor, Oxon, JP for Middlesex, acted as interme-
    diary between the ministry and the witnesses. 'Between the 18th & 31st of
    Jan. 80' (i.e. 1680/1), he writes in his journal (*EHR*, xl (1925), 249, ed.
    K. Feiling and F.R.D. Needham), 'I examined 18 Irish witnesses; delivered
    their examinations to counsel' (cf. Luttrell, i.66). On 6 Feb. he told Hyde
    of 'provision made for the 4 [?] Irish witnesses'. In the early summer of
    1682, Shaftesbury brought 'a scandalum magnatum against Mr. justice Warcup,

Mr. Ivy, and others of the Irish evidence', but desisted when their objection to being tried in Middlesex was upheld (Luttrell, i.190).

12. Pursuivant here means a royal or state officer with the power to execute warrants; for Messenger see 'Upon a Bookseller', l. 28 and n.

Horace B[ook] 4. Ode 13. imitated

From R218 f.

5. Cf. Rochester, 'Timon', ll. 53 f.:
> Though nothing else, she in despite of time
> Preserved the affectation of her prime.

8. In the margin, 'captive hearts', an alternative requiring (say) 'once' for 'heretofore'.

10: almost identical with the Morwent ode, l. 554, and 'To Cosmelia', l. 35.

Juvenal's 10 Satyr imitated

From R278. Had Oldham pursued his design, he would have furnished a precedent for Johnson's *The Vanity of Human Wishes*, as he did elsewhere for *London*.

[On the death of Charles I]

From R80. Followed by a draft for 'The Desk', clearly written later, the ll. must be prior to Oct. 1678. Were they intended to form part of an occasional poem upon the 30th of Jan., the annual fast on the anniversary of Charles I's execution? The 'execrable cause' which deprived the nation of her king (ll. 1 f.) is the Great Rebellion itself; it is Cromwell in whom (ll. 5 f.) later usurpers might find a model; and the 'Act of Amnesty' (ll. 7 f.) is the Act of Indemnity and Oblivion, passed by Charles II in 1660 (cf. the ode on Morwent, l. 237 and n.). L. 12 alludes to the Great Plague of 1665.

4. A harsh line, meaning 'What crimes forced him (Charles I) to heaven, and forced *those who forced him hence* (the regicides) to hell'.

[Cadmus and the Dragon's Teeth]

From R242: a copy without corrections. A space is left above, as for the addition of a preceding passage. There is no heading; the lines are, however, an expanded rendering of Ovid's *Metamorphoses*, III.106-15. Oldham translated the Byblis episode from Bk. IX.

Upon the Author of the Play called *Sodom*.

As for 'Sardanapalus', text and probable relationship with Rochester's circle are discussed in the Introduction, pp. xxviii, xlii-v, lxxiii, xcl f. and nn.

7. *Inch oth' Candle*. See 'Jesuits IV', l. 151 n.

10. *Without Press-money*: without the inducement of earnest-money, paid to soldier or sailor on enlistment (cf. 'the King's shilling'); properly, 'prest-money' (so Pepys, 27 Feb. 1666/7), from O. Fr. 'prester' (prêter), being 'loaned' or 'advanced' in respect of subsequent service. Men recruited by impressment received it; hence, no doubt, the erroneous 'press-money'.

39. *Moorfields*: notorious for its brothels.

44. Cf. Rochester, 'A Satyr on Charles II', ll. 29-31.

Sardanapalus: Ode

The text, the probable relationship to Rochester's circle and its libertine cult, and the topical but not central satire on Charles II, are discussed in the Introduction, pp. xxviii f., xliv, lxxiii-v, xcii and nn.

1 f. The echo of Virgil's oft-quoted apostrophe, *Georgics*, II.458, establishes the mock-heroic key. Oldham would recollect also Cowley's translation (*Essays*, p. 409): 'Oh happy (if his happiness he knows) ...'.

2 f. A sidenote in the MS reads: *See Strabo Ca: 14 & Clemens Alex: Stromat. l. 2.* Strabo (*Geography*, XIV.v.9) describes Sardanapalus' tomb; the inscription referred to his gesture, in effigy, snapping his fingers: 'Eat, drink, be merry: everything else is not worth that'. Clement of Alexandria (*Stromata*, Bk. II, ch. 20) quotes an epigram: his 'many objects of happiness', 'what I enjoyed wantonly / And the pleasures I felt in love', along with him are dust.

5 f. Cf. 'Boileau VIII', 124 f., 137-9.

9. *Undershrievalties of Life.* See Introduction, p. lxxv, and 'Counterpart', l. 178 and n.

18. *motion.* The H1, V reading, 'Master', is one of two (cf. l. 39 n.) in this pair of MSS which seem to be authentic but discarded. Though more pregnant than 'motion', it cannot be accepted from two inferior MSS, closely related, against the remainder, including Hv (the best authority).

22 f. A sidenote in the MS reads: *See Augustin. de Civitat. Dei l.* [sc. lib.] *3 c.20:* referring to Bk. XVIII, ch. 2 of Augustine's *De Civitate Dei*, where he records Ninus as ruling all Asia, except India, on which his widow Semiramis made war.

25. Legendary founders, Nimrod of Babylon, Ninus and Semiramis of the Assyrian empire: Nimrod, 'a mighty hunter' (Gen. x.9) of beasts—and men; Semiramis, quiver-bearing (Juvenal, II.108: in Stapylton's n. a 'manly-spirited' warrior-queen—*Juvenal's Sixteen Satyrs*, 1647, p. 28). According to Ovid, *Met.* IV.58, she fortified Babylon with walls of brick.

35. A variant of 'Dithyrambique', l. 50: see n., and Introduction, p. lxxxvii.

39. *Maids lye.* H1, V's 'Fair ones' is probably an authentic but discarded reading: see above, l. 18 n.

44. *Cabals.* See 'Jesuits I', 0.3 n.

45 f. A sidenote in the MS reads: *See Justin c 1* (properly l. [sc. lib.] 1). The *Historiae Philippicae* of Marcus Junianus Justinus, Bk. 1, ch. 3, tells how one of Sardanapalus' satraps, Arbaces, governor of Media, arriving thence, obtained admission to him only after much solicitation, and found him playing the woman. On this Oldham has founded his depiction of emissaries from abroad awaiting audience, evidently while the monarch is in sexual council with his eunuchs.

57. *unprohibited Commodities.* Cf. 'prohibited goods', 'Juvenal III', l. 126 and n.

58. *profess the Trade.* Cf. 'Jesuits IV', l. 215.

71 f. In the tradition studied by Maren-Sofie Røstvig, *The Happy Man*, 2 vols., 2nd edn. (1962, 1971). Cf. 'To a Friend', ll. 115-22, n.

72-4. Cf. 1[ib] 5 above, and Rochester, 'A Satyr on Charles II' (shortly before 20 Jan. 1673-4), ll. 5 f.:
                    Him no ambition moves to get renown
                    Like the French fool ...,
Louis XIV, whose activity hazards his crown.

75-8. A sidenote in the MS reads *See Orosius L 1. 1, C 19*. With relevance to
the 'Complaints' and 'Mutinies' of ll. 75, 77, one reads in Orosius' *His-
toriarum Adversus Paganos* how Arbatus (Justinus' Arbaces) having seen
Sardanapalus in drag among his harlots, cursed him, and how shortly the
Medes, under him, rose in revolt.

79 f. No doubt glancing at Charles II: see headnote.

86. Conceivably one of the parallels with Charles II; the subject of treasonous astrological prediction of the King's death engaged the government's
attention before Gadbury (see 'Juvenal III', ll. 60-2 n.) was accused of it;
cf. Coventry's search for David Walker, June 1677 (Kenyon, p. 53).

86 f. A sidenote in the MS reads: *See Suidas in voce Sardanap*. In his *Lexicon*,
'Suidas'' article on Sardanapalus does not seem to bear on ll. 86 f. Drawn
from several sources, it adds nothing to the material for which Oldham cites
others. Being comprehensive, it does, however, move from the monarch's com-
placent self-indulgence to his downfall, and at this point (though in a different tone regarding them) Oldham is preparing to do the same.

93-7. *Prerogative ... Laws and Liberties*. Among Oldham's topicalities: watch-
words of royalists exalting the rights of the crown, and of their opponents
exalting those of the subject.

99 f. A sidenote in the MS reads: *See Diodorus Siculus l[ib]. 2.*: who gives,
in his Βιβλιοθήκη ιστορικη, II.xxv.1-8, an account of Sardanapalus' three
victories over the rebels led by Arbaces and Belesys the Babylonian.

101, 103 ff. The injustice of Fate, stars, and Gods is reminiscent of Lucan's
'Victrix causa deis placuit, sed victa Catoni' (*Pharsalia*, i.128).

111, 114 f. Rochester, 'A Satyr on Charles II', ll. 11, 14, 15, 18 f., characterized Charles's 'prick' as sovereign:
                    His scepter and his prick are of a length ...
                    Poor prince! thy prick ... / Will govern thee ...
                    Though safety, law, religion, life lay on't,
                    'Twould break through all to make its way to cunt.

123 f. A sidenote in the MS reads: *see Atheneus C. 12 c 7 at large*. Athenaeus
(*Deipnosophistae*, Bk. XII, ch. 529) relates Sardanapalus' defeat by Arbaces,
and self-immolation, in a chamber specially constructed within the palace,
roofed with great beams, and on a huge pyre, accompanied by his queen, with
the concubines on other couches.

126. *Lust's Mosaic*. Hv, the best MS, has 'Lusts Mosaic' but it is all but
impossible that so harsh an inversion as this would be of 'mosaic Lusts' can
have been intended.

127. *Chapiters*: capitals (*OED* 3.).

143. *In Picture by*. Cf. 'Jesuits IV', ll. 31, 41: 'These Pictures ... Those
Tables by'.

147. *Aretine*. See 'Jesuits III', l. 423 and n.

149. *Priapus*. See 'Jesuits IV', ll. 16 ff., n.
           Banner hung. Oldham's reading, probably from the start, and clearly
retained. 'Triumphs shown', peculiar to H3, may be his also, tried in the
ancestor of that goodish MS, or it may be unauthorized. It attempts to

improve on the characteristic imperfect rhyme: the new imperfection may have
been thought less obtrusive.

169. *Hecatombs*. The superior correctness of 'hecatomb' (read only by the
related MSS H1, V) does not justify deserting Hv, with which all the rest
concur. A hecatomb is 'a sacrifice of many victims'; but the plural, which
should mean many such sacrifices, is frequent in the sense of the singular.

170. Cf. 'Jesuits III', ll. 635, 672 f.

180. *Thrust*. Only three MSS recognize the enjambement; even Hv brings the
phrase to a premature pause.

In Obitum ... Johañis Frend

John Freind, b. 12 Apr. 1656, matriculated 26 Mar. 1672 at St. Edmund Hall,
d. there of 'our Oxford Feaver', 20 Mar. 1672/3, and was buried on the 21st
in St. Peter's in the East. His father, Nathaniel Freind of Westerleigh near
Bristol, collected in a memoir every detail he could of the lad's Oxford life,
and describes the funeral: verses, which the scholars of the Hall composed
that morning, were tacked to the hearse-cloth. Oldham's are the earliest of
his we have. Besides transcribing them (for his source, see Introduction,
p. lxxvii and n. 184), Nathaniel, for the benefit of John's sisters, who would
never learn Latin, translated .them:
> Apollo's servant here now scales ye skie
> The nearer to enjoy the Deitie
> Slighting the Muses springs & such as these,
> None but ye heavenly water could thee please.
> Cheare Blessed Soule! Heaven gives thee thy degree,
> 'Mongst Quires of Angells now thou art to bee.
> Noe Lamblike downe [sc. of the BA hood] thee cloth'd yet Nevertheless
> The Lamb of God doth wth his Righteousness.
> A Feaver's good, ye Pile to imitate
> Living his funeral fires t'anticipate
> Fire purgeth (Papists say) in's Feaver sure
> Hee purged was, t'ascend to heaven more pure.

See Bodl. MS Top. Oxon. f. 31, pp. 222 f., 225-7, 287 f.

Epitaph on Dr. Abia Qui

Direct evidence that these lines are Oldham's is lacking: for reasons why the
tradition which ascribed them to him may well be correct, and for J.M. Moffatt's
report of it, in 1805, see Introduction, pp. xxvii, lxxvii, and nn. 11, 185,
186. Dr Qui's son Christopher (bapt. 17 June 1669) came to be closely associated with the Oldham family neighbourhood: he was married at Shipton Moyne in
1695, when Oldham's father was still alive there, and is of Tetbury in his
Will (1742: Gloucester Probate Registry).

Abia Qui, 'a man of great eminence' as a physician, d. 1675; the quatrain is
given by Moffatt from his tomb in Malmesbury Abbey churchyard.

John Spencer's Verse-Epistle to Oldham (R198-204),
to which 'A Letter from the Country' is a reply

Dear Sr March. 18th 167$\frac{7}{8}$

    I promisd poetry, t'is true,
By wine embolden'd, & inspir'd by you,
By you, who did mee with such notions store,
I ne er soe much as dream'd of being Poor;
Mine soe manur'd, all barren heads I scorn'd,   5
Till sober I to my dull self return'd,
And then I found my treasure was at most
But tracts in waters, footsteps in the Dust.
As Ecchos too far distanc'd, words repeat
With dying accents, inarticulate,   10
So those Idea's, tho' not wholy lost,
Yet what remain'd was aiery, like a Ghost.
Fool that I was! to' expect a perfect face,
When ther's no Quicksilver behind the Glasse!

Now my blood's Cool, my brain's a dark abysse,   15
Wher ther's nought legible but promises.

As anger to the arme more vigour giues,
And fear to th' foot more speed, than it receiues
At nature's dolt,[1] when to each part it's due
She measures out unbyass'd, As Love too   20
Dreins ery Garison a Turne to serve,
And musters all the Spirits in one Nerve,
So Wine, enfeebling all the rest of Man,
Holds it[2] Cheif Rendezvous within the brain.
Whether[3] each draught's a sumons to resort,   25
And keep a Revells in great Bacchus's Court.
These Nimble Operators, t'is, refine

---

[1] *Sc.* dole.
[2] A slip (contrast ll. 59, 218 f.), rather than the archaic genitive.
[3] *Sc.* Whither; the anomalous full-stop, preceding, is *sic.*

What ere the servile senses bring them in;
And what before like a dead stock did lye,
A burthen to th ore charged Memory,   30
Rough-hewn, & undigested, is by them
Stampt into witt, or Graver Apothegme.

This was my Case, & thus prepar'd was I,
When on my Soule you made y^r battery.
Wound to this pitch, from you I lessons took,   35
And Greedily devour'd what ere you spoke:
Nor did I doubt, my stomach was so good,
To haue digested such delicious food.

Then t'was I promis'd Verses, & had then
One took the Glasse, & t'other hand the Pen,   40
(Our souls exactly tun'd to the same key)
I must haue witty bin by Sympathy.

But as in Love, after the feirce attack,
The spirits to their proper posts goe back,
And wher the bloody battail late was fought,   45
Ther's nothing left alive upon the Spot.
Soe my Dull Head, when hot, of Raptures full,
Is now vnfurnish'd left, an Empty Skull!
And I retir'd am to th' worst Extream,
From extasy relaps'd again to phlegme,   50
The Tide gone out, my phansy ebbs so low,
Poetry dwindles into Crambo now.

For how shou'd Put-Case I, in mazes led,
Baffle'd with shuff'ling of the Alphabett,
Wher A, B, C, & D, in Changes rung,   55
Make the Amused Soul stand bent so long,
And that for nought but noyse, till it do'nt know
Which the first letter is o'th' Chris-Cros-Row;
Leaue those Rough Sounds, & weigh out in soft Rhime,
To ery line it's sense; each word its time?   60

51 ebbs] *revising* runs

Fetter'd with formes, to figure ty'd & mood, ⎫
A Notion, can't so much as stir, that's good, ⎬
But Plaintiffe, & Defendant, streight intrude ⎭

Witt treads no beaten Paths, observes no Rules,
The Ebullition is of Youthfull soules,   61
The Frisks & wanton Sally's of the mind
By maximes, nor examples yet confin'd;
Her steps unmanag'd, her Notes Wild, & Free,
And her sublimest flights ex-tempore.
(For when from such Caprichio's she's reclaym'd   70
Her motions are not witt, but Wisdome nam'd)
No wonder then, If I unactive bee   ⎫
And nothing's Gay, nor Volatile in mee ⎬
Scince Littelton has fix'd my Mercury. ⎭

Yet vrg'd by promise, I've recourse alone   75
To Oldham's name, that Tetragrammaton.
Beleiveing pow'r enough couch'd in that Spell,
Of an Old Hagg to make an Oracle.

As vnlearn'd Zealott kneel's him down to pray
With hands lift up, yet knows not what to say,   80
Till from propitious heaven he does receiue
Words fitt to ask what that intends to giue;
Just so to poetry doe I advance,
Equaling both his zeal, & ignorance,
Like him I wave, & rowle my self about,   85
Not till I think, but till tho'ts find me out:
And as he's ignorant what t'is he prayes,
Vntill his ears informe him what he sayes,
But actuated by a pow'r within,
Hee to the spirit is a meer machine,   90
Wher Mouth distorted, strein'd Eys, face awry,
But turne a Cock to spout Divinity.
Alike prepost'rously do I indite,
Nor know I, till I've read it, what I write.

And then I can no more a forme to't giue,   95
Than into th'mystery of Thinking dive,
For T'is as hard to polish & To dresse
A Naked Tho't, so as to make it please,
As 'tis to e'ry foot to fit one last,
Or cook a dish to answer ery Tast,   100

T'is plain, it does not from the fume arise,
Whether to me t'is sweet or otherwise,
But from the Pores to which it does adresse
Itself, that it does either hurt or please.
Marryage is only to that pair a sweet,   105
Whose passions, humours, & whose wishes hit,
Where that fits This—there truly may't be sayd
That two are one, When they're so Rivetted.
The pleasure thus of Witt does cheifely lye
In concord, vnion, & In Sympathy.   110

A soul that's amorous on Tiptoe waits,
Enjoys each kindnes, & each Rivall hates,
Is Ravish'd by each favourable Glance,
And fights his Hero's Combates in Romance

So wher a Temper spleen, & Envy sway   115
Conception meets detracting thot's half way.

Witts now are grown so Critically nice,
That Wholsome Cleanly diet wo'nt suffice,
And therfore, be the subject ne'er so pure,
Prophane, & Bawdy, make the Garniture,   120
As if the heigth of entertainment lay
In dishes rub'd with Assa Foetida.
Yet a weak stomach gets but little by't,
Wher the meat's spoyl'd, to whet the appetite.
From Beastly Rhimes that pleasure is but Dull,   125
Which tickles more the body, than the soule;
The poet, as a Bawd, wee cheifely court,
When t'is not Wit, but Leachery's the Sport,

An art, no more within my wish, than pow'r, ⎫
To season what insipid was before   ⎬   130
With Nasty pickle, fetch'd from comon Shore. ⎭

Nor skill I how to serve up in Disguise,
As those who think wit nothing but surprize,
Whose Lines, like Riddles, lead the Reader nye
To Nonsense & Impossibilyty,   135
And when he thinks Checkmate secure enough,
They find him a Remove, & show'——Goe Off.
To Mazes, & to streights our feet they doom,
'Cause they can turne within a narrow Room,
And to demonstrate they've a piercing Eye,   140
Are fond of Darknesse, Court Obscurity.
Such allwayes run at Top, and scorne to speak
Their Mother Tongue, haueing attain'd to Greek.
As If that either witt or Beauty had
Ere the more Charmes when dressd in Masquerade;   145
Wit's best enjoy'd when with her free Consent,
For strugg'ling's an alloy in Ravishment.
They to their phansyes do the greatest Right,
Who draw to th' life, & choose the truest light
For Witt, like pictures well plac'd in a Roome,   150
Come whence they will, still looks on all that come.
Words are but Cloggs to sense, then why shou'd Man
Affect the hardest words, the heavy'est chain?

Those phrases to conception giue most ease,
W^{ch} soonest bring the fairest Images.   155
By those wee nearest to that state arrive,
Wher all discourse shall bee Intuitive;
Wher Spirits sh'an't their Joys by Proxy tell,
But tho'ts reach tho'ts without a Vehicle.

Another sort of playhouse-Witt I scorne,   160
Witt that's not read, or heard, but seen, & worne,
That's couch'd in Habits, Gestures, Simple Lookes,

137 show] *for* so

And ows its being to a—Hains, or—Nokes.
These make us laugh, but with a double face,
At once wee slite the play, & actors prayse.   165
Such faiding Changeables may set it forth,
Like Gaudy cloths without intrinsick worth,
Till out of mode, but then they're of no use,
But to expose & make ridiculous.

So—Eke & Ay—our modern stomachs paule,   170
So Monkish rhimes, nay Cambridge puns Grow stale,
As well as Granhams Ruff & Farthingale.
Witt shou'd be durable, like w^t Ben writ,
wch was, is now, & ever will be witt.

Nor wou'd I ever to that stile attaine,   175
Which speaks good poets but Ill natur'd men;
Whose spightfull muses, passing by the good,
Forage on filth, & poyson choose for food.
Who Ransack ages, & all nations cull,
To furnish out a Debauchee, or fool,   180
And that he may the more deformd appeare,
Cram ery vice into one Character;
Make heat with cold, & drought with moysture dwell,
Compound of Mischeifes Incompatable!
Worse than Pindora's[1] Box! and then as if   185
he were our comon representative,
And those the only fruits that human bee,
They damn our whole race in Effigie,
So heathens heretofore their malice dress'd,
And bated Christians in y^e skins of beasts.   190

From oft Repulses, if we won't allow
Most virgins Chast, most wives, & widdows true,
From one successe, pray, why should wee conclude,
Ther's not a woman upon Earth but—wou'd?—

186 he] *for* He

_____

[1] *Sc.* Pandora's.

Yet these the measures of wild Satyr are,   195
Which does on single acts such maximes rear,
Meer scavinger! that dirt from each dore scrapes,
To lay it in some publique place on heapes!

Besides he must uneasy bee, whose muse,
Tho' fruitfull, still brings forth with pangs, &   200
For no one can in earnest rayle at ills,   [throws
Unlesse within himself their stings he feels,
Nor with delight malicious Satyr read,
Except its bitter'st gaul with gaul does meet.

In kenning vice, those most Quicksighted are,   205
Who in their brests its counterpart do wear,
Them it most scares, who worst remorses feel,
And no wher looks so Ghastly as in Hell.
In haunted houses so the Ghost appears,
Wher the Room's full, only to' his murderers   210

Now did such miscreants by satyr mean
To sett a mark where they had shipwract bin,
They'd brand the sin, but pity him that sin'd,
Not for on's folly lampoon all mankind:
As if again each peccadilio cou'd   215
Poyson diffuse threw our whole masse of blood.

T'is more Ingenious to bee drawn than driven;
More Irksome to decipher Hell, than Heauen;
Then why shou'd poets passe its beauty by,
And scare the world with its deformity?   220

Of vgly faces, drawn with greatest skill,
Altho' the picture's good, the object's ill;
And all that art serves for no better use
Than to Compleat—a Pimp for privy-house.

214 on's] *for* one's   216 threw] *for* through

Thus, S^r, you see, that fools sometimes spy faults;   225
And standers-by see better Gamesters blotts;
Yet few can mend, what all agree's amisse;
Most know what wit is not, none what it is;
This it has of divine, that it receiues
No true portraiture but by negatives.   230

Now to conclude, my debt I thus haue payd,
You haue in number, what you want in weight.
My next shall panagyrick bee, (if I
Ere venture ought beyond Apology)
And What, Dear S^r, your Influence shall rayse,   235
I'le pay you back in tributary Prayse:

And scince y^r merits justice can't receiue,
For want of words Supersuperlative;
(The hyghest Epethets the Mistris had
Being worn thredbare, vailes to chambermaid)   240
Scince on this churlish soyle noe lawrells grow
Soe fair, as to bee worthy of Your Brow;
I'l strip each poet Lawreat I meet,
And strew their wither'd wreths beneath y^r feet.

I'l plunder Dauenant, Shakespear, Ben, nay then S^r   245
Not spare the namesake of
                          Y^r Faithfull
                                   Spencer.

APPENDIX II

From autograph in MS R: passages destined for four poems, but
abandoned in the definitive texts, as published.

1. 'A Letter from the Country'. Drafts discarded (except as
    noted) in the final version. The arrangement is the editor's;[1]
    the line-numbers imply nothing about the order in which the
    fragments were composed; or about their sequence, so far as
    Oldham may have decided on it. Their order even in the same
    page of the MS is not necessarily that in which they were writ-
    ten down: Oldham habitually left gaps in his rough drafts of a
    passage, filling them later with drafts for other passages and
    other poems.
    (a) Addressing Spencer, and referring to his professional and
        metropolitan advantages: in the country, wit is condemned.
R89   (i) This double benefit I receive from you
             At once I'm pleasd & am Instructed too
             We guess what proofs your Genius would impart
             Did it employ you as it dos divert:
                     & sell your breath more dear
             Than Wind is by some Lapland Conjurer:[2]
        (ii) What governs Kingdoms, & distributes Right,[3]
             And sets th.' unerring Bounds of Just & Fit.
             Is your great Task, a large & fruitfull Soile
             To exercise & pay your learned Toile: 10
R93   (i)   a skilful Lawyer shows[4]
             That you defend so well so bad a Cause
        (ii) To you, who live so near ye Line of Wit.
             That dos dispense a warm, yet tempr'ate Heat:

    6 gainfull Rm   8 unpractic'd unlabour'd untaught. painless Rm
    11 smotherd with Praise Rm

---

    [1] The MS order of the passages from R93 is iii, i, iv, ii, v, and from R103,
    i, iii, ii.
    [2] In R, followed by draft of 'Letter' 53 f.
    [3] In R, preceded by draft of 'Letter' 57 f.
    [4] With 11Rm, cf. 'Letter' 33-7.

(iii) Wits here Prohibited Goods[1]

      or [erasure] put it in their Letany

No poetry, but w^t in Fairs is sung

And after on some Alehouse Cupboard hung

And bought by gaping & admiring Throng

   In Church or ye Gallows sung   20

Some pray against it as a crying sin.

(iv) Or wretched Sternholds viler Sence & Rhime,[2]

Fit to be set apart for Gallows-Hymn.

Fit for no use but making &c.

 (v) But w^t at Fairs we 2 a year have sung

The Wonder of a dull admiring Throng

R103   (i) Wear's it on's Knife, & cuts his Meat with Rhime.

You're not permitted, tis so high a Crime,

To wear't on Knives, or cut your Meat with Rhime.[3]

(ii) Others, not quite so superstitious grown,   30

Yet who as little its Protection own

Would have it wisely publick Nuisance made

Only prohibited like French Goods & Trade:[4]

Preserve thy Church, & us thy Shepfold fence

From spreading Knowledge & infectious Sence

Destroy vile Cowley, wicked Hudibras

And ye rhiming Antichristian Race:

One made a Clench, & (ye wise Town) thought fit

Next Sessions to indite him for a Wit.

As if there were some Inquisition here   40

I'm fain to write by stealth, & Rhime in fear

For fear, as once ye Thracian Poet was,[5]

I should be made a Martyr for ye Cause:

Be made a second Martyr &c.

22 wretched doggrel Rs   25 No P-[*sc.* Poetry] Rm   27 Now yt- Rm
29 Bellman Rm   30 grown R; their own Rs   32 Would R[2]; Would only R
cancelled   (only) R; wisely Rm   33 And thought Rm   38 lately Rs
(ye wise Town) R; 'twas Rs   42 Lest [*sc.* Lest I] Rs   44 second R;

[1] Echoing Dryden, Prologue to Shadwell's *True Widow* (produced Mar. 1677/8): 'Meantime poor Wit prohibited must lie / As if 'twere made some French Commodity.' Cf. Jonson ode, 104-7, 'Careless Good Fellow', 17 f., 'Juvenal III', 125 f., and nn.
[2] See *Some New Pieces* Advertisement, 77 and n.
[3] With 29 Rm, cf. 'Bookseller', 65.   [4] Cf. above, 1 n.
[5] Orpheus: cf. 'Lycidas', 58 ff.

Some fear like Popery it should creep in
And pray against as a crying sin: [*sic*]

(b) Apologia, in reply to Spencer's animadversions on Satire,
for dedicating himself to it; with lines towards a speech
by the poet's dissuading friends, or towards that in which
he forswears poetry ('A Letter' 11. 84 ff., 113-32).

R95   (i) Who would both Ends of Poetry unite
He equally must profit & delight.[1]
                    to let you know
Why most my Genius dos to Satyr bow: 50
Its Excellence your very Instance shows
When you its Strength so well against it use.

R103   (iii) If nature won't, yet very rage & spite
Will serve & make ye arrantst Withers write,[2]
When every where I'm shock'd by ugly Vice
And thousand nauseous Coxcombs make my Spirits rise.

R94   (i)   The Poet addressing himself to Satyr.
'Tis now four Years (if I well count ye time)
Since first I felt ye Lechery of Rhime;
And like young wanton Girle once enter'd in,
Nought could Reclaim me from ye pleasing Sin.[3]   60
Oft (I remember) did wise Friends disswade,
And bid me quit ye trifling barren Trade:[4]
Have you forgot (said they) grim Poverty
Entail'd a Curse on wretched Poetry?[5]
What Rhimer ever fin'd for Sheriff? who
By Wit did ere State-Secretary grow?[6]

(ii) Oft have I beg'd kind Heav'n to mortify
This vile & wicked Lust of Poetry:[7]
Be free of Tickets & ye Playhouses
To make some tawdry Actress there thy Prize   70

46 against [*sc.* against it] R   48-9 you use its strength against it
self Rm   53 won't R; fail Rs   54 & usher'd him &c. Rm   55 Change
Rm   56 Affronts my sight Ey Rm   67 I R; they Rs   69 Made Rm

---

[1] Cf. 'Art of Poetry', 536.   [2] Cf. 'Jesuits, Prologue', 30 f.
[3] Cf. 'Letter', 88 f.   [4] Cf. 'Letter', 84 f.
[5] Henry Vaughan ('To his Friend', *Olor Iscanus*, 1651) wonders 'such entails
of poverty / Are laid on poets'. Cf. 'Letter', 127.
[6] Cf. 'Spencer's Ghost', 165 f.   [7] Cf. 'Letter', 86 f.

And spend thy third day's Gains twixt her clap'd
To be an Author, have thy posted Name   [thighs
Fix'd up with Bills of Quack & public Sham.
To be ye stop of gazing Prentices,
And read by reeling Drunkards when they piss:
Or else to lie expos'd on trading stall
Or hire Gazets to say it cannot sell:
At best 'tis vain & empty Praise he gain [*sic*]
The great Rewards of all his fruitless Pains:[1]

R95   (ii) Poet! once thought an honourable Name,   80
And stood with First-rates in ye lists of Fame,[2]
Match'd Priests & Prophets, almost justled Kings,
Is now debas'd amongst ye meanest things.

    Tis now at length become an arrant Trade
O'th' Companies ere long like to be made[3]
    What is ye Credit, which he gains by it,
The Credit of a damn'd confounded Wit:
Tis what I know & think but cannot tell.

    Charm tawdry Abigails[4] in wretched Rhime,
    I envy not our witty bawdy Peer[5]   90
All ye loth'd wretched Fame he dos acquire
Which Hell, Debauches, Claps & Lust inspire.
                    & strait is grown
A man of Parts, of Rhiming & Renown
                    to please some idle few,
Who read thee when they've nothing els to do:
Wit, y^t luxurious Plant is often found
To bear most & best (Fruit) in moderate Ground,
If too much forc'd, it strait to rankness thrives
And turns to Branches all, & empty Leaves[6]   100

79 great R; poor R *underscript*   81 And R; That Rm[1]. stood R; plac'd Rm[2]
82 Sacred as y^t of Pro. Pr. & K. Rm   83 rank's Rm   84 Simony Rm
85 And shortly will— Rm   97 like some goodly Rm   98 y choicest Rm

---

[1] Cf. 'Spencer's Ghost', 224-6, 78-84, 116 f.   [2] 'Art of Poetry', 672 f.
[3] Cf. Dryden, 'Prologue to the University of Oxford', 1673, 'So Poetry, which is in *Oxford* made / An Art, in *London* onely is a Trade'; and Rochester, 'Artemisia', p. 60 ff; 'Companies': the City Companies (Grocers, Haberdashers &c).
[4] Predates by fifteen years *OED*'s earliest example of 'Abigail' (the waiting woman in Beaumont and Fletcher's *Scornful Lady*), used generically.
[5] Rochester: see Introduction, pp. xlii f. and n. 58.
[6] In R, between drafts of 'Letter', 25-30 and 31-7.

2. 'Upon the Works of Ben. Johnson Reprinted:' after 1. 4 of
    the definitive text (as fair-copied and published), lines from
    a draft opening (R224 f.), not retained. Ll. 1-4, 25, are util-
    ized in 'The Praise of Homer', 11. 1-4, 137; 11. 6-8 are the
    germ of 'Spencer's Ghost' 11. 17-20; cf. 11. 9 f. with 'In
    Praise of Poetry', 1. 36.

            Pardon, dread Poet, that I take in vain
                Thy glorious & eternal Name,
                And in unhallow'd Verse blaspheme
            Pardon, that with strange Fire thy Altar I profane:
            Let thy dead Ashes (like the Prophets Dust) produce   5
            Some Miracle, let them (for sure they can) infuse
            And blow the Heav'nly Spark into a lifeless Muse;
                Some of thy mighty Spirit I implore
                (But 'tis I fear too vain too bold a Prayer
                For me to make, or any God to hear)   10
            That I with just and equal Praise may Thee adore
            Like Men, that offer Heav'n but what it gave before:
                Grant I in this high Trial prove but fit
                I'll wait no greater Call then it
            But boldly here take on the sacred Ministry of Wit: 15

                        (   )
                As a bold Traveller on the Banks of Nile,
                    Led by loud Story to survey
            The boasted Monuments of proud Antiquity
            Where long since buried Kings never are thought to dy
            With wonder there ascends some great stupendious Pile   20
                        And thinks it Fame
                But to have seen & clim'd the glorious Frame
            So idle may that fond Ambition well be thought
                Which my advent'rous Steps has brought
            To clime thy vast erected Pyramids of Wit   25
            More durable then those, more lofty for their Height.

    16 a R²; some R¹   17 Led R²; Led (thither) R1 [*deletion by brackets*]
    21 thinks it R2; vainly thinks he merits equal R¹   22 have R [*omitted and
    inserted*] & ... Frame R²; as he that built the same R¹   24 f. Seem / Clime
    Rm [*alternative rhyme-words*]

3. 'A Dithyrambique on Drinking': ll. of the fair copy (R206-11,
    213), discarded in the definitive published text.
    After l. 21
    Th' ambitious busling Monarch of the times,[1] which now
        Keeps such a mighty stir, so much ado
            He, who with so much pains dos strive
                    To fill Gazets alive
    And after in some lying Annal to survive;   5
            For all his pomp, for all his pride
        For all his fame & victories beside,
        Is but at best a gay unpittied slave,
            A glorious drudge of tyrant Fate,
            That tugs and labours to be great   10
    While we exempt from all his toil & all his hate
        Creep silent & unenvied to the grave.
    After l. 50
    By thee the mighty Bacchus climb'd the blest Abode
            By thee he wore a Name Divine
        Deserved Altars, & deserv'd a shrine,   15
        He scorn'd to mount to Heav'n the common Road,
            No known & vulgar Paths he trod
    But stoutly he debauch'd & drunk himself into a God.
    After l. 80
    To him our Company, to him our Wine we ow,
            To him our Wit & Fame which thence must flow: 20

4. 'A Satyr, in Imitation of the Third of Juvenal': between the
    heading and a fair copy of ll. 1-35 (R226), an 'Argument',
    mostly discarded in the published version. 'A Friend of y[e]
    Poet's is brought in, giving him an account, why he removes
    from London, where by reason of y[e] favour given by great People
    to y[e] French, their Arts, Customs & Fashions, likewise y[e] Plot-
    tings, Factions, Perjuries, Knaveries & Villanies of our own
    Nation, together with y[e] Contempt of y[e] poor, y[e] continual
    Fires, Noises, Crowdings, Night-Robberies & other Outrages,
    no man of sence & honesty will endure to reside.'

[1] Louis XIV.

A P P E N D I X   I I I

From the drafts of 'Satyrs upon the Jesuits', principally as indicating Oldham's sources.

R164m   Codurius & Hosius died before Loyola

         foul brood

           <u>blest</u>
         & Faber[1]

R166m   Loyola born at Aspatheia in Biscay. founded ye Society in 1540.
The Interim. Heylin. Geogr. 1.2. p.67: Ausburg Confession ib.
Tolerācon of ye Protestants. A^o 1555. ib. Luther born at Isleben
in Mansfield 1483. died 1546: Xavier came to Japan. 1549. died
upon ye coasts of China 1552 Varen. p. 184 see more:

      Death of Caesar Borgia Heylin 1.1. p.211.
          Ignatius born 1491
             dyed. 1556
                ————
                 56
                  9
                ————
                65^2

R168m   Mithridates
          p.3.[3]

---

[1] For probable sources, see III.21 n. and IV.35 f., n.
[2] Notes for 'Jesuits III' from Heylin, and Varenius. On 'Biscay', see II.31;
on Xavier, see IV.170 and n., and III.137 n.
[3] Opposite draft of III.24-9. See n.

R169   Kill ye rank Piedmont weeds, as you've begun
            As mighty Francis at Chabrieres has done[1]

R171m   As mighty Annibal to his great father *swore*[2]

R172m   Crabs in a Chu*r*c*h*yard[3]

            Talmud. Petrus de Natalibus.[4]

            Sun stood still[5]

            Mattins

            Canonical Ho*urs*[6]

R173   What pennance tender-hearted Saint did pay
            For murder of assassinated flea:[7]

R176   Loaden with years, & sins, ready to spew
            His soul out of one Hell into a new.[8]

R178m   Hecubas Dream[9]

[1] Opposite draft of III.47 f. The massacre at Cabrières d'Avignon (20 Apr. 1545) is referred to in Hall (p. 117), Heylyn (i.193), and Burton, *Anatomy* (p. 661).

[2] Opposite draft of III.653-63. From Dryden, *MacFlecknoe*, ll. 112 f.

[3] Opposite draft of III.285 ff. From Erasmus: see III.333 f., n.

[4] Pietro de' Natali wrote his *Catalogus sanctorum* in 1369-72; it was printed in 1493. Foulis cites it in his side-notes.

[5] Opposite draft of III.311 f. from Foulis, p. 26: 'the *Sun* itself must return back, or stand still, at the desire of Father Xavier'. See III.321-4.

[6] Same draft. From G. Hall. See IV.306 f., n.

[7] Follows draft of III.315 f. From Foulis, p. 19, on Abbot Macarius mortification 'onely for killing a flea'. See III.315 f., n.

[8] Draft of III.5. 'Spew' and the second line are from Donne's 'Jealousie', ll. 7 f.

[9] The germ of II.43 f. In classical legend (see Seneca, *Troades*, 36-40), Hecuba dreamed she brought forth a firebrand (Paris, through whom Troy was

R180   Stride ore crowned Heads[1]

R183   Soveraign Priest.[2]

R188m   Lesser crimes deserve hard penance.

          Treason not worth confession or ha͟i͟r shirts[3]

R189m   Van͟i͟n͟u͟s He repented[4]

R191   Go foul
          ~~Hence vile~~ Impostors ~~to some duller soil~~,[5]

R192m   mild Nero. gentle Dioclesian! Busiris.[6]

R193m   See Morocco p. 56[7]

burned). Cf. R289: 'like the Trojan mother' Loyola's 'should have dreamd
                   That she with fire & conflagration teemd
                   That fire, which since has the whole globe enflam'd.'
_____

[1] Draft of II.177. Cf. R261 and R263. From Lee, *Sophonisba* (1676), I.i,
p. 4: 'strideing ore y^e dead' (R261).
[2] From Dryden, *Indian Emperour* (1667), p. 11. Cf. *'Sovereign Prelate'* (III.
503). See R197.
[3] Opposite draft of II.20-5. Idea from G. Hall, p. 122: 'from a venial sin,
not only a simple Priest in Confession but a meer Laick ... may absolve a
man'. Cf. II.124 f.
[4] See II.141.
[5] Draft for II.266; the unrevised form shows the debt to Cleveland, 'The
Rebell Scot', l. 111: 'Hence then, you proud Imposters'.
[6] Note for II.139. Alludes to G. Hall, p. 117, where he mentions that the
Catholics compared Queen Elizabeth with Busiris, who sacrificed foreigners to
Zeus, as Nero and Diocletian persecuted Christians.
[7] Opposite draft of III.233-6. The note alludes to Settle, *Empress of Morocco*
(1673), V, ll. 1-2, 4:
                   Though on the Blood of Kings my Throne I've built,
                   The World my Glory sees, but not my Guilt ...
                   They Vertuous seem whose Vices are unknown.
The lines suggested III.231 f.

R194 $\Big\{$ So Judas has not wanted worshippers $\Big\}$ vide Foulis
        And India yet to Fiends its altars rears.   p. 464[1]

R196   Heads yet untouch'd.[2] Reliques Varen. 189[3]

      Miracles. Xavier's Crab.[4] St Nicholas sucking[5]

       Wildefortis beard.[6]

        Exorcisms:[7] Jos. Anchieta. Jesuit. M^a

        Trentals Masses Cloysters[8] Foul. p.26[9]

         Tallies of Devotion[10] Ignatius Miracl. Foul.25

       Purlieus to outlying Consciences[11] 23

       Lengthen ye Tether.[12] Xavier's Miracles. Fouly. p. 26

       And Crabs made Converts to Church of Rome: Varen. p. 177[13]

       Carnevals.[14] Sanbenito Triump. of Pop. p. 117[15]

       Pageantry. Jubilee[14]

       Indulgence-Office.[16]

---

[1] Follows draft of II.142-50. See II.151 n. for Foulis passage.

[2] The 'heads' which follow are for 'Jesuits' III and IV. They are 'untouch'd' up to III.300 (though the reference to Xavier's companions etc., never used, is more akin to III.137 ff. than to III.321 ff. or IV.170), so perhaps the list was made at that point in the work of composition.

[3] See IV.148, 156 n.

[4] See III.321-4n., and cf. further 'heads' 6 lines below. Foulis and Varenius do not mention the crab. For Foulis, see R172(m)—'sun stood still' and n. *Bernardi Vareni ... Descriptio Regni Japoniae et Siam* (1673), p. 177, has 'Tursellinus 1 IV c iii describit miracula duo, quorum uno puella mortua in vitam sit revocata per Xavierium, altero leprosus curatus. Sed id credat, qui potest. Sanè ipse Xaverius ejus nè verbo meminit, nec Maffeus in historiam suam retulit.'

[5] From G. Hall, p. 47, who refers to the story of St. Nicholas, who 'when he was an Infant, did two days in the week (Wednesdays and Fridays) content himself with sucking but once a day'.   [6] See IV.181 n.

[7] Probably from Foulis (see n. 9), pp. 22, 446, and Hall, p. 38. Probably for III.327 ff.

[8] Probably suggested by Hall. See IV.306 f., n.

[9] The miracles performed by Joseph of Anchieta in Brazil are mentioned by Foulis on p. 26. See line above this head. Cf. III.343-50, 345 f., nn.

[10] Refers to G. Hall, p. 51, where the use of rosaries is mocked: 'the Beads knock, and keep just reckoning, let the eyes rove', etc. Cf. p. 49 (see IV. 133-5 n.). See also below, 'thraves and lasts of private Oraisons'. Cf. R247 (m).

[11] Used in III.466; see n.   [12] For III.465; not retained.

[13] See n. above on 'Xavier's Crab'.

[14] From G. Hall, p. 24, where he pretends to regret that the Protestants have 'No Jubilees, no Carnevals, no Pageants'. Cf. Oldham's n. (R164) 'A Jubilee in 25 Year'; IV.212 n.; and III.428 n.

[15] Refers to G. Hall: 'the ugly Devils painted on their *San-benitos*'. In the Inquisition a sanbenito was a penitential garment of yellow cloth.

[16] For III.455. See IV.236 ff. for Hall and Foulis on indulgences.

Rochets Chimers. surplice[1]

Juniper Christ's Buffoon:[2]

Annats. Advowsons. Peterpence[3]

Proses prayers panegyricks:

   Conclave.[4] Sanhedrin

Comites Xaverii

Frojus: Fernandus.

Turrianus. Villela.

Japanners Religion

agreable to ye Roman

in many things:[5]

Holy Medals. Blessed Grains.

priviledg'd Altars[6] thraves & lasts

                    of Oraisons[7]

               Offices

Vespers. Complins.

Tierces.[8] Piazza. The datary.

     woolward.[9]

R197+m   Who sawcily teach Monarchs to obey

          And ye wide world in narrow cloysters sway[10]

[1] From G. Hall, p. 21, where he refers to 'Chimers, Rockets, Surplices' as ecclesiastical vestments. See IV.304 f., n.

[2] From Foulis, p. 20; cf. G. Hall, p. 15. Never utilized.

[3] From G. Hall, p. 98: 'what should I mention the moneths reserved, the Annates Advowsons, Expectatives, and other perquisites of Rectories and other lower dignities?' For Peterpence, see also III.557 and n.

[4] See III.596 and n.

[5] Varenius mentions Frojus, Caspar Villela, Cosmus Turrianus and Joannes Fernandus as fellow-missionaries of Xavier's on pp. 170, 184. He writes (p. 202): 'Similitudo Japoniae religionis, etsi falsae, cum Christiana, inprimis verò cum Pontificia, procul dubio non parum ad hanc rem fecit, cum & Bonzii initio adventûs Jesuitarum Japoniis persuadere conati sint, suam religionem non esse differentem ab illorum, ut Xaverius testatur.'

[6] From *The Excommunicated Prince*, p. 39:

          Holy Medals, *Agnus Dei's*, Blessed Grains,
          Priviledg'd Altars, Beads, and Rosaries,
          Holy Oil, Tapers, Branches, Ashes, Crosses ...
          Do work supernatural Effects.

See III.124-37 and n.

[7] See above, 'Tallies of Devotion' and n.

[8] See IV.306 and n.

[9] From G. Hall, pp. 11, 66; never utilized.

[10] From Dryden, *Indian Emperour* (1667), p. 61. For III.503.

repentance ye vertue of weak minds[1]

conscience ye foolish pride of doing well[2]

burn ravish & destroy[3]

Indian Emp. p. 11.[4]

Religion do you frown Hast holy Avarice[5]

A ghost stain'd more sins than Hell can boast.[6]

R246m   Protestant Book contrary to ye Interest of Rome[7]

R247m   string devotion The tally of devotion[8]

R248   Ambition The Lust of Powr, y^t licences to kill
                   A strong Temptation to do bravely ill.
                   A Bait to draw ye bold & backward in
                   The dearbought Recompence of highest sin.[9]

---

[1] From ibid., p. 28: 'Repentance is the Vertue of weak minds'. Cf. II.213.
[2] From ibid., IV.iii, p. 47: 'Conscience the foolish pride of doing well'.
Cf. II.216.
[3] From ibid., p. 47: 'Burn, Ravish, and Destroy'. Cf. III.155.
[4] Probably refers to 'Sovereign Priest' (see R183). But see also III.558 n.
[5] From ibid., p. 60: 'How now, Religion do you frown? Haste holy Avarice,
and help him down'. The phrases are addressed to a cruel Christian priest who
has been trying to convert Montezuma on the rack. See III.141 f.
[6] From Settle, *Empress of Morocco* (1673), p. 63:
          To the infernal Shades Ile send a Ghost,
          Stain'd with more Sins than all their Hell can boast.
Cf. II.284 f.
[7] Opposite draft of I.106-9. From Hall; see I.108 n.
[8] From Hall; see above R196 ('Tallies ...') and n. See IV.133-5 n. Cf. Edwin Sandys, *Europae Speculum* (1629), p. 5: 'in the admeasuring of devotion
by tale on beads, they string up ten salutations of our Lady to one of our
Lords prayers'.
[9] Follows draft of I.1-30. From Lee's *Sophonisba* (1676), I.i, p. 5:
          Massina: What is Ambition, Sir?
          K. Massinissa: The Lust of Power.
                 Like Glory, Boy, it licenses to kill &c.

R249+m   Courage in you like y^r Blood runs cold.[1]

Senseless what Honour & Ambition means

And ignorantly drag their load of Chains.[2]

Too honest to be great[3]

usurp ye credit of [y^e] scorn & Fame[4]

Dull Cynick Morals Don. Carl p. 8. Aurengz. p. 29. Virtues path

too narrow for his vast Soul y^t start out wide[5]

R250   Ease a Monarch of Crown & Life

Let no dull Virtue get Entrance

there, but when Treason is not aware[6]

[1] Opposite draft of I.195 ff. From Otway, *Don Carlos* (1676), III.i, p. 23:
                All vertue in thee, like thy blood, runs cold ...
                Thy Villany talk'd all; Courage had not a word.
[2] Follows draft of I.95-103. Verbatim from Otway, *Don Carlos* (1676), IV.i,
p. 33.
[3] Opposite draft of I.95-103. From Dryden, *Tyrannick Love* (1670), IV.i,
p. 46. Germ of I.106.
[4] Opposite quotation from Otway ('Senseless ...') above. From Dryden, *Tyrannick Love* (1670), IV.i, p. 37. Porphyrio, says Valeria, 'would try / T' usurp
the credit of a scorn, and dye'. Germ of I.40, 45.
[5] These nn. opposite draft of I.104-9. The first is from Otway, *Don Carlos*
(1676), p. 4: 'Hence Cynick to dull Slaves thy Moral teach'. p. 8 includes
the following lines from Don John's rant:
                Why should dull Law rule Nature, who first made
                That Law by which her self is now betray'd ...
                Law was an Innovation brought in since,
                When Fools began to love Obedience,
                And called their slavery Safety and defence....
Dryden, *Aureng-Zebe* (1676), II.i, p. 29: the hero's famous rant begins 'How
vain is Virtue ...'. 'Virtues path ...' is from Dryden, *All for Love* (1678),
I.i, p. 5:
                Virtue's his path; but sometimes 'tis too narrow
                For his vast Soul; and then he starts out wide....
Cf. I.95-128, and II.239 ff.
[6] Notes for I.34 f. and I.112-14. First line is from Otway, *Don Carlos*
(1676), p. 47: 'You'd ease me of my Crown to give me peace'. The rest is
derived from p. 46:
                ——Submission, which way got it entrance here!
                ——Perhaps it came e'er Treason was aware....
See also R281 ('Let never silly Vertue ...').

Like a Granado Don C, p. 27. full-charg'd with rage & with my
vengeance hot[1]

                                    its
Storm Tempest Granado deal ~~its~~ wide Destruction[1]

R257+m+s stupidity   And well I may resemble him, for he

         dolt   As stupid was

         <u>Stock</u>   Was senseless & as much a block as I[2]

R260m   Let lazy Princes wait,
         Till their slow Crowns be given by Fate[3]

         Plagues rot ye tongue & blasted boldly be ye lungs Perish y^e
         Bodies[4]

R261+m   The Infernal Prayer[:]
         Now ye that dwell in Everlasting flame

         Hot with Revenge & strideing ore ye dead.[5]

[1] Opposite a draft of I.254-7. From Otway, *Don Carlos* (1676), III, p. 21:
                Full charg'd with rage and with my vengeance hot,
                Like a Granado from a Cannon shot,
                Which lights at last upon the Enemies ground,
                Then breaking deals destruction all around.
See SJ I.257, Textual Apparatus, and Introduction, pp. lxxxii f.
[2] Draft of IV.7 f. The sources are Fletcher and Hall. 'Stock' is Fletcher's
rhyme-word at *Locusts*, III.xxxvii.1 f.: 'a goodly stone or stock' is chosen:
                Ah who can tell which is the verier block
                His god, or he!
'Senseless' (for 'stupid') is from a translated pasquil in G. Hall, p. 78;
cf. p. 10 (with an inexact quotation from Juvenal, XIII.119): 'some of our
jeering companions shall scornfully ask what difference there is Effigies
inter vestras statuamq: Bathulli ? and shall tell us that all blocks are alike.'
[3] Before draft of 'Jesuits I'. Derived from Settle, *Cambyses King of Persia*
(1671), p. 8:
                Let dull successive Monarchs idly wait
                To be enthron'd by the slow hand of Fate.
[4] Opposite draft of I.341 f. From Lee, *Mithridates* (1678), III.ii, p. 36.
[5] 'The Infernal Prayer' is a n. for I.341. The 1st verse is from Otway,
Don Carlos (1676), IV.i, p. 44; the 2nd from Lee, *Sophonisba* (1676), I.i,
p. 4 (see R180 and n.).

Drunk with Death & steaming slaughter[1]

R262m   [on] ye brink of Life[2]

R263   Stride ore Crown—Kill in cool Blood—
           This rub remov'd—I love a sober Murderer—[3]

R265m   Matrons hanging on your knees with dying grasps.

           Make 'em do't themselves & save you ye drudgery of a Murder, Not
           Mercy's self adorn'd in Beau-tie's dress.[4]

           storms borrow Rage from me:[5]

               Ill kill with so much eager[ness] & hast
           As Fiends let loose, would lay all Nature wast[6]

           I love a sober Murderer—Luxury of Cruelty.[7]

---

[1] Opposite draft of I.315. From Lee, *Mithridates* (1678), p. 61: see I.121 n.
[2] Note for I.299. See n. in loc.
[3] Various notes. For 'Stride ore Crown', see R180, R260 and nn.; and II.177.
'Kill in cool Blood' and 'I love a sober Murderer' are from Dryden, *All For Love* (1678), III.i (see R265).
[4] Three notes relating to I.292-5. 'Matrons ...' is opposite draft of I.304-
10; the other two opposite a draft of I.292-7. The first and third derive from
Lee, *Mithridates* (1678), III.ii, p. 39:
               ... nor Mercy's self, adorn'd
               In all *Semandra*'s beauties, in her Tears
               Prostrate upon the Earth, and hanging on
               My Knees, nay, dying with her Grief, shall move me.
'Make 'em do't ...' comes from Dryden, *Aureng-Zebe* (1676), V.i, p. 75: the
virgin Indamora is adjured to 'Do't' (stab herself) so that the villainess
may relish her death 'without the drudgery'.
[5] Opposite draft of I.288-91. But cf. III.153. From Lee, *Sophonisba* (1676),
III.ii, p. 38.
[6] After draft of I.288-91. But cf. III.153 f. From Dryden, *Aureng-Zebe*
(1676), V.i, p. 75:
               I'll kill thee with such eagerness and haste,
               As Fiends etc.
[7] Opposite draft of I.279-310. Verbatim from *All for Love* (1678), III.i,
p. 32. Cf. II.98 ff. and R263.

Triumph'd & laugh'd to see ye issuing Flood. And wantonly have
bath'd my hands in blood.[1] He's ye coolest Murderer, so stanch.
He kills & keeps his temper.[2] deliberate malice I'th'midst of
groans & cries & gushing Tears I'd ravish.[3]

R267   Go on brave Prince![4]

R281   Let never silly Vertue enter there
            No not in Dream, not when you ar'nt aware[5]

R284m   Ignorance a mark of *Grace*

            Devout by Instinct[6]

R286m   raise their Ashes up in Arms against thee[7]

R288   Rough as a Storm[8]

---

[1] Opposite draft of I.281-4, 279. From Otway, *Don Carlos* (1676), p. 57.
[2] See p. 556, n. 7.
[3] Opposite draft of I.298-300. From Lee, *Mithridates* (1678), p. 29.
[4] Note for abortive draft opening of 'Jesuits I'. From Cleveland's 'To P.
Rupert', 1. 165. Oldham's attack on the Duke of York was soon discarded.
[5] Draft of I.112-14. Derived from Otway, *Don Carlos* (1676), p. 46 (for which
see R250, n. on 'Let no dull Virtue ...').
[6] Opposite draft of II.270-3. The notes and the lines allude to G. Hall,
p. 103: 'since ... ignorance is the mother of Devotion; it hath therefore been
the wisdom of our holy Mother to keep the common people blindfold; and to
cause them to take up with an implicite faith, ... as suspecting, that upon
more light of understanding, they would grow scrupulous, censorious, refrac-
tory, ...'; and cf. p. 138: 'they keep them alwayes blindfold, not suffering
them to have any glimpse of light either from Scriptures, or conferences, or
their own authors'. Cf. III.491, 497 f.; 493 f., nn.
[7] Opposite draft of I.313 f. From Lee, *Mithridates* (1678), IV.i, p. 60. Lee
has 'my' ashes.
[8] Follows (and relates to) draft of I.116/129. From Dryden, 1 *Conquest of
Granada* (1672), I.i, p. 9.

R290   Creighton. Abyrcrumby. Gourdon concern'd in ye Rebellion against
Jame. 6 of Scots, Allan. Sanders of Surrey in ye Irish R. against
Q E. Holt Walpool in Squires Plot Felton y^t fix'd up ye Bull.
433

Sanders died mad & miserably in Ireland. Desmond. Tyroen. O-neals[1]

R292   Some dreadful Comet should have hung ye sky
To bode thy birth
To bode thy birth, a greater Prodigy To forerun thee[2]

R293m   R.Q. p. 27.[3]

[1] Notes for 'Jesuits', never utilized. From Foulis, pp. 367, 377 f.; 390 f.;
463-6; 433; 390-3. Crichton, Gordon, Abercromby, Holt, and Walpole are specified as Jesuits by Foulis. On p. 433 he relates that the papal bull excom-
municating Elizabeth was 'convey'd into the hands of one John Felton, who ...
boldly sticks it up, on the Bishop of *London's* Palace-gates in Pauls Church-
yard [May 25, 1570]'. Nicholas Sanders the papal legate starved to death in
the woods after the defeat of the Irish rebellion of 1580. Tyroen is Tyrone:
Foulis calls him Tir-Oen.
[2] Follows draft of II.25-35. Derived from Cowley, *Discourse ... Concerning
... Cromwell* (*Essays*, pp. 353):
            Methinks at least some Prodigy,
            Some dreadful Comet from on high,
            Should terribly forewarn the Earth,
        As of good Princes Deaths, so of a Tyrants birth.
See also II.1-4 n.
[3] Opposite draft of I.332 f. Refers to Lee, *Rival Queens* (1677), p. 27:
            Let not Medea's dreadfull vengeance stand
            A pattern more, but draw your own so fierce,
            It may for ever be Original.

The Wiltshire Drum (*Satyrs upon the Jesuits* IV.106)

Cf. Abraham Miles's ballad, *A Wonder of Wonders; being a true
Relation of the strange and invisible beating of a Drum, at the
house of John Mompesson, Esquire, at Tidcomb in the County of
Wiltshire ... to the great admiration of ... many hundreds who
have gone from several parts to hear this miraculous Wonder,
since the first time it began to beat Roundheads and Cuckolds,
come dig, come dig....* Wood dated his copy 'februar: 1662'; Tidcomb is Tidworth (or Tedworth). According to the detailed account
added to Joseph Glanvill's *A Blow at Modern Sadducism* (1668),
pp. 91-141, the drum had been impounded, March 1661/2, from a
pretended militiaman. In April the racket began with 'a very
great knocking' at the 'Doors and the out-sides' of the house.
After a month, '*It*' entered, and among other worse pranks, would
beat 'several Points of Warre, and that as dexterously as any
Drummer'. The 'militiaman' was tried at Salisbury for some petty
felonies, 'and there those passages also were producd and urg'd'.
He was sentenced to transportation, but contrived to return, and
the disturbances, which had ceased, then recommenced. From *Mercurius Publicus,* 16-23 Apr. 1663, it appears that the drummer was
William Drury of Uscut, Wilts. See also *The Wiltshire Ballad*
(dated by Luttrell Feb. 1679/80), repr. Yale *POAS*, ii.312. Gough
(*British Topography*, i.387, ii.380) notes that 'This affair furnished the plot for Mr. Addison's Drummer', and that John Wesley
(*Journal*, 1768-1770, p. 6) believed the story—his eldest brother
was told by Mompesson's son that the published account was true.

INDEX TO THE INTRODUCTION, COMMENTARY,
AND APPENDIX III

A Note on the Arrangement and Cross-References

THE Index of Persons and Places is an alphabetical list of names;
but the Index of Topics combines an analytical procedure with its
alphabetical one.

To bring kindred items together is its first purpose, classify-
ing them in fairly wide categories, under main headings. For these,
for their subheadings, and under each for the items listed, alphabetical order is followed, except that the books of the Bible are
in biblical order, *Education* begins with Oldham's, and in *History,
political*, chronology governs subdivision into periods. Items are
delimited by semicolons; further clarification has occasionally
required brackets.

It is recognized that a reader may seek some topic items apart
from any classification to which they have been assigned: e.g.
'Gazette, the', 'Plague, Great'. As with those, it might be doubtful under which classificatory heading an item should be looked
for. 'Huguenots', an extreme case, is needed (to avoid an obvious
gap in each of four categories) in the entries under *French, the*;
History, political; *Massacres, Persecutions*; and *Religion*. To
confine the four cross-references to 'q.v.' and to record the
page-references only once, a single main heading, *Huguenots*, is
wanted. For one or more of these reasons, certain topic items are
given, in their alphabetical place, main entries of their own.
A reader may regret the absence of others, but a choice has to be
made; and within the criteria mentioned, it is bound to be to some
extent arbitrary.

In cross-referencing, 'see' designates the entry to be consulted for all information; 'see also', a source of *further* information; 'see' with page-reference, the page or pages (out of a
series, especially a long one as under 'Rochester') relevant to
the topic concerned. Italicized cross-references are to main
headings in the Index of Topics. All *names* in that Index will be

found, with page-references, in the Index of Persons and Places.
'Above', 'below', means 'in the entry under the present main
heading'.

I INDEX OF TOPICS

Aeronautics: see *Science*
Armada 365
Army, Navy: see *Professions*
Astrology: see also *Crime* ... *Punishment; Topical Allusions, Old-ham's*
almanacs, 385, 551-3
Authorship: see also *History, literary Hack-writers* q.v.; *Independence* ...
Authorial q.v.; miseries of scholars xxv, lxvii, 525;
MSS. q.v.; Oldham's disciple-ships: see Boileau, Cowley, Dryden, Horace, Juvenal, Rochester; *Patronage* q.v.; prospects xxvif., lxixf., 467, 477; *Publication* q.v.
copy-money, see *Book Trade*; dedications, see *Patronage*; third day, see *Drama, Theatre*, theatre terminology
Rochester's circle, cults of q.v.; vocation xlvi, xlviiif., livf., lix, lxviiif., 460

Ballads, Pamphlets
drinking-ballads 409, 473f., 475f.; individuals, on: see Blood, Buckingham, Fitzharris, Hobbes 447, Preston, Settle 488; murders, executions, on 360, 434, 451, 453, see also *Popish Terror*
Pope-burnings q.v.
social subjects
abuses, on 440, 470, 483; descriptive 412, 419, 437, 493
Bible references
Genesis v.24, 520f.; ix.21, 495, 502; x.9, 531; xviii.32, 446; xix.32, 495; xxv. 22f, 522; xl.9-13, 21, 495; Exodus iii.2, 522; viii-x, 366, 504; x.19, 373; xvii.5, 504; Leviticus xvii.10, 442; Numbers xxi, 445; Deuteronomy xxiv.4, 472; Judges xx, 454;

xxi.19-21, 427; I. Samuel ii, v, xi, xiii-v, xviif., II. Samuel i.16-21, 453f.; II. Kings 11, 520f.; Mark xv.43, Luke xxxiii 50, 521; Acts ii.13-18, 502; Hebrews xi.5, 520; Revelations ix, 3, 11, 373; I. Maccabees iii.58, 520
Book-Trade: see also *Ballads, Pamphlets*
advertisement 432, 463, 479; *Censorship, Licensing* q.v.; copy-money 479; frontispiece (portraits) 478; *Gazette, the* q.v.; *News-books* q.v.; piracy ci, cvii, 432; prices 464, 473; printing: see Clark (Mary), *Text*, *Oldham's*: printing, compositors; prosecutions 463; *Publication* q.v.; second-hand 480, 482; title-pages 463, 479;
Building
London Monument 447, 492f.; St James's Square 492; St Paul's 396, 491
Buildings: see also *History, social*; *London*
London's flimsy 496; Louvre, see *French, the*

Casuistry: see also *Catholicism* ... *attacked*, moral currency debased
Jesuits: Pascal li, cv, 355, 371, 384, 388
Catholicism, Roman, attacked: see also *Jesuits; Popish Plot: Popish Terror*
Bible, hostility to 361, 376f., 384-6, 553, 557
creed, doctrine
adoration of the Host 445; of the Virgin, saints 444; martyrs alleged, venerated 369-71; prayers for the dead 510; purgatory 381; transubstan-

*Capitalized, current 17th-century designations; uncapitalized, modern in-
vented ones; dirae (revived from Puttenham).

Law, the
  authorities, Coke (Common Law),
    Dalton (JP, on the); Bar 356,
    453; benefit of clergy 447;
    dress, bar-gown 436, coif
    433; Law Courts: Chancery
    407, 445, 447; Common Pleas,
    Exchequer, King's Bench 407,
    451; lawyers, ill-repute of
    445, 521; Lords Chief Jus-
    tices: see Pemberton, Saun-
    ders (Edmund), Scroggs;
    messenger 433, 530; perjury,
    see *Crime ... Punishment,
    Popish Terror*, false witnes-
    ses; pursuivant 465, 530; remu-
    nerative profession, a 429f.;
    serjeant-at-law 433, 487;
    Temple, Inner xxif., c, Ben-
    chers of, their ritual dance
    436; Temple Walks 449; West-
    minster Hall 445
Medicine
  see Lower, Richard
  course, in a, see *Glosses*
  diseases
    ague 451, 509; diabetes 415;
    disorders of brain, nerves
    414f., 423, of lungs 423,
    485; fevers cii, 485, 533;
    morphew 393; smallpox xxxiv,
    513
  domicile
    Essex (Hundreds), noxious, see
    Sheppey; salubrious, see
    Montpellier
  Hospitals: see Index II. *London
    and environs*
    Chelsea, St Bartholomew's, St
    Thomas's;
  licentiates 441f.; mortality,
    bills of, see *London*
  Physician's College 390; physi-
    cians, credentials to prac-
    tice 441; hallmarks, social
    486; stock gibes at 429, 486;
    v. apothecaries 441f.
  physiology 424, 449; quacks 445,
    479, 486, 492; quacks' nos-
    trums 392f.; quinine ('Jesu-
    its' powder') 355, 396
  remunerative profession, a 449
Publication xxxiii, lixf., cvii, 423,
    425, 435f.

Religion, Irreligion
  Anglican
    Church and King xxxiii, 487f.;

Charles the martyr 530,
  compared to Christ 452
Christian concepts
  angels, orders of 525; Creation,
    the xl, 428, 459; Deity as
    mirror 520, 523; Heaven, bliss
    464, 509, mode of knowledge
    in 520, the war in 360, 426,
    527; Hell 368, 370, 375f.,
    381, and *passim*, after Cow-
    ley, Fletcher (Phineas),
    Milton 527; Judgement, Last
    407; judgements, God's 452;
    martyrs, 519, see also *Mas-
    sacres, Persecutions*; Mosaic
    law 442; Righteousness, im-
    puted 553; Scripture and
    reason 457; Sin, Original,
    innocence (pre-lapsarian)
    471f., 512; soul, diffusion
    of the 500f., 521; Tempta-
    tion and Fall of Eve 407, 527
Dissent
  Covenanters, q.v.; 'enthusiasts'
    414, 456; *Huguenots* q.v.;
    Presbyterians xxxii, xcix
  Heterodoxy: see also Simon, Vanini,
    Vrats
    scepticism 401, 403, 436, 522
  Irreligion
    atheism 400; Cainani 369, 379,
    403f.; *Libertinism*, q.v.;
    Rochester's circle, cults of
    q.v.; town gallant 517;
    materialism, see Hobbes
  Politics, religion prostituted to
    378
  Religions, non-Christian
    Islam 377, see also Mahomet;
    Japanese 377, 552; Jewish,
    Talmud, 379; New World, devil-
    worship, 368; Philistine,
    Dagon 453
    polytheism, ancient
    Egyptian 444f.; Roman, Greek
    386, 403, 406, 427, 447, 452,
    510, 514
  Superstition
    Astrology q.v.; Catholic 377,
    379-82, 389-97; Witches' fan-
    tasy 431
Rochester's circle, cults of xlii-
    xlv, lxviii, 401, 403, 436,
    444
Royal Society
  aeronautics 492f.
  experiments
    air, with 442; barometric 493;
    blood-transfusion cii

Vulgar Errors, on (*cont.*)
    tails 395; murdered corpse
    bleeding afresh 407; poison-
    ing by the sacramental Host
    359; porcupine 405; taran-
    tula 398

War:
    operations of 365, 503, 506, 508;
    see also Drake, Raleigh,
    Lorraine, Louis XIV,
    Medina-Sidonia, William of
    Orange

II   PERSONS AND PLACES

Note: Post-Augustan scholars and critics are not indexed: nor are some common
classical allusions